The History of The Decline and Fall of the Roman Empire by Edward Gibbon

Volume I (of VI)

For decades, perhaps centuries, the standard work of reference on Roman History has been courtesy of Edward Gibbon. In its original printing it was a best-seller and a publishing sensation. History was brought to the masses in vivid detail.

Within its massive six volumes Gibbon put into context the entire sweep of this huge and complex Empire. We visit its far-flung regions, its most charismatic characters as we travel through centuries of its existence and its eternal influence on Western and, most probably, World culture.

Considering the times and the resources at his disposal it quite incredible what Gibbon has been able to put together, to distil, to formulate and precisely plot in this most seducing of histories.

Index of Contents
Preface by The Editor
Preface of The Author
Preface - To the First Volume
Preface - To the Fourth Volume of The Original Quarto Edition
CHAPTER I - The Extent of The Empire in The Age of The Antonines
CHAPTER II - The Internal Prosperity in The Age of The Antonines
CHAPTER III - The Constitution in The Age of The Antonines.
CHAPTER IV - The Cruelty, Follies and Murder of Commodus
CHAPTER V - Sale of The Empire to Didius Julianus
CHAPTER VI - Death of Severus, Tyranny of Caracalla, Usurpation of Marcinus
CHAPTER VII - Tyranny of Maximin, Rebellion, Civil Wars, Death of Maximin
CHAPTER VIII - State of Persion And Restoration of The Monarchy
CHAPTER IX - State of Germany Until the Barbarians
CHAPTER X - Emperors Decius, Gallus, Aemilianus, Valerian and Gallienus
CHAPTER XI - Reign of Claudius, Defeat of The Goths
CHAPTER XII - Reigns of Tacitus, Probus, Carus And His Sons
CHAPTER XIII - Reign of Diocletian And His Three Associates
CHAPTER XIV - Six Emperors At The Same Time, Reunion Of The Empire
CHAPTER XV - Progress of The Christian Religion
Edward Gibbon – A Short Biography
Edward Gibbon – A Concise Bibliography

PREFACE BY THE EDITOR

The great work of Gibbon is indispensable to the student of history. The literature of Europe offers no substitute for "The Decline and Fall of the Roman Empire." It has obtained undisputed possession, as rightful occupant, of the vast period which it comprehends. However some subjects, which it embraces, may have undergone more complete investigation, on the general view of the whole period, this history is the sole undisputed authority to which all defer, and from which few appeal to the original writers, or to more modern compilers. The inherent interest of the subject, the inexhaustible labor employed upon it; the immense condensation of matter; the luminous arrangement; the general accuracy; the style, which, however monotonous from its uniform stateliness, and sometimes wearisome from its elaborate ar., is throughout vigorous, animated, often picturesque always commands attention, always conveys its meaning with emphatic energy, describes with singular breadth and fidelity, and generalizes with unrivalled felicity of expression; all these high qualifications have secured, and seem likely to secure, its permanent place in historic literature.

This vast design of Gibbon, the magnificent whole into which he has cast the decay and ruin of the ancient civilization, the formation and birth of the new order of things, will of itself, independent of the laborious execution of his immense plan, render "The Decline and Fall of the Roman Empire" an unapproachable subject to the future historian: in the eloquent language of his recent French editor, M. Guizot:—

"The gradual decline of the most extraordinary dominion which has ever invaded and oppressed the world; the fall of that immense empire, erected on the ruins of so many kingdoms, republics, and states both barbarous and civilized; and forming in its turn, by its dismemberment, a multitude of states, republics, and kingdoms; the annihilation of the religion of Greece and Rome; the birth and the progress of the two new religions which have shared the most beautiful regions of the earth; the decrepitude of the ancient world, the spectacle of its expiring glory and degenerate manners; the infancy of the modern world, the picture of its first progress, of the new direction given to the mind and character of man—such a subject must necessarily fix the attention and excite the interest of men, who cannot behold with indifference those memorable epochs, during which, in the fine language of Corneille—'Un grand destin commence, un grand destin s'acheve.'"

This extent and harmony of design is unquestionably that which distinguishes the work of Gibbon from all other great historical compositions. He has first bridged the abyss between ancient and modern times, and connected together the two great worlds of history. The great advantage which the classical historians possess over those of modern times is in unity of plan, of course greatly facilitated by the narrower sphere to which their researches were confined. Except Herodotus, the great historians of Greece—we exclude the more modern compilers, like Diodorus Siculus—limited themselves to a single period, or at 'east to the contracted sphere of Grecian affairs. As far as the Barbarians trespassed within the Grecian boundary, or were necessarily mingled up with Grecian politics, they were admitted into the pale of Grecian history; but to Thucydides and to Xenophon, excepting in the Persian inroad of the latter, Greece was the world. Natural unity confined their narrative almost to chronological order, the episodes were of rare occurrence and extremely brief. To the Roman historians the course was equally clear and defined. Rome was their centre of unity; and the uniformity with which the circle of the Roman dominion spread around, the regularity with which their civil polity expanded, forced, as it were, upon the Roman historian that plan which Polybius announces as the subject of his history, the means and the manner by which the whole world became subject to the Roman sway. How different the complicated politics of the European kingdoms! Every national history, to be complete, must, in a certain sense, be the history of Europe; there is no knowing to how remote a quarter it may be necessary to trace our most domestic events; from a country, how apparently disconnected, may originate the impulse which gives its direction to the whole course of affairs.

In imitation of his classical models, Gibbon places Rome as the cardinal point from which his inquiries diverge, and to which they bear constant reference; yet how immeasurable the space over which those inquiries range; how complicated, how confused, how apparently inextricable the ca-\nuses which tend to the decline of the Roman empire! how countless the nations which swarm forth, in mingling and indistinct hordes, constantly changing the geographical limits—incessantly confounding the natural boundaries! At first sight, the whole period, the whole state of the world, seems to offer no more secure footing to an historical adventurer than the chaos of Milton—to be in a state of irreclaimable disorder, best described in the language of the poet:—

—"A dark
Illimitable ocean, without bound,
Without dimension, where length, breadth, and height,
And time, and place, are lost: where eldest Night
And Chaos, ancestors of Nature, hold
Eternal anarchy, amidst the noise
Of endless wars, and by confusion stand."

We feel that the unity and harmony of narrative, which shall comprehend this period of social disorganization, must be ascribed entirely to the skill and luminous disposition of the historian. It is in this sublime Gothic architecture of his work, in which the boundless range, the infinite variety, the, at first sight, incongruous gorgeousness of the separate parts, nevertheless are all subordinate to one main and predominant idea, that Gibbon is unrivalled. We cannot but admire the manner in which he masses his materials, and arranges his facts in successive groups, not according to chronological order, but to their moral or political connection; the distinctness with which he marks his periods of gradually increasing decay; and the skill with which, though advancing on separate parallels of history, he shows the common tendency of the slower or more rapid religious or civil innovations. However these principles of composition may demand more than ordinary attention on the part of the reader, they can alone impress upon the memory the real course, and the relative importance of the events. Whoever would justly appreciate the superiority of Gibbon's lucid arrangement, should attempt to make his way through the regular but wearisome annals of Tillemont, or even the less ponderous volumes of Le Beau. Both these writers adhere, almost entirely, to chronological order; the consequence is, that we are twenty times called upon to break off, and resume the thread of six or eight wars in different parts of the empire; to suspend the operations of a military expedition for a court intrigue; to hurry away from a siege to a council; and the same page places us in the middle of a campaign against the barbarians, and in the depths of the Monophysite controversy. In Gibbon it is not always easy to bear in mind the exact dates but the course of events is ever clear and distinct; like a skilful general, though his troops advance from the most remote and opposite quarters, they are constantly bearing down and concentrating themselves on one point—that which is still occupied by the name, and by the waning power of Rome. Whether he traces the progress of hostile religions, or leads from the shores of the Baltic, or the verge of the Chinese empire, the successive hosts of barbarians—though one wave has hardly burst and discharged itself, before another swells up and approaches—all is made to flow in the same direction, and the impression which each makes upon the tottering fabric of the Roman greatness, connects their distant movements, and measures the relative importance assigned to them in the panoramic history. The more peaceful and didactic episodes on the development of the Roman law, or even on the details of ecclesiastical history, interpose themselves as resting-places or divisions between the periods of barbaric invasion. In short, though distracted first by the two capitals, and afterwards by the formal partition of the empire, the extraordinary felicity of arrangement maintains an order and a regular progression. As our horizon expands to reveal to us the gathering tempests which are forming far beyond the boundaries of the civilized world—as we follow their successive approach to the trembling frontier—the compressed and receding line is still distinctly visible; though gradually dismembered and the broken fragments assuming the form of regular states and kingdoms, the real relation of those kingdoms to the empire is maintained and defined; and even when the Roman dominion has shrunk into little more than the province of Thrace—when the name of Rome, confined, in Italy, to the walls of the city—yet it is still the memory, the shade of the Roman greatness, which extends over the wide sphere into which the historian expands his later narrative; the whole blends into the unity, and is manifestly essential to the double catastrophe of his tragic drama.

But the amplitude, the magnificence, or the harmony of design, are, though imposing, yet unworthy claims on our admiration, unless the details are filled up with correctness and accuracy. No writer has been more severely tried on this point than Gibbon. He has undergone the triple scrutiny of theological zeal quickened by just resentment, of literary emulation, and of that mean and invidious vanity which delights in detecting errors in writers of established fame. On the result of the trial, we may be permitted to summon competent witnesses before we deliver our own judgment.

M. Guizot, in his preface, after stating that in France and Germany, as well as in England, in the most enlightened countries of Europe, Gibbon is constantly cited as an authority, thus proceeds:—

"I have had occasion, during my labors, to consult the writings of philosophers, who have treated on the finances of the Roman empire; of scholars, who have investigated the chronology; of theologians, who have searched the depths of ecclesiastical history; of writers on law, who have studied with care the Roman jurisprudence; of Orientalists, who have occupied themselves with the Arabians and the Koran; of modern historians, who have entered upon extensive researches touching the crusades and their influence; each of these writers has remarked and pointed out, in the 'History of the Decline and Fall of the Roman Empire,' some negligences, some false or imperfect views some omissions, which it is impossible not to suppose voluntary; they have rectified some facts combated with advantage some assertions; but in general they have taken the researches and the ideas of Gibbon, as points of departure, or as proofs of the researches or of the new opinions which they have advanced."

M. Guizot goes on to state his own impressions on reading Gibbon's history, and no authority will have greater weight with those to whom the extent and accuracy of his historical researches are known:—

"After a first rapid perusal, which allowed me to feel nothing but the interest of a narrative, always animated, and, notwithstanding its extent and the variety of objects which it makes to pass before the view, always perspicuous, I entered upon a minute examination of the details of which it was composed; and the opinion which I then formed was, I confess, singularly severe. I discovered, in certain chapters, errors which appeared to me sufficiently important and numerous to make me believe that they had been written with extreme negligence; in others, I was struck with a certain tinge of partiality and prejudice, which imparted to the exposition of the facts that want of truth and justice, which the English express by their happy term misrepresentation. Some imperfect (tronquees) quotations; some passages, omitted unintentionally or designedly cast a suspicion on the honesty (bonne foi) of the author; and his violation of the first law of history—increased to my eye by the prolonged attention with which I occupied myself with every phrase, every note, every reflection—caused me to form upon the whole work, a judgment far too rigorous. After having finished my labors, I allowed some time to elapse before I reviewed the whole. A second attentive and regular perusal of the entire work, of the notes of the author, and of those which I had thought it right to subjoin, showed me how much I had exaggerated the importance of the reproaches which Gibbon really deserved; I was struck with the same errors, the same partiality on certain subjects; but I had been far from doing adequate justice to the immensity of his researches, the variety of his knowledge, and above all, to that truly philosophical discrimination (justesse d'esprit) which judges the past as it would judge the present; which does not permit itself to be blinded by the clouds which time gathers around the dead, and which prevent us from seeing that, under the toga, as under the modern dress, in the senate as in our councils, men were what they still are, and that events took place eighteen centuries ago, as they take place in our days. I then felt that his book, in spite of its faults, will always be a noble work—and that we may correct his errors and combat his prejudices, without ceasing to admit that few men have combined, if we are not to say in so high a degree, at least in a manner so complete, and so well regulated, the necessary qualifications for a writer of history."

The present editor has followed the track of Gibbon through many parts of his work; he has read his authorities with constant reference to his pages, and must pronounce his deliberate judgment, in terms of the highest admiration as to his general accuracy. Many of his seeming errors are almost inevitable from the close condensation of his matter. From the immense range of his history, it was sometimes necessary to compress into a single sentence, a whole vague and diffuse page of a Byzantine chronicler. Perhaps something of importance may have thus escaped, and his expressions may not quite contain the whole substance of the passage from which they are taken. His limits, at times, compel him to sketch; where that is the case, it is not fair to expect the full details of the finished picture. At times he can only deal with important results; and in his account of a war, it sometimes requires great attention to discover that the events which seem to be comprehended in a single campaign, occupy several years. But this admirable skill in selecting and giving prominence to the points which are of real weight and importance—this distribution of light and shade—though perhaps it may occasionally betray him into vague and imperfect statements, is one of the highest excellencies of Gibbon's historic manner. It is the more striking, when we pass from the works of his chief authorities, where, after laboring through long, minute, and wearisome descriptions of the accessary and subordinate circumstances, a single unmarked and undistinguished sentence, which we may overlook from the inattention of fatigue, contains the great moral and political result.

Gibbon's method of arrangement, though on the whole most favorable to the clear comprehension of the events, leads likewise to apparent inaccuracy. That which we expect to find in one part is reserved for another. The estimate which we are to form, depends on the accurate balance of statements in remote parts of the work; and we have sometimes to correct and modify opinions, formed from one chapter by those of another. Yet, on the other hand, it is astonishing how rarely we detect contradiction; the mind of the author has already harmonized the whole result to truth and probability; the general impression is almost invariably the same. The quotations of Gibbon have likewise been called in question;—I have, in general, been more inclined to admire their exactitude, than to complain of their indistinctness, or incompleteness. Where they are imperfect, it is commonly from the study of brevity, and rather from the desire of compressing the substance of his notes into pointed and emphatic sentences, than from dishonesty, or uncandid suppression of truth.

These observations apply more particularly to the accuracy and fidelity of the historian as to his facts; his inferences, of course, are more liable to exception. It is almost impossible to trace the line between unfairness and unfaithfulness; between intentional misrepresentation and undesigned false coloring. The relative magnitude and importance of events must, in some respect, depend upon the mind before which they are presented; the estimate of character, on the habits and feelings of the reader. Christians, like M. Guizot and ourselves, will see some things, and some persons, in a different light from the historian of the Decline and Fall. We may deplore the bias of his mind; we may ourselves be on our guard against the danger of being misled, and be anxious to warn less wary readers against the same perils; but we must not confound this secret and unconscious departure from truth, with the deliberate violation of that veracity which is the only title of an historian to our confidence. Gibbon, it may be fearlessly asserted, is rarely chargeable even with the suppression of any material fact, which bears upon individual character; he may, with apparently invidious hostility, enhance the errors and crimes, and disparage the virtues of certain persons; yet, in general, he leaves us the materials for forming a fairer judgment; and if he is not exempt from his own prejudices, perhaps we might write passions, yet it must be candidly acknowledged, that his philosophical bigotry is not more unjust than the theological partialities of those ecclesiastical writers who were before in undisputed possession of this province of history.

We are thus naturally led to that great misrepresentation which pervades his history—his false estimate of the nature and influence of Christianity.

But on this subject some preliminary caution is necessary, lest that should be expected from a new edition, which it is impossible that it should completely accomplish. We must first be prepared with the only sound preservative against the false impression likely to be produced by the perusal of Gibbon; and we must see clearly the real cause of that false impression. The former of these cautions will be briefly suggested in its proper place, but it may be as well to state it, here, somewhat more at length. The art of Gibbon, or at least the unfair impression produced by his two memorable chapters, consists in his confounding together, in one indistinguishable mass, the origin and apostolic propagation of the new religion, with its later progress. No argument for the divine authority of Christianity has been urged with greater force, or traced with higher eloquence, than that deduced from its primary development, explicable on no other hypothesis than a heavenly origin, and from its rapid extension through great part of the Roman empire. But this argument—one, when confined within reasonable limits, of unanswerable force—becomes more feeble and disputable in proportion as it recedes from the birthplace, as it were, of the religion. The further Christianity advanced, the more causes purely human were enlisted in its favor; nor can it be doubted that those developed with such artful exclusiveness by Gibbon did concur most essentially to its establishment. It is in the Christian dispensation, as in the material world. In both it is as the great First Cause, that the Deity is most undeniably manifest. When once launched in regular motion upon the bosom of space, and endowed with all their properties and relations of weight and mutual attraction, the heavenly bodies appear to pursue their courses according to secondary laws, which account for all their sublime regularity. So Christianity proclaims its Divine Author chiefly in its first origin and development. When it had once received its impulse from above—when it had once been infused into the minds of its first teachers—when it had gained full possession of the reason and affections of the favored few—it might be—and to the Protestant, the rationa Christian, it is impossible to define when it really was—left to make its way by its native force, under the ordinary secret agencies of all-ruling Providence. The main question, the divine origin of the religion, was dexterously eluded, or speciously conceded by Gibbon; his plan enabled him to commence his account, in most parts, below the apostolic times; and it was only by the strength of the dark coloring with which he brought out the failings and the follies of the succeeding ages, that a shadow of doubt and suspicion was thrown back upon the primitive period of Christianity.

"The theologian," says Gibbon, "may indulge the pleasing task of describing religion as she descended from heaven, arrayed in her native purity; a more melancholy duty is imposed upon the historian:—he must discover the inevitable mixture of error and corruption which she contracted in a long residence upon earth among a weak and degenerate race of beings." Divest this passage of the latent sarcasm betrayed by the subsequent tone of the whole disquisition, and it might commence a Christian history written in the most Christian spirit of candor. But as the historian, by seeming to respect, yet by dexterously confounding the limits of the sacred land, contrived to insinuate that it was an Utopia which had no existence but in the imagination of the theologian—as he suggested rather than affirmed that the days of Christian purity were a kind of poetic golden age;—so the theologian, by venturing too far into the domain of the historian, has been perpetually obliged to contest points on which he had little chance of victory—to deny facts established on unshaken evidence—and thence, to retire, if not with the shame of defeat, yet with but doubtful and imperfect success. Paley, with his intuitive sagacity, saw through the difficulty of answering Gibbon by the ordinary arts of controversy; his emphatic sentence, "Who can refute a sneer?" contains as much truth as point. But full and pregnant as this phrase is, it is not quite the whole truth; it is the tone in which the progress of Christianity is traced, in comparison with the rest of the splendid and prodigally ornamented work, which is the radical defect in the "Decline and Fall." Christianity alone receives no embellishment from the magic of Gibbon's language; his imagination is dead to its moral dignity; it is kept down by a general zone of jealous disparagement, or neutralized by a painfully elaborate exposition of its darker and degenerate periods. There are occasions, indeed, when its pure and exalted humanity, when its manifestly beneficial influence, can compel even him, as it were, to fairness, and kindle his unguarded eloquence to its usual fervor; but, in general, he soon relapses into a frigid apathy; affects an ostentatiously severe impartiality; notes all the faults of Christians in every age with bitter and almost malignant sarcasm; reluctantly, and with exception and reservation, admits their claim to admiration. This inextricable bias appears even to influence his manner of composition. While all the other assailants of the Roman empire, whether warlike or religious, the Goth, the Hun, the Arab, the Tartar, Alaric and Attila, Mahomet, and Zengis, and Tamerlane, are each introduced upon the scene almost with dramatic animation—their progress related in a full, complete, and unbroken narrative—the triumph of Christianity alone takes the form of a cold and critical disquisition. The successes of barbarous energy and brute force call forth all the consummate skill of composition; while the moral triumphs of Christian benevolence—the tranquil heroism of endurance, the blameless purity, the contempt of guilty fame and of honors destructive to the human race, which, had they assumed the proud name of philosophy, would have been blazoned in his brightest words, because they own religion as their principle—sink into narrow asceticism. The glories of Christianity, in short, touch on no chord in the heart of the writer; his imagination remains unkindled; his words, though they maintain their stately and measured march, have become cool, argumentative, and inanimate. Who would obscure one hue of that gorgeous coloring in which Gibbon has invested the dying forms of Paganism, or darken one paragraph in his splendid view of the rise and progress of Mahometanism? But who would not have wished that the same equal justice had been done to Christianity; that its real character and deeply penetrating influence had been traced with the same philosophical sagacity, and represented with more sober, as would become its quiet course, and perhaps less picturesque, but still with lively and attractive, descriptiveness? He might have thrown aside, with the same scorn, the mass of ecclesiastical fiction which envelops the early history of the church, stripped off the legendary romance, and brought out the facts in their primitive nakedness and simplicity—if he had but allowed those facts the benefit of the glowing eloquence which he denied to them alone. He might have annihilated the whole fabric of post-apostolic miracles, if he had left uninjured by sarcastic insinuation those of the New Testament; he might have cashiered, with Dodwell, the whole host of martyrs, which owe their existence to the prodigal invention of later days, had he but bestowed fair room, and dwelt with his ordinary energy on the sufferings of the genuine witnesses to the truth of Christianity, the Polycarps, or the martyrs of Vienne. And indeed, if, after all, the view of the early progress of Christianity be melancholy and humiliating we must beware lest we charge the whole of this on the infidelity of the historian. It is idle, it is disingenuous, to deny or to dissemble the early depravations of Christianity, its gradual but rapid departure from its primitive simplicity and purity, still more, from its spirit of universal love. It may be no unsalutary lesson to the Christian world, that this silent, this unavoidable, perhaps, yet fatal change shall have been drawn by an impartial, or even an hostile hand. The Christianity of every age may take warning, lest by its own narrow views, its want of wisdom, and its want of charity, it give the same advantage to the future unfriendly historian, and disparage the cause of true religion.

The design of the present edition is partly corrective, partly supplementary: corrective, by notes, which point out (it is hoped, in a perfectly candid and dispassionate spirit with no desire but to establish the truth) such inaccuracies or misstatements as may have been detected, particularly with regard to Christianity; and which thus, with the previous caution, may counteract to a considerable extent the unfair and unfavorable impression created against rational religion: supplementary, by adding such additional information as the editor's reading may have been able to furnish, from original documents or books, not accessible at the time when Gibbon wrote.

The work originated in the editor's habit of noting on the margin of his copy of Gibbon references to such authors as had discovered errors, or thrown new light on the subjects treated by Gibbon. These had grown to some extent, and seemed to him likely to be of use to others. The annotations of M. Guizot also appeared to him worthy of being better known to the English public than they were likely to be, as appended to the French translation.

The chief works from which the editor has derived his materials are, I. The French translation, with notes by M. Guizot; 2d edition, Paris, 1828. The editor has translated almost all the notes of M. Guizot. Where he has not altogether agreed with him, his respect for the learning and judgment of that writer has, in general, induced him to retain the statement from which he has ventured to differ, with the grounds on which he formed his own opinion. In the notes on Christianity, he has retained all those of M. Guizot, with his own, from the conviction, that on such a subject, to many, the authority of a French statesman, a Protestant, and a rational and sincere Christian, would appear more independent and unbiassed, and therefore be more commanding, than that of an English clergyman.

The editor has not scrupled to transfer the notes of M. Guizot to the present work. The well-known zeal for knowledge, displayed in all the writings of that distinguished historian, has led to the natural inference, that he would not be displeased at the attempt to make them of use to the English readers of Gibbon. The notes of M. Guizot are signed with the letter G.

II. The German translation, with the notes of Wenck. Unfortunately this learned translator died, after having completed only the first volume; the rest of the work was executed by a very inferior hand.

The notes of Wenck are extremely valuable; many of them have been adopted by M. Guizot; they are distinguished by the letter W. [*]

[* The editor regrets that he has not been able to find the Italian translation, mentioned by Gibbon himself with some respect. It is not in our great libraries, the Museum or the Bodleian; and he has never found any bookseller in London who has seen it.]

III. The new edition of Le Beau's "Histoire du Bas Empire, with notes by M. St. Martin, and M. Brosset." That distinguished Armenian scholar, M. St. Martin (now, unhappily, deceased) had added much information from Oriental writers, particularly from those of Armenia, as well as from more general sources. Many of his observations have been found as applicable to the work of Gibbon as to that of Le Beau.

IV. The editor has consulted the various answers made to Gibbon on the first appearance of his work; he must confess, with little profit. They were, in general, hastily compiled by inferior and now forgotten writers, with the exception of Bishop Watson, whose able apology is rather a general argument, than an examination of misstatements. The name of Milner stands higher with a certain class of readers, but will not carry much weight with the severe investigator of history.

V. Some few classical works and fragments have come to light, since the appearance of Gibbon's History, and have been noticed in their respective places; and much use has been made, in the latter volumes particularly, of the increase to our stores of Oriental literature. The editor cannot, indeed, pretend to have followed his author, in these gleanings, over the whole vast field of his inquiries; he may have overlooked or may not have been able to command some works, which might have thrown still further light on these subjects; but he trusts that what he has adduced will be of use to the student of historic truth.

The editor would further observe, that with regard to some other objectionable passages, which do not involve misstatement or inaccuracy, he has intentionally abstained from directing particular attention towards them by any special protest.

The editor's notes are marked M.

A considerable part of the quotations (some of which in the later editions had fallen into great confusion) have been verified, and have been corrected by the latest and best editions of the authors.

June, 1845.

PREFACE OF THE AUTHOR

It is not my intention to detain the reader by expatiating on the variety or the importance of the subject, which I have undertaken to treat; since the merit of the choice would serve to render the weakness of the execution still more apparent, and still less excusable. But as I have presumed to lay before the public a first volume only [1] of the History of the Decline and Fall of the Roman Empire, it will, perhaps, be expected that I should explain, in a few words, the nature and limits of my general plan.

[Footnote 1: The first volume of the quarto, which contained the sixteen first chapters.]

The memorable series of revolutions, which in the course of about thirteen centuries gradually undermined, and at length destroyed, the solid fabric of human greatness, may, with some propriety, be divided into the three following periods:

I. The first of these periods may be traced from the age of Trajan and the Antonines, when the Roman monarchy, having attained its full strength and maturity, began to verge towards its decline; and will extend to the subversion of the Western Empire, by the barbarians of Germany and Scythia, the rude ancestors of the most polished nations of modern Europe. This extraordinary revolution, which subjected Rome to the power of a Gothic conqueror, was completed about the beginning of the sixth century.

II. The second period of the Decline and Fall of Rome may be supposed to commence with the reign of Justinian, who, by his laws, as well as by his victories, restored a transient splendor to the Eastern Empire. It will comprehend the invasion of Italy by the Lombards; the conquest of the Asiatic and African provinces by the Arabs, who embraced the religion of Mahomet; the revolt of the Roman people against the feeble princes of Constantinople; and the elevation of Charlemagne, who, in the year eight hundred, established the second, or German Empire of the West

III. The last and longest of these periods includes about six centuries and a half; from the revival of the Western Empire, till the taking of Constantinople by the Turks, and the extinction of a degenerate race of princes, who continued to assume the titles of Caesar and Augustus, after their dominions were contracted to the limits of a single city; in which the language, as well as manners, of the ancient Romans, had been long since forgotten. The writer who should undertake to relate the events of this period, would find himself obliged to enter into the general history of the Crusades, as far as they contributed to the ruin of the Greek Empire; and he would scarcely be able to restrain his curiosity from making some inquiry into the state of the city of Rome, during the darkness and confusion of the middle ages.

As I have ventured, perhaps too hastily, to commit to the press a work which in every sense of the word, deserves the epithet of imperfect. I consider myself as contracting an engagement to finish, most probably in a second volume, [2] the first of these memorable periods; and to deliver to the Public the complete History of the Decline and Fall of Rome, from the age of the Antonines to the subversion of the Western Empire. With regard to the subsequent periods, though I may entertain some hopes, I dare not presume to give any assurances. The execution of the extensive plan which I have described, would connect the ancient and modern history of the world; but it would require many years of health, of leisure, and of perseverance.

[Footnote 2: The Author, as it frequently happens, took an inadequate measure of his growing work. The remainder of the first period has filled two volumes in quarto, being the third, fourth, fifth, and sixth volumes of the octavo edition.]

Bentinck Street, February 1, 1776.

P. S. The entire History, which is now published, of the Decline and Fall of the Roman Empire in the West, abundantly discharges my engagements with the Public. Perhaps their favorable opinion may encourage me to prosecute a work, which, however laborious it may seem, is the most agreeable occupation of my leisure hours.

Bentinck Street, March 1, 1781.

An Author easily persuades himself that the public opinion is still favorable to his labors; and I have now embraced the serious resolution of proceeding to the last period of my original design, and of the Roman Empire, the taking of Constantinople by the Turks, in the year one thousand four hundred and fifty-three. The most patient Reader, who computes that three ponderous [3] volumes have been already employed on the events of four centuries, may, perhaps, be alarmed at the long prospect of nine hundred years. But it is not my intention to expatiate with the same minuteness on the whole series of the Byzantine history. At our entrance into this period, the reign of Justinian, and the conquests of the Mahometans, will deserve and detain our attention, and the last age of Constantinople (the Crusades and the Turks) is connected with the revolutions of Modern Europe. From the seventh to the eleventh century, the obscure interval will be supplied by a concise narrative of such facts as may still appear either interesting or important.

[Footnote 3: The first six volumes of the octavo edition.] Bentinck Street, March 1, 1782.

PREFACE TO THE FIRST VOLUME

Diligence and accuracy are the only merits which an historical writer may ascribe to himself; if any merit, indeed, can be assumed from the performance of an indispensable duty. I may therefore be allowed to say, that I have carefully examined all the original materials that could illustrate the subject which I had undertaken to treat. Should I ever complete the extensive design which has been sketched out in the Preface, I might perhaps conclude it with a critical account of the authors consulted during the progress of the whole work; and however such an attempt might incur the censure of ostentation, I am persuaded that it would be susceptible of entertainment, as well as information.

At present I shall content myself with a single observation.

The biographers, who, under the reigns of Diocletian and Constantine, composed, or rather compiled, the lives of the Emperors, from Hadrian to the sons of Carus, are usually mentioned under the names of Aelius Spartianus, Julius Capitolinus, Aelius Lampridius, Vulcatius Gallicanus, Trebellius Pollio and Flavius Vopiscus. But there is so much perplexity in the titles of the MSS., and so many disputes have arisen among the critics (see Fabricius, Biblioth. Latin. l. iii. c. 6) concerning their number, their names, and their respective property, that for the most part I have quoted them without distinction, under the general and well-known title of the Augustan History.

PREFACE TO THE FOURTH VOLUME OF THEORIGINAL QUARTO EDITION

I now discharge my promise, and complete my design, of writing the History of the Decline and Fall of the Roman Empire, both in the West and the East. The whole period extends from the age of Trajan and the Antonines, to the taking of Constantinople by Mahomet the Second; and includes a review of the Crusades, and the state of Rome during the middle ages. Since the publication of the first volume, twelve years have elapsed; twelve years, according to my wish, "of health, of leisure, and of perseverance." I may now congratulate my deliverance from a long and laborious service, and my satisfaction will be pure and perfect, if the public favor should be extended to the conclusion of my work.

It was my first intention to have collected, under one view, the numerous authors, of every age and language, from whom I have derived the materials of this history; and I am still convinced that the apparent ostentation would be more than compensated by real use. If I have renounced this idea, if I have declined an undertaking which had obtained the approbation of a master-artist, [4] my excuse may be found in the extreme difficulty of assigning a proper measure to such a catalogue. A naked list of names and editions would not be satisfactory either to myself or my readers: the characters of the principal Authors of the Roman and Byzantine History have been occasionally connected with the events which they describe; a more copious and critical inquiry might indeed deserve, but it would demand, an elaborate volume, which might swell by degrees into a general library of historical writers. For the present, I shall content myself with renewing my serious protestation, that I have always endeavored to draw from the fountain-head; that my curiosity, as well as a sense of duty, has always urged me to study the originals; and that, if they have sometimes eluded my search, I have carefully marked the secondary evidence, on whose faith a passage or a fact were reduced to depend.

[Footnote 4: See Dr. Robertson's Preface to his History of America.]

I shall soon revisit the banks of the Lake of Lausanne, a country which I have known and loved from my early youth. Under a mild government, amidst a beauteous landscape, in a life of leisure and independence, and among a people of easy and elegant manners, I have enjoyed, and may again hope to enjoy, the varied pleasures of retirement and society. But I shall ever glory in the name and character of an Englishman: I am proud of my birth in a free and enlightened country; and the approbation of that country is the best and most honorable reward of my labors. Were I ambitious of any other Patron than the Public, I would inscribe this work to a Statesman, who, in a long, a stormy, and at length an unfortunate administration, had many political opponents, almost without a personal enemy; who has retained, in his fall from power, many faithful and disinterested friends; and who, under the pressure of severe infirmity, enjoys the lively vigor of his mind, and the felicity of his incomparable temper. Lord North will permit me to express the feelings of friendship in the language of truth: but even truth and friendship should be silent, if he still dispensed the favors of the crown.

In a remote solitude, vanity may still whisper in my ear, that my readers, perhaps, may inquire whether, in the conclusion of the present work, I am now taking an everlasting farewell. They shall hear all that I know myself, and all that I could reveal to the most intimate friend. The motives of action or silence are now equally balanced; nor can I pronounce, in my most secret thoughts, on which side the scale will preponderate. I cannot dissemble that six quartos must have tried, and may have exhausted, the indulgence of the Public; that, in the repetition of similar attempts, a successful Author has much more to lose than he can hope to gain; that I am now descending into the vale of years; and that the most respectable of my countrymen, the men whom I aspire to imitate, have resigned the pen of history about the same period of their lives. Yet I consider that the annals of ancient and modern times may afford many rich and interesting subjects; that I am still possessed of health and leisure; that by the practice of writing, some skill and facility must be acquired; and that, in the ardent pursuit of truth and knowledge, I am not conscious of decay. To an active mind, indolence is more painful than labor; and the first months of my liberty will be occupied and amused in the excursions of curiosity and taste. By such temptations, I have been sometimes seduced from the rigid duty even of a pleasing and voluntary task: but my time will now be my own; and in the use or abuse of independence, I shall no longer fear my own reproaches or those of my friends. I am fairly entitled to a year of jubilee: next summer and the following winter will rapidly pass away; and experience only can determine whether I shall still prefer the freedom and variety of study to the design and composition of a regular work, which animates, while it confines, the daily application of the Author.

Caprice and accident may influence my choice; but the dexterity of self-love will contrive to applaud either active industry or philosophic repose.

Downing Street, May 1, 1788.

P. S. I shall embrace this opportunity of introducing two verbal remarks, which have not conveniently offered themselves to my notice. 1. As often as I use the definitions of beyond the Alps, the Rhine, the

Danube, &c., I generally suppose myself at Rome, and afterwards at Constantinople; without observing whether this relative geography may agree with the local, but variable, situation of the reader, or the historian. 2. In proper names of foreign, and especially of Oriental origin, it should be always our aim to express, in our English version, a faithful copy of the original. But this rule, which is founded on a just regard to uniformity and truth, must often be relaxed; and the exceptions will be limited or enlarged by the custom of the language and the taste of the interpreter. Our alphabets may be often defective; a harsh sound, an uncouth spelling, might offend the ear or the eye of our countrymen; and some words, notoriously corrupt, are fixed, and, as it were, naturalized in the vulgar tongue. The prophet Mohammed can no longer be stripped of the famous, though improper, appellation of Mahomet: the well-known cities of Aleppo, Damascus, and Cairo, would almost be lost in the strange descriptions of Haleb, Demashk, and Al Cahira: the titles and offices of the Ottoman empire are fashioned by the practice of three hundred years; and we are pleased to blend the three Chinese monosyllables, Con-fu-tzee, in the respectable name of Confucius, or even to adopt the Portuguese corruption of Mandarin. But I would vary the use of Zoroaster and Zerdusht, as I drew my information from Greece or Persia: since our connection with India, the genuine Timour is restored to the throne of Tamerlane: our most correct writers have retrenched the Al, the superfluous article, from the Koran; and we escape an ambiguous termination, by adopting Moslem instead of Musulman, in the plural number. In these, and in a thousand examples, the shades of distinction are often minute; and I can feel, where I cannot explain, the motives of my choice.

CHAPTER I

THE EXTENT OF THE EMPIRE IN THE AGE OF ANTONINES

PART I

In the second century of the Christian Aera, the empire of Rome comprehended the fairest part of the earth, and the most civilized portion of mankind. The frontiers of that extensive monarchy were guarded by ancient renown and disciplined valor. The gentle but powerful influence of laws and manners had gradually cemented the union of the provinces. Their peaceful inhabitants enjoyed and abused the advantages of wealth and luxury. The image of a free constitution was preserved with decent reverence: the Roman senate appeared to possess the sovereign authority, and devolved on the emperors all the executive powers of government. During a happy period of more than fourscore years, the public administration was conducted by the virtue and abilities of Nerva, Trajan, Hadrian, and the two Antonines. It is the design of this, and of the two succeeding chapters, to describe the prosperous condition of their empire; and after wards, from the death of Marcus Antoninus, to deduce the most important circumstances of its decline and fall; a revolution which will ever be remembered, and is still felt by the nations of the earth.

The principal conquests of the Romans were achieved under the republic; and the emperors, for the most part, were satisfied with preserving those dominions which had been acquired by the policy of the senate, the active emulations of the consuls, and the martial enthusiasm of the people. The seven first centuries were filled with a rapid succession of triumphs; but it was reserved for Augustus to relinquish the ambitious design of subduing the whole earth, and to introduce a spirit of moderation into the public councils. Inclined to peace by his temper and situation, it was easy for him to discover that Rome, in her present exalted situation, had much less to hope than to fear from the chance of arms; and that, in the prosecution of remote wars, the undertaking became every day more difficult, the event more doubtful, and the possession more precarious, and less beneficial. The experience of Augustus added weight to these salutary reflections, and effectually convinced him that, by the prudent vigor of his counsels, it would be easy to secure every concession which the safety or the dignity of Rome might require from the most formidable barbarians. Instead of exposing his person and his legions to the arrows of the Parthians, he obtained, by an honorable treaty, the restitution of the standards and prisoners which had been taken in the defeat of Crassus. [1]

[Footnote 1: Dion Cassius, (l. liv. p. 736,) with the annotations of Reimar, who has collected all that Roman vanity has left upon the subject. The marble of Ancyra, on which Augustus recorded his own exploits, asserted that he compelled the Parthians to restore the ensigns of Crassus.]

His generals, in the early part of his reign, attempted the reduction of Ethiopia and Arabia Felix. They marched near a thousand miles to the south of the tropic; but the heat of the climate soon repelled the invaders, and protected the un-warlike natives of those sequestered regions. [2] The northern countries of Europe scarcely deserved the expense and labor of conquest. The forests and morasses of Germany were filled with a hardy race of barbarians, who despised life when it was separated from freedom; and though, on the first attack, they seemed to yield to the weight of the Roman power, they soon, by a signal act of despair, regained their independence, and reminded Augustus of the vicissitude of fortune. [3] On the death of that emperor, his testament was publicly read in the senate. He bequeathed, as a valuable legacy to his successors, the advice of confining the empire within those limits which nature seemed to have placed as its permanent bulwarks and boundaries: on the west, the Atlantic Ocean; the Rhine and Danube on the north; the Euphrates on the east; and towards the south, the sandy deserts of Arabia and Africa. [4]

[Footnote 2: Strabo, (l. xvi. p. 780,) Pliny the elder, (Hist. Natur. l. vi. c. 32, 35, [28, 29,]) and Dion Cassius, (l. liii. p. 723, and l. liv. p. 734,) have left us very curious details concerning these wars. The Romans made themselves masters of Mariaba, or Merab, a city of Arabia Felix, well known to the Orientals. (See Abulfeda and the Nubian geography, p. 52) They were arrived within three days' journey of the spice country, the rich object of their invasion.

Note: It is the city of Merab that the Arabs say was the residence of Belkis, queen of Saba, who desired to see Solomon. A dam, by which the waters collected in its neighborhood were kept back, having been swept away, the sudden inundation destroyed this city, of which, nevertheless, vestiges remain. It bordered on a country called Adramout, where a particular aromatic plant grows: it is for this reason that we read in the history of the Roman expedition, that they were arrived within three days' journey of the spice country.—G. Compare Malte-Brun, Geogr. Eng. trans. vol. ii. p. 215. The period of this flood has been copiously discussed by Reiske, (Program. de vetusta Epocha Arabum, ruptura cataractae Merabensis.) Add. Johannsen, Hist. Yemanae, p. 282. Bonn, 1828; and see Gibbon, note 16. to Chap. L.—M.

Note: Two, according to Strabo. The detailed account of Strabo makes the invaders fail before Marsuabae: this cannot be the same place as Mariaba. Ukert observes, that Aelius Gallus would not have failed for want of water before Mariaba. (See M. Guizot's note above.) "Either, therefore, they were different places, or Strabo is mistaken." (Ukert, Geographic der Griechen und Romer, vol. i. p. 181.) Strabo, indeed, mentions Mariaba distinct from Marsuabae. Gibbon has followed Pliny in reckoning Mariaba among the conquests of Gallus. There can be little doubt that he is wrong, as Gallus did not approach the capital of Sabaea. Compare the note of the Oxford editor of Strabo.—M.]

[Footnote 3: By the slaughter of Varus and his three legions. See the first book of the Annals of Tacitus. Sueton. in August. c. 23, and Velleius Paterculus, l. ii. c. 117, &c. Augustus did not receive the melancholy news with all the temper and firmness that might have been expected from his character.]

[Footnote 4: Tacit. Annal. l. ii. Dion Cassius, l. lvi. p. 833, and the speech of Augustus himself, in Julian's Caesars. It receives great light from the learned notes of his French translator, M. Spanheim.]

Happily for the repose of mankind, the moderate system recommended by the wisdom of Augustus, was adopted by the fears and vices of his immediate successors. Engaged in the pursuit of pleasure, or in the exercise of tyranny, the first Caesars seldom showed themselves to the armies, or to the provinces; nor were they disposed to suffer, that those triumphs which their indolence neglected, should be usurped by the conduct and valor of their lieutenants. The military fame of a subject was considered as an insolent invasion of the Imperial prerogative; and it became the duty, as well as interest, of every Roman general, to guard the frontiers intrusted to his care, without aspiring to conquests which might have proved no less fatal to himself than to the vanquished barbarians. [5]

[Footnote 5: Germanicus, Suetonius Paulinus, and Agricola were checked and recalled in the course of their victories. Corbulo was put to death. Military merit, as it is admirably expressed by Tacitus, was, in the strictest sense of the word, imperatoria virtus.]

The only accession which the Roman empire received, during the first century of the Christian Aera, was the province of Britain. In this single instance, the successors of Caesar and Augustus were persuaded to follow the example of the former, rather than the precept of the latter. The proximity of its situation to the coast of Gaul seemed to invite their arms; the pleasing though doubtful intelligence of a pearl fishery, attracted their avarice; [6] and as Britain was viewed in the light of a distinct and insulated world, the conquest scarcely formed any exception to the general system of continental measures. After a war of about forty years, undertaken by the most stupid, [7] maintained by the most dissolute, and terminated by the most timid of all the emperors, the far greater part of the island submitted to the Roman yoke. [8] The various tribes of Britain possessed valor without conduct, and the love of freedom without the spirit of union. They took up arms with savage fierceness; they laid them down, or turned them against each other, with wild inconsistency; and while they fought singly, they were successively subdued. Neither the fortitude of Caractacus, nor the despair of Boadicea, nor the fanaticism of the Druids, could avert the slavery of their country, or resist the steady progress of the Imperial generals, who maintained the national glory, when the throne was disgraced by the weakest, or the most vicious of mankind. At the very time when Domitian, confined to his palace, felt the terrors which he inspired, his legions, under the command of the virtuous Agricola, defeated the collected force of the Caledonians, at the foot of the Grampian Hills; and his fleets, venturing to explore an unknown and dangerous navigation, displayed the Roman arms round every part of the island. The conquest of Britain was considered as already achieved; and it was the design of Agricola to complete and insure his success, by the easy reduction of Ireland, for which, in his opinion, one legion and a few auxiliaries were sufficient. [9] The western isle might be improved into a valuable possession, and the Britons would wear their chains with the less reluctance, if the prospect and example of freedom were on every side removed from before their eyes.

[Footnote 6: Caesar himself conceals that ignoble motive; but it is mentioned by Suetonius, c. 47. The British pearls proved, however, of little value, on account of their dark and livid color. Tacitus observes, with reason, (in Agricola, c. 12,) that it was an inherent defect. "Ego facilius crediderim, naturam margaritis deesse quam nobis avaritiam."]

[Footnote 7: Claudius, Nero, and Domitian. A hope is expressed by Pomponius Mela, l. iii. c. 6, (he wrote under Claudius,) that, by the success of the Roman arms, the island and its savage inhabitants would soon be better known. It is amusing enough to peruse such passages in the midst of London.]

[Footnote 8: See the admirable abridgment given by Tacitus, in the life of Agricola, and copiously, though perhaps not completely, illustrated by our own antiquarians, Camden and Horsley.]

[Footnote 9: The Irish writers, jealous of their national honor, are extremely provoked on this occasion, both with Tacitus and with Agricola.]

But the superior merit of Agricola soon occasioned his removal from the government of Britain; and forever disappointed this rational, though extensive scheme of conquest. Before his departure, the prudent general had provided for security as well as for dominion. He had observed, that the island is almost divided into two unequal parts by the opposite gulfs, or, as they are now called, the Friths of Scotland. Across the narrow interval of about forty miles, he had drawn a line of military stations, which was afterwards fortified, in the reign of Antoninus Pius, by a turf rampart, erected on foundations of stone. [10] This wall of Antoninus, at a small distance beyond the modern cities of Edinburgh and Glasgow, was fixed as the limit of the Roman province. The native Caledonians preserved, in the northern extremity of the island, their wild independence, for which they were not less indebted to their poverty than to their valor. Their incursions were frequently repelled and chastised; but their country was never subdued. [11] The masters of the fairest and most wealthy climates of the globe turned with contempt from gloomy hills, assailed by the winter tempest, from lakes concealed in a blue mist, and from cold and lonely heaths, over which the deer of the forest were chased by a troop of naked barbarians. [12]

[Footnote 10: See Horsley's Britannia Romana, l. i. c. 10. Note: Agricola fortified the line from Dumbarton to Edinburgh, consequently within Scotland. The emperor Hadrian, during his residence in Britain, about the year 121, caused a rampart of earth to be raised between Newcastle and Carlisle. Antoninus Pius, having gained new victories over the Caledonians, by the ability of his general, Lollius, Urbicus, caused a new rampart of earth to be constructed between Edinburgh and Dumbarton. Lastly, Septimius Severus caused a wall of stone to be built parallel to the rampart of Hadrian, and on the same locality. See John Warburton's Vallum Romanum, or the History and Antiquities of the Roman Wall. London, 1754, 4to.—W. See likewise a good note on the Roman wall in Lingard's History of England, vol. i. p. 40, 4to edit—M.]

[Footnote 11: The poet Buchanan celebrates with elegance and spirit (see his Sylvae, v.) the unviolated independence of his native country. But, if the single testimony of Richard of Cirencester was sufficient to create a Roman province of Vespasiana to the north of the wall, that independence would be reduced within very narrow limits.]

[Footnote 12: See Appian (in Prooem.) and the uniform imagery of Ossian's Poems, which, according to every hypothesis, were composed by a native Caledonian.]

Such was the state of the Roman frontiers, and such the maxims of Imperial policy, from the death of Augustus to the accession of Trajan. That virtuous and active prince had received the education of a soldier, and possessed the talents of a general. [13] The peaceful system of his predecessors was interrupted by scenes of war and conquest; and the legions, after a long interval, beheld a military emperor at their head. The first exploits of Trajan were against the Dacians, the most warlike of men, who dwelt beyond the Danube, and who, during the reign of Domitian, had insulted, with impunity, the Majesty of Rome. [14] To the strength and fierceness of barbarians they added a contempt for life, which was derived from a warm persuasion of the immortality and transmigration of the soul. [15] Decebalus, the Dacian king, approved himself a rival not unworthy of Trajan; nor did he despair of his own and the public fortune, till, by the confession of his enemies, he had exhausted every resource both of valor and policy. [16] This memorable war, with a very short suspension of hostilities, lasted five years; and as the emperor could exert, without control, the whole force of the state, it was terminated by an absolute submission of the barbarians. [17] The new province of Dacia, which formed a second exception to the precept of Augustus, was about thirteen hundred miles in circumference. Its natural boundaries were the Niester, the Teyss or Tibiscus, the Lower Danube, and the Euxine Sea. The vestiges of a military road may still be traced from the banks of the Danube to the neighborhood of Bender, a place famous in modern history, and the actual frontier of the Turkish and Russian empires. [18]

[Footnote 13: See Pliny's Panegyric, which seems founded on facts.]

[Footnote 14: Dion Cassius, l. lxvii.]

[Footnote 15: Herodotus, l. iv. c. 94. Julian in the Caesars, with Spanheims observations.]

[Footnote 16: Plin. Epist. viii. 9.]

[Footnote 17: Dion Cassius, l. lxviii. p. 1123, 1131. Julian in Caesaribus Eutropius, viii. 2, 6. Aurelius Victor in Epitome.]

[Footnote 18: See a Memoir of M. d'Anville, on the Province of Dacia, in the Academie des Inscriptions, tom. xxviii. p. 444—468.]

Trajan was ambitious of fame; and as long as mankind shall continue to bestow more liberal applause on their destroyers than on their benefactors, the thirst of military glory will ever be the vice of the most exalted characters. The praises of Alexander, transmitted by a succession of poets and historians, had kindled a dangerous emulation in the mind of Trajan. Like him, the Roman emperor undertook an expedition against the nations of the East; but he lamented with a sigh, that his advanced age scarcely left him any hopes of equalling the renown of the son of Philip. [19] Yet the success of Trajan, however transient, was rapid and specious. The degenerate Parthians, broken by intestine discord, fled before his arms. He descended the River Tigris in triumph, from the mountains of Armenia to the Persian Gulf. He enjoyed the honor of being the first, as he was the last, of the Roman generals, who ever navigated that remote sea. His fleets ravaged the coast of Arabia; and Trajan vainly flattered himself that he was approaching towards the confines of India. [20] Every day the astonished senate received the intelligence of new names and new nations, that acknowledged his sway. They were informed that the kings of Bosphorus, Colchos, Iberia, Albania, Osrhoene, and even the Parthian monarch himself, had accepted their diadems from the hands of the emperor; that the independent tribes of the Median and Carduchian hills had implored his protection; and that the rich countries of Armenia, Mesopotamia, and Assyria, were reduced into the state of provinces. [21] But the death of Trajan soon clouded the splendid prospect; and it was justly to be dreaded, that so many distant nations would throw off the unaccustomed yoke, when they were no longer restrained by the powerful hand which had imposed it.

[Footnote 19: Trajan's sentiments are represented in a very just and lively manner in the Caesars of Julian.]

[Footnote 20: Eutropius and Sextus Rufus have endeavored to perpetuate the illusion. See a very sensible dissertation of M. Freret in the Academie des Inscriptions, tom. xxi. p. 55.]

[Footnote 21: Dion Cassius, l. lxviii.; and the Abbreviators.]

It was an ancient tradition, that when the Capitol was founded by one of the Roman kings, the god Terminus (who presided over boundaries, and was represented, according to the fashion of that age, by a large stone) alone, among all the inferior deities, refused to yield his place to Jupiter himself. A favorable inference was drawn from his obstinacy, which was interpreted by the augurs as a sure presage that the boundaries of the Roman power would never recede. [22] During many ages, the prediction, as it is usual, contributed to its own accomplishment. But though Terminus had resisted the Majesty of Jupiter, he submitted to the authority of the emperor Hadrian. [23] The resignation of all the eastern conquests of Trajan was the first measure of his reign. He restored to the Parthians the election of an independent sovereign; withdrew the Roman garrisons from the provinces of Armenia, Mesopotamia, and Assyria; and, in compliance with the precept of Augustus, once more established the Euphrates as the frontier of the empire. [24] Censure, which arraigns the public actions and the private motives of princes, has ascribed to envy, a conduct which might be attributed to the prudence and moderation of Hadrian. The various character of that emperor, capable, by turns, of the meanest and the most generous sentiments, may afford some color to the suspicion. It was, however, scarcely in his power to place the superiority of his predecessor in a more conspicuous light, than by thus confessing himself unequal to the task of defending the conquests of Trajan.

[Footnote 22: Ovid. Fast. l. ii. ver. 667. See Livy, and Dionysius of Halicarnassus, under the reign of Tarquin.]

[Footnote 23: St. Augustin is highly delighted with the proof of the weakness of Terminus, and the vanity of the Augurs. See De Civitate Dei, iv. 29. Note: The turn of Gibbon's sentence is Augustin's: "Plus Hadrianum regem hominum, quam regem Deorum timuisse videatur."—M]

[Footnote 24: See the Augustan History, p. 5, Jerome's Chronicle, and all the Epitomizers. It is somewhat surprising, that this memorable event should be omitted by Dion, or rather by Xiphilin.]

The martial and ambitious of spirit Trajan formed a very singular contrast with the moderation of his successor. The restless activity of Hadrian was not less remarkable when compared with the gentle repose of Antoninus Pius. The life of the former was almost a perpetual journey; and as he possessed the various talents of the soldier, the statesman, and the scholar, he gratified his curiosity in the discharge of his duty.

Careless of the difference of seasons and of climates, he marched on foot, and bare-headed, over the snows of Caledonia, and the sultry plains of the Upper Egypt; nor was there a province of the empire which, in the course of his reign, was not honored with the presence of the monarch. [25] But the tranquil life of Antoninus Pius was spent in the bosom of Italy, and, during the twenty-three years that he directed the public administration, the longest journeys of that amiable prince extended no farther than from his palace in Rome to the retirement of his Lanuvian villa. [26]

[Footnote 25: Dion, l. lxix. p. 1158. Hist. August. p. 5, 8. If all our historians were lost, medals, inscriptions, and other monuments, would be sufficient to record the travels of Hadrian. Note: The journeys of Hadrian are traced in a note on Solvet's translation of Hegewisch, Essai sur l'Epoque de Histoire Romaine la plus heureuse pour Genre Humain Paris, 1834, p. 123.—M.]

[Footnote 26: See the Augustan History and the Epitomes.]

Notwithstanding this difference in their personal conduct, the general system of Augustus was equally adopted and uniformly pursued by Hadrian and by the two Antonines. They persisted in the design of maintaining the dignity of the empire, without attempting to enlarge its limits. By every honorable expedient they invited the friendship of the barbarians; and endeavored to convince mankind that the Roman power, raised above the temptation of conquest, was actuated only by the love of order and justice. During a long period of forty-three years, their virtuous labors were crowned with success; and if we except a few slight hostilities, that served to exercise the legions of the frontier, the reigns of Hadrian and Antoninus Pius offer the fair prospect of universal peace. [27] The Roman name was revered among the most remote nations of the earth. The fiercest barbarians frequently submitted their differences to the arbitration of the emperor; and we are informed by a contemporary historian that he had seen ambassadors who were refused the honor which they came to solicit of being admitted into the rank of subjects. [28]

[Footnote 27: We must, however, remember, that in the time of Hadrian, a rebellion of the Jews raged with religious fury, though only in a single province. Pausanias (l. viii. c. 43) mentions two necessary and successful wars, conducted by the generals of Pius: 1st. Against the wandering Moors, who were driven into the solitudes of Atlas. 2d. Against the Brigantes of Britain, who had invaded the Roman province. Both these wars (with several other hostilities) are mentioned in the Augustan History, p. 19.]

[Footnote 28: Appian of Alexandria, in the preface to his History of the Roman Wars.]

PART II

The terror of the Roman arms added weight and dignity to the moderation of the emperors. They preserved peace by a constant preparation for war; and while justice regulated their conduct, they announced to the nations on their confines, that they were as little disposed to endure, as to offer an injury. The military strength, which it had been sufficient for Hadrian and the elder Antoninus to display, was exerted against the Parthians and the Germans by the emperor Marcus. The hostilities of the barbarians provoked the resentment of that philosophic monarch, and, in the prosecution of a just defence, Marcus and his generals obtained many signal victories, both on the Euphrates and on the Danube. [29] The military establishment of the Roman empire, which thus assured either its tranquillity or success, will now become the proper and important object of our attention.

[Footnote 29: Dion, l. lxxi. Hist. August. in Marco. The Parthian victories gave birth to a crowd of contemptible historians, whose memory has been rescued from oblivion and exposed to ridicule, in a very lively piece of criticism of Lucian.]

In the purer ages of the commonwealth, the use of arms was reserved for those ranks of citizens who had a country to love, a property to defend, and some share in enacting those laws, which it was their interest as well as duty to maintain. But in proportion as the public freedom was lost in extent of conquest, war was gradually improved into an art, and degraded into a trade. [30] The legions themselves, even at the time when they were recruited in the most distant provinces, were supposed to consist of Roman citizens. That distinction was generally considered, either as a legal qualification or as a proper recompense for the soldier; but a more serious regard was paid to the essential merit of age, strength, and military stature. [31] In all levies, a just preference was given to the climates of the North over those of the South: the race of men born to the exercise of arms was sought for in the country rather than in cities; and it was very reasonably presumed, that the hardy occupations of smiths, carpenters, and huntsmen, would supply more vigor and resolution than the sedentary trades which are employed in the service of luxury. [32] After every qualification of property had been laid aside, the armies of the Roman emperors were still commanded, for the most part, by officers of liberal birth and education; but the common soldiers, like the mercenary troops of modern Europe, were drawn from the meanest, and very frequently from the most profligate, of mankind.

[Footnote 30: The poorest rank of soldiers possessed above forty pounds sterling, (Dionys. Halicarn. iv. 17,) a very high qualification at a time when money was so scarce, that an ounce of silver was equivalent to seventy pounds weight of brass. The populace, excluded by the ancient constitution, were indiscriminately admitted by Marius. See Sallust. de Bell. Jugurth. c. 91. Note: On the uncertainty of all these estimates, and the difficulty of fixing the relative value of brass and silver, compare Niebuhr, vol. i. p. 473, &c. Eng. trans. p. 452. According to Niebuhr, the relative disproportion in value, between the two metals, arose, in a great degree from the abundance of brass or copper.—M. Compare also Dureau 'de la Malle Economie Politique des Romains especially L. l. c. ix.—M. 1845.]

[Footnote 31: Caesar formed his legion Alauda of Gauls and strangers; but it was during the license of civil war; and after the victory, he gave them the freedom of the city for their reward.]

[Footnote 32: See Vegetius, de Re Militari, l. i. c. 2—7.]

That public virtue, which among the ancients was denominated patriotism, is derived from a strong sense of our own interest in the preservation and prosperity of the free government of which we are members. Such a sentiment, which had rendered the legions of the republic almost invincible, could make but a very feeble impression on the mercenary servants of a despotic prince; and it became necessary to supply that defect by other motives, of a different, but not less forcible nature—honor and religion. The peasant, or mechanic, imbibed the useful prejudice that he was advanced to the more dignified profession of arms, in which his rank and reputation would depend on his own valor; and that, although the prowess of a private soldier must often escape the notice of fame, his own behavior might sometimes confer glory or disgrace on the company, the legion, or even the army, to whose honors he was associated. On his first entrance into the service, an oath was administered to him with every circumstance of solemnity. He promised never to desert his standard, to submit his own will to the commands of his leaders, and to sacrifice his life for the safety of the emperor and the empire. [33] The attachment of the Roman troops to their standards was inspired by the united influence of religion and of honor. The golden eagle, which glittered in the front of the legion, was the object of their fondest devotion; nor was it esteemed less impious than it was ignominious, to abandon that sacred ensign in the hour of danger. [34] These motives, which derived their strength from the imagination, were enforced by fears and hopes of a more substantial kind. Regular pay, occasional donatives, and a stated recompense, after the appointed time of service, alleviated the hardships of the military life, [35] whilst, on the other hand, it was impossible for cowardice or disobedience to escape the severest punishment. The centurions were authorized to chastise with blows, the generals had a right to punish with death;

and it was an inflexible maxim of Roman discipline, that a good soldier should dread his officers far more than the enemy. From such laudable arts did the valor of the Imperial troops receive a degree of firmness and docility unattainable by the impetuous and irregular passions of barbarians.

[Footnote 33: The oath of service and fidelity to the emperor was annually renewed by the troops on the first of January.]

[Footnote 34: Tacitus calls the Roman eagles, Bellorum Deos. They were placed in a chapel in the camp, and with the other deities received the religious worship of the troops. Note: See also Dio. Cass. xl. c. 18. —M.]

[Footnote 35: See Gronovius de Pecunia vetere, l. iii. p. 120, &c. The emperor Domitian raised the annual stipend of the legionaries to twelve pieces of gold, which, in his time, was equivalent to about ten of our guineas. This pay, somewhat higher than our own, had been, and was afterwards, gradually increased, according to the progress of wealth and military government. After twenty years' service, the veteran received three thousand denarii, (about one hundred pounds sterling,) or a proportionable allowance of land. The pay and advantages of the guards were, in general, about double those of the legions.]

And yet so sensible were the Romans of the imperfection of valor without skill and practice, that, in their language, the name of an army was borrowed from the word which signified exercise. [36] Military exercises were the important and unremitted object of their discipline. The recruits and young soldiers were constantly trained, both in the morning and in the evening, nor was age or knowledge allowed to excuse the veterans from the daily repetition of what they had completely learnt. Large sheds were erected in the winter-quarters of the troops, that their useful labors might not receive any interruption from the most tempestuous weather; and it was carefully observed, that the arms destined to this imitation of war, should be of double the weight which was required in real action. [37] It is not the purpose of this work to enter into any minute description of the Roman exercises. We shall only remark, that they comprehended whatever could add strength to the body, activity to the limbs, or grace to the motions. The soldiers were diligently instructed to march, to run, to leap, to swim, to carry heavy burdens, to handle every species of arms that was used either for offence or for defence, either in distant engagement or in a closer onset; to form a variety of evolutions; and to move to the sound of flutes in the Pyrrhic or martial dance. [38] In the midst of peace, the Roman troops familiarized themselves with the practice of war; and it is prettily remarked by an ancient historian who had fought against them, that the effusion of blood was the only circumstance which distinguished a field of battle from a field of exercise. [39] It was the policy of the ablest generals, and even of the emperors themselves, to encourage these military studies by their presence and example; and we are informed that Hadrian, as well as Trajan, frequently condescended to instruct the unexperienced soldiers, to reward the diligent, and sometimes to dispute with them the prize of superior strength or dexterity. [40] Under the reigns of those princes, the science of tactics was cultivated with success; and as long as the empire retained any vigor, their military instructions were respected as the most perfect model of Roman discipline.

[Footnote 36: Exercitus ab exercitando, Varro de Lingua Latina, l. iv. Cicero in Tusculan. l. ii. 37. 15. There is room for a very interesting work, which should lay open the connection between the languages and manners of nations. Note I am not aware of the existence, at present, of such a work; but the profound observations of the late William von Humboldt, in the introduction to his posthumously published Essay on the Language of the Island of Java, (uber die Kawi-sprache, Berlin, 1836,) may cause regret that this task was not completed by that accomplished and universal scholar.—M.]

[Footnote 37: Vegatius, l. ii. and the rest of his first book.]

[Footnote 38: The Pyrrhic dance is extremely well illustrated by M. le Beau, in the Academie des Inscriptions, tom. xxxv. p. 262, &c. That learned academician, in a series of memoirs, has collected all the passages of the ancients that relate to the Roman legion.]

[Footnote 39: Joseph. de Bell. Judaico, l. iii. c. 5. We are indebted to this Jew for some very curious details of Roman discipline.]

[Footnote 40: Plin. Panegyr. c. 13. Life of Hadrian, in the Augustan History.]

Nine centuries of war had gradually introduced into the service many alterations and improvements. The legions, as they are described by Polybius, [41] in the time of the Punic wars, differed very materially from those which achieved the victories of Caesar, or defended the monarchy of Hadrian and the Antonines.

The constitution of the Imperial legion may be described in a few words. [42] The heavy-armed infantry, which composed its principal strength, [43] was divided into ten cohorts, and fifty-five companies, under the orders of a correspondent number of tribunes and centurions. The first cohort, which always claimed the post of honor and the custody of the eagle, was formed of eleven hundred and five soldiers, the most approved for valor and fidelity. The remaining nine cohorts consisted each of five hundred and fifty-five; and the whole body of legionary infantry amounted to six thousand one hundred men. Their arms were uniform, and admirably adapted to the nature of their service: an open helmet, with a lofty crest; a breastplate, or coat of mail; greaves on their legs, and an ample buckler on their left arm. The buckler was of an oblong and concave figure, four feet in length, and two and a half in breadth, framed of a light wood, covered with a bull's hide, and strongly guarded with plates of brass. Besides a lighter spear, the legionary soldier grasped in his right hand the formidable pilum, a ponderous javelin, whose utmost length was about six feet, and which was terminated by a massy triangular point of steel of eighteen inches. [44] This instrument was indeed much inferior to our modern fire-arms; since it was exhausted by a single discharge, at the distance of only ten or twelve paces. Yet when it was launched by a firm and skilful hand, there was not any cavalry that durst venture within its reach, nor any shield or corselet that could sustain the impetuosity of its weight. As soon as the Roman had darted his pilum, he drew his sword, and rushed forwards to close with the enemy. His sword was a short well-tempered Spanish blade, that carried a double edge, and was alike suited to the purpose of striking or of pushing; but the soldier was always instructed to prefer the latter use of his weapon, as his own body remained less exposed, whilst he inflicted a more dangerous wound on his adversary. [45] The legion was usually drawn up eight deep; and the regular distance of three feet was left between the files as well as ranks. [46] A body of troops, habituated to preserve this open order, in a long front and a rapid charge, found themselves prepared to execute every disposition which the circumstances of war, or the skill of their leader, might suggest. The soldier possessed a free space for his arms and motions, and sufficient intervals were allowed, through which seasonable reenforcements might be introduced to the relief of the exhausted combatants. [47] The tactics of the Greeks and Macedonians were formed on very different principles. The strength of the phalanx depended on sixteen ranks of long pikes, wedged together in the closest array. [48] But it was soon discovered by reflection, as well as by the event, that the strength of the phalanx was unable to contend with the activity of the legion. [49

[Footnote 41: See an admirable digression on the Roman discipline, in the sixth book of his History.]

[Footnote 42: Vegetius de Re Militari, l. ii. c. 4, &c. Considerable part of his very perplexed abridgment was taken from the regulations of Trajan and Hadrian; and the legion, as he describes it, cannot suit any other age of the Roman empire.]

[Footnote 43: Vegetius de Re Militari, l. ii. c. 1. In the purer age of Caesar and Cicero, the word miles was almost confined to the infantry. Under the lower empire, and the times of chivalry, it was appropriated almost as exclusively to the men at arms, who fought on horseback.]

[Footnote 44: In the time of Polybius and Dionysius of Halicarnassus, (l. v. c. 45,) the steel point of the pilum seems to have been much longer. In the time of Vegetius, it was reduced to a foot, or even nine inches. I have chosen a medium.]

[Footnote 45: For the legionary arms, see Lipsius de Militia Romana, l. iii. c. 2—7.]

[Footnote 46: See the beautiful comparison of Virgil, Georgic ii. v. 279.]

[Footnote 47: M. Guichard, Memoires Militaires, tom. i. c. 4, and Nouveaux Memoires, tom. i. p. 293—311, has treated the subject like a scholar and an officer.]

[Footnote 48: See Arrian's Tactics. With the true partiality of a Greek, Arrian rather chose to describe the phalanx, of which he had read, than the legions which he had commanded.]

[Footnote 49: Polyb. l. xvii. (xviii. 9.)]

The cavalry, without which the force of the legion would have remained imperfect, was divided into ten troops or squadrons; the first, as the companion of the first cohort, consisted of a hundred and thirty-two men; whilst each of the other nine amounted only to sixty-six. The entire establishment formed a regiment, if we may use the modern expression, of seven hundred and twenty-six horse, naturally connected with its respective legion, but occasionally separated to act in the line, and to compose a part of the wings of the army. [50] The cavalry of the emperors was no longer composed, like that of the ancient republic, of the noblest youths of Rome and Italy, who, by performing their military service on horseback, prepared themselves for the offices of senator and consul; and solicited, by deeds of valor, the future suffrages of their countrymen. [51] Since the alteration of manners and government, the most wealthy of the equestrian order were engaged in the administration of justice, and of the revenue; [52] and whenever they embraced the profession of arms, they were immediately intrusted with a troop of horse, or a cohort of foot. [53] Trajan and Hadrian formed their cavalry from the same provinces, and the same class of their subjects, which recruited the ranks of the legion. The horses were bred, for the most part, in Spain or Cappadocia. The Roman troopers despised the complete armor with which the cavalry of the East was encumbered. Their more useful arms consisted in a helmet, an oblong shield, light boots, and a coat of mail. A javelin, and a long broad sword, were their principal weapons of offence. The use of lances and of iron maces they seem to have borrowed from the barbarians. [54]

[Footnote 50: Veget. de Re Militari, l. ii. c. 6. His positive testimony, which might be supported by circumstantial evidence, ought surely to silence those critics who refuse the Imperial legion its proper body of cavalry. Note: See also Joseph. B. J. iii. vi. 2.—M.]

[Footnote 51: See Livy almost throughout, particularly xlii. 61.]

[Footnote 52: Plin. Hist. Natur. xxxiii. 2. The true sense of that very curious passage was first discovered and illustrated by M. de Beaufort, Republique Romaine, l. ii. c. 2.]

[Footnote 53: As in the instance of Horace and Agricola. This appears to have been a defect in the Roman discipline; which Hadrian endeavored to remedy by ascertaining the legal age of a tribune. Note: These details are not altogether accurate. Although, in the latter days of the republic, and under the first emperors, the young Roman nobles obtained the command of a squadron or a cohort with greater facility than in the former times, they never obtained it without passing through a tolerably long military service. Usually they served first in the praetorian cohort, which was intrusted with the guard of the general: they were received into the companionship (contubernium) of some superior officer, and were there formed for duty. Thus Julius Caesar, though sprung from a great family, served first as contubernalis under the praetor, M. Thermus, and later under Servilius the Isaurian. (Suet. Jul. 2, 5. Plut. in Par. p. 516. Ed. Froben.) The example of Horace, which Gibbon adduces to prove that young knights were made tribunes immediately on entering the service, proves nothing. In the first place, Horace was not a knight; he was the son of a freedman of Venusia, in Apulia, who exercised the humble office of coactor exauctionum, (collector of payments at auctions.) (Sat. i. vi. 45, or 86.) Moreover, when the poet was made tribune, Brutus, whose army was nearly entirely composed of Orientals, gave this title to all the Romans of consideration who joined him. The emperors were still less difficult in their choice; the number of tribunes was augmented; the title and honors were conferred on persons whom they wished to attack to the court. Augustus conferred on the sons of senators, sometimes the tribunate, sometimes the command of a squadron. Claudius gave to the knights who entered into the service, first the command of a cohort of auxiliaries, later that of a squadron, and at length, for the first time, the tribunate. (Suet in Claud. with the notes of Ernesti.) The abuses that arose caused by the edict of Hadrian, which fixed the age at which that honor could be attained. (Spart. in Had. &c.) This edict was subsequently obeyed; for the emperor Valerian, in a letter addressed to Mulvius Gallinnus, praetorian praefect, excuses himself for having violated it in favor of the young Probus afterwards emperor, on whom he had conferred the tribunate at an earlier age on account of his rare talents. (Vopisc. in Prob. iv.)—W. and G. Agricola, though already invested with the title of tribune, was contubernalis in Britain with Suetonius Paulinus. Tac. Agr. v.—M.]

[Footnote 54: See Arrian's Tactics.]

The safety and honor of the empire was principally intrusted to the legions, but the policy of Rome condescended to adopt every useful instrument of war. Considerable levies were regularly made among the provincials, who had not yet deserved the honorable distinction of Romans. Many dependent princes and communities, dispersed round the frontiers, were permitted, for a while, to hold their freedom and security by the tenure of military service. [55] Even select troops of hostile barbarians were frequently compelled or persuaded to consume their dangerous valor in remote climates, and for the benefit of the state. [56] All these were included under the general name of auxiliaries; and howsoever they might vary according to the difference of times and circumstances, their numbers were seldom much inferior to those of the legions themselves. [57] Among the auxiliaries, the bravest and most faithful bands were placed under the command of praefects and centurions, and severely trained in the arts of Roman discipline; but the far greater part retained those arms, to which the nature of their country, or their early habits of life, more peculiarly adapted them. By this institution, each legion, to whom a certain proportion of auxiliaries was allotted, contained within itself every species of lighter troops, and of missile weapons; and was capable of encountering every nation, with the advantages of its respective arms and discipline. [58] Nor was the legion destitute of what, in modern language, would be styled a train of artillery. It consisted in ten military engines of the largest, and fifty-five of a smaller size; but all of which, either in an oblique or horizontal manner, discharged stones and darts with irresistible violence. [59]

[Footnote 55: Such, in particular, was the state of the Batavians. Tacit. Germania, c. 29.]

[Footnote 56: Marcus Antoninus obliged the vanquished Quadi and Marcomanni to supply him with a large body of troops, which he immediately sent into Britain. Dion Cassius, l. lxxi. (c. 16.)]

[Footnote 57: Tacit. Annal. iv. 5. Those who fix a regular proportion of as many foot, and twice as many horse, confound the auxiliaries of the emperors with the Italian allies of the republic.]

[Footnote 58: Vegetius, ii. 2. Arrian, in his order of march and battle against the Alani.]

[Footnote 59: The subject of the ancient machines is treated with great knowledge and ingenuity by the Chevalier Folard, (Polybe, tom. ii. p. 233-290.) He prefers them in many respects to our modern cannon and mortars. We may observe, that the use of them in the field gradually became more prevalent, in proportion as personal valor and military skill declined with the Roman empire. When men were no longer found, their place was supplied by machines. See Vegetius, ii. 25. Arrian.]

PART III

The camp of a Roman legion presented the appearance of a fortified city. [60] As soon as the space was marked out, the pioneers carefully levelled the ground, and removed every impediment that might interrupt its perfect regularity. Its form was an exact quadrangle; and we may calculate, that a square of about seven hundred yards was sufficient for the encampment of twenty thousand Romans; though a similar number of our own troops would expose to the enemy a front of more than treble that extent. In the midst of the camp, the praetorium, or general's quarters, rose above the others; the cavalry, the infantry, and the auxiliaries occupied their respective stations; the streets were broad and perfectly straight, and a vacant space of two hundred feet was left on all sides between the tents and the rampart. The rampart itself was usually twelve feet high, armed with a line of strong and intricate palisades, and defended by a ditch of twelve feet in depth as well as in breadth. This important labor was performed by the hands of the legionaries themselves; to whom the use of the spade and the pickaxe was no less familiar than that of the sword or pilum. Active valor may often be the present of nature; but such patient diligence can be the fruit only of habit and discipline. [61]

[Footnote 60: Vegetius finishes his second book, and the description of the legion, with the following emphatic words:—"Universa quae ix quoque belli genere necessaria esse creduntur, secum Jegio debet ubique portare, ut in quovis loco fixerit castra, arma'am faciat civitatem."]

[Footnote 61: For the Roman Castrametation, see Polybius, l. vi. with Lipsius de Militia Romana, Joseph. de Bell. Jud. l. iii. c. 5. Vegetius, i. 21—25, iii. 9, and Memoires de Guichard, tom. i. c. 1.]

Whenever the trumpet gave the signal of departure, the camp was almost instantly broke up, and the troops fell into their ranks without delay or confusion. Besides their arms, which the legendaries scarcely considered as an encumbrance, they were laden with their kitchen furniture, the instruments of fortification, and the provision of many days. [62] Under this weight, which would oppress the delicacy of a modern soldier, they were trained by a regular step to advance, in about six hours, near twenty miles. [63] On the appearance of an enemy, they threw aside their baggage, and by easy and rapid evolutions converted the column of march into an order of battle. [64] The slingers and archers skirmished in the front; the auxiliaries formed the first line, and were seconded or sustained by the strength of the legions; the cavalry covered the flanks, and the military engines were placed in the rear.

[Footnote 62: Cicero in Tusculan. ii. 37, [15.]—Joseph. de Bell. Jud. l. iii. 5, Frontinus, iv. 1.]

[Footnote 63: Vegetius, i. 9. See Memoires de l'Academie des Inscriptions, tom. xxv. p. 187.]

[Footnote 64: See those evolutions admirably well explained by M. Guichard Nouveaux Memoires, tom. i. p. 141—234.]

Such were the arts of war, by which the Roman emperors defended their extensive conquests, and preserved a military spirit, at a time when every other virtue was oppressed by luxury and despotism. If, in the consideration of their armies, we pass from their discipline to their numbers, we shall not find it easy to define them with any tolerable accuracy. We may compute, however, that the legion, which was itself a body of six thousand eight hundred and thirty-one Romans, might, with its attendant auxiliaries, amount to about twelve thousand five hundred men. The peace establishment of Hadrian and his successors was composed of no less than thirty of these formidable brigades; and most probably formed a standing force of three hundred and seventy-five thousand men. Instead of being confined within the walls of fortified cities, which the Romans considered as the refuge of weakness or pusillanimity, the legions were encamped on the banks of the great rivers, and along the frontiers of the barbarians. As their stations, for the most part, remained fixed and permanent, we may venture to describe the distribution of the troops. Three legions were sufficient for Britain. The principal strength lay upon the Rhine and Danube, and consisted of sixteen legions, in the following proportions: two in the Lower, and three in the Upper Germany; one in Rhaetia, one in Noricum, four in Pannonia, three in Maesia, and two in Dacia. The defence of the Euphrates was intrusted to eight legions, six of whom were planted in Syria, and the other two in Cappadocia. With regard to Egypt, Africa, and Spain, as they were far removed from any important scene of war, a single legion maintained the domestic tranquillity of each of those great provinces. Even Italy was not left destitute of a military force. Above twenty thousand chosen soldiers, distinguished by the titles of City Cohorts and Praetorian Guards, watched over the safety of the monarch and the capital. As the authors of almost every revolution that distracted the empire, the Praetorians will, very soon, and very loudly, demand our attention; but, in their arms and institutions, we cannot find any circumstance which discriminated them from the legions, unless it were a more splendid appearance, and a less rigid discipline. [65]

[Footnote 65: Tacitus (Annal. iv. 5) has given us a state of the legions under Tiberius; and Dion Cassius (l. lv. p. 794) under Alexander Severus. I have endeavored to fix on the proper medium between these two periods. See likewise Lipsius de Magnitudine Romana, l. i. c. 4, 5.]

The navy maintained by the emperors might seem inadequate to their greatness; but it was fully sufficient for every useful purpose of government. The ambition of the Romans was confined to the land; nor was that warlike people ever actuated by the enterprising spirit which had prompted the navigators of Tyre, of Carthage, and even of Marseilles, to enlarge the bounds of the world, and to explore the most remote coasts of the ocean. To the Romans the ocean remained an object of terror rather than of curiosity; [66] the whole extent of the Mediterranean, after the destruction of Carthage, and the extirpation of the pirates, was included within their provinces. The policy of the emperors was directed only to preserve the peaceful dominion of that sea, and to protect the commerce of their subjects. With these moderate views, Augustus stationed two permanent fleets in the most convenient ports of Italy, the one at Ravenna, on the Adriatic, the other at Misenum, in the Bay of Naples. Experience seems at length to have convinced the ancients, that as soon as their galleys exceeded two, or at the most three ranks of oars, they were suited rather for vain pomp than for real service. Augustus himself, in the victory of Actium, had seen the superiority of his own light frigates (they were called Liburnians) over the lofty but unwieldy castles of his rival. [67] Of these Liburnians he composed the two fleets of Ravenna and Misenum, destined to command, the one the eastern, the other the western division of the Mediterranean; and to each of the squadrons he attached a body of several thousand marines. Besides these two ports, which may be considered as the principal seats of the Roman navy, a very considerable force was stationed at Frejus, on the coast of Provence, and the Euxine was guarded by forty ships, and three thousand soldiers. To all these we add the fleet which preserved the communication between Gaul and Britain, and a great number of vessels constantly maintained on the Rhine and Danube, to harass the country, or to intercept the passage of the barbarians. [68] If we review this general state of the Imperial forces; of the cavalry as well as infantry; of the legions, the auxiliaries, the guards, and the navy; the most liberal computation will not allow us to fix the entire establishment by sea and by land at more than four hundred and fifty thousand men: a military power, which, however formidable it may seem, was equalled by a monarch of the last century, whose kingdom was confined within a single province of the Roman empire. [69]

[Footnote 66: The Romans tried to disguise, by the pretence of religious awe their ignorance and terror. See Tacit. Germania, c. 34.]

[Footnote 67: Plutarch, in Marc. Anton. [c. 67.] And yet, if we may credit Orosius, these monstrous castles were no more than ten feet above the water, vi. 19.]

[Footnote 68: See Lipsius, de Magnitud. Rom. l. i. c. 5. The sixteen last chapters of Vegetius relate to naval affairs.]

[Footnote 69: Voltaire, Siecle de Louis XIV. c. 29. It must, however, be remembered, that France still feels that extraordinary effort.]

We have attempted to explain the spirit which moderated, and the strength which supported, the power of Hadrian and the Antonines. We shall now endeavor, with clearness and precision, to describe the provinces once united under their sway, but, at present, divided into so many independent and hostile states. Spain, the western extremity of the empire, of Europe, and of the ancient world, has, in every age, invariably preserved the same natural limits; the Pyrenaean Mountains, the Mediterranean, and the Atlantic Ocean. That great peninsula, at present so unequally divided between two sovereigns, was distributed by Augustus into three provinces, Lusitania, Baetica, and Tarraconensis. The kingdom of Portugal now fills the place of the warlike country of the Lusitanians; and the loss sustained by the former on the side of the East, is compensated by an accession of territory towards the North. The confines of Grenada and Andalusia correspond with those of ancient Baetica. The remainder of Spain, Gallicia, and the Asturias, Biscay, and Navarre, Leon, and the two Castiles, Murcia, Valencia, Catalonia, and Arragon, all contributed to form the third and most considerable of the Roman governments, which, from the name of its capital, was styled the province of Tarragona. [70] Of the native barbarians, the Celtiberians were the most powerful, as the Cantabrians and Asturians proved the most obstinate.

Confident in the strength of their mountains, they were the last who submitted to the arms of Rome, and the first who threw off the yoke of the Arabs.

[Footnote 70: See Strabo, l. ii. It is natural enough to suppose, that Arragon is derived from Tarraconensis, and several moderns who have written in Latin use those words as synonymous. It is, however, certain, that the Arragon, a little stream which falls from the Pyrenees into the Ebro, first gave its name to a country, and gradually to a kingdom. See d'Anville, Geographie du Moyen Age, p. 181.]

Ancient Gaul, as it contained the whole country between the Pyrenees, the Alps, the Rhine, and the Ocean, was of greater extent than modern France. To the dominions of that powerful monarchy, with its recent acquisitions of Alsace and Lorraine, we must add the duchy of Savoy, the cantons of Switzerland, the four electorates of the Rhine, and the territories of Liege, Luxemburgh, Hainault, Flanders, and Brabant. When Augustus gave laws to the conquests of his father, he introduced a division of Gaul, equally adapted to the progress of the legions, to the course of the rivers, and to the principal national distinctions, which had comprehended above a hundred independent states. [71] The sea-coast of the Mediterranean, Languedoc, Provence, and Dauphine, received their provincial appellation from the colony of Narbonne. The government of Aquitaine was extended from the Pyrenees to the Loire. The country between the Loire and the Seine was styled the Celtic Gaul, and soon borrowed a new denomination from the celebrated colony of Lugdunum, or Lyons. The Belgic lay beyond the Seine, and in more ancient times had been bounded only by the Rhine; but a little before the age of Caesar, the Germans, abusing their superiority of valor, had occupied a considerable portion of the Belgic territory. The Roman conquerors very eagerly embraced so flattering a circumstance, and the Gallic frontier of the Rhine, from Basil to Leyden, received the pompous names of the Upper and the Lower Germany. [72] Such, under the reign of the Antonines, were the six provinces of Gaul; the Narbonnese, Aquitaine, the Celtic, or Lyonnese, the Belgic, and the two Germanies.

[Footnote 71: One hundred and fifteen cities appear in the Notitia of Gaul; and it is well known that this appellation was applied not only to the capital town, but to the whole territory of each state. But Plutarch and Appian increase the number of tribes to three or four hundred.]

[Footnote 72: D'Anville. Notice de l'Ancienne Gaule.]

We have already had occasion to mention the conquest of Britain, and to fix the boundary of the Roman Province in this island. It comprehended all England, Wales, and the Lowlands of Scotland, as far as the Friths of Dumbarton and Edinburgh. Before Britain lost her freedom, the country was irregularly divided between thirty tribes of barbarians, of whom the most considerable were the Belgae in the West, the Brigantes in the North, the Silures in South Wales, and the Iceni in Norfolk and Suffolk. [73] As far as we can either trace or credit the resemblance of manners and language, Spain, Gaul, and Britain were peopled by the same hardy race of savages. Before they yielded to the Roman arms, they often disputed the field, and often renewed the contest. After their submission, they constituted the western division of the European provinces, which extended from the columns of Hercules to the wall of Antoninus, and from the mouth of the Tagus to the sources of the Rhine and Danube.

[Footnote 73: Whittaker's History of Manchester, vol. i. c. 3.]

Before the Roman conquest, the country which is now called Lombardy, was not considered as a part of Italy. It had been occupied by a powerful colony of Gauls, who, settling themselves along the banks of the Po, from Piedmont to Romagna, carried their arms and diffused their name from the Alps to the Apennine.

The Ligurians dwelt on the rocky coast which now forms the republic of Genoa. Venice was yet unborn; but the territories of that state, which lie to the east of the Adige, were inhabited by the Venetians. [74] The middle part of the peninsula, that now composes the duchy of Tuscany and the ecclesiastical state, was the ancient seat of the Etruscans and Umbrians; to the former of whom Italy was indebted for the first rudiments of civilized life. [75] The Tyber rolled at the foot of the seven hills of Rome, and the country of the Sabines, the Latins, and the Volsci, from that river to the frontiers of Naples, was the theatre of her infant victories. On that celebrated ground the first consuls deserved triumphs, their successors adorned villas, and their posterity have erected convents. [76] Capua and Campania possessed the immediate territory of Naples; the rest of the kingdom was inhabited by many warlike nations, the Marsi, the Samnites, the Apulians, and the Lucanians; and the sea-coasts had been covered by the flourishing colonies of the Greeks. We may remark, that when Augustus divided Italy into eleven regions, the little province of Istria was annexed to that seat of Roman sovereignty. [77]

[Footnote 74: The Italian Veneti, though often confounded with the Gauls, were more probably of Illyrian origin. See M. Freret, Memoires de l'Academie des Inscriptions, tom. xviii. Note: Or Liburnian, according to Niebuhr. Vol. i. p. 172.—M.]

[Footnote 75: See Maffei Verona illustrata, l. i. Note: Add Niebuhr, vol. i., and Otfried Muller, die Etrusker, which contains much that is known, and much that is conjectured, about this remarkable people. Also Micali, Storia degli antichi popoli Italiani. Florence, 1832—M.]

[Footnote 76: The first contrast was observed by the ancients. See Florus, i. 11. The second must strike every modern traveller.]

[Footnote 77: Pliny (Hist. Natur. l. iii.) follows the division of Italy by Augustus.]

The European provinces of Rome were protected by the course of the Rhine and the Danube. The latter of those mighty streams, which rises at the distance of only thirty miles from the former, flows above thirteen hundred miles, for the most part to the south-east, collects the tribute of sixty navigable rivers, and is, at length, through six mouths, received into the Euxine, which appears scarcely equal to such an accession of waters. [78] The provinces of the Danube soon acquired the general appellation of Illyricum, or the Illyrian frontier, [79] and were esteemed the most warlike of the empire; but they deserve to be more particularly considered under the names of Rhaetia, Noricum, Pannonia, Dalmatia, Dacia, Maesia, Thrace, Macedonia, and Greece.

[Footnote 78: Tournefort, Voyages en Grece et Asie Mineure, lettre xviii.]

[Footnote 79: The name of Illyricum originally belonged to the sea-coast of the Adriatic, and was gradually extended by the Romans from the Alps to the Euxine Sea. See Severini Pannonia, l. i. c. 3.]

The province of Rhaetia, which soon extinguished the name of the Vindelicians, extended from the summit of the Alps to the banks of the Danube; from its source, as far as its conflux with the Inn. The greatest part of the flat country is subject to the elector of Bavaria; the city of Augsburg is protected by the constitution of the German empire; the Grisons are safe in their mountains, and the country of Tirol is ranked among the numerous provinces of the house of Austria.

The wide extent of territory which is included between the Inn, the Danube, and the Save,—Austria, Styria, Carinthia, Carniola, the Lower Hungary, and Sclavonia,—was known to the ancients under the names of Noricum and Pannonia. In their original state of independence, their fierce inhabitants were intimately connected. Under the Roman government they were frequently united, and they still remain the patrimony of a single family. They now contain the residence of a German prince, who styles himself Emperor of the Romans, and form the centre, as well as strength, of the Austrian power. It may not be improper to observe, that if we except Bohemia, Moravia, the northern skirts of Austria, and a part of Hungary between the Teyss and the Danube, all the other dominions of the House of Austria were comprised within the limits of the Roman Empire.

Dalmatia, to which the name of Illyricum more properly belonged, was a long, but narrow tract, between the Save and the Adriatic. The best part of the sea-coast, which still retains its ancient appellation, is a province of the Venetian state, and the seat of the little republic of Ragusa. The inland parts have assumed the Sclavonian names of Croatia and Bosnia; the former obeys an Austrian governor, the latter a Turkish pacha; but the whole country is still infested by tribes of barbarians, whose savage independence irregularly marks the doubtful limit of the Christian and Mahometan power. [80]

[Footnote 80: A Venetian traveller, the Abbate Fortis, has lately given us some account of those very obscure countries. But the geography and antiquities of the western Illyricum can be expected only from the munificence of the emperor, its sovereign.]

After the Danube had received the waters of the Teyss and the Save, it acquired, at least among the Greeks, the name of Ister. [81] It formerly divided Maesia and Dacia, the latter of which, as we have already seen, was a conquest of Trajan, and the only province beyond the river. If we inquire into the present state of those countries, we shall find that, on the left hand of the Danube, Temeswar and Transylvania have been annexed, after many revolutions, to the crown of Hungary; whilst the principalities of Moldavia and Wallachia acknowledge the supremacy of the Ottoman Porte. On the right hand of the Danube, Maesia, which, during the middle ages, was broken into the barbarian kingdoms of Servia and Bulgaria, is again united in Turkish slavery.

[Footnote 81: The Save rises near the confines of Istria, and was considered by the more early Greeks as the principal stream of the Danube.]

The appellation of Roumelia, which is still bestowed by the Turks on the extensive countries of Thrace, Macedonia, and Greece, preserves the memory of their ancient state under the Roman empire. In the time of the Antonines, the martial regions of Thrace, from the mountains of Haemus and Rhodope, to the Bosphorus and the Hellespont, had assumed the form of a province. Notwithstanding the change of masters and of religion, the new city of Rome, founded by Constantine on the banks of the Bosphorus, has ever since remained the capital of a great monarchy. The kingdom of Macedonia, which, under the reign of Alexander, gave laws to Asia, derived more solid advantages from the policy of the two Philips; and with its dependencies of Epirus and Thessaly, extended from the Aegean to the Ionian Sea. When we reflect on the fame of Thebes and Argos, of Sparta and Athens, we can scarcely persuade ourselves, that so many immortal republics of ancient Greece were lost in a single province of the Roman empire, which, from the superior influence of the Achaean league, was usually denominated the province of Achaia.

Such was the state of Europe under the Roman emperors. The provinces of Asia, without excepting the transient conquests of Trajan, are all comprehended within the limits of the Turkish power. But, instead of following the arbitrary divisions of despotism and ignorance, it will be safer for us, as well as more agreeable, to observe the indelible characters of nature. The name of Asia Minor is attributed with some propriety to the peninsula, which, confined betwixt the Euxine and the Mediterranean, advances from the Euphrates towards Europe. The most extensive and flourishing district, westward of Mount Taurus and the River Halys, was dignified by the Romans with the exclusive title of Asia. The jurisdiction of that province extended over the ancient monarchies of Troy, Lydia, and Phrygia, the maritime countries of the Pamphylians, Lycians, and Carians, and the Grecian colonies of Ionia, which equalled in arts, though not in arms, the glory of their parent. The kingdoms of Bithynia and Pontus possessed the northern side of the peninsula from Constantinople to Trebizond. On the opposite side, the province of Cilicia was terminated by the mountains of Syria: the inland country, separated from the Roman Asia by the River Halys, and from Armenia by the Euphrates, had once formed the independent kingdom of Cappadocia. In this place we may observe, that the northern shores of the Euxine, beyond Trebizond in Asia, and beyond the Danube in Europe, acknowledged the sovereignty of the emperors, and received at their hands either tributary princes or Roman garrisons. Budzak, Crim Tartary, Circassia, and Mingrelia, are the modern appellations of those savage countries. [82]

[Footnote 82: See the Periplus of Arrian. He examined the coasts of the Euxine, when he was governor of Cappadocia.]

Under the successors of Alexander, Syria was the seat of the Seleucidae, who reigned over Upper Asia, till the successful revolt of the Parthians confined their dominions between the Euphrates and the Mediterranean. When Syria became subject to the Romans, it formed the eastern frontier of their empire: nor did that province, in its utmost latitude, know any other bounds than the mountains of Cappadocia to the north, and towards the south, the confines of Egypt, and the Red Sea. Phoenicia and Palestine were sometimes annexed to, and sometimes separated from, the jurisdiction of Syria. The former of these was a narrow and rocky coast; the latter was a territory scarcely superior to Wales, either in fertility or extent. [82/1] Yet Phoenicia and Palestine will forever live in the memory of mankind; since America, as well as Europe, has received letters from the one, and religion from the other. [83] A sandy desert, alike destitute of wood and water, skirts along the doubtful confine of Syria, from the Euphrates to the Red Sea. The wandering life of the Arabs was inseparably connected with their independence; and wherever, on some spots less barren than the rest, they ventured to for many settled habitations, they soon became subjects to the Roman empire. [84]

[Footnote 82/1: This comparison is exaggerated, with the intention, no doubt, of attacking the authority of the Bible, which boasts of the fertility of Palestine. Gibbon's only authorities were that of Strabo (l. xvi. 1104) and the present state of the country. But Strabo only speaks of the neighborhood of Jerusalem, which he calls barren and arid to the extent of sixty stadia round the city: in other parts he gives a favorable testimony to the fertility of many parts of Palestine: thus he says, "Near Jericho there is a grove of palms, and a country of a hundred stadia, full of springs, and well peopled." Moreover, Strabo had never seen Palestine; he spoke only after reports, which may be as inaccurate as those according to which he has composed that description of Germany, in which Gluverius has detected so many errors. (Gluv. Germ. iii. 1.) Finally, his testimony is contradicted and refuted by that of other ancient authors, and by medals. Tacitus says, in speaking of Palestine, "The inhabitants are healthy and robust; the rains moderate; the soil fertile." (Hist. v. 6.) Ammianus Macellinus says also, "The last of the Syrias is Palestine, a country of considerable extent, abounding in clean and well-cultivated land, and containing some fine cities, none of which yields to the other; but, as it were, being on a parallel, are rivals."—xiv. 8. See also the historian Josephus, Hist. vi. 1. Procopius of Caeserea, who lived in the sixth century, says that Chosroes, king of Persia, had a great desire to make himself master of Palestine, on account of its extraordinary fertility, its opulence, and the great number of its inhabitants. The Saracens thought the same, and were afraid that Omar. when he went to Jerusalem, charmed with the fertility of the soil and the purity of the air, would never return to Medina. (Ockley, Hist. of Sarac. i. 232.) The importance attached by the Romans to the conquest of Palestine, and the obstacles they encountered, prove also the richness and population of the country. Vespasian and Titus caused medals to be struck with trophies, in which Palestine is represented by a female under a palm-tree, to signify the richness of he country, with this legend: Judea capta. Other medals also indicate this fertility; for instance, that of Herod holding a bunch of grapes, and that of the young Agrippa displaying fruit. As to the present state of he country, one perceives that it is not fair to draw any inference against its ancient fertility: the disasters through which it has passed, the government to which it is subject, the disposition of the inhabitants, explain sufficiently the wild and uncultivated appearance of the land, where, nevertheless, fertile and cultivated districts are still found, according to the testimony of travellers; among others, of Shaw, Maundrel, La Rocque, &c.—G. The Abbe Guenee, in his Lettres de quelques Juifs a Mons. de Voltaire, has exhausted the subject of the fertility of Palestine; for Voltaire had likewise indulged in sarcasm on this subject. Gibbon was assailed on this point, not, indeed, by Mr. Davis, who, he slyly insinuates, was prevented by his patriotism as a Welshman from resenting the comparison with Wales, but by other writers. In his Vindication, he first established the correctness of his measurement of Palestine, which he estimates as 7600 square English miles, while Wales is about 7011. As to fertility, he proceeds in the following dexterously composed and splendid passage: "The emperor Frederick II., the enemy and the victim of the clergy, is accused of saying, after his return from his crusade, that the God of the Jews would have despised his promised land, if he had once seen the fruitful realms of Sicily and Naples." (See Giannone, Istor. Civ. del R. di Napoli, ii. 245.) This raillery, which malice has, perhaps, falsely imputed to Frederick, is inconsistent with truth and piety; yet it must be confessed that the soil of Palestine does not contain that inexhaustible, and, as it were, spontaneous principle of fertility, which, under the most unfavorable circumstances, has covered with rich harvests the banks of the Nile, the fields of Sicily, or the plains of Poland. The Jordan is the only navigable river of Palestine: a considerable part of the narrow space is occupied, or rather lost, in the Dead Sea whose horrid aspect inspires every sensation of disgust, and countenances every tale of horror. The districts which border on Arabia partake of the sandy quality of the adjacent desert. The face of the country, except the sea-coast, and the valley of the Jordan, is covered with mountains, which appear, for the most part, as naked and barren rocks; and in the neighborhood of Jerusalem, there is a real scarcity of the two elements of earth and water. (See Maundrel's Travels, p. 65, and Reland's Palestin. i. 238, 395.) These disadvantages, which now operate in their fullest extent, were formerly corrected by the labors of a numerous people, and the active protection of a wise government. The hills were clothed with rich beds of artificial mould, the rain was collected in vast cisterns, a supply of fresh water was conveyed by pipes and aqueducts to the dry lands. The breed of cattle was encouraged in those parts which were not adapted for tillage, and almost every spot was compelled to yield some production for the use of the inhabitants.

Pater ispe colendi Haud facilem esse viam voluit, primusque par artem Movit agros; curis acuens mortalia corda, Nec torpere gravi passus sua Regna veterno. Gibbon, Misc. Works, iv. 540.

But Gibbon has here eluded the question about the land "flowing with milk and honey." He is describing Judaea only, without comprehending Galilee, or the rich pastures beyond the Jordan, even now proverbial for their flocks and herds. (See Burckhardt's Travels, and Hist of Jews, i. 178.) The following is believed to be a fair statement: "The extraordinary fertility of the whole country must be taken into the account. No part was waste; very little was occupied by unprofitable wood; the more fertile hills were cultivated in artificial terraces, others were hung with orchards of fruit trees the more rocky and barren districts were covered with vineyards. " Even in the present day, the wars and misgovernment of ages have not exhausted the natural richness of the soil. "Galilee," says Malte Brun, "would be a paradise were it inhabited by an industrious people under an enlightened government. No land could be less dependent on foreign importation; it bore within itself every thing that could be necessary for the subsistence and comfort of a simple agricultural people. The climate was healthy, the seasons regular; the former rains, which fell about October, after the vintage, prepared the ground for the seed; that latter, which prevailed during March and the beginning of April, made it grow rapidly. Directly the rains ceased, the grain ripened with still greater rapidity, and was gathered in before the end of May. The summer months were dry and very hot, but the nights cool and refreshed by copious dews. In September, the vintage was gathered. Grain of all kinds, wheat, barley, millet, zea, and other sorts, grew in abundance; the wheat commonly yielded thirty for one. Besides the vine and the olive, the almond, the date, figs of many kinds, the orange, the pomegranate, and many other fruit trees, flourished in the greatest luxuriance. Great quantity of honey was collected. The balm-tree, which produced the opobalsamum,a great object of trade, was probably introduced from Arabia, in the time of Solomon. It flourished about Jericho and in Gilead."—Milman's Hist. of Jews. i. 177.—M.]

[Footnote 83: The progress of religion is well known. The use of letter was introduced among the savages of Europe about fifteen hundred years before Christ; and the Europeans carried them to America about fifteen centuries after the Christian Aera. But in a period of three thousand years, the Phoenician alphabet received considerable alterations, as it passed through the hands of the Greeks and Romans.]

[Footnote 84: Dion Cassius, lib. lxviii. p. 1131.]

The geographers of antiquity have frequently hesitated to what portion of the globe they should ascribe Egypt. [85] By its situation that celebrated kingdom is included within the immense peninsula of Africa; but it is accessible only on the side of Asia, whose revolutions, in almost every period of history, Egypt has humbly obeyed. A Roman praefect was seated on the splendid throne of the Ptolemies; and the iron sceptre of the Mamelukes is now in the hands of a Turkish pacha. The Nile flows down the country, above five hundred miles from the tropic of Cancer to the Mediterranean, and marks on either side of the extent of fertility by the measure of its inundations. Cyrene, situate towards the west, and along the sea-coast, was first a Greek colony, afterwards a province of Egypt, and is now lost in the desert of Barca. [85/1]

[Footnote 85: Ptolemy and Strabo, with the modern geographers, fix the Isthmus of Suez as the boundary of Asia and Africa. Dionysius, Mela, Pliny, Sallust, Hirtius, and Solinus, have preferred for that purpose the western branch of the Nile, or even the great Catabathmus, or descent, which last would assign to Asia, not only Egypt, but part of Libya.]

[Footnote 85/1: The French editor has a long and unnecessary note on the History of Cyrene. For the present state of that coast and country, the volume of Captain Beechey is full of interesting details. Egypt, now an independent and improving kingdom, appears, under the enterprising rule of Mahommed Ali, likely to revenge its former oppression upon the decrepit power of the Turkish empire.—M.—This note was written in 1838. The future destiny of Egypt is an important problem, only to be solved by time. This observation will also apply to the new French colony in Algiers.—M. 1845.]

From Cyrene to the ocean, the coast of Africa extends above fifteen hundred miles; yet so closely is it pressed between the Mediterranean and the Sahara, or sandy desert, that its breadth seldom exceeds fourscore or a hundred miles. The eastern division was considered by the Romans as the more peculiar and proper province of Africa. Till the arrival of the Phoenician colonies, that fertile country was inhabited by the Libyans, the most savage of mankind. Under the immediate jurisdiction of Carthage, it became the centre of commerce and empire; but the republic of Carthage is now degenerated into the feeble and disorderly states of Tripoli and Tunis. The military government of Algiers oppresses the wide extent of Numidia, as it was once united under Massinissa and Jugurtha; but in the time of Augustus, the limits of Numidia were contracted; and, at least, two thirds of the country acquiesced in the name of Mauritania, with the epithet of Caesariensis. The genuine Mauritania, or country of the Moors, which, from the ancient city of Tingi, or Tangier, was distinguished by the appellation of Tingitana, is represented by the modern kingdom of Fez. Salle, on the Ocean, so infamous at present for its piratical depredations, was noticed by the Romans, as the extreme object of their power, and almost of their geography. A city of their foundation may still be discovered near Mequinez, the residence of the barbarian whom we condescend to style the Emperor of Morocco; but it does not appear, that his more southern dominions, Morocco itself, and Segelmessa, were ever comprehended within the Roman province. The western parts of Africa are intersected by the branches of Mount Atlas, a name so idly celebrated by the fancy of poets; [86] but which is now diffused over the immense ocean that rolls between the ancient and the new continent. [87]

[Footnote 86: *The long range, moderate height, and gentle declivity of Mount Atlas, (see Shaw's Travels, p. 5,) are very unlike a solitary mountain which rears its head into the clouds, and seems to support the heavens. The peak of Teneriff, on the contrary, rises a league and a half above the surface of the sea; and, as it was frequently visited by the Phoenicians, might engage the notice of the Greek poets. See Buffon, Histoire Naturelle, tom. i. p. 312. Histoire des Voyages, tom. ii.*]

[Footnote 87: *M. de Voltaire, tom. xiv. p. 297, unsupported by either fact or probability, has generously bestowed the Canary Islands on the Roman empire.*]

Having now finished the circuit of the Roman empire, we may observe, that Africa is divided from Spain by a narrow strait of about twelve miles, through which the Atlantic flows into the Mediterranean. The columns of Hercules, so famous among the ancients, were two mountains which seemed to have been torn asunder by some convulsion of the elements; and at the foot of the European mountain, the fortress of Gibraltar is now seated. The whole extent of the Mediterranean Sea, its coasts and its islands, were comprised within the Roman dominion. Of the larger islands, the two Baleares, which derive their name of Majorca and Minorca from their respective size, are subject at present, the former to Spain, the latter to Great Britain. [87/1] It is easier to deplore the fate, than to describe the actual condition, of Corsica. [87/2] Two Italian sovereigns assume a regal title from Sardinia and Sicily. Crete, or Candia, with Cyprus, and most of the smaller islands of Greece and Asia, have been subdued by the Turkish arms, whilst the little rock of Malta defies their power, and has emerged, under the government of its military Order, into fame and opulence. [87/3]

[Footnote 87/1: *Minorca was lost to Great Britain in 1782. Ann. Register for that year.—M.*]

[Footnote 87/2: *The gallant struggles of the Corsicans for their independence, under Paoli, were brought to a close in the year 1769. This volume was published in 1776. See Botta, Storia d'Italia, vol. xiv.—M.*]

[Footnote 87/3: *Malta, it need scarcely be said, is now in the possession of the English. We have not, however, thought it necessary to notice every change in the political state of the world, since the time of Gibbon.—M*]

This long enumeration of provinces, whose broken fragments have formed so many powerful kingdoms, might almost induce us to forgive the vanity or ignorance of the ancients. Dazzled with the extensive sway, the irresistible strength, and the real or affected moderation of the emperors, they permitted themselves to despise, and sometimes to forget, the outlying countries which had been left in the enjoyment of a barbarous independence; and they gradually usurped the license of confounding the Roman monarchy with the globe of the earth. [88] But the temper, as well as knowledge, of a modern historian, require a more sober and accurate language. He may impress a juster image of the greatness of Rome, by observing that the empire was above two thousand miles in breadth, from the wall of Antoninus and the northern limits of Dacia, to Mount Atlas and the tropic of Cancer; that it extended in length more than three thousand miles from the Western Ocean to the Euphrates; that it was situated in the finest part of the Temperate Zone, between the twenty-fourth and fifty-sixth degrees of northern latitude; and that it was supposed to contain above sixteen hundred thousand square miles, for the most part of fertile and well-cultivated land. [89]

[Footnote 88: Bergier, Hist. des Grands Chemins, l. iii. c. 1, 2, 3, 4, a very useful collection.]

[Footnote 89: See Templeman's Survey of the Globe; but I distrust both the Doctor's learning and his maps.]

CHAPTER II

THE INTERNAL PROSPERITY IN THE AGE OF THE ANTONINES

PART I

Of THE UNION & INTERNAL PROSPERITY OF THE ROMAN EMPIRE IN THE AGE OF THE ANTONINES

It is not alone by the rapidity, or extent of conquest, that we should estimate the greatness of Rome. The sovereign of the Russian deserts commands a larger portion of the globe. In the seventh summer after his passage of the Hellespont, Alexander erected the Macedonian trophies on the banks of the Hyphasis. [1] Within less than a century, the irresistible Zingis, and the Mogul princes of his race, spread their cruel devastations and transient empire from the Sea of China, to the confines of Egypt and Germany. [2] But the firm edifice of Roman power was raised and preserved by the wisdom of ages. The obedient provinces of Trajan and the Antonines were united by laws, and adorned by arts. They might occasionally suffer from the partial abuse of delegated authority; but the general principle of government was wise, simple, and beneficent. They enjoyed the religion of their ancestors, whilst in civil honors and advantages they were exalted, by just degrees, to an equality with their conquerors.

[Footnote 1: They were erected about the midway between Lahor and Delhi. The conquests of Alexander in Hindostan were confined to the Punjab, a country watered by the five great streams of the Indus. Note: The Hyphasis is one of the five rivers which join the Indus or the Sind, after having traversed the province of the Pendj-ab—a name which in Persian, signifies five rivers. —G. The five rivers were, 1. The Hydaspes, now the Chelum, Behni, or Bedusta, (Sanscrit, Vitastha, Arrow-swift.) 2. The Acesines, the Chenab, (Sanscrit, Chandrabhaga, Moon-gift.) 3. Hydraotes, the Ravey, or Iraoty, (Sanscrit, Iravati.) 4. Hyphasis, the Beyah, (Sanscrit, Vepasa, Fetterless.) 5. The Satadru, (Sanscrit, the Hundred Streamed,) the

Sutledj, known first to the Greeks in the time of Ptolemy. Rennel. Vincent, Commerce of Anc. book 2. Lassen, Pentapotam. Ind. Wilson's Sanscrit Dict., and the valuable memoir of Lieut. Burnes, Journal of London Geogr. Society, vol. iii. p. 2, with the travels of that very able writer. Compare Gibbon's own note, c. lxv. note 25.—M substit. for G.]

[Footnote 2: See M. de Guignes, Histoire des Huns, l. xv. xvi. and xvii.]

I. The policy of the emperors and the senate, as far as it concerned religion, was happily seconded by the reflections of the enlightened, and by the habits of the superstitious, part of their subjects. The various modes of worship, which prevailed in the Roman world, were all considered by the people, as equally true; by the philosopher, as equally false; and by the magistrate, as equally useful. And thus toleration produced not only mutual indulgence, but even religious concord.

The superstition of the people was not imbittered by any mixture of theological rancor; nor was it confined by the chains of any speculative system. The devout polytheist, though fondly attached to his national rites, admitted with implicit faith the different religions of the earth. [3] Fear, gratitude, and curiosity, a dream or an omen, a singular disorder, or a distant journey, perpetually disposed him to multiply the articles of his belief, and to enlarge the list of his protectors. The thin texture of the Pagan mythology was interwoven with various but not discordant materials. As soon as it was allowed that sages and heroes, who had lived or who had died for the benefit of their country, were exalted to a state of power and immortality, it was universally confessed, that they deserved, if not the adoration, at least the reverence, of all mankind. The deities of a thousand groves and a thousand streams possessed, in peace, their local and respective influence; nor could the Romans who deprecated the wrath of the Tiber, deride the Egyptian who presented his offering to the beneficent genius of the Nile. The visible powers of nature, the planets, and the elements were the same throughout the universe. The invisible governors of the moral world were inevitably cast in a similar mould of fiction and allegory. Every virtue, and even vice, acquired its divine representative; every art and profession its patron, whose attributes, in the most distant ages and countries, were uniformly derived from the character of their peculiar votaries. A republic of gods of such opposite tempers and interests required, in every system, the moderating hand of a supreme magistrate, who, by the progress of knowledge and flattery, was gradually invested with the sublime perfections of an Eternal Parent, and an Omnipotent Monarch. [4] Such was the mild spirit of antiquity, that the nations were less attentive to the difference, than to the resemblance, of their religious worship. The Greek, the Roman, and the Barbarian, as they met before their respective altars, easily persuaded themselves, that under various names, and with various ceremonies, they adored the same deities. [5] The elegant mythology of Homer gave a beautiful, and almost a regular form, to the polytheism of the ancient world.

[Footnote 3: There is not any writer who describes in so lively a manner as Herodotus the true genius of polytheism. The best commentary may be found in Mr. Hume's Natural History of Religion; and the best contrast in Bossuet's Universal History. Some obscure traces of an intolerant spirit appear in the conduct of the Egyptians, (see Juvenal, Sat. xv.;) and the Christians, as well as Jews, who lived under the Roman empire, formed a very important exception; so important indeed, that the discussion will require a distinct chapter of this work. Note: M. Constant, in his very learned and eloquent work, "Sur la Religion," with the two additional volumes, "Du Polytheisme Romain," has considered the whole history of polytheism in a tone of philosophy, which, without subscribing to all his opinions, we may be permitted to admire. "The boasted tolerance of polytheism did not rest upon the respect due from society to the freedom of individual opinion. The polytheistic nations, tolerant as they were towards each other, as separate states, were not the less ignorant of the eternal principle, the only basis of enlightened

toleration, that every one has a right to worship God in the manner which seems to him the best. Citizens, on the contrary, were bound to conform to the religion of the state; they had not the liberty to adopt a foreign religion, though that religion might be legally recognized in their own city, for the strangers who were its votaries." —Sur la Religion, v. 184. Du. Polyth. Rom. ii. 308. At this time, the growing religious indifference, and the general administration of the empire by Romans, who, being strangers, would do no more than protect, not enlist themselves in the cause of the local superstitions, had introduced great laxity. But intolerance was clearly the theory both of the Greek and Roman law. The subject is more fully considered in another place.—M.]

[Footnote 4: The rights, powers, and pretensions of the sovereign of Olympus are very clearly described in the xvth book of the Iliad; in the Greek original, I mean; for Mr. Pope, without perceiving it, has improved the theology of Homer. Note: There is a curious coincidence between Gibbon's expressions and those of the newly-recovered "De Republica" of Cicero, though the argument is rather the converse, lib. i. c. 36. "Sive haec ad utilitatem vitae constitute sint a principibus rerum publicarum, ut rex putaretur unus esse in coelo, qui nutu, ut ait Homerus, totum Olympum converteret, idemque et rex et patos haberetur omnium."—M.]

[Footnote 5: See, for instance, Caesar de Bell. Gall. vi. 17. Within a century or two, the Gauls themselves applied to their gods the names of Mercury, Mars, Apollo, &c.]

The philosophers of Greece deduced their morals from the nature of man, rather than from that of God. They meditated, however, on the Divine Nature, as a very curious and important speculation; and in the profound inquiry, they displayed the strength and weakness of the human understanding. [6] Of the four most celebrated schools, the Stoics and the Platonists endeavored to reconcile the jaring interests of reason and piety. They have left us the most sublime proofs of the existence and perfections of the first cause; but, as it was impossible for them to conceive the creation of matter, the workman in the Stoic philosophy was not sufficiently distinguished from the work; whilst, on the contrary, the spiritual God of Plato and his disciples resembled an idea, rather than a substance. The opinions of the Academics and Epicureans were of a less religious cast; but whilst the modest science of the former induced them to doubt, the positive ignorance of the latter urged them to deny, the providence of a Supreme Ruler. The spirit of inquiry, prompted by emulation, and supported by freedom, had divided the public teachers of philosophy into a variety of contending sects; but the ingenious youth, who, from every part, resorted to Athens, and the other seats of learning in the Roman empire, were alike instructed in every school to reject and to despise the religion of the multitude. How, indeed, was it possible that a philosopher should accept, as divine truths, the idle tales of the poets, and the incoherent traditions of antiquity; or that he should adore, as gods, those imperfect beings whom he must have despised, as men? Against such unworthy adversaries, Cicero condescended to employ the arms of reason and eloquence; but the satire of Lucian was a much more adequate, as well as more efficacious, weapon. We may be well assured, that a writer, conversant with the world, would never have ventured to expose the gods of his country to public ridicule, had they not already been the objects of secret contempt among the polished and enlightened orders of society. [7]

[Footnote 6: The admirable work of Cicero de Natura Deorum is the best clew we have to guide us through the dark and profound abyss. He represents with candor, and confutes with subtlety, the opinions of the philosophers.]

[Footnote 7: I do not pretend to assert, that, in this irreligious age, the natural terrors of superstition, dreams, omens, apparitions, &c., had lost their efficacy.]

Notwithstanding the fashionable irreligion which prevailed in the age of the Antonines, both the interest of the priests and the credulity of the people were sufficiently respected. In their writings and conversation, the philosophers of antiquity asserted the independent dignity of reason; but they resigned their actions to the commands of law and of custom. Viewing, with a smile of pity and indulgence, the various errors of the vulgar, they diligently practised the ceremonies of their fathers, devoutly frequented the temples of the gods; and sometimes condescending to act a part on the theatre of superstition, they concealed the sentiments of an atheist under the sacerdotal robes. Reasoners of such a temper were scarcely inclined to wrangle about their respective modes of faith, or of worship. It was indifferent to them what shape the folly of the multitude might choose to assume; and they approached with the same inward contempt, and the same external reverence, the altars of the Libyan, the Olympian, or the Capitoline Jupiter. [8]

[Footnote 8: Socrates, Epicurus, Cicero, and Plutarch always inculcated a decent reverence for the religion of their own country, and of mankind. The devotion of Epicurus was assiduous and exemplary. Diogen. Laert. x. 10.]

It is not easy to conceive from what motives a spirit of persecution could introduce itself into the Roman councils. The magistrates could not be actuated by a blind, though honest bigotry, since the magistrates were themselves philosophers; and the schools of Athens had given laws to the senate. They could not be impelled by ambition or avarice, as the temporal and ecclesiastical powers were united in the same hands. The pontiffs were chosen among the most illustrious of the senators; and the office of Supreme Pontiff was constantly exercised by the emperors themselves. They knew and valued the advantages of religion, as it is connected with civil government. They encouraged the public festivals which humanize the manners of the people. They managed the arts of divination as a convenient instrument of policy; and they respected, as the firmest bond of society, the useful persuasion, that, either in this or in a future life, the crime of perjury is most assuredly punished by the avenging gods. [9] But whilst they acknowledged the general advantages of religion, they were convinced that the various modes of worship contributed alike to the same salutary purposes; and that, in every country, the form of superstition, which had received the sanction of time and experience, was the best adapted to the climate, and to its inhabitants. Avarice and taste very frequently despoiled the vanquished nations of the elegant statues of their gods, and the rich ornaments of their temples; [10] but, in the exercise of the religion which they derived from their ancestors, they uniformly experienced the indulgence, and even protection, of the Roman conquerors. The province of Gaul seems, and indeed only seems, an exception to this universal toleration. Under the specious pretext of abolishing human sacrifices, the emperors Tiberius and Claudius suppressed the dangerous power of the Druids: [11] but the priests themselves, their gods and their altars, subsisted in peaceful obscurity till the final destruction of Paganism. [12]

[Footnote 9: Polybius, l. vi. c. 53, 54. Juvenal, Sat. xiii. laments that in his time this apprehension had lost much of its effect.]

[Footnote 10: See the fate of Syracuse, Tarentum, Ambracia, Corinth, &c., the conduct of Verres, in Cicero, (Actio ii. Orat. 4,) and the usual practice of governors, in the viiith Satire of Juvenal.]

[Footnote 11: Seuton. in Claud.—Plin. Hist. Nat. xxx. 1.]

[Footnote 12: Pelloutier, Histoire des Celtes, tom. vi. p. 230—252.]

Rome, the capital of a great monarchy, was incessantly filled with subjects and strangers from every part of the world, [13] who all introduced and enjoyed the favorite superstitions of their native country. [14] Every city in the empire was justified in maintaining the purity of its ancient ceremonies; and the Roman senate, using the common privilege, sometimes interposed, to check this inundation of foreign rites. [14/1] The Egyptian superstition, of all the most contemptible and abject, was frequently prohibited: the temples of Serapis and Isis demolished, and their worshippers banished from Rome and Italy. [15] But the zeal of fanaticism prevailed over the cold and feeble efforts of policy. The exiles returned, the proselytes multiplied, the temples were restored with increasing splendor, and Isis and Serapis at length assumed their place among the Roman Deities. [151] [16] Nor was this indulgence a departure from the old maxims of government. In the purest ages of the commonwealth, Cybele and Aesculapius had been invited by solemn embassies; [17] and it was customary to tempt the protectors of besieged cities, by the promise of more distinguished honors than they possessed in their native country. [18] Rome gradually became the common temple of her subjects; and the freedom of the city was bestowed on all the gods of mankind. [19]

[Footnote 13: Seneca, Consolat. ad Helviam, p. 74. Edit., Lips.]

[Footnote 14: Dionysius Halicarn. Antiquitat. Roman. l. ii. (vol. i. p. 275, edit. Reiske.)]

[Footnote 14/1: Yet the worship of foreign gods at Rome was only guaranteed to the natives of those countries from whence they came. The Romans administered the priestly offices only to the gods of their fathers. Gibbon, throughout the whole preceding sketch of the opinions of the Romans and their subjects, has shown through what causes they were free from religious hatred and its consequences. But, on the other hand the internal state of these religions, the infidelity and hypocrisy of the upper orders, the indifference towards all religion, in even the better part of the common people, during the last days of the republic, and under the Caesars, and the corrupting principles of the philosophers, had exercised a very pernicious influence on the manners, and even on the constitution.—W.]

[Footnote 15: In the year of Rome 701, the temple of Isis and Serapis was demolished by the order of the Senate, (Dion Cassius, l. xl. p. 252,) and even by the hands of the consul, (Valerius Maximus, l. 3.) After the death of Caesar it was restored at the public expense, (Dion. l. xlvii. p. 501.) When Augustus was in Egypt, he revered the majesty of Serapis, (Dion, l. li. p. 647;) but in the Pomaerium of Rome, and a mile round it, he prohibited the worship of the Egyptian gods, (Dion, l. liii. p. 679; l. liv. p. 735.) They remained, however, very fashionable under his reign (Ovid. de Art. Amand. l. i.) and that of his successor, till the justice of Tiberius was provoked to some acts of severity. (See Tacit. Annal. ii. 85. Joseph. Antiquit. l. xviii. c. 3.) Note: See, in the pictures from the walls of Pompeii, the representation of an Isiac temple and worship. Vestiges of Egyptian worship have been traced in Gaul, and, I am informed, recently in Britain, in excavations at York.— M.]

[Footnote 15/1: Gibbon here blends into one, two events, distant a hundred and sixty-six years from each other. It was in the year of Rome 535, that the senate having ordered the destruction of the temples of Isis and Serapis, the workman would lend his hand; and the consul, L. Paulus himself (Valer. Max. 1, 3) seized the axe, to give the first blow. Gibbon attribute this circumstance to the second demolition, which took place in the year 701 and which he considers as the first.—W.]

[Footnote 16: Tertullian in Apologetic. c. 6, p. 74. Edit. Havercamp. I am inclined to attribute their establishment to the devotion of the Flavian family.]

[Footnote 17: See Livy, l. xi. [Suppl.] and xxix.]

[Footnote 18: Macrob. Saturnalia, l. iii. c. 9. He gives us a form of evocation.]

[Footnote 19: Minutius Faelix in Octavio, p. 54. Arnobius, l. vi. p. 115.]

II. The narrow policy of preserving, without any foreign mixture, the pure blood of the ancient citizens, had checked the fortune, and hastened the ruin, of Athens and Sparta. The aspiring genius of Rome sacrificed vanity to ambition, and deemed it more prudent, as well as honorable, to adopt virtue and merit for her own wheresoever they were found, among slaves or strangers, enemies or barbarians. [20] During the most flourishing aera of the Athenian commonwealth, the number of citizens gradually decreased from about thirty [21] to twenty-one thousand. [22] If, on the contrary, we study the growth of the Roman republic, we may discover, that, notwithstanding the incessant demands of wars and colonies, the citizens, who, in the first census of Servius Tullius, amounted to no more than eighty-three thousand, were multiplied, before the commencement of the social war, to the number of four hundred and sixty-three thousand men, able to bear arms in the service of their country. [23] When the allies of Rome claimed an equal share of honors and privileges, the senate indeed preferred the chance of arms to an ignominious concession. The Samnites and the Lucanians paid the severe penalty of their rashness; but the rest of the Italian states, as they successively returned to their duty, were admitted into the bosom of the republic, [24] and soon contributed to the ruin of public freedom. Under a democratical government, the citizens exercise the powers of sovereignty; and those powers will be first abused, and afterwards lost, if they are committed to an unwieldy multitude. But when the popular assemblies had been suppressed by the administration of the emperors, the conquerors were distinguished from the vanquished nations, only as the first and most honorable order of subjects; and their increase, however rapid, was no longer exposed to the same dangers. Yet the wisest princes, who adopted the maxims of Augustus, guarded with the strictest care the dignity of the Roman name, and diffused the freedom of the city with a prudent liberality. [25]

[Footnote 20: Tacit. Annal. xi. 24. The Orbis Romanus of the learned Spanheim is a complete history of the progressive admission of Latium, Italy, and the provinces, to the freedom of Rome. Note: Democratic states, observes Denina, (delle Revoluz. d' Italia, l. ii. c. l.), are most jealous of communication the privileges of citizenship; monarchies or oligarchies willingly multiply the numbers of their free subjects. The most remarkable accessions to the strength of Rome, by the aggregation of conquered and foreign nations, took place under the regal and patrician—we may add, the Imperial government.—M.]

[Footnote 21: Herodotus, v. 97. It should seem, however, that he followed a large and popular estimation.]

[Footnote 22: Athenaeus, Deipnosophist. l. vi. p. 272. Edit. Casaubon. Meursius de Fortuna Attica, c. 4. Note: On the number of citizens in Athens, compare Boeckh, Public Economy of Athens, (English Tr.,) p. 45, et seq. Fynes Clinton, Essay in Fasti Hel lenici, vol. i. 381.—M.]

[Footnote 23: See a very accurate collection of the numbers of each Lustrum in M. de Beaufort, Republique Romaine, l. iv. c. 4. Note: All these questions are placed in an entirely new point of view by Nicbuhr, (Romische Geschichte, vol. i. p. 464.) He rejects the census of Servius fullius as unhistoric, (vol. ii. p. 78, et seq.,) and he establishes the principle that the census comprehended all the confederate cities which had the right of Isopolity.—M.]

[Footnote 24: Appian. de Bell. Civil. l. i. Velleius Paterculus, l. ii. c. 15, 16, 17.]

[Footnote 25: Maecenas had advised him to declare, by one edict, all his subjects citizens. But we may justly suspect that the historian Dion was the author of a counsel so much adapted to the practice of his own age, and so little to that of Augustus.]

PART II

Till the privileges of Romans had been progressively extended to all the inhabitants of the empire, an important distinction was preserved between Italy and the provinces. The former was esteemed the centre of public unity, and the firm basis of the constitution. Italy claimed the birth, or at least the residence, of the emperors and the senate. [26] The estates of the Italians were exempt from taxes, their persons from the arbitrary jurisdiction of governors. Their municipal corporations, formed after the perfect model of the capital, [26/1] were intrusted, under the immediate eye of the supreme power, with the execution of the laws. From the foot of the Alps to the extremity of Calabria, all the natives of Italy were born citizens of Rome. Their partial distinctions were obliterated, and they insensibly coalesced into one great nation, united by language, manners, and civil institutions, and equal to the weight of a powerful empire. The republic gloried in her generous policy, and was frequently rewarded by the merit and services of her adopted sons. Had she always confined the distinction of Romans to the ancient families within the walls of the city, that immortal name would have been deprived of some of its noblest ornaments. Virgil was a native of Mantua; Horace was inclined to doubt whether he should call himself an Apulian or a Lucanian; it was in Padua that an historian was found worthy to record the majestic series of Roman victories. The patriot family of the Catos emerged from Tusculum; and the little town of Arpinum claimed the double honor of producing Marius and Cicero, the former of whom deserved, after Romulus and Camillus, to be styled the Third Founder of Rome; and the latter, after saving his country from the designs of Catiline, enabled her to contend with Athens for the palm of eloquence. [27]

[Footnote 26: The senators were obliged to have one third of their own landed property in Italy. See Plin. l. vi. ep. 19. The qualification was reduced by Marcus to one fourth. Since the reign of Trajan, Italy had sunk nearer to the level of the provinces.]

[Footnote 26/1: It may be doubted whether the municipal government of the cities was not the old Italian constitution rather than a transcript from that of Rome. The free government of the cities, observes Savigny, was the leading characteristic of Italy. Geschichte des Romischen Rechts, i. p. G.—M.]

[Footnote 27: The first part of the Verona Illustrata of the Marquis Maffei gives the clearest and most comprehensive view of the state of Italy under the Caesars. Note: Compare Denina, Revol. d' Italia, l. ii. c. 6, p. 100, 4 to edit.]

The provinces of the empire (as they have been described in the preceding chapter) were destitute of any public force, or constitutional freedom. In Etruria, in Greece, [28] and in Gaul, [29] it was the first care of the senate to dissolve those dangerous confederacies, which taught mankind that, as the Roman arms prevailed by division, they might be resisted by union. Those princes, whom the ostentation of gratitude or generosity permitted for a while to hold a precarious sceptre, were dismissed from their thrones, as soon as they had per formed their appointed task of fashioning to the yoke the vanquished nations. The free states and cities which had embraced the cause of Rome were rewarded with a nominal alliance, and insensibly sunk into real servitude. The public authority was every where exercised by the ministers of the senate and of the emperors, and that authority was absolute, and without control. [29/1] But the same salutary maxims of government, which had secured the peace and obedience of Italy were extended to the most distant conquests. A nation of Romans was gradually formed in the provinces, by the double expedient of introducing colonies, and of admitting the most faithful and deserving of the provincials to the freedom of Rome.

[Footnote 28: See Pausanias, l. vii. The Romans condescended to restore the names of those assemblies, when they could no longer be dangerous.]

[Footnote 29: They are frequently mentioned by Caesar. The Abbe Dubos attempts, with very little success, to prove that the assemblies of Gaul were continued under the emperors. Histoire de l'Etablissement de la Monarchie Francoise, l. i. c. 4.]

[Footnote 29/1: This is, perhaps, rather overstated. Most cities retained the choice of their municipal officers: some retained valuable privileges; Athens, for instance, in form was still a confederate city. (Tac. Ann. ii. 53.) These privileges, indeed, depended entirely on the arbitrary will of the emperor, who revoked or restored them according to his caprice. See Walther Geschichte les Romischen Rechts, i. 324—an admirable summary of the Roman constitutional history.—M.]

"Wheresoever the Roman conquers, he inhabits," is a very just observation of Seneca, [30] confirmed by history and experience. The natives of Italy, allured by pleasure or by interest, hastened to enjoy the advantages of victory; and we may remark, that, about forty years after the reduction of Asia, eighty thousand Romans were massacred in one day, by the cruel orders of Mithridates. [31] These voluntary exiles were engaged, for the most part, in the occupations of commerce, agriculture, and the farm of the revenue. But after the legions were rendered permanent by the emperors, the provinces were peopled by a race of soldiers; and the veterans, whether they received the reward of their service in land or in money, usually settled with their families in the country, where they had honorably spent their youth. Throughout the empire, but more particularly in the western parts, the most fertile districts, and the most convenient situations, were reserved for the establishment of colonies; some of which were of a civil, and others of a military nature. In their manners and internal policy, the colonies formed a perfect representation of their great parent; and they were soon endeared to the natives by the ties of friendship and alliance, they effectually diffused a reverence for the Roman name, and a desire, which was seldom disappointed, of sharing, in due time, its honors and advantages. [32] The municipal cities insensibly equalled the rank and splendor of the colonies; and in the reign of Hadrian, it was disputed which was the preferable condition, of those societies which had issued from, or those which had been received into, the bosom of Rome. [33] The right of Latium, as it was called, [33/1] conferred on the cities to which it had been granted, a more partial favor. The magistrates only, at the expiration of their office, assumed the quality of Roman citizens; but as those offices were annual, in a few years they circulated round the principal families. [34] Those of the provincials who were permitted to bear arms in the legions; [35] those who exercised any civil employment; all, in a word, who performed any public service, or displayed any personal talents, were rewarded with a present, whose value was continually diminished by the increasing liberality of the emperors. Yet even, in the age of the Antonines, when the freedom of the city had been bestowed on the greater number of their subjects, it was still accompanied with very solid advantages. The bulk of the people acquired, with that title, the benefit of the Roman laws, particularly in the interesting articles of marriage, testaments, and inheritances; and the road of fortune was open to those whose pretensions were seconded by favor or merit. The grandsons of the Gauls, who had besieged Julius Caesar in Alcsia, commanded legions, governed provinces, and were admitted into the senate of Rome. [36] Their ambition, instead of disturbing the tranquillity of the state, was intimately connected with its safety and greatness.

[Footnote 30: Seneca in Consolat. ad Helviam, c. 6.]

[Footnote 31: Memnon apud Photium, (c. 33,) [c. 224, p. 231, ed Bekker.] Valer. Maxim. ix. 2. Plutarch and Dion Cassius swell the massacre to 150,000 citizens; but I should esteem the smaller number to be more than sufficient.]

[Footnote 32: Twenty-five colonies were settled in Spain, (see Plin. Hist. Nat. iii. 3, 4; iv. 35;) and nine in Britain, of which London, Colchester, Lincoln, Chester, Gloucester, and Bath still remain considerable cities. (See Richard of Cirencester, p. 36, and Whittaker's History of Manchester, l. i. c. 3.)]

[Footnote 33: Aul. Gel. Noctes Atticae, xvi 13. The Emperor Hadrian expressed his surprise, that the cities of Utica, Gades, and Italica, which already enjoyed the rights of Municipia, should solicit the title of colonies. Their example, however, became fashionable, and the empire was filled with honorary colonies. See Spanheim, de Usu Numismatum Dissertat. xiii.]

[Footnote 33/1: The right of Latium conferred an exemption from the government of the Roman praefect. Strabo states this distinctly, l. iv. p. 295, edit. Caesar's. See also Walther, p. 233.—M]

[Footnote 34: Spanheim, Orbis Roman. c. 8, p. 62.]

[Footnote 35: Aristid. in Romae Encomio. tom. i. p. 218, edit. Jebb.]

[Footnote 36: Tacit. Annal. xi. 23, 24. Hist. iv. 74.]

So sensible were the Romans of the influence of language over national manners, that it was their most serious care to extend, with the progress of their arms, the use of the Latin tongue. [37] The ancient dialects of Italy, the Sabine, the Etruscan, and the Venetian, sunk into oblivion; but in the provinces, the east was less docile than the west to the voice of its victorious preceptors. This obvious difference marked the two portions of the empire with a distinction of colors, which, though it was in some degree concealed during the meridian splendor of prosperity, became gradually more visible, as the shades of night descended upon the Roman world. The western countries were civilized by the same hands which subdued them. As soon as the barbarians were reconciled to obedience, their minds were open to any new impressions of knowledge and politeness. The language of Virgil and Cicero, though with some inevitable mixture of corruption, was so universally adopted in Africa, Spain, Gaul Britain, and Pannonia, [38] that the faint traces of the Punic or Celtic idioms were preserved only in the mountains, or among the peasants. [39] Education and study insensibly inspired the natives of those countries with the sentiments of Romans; and Italy gave fashions, as well as laws, to her Latin provincials. They solicited with more ardor, and obtained with more facility, the freedom and honors of the state; supported the national dignity in letters [40] and in arms; and at length, in the person of Trajan, produced an emperor whom the Scipios would not have disowned for their countryman. The situation of the Greeks was very different from that of the barbarians. The former had been long since civilized and corrupted. They had too much taste to relinquish their language, and too much vanity to adopt any foreign institutions. Still preserving the prejudices, after they had lost the virtues, of their ancestors, they affected to despise the unpolished manners of the Roman conquerors, whilst they were compelled to respect their superior wisdom and power. [41] Nor was the influence of the Grecian language and sentiments confined to the narrow limits of that once celebrated country. Their empire, by the progress of colonies and conquest, had been diffused from the Adriatic to the Euphrates and the Nile. Asia was covered with Greek cities, and the long reign of the Macedonian kings had introduced a silent revolution into Syria and Egypt. In their pompous courts, those princes united the elegance of Athens with the luxury of the East, and the example of the court was imitated, at an humble distance, by the higher ranks of their subjects. Such was the general division of the Roman empire into the Latin and Greek languages. To these we may add a third distinction for the body of the natives in Syria, and especially in Egypt, the use of their ancient dialects, by secluding them from the commerce of mankind, checked the improvements of those barbarians. [42] The slothful effeminacy of the former exposed them to the contempt, the sullen ferociousness of the latter excited the aversion, of the conquerors. [43] Those nations had submitted to the Roman power, but they seldom desired or deserved the freedom of the city: and it was remarked, that more than two hundred and thirty years elapsed after the ruin of the Ptolemies, before an Egyptian was admitted into the senate of Rome. [44]

[Footnote 37: See Plin. Hist. Natur. iii. 5. Augustin. de Civitate Dei, xix 7 Lipsius de Pronunciatione Linguae Latinae, c. 3.]

[Footnote 38: Apuleius and Augustin will answer for Africa; Strabo for Spain and Gaul; Tacitus, in the life of Agricola, for Britain; and Velleius Paterculus, for Pannonia. To them we may add the language of the Inscriptions. Note: Mr. Hallam contests this assertion as regards Britain. "Nor did the Romans ever establish their language—I know not whether they wished to do so—in this island, as we perceive by that stubborn British tongue which has survived two conquests." In his note, Mr. Hallam examines the passage from Tacitus (Agric. xxi.) to which Gibbon refers. It merely asserts the progress of Latin studies among the higher orders. (Midd. Ages, iii. 314.) Probably it was a kind of court language, and that of public affairs and prevailed in the Roman colonies.—M.]

[Footnote 39: The Celtic was preserved in the mountains of Wales, Cornwall, and Armorica. We may observe, that Apuleius reproaches an African youth, who lived among the populace, with the use of the Punic; whilst he had almost forgot Greek, and neither could nor would speak Latin, (Apolog. p. 596.) The greater part of St. Austin's congregations were strangers to the Punic.]

[Footnote 40: Spain alone produced Columella, the Senecas, Lucan, Martial, and Quintilian.]

[Footnote 41: There is not, I believe, from Dionysius to Libanus, a single Greek critic who mentions Virgil or Horace. They seem ignorant that the Romans had any good writers.]

[Footnote 42: The curious reader may see in Dupin, (Bibliotheque Ecclesiastique, tom. xix. p. 1, c. 8,) how much the use of the Syriac and Egyptian languages was still preserved.]

[Footnote 43: See Juvenal, Sat. iii. and xv. Ammian. Marcellin. xxii. 16.]

[Footnote 44: Dion Cassius, l. lxxvii. p. 1275. The first instance happened under the reign of Septimius Severus.]

It is a just though trite observation, that victorious Rome was herself subdued by the arts of Greece. Those immortal writers who still command the admiration of modern Europe, soon became the favorite object of study and imitation in Italy and the western provinces. But the elegant amusements of the Romans were not suffered to interfere with their sound maxims of policy. Whilst they acknowledged the charms of the Greek, they asserted the dignity of the Latin tongue, and the exclusive use of the latter was inflexibly maintained in the administration of civil as well as military government. [45] The two languages exercised at the same time their separate jurisdiction throughout the empire: the former, as the natural idiom of science; the latter, as the legal dialect of public transactions. Those who united letters with business were equally conversant with both; and it was almost impossible, in any province, to find a Roman subject, of a liberal education, who was at once a stranger to the Greek and to the Latin language.

[Footnote 45: See Valerius Maximus, l. ii. c. 2, n. 2. The emperor Claudius disfranchised an eminent Grecian for not understanding Latin. He was probably in some public office. Suetonius in Claud. c. 16. Note: Causes seem to have been pleaded, even in the senate, in both languages. Val. Max. loc. cit. Dion. l. lvii. c. 15.—M]

It was by such institutions that the nations of the empire insensibly melted away into the Roman name and people. But there still remained, in the centre of every province and of every family, an unhappy condition of men who endured the weight, without sharing the benefits, of society. In the free states of antiquity, the domestic slaves were exposed to the wanton rigor of despotism. The perfect settlement of the Roman empire was preceded by ages of violence and rapine. The slaves consisted, for the most part, of barbarian captives, [45/1] taken in thousands by the chance of war, purchased at a vile price, [46] accustomed to a life of independence, and impatient to break and to revenge their fetters. Against such internal enemies, whose desperate insurrections had more than once reduced the republic to the brink of destruction, [47] the most severe [47/1] regulations, [48] and the most cruel treatment, seemed almost justified by the great law of self-preservation. But when the principal nations of Europe, Asia, and Africa were united under the laws of one sovereign, the source of foreign supplies flowed with much less abundance, and the Romans were reduced to the milder but more tedious method of propagation. [48/1] In their numerous families, and particularly in their country estates, they encouraged the marriage of their slaves. [48/2] The sentiments of nature, the habits of education, and the possession of a dependent species of property, contributed to alleviate the hardships of servitude. [49] The existence of a slave became an object of greater value, and though his happiness still depended on the temper and circumstances of the master, the humanity of the latter, instead of being restrained by fear, was encouraged by the sense of his own interest. The progress of manners was accelerated by the virtue or policy of the emperors; and by the edicts of Hadrian and the Antonines, the protection of the laws was extended to the most abject part of mankind. The jurisdiction of life and death over the slaves, a power long exercised and often abused, was taken out of private hands, and reserved to the magistrates alone. The subterraneous prisons were abolished; and, upon a just complaint of intolerable treatment, the injured slave obtained either his deliverance, or a less cruel master. [50]

[Footnote 45/1: It was this which rendered the wars so sanguinary, and the battles so obstinate. The immortal Robertson, in an excellent discourse on the state of the world at the period of the establishment of Christianity, has traced a picture of the melancholy effects of slavery, in which we find all the depth of his views and the strength of his mind. I shall oppose successively some passages to the reflections of Gibbon. The reader will see, not without interest, the truths which Gibbon appears to have mistaken or voluntarily neglected, developed by one of the best of modern historians. It is important to call them to mind here, in order to establish the facts and their consequences with accuracy. I shall more than once have occasion to employ, for this purpose, the discourse of Robertson. "Captives taken in war were, in all probability, the first persons subjected to perpetual servitude; and, when the necessities or luxury of mankind increased the demand for slaves, every new war recruited their number, by reducing the vanquished to that wretched condition. Hence proceeded the fierce and desperate spirit with which wars were carried on among ancient nations. While chains and slavery were the certain lot of the conquered, battles were fought, and towns defended with a rage and obstinacy which nothing but horror at such a fate could have inspired; but, putting an end to the cruel institution of slavery, Christianity extended its mild influences to the practice of war, and that barbarous art, softened by its humane spirit, ceased to be so destructive. Secure, in every event, of personal liberty, the resistance of the vanquished became less obstinate, and the triumph of the victor less cruel. Thus humanity was introduced into the exercise of war, with which it appears to be almost incompatible; and it is to the merciful maxims of Christianity, much more than to any other cause, that we must ascribe the little ferocity and bloodshed which accompany modern victories."—G.]

[Footnote 46: In the camp of Lucullus, an ox sold for a drachma, and a slave for four drachmae, or about three shillings. Plutarch. in Lucull. p. 580. Note: Above 100,000 prisoners were taken in the Jewish war.—G. Hist. of Jews, iii. 71. According to a tradition preserved by S. Jerom, after the insurrection in the time of Hadrian, they were sold as cheap as horse. Ibid. 124. Compare Blair on Roman Slavery, p. 19.—M., and Dureau de la blalle, Economie Politique des Romains, l. i. c. 15. But I cannot think that this writer has made out his case as to the common price of an agricultural slave being from 2000 to 2500 francs, (80l. to 100l.) He has overlooked the passages which show the ordinary prices, (i. e. Hor. Sat. ii. vii. 45,) and argued from extraordinary and exceptional cases.—M. 1845.]

[Footnote 47: Diodorus Siculus in Eclog. Hist. l. xxxiv. and xxxvi. Florus, iii. 19, 20.]

[Footnote 47/1: The following is the example: we shall see whether the word "severe" is here in its place. "At the time in which L. Domitius was praetor in Sicily, a slave killed a wild boar of extraordinary size. The praetor, struck by the dexterity and courage of the man, desired to see him. The poor wretch, highly gratified with the distinction, came to present himself before the praetor, in hopes, no doubt, of praise and reward; but Domitius, on learning that he had only a javelin to attack and kill the boar, ordered him to be instantly crucified, under the barbarous pretext that the law prohibited the use of this weapon, as of all others, to slaves." Perhaps the cruelty of Domitius is less astonishing than the indifference with which the Roman orator relates this circumstance, which affects him so little that he thus expresses himself: "Durum hoc fortasse videatur, neque ego in ullam partem disputo." "This may appear harsh, nor do I give any opinion on the subject." And it is the same orator who exclaims in the same oration, "Facinus est cruciare civem Romanum; scelus verberare; prope parricidium necare: quid dicam in crucem tollere?" "It is a crime to imprison a Roman citizen; wickedness to scourge; next to parricide to put to death, what shall I call it to crucify?"

In general, this passage of Gibbon on slavery, is full, not only of blamable indifference, but of an exaggeration of impartiality which resembles dishonesty. He endeavors to extenuate all that is appalling in the condition and treatment of the slaves; he would make us consider those cruelties as possibly "justified by necessity." He then describes, with minute accuracy, the slightest mitigations of their deplorable condition; he attributes to the virtue or the policy of the emperors the progressive amelioration in the lot of the slaves; and he passes over in silence the most influential cause, that which, after rendering the slaves less miserable, has contributed at length entirely to enfranchise them from their sufferings and their chains,—Christianity. It would be easy to accumulate the most frightful, the most agonizing details, of the manner in which the Romans treated their slaves; whole works have been devoted to the description. I content myself with referring to them. Some reflections of Robertson, taken from the discourse already quoted, will make us feel that Gibbon, in tracing the mitigation of the condition of the slaves, up to a period little later than that which witnessed the establishment of Christianity in the world, could not have avoided the acknowledgment of the influence of that beneficent cause, if he had not already determined not to speak of it.

"Upon establishing despotic government in the Roman empire, domestic tyranny rose, in a short time, to an astonishing height. In that rank soil, every vice, which power nourishes in the great, or oppression engenders in the mean, thrived and grew up apace. It is not the authority of any single detached precept in the gospel, but the spirit and genius of the Christian religion, more powerful than any particular command, which hath abolished the practice of slavery throughout the world. The temper which Christianity inspired was mild and gentle; and the doctrines it taught added such dignity and lustre to human nature, as rescued it from the dishonorable servitude into which it was sunk."

It is in vain, then, that Gibbon pretends to attribute solely to the desire of keeping up the number of slaves, the milder conduct which the Romans began to adopt in their favor at the time of the emperors. This cause had hitherto acted in an opposite direction; how came it on a sudden to have a different influence? "The masters," he says, "encouraged the marriage of their slaves; the sentiments of nature, the habits of education, contributed to alleviate the hardships of servitude." The children of slaves were the property of their master, who could dispose of or alienate them like the rest of his property. Is it in such a situation, with such notions, that the sentiments of nature unfold themselves, or habits of education become mild and peaceful? We must not attribute to causes inadequate or altogether without force, effects which require to explain them a reference to more influential causes; and even if these slighter causes had in effect a manifest influence, we must not forget that they are themselves the effect of a primary, a higher, and more extensive cause, which, in giving to the mind and to the character a more disinterested and more humane bias, disposed men to second or themselves to advance, by their conduct, and by the change of manners, the happy results which it tended to produce.—G.

I have retained the whole of M. Guizot's note, though, in his zeal for the invaluable blessings of freedom and Christianity, he has done Gibbon injustice. The condition of the slaves was undoubtedly improved under the emperors. What a great authority has said, "The condition of a slave is better under an arbitrary than under a free government," (Smith's Wealth of Nations, iv. 7,) is, I believe, supported by the history of all ages and nations. The protecting edicts of Hadrian and the Antonines are historical facts, and can as little be attributed to the influence of Christianity, as the milder language of heathen writers, of Seneca, (particularly Ep. 47,) of Pliny, and of Plutarch. The latter influence of Christianity is admitted by Gibbon himself. The subject of Roman slavery has recently been investigated with great diligence in a very modest but valuable volume, by Wm. Blair, Esq., Edin. 1833. May we be permitted, while on the subject, to refer to the most splendid passage extant of Mr. Pitt's eloquence, the description of the Roman slave-dealer. on the shores of Britain, condemning the island to irreclaimable barbarism, as a perpetual and prolific nursery of slaves? Speeches, vol. ii. p. 80.

Gibbon, it should be added, was one of the first and most consistent opponents of the African slave-trade. (See Hist. ch. xxv. and Letters to Lor Sheffield, Misc. Works)—M.]

[Footnote 48: See a remarkable instance of severity in Cicero in Verrem, v. 3.]

[Footnote 48/1: An active slave-trade, which was carried on in many quarters, particularly the Euxine, the eastern provinces, the coast of Africa, and British must be taken into the account. Blair, 23—32.—M.]

[Footnote 48/2: The Romans, as well in the first ages of the republic as later, allowed to their slaves a kind of marriage, (contubernium:) notwithstanding this, luxury made a greater number of slaves in demand. The increase in their population was not sufficient, and recourse was had to the purchase of slaves, which was made even in the provinces of the East subject to the Romans. It is, moreover, known that slavery is a state little favorable to population. (See Hume's Essay, and Malthus on population, i. 334.—G.) The testimony of Appian (B.C. l. i. c. 7) is decisive in favor of the rapid multiplication of the agricultural slaves; it is confirmed by the numbers engaged in the servile wars. Compare also Blair, p. 119; likewise Columella l. viii.—M.]

[Footnote 49: See in Gruter, and the other collectors, a great number of inscriptions addressed by slaves to their wives, children, fellow-servants, masters, &c. They are all most probably of the Imperial age.]

[Footnote 50: See the Augustan History, and a Dissertation of M. de Burigny, in the xxxvth volume of the Academy of Inscriptions, upon the Roman slaves.]

Hope, the best comfort of our imperfect condition, was not denied to the Roman slave; and if he had any opportunity of rendering himself either useful or agreeable, he might very naturally expect that the diligence and fidelity of a few years would be rewarded with the inestimable gift of freedom. The benevolence of the master was so frequently prompted by the meaner suggestions of vanity and avarice, that the laws found it more necessary to restrain than to encourage a profuse and undistinguishing liberality, which might degenerate into a very dangerous abuse. [51] It was a maxim of ancient jurisprudence, that a slave had not any country of his own; he acquired with his liberty an admission into the political society of which his patron was a member. The consequences of this maxim would have prostituted the privileges of the Roman city to a mean and promiscuous multitude. Some seasonable exceptions were therefore provided; and the honorable distinction was confined to such slaves only as, for just causes, and with the approbation of the magistrate, should receive a solemn and legal manumission. Even these chosen freedmen obtained no more than the private rights of citizens, and were rigorously excluded from civil or military honors. Whatever might be the merit or fortune of their sons, they likewise were esteemed unworthy of a seat in the senate; nor were the traces of a servile origin allowed to be completely obliterated till the third or fourth generation. [52] Without destroying the distinction of ranks, a distant prospect of freedom and honors was presented, even to those whom pride and prejudice almost disdained to number among the human species.

[Footnote 51: See another Dissertation of M. de Burigny, in the xxxviith volume, on the Roman freedmen.]

[Footnote 52: Spanheim, Orbis Roman. l. i. c. 16, p. 124, &c.] It was once proposed to discriminate the slaves by a peculiar habit; but it was justly apprehended that there might be some danger in acquainting them with their own numbers. [53] Without interpreting, in their utmost strictness, the liberal appellations of legions and myriads, [54] we may venture to pronounce, that the proportion of slaves, who were valued as property, was more considerable than that of servants, who can be computed only as an expense. [55] The youths of a promising genius were instructed in the arts and sciences, and their price was ascertained by the degree of their skill and talents. [56] Almost every profession, either liberal [57] or mechanical, might be found in the household of an opulent senator. The ministers of pomp and sensuality were multiplied beyond the conception of modern luxury. [58] It was more for the interest of the merchant or manufacturer to purchase, than to hire his workmen; and in the country, slaves were employed as the cheapest and most laborious instruments of agriculture. To confirm the general observation, and to display the multitude of slaves, we might allege a variety of particular instances. It was discovered, on a very melancholy occasion, that four hundred slaves were maintained in a single palace of Rome. [59] The same number of four hundred belonged to an estate which an African widow, of a very private condition, resigned to her son, whilst she reserved for herself a much larger share of her property. [60] A freedman, under the name of Augustus, though his fortune had suffered great losses in the civil wars, left behind him three thousand six hundred yoke of oxen, two hundred and fifty thousand head of smaller cattle, and what was almost included in the description of cattle, four thousand one hundred and sixteen slaves. [61]

[Footnote 53: Seneca de Clementia, l. i. c. 24. The original is much stronger, "Quantum periculum immineret si servi nostri numerare nos coepissent."]

[Footnote 54: See Pliny (Hist. Natur. l. xxxiii.) and Athenaeus (Deipnosophist. l. vi. p. 272.) The latter boldly asserts, that he knew very many Romans who possessed, not for use, but ostentation, ten and even twenty thousand slaves.]

[Footnote 55: In Paris there are not more than 43,000 domestics of every sort, and not a twelfth part of the inhabitants. Messange, Recherches sui la Population, p. 186.]

[Footnote 56: A learned slave sold for many hundred pounds sterling: Atticus always bred and taught them himself. Cornel. Nepos in Vit. c. 13, [on the prices of slaves. Blair, 149.]—M.]

[Footnote 57: Many of the Roman physicians were slaves. See Dr. Middleton's Dissertation and Defence.]

[Footnote 58: Their ranks and offices are very copiously enumerated by Pignorius de Servis.]

[Footnote 59: Tacit. Annal. xiv. 43. They were all executed for not preventing their master's murder. Note: The remarkable speech of Cassius shows the proud feelings of the Roman aristocracy on this subject.—M]

[Footnote 60: Apuleius in Apolog. p. 548. edit. Delphin]

[Footnote 61: Plin. Hist. Natur. l. xxxiii. 47.]

The number of subjects who acknowledged the laws of Rome, of citizens, of provincials, and of slaves, cannot now be fixed with such a degree of accuracy, as the importance of the object would deserve. We are informed, that when the Emperor Claudius exercised the office of censor, he took an account of six millions nine hundred and forty-five thousand Roman citizens, who, with the proportion of women and children, must have amounted to about twenty millions of souls. The multitude of subjects of an inferior rank was uncertain and fluctuating. But, after weighing with attention every circumstance which could influence the balance, it seems probable that there existed, in the time of Claudius, about twice as many provincials as there were citizens, of either sex, and of every age; and that the slaves were at least equal in number to the free inhabitants of the Roman world. [611] The total amount of this imperfect calculation would rise to about one hundred and twenty millions of persons; a degree of population which possibly exceeds that of modern Europe, [62] and forms the most numerous society that has ever been united under the same system of government.

[Footnote 61/1]: According to Robertson, there were twice as many slaves as free citizens.—G. Mr. Blair (p. 15) estimates three slaves to one freeman, between the conquest of Greece, B.C. 146, and the reign of

Alexander Severus, A. D. 222, 235. The proportion was probably larger in Italy than in the provinces.—M. On the other hand, Zumpt, in his Dissertation quoted below, (p. 86,) asserts it to be a gross error in Gibbon to reckon the number of slaves equal to that of the free population. The luxury and magnificence of the great, (he observes,) at the commencement of the empire, must not be taken as the groundwork of calculations for the whole Roman world. "The agricultural laborer, and the artisan, in Spain, Gaul, Britain, Syria, and Egypt, maintained himself, as in the present day, by his own labor and that of his household, without possessing a single slave." The latter part of my note was intended to suggest this consideration. Yet so completely was slavery rooted in the social system, both in the east and the west, that in the great diffusion of wealth at this time, every one, I doubt not, who could afford a domestic slave, kept one; and generally, the number of slaves was in proportion to the wealth. I do not believe that the cultivation of the soil by slaves was confined to Italy; the holders of large estates in the provinces would probably, either from choice or necessity, adopt the same mode of cultivation. The latifundia, says Pliny, had ruined Italy, and had begun to ruin the provinces. Slaves were no doubt employed in agricultural labor to a great extent in Sicily, and were the estates of those six enormous landholders who were said to have possessed the whole province of Africa, cultivated altogether by free coloni? Whatever may have been the case in the rural districts, in the towns and cities the household duties were almost entirely discharged by slaves, and vast numbers belonged to the public establishments. I do not, however, differ so far from Zumpt, and from M. Dureau de la Malle, as to adopt the higher and bolder estimate of Robertson and Mr. Blair, rather than the more cautious suggestions of Gibbon. I would reduce rather than increase the proportion of the slave population. The very ingenious and elaborate calculations of the French writer, by which he deduces the amount of the population from the produce and consumption of corn in Italy, appear to me neither precise nor satisfactory bases for such complicated political arithmetic. I am least satisfied with his views as to the population of the city of Rome; but this point will be more fitly reserved for a note on the thirty-first chapter of Gibbon. The work, however, of M. Dureau de la Malle is very curious and full on some of the minuter points of Roman statistics.—M. 1845.]

[Footnote 62: Compute twenty millions in France, twenty-two in Germany, four in Hungary, ten in Italy with its islands, eight in Great Britain and Ireland, eight in Spain and Portugal, ten or twelve in the European Russia, six in Poland, six in Greece and Turkey, four in Sweden, three in Denmark and Norway, four in the Low Countries. The whole would amount to one hundred and five, or one hundred and seven millions. See Voltaire, de l'Histoire Generale. Note: The present population of Europe is estimated at 227,700,000. Malts Bran, Geogr. Trans edit. 1832 See details in the different volumes Another authority, (Almanach de Gotha,) quoted in a recent English publication, gives the following details:—

France, 32,897,521 Germany, (including Hungary, Prussian and Austrian Poland,) 56,136,213 Italy, 20,548,616 Great Britain and Ireland, 24,062,947 Spain and Portugal, 13,953,959. 3,144,000 Russia, including Poland, 44,220,600 Cracow, 128,480 Turkey, (including Pachalic of Dschesair,) 9,545,300 Greece, 637,700 Ionian Islands, 208,100 Sweden and Norway, 3,914,963 Denmark, 2,012,998 Belgium, 3,533,538 Holland, 2,444,550 Switzerland, 985,000. Total, 219,344,116

Since the publication of my first annotated edition of Gibbon, the subject of the population of the Roman empire has been investigated by two writers of great industry and learning; Mons. Dureau de la Malle, in his Economie Politique des Romains, liv. ii. c. 1. to 8, and M. Zumpt, in a dissertation printed in the Transactions of the Berlin Academy, 1840. M. Dureau de la Malle confines his inquiry almost entirely to the city of Rome, and Roman Italy. Zumpt examines at greater length the axiom, which he supposes to have been assumed by Gibbon as unquestionable, "that Italy and the Roman world was never so populous as in the time of the Antonines." Though this probably was Gibbon's opinion, he has not stated it so peremptorily as asserted by Mr. Zumpt. It had before been expressly laid down by Hume, and his statement was controverted by Wallace and by Malthus. Gibbon says (p. 84) that there is no reason to believe the country (of Italy) less populous in the age of the Antonines, than in that of Romulus; and Zumpt acknowledges that we have no satisfactory knowledge of the state of Italy at that early age. Zumpt, in my opinion with some reason, takes the period just before the first Punic war, as that in which Roman Italy (all south of the Rubicon) was most populous. From that time, the numbers began to diminish, at first from the enormous waste of life out of the free population in the foreign, and afterwards in the civil wars; from the cultivation of the soil by slaves; towards the close of the republic, from the repugnance to marriage, which resisted alike the dread of legal punishment and the offer of legal immunity and privilege; and from the depravity of manners, which interfered with the procreation, the birth, and the rearing of children. The arguments and the authorities of Zumpt are equally conclusive as to the decline of population in Greece. Still the details, which he himself adduces as to the prosperity and populousness of Asia Minor, and the whole of the Roman East, with the advancement of the European provinces, especially Gaul, Spain, and Britain, in civilization, and therefore in populousness, (for I have no confidence in the vast numbers sometimes assigned to the barbarous inhabitants of these countries,) may, I think, fairly compensate for any deduction to be made from Gibbon's general estimate on account of Greece and Italy. Gibbon himself acknowledges his own estimate to be vague and conjectural; and I may venture to recommend the dissertation of Zumpt as deserving respectful consideration.—M 1815.]

PART III

Domestic peace and union were the natural consequences of the moderate and comprehensive policy embraced by the Romans. If we turn our eyes towards the monarchies of Asia, we shall behold despotism in the centre, and weakness in the extremities; the collection of the revenue, or the administration of justice, enforced by the presence of an army; hostile barbarians established in the heart of the country, hereditary satraps usurping the dominion of the provinces, and subjects inclined to rebellion, though incapable of freedom. But the obedience of the Roman world was uniform, voluntary, and permanent. The vanquished nations, blended into one great people, resigned the hope, nay, even the wish, of resuming their independence, and scarcely considered their own existence as distinct from the existence of Rome. The established authority of the emperors pervaded without an effort the wide extent of their dominions, and was exercised with the same facility on the banks of the Thames, or of the Nile, as on those of the Tyber. The legions were destined to serve against the public enemy, and the civil magistrate seldom required the aid of a military force. [63] In this state of general security, the leisure, as well as opulence, both of the prince and people, were devoted to improve and to adorn the Roman empire.

[Footnote 63: Joseph. de Bell. Judaico, l. ii. c. 16. The oration of Agrippa, or rather of the historian, is a fine picture of the Roman empire.]

Among the innumerable monuments of architecture constructed by the Romans, how many have escaped the notice of history, how few have resisted the ravages of time and barbarism! And yet, even the majestic ruins that are still scattered over Italy and the provinces, would be sufficient to prove that those countries were once the seat of a polite and powerful empire. Their greatness alone, or their beauty, might deserve our attention: but they are rendered more interesting, by two important circumstances, which connect the agreeable history of the arts with the more useful history of human manners. Many of those works were erected at private expense, and almost all were intended for public benefit.

It is natural to suppose that the greatest number, as well as the most considerable of the Roman edifices, were raised by the emperors, who possessed so unbounded a command both of men and money. Augustus was accustomed to boast that he had found his capital of brick, and that he had left it of marble. [64] The strict economy of Vespasian was the source of his magnificence. The works of Trajan bear the stamp of his genius. The public monuments with which Hadrian adorned every province of the empire, were executed not only by his orders, but under his immediate inspection. He was himself an artist; and he loved the arts, as they conduced to the glory of the monarch. They were encouraged by the Antonines, as they contributed to the happiness of the people. But if the emperors were the first, they were not the only architects of their dominions. Their example was universally imitated by their principal subjects, who were not afraid of declaring to the world that they had spirit to conceive, and wealth to accomplish, the noblest undertakings. Scarcely had the proud structure of the Coliseum been dedicated at Rome, before the edifices, of a smaller scale indeed, but of the same design and materials, were erected for the use, and at the expense, of the cities of Capua and Verona. [65] The inscription of the stupendous bridge of Alcantara attests that it was thrown over the Tagus by the contribution of a few Lusitanian communities. When Pliny was intrusted with the government of Bithynia and Pontus, provinces by no means the richest or most considerable of the empire, he found the cities within his jurisdiction striving with each other in every useful and ornamental work, that might deserve the curiosity of strangers, or the gratitude of their citizens. It was the duty of the proconsul to supply their deficiencies, to direct their taste, and sometimes to moderate their emulation. [66] The opulent senators of Rome and the provinces esteemed it an honor, and almost an obligation, to adorn the splendor of their age and country; and the influence of fashion very frequently supplied the want of taste or generosity. Among a crowd of these private benefactors, we may select Herodes Atticus, an Athenian citizen, who lived in the age of the Antonines. Whatever might be the motive of his conduct, his magnificence would have been worthy of the greatest kings.

[Footnote 64: Sueton. in August. c. 28. Augustus built in Rome the temple and forum of Mars the Avenger; the temple of Jupiter Tonans in the Capitol; that of Apollo Palatine, with public libraries; the portico and basilica of Caius and Lucius; the porticos of Livia and Octavia; and the theatre of Marcellus. The example of the sovereign was imitated by his ministers and generals; and his friend Agrippa left behind him the immortal monument of the Pantheon.] [See Theatre Of Marcellus: Augustus built in Rome the theatre of Marcellus.]

[Footnote 65: See Maffei, Veroni Illustrata, l. iv. p. 68.]

[Footnote 66: See the xth book of Pliny's Epistles. He mentions the following works carried on at the expense of the cities. At Nicomedia, a new forum, an aqueduct, and a canal, left unfinished by a king; at Nice, a gymnasium, and a theatre, which had already cost near ninety thousand pounds; baths at Prusa and Claudiopolis, and an aqueduct of sixteen miles in length for the use of Sinope.]

The family of Herod, at least after it had been favored by fortune, was lineally descended from Cimon and Miltiades, Theseus and Cecrops, Aeacus and Jupiter. But the posterity of so many gods and heroes was fallen into the most abject state. His grandfather had suffered by the hands of justice, and Julius Atticus, his father, must have ended his life in poverty and contempt, had he not discovered an immense treasure buried under an old house, the last remains of his patrimony. According to the rigor of the law, the emperor might have asserted his claim, and the prudent Atticus prevented, by a frank confession, the officiousness of informers. But the equitable Nerva, who then filled the throne, refused to accept any part of it, and commanded him to use, without scruple, the present of fortune. The cautious Athenian still insisted, that the treasure was too considerable for a subject, and that he knew not how to use it. Abuse it then, replied the monarch, with a good-natured peevishness; for it is your own. [67] Many will be of opinion, that Atticus literally obeyed the emperor's last instructions; since he expended the greatest part of his fortune, which was much increased by an advantageous marriage, in the service of the public. He had obtained for his son Herod the prefecture of the free cities of Asia; and the young magistrate, observing that the town of Troas was indifferently supplied with water, obtained from the munificence of Hadrian three hundred myriads of drachms, (about a hundred thousand pounds,) for the construction of a new aqueduct. But in the execution of the work, the charge amounted to more than double the estimate, and the officers of the revenue began to murmur, till the generous Atticus silenced their complaints, by requesting that he might be permitted to take upon himself the whole additional expense. [68]

[Footnote 67: Hadrian afterwards made a very equitable regulation, which divided all treasure-trove between the right of property and that of discovery. Hist. August. p. 9.]

[Footnote 68: Philostrat. in Vit. Sophist. l. ii. p. 548.]

The ablest preceptors of Greece and Asia had been invited by liberal rewards to direct the education of young Herod. Their pupil soon became a celebrated orator, according to the useless rhetoric of that age, which, confining itself to the schools, disdained to visit either the Forum or the Senate.

He was honored with the consulship at Rome: but the greatest part of his life was spent in a philosophic retirement at Athens, and his adjacent villas; perpetually surrounded by sophists, who acknowledged, without reluctance, the superiority of a rich and generous rival. [69] The monuments of his genius have perished; some considerable ruins still preserve the fame of his taste and munificence: modern travellers have measured the remains of the stadium which he constructed at Athens. It was six hundred feet in length, built entirely of white marble, capable of admitting the whole body of the people, and finished in four years, whilst Herod was president of the Athenian games. To the memory of his wife Regilla he dedicated a theatre, scarcely to be paralleled in the empire: no wood except cedar, very curiously carved, was employed in any part of the building. The Odeum, [69/1] designed by Pericles for musical performances, and the rehearsal of new tragedies, had been a trophy of the victory of the arts over barbaric greatness; as the timbers employed in the construction consisted chiefly of the masts of the Persian vessels. Notwithstanding the repairs bestowed on that ancient edifice by a king of Cappadocia, it was again fallen to decay. Herod restored its ancient beauty and magnificence. Nor was the liberality of that illustrious citizen confined to the walls of Athens. The most splendid ornaments bestowed on the temple of Neptune in the Isthmus, a theatre at Corinth, a stadium at Delphi, a bath at Thermopylae, and an aqueduct at Canusium in Italy, were insufficient to exhaust his treasures. The people of Epirus, Thessaly, Euboea, Boeotia, and Peloponnesus, experienced his favors; and many inscriptions of the cities of Greece and Asia gratefully style Herodes Atticus their patron and benefactor. [70]

[Footnote 69: Aulus Gellius, in Noct. Attic. i. 2, ix. 2, xviii. 10, xix. 12. Phil ostrat. p. 564.]

[Footnote 69/1: The Odeum served for the rehearsal of new comedies as well as tragedies; they were read or repeated, before representation, without music or decorations, &c. No piece could be represented in the theatre if it had not been previously approved by judges for this purpose. The king of

Cappadocia who restored the Odeum, which had been burnt by Sylla, was Araobarzanes. See Martini, Dissertation on the Odeons of the Ancients, Leipsic. 1767, p. 10—91.—W.]

[Footnote 70: See Philostrat. l. ii. p. 548, 560. Pausanias, l. i. and vii. 10. The life of Herodes, in the xxxth volume of the Memoirs of the Academy of Inscriptions.]

In the commonwealths of Athens and Rome, the modest simplicity of private houses announced the equal condition of freedom; whilst the sovereignty of the people was represented in the majestic edifices designed to the public use; [71] nor was this republican spirit totally extinguished by the introduction of wealth and monarchy. It was in works of national honor and benefit, that the most virtuous of the emperors affected to display their magnificence. The golden palace of Nero excited a just indignation, but the vast extent of ground which had been usurped by his selfish luxury was more nobly filled under the succeeding reigns by the Coliseum, the baths of Titus, the Claudian portico, and the temples dedicated to the goddess of Peace, and to the genius of Rome. [72] These monuments of architecture, the property of the Roman people, were adorned with the most beautiful productions of Grecian painting and sculpture; and in the temple of Peace, a very curious library was open to the curiosity of the learned. [72/1] At a small distance from thence was situated the Forum of Trajan. It was surrounded by a lofty portico, in the form of a quadrangle, into which four triumphal arches opened a noble and spacious entrance: in the centre arose a column of marble, whose height, of one hundred and ten feet, denoted the elevation of the hill that had been cut away. This column, which still subsists in its ancient beauty, exhibited an exact representation of the Dacian victories of its founder. The veteran soldier contemplated the story of his own campaigns, and by an easy illusion of national vanity, the peaceful citizen associated himself to the honors of the triumph. All the other quarters of the capital, and all the provinces of the empire, were embellished by the same liberal spirit of public magnificence, and were filled with amphi theatres, theatres, temples, porticoes, triumphal arches, baths and aqueducts, all variously conducive to the health, the devotion, and the pleasures of the meanest citizen. The last mentioned of those edifices deserve our peculiar attention. The boldness of the enterprise, the solidity of the execution, and the uses to which they were subservient, rank the aqueducts among the noblest monuments of Roman genius and power. The aqueducts of the capital claim a just preeminence; but the curious traveller, who, without the light of history, should examine those of Spoleto, of Metz, or of Segovia, would very naturally conclude that those provincial towns had formerly been the residence of some potent monarch. The solitudes of Asia and Africa were once covered with flourishing cities, whose populousness, and even whose existence, was derived from such artificial supplies of a perennial stream of fresh water. [73]

[Footnote 71: It is particularly remarked of Athens by Dicaearchus, de Statu Graeciae, p. 8, inter Geographos Minores, edit. Hudson.]

[Footnote 72: Donatus de Roma Vetere, l. iii. c. 4, 5, 6. Nardini Roma Antica, l. iii. 11, 12, 13, and a Ms. description of ancient Rome, by Bernardus Oricellarius, or Rucellai, of which I obtained a copy from the library of the Canon Ricardi at Florence. Two celebrated pictures of Timanthes and of Protogenes are mentioned by Pliny, as in the Temple of Peace; and the Laocoon was found in the baths of Titus.]

[Footnote 72/1: The Emperor Vespasian, who had caused the Temple of Peace to be built, transported to it the greatest part of the pictures, statues, and other works of art which had escaped the civil tumults. It was there that every day the artists and the learned of Rome assembled; and it is on the site of this temple that a multitude of antiques have been dug up. See notes of Reimar on Dion Cassius, lxvi. c. 15, p. 1083.—W.]

[Footnote 73: Montfaucon l'Antiquite Expliquee, tom. iv. p. 2, l. i. c. 9. Fabretti has composed a very learned treatise on the aqueducts of Rome.]

We have computed the inhabitants, and contemplated the public works, of the Roman empire. The observation of the number and greatness of its cities will serve to confirm the former, and to multiply the latter. It may not be unpleasing to collect a few scattered instances relative to that subject without forgetting, however, that from the vanity of nations and the poverty of language, the vague appellation of city has been indifferently bestowed on Rome and upon Laurentum.

I. Ancient Italy is said to have contained eleven hundred and ninety-seven cities; and for whatsoever aera of antiquity the expression might be intended, [74] there is not any reason to believe the country less populous in the age of the Antonines, than in that of Romulus. The petty states of Latium were contained within the metropolis of the empire, by whose superior influence they had been attracted. [74/1] Those parts of Italy which have so long languished under the lazy tyranny of priests and viceroys, had been afflicted only by the more tolerable calamities of war; and the first symptoms of decay which they experienced, were amply compensated by the rapid improvements of the Cisalpine Gaul. The splendor of Verona may be traced in its remains: yet Verona was less celebrated than Aquileia or Padua, Milan or Ravenna. II. The spirit of improvement had passed the Alps, and been felt even in the woods of Britain, which were gradually cleared away to open a free space for convenient and elegant habitations. York was the seat of government; London was already enriched by commerce; and Bath was celebrated for the salutary effects of its medicinal waters. Gaul could boast of her twelve hundred cities; [75] and though, in the northern parts, many of them, without excepting Paris itself, were little more than the rude and imperfect townships of a rising people, the southern provinces imitated the wealth and elegance of Italy. [76] Many were the cities of Gaul, Marseilles, Arles, Nismes, Narbonne, Thoulouse, Bourdeaux, Autun, Vienna, Lyons, Langres, and Treves, whose ancient condition might sustain an equal, and perhaps advantageous comparison with their present state. With regard to Spain, that country flourished as a province, and has declined as a kingdom. Exhausted by the abuse of her strength, by America, and by superstition, her pride might possibly be confounded, if we required such a list of three hundred and sixty cities, as Pliny has exhibited under the reign of Vespasian. [77] III. Three hundred African cities had once acknowledged the authority of Carthage, [78] nor is it likely that their numbers diminished under the administration of the emperors: Carthage itself rose with new splendor from its ashes; and that capital, as well as Capua and Corinth, soon recovered all the advantages which can be separated from independent sovereignty. IV. The provinces of the East present the contrast of Roman magnificence with Turkish barbarism. The ruins of antiquity scattered over uncultivated fields, and ascribed, by ignorance to the power of magic, scarcely afford a shelter to the oppressed peasant or wandering Arab. Under the reign of the Caesars, the proper Asia alone contained five hundred populous cities, [79] enriched with all the gifts of nature, and adorned with all the refinements of art. Eleven cities of Asia had once disputed the honor of dedicating a temple of Tiberius, and their respective merits were examined by the senate. [80] Four of them were immediately rejected as unequal to the burden; and among these was Laodicea, whose splendor is still displayed in its ruins. [81] Laodicea collected a very considerable revenue from its flocks of sheep, celebrated for the fineness of their wool, and had received, a little before the contest, a legacy of above four hundred thousand pounds by the testament of a generous citizen. [82] If such was the poverty of Laodicea, what must have been the wealth of those cities, whose claim appeared preferable, and particularly of Pergamus, of Smyrna, and of Ephesus, who so long disputed with each other the titular primacy of Asia? [83] The capitals of Syria and Egypt held a still superior rank in the empire; Antioch and Alexandria looked down with disdain on a crowd of dependent cities, [84] and yielded, with reluctance, to the majesty of Rome itself.

[Footnote 74: Aelian. Hist. Var. lib. ix. c. 16. He lived in the time of Alexander Severus. See Fabricius, Biblioth. Graeca, l. iv. c. 21.]

[Footnote 74/1: This may in some degree account for the difficulty started by Livy, as to the incredibly numerous armies raised by the small states around Rome where, in his time, a scanty stock of free soldiers among a larger population of Roman slaves broke the solitude. Vix seminario exiguo militum relicto servitia Romana ab solitudine vindicant, Liv. vi. vii. Compare Appian Bel Civ. i. 7.—M. subst. for G.]

[Footnote 75: Joseph. de Bell. Jud. ii. 16. The number, however, is mentioned, and should be received with a degree of latitude. Note: Without doubt no reliance can be placed on this passage of Josephus. The historian makes Agrippa give advice to the Jews, as to the power of the Romans; and the speech is full of declamation which can furnish no conclusions to history. While enumerating the nations subject to the Romans, he speaks of the Gauls as submitting to 1200 soldiers, (which is false, as there were eight legions in Gaul, Tac. iv. 5,) while there are nearly twelve hundred cities.—G. Josephus (infra) places these eight legions on the Rhine, as Tacitus does.—M.]

[Footnote 76: Plin. Hist. Natur. iii. 5.]

[Footnote 77: Plin. Hist. Natur. iii. 3, 4, iv. 35. The list seems authentic and accurate; the division of the provinces, and the different condition of the cities, are minutely distinguished.]

[Footnote 78: Strabon. Geograph. l. xvii. p. 1189.]

[Footnote 79: Joseph. de Bell. Jud. ii. 16. Philostrat. in Vit. Sophist. l. ii. p. 548, edit. Olear.]

[Footnote 80: Tacit. Annal. iv. 55. I have taken some pains in consulting and comparing modern travellers, with regard to the fate of those eleven cities of Asia. Seven or eight are totally destroyed: Hypaepe, Tralles, Laodicea, Hium, Halicarnassus, Miletus, Ephesus, and we may add Sardes. Of the remaining three, Pergamus is a straggling village of two or three thousand inhabitants; Magnesia, under the name of Guzelhissar, a town of some consequence; and Smyrna, a great city, peopled by a hundred thousand souls. But even at Smyrna, while the Franks have maintained a commerce, the Turks have ruined the arts.]

[Footnote 81: See a very exact and pleasing description of the ruins of Laodicea, in Chandler's Travels through Asia Minor, p. 225, &c.]

[Footnote 82: Strabo, l. xii. p. 866. He had studied at Tralles.]

[Footnote 83: See a Dissertation of M. de Boze, Mem. de l'Academie, tom. xviii. Aristides pronounced an oration, which is still extant, to recommend concord to the rival cities.]

[Footnote 84: The inhabitants of Egypt, exclusive of Alexandria, amounted to seven millions and a half, (Joseph. de Bell. Jud. ii. 16.) Under the military government of the Mamelukes, Syria was supposed to contain sixty thousand villages, (Histoire de Timur Bec, l. v. c. 20.)]

PART IV

All these cities were connected with each other, and with the capital, by the public highways, which, issuing from the Forum of Rome, traversed Italy, pervaded the provinces, and were terminated only by the frontiers of the empire. If we carefully trace the distance from the wall of Antoninus to Rome, and from thence to Jerusalem, it will be found that the great chain of communication, from the north-west to the south-east point of the empire, was drawn out to the length of four thousand and eighty Roman miles. [85] The public roads were accurately divided by mile-stones, and ran in a direct line from one city to another, with very little respect for the obstacles either of nature or private property. Mountains were perforated, and bold arches thrown over the broadest and most rapid streams. [86] The middle part of the road was raised into a terrace which commanded the adjacent country, consisted of several strata of sand, gravel, and cement, and was paved with large stones, or, in some places near the capital, with granite. [87] Such was the solid construction of the Roman highways, whose firmness has not entirely yielded to the effort of fifteen centuries. They united the subjects of the most distant provinces by an easy and familiar intercourse; out their primary object had been to facilitate the marches of the legions; nor was any country considered as completely subdued, till it had been rendered, in all its parts, pervious to the arms and authority of the conqueror. The advantage of receiving the earliest intelligence, and of conveying their orders with celerity, induced the emperors to establish, throughout their extensive dominions, the regular institution of posts. [88] Houses were every where erected at the distance only of five or six miles; each of them was constantly provided with forty horses, and by the help of these relays, it was easy to travel a hundred miles in a day along the Roman roads. [89] [89/1] The use of posts was allowed to those who claimed it by an Imperial mandate; but though originally intended for the public service, it was sometimes indulged to the business or conveniency of private citizens. [90] Nor was the communication of the Roman empire less free and open by sea than it was by land. The provinces surrounded and enclosed the Mediterranean: and Italy, in the shape of an immense promontory, advanced into the midst of that great lake. The coasts of Italy are, in general, destitute of safe harbors; but human industry had corrected the deficiencies of nature; and the artificial port of Ostia, in particular, situate at the mouth of the Tyber, and formed by the emperor Claudius, was a useful monument of Roman greatness. [91] From this port, which was only sixteen miles from the capital, a favorable breeze frequently carried vessels in seven days to the columns of Hercules, and in nine or ten, to Alexandria in Egypt. [92]

[See Remains Of Claudian Aquaduct]

[Footnote 85: The following Itinerary may serve to convey some idea of the direction of the road, and of the distance between the principal towns. I. From the wall of Antoninus to York, 222 Roman miles. II. London, 227. III. Rhutupiae or Sandwich, 67. IV. The navigation to Boulogne, 45. V. Rheims, 174. VI. Lyons, 330. VII. Milan, 324. VIII. Rome, 426. IX. Brundusium, 360. X. The navigation to Dyrrachium, 40. XI. Byzantium, 711. XII. Ancyra, 283. XIII. Tarsus, 301. XIV. Antioch, 141. XV. Tyre, 252. XVI. Jerusalem, 168. In all 4080 Roman, or 3740 English miles. See the Itineraries published by Wesseling, his annotations; Gale and Stukeley for Britain, and M. d'Anville for Gaul and Italy.]

[Footnote 86: Montfaucon, l'Antiquite Expliquee, (tom. 4, p. 2, l. i. c. 5,) has described the bridges of Narni, Alcantara, Nismes, &c.]

[Footnote 87: Bergier, Histoire des grands Chemins de l'Empire Romain, l. ii. c. l. I—28.]

[Footnote 88: Procopius in Hist. Arcana, c. 30. Bergier, Hist. des grands Chemins, l. iv. Codex Theodosian. l. viii. tit. v. vol. ii. p. 506—563 with Godefroy's learned commentary.]

[Footnote 89: In the time of Theodosius, Caesarius, a magistrate of high rank, went post from Antioch to Constantinople. He began his journey at night, was in Cappadocia (165 miles from Antioch) the ensuing evening, and arrived at Constantinople the sixth day about noon. The whole distance was 725 Roman, or 665 English miles. See Libanius, Orat. xxii., and the Itineria, p. 572—581. Note: A courier is mentioned in Walpole's Travels, ii. 335, who was to travel from Aleppo to Constantinople, more than 700 miles, in eight days, an unusually short journey.—M.]

[Footnote 89/1: Posts for the conveyance of intelligence were established by Augustus. Suet. Aug. 49. The couriers travelled with amazing speed. Blair on Roman Slavery, note, p. 261. It is probable that the posts, from the time of Augustus, were confined to the public service, and supplied by impressment Nerva, as it appears from a coin of his reign, made an important change; "he established posts upon all the public roads of Italy, and made the service chargeable upon his own exchequer. Hadrian, perceiving the advantage of this improvement, extended it to all the provinces of the empire." Cardwell on Coins, p. 220.—M.]

[Footnote 90: Pliny, though a favorite and a minister, made an apology for granting post-horses to his wife on the most urgent business. Epist. x. 121, 122.]

[Footnote 91: Bergier, Hist. des grands Chemins, l. iv. c. 49.]

[Footnote 92: Plin. Hist. Natur. xix. i. [In Prooem.] Note: Pliny says Puteoli, which seems to have been the usual landing place from the East. See the voyages of St. Paul, Acts xxviii. 13, and of Josephus, Vita, c. 3—M.]

Whatever evils either reason or declamation have imputed to extensive empire, the power of Rome was attended with some beneficial consequences to mankind; and the same freedom of intercourse which extended the vices, diffused likewise the improvements, of social life. In the more remote ages of antiquity, the world was unequally divided. The East was in the immemorial possession of arts and luxury; whilst the West was inhabited by rude and warlike barbarians, who either disdained agriculture, or to whom it was totally unknown. Under the protection of an established government, the productions of happier climates, and the industry of more civilized nations, were gradually introduced into the western countries of Europe; and the natives were encouraged, by an open and profitable commerce, to multiply the former, as well as to improve the latter. It would be almost impossible to enumerate all the articles, either of the animal or the vegetable reign, which were successively imported into Europe from Asia and Egypt: [93] but it will not be unworthy of the dignity, and much less of the utility, of an historical work, slightly to touch on a few of the principal heads. 1. Almost all the flowers, the herbs, and the fruits, that grow in our European gardens, are of foreign extraction, which, in many cases, is betrayed even by their names: the apple was a native of Italy, and when the Romans had tasted the richer flavor of the apricot, the peach, the pomegranate, the citron, and the orange, they contented themselves with applying to all these new fruits the common denomination of apple, discriminating them from each other by the additional epithet of their country. 2. In the time of Homer, the vine grew wild in the island of Sicily, and most probably in the adjacent continent; but it was not improved by the skill, nor did it afford a liquor grateful to the taste, of the savage inhabitants. [94] A thousand years afterwards, Italy could boast, that of the fourscore most generous and celebrated wines, more than two thirds were produced from her soil. [95] The blessing was soon communicated to the Narbonnese province of Gaul; but so intense was the cold to the north of the Cevennes, that, in the time of Strabo, it was thought impossible to ripen the grapes in those parts of Gaul. [96] This difficulty, however, was gradually vanquished; and there is some reason to believe, that the vineyards of Burgundy are as old as the age of the Antonines. [97] 3. The olive, in the western world, followed the progress of peace, of which it was considered as the symbol. Two centuries after the foundation of Rome, both Italy and Africa were strangers to that useful plant: it was naturalized in those countries; and at length carried into the heart of Spain and Gaul. The timid errors of the ancients, that it required a certain degree of heat, and could only flourish in the neighborhood of the sea, were insensibly exploded by industry and experience. [98] 4. The cultivation of flax was transported from Egypt to Gaul, and enriched the whole country, however it might impoverish the particular lands on which it was sown. [99] 5. The use of artificial grasses became familiar to the farmers both of Italy and the provinces, particularly the Lucerne, which derived its name and origin from Media. [100] The assured supply of wholesome and plentiful food for the cattle during winter, multiplied the number of the docks and herds, which in their turn contributed to the fertility of the soil. To all these improvements may be added an assiduous attention to mines and fisheries, which, by employing a multitude of laborious hands, serve to increase the pleasures of the rich and the subsistence of the poor. The elegant treatise of Columella describes the advanced state of the Spanish husbandry under the reign of Tiberius; and it may be observed, that those famines, which so frequently afflicted the infant republic, were seldom or never experienced by the extensive empire of Rome. The accidental scarcity, in any single province, was immediately relieved by the plenty of its more fortunate neighbors.

[Footnote 93: It is not improbable that the Greeks and Phoenicians introduced some new arts and productions into the neighborhood of Marseilles and Gades.]

[Footnote 94: See Homer, Odyss. l. ix. v. 358.]

[Footnote 95: Plin. Hist. Natur. l. xiv.]

[Footnote 96: Strab. Geograph. l. iv. p. 269. The intense cold of a Gallic winter was almost proverbial among the ancients. Note: Strabo only says that the grape does not ripen. Attempts had been made in the time of Augustus to naturalize the vine in the north of Gaul; but the cold was too great. Diod. Sic. edit. Rhodom. p. 304.—W. Diodorus (lib. v. 26) gives a curious picture of the Italian traders bartering, with the savages of Gaul, a cask of wine for a slave.—M. —It appears from the newly discovered treatise of Cicero de Republica, that there was a law of the republic prohibiting the culture of the vine and olive beyond the Alps, in order to keep up the value of those in Italy. Nos justissimi homines, qui transalpinas gentes oleam et vitem serere non sinimus, quo pluris sint nostra oliveta nostraeque vineae. Lib. iii. 9. The restrictive law of Domitian was veiled under the decent pretext of encouraging the cultivation of grain. Suet. Dom. vii. It was repealed by Probus Vopis Strobus, 18.—M.]

[Footnote 97: In the beginning of the fourth century, the orator Eumenius (Panegyr. Veter. viii. 6, edit. Delphin.) speaks of the vines in the territory of Autun, which were decayed through age, and the first plantation of which was totally unknown. The Pagus Arebrignus is supposed by M. d'Anville to be the district of Beaune, celebrated, even at present for one of the first growths of Burgundy. Note: This is proved by a passage of Pliny the Elder, where he speaks of a certain kind of grape (vitis picata. vinum picatum) which grows naturally to the district of Vienne, and had recently been transplanted into the country of the Arverni, (Auvergne,) of the Helvii, (the Vivarias.) and the Burgundy and Franche Compte. Pliny wrote A.D. 77. Hist. Nat. xiv. 1.— W.]

[Footnote 98: Plin. Hist. Natur. l. xv.]

[Footnote 99: Plin. Hist. Natur. l. xix.]

[Footnote 100: See the agreeable Essays on Agriculture by Mr. Harte, in which he has collected all that the ancients and moderns have said of Lucerne.]

Agriculture is the foundation of manufactures; since the productions of nature are the materials of art. Under the Roman empire, the labor of an industrious and ingenious people was variously, but incessantly, employed in the service of the rich. In their dress, their table, their houses, and their furniture, the favorites of fortune united every refinement of conveniency, of elegance, and of splendor, whatever could soothe their pride or gratify their sensuality. Such refinements, under the odious name of luxury, have been severely arraigned by the moralists of every age; and it might perhaps be more conducive to the virtue, as well as happiness, of mankind, if all possessed the necessaries, and none the superfluities, of life. But in the present imperfect condition of society, luxury, though it may proceed from vice or folly, seems to be the only means that can correct the unequal distribution of property. The diligent mechanic, and the skilful artist, who have obtained no share in the division of the earth, receive a voluntary tax from the possessors of land; and the latter are prompted, by a sense of interest, to improve those estates, with whose produce they may purchase additional pleasures. This operation, the particular effects of which are felt in every society, acted with much more diffusive energy in the Roman world. The provinces would soon have been exhausted of their wealth, if the manufactures and commerce of luxury had not insensibly restored to the industrious subjects the sums which were exacted from them by the arms and authority of Rome. As long as the circulation was confined within the bounds of the empire, it impressed the political machine with a new degree of activity, and its consequences, sometimes beneficial, could never become pernicious.

But it is no easy task to confine luxury within the limits of an empire. The most remote countries of the ancient world were ransacked to supply the pomp and delicacy of Rome. The forests of Scythia afforded some valuable furs. Amber was brought over land from the shores of the Baltic to the Danube; and the barbarians were astonished at the price which they received in exchange for so useless a commodity. [101] There was a considerable demand for Babylonian carpets, and other manufactures of the East; but the most important and unpopular branch of foreign trade was carried on with Arabia and India. Every year, about the time of the summer solstice, a fleet of a hundred and twenty vessels sailed from Myoshormos, a port of Egypt, on the Red Sea. By the periodical assistance of the monsoons, they traversed the ocean in about forty days. The coast of Malabar, or the island of Ceylon, [102] was the usual term of their navigation, and it was in those markets that the merchants from the more remote countries of Asia expected their arrival. The return of the fleet of Egypt was fixed to the months of December or January; and as soon as their rich cargo had been transported on the backs of camels, from the Red Sea to the Nile, and had descended that river as far as Alexandria, it was poured, without delay, into the capital of the empire. [103] The objects of oriental traffic were splendid and trifling; silk, a pound of which was esteemed not inferior in value to a pound of gold; [104] precious stones, among which the pearl claimed the first rank after the diamond; [105] and a variety of aromatics, that were consumed in religious worship and the pomp of funerals. The labor and risk of the voyage was rewarded with almost incredible profit; but the profit was made upon Roman subjects, and a few individuals were enriched at the expense of the public. As the natives of Arabia and India were contented with the productions and manufactures of their own country, silver, on the side of the Romans, was the principal, if not the only [105/1] instrument of commerce. It was a complaint worthy of the gravity of the senate, that, in the purchase of female ornaments, the wealth of the state was irrecoverably given away to foreign and hostile nations. [106] The annual loss is computed, by a writer of an inquisitive but censorious temper, at upwards of eight hundred thousand pounds sterling. [107] Such was the style of discontent, brooding over the dark prospect of approaching poverty. And yet, if we compare the proportion between gold and silver, as it stood in the time of Pliny, and as it was fixed in the reign of Constantine, we shall discover within that period a very considerable increase. [108] There is not the least reason to suppose that gold was become more scarce; it is therefore evident that silver was grown more common; that whatever might be the amount of the Indian and Arabian exports, they were far from exhausting the wealth of the Roman world; and that the produce of the mines abundantly supplied the demands of commerce.

[Footnote 101: Tacit. Germania, c. 45. Plin. Hist. Nat. xxxvii. 13. The latter observed, with some humor, that even fashion had not yet found out the use of amber. Nero sent a Roman knight to purchase great quantities on the spot where it was produced, the coast of modern Prussia.]

[Footnote 102: Called Taprobana by the Romans, and Serindib by the Arabs. It was discovered under the reign of Claudius, and gradually became the principal mart of the East.]

[Footnote 103: Plin. Hist. Natur. l. vi. Strabo, l. xvii.]

[Footnote 104: Hist. August. p. 224. A silk garment was considered as an ornament to a woman, but as a disgrace to a man.]

[Footnote 105: The two great pearl fisheries were the same as at present, Ormuz and Cape Comorin. As well as we can compare ancient with modern geography, Rome was supplied with diamonds from the mine of Jumelpur, in Bengal, which is described in the Voyages de Tavernier, tom. ii. p. 281.]

[Footnote 105/1: Certainly not the only one. The Indians were not so contented with regard to foreign productions. Arrian has a long list of European wares, which they received in exchange for their own; Italian and other wines, brass, tin, lead, coral, chrysolith, storax, glass, dresses of one or many colors, zones, &c. See Periplus Maris Erythraei in Hudson, Geogr. Min. i. p. 27.—W. The German translator observes that Gibbon has confined the use of aromatics to religious worship and funerals. His error seems the omission of other spices, of which the Romans must have consumed great quantities in their cookery. Wenck, however, admits that silver was the chief article of exchange.—M. In 1787, a peasant (near Nellore in the Carnatic) struck, in digging, on the remains of a Hindu temple; he found, also, a pot which contained Roman coins and medals of the second century, mostly Trajans, Adrians, and Faustinas, all of gold, many of them fresh and beautiful, others defaced or perforated, as if they had been worn as ornaments. (Asiatic Researches, ii. 19.)—M.]

[Footnote 106: Tacit. Annal. iii. 53. In a speech of Tiberius.]

[Footnote 107: Plin. Hist. Natur. xii. 18. In another place he computes half that sum; Quingenties H. S. for India exclusive of Arabia.]

[Footnote 108: The proportion, which was 1 to 10, and 12 1/2, rose to 14 2/5, the legal regulation of Constantine. See Arbuthnot's Tables of ancient Coins, c. 5.]

Notwithstanding the propensity of mankind to exalt the past, and to depreciate the present, the tranquil and prosperous state of the empire was warmly felt, and honestly confessed, by the provincials as well as Romans. "They acknowledged that the true principles of social life, laws, agriculture, and science, which had been first invented by the wisdom of Athens, were now firmly established by the power of Rome, under whose auspicious influence the fiercest barbarians were united by an equal government and common language. They affirm, that with the improvement of arts, the human species were visibly multiplied. They celebrate the increasing splendor of the cities, the beautiful face of the country, cultivated and adorned like an immense garden; and the long festival of peace which was enjoyed by so many nations, forgetful of the ancient animosities, and delivered from the apprehension of future danger." [109] Whatever suspicions may be suggested by the air of rhetoric and declamation, which seems to prevail in these passages, the substance of them is perfectly agreeable to historic truth.

[Footnote 109: Among many other passages, see Pliny, (Hist. Natur. iii. 5.) Aristides, (de Urbe Roma,) and Tertullian, (de Anima, c. 30.)]

It was scarcely possible that the eyes of contemporaries should discover in the public felicity the latent causes of decay and corruption. This long peace, and the uniform government of the Romans, introduced a slow and secret poison into the vitals of the empire. The minds of men were gradually reduced to the same level, the fire of genius was extinguished, and even the military spirit evaporated. The natives of Europe were brave and robust. Spain, Gaul, Britain, and Illyricum supplied the legions with excellent soldiers, and constituted the real strength of the monarchy. Their personal valor remained, but they no longer possessed that public courage which is nourished by the love of independence, the sense of national honor, the presence of danger, and the habit of command. They received laws and governors from the will of their sovereign, and trusted for their defence to a mercenary army. The posterity of their boldest leaders was contented with the rank of citizens and subjects. The most aspiring spirits resorted to the court or standard of the emperors; and the deserted provinces, deprived of political strength or union, insensibly sunk into the languid indifference of private life.

The love of letters, almost inseparable from peace and refinement, was fashionable among the subjects of Hadrian and the Antonines, who were themselves men of learning and curiosity. It was diffused over the whole extent of their empire; the most northern tribes of Britons had acquired a taste for rhetoric; Homer as well as Virgil were transcribed and studied on the banks of the Rhine and Danube; and the most liberal rewards sought out the faintest glimmerings of literary merit. [110] The sciences of physic and astronomy were successfully cultivated by the Greeks; the observations of Ptolemy and the writings of Galen are studied by those who have improved their discoveries and corrected their errors; but if we except the inimitable Lucian, this age of indolence passed away without having produced a single writer of original genius, or who excelled in the arts of elegant composition. The authority of Plato and Aristotle, of Zeno and Epicurus, still reigned in the schools; and their systems, transmitted with blind deference from one generation of disciples to another, precluded every generous attempt to exercise the powers, or enlarge the limits, of the human mind. The beauties of the poets and orators, instead of kindling a fire like their own, inspired only cold and servile mitations: or if any ventured to deviate from those models, they deviated at the same time from good sense and propriety. On the revival of letters, the youthful vigor of the imagination, after a long repose, national emulation, a new religion, new languages, and a new world, called forth the genius of Europe. But the provincials of Rome, trained by a uniform artificial foreign education, were engaged in a very unequal competition with those bold ancients, who, by expressing their genuine feelings in their native tongue, had already occupied every place of honor. The name of Poet was almost forgotten; that of Orator was usurped by the sophists. A cloud of critics, of compilers, of commentators, darkened the face of learning, and the decline of genius was soon followed by the corruption of taste.[110/1]

[Footnote 110: Herodes Atticus gave the sophist Polemo above eight thousand pounds for three declamations. See Philostrat. l. i. p. 538. The Antonines founded a school at Athens, in which professors of grammar, rhetoric, politics, and the four great sects of philosophy were maintained at the public expense for the instruction of youth. The salary of a philosopher was ten thousand drachmae, between three and four hundred pounds a year. Similar establishments were formed in the other great cities of the empire. See Lucian in Eunuch. tom. ii. p. 352, edit. Reitz. Philostrat. l. ii. p. 566. Hist. August. p. 21. Dion Cassius, l. lxxi. p. 1195. Juvenal himself, in a morose satire, which in every line betrays his own disappointment and envy, is obliged, however, to say,—"—O Juvenes, circumspicit et stimulat vos. Materiamque sibi Ducis indulgentia quaerit."—Satir. vii. 20. Note: Vespasian first gave a salary to professors: he assigned to each professor of rhetoric, Greek and Roman, centena sestertia. (Sueton. in Vesp. 18). Hadrian and the Antonines, though still liberal, were less profuse.—G. from W. Suetonius wrote annua centena L. 807, 5, 10.—M.]

[Footnote 110/1: This judgment is rather severe: besides the physicians, astronomers, and grammarians, among whom there were some very distinguished men, there were still, under Hadrian, Suetonius, Florus, Plutarch; under the Antonines, Arrian, Pausanias, Appian, Marcus Aurelius himself, Sextus Empiricus, &c. Jurisprudence gained much by the labors of Salvius Julianus, Julius Celsus, Sex. Pomponius, Caius, and others.—G. from W. Yet where, among these, is the writer of original genius, unless, perhaps Plutarch? or even of a style really elegant?— M.]

The sublime Longinus, who, in somewhat a later period, and in the court of a Syrian queen, preserved the spirit of ancient Athens, observes and laments this degeneracy of his contemporaries, which debased their sentiments, enervated their courage, and depressed their talents. "In the same manner," says he, "as some children always remain pygmies, whose infant limbs have been too closely confined, thus our tender minds, fettered by the prejudices and habits of a just servitude, are unable to expand themselves, or to attain that well-proportioned greatness which we admire in the ancients; who, living under a popular government, wrote with the same freedom as they acted." [111] This diminutive stature of mankind, if we pursue the metaphor, was daily sinking below the old standard, and the Roman world was indeed peopled by a race of pygmies; when the fierce giants of the north broke in, and mended the puny breed. They restored a manly spirit of freedom; and after the revolution of ten centuries, freedom became the happy parent of taste and science.

[Footnote 111: Longin. de Sublim. c. 44, p. 229, edit. Toll. Here, too, we may say of Longinus, "his own example strengthens all his laws." Instead of proposing his sentiments with a manly boldness, he insinuates them with the most guarded caution; puts them into the mouth of a friend, and as far as we can collect from a corrupted text, makes a show of refuting them himself.]

CHAPTER III

THE CONSTITUTION IN THE AGE OF ANTONINES

PART I

OF THE CONSTITUTION OF THE ROMAN EMPIREIN THE AGE OF THE ANTONINES

The obvious definition of a monarchy seems to be that of a state, in which a single person, by whatsoever name he may be distinguished, is intrusted with the execution of the laws, the management of the revenue, and the command of the army. But, unless public liberty is protected by intrepid and vigilant guardians, the authority of so formidable a magistrate will soon degenerate into despotism. The influence of the clergy, in an age of superstition, might be usefully employed to assert the rights of mankind; but so intimate is the connection between the throne and the altar, that the banner of the church has very seldom been seen on the side of the people. [101] A martial nobility and stubborn commons, possessed of arms, tenacious of property, and collected into constitutional assemblies, form the only balance capable of preserving a free constitution against enterprises of an aspiring prince.

[Footnote 101: Often enough in the ages of superstition, but not in the interest of the people or the state, but in that of the church to which all others were subordinate. Yet the power of the pope has often been of great service in repressing the excesses of sovereigns, and in softening manners.—W. The history of the Italian republics proves the error of Gibbon, and the justice of his German translator's comment.—M.]

Every barrier of the Roman constitution had been levelled by the vast ambition of the dictator; every fence had been extirpated by the cruel hand of the triumvir. After the victory of Actium, the fate of the Roman world depended on the will of Octavianus, surnamed Caesar, by his uncle's adoption, and afterwards Augustus, by the flattery of the senate. The conqueror was at the head of forty-four veteran legions, [1] conscious of their own strength, and of the weakness of the constitution, habituated, during twenty years' civil war, to every act of blood and violence, and passionately devoted to the house of Caesar, from whence alone they had received, and expected the most lavish rewards. The provinces, long oppressed by the ministers of the republic, sighed for the government of a single person, who would be the master, not the accomplice, of those petty tyrants. The people of Rome, viewing, with a secret pleasure, the humiliation of the aristocracy, demanded only bread and public shows; and were supplied with both by the liberal hand of Augustus. The rich and polite Italians, who had almost universally embraced the philosophy of Epicurus, enjoyed the present blessings of ease and tranquillity, and suffered not the pleasing dream to be interrupted by the memory of their old tumultuous freedom. With its power, the senate had lost its dignity; many of the most noble families were extinct. The republicans of spirit and ability had perished in the field of battle, or in the proscription. The door of the assembly had been designedly left open, for a mixed multitude of more than a thousand persons, who reflected disgrace upon their rank, instead of deriving honor from it. [2]

[Footnote 1: Orosius, vi. 18. Note: Dion says twenty-five, (or three,) (lv. 23.) The united triumvirs had but forty-three. (Appian. Bell. Civ. iv. 3.) The testimony of Orosius is of little value when more certain may be had.—W. But all the legions, doubtless, submitted to Augustus after the battle of Actium.—M.]

[Footnote 2: Julius Caesar introduced soldiers, strangers, and half-barbarians into the senate (Sueton. in Caesar. c. 77, 80.) The abuse became still more scandalous after his death.]

The reformation of the senate was one of the first steps in which Augustus laid aside the tyrant, and professed himself the father of his country. He was elected censor; and, in concert with his faithful Agrippa, he examined the list of the senators, expelled a few members, [201] whose vices or whose obstinacy required a public example, persuaded near two hundred to prevent the shame of an expulsion by a voluntary retreat, raised the qualification of a senator to about ten thousand pounds, created a sufficient number of patrician families, and accepted for himself the honorable title of Prince of the Senate, [202] which had always been bestowed, by the censors, on the citizen the most eminent for his honors and services. [3] But whilst he thus restored the dignity, he destroyed the independence, of the senate. The principles of a free constitution are irrecoverably lost, when the legislative power is nominated by the executive.

[Footnote 201: Of these Dion and Suetonius knew nothing.—W. Dion says the contrary.—M.]

[Footnote 202: But Augustus, then Octavius, was censor, and in virtue of that office, even according to the constitution of the free republic, could reform the senate, expel unworthy members, name the Princeps Senatus, &c. That was called, as is well known, Senatum legere. It was customary, during the free republic, for the censor to be named Princeps Senatus, (S. Liv. l. xxvii. c. 11, l. xl. c. 51;) and Dion expressly says, that this was done according to ancient usage. He was empowered by a decree of the senate to admit a number of families among the patricians. Finally, the senate was not the legislative power.—W]

[Footnote 3: Dion Cassius, l. liii. p. 693. Suetonius in August. c. 35.]

Before an assembly thus modelled and prepared, Augustus pronounced a studied oration, which displayed his patriotism, and disguised his ambition. "He lamented, yet excused, his past conduct. Filial piety had required at his hands the revenge of his father's murder; the humanity of his own nature had sometimes given way to the stern laws of necessity, and to a forced connection with two unworthy colleagues: as long as Antony lived, the republic forbade him to abandon her to a degenerate Roman, and a barbarian queen. He was now at liberty to satisfy his duty and his inclination. He solemnly restored the senate and people to all their ancient rights; and wished only to mingle with the crowd of his fellow-citizens, and to share the blessings which he had obtained for his country." [4]

[Footnote 4: Dion (l. liii. p. 698) gives us a prolix and bombast speech on this great occasion. I have borrowed from Suetonius and Tacitus the general language of Augustus.]

It would require the pen of Tacitus (if Tacitus had assisted at this assembly) to describe the various emotions of the senate, those that were suppressed, and those that were affected. It was dangerous to trust the sincerity of Augustus; to seem to distrust it was still more dangerous. The respective advantages of monarchy and a republic have often divided speculative inquirers; the present greatness of the Roman state, the corruption of manners, and the license of the soldiers, supplied new arguments to the advocates of monarchy; and these general views of government were again warped by the hopes and fears of each individual. Amidst this confusion of sentiments, the answer of the senate was unanimous and decisive. They refused to accept the resignation of Augustus; they conjured him not to desert the republic, which he had saved. After a decent resistance, the crafty tyrant submitted to the orders of the senate; and consented to receive the government of the provinces, and the general command of the Roman armies, under the well-known names of Proconsul and Imperator. [5] But he would receive them only for ten years. Even before the expiration of that period, he hope that the wounds of civil discord would be completely healed, and that the republic, restored to its pristine health and vigor, would no longer require the dangerous interposition of so extraordinary a magistrate. The memory of this comedy, repeated several times during the life of Augustus, was preserved to the last ages of the empire, by the peculiar pomp with which the perpetual monarchs of Rome always solemnized the tenth years of their reign. [6]

[Footnote 5: Imperator (from which we have derived Emperor) signified under her republic no more than general, and was emphatically bestowed by the soldiers, when on the field of battle they proclaimed their victorious leader worthy of that title. When the Roman emperors assumed it in that sense, they placed it after their name, and marked how often they had taken it.]

[Footnote 6: Dion. l. liii. p. 703, &c.]

Without any violation of the principles of the constitution, the general of the Roman armies might receive and exercise an authority almost despotic over the soldiers, the enemies, and the subjects of the republic. With regard to the soldiers, the jealousy of freedom had, even from the earliest ages of Rome, given way to the hopes of conquest, and a just sense of military discipline. The dictator, or consul, had a right to command the service of the Roman youth; and to punish an obstinate or cowardly disobedience by the most severe and ignominious penalties, by striking the offender out of the list of citizens, by confiscating his property, and by selling his person into slavery. [7] The most sacred rights of freedom, confirmed by the Porcian and Sempronian laws, were suspended by the military engagement. In his camp the general exercised an absolute power of life and death; his jurisdiction was not confined by any forms of trial, or rules of proceeding, and the execution of the sentence was immediate and without appeal. [8] The choice of the enemies of Rome was regularly decided by the legislative authority. The most important resolutions of peace and war were seriously debated in the senate, and solemnly ratified by the people. But when the arms of the legions were carried to a great distance from Italy, the general assumed the liberty of directing them against whatever people, and in whatever manner, they judged most advantageous for the public service. It was from the success, not from the justice, of their enterprises, that they expected the honors of a triumph. In the use of victory, especially after they were no longer controlled by the commissioners of the senate, they exercised the most unbounded despotism. When Pompey commanded in the East, he rewarded his soldiers and allies, dethroned princes, divided kingdoms, founded colonies, and distributed the treasures of Mithridates. On his return to Rome, he obtained, by a single act of the senate and people, the universal ratification of all his proceedings. [9] Such was the power over the soldiers, and over the enemies of Rome, which was either granted to, or assumed by, the generals of the republic. They were, at the same time, the governors, or rather monarchs, of the conquered provinces, united the civil with the military character, administered justice as well as the finances, and exercised both the executive and legislative power of the state.

[Footnote 7: Livy Epitom. l. xiv. [c. 27.] Valer. Maxim. vi. 3.]

[Footnote 8: See, in the viiith book of Livy, the conduct of Manlius Torquatus and Papirius Cursor. They violated the laws of nature and humanity, but they asserted those of military discipline; and the people, who abhorred the action, was obliged to respect the principle.]

[Footnote 9: By the lavish but unconstrained suffrages of the people, Pompey had obtained a military command scarcely inferior to that of Augustus. Among the extraordinary acts of power executed by the former we may remark the foundation of twenty-nine cities, and the distribution of three or four millions sterling to his troops. The ratification of his acts met with some opposition and delays in the senate See Plutarch, Appian, Dion Cassius, and the first book of the epistles to Atticus.]

From what has already been observed in the first chapter of this work, some notion may be formed of the armies and provinces thus intrusted to the ruling hand of Augustus. But as it was impossible that he could personally command the regions of so many distant frontiers, he was indulged by the senate, as Pompey had already been, in the permission of devolving the execution of his great office on a sufficient number of lieutenants. In rank and authority these officers seemed not inferior to the ancient proconsuls; but their station was dependent and precarious. They received and held their commissions at the will of a superior, to whose auspicious influence the merit of their action was legally attributed. [10] They were the representatives of the emperor. The emperor alone was the general of the republic, and his jurisdiction, civil as well as military, extended over all the conquests of Rome. It was some satisfaction, however, to the senate, that he always delegated his power to the members of their body. The imperial lieutenants were of consular or praetorian dignity; the legions were commanded by senators, and the praefecture of Egypt was the only important trust committed to a Roman knight.

[Footnote 10: *Under the commonwealth, a triumph could only be claimed by the general, who was authorized to take the Auspices in the name of the people. By an exact consequence, drawn from this principle of policy and religion, the triumph was reserved to the emperor; and his most successful lieutenants were satisfied with some marks of distinction, which, under the name of triumphal honors, were invented in their favor.*]

Within six days after Augustus had been compelled to accept so very liberal a grant, he resolved to gratify the pride of the senate by an easy sacrifice. He represented to them, that they had enlarged his powers, even beyond that degree which might be required by the melancholy condition of the times. They had not permitted him to refuse the laborious command of the armies and the frontiers; but he must insist on being allowed to restore the more peaceful and secure provinces to the mild administration of the civil magistrate. In the division of the provinces, Augustus provided for his own power and for the dignity of the republic. The proconsuls of the senate, particularly those of Asia, Greece, and Africa, enjoyed a more honorable character than the lieutenants of the emperor, who commanded in Gaul or Syria. The former were attended by lictors, the latter by soldiers. [105] A law was passed, that wherever the emperor was present, his extraordinary commission should supersede the ordinary jurisdiction of the governor; a custom was introduced, that the new conquests belonged to the imperial portion; and it was soon discovered that the authority of the Prince, the favorite epithet of Augustus, was the same in every part of the empire.

[Footnote 105: *This distinction is without foundation. The lieutenants of the emperor, who were called Propraetors, whether they had been praetors or consuls, were attended by six lictors; those who had the right of the sword, (of life and death over the soldiers.—M.) bore the military habit (paludamentum) and the sword. The provincial governors commissioned by the senate, who, whether they had been consuls or not, were called Pronconsuls, had twelve lictors when they had been consuls, and six only when they had but been praetors. The provinces of Africa and Asia were only given to ex-consuls. See, on the Organization of the Provinces, Dion, liii. 12, 16 Strabo, xvii 840.—W*]

In return for this imaginary concession, Augustus obtained an important privilege, which rendered him master of Rome and Italy. By a dangerous exception to the ancient maxims, he was authorized to preserve his military command, supported by a numerous body of guards, even in time of peace, and in the heart of the capital. His command, indeed, was confined to those citizens who were engaged in the service by the military oath; but such was the propensity of the Romans to servitude, that the oath was voluntarily taken by the magistrates, the senators, and the equestrian order, till the homage of flattery was insensibly converted into an annual and solemn protestation of fidelity.

Although Augustus considered a military force as the firmest foundation, he wisely rejected it, as a very odious instrument of government. It was more agreeable to his temper, as well as to his policy, to reign under the venerable names of ancient magistracy, and artfully to collect, in his own person, all the scattered rays of civil jurisdiction. With this view, he permitted the senate to confer upon him, for his life, the powers of the consular [11] and tribunitian offices, [12] which were, in the same manner, continued to all his successors. The consuls had succeeded to the kings of Rome, and represented the dignity of the state. They superintended the ceremonies of religion, levied and commanded the legions, gave audience to foreign ambassadors, and presided in the assemblies both of the senate and people. The general control of the finances was intrusted to their care; and though they seldom had leisure to administer justice in person, they were considered as the supreme guardians of law, equity, and the public peace. Such was their ordinary jurisdiction; but whenever the senate empowered the first magistrate to consult the safety of the commonwealth, he was raised by that decree above the laws, and exercised, in the defence of liberty, a temporary despotism. [13] The character of the tribunes was, in every respect, different from that of the consuls. The appearance of the former was modest and humble; but their persons were sacred and inviolable. Their force was suited rather for opposition than for action. They were instituted to defend the oppressed, to pardon offences, to arraign the enemies of the people, and, when they judged it necessary, to stop, by a single word, the whole machine of government. As long as the republic subsisted, the dangerous influence, which either the consul or the tribune might derive from their respective jurisdiction, was diminished by several important restrictions. Their authority expired with the year in which they were elected; the former office was divided between two, the latter among ten persons; and, as both in their private and public interest they were averse to each other, their mutual conflicts contributed, for the most part, to strengthen rather than to destroy the balance of the constitution. [13/1] But when the consular and tribunitian powers were united, when they were vested for life in a single person, when the general of the army was, at the same time, the minister of the senate and the representative of the Roman people, it was impossible to resist the exercise, nor was it easy to define the limits, of his imperial prerogative.

[Footnote 11: Cicero (de Legibus, iii. 3) gives the consular office the name of egia potestas; and Polybius (l. vi. c. 3) observes three powers in the Roman constitution. The monarchical was represented and exercised by the consuls.]

[Footnote 12: As the tribunitian power (distinct from the annual office) was first invented by the dictator Caesar, (Dion, l. xliv. p. 384,) we may easily conceive, that it was given as a reward for having so nobly asserted, by arms, the sacred rights of the tribunes and people. See his own Commentaries, de Bell. Civil. l. i.]

[Footnote 13: Augustus exercised nine annual consulships without interruption. He then most artfully refused the magistracy, as well as the dictatorship, absented himself from Rome, and waited till the fatal effects of tumult and faction forced the senate to invest him with a perpetual consulship. Augustus, as well as his successors, affected, however, to conceal so invidious a title.]

[Footnote 13/1: The note of M. Guizot on the tribunitian power applies to the French translation rather than to the original. The former has, maintenir la balance toujours egale, which implies much more than Gibbon's general expression. The note belongs rather to the history of the Republic than that of the Empire.—M]

To these accumulated honors, the policy of Augustus soon added the splendid as well as important dignities of supreme pontiff, and of censor. By the former he acquired the management of the religion, and by the latter a legal inspection over the manners and fortunes, of the Roman people. If so many distinct and independent powers did not exactly unite with each other, the complaisance of the senate was prepared to supply every deficiency by the most ample and extraordinary concessions. The emperors, as the first ministers of the republic, were exempted from the obligation and penalty of many inconvenient laws: they were authorized to convoke the senate, to make several motions in the same day, to recommend candidates for the honors of the state, to enlarge the bounds of the city, to employ the revenue at their discretion, to declare peace and war, to ratify treaties; and by a most comprehensive clause, they were empowered to execute whatsoever they should judge advantageous to the empire, and agreeable to the majesty of things private or public, human of divine. [14]

[Footnote 14: See a fragment of a Decree of the Senate, conferring on the emperor Vespasian all the powers granted to his predecessors, Augustus, Tiberius, and Claudius. This curious and important monument is published in Gruter's Inscriptions, No. ccxlii. Note: It is also in the editions of Tacitus by Ryck, (Annal. p. 420, 421,) and Ernesti, (Excurs. ad lib. iv. 6;) but this fragment contains so many inconsistencies, both in matter and form, that its authenticity may be doubted—W.]

When all the various powers of executive government were committed to the Imperial magistrate, the ordinary magistrates of the commonwealth languished in obscurity, without vigor, and almost without business. The names and forms of the ancient administration were preserved by Augustus with the most anxious care. The usual number of consuls, praetors, and tribunes, [15] were annually invested with their respective ensigns of office, and continued to discharge some of their least important functions. Those honors still attracted the vain ambition of the Romans; and the emperors themselves, though invested for life with the powers of the consul ship, frequently aspired to the title of that annual dignity, which they condescended to share with the most illustrious of their fellow-citizens. [16] In the election of these magistrates, the people, during the reign of Augustus, were permitted to expose all the inconveniences of a wild democracy. That artful prince, instead of discovering the least symptom of impatience, humbly solicited their suffrages for himself or his friends, and scrupulously practised all the duties of an ordinary candidate. [17] But we may venture to ascribe to his councils the first measure of the succeeding reign, by which the elections were transferred to the senate. [18] The assemblies of the people were forever abolished, and the emperors were delivered from a dangerous multitude, who, without restoring liberty, might have disturbed, and perhaps endangered, the established government.

[Footnote 15: Two consuls were created on the Calends of January; but in the course of the year others were substituted in their places, till the annual number seems to have amounted to no less than twelve. The praetors were usually sixteen or eighteen, (Lipsius in Excurs. D. ad Tacit. Annal. l. i.) I have not mentioned the Aediles or Quaestors Officers of the police or revenue easily adapt themselves to any form of government. In the time of Nero, the tribunes legally possessed the right of intercession, though it might be dangerous to exercise it (Tacit. Annal. xvi. 26.) In the time of Trajan, it was doubtful whether the tribuneship was an office or a name, (Plin. Epist. i. 23.)]

[Footnote 16: The tyrants themselves were ambitious of the consulship. The virtuous princes were moderate in the pursuit, and exact in the discharge of it. Trajan revived the ancient oath, and swore before the consul's tribunal that he would observe the laws, (Plin. Panegyric c. 64.)]

[Footnote 17: Quoties Magistratuum Comitiis interesset. Tribus cum candidatis suis circunbat: supplicabatque more solemni. Ferebat et ipse suffragium in tribubus, ut unus e populo. Suetonius in August c. 56.]

[Footnote 18: Tum primum Comitia e campo ad patres translata sunt. Tacit. Annal. i. 15. The word primum seems to allude to some faint and unsuccessful efforts which were made towards restoring them to the people. Note: The emperor Caligula made the attempt: he rest red the Comitia to the people, but, in a short time, took them away again. Suet. in Caio. c. 16. Dion. lix. 9, 20. Nevertheless, at the time of Dion, they preserved still the form of the Comitia. Dion. lviii. 20.—W.]

By declaring themselves the protectors of the people, Marius and Caesar had subverted the constitution of their country. But as soon as the senate had been humbled and disarmed, such an assembly, consisting of five or six hundred persons, was found a much more tractable and useful instrument of dominion. It was on the dignity of the senate that Augustus and his successors founded their new empire; and they affected, on every occasion, to adopt the language and principles of Patricians. In the administration of their own powers, they frequently consulted the great national council, and seemed to refer to its decision the most important concerns of peace and war. Rome, Italy, and the internal provinces, were subject to the immediate jurisdiction of the senate. With regard to civil objects, it was the supreme court of appeal; with regard to criminal matters, a tribunal, constituted for the trial of all offences that were committed by men in any public station, or that affected the peace and majesty of the Roman people. The exercise of the judicial power became the most frequent and serious occupation of the senate; and the important causes that were pleaded before them afforded a last refuge to the spirit of ancient eloquence. As a council of state, and as a court of justice, the senate possessed very considerable prerogatives; but in its legislative capacity, in which it was supposed virtually to represent the people, the rights of sovereignty were acknowledged to reside in that assembly. Every power was derived from their authority, every law was ratified by their sanction. Their regular meetings were held on three stated days in every month, the Calends, the Nones, and the Ides. The debates were conducted with decent freedom; and the emperors themselves, who gloried in the name of senators, sat, voted, and divided with their equals. To resume, in a few words, the system of the Imperial government; as it was instituted by Augustus, and maintained by those princes who understood their own interest and that of the people, it may be defined an absolute monarchy disguised by the forms of a commonwealth. The masters of the Roman world surrounded their throne with darkness, concealed their irresistible strength, and humbly professed themselves the accountable ministers of the senate, whose supreme decrees they dictated and obeyed. [19]

[Footnote 19: Dion Cassius (l. liii. p. 703—714) has given a very loose and partial sketch of the Imperial system. To illustrate and often to correct him, I have meditated Tacitus, examined Suetonius, and consulted the following moderns: the Abbe de la Bleterie, in the Memoires de l'Academie des Inscriptions, tom. xix. xxi. xxiv. xxv. xxvii. Beaufort Republique Romaine, tom. i. p. 255—275. The Dissertations of Noodt and Gronovius de lege Regia, printed at Leyden, in the year 1731 Gravina de Imperio Romano, p. 479—544 of his Opuscula. Maffei, Verona Illustrata, p. i. p. 245, &c.] The face of the court corresponded with the forms of the administration. The emperors, if we except those tyrants whose capricious folly violated every law of nature and decency, disdained that pomp and ceremony which might offend their countrymen, but could add nothing to their real power. In all the offices of life, they affected to confound themselves with their subjects, and maintained with them an equal intercourse of visits and entertainments. Their habit, their palace, their table, were suited only to the rank of an opulent senator. Their family, however numerous or splendid, was composed entirely of their domestic slaves and freedmen. [20] Augustus or Trajan would have blushed at employing the meanest of the Romans in those menial offices, which, in the household and bedchamber of a limited monarch, are so eagerly solicited by the proudest nobles of Britain.]

[Footnote 20: A weak prince will always be governed by his domestics. The power of slaves aggravated the shame of the Romans; and the senate paid court to a Pallas or a Narcissus. There is a chance that a modern favorite may be a gentleman.]

The deification of the emperors [21] is the only instance in which they departed from their accustomed prudence and modesty. The Asiatic Greeks were the first inventors, the successors of Alexander the first objects, of this servile and impious mode of adulation. [21/1] It was easily transferred from the kings to the governors of Asia; and the Roman magistrates very frequently were adored as provincial deities, with the pomp of altars and temples, of festivals and sacrifices. [22] It was natural that the emperors should not refuse what the proconsuls had accepted; and the divine honors which both the one and the other received from the provinces, attested rather the despotism than the servitude of Rome. But the conquerors soon imitated the vanquished nations in the arts of flattery; and the imperious spirit of the first Caesar too easily consented to assume, during his lifetime, a place among the tutelar deities of Rome. The milder temper of his successor declined so dangerous an ambition, which was never afterwards revived, except by the madness of Caligula and Domitian. Augustus permitted indeed some of the provincial cities to erect temples to his honor, on condition that they should associate the worship of Rome with that of the sovereign; he tolerated private superstition, of which he might be the object; [23] but he contented himself with being revered by the senate and the people in his human character, and wisely left to his successor the care of his public deification. A regular custom was introduced, that on the decease of every emperor who had neither lived nor died like a tyrant, the senate by a solemn decree should place him in the number of the gods: and the ceremonies of his apotheosis were blended with those of his funeral. [23/1] This legal, and, as it should seem, injudicious profanation, so abhorrent to our stricter principles, was received with a very faint murmur, [24] by the easy nature of Polytheism; but it was received as an institution, not of religion, but of policy. We should disgrace the virtues of the Antonines by comparing them with the vices of Hercules or Jupiter. Even the characters of Caesar or Augustus were far superior to those of the popular deities. But it was the misfortune of the former to live in an enlightened age, and their actions were too faithfully recorded to admit of such a mixture of fable and mystery, as the devotion of the vulgar requires. As soon as their divinity was established by law, it sunk into oblivion, without contributing either to their own fame, or to the dignity of succeeding princes.

[Footnote 21: See a treatise of Vandale de Consecratione Principium. It would be easier for me to copy, than it has been to verify, the quotations of that learned Dutchman.]

[Footnote 21/1: This is inaccurate. The successors of Alexander were not the first deified sovereigns; the Egyptians had deified and worshipped many of their kings; the Olympus of the Greeks was peopled with divinities who had reigned on earth; finally, Romulus himself had received the honors of an apotheosis (Tit. Liv. i. 16) a long time before Alexander and his successors. It is also an inaccuracy to confound the honors offered in the provinces to the Roman governors, by temples and altars, with the true apotheosis of the emperors; it was not a religious worship, for it had neither priests nor sacrifices. Augustus was severely blamed for having permitted himself to be worshipped as a god in the provinces, (Tac. Ann. i. 10:) he would not have incurred that blame if he had only done what the governors were accustomed to do.—G. from W. M. Guizot has been guilty of a still greater inaccuracy in confounding the deification of the living with the apotheosis of the dead emperors. The nature of the king-worship of Egypt is still very obscure; the hero-worship of the Greeks very different from the adoration of the "praesens numen" in the reigning sovereign.—M.]

[Footnote 22: See a dissertation of the Abbe Mongault in the first volume of the Academy of Inscriptions.]

[Footnote 23: Jurandasque tuum per nomen ponimus aras, says Horace to the emperor himself, and Horace was well acquainted with the court of Augustus. Note: The good princes were not those who alone obtained the honors of an apotheosis: it was conferred on many tyrants. See an excellent treatise of Schaepflin, de Consecratione Imperatorum Romanorum, in his Commentationes historicae et criticae. Bale, 1741, p. 184.—W.]

[Footnote 23/1: The curious satire in the works of Seneca, is the strongest remonstrance of profaned religion.—M.]

[Footnote 24: See Cicero in Philippic. i. 6. Julian in Caesaribus. Inque Deum templis jurabit Roma per umbras, is the indignant expression of Lucan; but it is a patriotic rather than a devout indignation.]

In the consideration of the Imperial government, we have frequently mentioned the artful founder, under his well-known title of Augustus, which was not, however, conferred upon him till the edifice was almost completed. The obscure name of Octavianus he derived from a mean family, in the little town of Aricia. [24/1] It was stained with the blood of the proscription; and he was desirous, had it been possible, to erase all memory of his former life. The illustrious surname of Caesar he had assumed, as the adopted son of the dictator: but he had too much good sense, either to hope to be confounded, or to wish to be compared with that extraordinary man. It was proposed in the senate to dignify their minister with a new appellation; and after a serious discussion, that of Augustus was chosen, among several others, as being the most expressive of the character of peace and sanctity, which he uniformly affected. [25] Augustus was therefore a personal, Caesar a family distinction. The former should naturally have expired with the prince on whom it was bestowed; and however the latter was diffused by adoption and female alliance, Nero was the last prince who could allege any hereditary claim to the honors of the Julian line. But, at the time of his death, the practice of a century had inseparably connected those appellations with the Imperial dignity, and they have been preserved by a long succession of emperors, Romans, Greeks, Franks, and Germans, from the fall of the republic to the present time. A distinction was, however, soon introduced. The sacred title of Augustus was always reserved for the monarch, whilst the name of Caesar was more freely communicated to his relations; and, from the reign of Hadrian, at least, was appropriated to the second person in the state, who was considered as the presumptive heir of the empire. [25/1]

[Footnote 24/1: Octavius was not of an obscure family, but of a considerable one of the equestrian order. His father, C. Octavius, who possessed great property, had been praetor, governor of Macedonia, adorned with the title of Imperator, and was on the point of becoming consul when he died. His mother Attia, was daughter of M. Attius Balbus, who had also been praetor. M. Anthony reproached Octavius with having been born in Aricia, which, nevertheless, was a considerable municipal city: he was vigorously refuted by Cicero. Philip. iii. c. 6.—W. Gibbon probably meant that the family had but recently emerged into notice.—M.]

[Footnote 25: Dion. Cassius, l. liii. p. 710, with the curious Annotations of Reimar.]

[Footnote 25/1: The princes who by their birth or their adoption belonged to the family of the Caesars, took the name of Caesar. After the death of Nero, this name designated the Imperial dignity itself, and afterwards the appointed successor. The time at which it was employed in the latter sense, cannot be fixed with certainty. Bach (Hist. Jurisprud. Rom. 304) affirms from Tacitus, H. i. 15, and Suetonius, Galba, 17, that Galba conferred on Piso Lucinianus the title of Caesar, and from that time the term had this meaning: but these two historians simply say that he appointed Piso his successor, and do not mention the word Caesar. Aurelius Victor (in Traj. 348, ed. Artzen) says that Hadrian first received this title on his adoption; but as the adoption of Hadrian is still doubtful, and besides this, as Trajan, on his death-bed, was not likely to have created a new title for his successor, it is more probable that Aelius Verus was the first who was called Caesar when adopted by Hadrian. Spart. in Aelio Vero, 102.—W.]

PART II

The tender respect of Augustus for a free constitution which he had destroyed, can only be explained by an attentive consideration of the character of that subtle tyrant. A cool head, an unfeeling heart, and a cowardly disposition, prompted him at the age of nineteen to assume the mask of hypocrisy, which he never afterwards laid aside. With the same hand, and probably with the same temper, he signed the proscription of Cicero, and the pardon of Cinna. His virtues, and even his vices, were artificial; and according to the various dictates of his interest, he was at first the enemy, and at last the father, of the Roman world. [26] When he framed the artful system of the Imperial authority, his moderation was inspired by his fears. He wished to deceive the people by an image of civil liberty, and the armies by an image of civil government.

[Footnote 26: As Octavianus advanced to the banquet of the Caesars, his color changed like that of the chameleon; pale at first, then red, afterwards black, he at last assumed the mild livery of Venus and the Graces, (Caesars, p. 309.) This image, employed by Julian in his ingenious fiction, is just and elegant; but when he considers this change of character as real and ascribes it to the power of philosophy, he does too much honor to philosophy and to Octavianus.]

I. The death of Caesar was ever before his eyes. He had lavished wealth and honors on his adherents; but the most favored friends of his uncle were in the number of the conspirators. The fidelity of the legions might defend his authority against open rebellion; but their vigilance could not secure his person from the dagger of a determined republican; and the Romans, who revered the memory of Brutus, [27] would applaud the imitation of his virtue. Caesar had provoked his fate, as much as by the ostentation of his power, as by his power itself. The consul or the tribune might have reigned in peace. The title of king had armed the Romans against his life. Augustus was sensible that mankind is governed by names; nor was he deceived in his expectation, that the senate and people would submit to slavery, provided they were respectfully assured that they still enjoyed their ancient freedom. A feeble senate and enervated people cheerfully acquiesced in the pleasing illusion, as long as it was supported by the virtue, or even by the prudence, of the successors of Augustus. It was a motive of self-preservation, not a principle of liberty, that animated the conspirators against Caligula, Nero, and Domitian. They attacked the person of the tyrant, without aiming their blow at the authority of the emperor.

[Footnote 27: Two centuries after the establishment of monarchy, the emperor Marcus Antoninus recommends the character of Brutus as a perfect model of Roman virtue. Note: In a very ingenious essay, Gibbon has ventured to call in question the preeminent virtue of Brutus. Misc Works, iv. 95.—M.]

There appears, indeed, one memorable occasion, in which the senate, after seventy years of patience, made an ineffectual attempt to re-assume its long-forgotten rights. When the throne was vacant by the murder of Caligula, the consuls convoked that assembly in the Capitol, condemned the memory of the Caesars, gave the watchword liberty to the few cohorts who faintly adhered to their standard, and during eight-and-forty hours acted as the independent chiefs of a free commonwealth. But while they deliberated, the praetorian guards had resolved. The stupid Claudius, brother of Germanicus, was already in their camp, invested with the Imperial purple, and prepared to support his election by arms.

The dream of liberty was at an end; and the senate awoke to all the horrors of inevitable servitude. Deserted by the people, and threatened by a military force, that feeble assembly was compelled to ratify the choice of the praetorians, and to embrace the benefit of an amnesty, which Claudius had the prudence to offer, and the generosity to observe. [28]

[See The Capitol: When the throne was vacant by the murder of Caligula, the consuls convoked that assembly in the Capitol.]

[Footnote 28: It is much to be regretted that we have lost the part of Tacitus which treated of that transaction. We are forced to content ourselves with the popular rumors of Josephus, and the imperfect hints of Dion and Suetonius.]

II. The insolence of the armies inspired Augustus with fears of a still more alarming nature. The despair of the citizens could only attempt, what the power of the soldiers was, at any time, able to execute. How precarious was his own authority over men whom he had taught to violate every social duty! He had heard their seditious clamors; he dreaded their calmer moments of reflection. One revolution had been purchased by immense rewards; but a second revolution might double those rewards. The troops professed the fondest attachment to the house of Caesar; but the attachments of the multitude are capricious and inconstant. Augustus summoned to his aid whatever remained in those fierce minds of Roman prejudices; enforced the rigor of discipline by the sanction of law; and, interposing the majesty of the senate between the emperor and the army, boldly claimed their allegiance, as the first magistrate of the republic.

During a long period of two hundred and twenty years from the establishment of this artful system to the death of Commodus, the dangers inherent to a military government were, in a great measure, suspended. The soldiers were seldom roused to that fatal sense of their own strength, and of the weakness of the civil authority, which was, before and afterwards, productive of such dreadful calamities. Caligula and Domitian were assassinated in their palace by their own domestics: [281] the convulsions which agitated Rome on the death of the former, were confined to the walls of the city. But Nero involved the whole empire in his ruin. In the space of eighteen months, four princes perished by the sword; and the Roman world was shaken by the fury of the contending armies. Excepting only this short, though violent eruption of military license, the two centuries from Augustus [29] to Commodus passed away unstained with civil blood, and undisturbed by revolutions. The emperor was elected by the authority of the senate, and the consent of the soldiers. [30] The legions respected their oath of fidelity; and it requires a minute inspection of the Roman annals to discover three inconsiderable rebellions, which were all suppressed in a few months, and without even the hazard of a battle. [31]

[Footnote 28/1: Caligula perished by a conspiracy formed by the officers of the praetorian troops, and Domitian would not, perhaps, have been assassinated without the participation of the two chiefs of that guard in his death.—W.]

[Footnote 29: Augustus restored the ancient severity of discipline. After the civil wars, he dropped the endearing name of Fellow-Soldiers, and called them only Soldiers, (Sueton. in August. c. 25.) See the use Tiberius made of the Senate in the mutiny of the Pannonian legions, (Tacit. Annal. i.)]

[Footnote 30: These words seem to have been the constitutional language. See Tacit. Annal. xiii. 4. Note: This panegyric on the soldiery is rather too liberal. Claudius was obliged to purchase their consent to his coronation: the presents which he made, and those which the praetorians received on other occasions, *considerably embarrassed the finances. Moreover, this formidable guard favored, in general, the cruelties of the tyrants. The distant revolts were more frequent than Gibbon thinks: already, under Tiberius, the legions of Germany would have seditiously constrained Germanicus to assume the Imperial purple. On the revolt of Claudius Civilis, under Vespasian, the legions of Gaul murdered their general, and offered their assistance to the Gauls who were in insurrection. Julius Sabinus made himself be proclaimed emperor, &c. The wars, the merit, and the severe discipline of Trajan, Hadrian, and the two Antonines, established, for some time, a greater degree of subordination.—W]*

[Footnote 31: The first was Camillus Scribonianus, who took up arms in Dalmatia against Claudius, and was deserted by his own troops in five days, the second, L. Antonius, in Germany, who rebelled against Domitian; and the third, Avidius Cassius, in the reign of M. Antoninus. The two last reigned but a few months, and were cut off by their own adherents. We may observe, that both Camillus and Cassius colored their ambition with the design of restoring the republic; a task, said Cassius peculiarly reserved for his name and family.]

In elective monarchies, the vacancy of the throne is a moment big with danger and mischief. The Roman emperors, desirous to spare the legions that interval of suspense, and the temptation of an irregular choice, invested their designed successor with so large a share of present power, as should enable him, after their decease, to assume the remainder, without suffering the empire to perceive the change of masters. Thus Augustus, after all his fairer prospects had been snatched from him by untimely deaths, rested his last hopes on Tiberius, obtained for his adopted son the censorial and tribunitian powers, and dictated a law, by which the future prince was invested with an authority equal to his own, over the provinces and the armies. [32] Thus Vespasian subdued the generous mind of his eldest son. Titus was adored by the eastern legions, which, under his command, had recently achieved the conquest of Judaea. His power was dreaded, and, as his virtues were clouded by the intemperance of youth, his designs were suspected. Instead of listening to such unworthy suspicions, the prudent monarch associated Titus to the full powers of the Imperial dignity; and the grateful son ever approved himself the humble and faithful minister of so indulgent a father. [33]

[Footnote 32: Velleius Paterculus, l. ii. c. 121. Sueton. in Tiber. c. 26.]

[Footnote 33: Sueton. in Tit. c. 6. Plin. in Praefat. Hist. Natur.]

The good sense of Vespasian engaged him indeed to embrace every measure that might confirm his recent and precarious elevation. The military oath, and the fidelity of the troops, had been consecrated, by the habits of a hundred years, to the name and family of the Caesars; and although that family had been continued only by the fictitious rite of adoption, the Romans still revered, in the person of Nero, the grandson of Germanicus, and the lineal successor of Augustus. It was not without reluctance and remorse, that the praetorian guards had been persuaded to abandon the cause of the tyrant. [34] The rapid downfall of Galba, Otho, and Vitellus, taught the armies to consider the emperors as the creatures of their will, and the instruments of their license. The birth of Vespasian was mean: his grandfather had been a private soldier, his father a petty officer of the revenue; [35] his own merit had raised him, in an advanced age, to the empire; but his merit was rather useful than shining, and his virtues were disgraced by a strict and even sordid parsimony. Such a prince consulted his true interest by the association of a son, whose more splendid and amiable character might turn the public attention from the obscure origin, to the future glories, of the Flavian house. Under the mild administration of Titus, the Roman world enjoyed a transient felicity, and his beloved memory served to protect, above fifteen years, the vices of his brother Domitian.

[Footnote 34: This idea is frequently and strongly inculcated by Tacitus. See Hist. i. 5, 16, ii. 76.]

[Footnote 35: The emperor Vespasian, with his usual good sense, laughed at the genealogists, who deduced his family from Flavius, the founder of Reate, (his native country,) and one of the companions of Hercules Suet in Vespasian, c. 12.]

Nerva had scarcely accepted the purple from the assassins of Domitian, before he discovered that his feeble age was unable to stem the torrent of public disorders, which had multiplied under the long tyranny of his predecessor. His mild disposition was respected by the good; but the degenerate Romans required a more vigorous character, whose justice should strike terror into the guilty. Though he had several relations, he fixed his choice on a stranger. He adopted Trajan, then about forty years of age, and who commanded a powerful army in the Lower Germany; and immediately, by a decree of the senate, declared him his colleague and successor in the empire. [36] It is sincerely to be lamented, that whilst we are fatigued with the disgustful relation of Nero's crimes and follies, we are reduced to collect the actions of Trajan from the glimmerings of an abridgment, or the doubtful light of a panegyric. There remains, however, one panegyric far removed beyond the suspicion of flattery. Above two hundred and fifty years after the death of Trajan, the senate, in pouring out the customary acclamations on the accession of a new emperor, wished that he might surpass the felicity of Augustus, and the virtue of Trajan. [37]

[Footnote 36: Dion, l. lxviii. p. 1121. Plin. Secund. in Panegyric.]

[Footnote 37: Felicior Augusto, Melior Trajano. Eutrop. viii. 5.]

We may readily believe, that the father of his country hesitated whether he ought to intrust the various and doubtful character of his kinsman Hadrian with sovereign power. In his last moments the arts of the empress Plotina either fixed the irresolution of Trajan, or boldly supposed a fictitious adoption; [38] the truth of which could not be safely disputed, and Hadrian was peaceably acknowledged as his lawful successor. Under his reign, as has been already mentioned, the empire flourished in peace and prosperity. He encouraged the arts, reformed the laws, asserted military discipline, and visited all his provinces in person. His vast and active genius was equally suited to the most enlarged views, and the minute details of civil policy. But the ruling passions of his soul were curiosity and vanity. As they prevailed, and as they were attracted by different objects, Hadrian was, by turns, an excellent prince, a ridiculous sophist, and a jealous tyrant. The general tenor of his conduct deserved praise for its equity and moderation. Yet in the first days of his reign, he put to death four consular senators, his personal enemies, and men who had been judged worthy of empire; and the tediousness of a painful illness rendered him, at last, peevish and cruel. The senate doubted whether they should pronounce him a god or a tyrant; and the honors decreed to his memory were granted to the prayers of the pious Antoninus. [39]

[Footnote 38: Dion (l. lxix. p. 1249) affirms the whole to have been a fiction, on the authority of his father, who, being governor of the province where Trajan died, had very good opportunities of sifting this mysterious transaction. Yet Dodwell (Praelect. Camden. xvii.) has maintained that Hadrian was called to the certain hope of the empire, during the lifetime of Trajan.]

[Footnote 39: Dion, (l. lxx. p. 1171.) Aurel. Victor.]

The caprice of Hadrian influenced his choice of a successor.

After revolving in his mind several men of distinguished merit, whom he esteemed and hated, he adopted Aelius Verus a gay and voluptuous nobleman, recommended by uncommon beauty to the lover of Antinous. [40] But whilst Hadrian was delighting himself with his own applause, and the acclamations of the soldiers, whose consent had been secured by an immense donative, the new Caesar [41] was ravished from his embraces by an untimely death. He left only one son. Hadrian commended the boy to the gratitude of the Antonines. He was adopted by Pius; and, on the accession of Marcus, was invested with an equal share of sovereign power. Among the many vices of this younger Verus, he possessed one virtue; a dutiful reverence for his wiser colleague, to whom he willingly abandoned the ruder cares of empire. The philosophic emperor dissembled his follies, lamented his early death, and cast a decent veil over his memory.

[Footnote 40: The deification of Antinous, his medals, his statues, temples, city, oracles, and constellation, are well known, and still dishonor the memory of Hadrian. Yet we may remark, that of the first fifteen emperors, Claudius was the only one whose taste in love was entirely correct. For the honors of Antinous, see Spanheim, Commentaire sui les Caesars de Julien, p. 80.]

[Footnote 41: Hist. August. p. 13. Aurelius Victor in Epitom.]

As soon as Hadrian's passion was either gratified or disappointed, he resolved to deserve the thanks of posterity, by placing the most exalted merit on the Roman throne. His discerning eye easily discovered a senator about fifty years of age, clameless in all the offices of life; and a youth of about seventeen, whose riper years opened a fair prospect of every virtue: the elder of these was declared the son and successor of Hadrian, on condition, however, that he himself should immediately adopt the younger. The two Antonines (for it is of them that we are now peaking,) governed the Roman world forty-two years, with the same invariable spirit of wisdom and virtue. Although Pius had two sons, [42] he preferred the welfare of Rome to the interest of his family, gave his daughter Faustina, in marriage to young Marcus, obtained from the senate the tribunitian and proconsular powers, and, with a noble disdain, or rather ignorance of jealousy, associated him to all the labors of government. Marcus, on the other hand, revered the character of his benefactor, loved him as a parent, obeyed him as his sovereign, [43] and, after he was no more, regulated his own administration by the example and maxims of his predecessor. Their united reigns are possibly the only period of history in which the happiness of a great people was the sole object of government.

[Footnote 42: Without the help of medals and inscriptions, we should be ignorant of this fact, so honorable to the memory of Pius. Note: Gibbon attributes to Antoninus Pius a merit which he either did not possess, or was not in a situation to display.

1. He was adopted only on the condition that he would adopt, in his turn, Marcus Aurelius and L. Verus.

2. His two sons died children, and one of them, M. Galerius, alone, appears to have survived, for a few years, his father's coronation. Gibbon is also mistaken when he says (note 42) that "without the help of medals and inscriptions, we should be ignorant that Antoninus had two sons." Capitolinus says expressly, (c. 1,) Filii mares duo, duae-foeminae; we only owe their names to the medals. Pagi. Cont. Baron, i. 33, edit Paris.—W.]

[Footnote 43: During the twenty-three years of Pius's reign, Marcus was only two nights absent from the palace, and even those were at different times. Hist. August. p. 25.]

Titus Antoninus Pius has been justly denominated a second Numa. The same love of religion, justice, and peace, was the distinguishing characteristic of both princes. But the situation of the latter opened a much larger field for the exercise of those virtues. Numa could only prevent a few neighboring villages from plundering each other's harvests. Antoninus diffused order and tranquillity over the greatest part of the earth. His reign is marked by the rare advantage of furnishing very few materials for history; which is, indeed, little more than the register of the crimes, follies, and misfortunes of mankind. In private life, he was an amiable, as well as a good man. The native simplicity of his virtue was a stranger to vanity or affectation. He enjoyed with moderation the conveniences of his fortune, and the innocent pleasures of society; [44] and the benevolence of his soul displayed itself in a cheerful serenity of temper.

[Footnote 44: He was fond of the theatre, and not insensible to the charms of the fair sex. Marcus Antoninus, i. 16. Hist. August. p. 20, 21. Julian in Caesar.]

The virtue of Marcus Aurelius Antoninus was of severer and more laborious kind. [45] It was the well-earned harvest of many a learned conference, of many a patient lecture, and many a midnight lucubration. At the age of twelve years he embraced the rigid system of the Stoics, which taught him to submit his body to his mind, his passions to his reason; to consider virtue as the only good, vice as the only evil, all things external as things indifferent. [46] His meditations, composed in the tumult of the camp, are still extant; and he even condescended to give lessons of philosophy, in a more public manner than was perhaps consistent with the modesty of sage, or the dignity of an emperor. [47] But his life was the noblest commentary on the precepts of Zeno. He was severe to himself, indulgent to the imperfections of others, just and beneficent to all mankind. He regretted that Avidius Cassius, who excited a rebellion in Syria, had disappointed him, by a voluntary death, [47/1] of the pleasure of converting an enemy into a friend;; and he justified the sincerity of that sentiment, by moderating the zeal of the senate against the adherents of the traitor. [48] War he detested, as the disgrace and calamity of human nature; [48/1] but when the necessity of a just defence called upon him to take up arms, he readily exposed his person to eight winter campaigns, on the frozen banks of the Danube, the severity of which was at last fatal to the weakness of his constitution. His memory was revered by a grateful posterity, and above a century after his death, many persons preserved the image of Marcus Antoninus among those of their household gods. [49]

[Footnote 45: The enemies of Marcus charged him with hypocrisy, and with a want of that simplicity which distinguished Pius and even Verus. (Hist. August. 6, 34.) This suspicions, unjust as it was, may serve to account for the superior applause bestowed upon personal qualifications, in preference to the social virtues. Even Marcus Antoninus has been called a hypocrite; but the wildest scepticism never insinuated that Caesar might probably be a coward, or Tully a fool. Wit and valor are qualifications more easily ascertained than humanity or the love of justice.]

[Footnote 46: Tacitus has characterized, in a few words, the principles of the portico: Doctores sapientiae secutus est, qui sola bona quae honesta, main tantum quae turpia; potentiam, nobilitatem, aeteraque extra... bonis neque malis adnumerant. Tacit. Hist. iv. 5.]

[Footnote 47: Before he went on the second expedition against the Germans, he read lectures of philosophy to the Roman people, during three days. He had already done the same in the cities of Greece and Asia. Hist. August. in Cassio, c. 3.]

[Footnote 47/1: Cassius was murdered by his own partisans. Vulcat. Gallic. in Cassio, c. 7. Dion, lxxi. c. 27.—W.]

[Footnote 48: Dion, l. lxxi. p. 1190. Hist. August. in Avid. Cassio. Note: See one of the newly discovered passages of Dion Cassius. Marcus wrote to the senate, who urged the execution of the partisans of Cassius, in these words: "I entreat and beseech you to preserve my reign unstained by senatorial blood. None of your order must perish either by your desire or mine." Mai. Fragm. Vatican. ii. p. 224.—M.]

[Footnote 48/1: Marcus would not accept the services of any of the barbarian allies who crowded to his standard in the war against Avidius Cassius. "Barbarians," he said, with wise but vain sagacity, "must not become acquainted with the dissensions of the Roman people." Mai. Fragm Vatican l. 224.—M.]

[Footnote 49: Hist. August. in Marc. Antonin. c. 18.]

If a man were called to fix the period in the history of the world, during which the condition of the human race was most happy and prosperous, he would, without hesitation, name that which elapsed from the death of Domitian to the accession of Commodus. The vast extent of the Roman empire was governed by absolute power, under the guidance of virtue and wisdom. The armies were restrained by the firm but gentle hand of four successive emperors, whose characters and authority commanded involuntary respect. The forms of the civil administration were carefully preserved by Nerva, Trajan, Hadrian, and the Antonines, who delighted in the image of liberty, and were pleased with considering themselves as the accountable ministers of the laws. Such princes deserved the honor of restoring the republic, had the Romans of their days been capable of enjoying a rational freedom.

The labors of these monarchs were overpaid by the immense reward that inseparably waited on their success; by the honest pride of virtue, and by the exquisite delight of beholding the general happiness of which they were the authors. A just but melancholy reflection imbittered, however, the noblest of human enjoyments. They must often have recollected the instability of a happiness which depended on the character of single man. The fatal moment was perhaps approaching, when some licentious youth, or some jealous tyrant, would abuse, to the destruction, that absolute power, which they had exerted for the benefit of their people. The ideal restraints of the senate and the laws might serve to display the virtues, but could never correct the vices, of the emperor. The military force was a blind and irresistible instrument of oppression; and the corruption of Roman manners would always supply flatterers eager to applaud, and ministers prepared to serve, the fear or the avarice, the lust or the cruelty, of their master. These gloomy apprehensions had been already justified by the experience of the Romans. The annals of the emperors exhibit a strong and various picture of human nature, which we should vainly seek among the mixed and doubtful characters of modern history. In the conduct of those monarchs we may trace the utmost lines of vice and virtue; the most exalted perfection, and the meanest degeneracy of our own species. The golden age of Trajan and the Antonines had been preceded by an age of iron. It is almost superfluous to enumerate the unworthy successors of Augustus. Their unparalleled vices, and the splendid theatre on which they were acted, have saved them from oblivion. The dark, unrelenting Tiberius, the furious Caligula, the feeble Claudius, the profligate and cruel Nero, the beastly Vitellius, [50] and the timid, inhuman Domitian, are condemned to everlasting infamy. During fourscore years (excepting only the short and doubtful respite of Vespasian's reign) [51] Rome groaned beneath an unremitting tyranny, which exterminated the ancient families of the republic, and was fatal to almost every virtue and every talent that arose in that unhappy period.

[Footnote 50: Vitellius consumed in mere eating at least six millions of our money in about seven months. It is not easy to express his vices with dignity, or even decency. Tacitus fairly calls him a hog, but it is by substituting for a coarse word a very fine image. "At Vitellius, umbraculis hortorum abditus, ut ignava animalia, quibus si cibum suggeras, jacent torpentque, praeterita, instantia, futura, pari oblivione dimiserat. Atque illum nemore Aricino desidem et marcentum," &c. Tacit. Hist. iii. 36, ii. 95. Sueton. in Vitell. c. 13. Dion. Cassius, l xv. p. 1062.]

[Footnote 51: The execution of Helvidius Priscus, and of the virtuous Eponina, disgraced the reign of Vespasian.]

Under the reign of these monsters, the slavery of the Romans was accompanied with two peculiar circumstances, the one occasioned by their former liberty, the other by their extensive conquests, which rendered their condition more completely wretched than that of the victims of tyranny in any other age or country. From these causes were derived, 1. The exquisite sensibility of the sufferers; and, 2. The impossibility of escaping from the hand of the oppressor.

I. When Persia was governed by the descendants of Sefi, a race of princes whose wanton cruelty often stained their divan, their table, and their bed, with the blood of their favorites, there is a saying recorded of a young nobleman, that he never departed from the sultan's presence, without satisfying himself whether his head was still on his shoulders. The experience of every day might almost justify the scepticism of Rustan. [52] Yet the fatal sword, suspended above him by a single thread, seems not to have disturbed the slumbers, or interrupted the tranquillity, of the Persian. The monarch's frown, he well knew, could level him with the dust; but the stroke of lightning or apoplexy might be equally fatal; and it was the part of a wise man to forget the inevitable calamities of human life in the enjoyment of the fleeting hour. He was dignified with the appellation of the king's slave; had, perhaps, been purchased from obscure parents, in a country which he had never known; and was trained up from his infancy in the severe discipline of the seraglio. [53] His name, his wealth, his honors, were the gift of a master, who might, without injustice, resume what he had bestowed. Rustan's knowledge, if he possessed any, could only serve to confirm his habits by prejudices. His language afforded not words for any form of government, except absolute monarchy. The history of the East informed him, that such had ever been the condition of mankind. [54] The Koran, and the interpreters of that divine book, inculcated to him, that the sultan was the descendant of the prophet, and the vicegerent of heaven; that patience was the first virtue of a Mussulman, and unlimited obedience the great duty of a subject.

[Footnote 52: Voyage de Chardin en Perse, vol. iii. p. 293.]

[Footnote 53: The practice of raising slaves to the great offices of state is still more common among the Turks than among the Persians. The miserable countries of Georgia and Circassia supply rulers to the greatest part of the East.]

[Footnote 54: Chardin says, that European travellers have diffused among the Persians some ideas of the freedom and mildness of our governments. They have done them a very ill office.]

The minds of the Romans were very differently prepared for slavery. Oppressed beneath the weight of their own corruption and of military violence, they for a long while preserved the sentiments, or at least the ideas, of their free-born ancestors. The education of Helvidius and Thrasea, of Tacitus and Pliny, was the same as that of Cato and Cicero. From Grecian philosophy, they had imbibed the justest and most liberal notions of the dignity of human nature, and the origin of civil society. The history of their own country had taught them to revere a free, a virtuous, and a victorious commonwealth; to abhor the successful crimes of Caesar and Augustus; and inwardly to despise those tyrants whom they adored with the most abject flattery. As magistrates and senators they were admitted into the great council, which had once dictated laws to the earth, whose authority was so often prostituted to the vilest purposes of tyranny. Tiberius, and those emperors who adopted his maxims, attempted to disguise their murders by the formalities of justice, and perhaps enjoyed a secret pleasure in rendering the senate their accomplice as well as their victim. By this assembly, the last of the Romans were condemned for imaginary crimes and real virtues. Their infamous accusers assumed the language of independent patriots, who arraigned a dangerous citizen before the tribunal of his country; and the public service was rewarded by riches and honors. [55] The servile judges professed to assert the majesty of the commonwealth, violated in the person of its first magistrate, [56] whose clemency they most applauded when they trembled the most at his inexorable and impending cruelty. [57] The tyrant beheld their baseness with just contempt, and encountered their secret sentiments of detestation with sincere and avowed hatred for the whole body of the senate.

[Footnote 55: They alleged the example of Scipio and Cato, (Tacit. Annal. iii. 66.) Marcellus Epirus and Crispus Vibius had acquired two millions and a half under Nero. Their wealth, which aggravated their crimes, protected them under Vespasian. See Tacit. Hist. iv. 43. Dialog. de Orator. c. 8. For one accusation, Regulus, the just object of Pliny's satire, received from the senate the consular ornaments, and a present of sixty thousand pounds.]

[Footnote 56: The crime of majesty was formerly a treasonable offence against the Roman people. As tribunes of the people, Augustus and Tiberius applied tit to their own persons, and extended it to an infinite latitude. Note: It was Tiberius, not Augustus, who first took in this sense the words crimen laesae majestatis. Bachii Trajanus, 27. —W.]

[Footnote 57: After the virtuous and unfortunate widow of Germanicus had been put to death, Tiberius received the thanks of the senate for his clemency. she had not been publicly strangled; nor was the body drawn with a hook to the Gemoniae, where those of common male factors were exposed. See Tacit. Annal. vi. 25. Sueton. in Tiberio c. 53.]

II. The division of Europe into a number of independent states, connected, however, with each other by the general resemblance of religion, language, and manners, is productive of the most beneficial consequences to the liberty of mankind. A modern tyrant, who should find no resistance either in his own breast, or in his people, would soon experience a gentle restrain from the example of his equals, the dread of present censure, the advice of his allies, and the apprehension of his enemies. The object of his displeasure, escaping from the narrow limits of his dominions, would easily obtain, in a happier climate, a secure refuge, a new fortune adequate to his merit, the freedom of complaint, and perhaps the means of revenge. But the empire of the Romans filled the world, and when the empire fell into the hands of a single person, he would became a safe and dreary prison for his enemies. The slave of Imperial despotism, whether he was condemned to drag his gilded chain in rome and the senate, or to were out a life of exile on the barren rock of Seriphus, or the frozen bank of the Danube, expected his fate in silent despair. [58] To resist was fatal, and it was impossible to fly. On every side he was encompassed with a vast extent of sea and land, which he could never hope to traverse without being discovered, seized, and restored to his irritated master. Beyond the frontiers, his anxious view could discover nothing, except the ocean, inhospitable deserts, hostile tribes of barbarians, of fierce manners and unknown language, or dependent kings, who would gladly purchase the emperor's protection by the sacrifice of an obnoxious fugitive. [59] "Wherever you are," said Cicero to the exiled Marcellus, "remember that you are equally within the power of the conqueror." [60]

[Footnote 58: Seriphus was a small rocky island in the Aegean Sea, the inhabitants of which were despised for their ignorance and obscurity. The place of Ovid's exile is well known, by his just, but unmanly lamentations. It should seem, that he only received an order to leave rome in so many days, and to transport himself to Tomi. Guards and jailers were unnecessary.]

[Footnote 59: Under Tiberius, a Roman knight attempted to fly to the Parthians. He was stopped in the straits of Sicily; but so little danger did there appear in the example, that the most jealous of tyrants disdained to punish it. Tacit. Annal. vi. 14.]

[Footnote 60: Cicero ad Familiares, iv. 7.]

CHAPTER IV

THE CRUELTY, FOLLIES AND MURDER OF COMMODUS

PART I

THE CRUELTY, FOLLIES AND MURDER OF COMMODUS—ELECTION OF PERTINAX—HIS ATTEMPTS TO REFORM THE STATE—HIS ASSINATION BY THE PRAETORIAN GUARDS

The mildness of Marcus, which the rigid discipline of the Stoics was unable to eradicate, formed, at the same time, the most amiable, and the only defective part of his character. His excellent understanding was often deceived by the unsuspecting goodness of his heart. Artful men, who study the passions of princes, and conceal their own, approached his person in the disguise of philosophic sanctity, and acquired riches and honors by affecting to despise them. [1] His excessive indulgence to his brother, [105] his wife, and his son, exceeded the bounds of private virtue, and became a public injury, by the example and consequences of their vices.

[Footnote 1: See the complaints of Avidius Cassius, Hist. August. p. 45. These are, it is true, the complaints of faction; but even faction exaggerates, rather than invents.]

[Footnote 105: His brother by adoption, and his colleague, L. Verus. Marcus Aurelius had no other brother.—W.]

Faustina, the daughter of Pius and the wife of Marcus, has been as much celebrated for her gallantries as for her beauty. The grave simplicity of the philosopher was ill calculated to engage her wanton levity, or to fix that unbounded passion for variety, which often discovered personal merit in the meanest of mankind. [2] The Cupid of the ancients was, in general, a very sensual deity; and the amours of an empress, as they exact on her side the plainest advances, are seldom susceptible of much sentimental delicacy. Marcus was the only man in the empire who seemed ignorant or insensible of the irregularities of Faustina; which, according to the prejudices of every age, reflected some disgrace on the injured husband. He promoted several of her lovers to posts of honor and profit, [3] and during a connection of thirty years, invariably gave her proofs of the most tender confidence, and of a respect which ended not with her life. In his Meditations, he thanks the gods, who had bestowed on him a wife so faithful, so gentle, and of such a wonderful simplicity of manners. [4] The obsequious senate, at his earnest request, declared her a goddess. She was represented in her temples, with the attributes of Juno, Venus, and Ceres; and it was decreed, that, on the day of their nuptials, the youth of either sex should pay their vows before the altar of their chaste patroness. [5]

[Footnote 2: Faustinam satis constat apud Cajetam conditiones sibi et nauticas et gladiatorias, elegisse. Hist. August. p. 30. Lampridius explains the sort of merit which Faustina chose, and the conditions which she exacted. Hist. August. p. 102.]

[Footnote 3: Hist. August. p. 34.]

[Footnote 4: Meditat. l. i. The world has laughed at the credulity of Marcus but Madam Dacier assures us, (and we may credit a lady,) that the husband will always be deceived, if the wife condescends to dissemble.] [Footnote 5: Dion Cassius, l. lxxi. [c. 31,] p. 1195. Hist. August. p. 33. Commentaire de Spanheim sur les Caesars de Julien, p. 289. The deification of Faustina is the only defect which Julian's criticism is able to discover in the all-accomplished character of Marcus.]

The monstrous vices of the son have cast a shade on the purity of the father's virtues. It has been objected to Marcus, that he sacrificed the happiness of millions to a fond partiality for a worthless boy; and that he chose a successor in his own family, rather than in the republic. Nothing however, was neglected by the anxious father, and by the men of virtue and learning whom he summoned to his assistance, to expand the narrow mind of young Commodus, to correct his growing vices, and to render him worthy of the throne for which he was designed. But the power of instruction is seldom of much efficacy, except in those happy dispositions where it is almost superfluous. The distasteful lesson of a grave philosopher was, in a moment, obliterated by the whisper of a profligate favorite; and Marcus himself blasted the fruits of this labored education, by admitting his son, at the age of fourteen or fifteen, to a full participation of the Imperial power. He lived but four years afterwards: but he lived long enough to repent a rash measure, which raised the impetuous youth above the restraint of reason and authority.

Most of the crimes which disturb the internal peace of society, are produced by the restraints which the necessary but unequal laws of property have imposed on the appetites of mankind, by confining to a few the possession of those objects that are coveted by many. Of all our passions and appetites, the love of power is of the most imperious and unsociable nature, since the pride of one man requires the submission of the multitude. In the tumult of civil discord, the laws of society lose their force, and their place is seldom supplied by those of humanity. The ardor of contention, the pride of victory, the despair of success, the memory of past injuries, and the fear of future dangers, all contribute to inflame the mind, and to silence the voice of pity. From such motives almost every page of history has been stained with civil blood; but these motives will not account for the unprovoked cruelties of Commodus, who had nothing to wish and every thing to enjoy. The beloved son of Marcus succeeded to his father, amidst the acclamations of the senate and armies; [6] and when he ascended the throne, the happy youth saw round him neither competitor to remove, nor enemies to punish. In this calm, elevated station, it was surely natural that he should prefer the love of mankind to their detestation, the mild glories of his five predecessors to the ignominious fate of Nero and Domitian.

[Footnote 6: Commodus was the first Porphyrogenitus, (born since his father's accession to the throne.) By a new strain of flattery, the Egyptian medals date by the years of his life; as if they were synonymous to those of his reign. Tillemont, Hist. des Empereurs, tom. ii. p. 752.]

Yet Commodus was not, as he has been represented, a tiger born with an insatiate thirst of human blood, and capable, from his infancy, of the most inhuman actions. [7] Nature had formed him of a weak rather than a wicked disposition. His simplicity and timidity rendered him the slave of his attendants, who gradually corrupted his mind. His cruelty, which at first obeyed the dictates of others, degenerated into habit, and at length became the ruling passion of his soul. [8]

[Footnote 7: Hist. August. p. 46.]

[Footnote 8: Dion Cassius, l. lxxii. p. 1203.]

Upon the death of his father, Commodus found himself embarrassed with the command of a great army, and the conduct of a difficult war against the Quadi and Marcomanni. [9] The servile and profligate youths whom Marcus had banished, soon regained their station and influence about the new emperor. They exaggerated the hardships and dangers of a campaign in the wild countries beyond the Danube; and they assured the indolent prince that the terror of his name, and the arms of his lieutenants, would be sufficient to complete the conquest of the dismayed barbarians, or to impose such conditions as were more advantageous than any conquest. By a dexterous application to his sensual appetites, they compared the tranquillity, the splendor, the refined pleasures of Rome, with the tumult of a Pannonian camp, which afforded neither leisure nor materials for luxury. [10] Commodus listened to the pleasing advice; but whilst he hesitated between his own inclination and the awe which he still retained for his father's counsellors, the summer insensibly elapsed, and his triumphal entry into the capital was deferred till the autumn. His graceful person, [11] popular address, and imagined virtues, attracted the public favor; the honorable peace which he had recently granted to the barbarians, diffused a universal joy; [12] his impatience to revisit Rome was fondly ascribed to the love of his country; and his dissolute course of amusements was faintly condemned in a prince of nineteen years of age.

[Footnote 9: According to Tertullian, (Apolog. c. 25,) he died at Sirmium. But the situation of Vindobona, or Vienna, where both the Victors place his death, is better adapted to the operations of the war against the Marcomanni and Quadi.]

[Footnote 10: Herodian, l. i. p. 12.]

[Footnote 11: Herodian, l. i. p. 16.]

[Footnote 12: This universal joy is well described (from the medals as well as historians) by Mr. Wotton, Hist. of Rome, p. 192, 193.] During the three first years of his reign, the forms, and even the spirit, of the old administration, were maintained by those faithful counsellors, to whom Marcus had recommended his son, and for whose wisdom and integrity Commodus still entertained a reluctant esteem. The young prince and his profligate favorites revelled in all the license of sovereign power; but his hands were yet unstained with blood; and he had even displayed a generosity of sentiment, which might perhaps have ripened into solid virtue. [13] A fatal incident decided his fluctuating character.

[Footnote 13: Manilius, the confidential secretary of Avidius Cassius, was discovered after he had lain concealed several years. The emperor nobly relieved the public anxiety by refusing to see him, and burning his papers without opening them. Dion Cassius, l. lxxii. p. 1209.]

One evening, as the emperor was returning to the palace, through a dark and narrow portico in the amphitheatre, [14] an assassin, who waited his passage, rushed upon him with a drawn sword, loudly exclaiming, "The senate sends you this." The menace prevented the deed; the assassin was seized by the guards, and immediately revealed the authors of the conspiracy. It had been formed, not in the state, but within the walls of the palace. Lucilla, the emperor's sister, and widow of Lucius Verus, impatient of the second rank, and jealous of the reigning empress, had armed the murderer against her brother's life. She had not ventured to communicate the black design to her second husband, Claudius Pompeianus, a senator of distinguished merit and unshaken loyalty; but among the crowd of her lovers (for she imitated the manners of Faustina) she found men of desperate fortunes and wild ambition, who were prepared to serve her more violent, as well as her tender passions. The conspirators experienced the rigor of justice, and the abandoned princess was punished, first with exile, and afterwards with death. [15]

[Footnote 14: See Maffei degli Amphitheatri, p. 126.]

[Footnote 15: Dion, l. lxxi. p. 1205 Herodian, l. i. p. 16 Hist. August p. 46.]

But the words of the assassin sunk deep into the mind of Commodus, and left an indelible impression of fear and hatred against the whole body of the senate. [15/1] Those whom he had dreaded as importunate ministers, he now suspected as secret enemies. The Delators, a race of men discouraged, and almost extinguished, under the former reigns, again became formidable, as soon as they discovered that the emperor was desirous of finding disaffection and treason in the senate. That assembly, whom Marcus had ever considered as the great council of the nation, was composed of the most distinguished of the Romans; and distinction of every kind soon became criminal. The possession of wealth stimulated the diligence of the informers; rigid virtue implied a tacit censure of the irregularities of Commodus; important services implied a dangerous superiority of merit; and the friendship of the father always insured the aversion of the son. Suspicion was equivalent to proof; trial to condemnation. The execution of a considerable senator was attended with the death of all who might lament or revenge his fate; and when Commodus had once tasted human blood, he became incapable of pity or remorse.

[Footnote 15/1: The conspirators were senators, even the assassin himself. Herod. 81.—G.]

Of these innocent victims of tyranny, none died more lamented than the two brothers of the Quintilian family, Maximus and Condianus; whose fraternal love has saved their names from oblivion, and endeared their memory to posterity. Their studies and their occupations, their pursuits and their pleasures, were still the same. In the enjoyment of a great estate, they never admitted the idea of a separate interest: some fragments are now extant of a treatise which they composed in common; [15/2] and in every action of life it was observed that their two bodies were animated by one soul. The Antonines, who valued their virtues, and delighted in their union, raised them, in the same year, to the consulship; and Marcus afterwards intrusted to their joint care the civil administration of Greece, and a great military command, in which they obtained a signal victory over the Germans. The kind cruelty of Commodus united them in death. [16]

[Footnote 15/2: This work was on agriculture, and is often quoted by later writers. See P. Needham, Proleg. ad Geoponic. Camb. 1704.—W.]

[Footnote 16: In a note upon the Augustan History, Casaubon has collected a number of particulars concerning these celebrated brothers. See p. 96 of his learned commentary.]

The tyrant's rage, after having shed the noblest blood of the senate, at length recoiled on the principal instrument of his cruelty. Whilst Commodus was immersed in blood and luxury, he devolved the detail of the public business on Perennis, a servile and ambitious minister, who had obtained his post by the murder of his predecessor, but who possessed a considerable share of vigor and ability. By acts of extortion, and the forfeited estates of the nobles sacrificed to his avarice, he had accumulated an immense treasure. The Praetorian guards were under his immediate command; and his son, who already discovered a military genius, was at the head of the Illyrian legions. Perennis aspired to the empire; or what, in the eyes of Commodus, amounted to the same crime, he was capable of aspiring to it, had he not been prevented, surprised, and put to death. The fall of a minister is a very trifling incident in the general history of the empire; but it was hastened by an extraordinary circumstance, which proved how much the nerves of discipline were already relaxed. The legions of Britain, discontented with the administration of Perennis, formed a deputation of fifteen hundred select men, with instructions to march to Rome, and lay their complaints before the emperor. These military petitioners, by their own determined behaviour, by inflaming the divisions of the guards, by exaggerating the strength of the British army, and by alarming the fears of Commodus, exacted and obtained the minister's death, as the only redress of their grievances. [17] This presumption of a distant army, and their discovery of the weakness of government, was a sure presage of the most dreadful convulsions.

[Footnote 17: Dion, l. lxxii. p. 1210. Herodian, l. i. p. 22. Hist. August. p. 48. Dion gives a much less odious character of Perennis, than the other historians. His moderation is almost a pledge of his veracity. Note: Gibbon praises Dion for the moderation with which he speaks of Perennis: he follows, nevertheless, in his own narrative, Herodian and Lampridius. Dion speaks of Perennis not only with moderation, but with admiration; he represents him as a great man, virtuous in his life, and blameless in his death: perhaps he may be suspected of partiality; but it is singular that Gibbon, having adopted, from Herodian and Lampridius, their judgment on this minister, follows Dion's improbable account of his death. What likelihood, in fact, that fifteen hundred men should have traversed Gaul and Italy, and have arrived at Rome without any understanding with the Praetorians, or without detection or opposition from Perennis, the Praetorian praefect? Gibbon, foreseeing, perhaps, this difficulty, has added, that the military deputation inflamed the divisions of the guards; but Dion says expressly that they did not reach Rome, but that the emperor went out to meet them: he even reproaches him for not having opposed them with the guards, who were superior in number. Herodian relates that Commodus, having learned, from a soldier, the ambitious designs of Perennis and his son, caused them to be attacked and massacred by night.—G. from W. Dion's narrative is remarkably circumstantial, and his authority higher than either of the other writers. He hints that Cleander, a new favorite, had already undermined the influence of Perennis.—M.]

The negligence of the public administration was betrayed, soon afterwards, by a new disorder, which arose from the smallest beginnings. A spirit of desertion began to prevail among the troops: and the deserters, instead of seeking their safety in flight or concealment, infested the highways. Maternus, a private soldier, of a daring boldness above his station, collected these bands of robbers into a little army, set open the prisons, invited the slaves to assert their freedom, and plundered with impunity the rich and defenceless cities of Gaul and Spain. The governors of the provinces, who had long been the spectators, and perhaps the partners, of his depredations, were, at length, roused from their supine indolence by the threatening commands of the emperor. Maternus found that he was encompassed, and foresaw that he must be overpowered. A great effort of despair was his last resource. He ordered his followers to disperse, to pass the Alps in small parties and various disguises, and to assemble at Rome, during the licentious tumult of the festival of Cybele. [18] To murder Commodus, and to ascend the vacant throne, was the ambition of no vulgar robber. His measures were so ably concerted that his concealed troops already filled the streets of Rome. The envy of an accomplice discovered and ruined this singular enterprise, in a moment when it was ripe for execution. [19]

[Footnote 18: During the second Punic war, the Romans imported from Asia the worship of the mother of the gods. Her festival, the Megalesia, began on the fourth of April, and lasted six days. The streets were crowded with mad processions, the theatres with spectators, and the public tables with unbidden guests. Order and police were suspended, and pleasure was the only serious business of the city. See Ovid. de Fastis, l. iv. 189, &c.]

[Footnote 19: Herodian, l. i. p. 23, 23.]

Suspicious princes often promote the last of mankind, from a vain persuasion, that those who have no dependence, except on their favor, will have no attachment, except to the person of their benefactor. Cleander, the successor of Perennis, was a Phrygian by birth; of a nation over whose stubborn, but servile temper, blows only could prevail. [20] He had been sent from his native country to Rome, in the capacity of a slave. As a slave he entered the Imperial palace, rendered himself useful to his master's passions, and rapidly ascended to the most exalted station which a subject could enjoy. His influence over the mind of Commodus was much greater than that of his predecessor; for Cleander was devoid of any ability or virtue which could inspire the emperor with envy or distrust. Avarice was the reigning passion of his soul, and the great principle of his administration. The rank of Consul, of Patrician, of Senator, was exposed to public sale; and it would have been considered as disaffection, if any one had refused to purchase these empty and disgraceful honors with the greatest part of his fortune. [21] In the lucrative provincial employments, the minister shared with the governor the spoils of the people. The execution of the laws was penal and arbitrary. A wealthy criminal might obtain, not only the reversal of the sentence by which he was justly condemned, but might likewise inflict whatever punishment he pleased on the accuser, the witnesses, and the judge.

[Footnote 20: Cicero pro Flacco, c. 27.]

[Footnote 21: One of these dear-bought promotions occasioned a current... that Julius Solon was banished into the senate.]

By these means, Cleander, in the space of three years, had accumulated more wealth than had ever yet been possessed by any freedman. [22] Commodus was perfectly satisfied with the magnificent presents which the artful courtier laid at his feet in the most seasonable moments. To divert the public envy, Cleander, under the emperor's name, erected baths, porticos, and places of exercise, for the use of the people. [23] He flattered himself that the Romans, dazzled and amused by this apparent liberality, would be less affected by the bloody scenes which were daily exhibited; that they would forget the death of Byrrhus, a senator to whose superior merit the late emperor had granted one of his daughters; and that they would forgive the execution of Arrius Antoninus, the last representative of the name and virtues of the Antonines. The former, with more integrity than prudence, had attempted to disclose, to his brother-in-law, the true character of Cleander. An equitable sentence pronounced by the latter, when proconsul of Asia, against a worthless creature of the favorite, proved fatal to him. [24] After the fall of Perennis, the terrors of Commodus had, for a short time, assumed the appearance of a return to virtue. He repealed the most odious of his acts; loaded his memory with the public execration, and ascribed to the pernicious counsels of that wicked minister all the errors of his inexperienced youth. But his repentance lasted only thirty days; and, under Cleander's tyranny, the administration of Perennis was often regretted.

[Footnote 22: Dion (l. lxxii. p. 12, 13) observes, that no freedman had possessed riches equal to those of Cleander. The fortune of Pallas amounted, however, to upwards of five and twenty hundred thousand pounds; Ter millies.]

[Footnote 23: Dion, l. lxxii. p. 12, 13. Herodian, l. i. p. 29. Hist. August. p. 52. These baths were situated near the Porta Capena. See Nardini Roma Antica, p. 79.]

[Footnote 24: Hist. August. p. 79.]

PART II

Pestilence and famine contributed to fill up the measure of the calamities of Rome. [25] The first could be only imputed to the just indignation of the gods; but a monopoly of corn, supported by the riches and power of the minister, was considered as the immediate cause of the second. The popular discontent, after it had long circulated in whispers, broke out in the assembled circus. The people quitted their favorite amusements for the more delicious pleasure of revenge, rushed in crowds towards a palace in the suburbs, one of the emperor's retirements, and demanded, with angry clamors, the head of the public enemy. Cleander, who commanded the Praetorian guards, [26] ordered a body of cavalry to sally forth, and disperse the seditious multitude. The multitude fled with precipitation towards the city; several were slain, and many more were trampled to death; but when the cavalry entered the streets, their pursuit was checked by a shower of stones and darts from the roofs and windows of the houses. The foot guards, [27] who had been long jealous of the prerogatives and insolence of the Praetorian cavalry, embraced the party of the people. The tumult became a regular engagement, and threatened a general massacre. The Praetorians, at length, gave way, oppressed with numbers; and the tide of popular fury returned with redoubled violence against the gates of the palace, where Commodus lay, dissolved in luxury, and alone unconscious of the civil war. It was death to approach his person with the unwelcome news. He would have perished in this supine security, had not two women, his eldest sister Fadilla, and Marcia, the most favored of his concubines, ventured to break into his presence. Bathed in tears, and with dishevelled hair, they threw themselves at his feet; and with all the pressing eloquence of fear, discovered to the affrighted emperor the crimes of the minister, the rage of the people, and the impending ruin, which, in a few minutes, would burst over his palace and person. Commodus started from his dream of pleasure, and commanded that the head of Cleander should be thrown out to the people. The desired spectacle instantly appeased the tumult; and the son of Marcus might even yet have regained the affection and confidence of his subjects. [28]

[Footnote 25: Herodian, l. i. p. 28. Dion, l. lxxii. p. 1215. The latter says that two thousand persons died every day at Rome, during a considerable length of time.]

[Footnote 26: Tuneque primum tres praefecti praetorio fuere: inter quos libertinus. From some remains of modesty, Cleander declined the title, whilst he assumed the powers, of Praetorian praefect. As the other freedmen were styled, from their several departments, a rationibus, ab epistolis, Cleander called himself a pugione, as intrusted with the defence of his master's person. Salmasius and Casaubon seem to have talked very idly upon this passage. Note: M. Guizot denies that Lampridius means Cleander as praefect a pugione. The Libertinus seems to me to mean him.—M.]

[Footnote 27: Herodian, l. i. p. 31. It is doubtful whether he means the Praetorian infantry, or the cohortes urbanae, a body of six thousand men, but whose rank and discipline were not equal to their numbers. Neither Tillemont nor Wotton choose to decide this question.]

[Footnote 28: Dion Cassius, l. lxxii. p. 1215. Herodian, l. i. p. 32. Hist. August. p. 48.]

But every sentiment of virtue and humanity was extinct in the mind of Commodus. Whilst he thus abandoned the reins of empire to these unworthy favorites, he valued nothing in sovereign power, except the unbounded license of indulging his sensual appetites. His hours were spent in a seraglio of three hundred beautiful women, and as many boys, of every rank, and of every province; and, wherever the arts of seduction proved ineffectual, the brutal lover had recourse to violence. The ancient historians [29] have expatiated on these abandoned scenes of prostitution, which scorned every restraint of nature or modesty; but it would not be easy to translate their too faithful descriptions into the decency of modern language. The intervals of lust were filled up with the basest amusements. The influence of a polite age, and the labor of an attentive education, had never been able to infuse into his rude and brutish mind the least tincture of learning; and he was the first of the Roman emperors totally devoid of taste for the pleasures of the understanding. Nero himself excelled, or affected to excel, in the elegant arts of music and poetry: nor should we despise his pursuits, had he not converted the pleasing relaxation of a leisure hour into the serious business and ambition of his life. But Commodus, from his earliest infancy, discovered an aversion to whatever was rational or liberal, and a fond attachment to the amusements of the populace; the sports of the circus and amphitheatre, the combats of gladiators, and the hunting of wild beasts. The masters in every branch of learning, whom Marcus provided for his son, were heard with inattention and disgust; whilst the Moors and Parthians, who taught him to dart the javelin and to shoot with the bow, found a disciple who delighted in his application, and soon equalled the most skilful of his instructors in the steadiness of the eye and the dexterity of the hand.

[Footnote 29: Sororibus suis constupratis. Ipsas concubinas suas sub oculis...stuprari jubebat. Nec irruentium in se juvenum carebat infamia, omni parte corporis atque ore in sexum utrumque pollutus. Hist. Aug. p. 47.]

The servile crowd, whose fortune depended on their master's vices, applauded these ignoble pursuits. The perfidious voice of flattery reminded him, that by exploits of the same nature, by the defeat of the Nemaean lion, and the slaughter of the wild boar of Erymanthus, the Grecian Hercules had acquired a place among the gods, and an immortal memory among men. They only forgot to observe, that, in the first ages of society, when the fiercer animals often dispute with man the possession of an unsettled country, a successful war against those savages is one of the most innocent and beneficial labors of heroism. In the civilized state of the Roman empire, the wild beasts had long since retired from the face of man, and the neighborhood of populous cities. To surprise them in their solitary haunts, and to transport them to Rome, that they might be slain in pomp by the hand of an emperor, was an enterprise equally ridiculous for the prince and oppressive for the people. [30] Ignorant of these distinctions, Commodus eagerly embraced the glorious resemblance, and styled himself (as we still read on his medals [31] the Roman Hercules. [31/1] The club and the lion's hide were placed by the side of the throne, amongst the ensigns of sovereignty; and statues were erected, in which Commodus was represented in the character, and with the attributes, of the god, whose valor and dexterity he endeavored to emulate in the daily course of his ferocious amusements. [32]

[Footnote 30: The African lions, when pressed by hunger, infested the open villages and cultivated country; and they infested them with impunity. The royal beast was reserved for the pleasures of the emperor and the capital; and the unfortunate peasant who killed one of them though in his own defence, incurred a very heavy penalty. This extraordinary game-law was mitigated by Honorius, and finally repealed by Justinian. Codex Theodos. tom. v. p. 92, et Comment Gothofred.]

[Footnote 31: Spanheim de Numismat. Dissertat. xii. tom. ii. p. 493.]

[Footnote 31/1: Commodus placed his own head on the colossal statue of Hercules with the inscription, Lucius Commodus Hercules. The wits of Rome, according to a new fragment of Dion, published an epigram, of which, like many other ancient jests, the point is not very clear. It seems to be a protest of the god against being confounded with the emperor. Mai Fragm. Vatican. ii. 225.—M.]

[Footnote 32: Dion, l. lxxii. p. 1216. Hist. August. p. 49.]

Elated with these praises, which gradually extinguished the innate sense of shame, Commodus resolved to exhibit before the eyes of the Roman people those exercises, which till then he had decently confined within the walls of his palace, and to the presence of a few favorites. On the appointed day, the various motives of flattery, fear, and curiosity, attracted to the amphitheatre an innumerable multitude of spectators; and some degree of applause was deservedly bestowed on the uncommon skill of the Imperial performer. Whether he aimed at the head or heart of the animal, the wound was alike certain and mortal. With arrows whose point was shaped into the form of crescent, Commodus often intercepted the rapid career, and cut asunder the long, bony neck of the ostrich. [33] A panther was let loose; and the archer waited till he had leaped upon a trembling malefactor. In the same instant the shaft flew, the beast dropped dead, and the man remained unhurt. The dens of the amphitheatre disgorged at once a hundred lions: a hundred darts from the unerring hand of Commodus laid them dead as they run raging round the Arena. Neither the huge bulk of the elephant, nor the scaly hide of the rhinoceros, could defend them from his stroke. Aethiopia and India yielded their most extraordinary productions; and several animals were slain in the amphitheatre, which had been seen only in the representations of art, or perhaps of fancy. [34] In all these exhibitions, the securest precautions were used to protect the person of the Roman Hercules from the desperate spring of any savage, who might possibly disregard the dignity of the emperor and the sanctity of the god. [35]

[Footnote 33: The ostrich's neck is three feet long, and composed of seventeen vertebrae. See Buffon, Hist. Naturelle.]

[Footnote 34: Commodus killed a camelopardalis or Giraffe, (Dion, l. lxxii. p. 1211,) the tallest, the most gentle, and the most useless of the large quadrupeds. This singular animal, a native only of the interior parts of Africa, has not been seen in Europe since the revival of letters; and though M. de Buffon (Hist. Naturelle, tom. xiii.) has endeavored to describe, he has not ventured to delineate, the Giraffe. Note: The naturalists of our days have been more fortunate. London probably now contains more specimens of this animal than have been seen in Europe since the fall of the Roman empire, unless in the pleasure gardens of the emperor Frederic II., in Sicily, which possessed several. Frederic's collections of wild beasts were *exhibited, for the popular amusement, in many parts of Italy. Raumer, Geschichte der Hohenstaufen, v. iii. p. 571. Gibbon, moreover, is mistaken; as a giraffe was presented to Lorenzo de Medici, either by the sultan of Egypt or the king of Tunis. Contemporary authorities are quoted in the old work, Gesner de Quadrupedibum p. 162.—M.]*

[Footnote 35: Herodian, l. i. p. 37. Hist. August. p. 50.]

But the meanest of the populace were affected with shame and indignation when they beheld their sovereign enter the lists as a gladiator, and glory in a profession which the laws and manners of the Romans had branded with the justest note of infamy. [36] He chose the habit and arms of the Secutor, whose combat with the Retiarius formed one of the most lively scenes in the bloody sports of the amphitheatre. The Secutor was armed with a helmet, sword, and buckler; his naked antagonist had only a large net and a trident; with the one he endeavored to entangle, with the other to despatch his enemy. If he missed the first throw, he was obliged to fly from the pursuit of the Secutor, till he had prepared his net for a second cast. [37] The emperor fought in this character seven hundred and thirty-five several times. These glorious achievements were carefully recorded in the public acts of the empire; and that he might omit no circumstance of infamy, he received from the common fund of gladiators a stipend so exorbitant that it became a new and most ignominious tax upon the Roman people. [38] It may be easily supposed, that in these engagements the master of the world was always successful; in the amphitheatre, his victories were not often sanguinary; but when he exercised his skill in the school of gladiators, or his own palace, his wretched antagonists were frequently honored with a mortal wound from the hand of Commodus, and obliged to seal their flattery with their blood. [39] He now disdained the appellation of Hercules. The name of Paulus, a celebrated Secutor, was the only one which delighted his ear. It was inscribed on his colossal statues, and repeated in the redoubled acclamations [40] of the mournful and applauding senate. [41] Claudius Pompeianus, the virtuous husband of Lucilla, was the only senator who asserted the honor of his rank. As a father, he permitted his sons to consult their safety by attending the amphitheatre. As a Roman, he declared, that his own life was in the emperor's hands, but that he would never behold the son of Marcus prostituting his person and dignity. Notwithstanding his manly resolution Pompeianus escaped the resentment of the tyrant, and, with his honor, had the good fortune to preserve his life. [42]

[Footnote 36: The virtuous and even the wise princes forbade the senators and knights to embrace this scandalous profession, under pain of infamy, or, what was more dreaded by those profligate wretches, of exile. The tyrants allured them to dishonor by threats and rewards. Nero once produced in the arena forty senators and sixty knights. See Lipsius, Saturnalia, l. ii. c. 2. He has happily corrected a passage of Suetonius in Nerone, c. 12.]

[Footnote 37: Lipsius, l. ii. c. 7, 8. Juvenal, in the eighth satire, gives a picturesque description of this combat.]

[Footnote 38: Hist. August. p. 50. Dion, l. lxxii. p. 1220. He received, for each time, decies, about 8000l. sterling.]

[Footnote 39: Victor tells us, that Commodus only allowed his antagonists a...weapon, dreading most probably the consequences of their despair.]

[Footnote 40: They were obliged to repeat, six hundred and twenty-six times, Paolus first of the Secutors, &c.]

[Footnote 41: Dion, l. lxxii. p. 1221. He speaks of his own baseness and danger.]

[Footnote 42: He mixed, however, some prudence with his courage, and passed the greatest part of his time in a country retirement; alleging his advanced age, and the weakness of his eyes. "I never saw him in the senate," says Dion, "except during the short reign of Pertinax." All his infirmities had suddenly left him, and they returned as suddenly upon the murder of that excellent prince. Dion, l. lxxiii. p. 1227.]

Commodus had now attained the summit of vice and infamy. Amidst the acclamations of a flattering court, he was unable to disguise from himself, that he had deserved the contempt and hatred of every man of sense and virtue in his empire. His ferocious spirit was irritated by the consciousness of that hatred, by the envy of every kind of merit, by the just apprehension of danger, and by the habit of slaughter, which he contracted in his daily amusements. History has preserved a long list of consular senators sacrificed to his wanton suspicion, which sought out, with peculiar anxiety, those unfortunate persons connected, however remotely, with the family of the Antonines, without sparing even the ministers of his crimes or pleasures. [43] His cruelty proved at last fatal to himself. He had shed with impunity the noblest blood of Rome: he perished as soon as he was dreaded by his own domestics. Marcia, his favorite concubine, Eclectus, his chamberlain, and Laetus, his Praetorian praefect, alarmed by the fate of their companions and predecessors, resolved to prevent the destruction which every hour hung over their heads, either from the mad caprice of the tyrant, [43/1] or the sudden indignation of the people. Marcia seized the occasion of presenting a draught of wine to her lover, after he had fatigued himself with hunting some wild beasts. Commodus retired to sleep; but whilst he was laboring with the effects of poison and drunkenness, a robust youth, by profession a wrestler, entered his chamber, and strangled him without resistance. The body was secretly conveyed out of the palace, before the least suspicion was entertained in the city, or even in the court, of the emperor's death. Such was the fate of the son of Marcus, and so easy was it to destroy a hated tyrant, who, by the artificial powers of government, had oppressed, during thirteen years, so many millions of subjects, each of whom was equal to their master in personal strength and personal abilities. [44]

[Footnote 43: The prefects were changed almost hourly or daily; and the caprice of Commodus was often fatal to his most favored chamberlains. Hist. August. p. 46, 51.]

[Footnote 43/1: Commodus had already resolved to massacre them the following night they determined o anticipate his design. Herod. i. 17.—W.]

[Footnote 44: Dion, l. lxxii. p. 1222. Herodian, l. i. p. 43. Hist. August. p. 52.]

The measures of the conspirators were conducted with the deliberate coolness and celerity which the greatness of the occasion required. They resolved instantly to fill the vacant throne with an emperor whose character would justify and maintain the action that had been committed. They fixed on Pertinax, praefect of the city, an ancient senator of consular rank, whose conspicuous merit had broke through the obscurity of his birth, and raised him to the first honors of the state. He had successively governed most of the provinces of the empire; and in all his great employments, military as well as civil, he had uniformly distinguished himself by the firmness, the prudence, and the integrity of his conduct. [45] He now remained almost alone of the friends and ministers of Marcus; and when, at a late hour of the night, he was awakened with the news, that the chamberlain and the praefect were at his door, he received them with intrepid resignation, and desired they would execute their master's orders. Instead of death, they offered him the throne of the Roman world. During some moments he distrusted their intentions and assurances. Convinced at length of the death of Commodus, he accepted the purple with a sincere reluctance, the natural effect of his knowledge both of the duties and of the dangers of the supreme rank. [46]

[Footnote 45: Pertinax was a native of Alba Pompeia, in Piedmont, and son of a timber merchant. The order of his employments (it is marked by Capitolinus) well deserves to be set down, as expressive of the form of government and manners of the age. 1. He was a centurion. 2. Praefect of a cohort in Syria, in the Parthian war, and in Britain. 3. He obtained an Ala, or squadron of horse, in Maesia. 4. He was commissary of provisions on the Aemilian way. 5. He commanded the fleet upon the Rhine. 6. He was procurator of Dacia, with a salary of about 1600l. a year. 7. He commanded the veterans of a legion. 8. He obtained the rank of senator. 9. Of praetor. 10. With the command of the first legion in Rhaetia and Noricum. 11. He was consul about the year 175. 12. He attended Marcus into the East. 13. He commanded an army on the Danube. 14. He was consular legate of Maesia. 15. Of Dacia. 16. Of Syria. 17. Of Britain. 18. He had the care of the public provisions at Rome. 19. He was proconsul of Africa. 20. Praefect of the city. Herodian (l. i. p. 48) does justice to his disinterested spirit; but Capitolinus, who collected every popular rumor, charges him with a great fortune acquired by bribery and corruption.]

[Footnote 46: Julian, in the Caesars, taxes him with being accessory to the death of Commodus.]

Laetus conducted without delay his new emperor to the camp of the Praetorians, diffusing at the same time through the city a seasonable report that Commodus died suddenly of an apoplexy; and that the virtuous Pertinax had already succeeded to the throne. The guards were rather surprised than pleased with the suspicious death of a prince, whose indulgence and liberality they alone had experienced; but the emergency of the occasion, the authority of their praefect, the reputation of Pertinax, and the clamors of the people, obliged them to stifle their secret discontents, to accept the donative promised by the new emperor, to swear allegiance to him, and with joyful acclamations and laurels in their hands to conduct him to the senate house, that the military consent might be ratified by the civil authority. This important night was now far spent; with the dawn of day, and the commencement of the new year, the senators expected a summons to attend an ignominious ceremony. [461] In spite of all remonstrances, even of those of his creatures who yet preserved any regard for prudence or decency, Commodus had resolved to pass the night in the gladiators' school, and from thence to take possession of the consulship, in the habit and with the attendance of that infamous crew. On a sudden, before the break of day, the senate was called together in the temple of Concord, to meet the guards, and to ratify the election of a new emperor. For a few minutes they sat in silent suspense, doubtful of their unexpected deliverance, and suspicious of the cruel artifices of Commodus: but when at length they were assured that the tyrant was no more, they resigned themselves to all the transports of joy and indignation. Pertinax, who modestly represented the meanness of his extraction, and pointed out several noble senators more deserving than himself of the empire, was constrained by their dutiful violence to ascend the throne, and received all the titles of Imperial power, confirmed by the most sincere vows of fidelity. The memory of Commodus was branded with eternal infamy. The names of tyrant, of gladiator, of public enemy resounded in every corner of the house. They decreed in tumultuous votes, [462] that his honors should be reversed, his titles erased from the public monuments, his statues thrown down, his body dragged with a hook into the stripping room of the gladiators, to satiate the public fury; and they expressed some indignation against those officious servants who had already presumed to screen his remains from the justice of the senate. But Pertinax could not refuse those last rites to the memory of Marcus, and the tears of his first protector Claudius Pompeianus, who lamented the cruel fate of his brother-in-law, and lamented still more that he had deserved it. [47]

[Footnote 46/1: The senate always assembled at the beginning of the year, on the night of the 1st January, (see Savaron on Sid. Apoll. viii. 6,) and this happened the present year, as usual, without any particular order.—G from W.]

[Footnote 46/2: What Gibbon improperly calls, both here and in the note, tumultuous decrees, were no more than the applauses and acclamations which recur so often in the history of the emperors. The custom passed from the theatre to the forum, from the forum to the senate. Applauses on the adoption of the Imperial decrees were first introduced under Trajan. (Plin. jun. Panegyr. 75.) One senator read the form of the decree, and all the rest answered by acclamations, accompanied with a kind of chant or rhythm. These were some of the acclamations addressed to Pertinax, and against the memory of Commodus. Hosti patriae honores detrahantur. Parricidae honores detrahantur. Ut salvi simus, Jupiter, optime, maxime, serva nobis Pertinacem. This custom prevailed not only in the councils of state, but in all the meetings of the senate. However inconsistent it may appear with the solemnity of a religious assembly, the early Christians adopted and introduced it into their synods, notwithstanding the opposition of some of the Fathers, particularly of St. Chrysostom. See the Coll. of Franc. Bern. Ferrarius de veterum acclamatione in Graevii Thesaur. Antiq. Rom. i. 6.—W. This note is rather hypercritical, as regards Gibbon, but appears to be worthy of preservation.—M.]

[Footnote 47: Capitolinus gives us the particulars of these tumultuary votes, which were moved by one senator, and repeated, or rather chanted by the whole body. Hist. August. p. 52.]

These effusions of impotent rage against a dead emperor, whom the senate had flattered when alive with the most abject servility, betrayed a just but ungenerous spirit of revenge.

The legality of these decrees was, however, supported by the principles of the Imperial constitution. To censure, to depose, or to punish with death, the first magistrate of the republic, who had abused his delegated trust, was the ancient and undoubted prerogative of the Roman senate; [48] but the feeble assembly was obliged to content itself with inflicting on a fallen tyrant that public justice, from which, during his life and reign, he had been shielded by the strong arm of military despotism. [48/1]

[Footnote 48: The senate condemned Nero to be put to death more majorum. Sueton. c. 49.]

[Footnote 48/1: No particular law assigned this right to the senate: it was deduced from the ancient principles of the republic. Gibbon appears to infer, from the passage of Suetonius, that the senate, according to its ancient right, punished Nero with death. The words, however, more majerum refer not to the decree of the senate, but to the kind of death, which was taken from an old law of Romulus. (See Victor. Epit. Ed. Artzen p. 484, n. 7.)—W.]

Pertinax found a nobler way of condemning his predecessor's memory; by the contrast of his own virtues with the vices of Commodus. On the day of his accession, he resigned over to his wife and son his whole private fortune; that they might have no pretence to solicit favors at the expense of the state. He refused to flatter the vanity of the former with the title of Augusta; or to corrupt the inexperienced youth of the latter by the rank of Caesar. Accurately distinguishing between the duties of a parent and those of a sovereign, he educated his son with a severe simplicity, which, while it gave him no assured prospect of the throne, might in time have rendered him worthy of it. In public, the behavior of Pertinax was grave and affable. He lived with the virtuous part of the senate, (and, in a private station, he had been acquainted with the true character of each individual,) without either pride or jealousy; considered them as friends and companions, with whom he had shared the danger of the tyranny, and with whom he wished to enjoy the security of the present time. He very frequently invited them to familiar entertainments, the frugality of which was ridiculed by those who remembered and regretted the luxurious prodigality of Commodus. [49]

[Footnote 49: Dion (l. lxxiii. p. 1223) speaks of these entertainments, as a senator who had supped with the emperor; Capitolinus, (Hist. August. p. 58,) like a slave, who had received his intelligence from one the scullions.]

To heal, as far as it was possible, the wounds inflicted by the hand of tyranny, was the pleasing, but melancholy, task of Pertinax. The innocent victims, who yet survived, were recalled from exile, released from prison, and restored to the full possession of their honors and fortunes. The unburied bodies of murdered senators (for the cruelty of Commodus endeavored to extend itself beyond death) were deposited in the sepulchres of their ancestors; their memory was justified and every consolation was bestowed on their ruined and afflicted families. Among these consolations, one of the most grateful was the punishment of the Delators; the common enemies of their master, of virtue, and of their country. Yet even in the inquisition of these legal assassins, Pertinax proceeded with a steady temper, which gave every thing to justice, and nothing to popular prejudice and resentment. The finances of the state demanded the most vigilant care of the emperor. Though every measure of injustice and extortion had been adopted, which could collect the property of the subject into the coffers of the prince, the rapaciousness of Commodus had been so very inadequate to his extravagance, that, upon his death, no more than eight thousand pounds were found in the exhausted treasury, [50] to defray the current expenses of government, and to discharge the pressing demand of a liberal donative, which the new emperor had been obliged to promise to the Praetorian guards. Yet under these distressed circumstances, Pertinax had the generous firmness to remit all the oppressive taxes invented by Commodus, and to cancel all the unjust claims of the treasury; declaring, in a decree of the senate, "that he was better satisfied to administer a poor republic with innocence, than to acquire riches by the ways of tyranny and dishonor. Economy and industry he considered as the pure and genuine sources of wealth; and from them he soon derived a copious supply for the public necessities. The expense of the household was immediately reduced to one half. All the instruments of luxury Pertinax exposed to public auction, [51] gold and silver plate, chariots of a singular construction, a superfluous wardrobe of silk and embroidery, and a great number of beautiful slaves of both sexes; excepting only, with attentive humanity, those who were born in a state of freedom, and had been ravished from the arms of their weeping parents. At the same time that he obliged the worthless favorites of the tyrant to resign a part of their ill-gotten wealth, he satisfied the just creditors of the state, and unexpectedly discharged the long arrears of honest services. He removed the oppressive restrictions which had been laid upon commerce, and granted all the uncultivated lands in Italy and the provinces to those who would improve them; with an exemption from tribute during the term of ten years. [52]

[Footnote 50: Decies. The blameless economy of Pius left his successors a treasure of vicies septies millies, above two and twenty millions sterling. Dion, l. lxxiii. p. 1231.]

[Footnote 51: Besides the design of converting these useless ornaments into money, Dion (l. lxxiii. p. 1229) assigns two secret motives of Pertinax. He wished to expose the vices of Commodus, and to discover by the purchasers those who most resembled him.]

[Footnote 52: Though Capitolinus has picked up many idle tales of the private life of Pertinax, he joins with Dion and Herodian in admiring his public conduct.]

Such a uniform conduct had already secured to Pertinax the noblest reward of a sovereign, the love and esteem of his people.

Those who remembered the virtues of Marcus were happy to contemplate in their new emperor the features of that bright original; and flattered themselves, that they should long enjoy the benign influence of his administration. A hasty zeal to reform the corrupted state, accompanied with less prudence than might have been expected from the years and experience of Pertinax, proved fatal to himself and to his country. His honest indiscretion united against him the servile crowd, who found their private benefit in the public disorders, and who preferred the favor of a tyrant to the inexorable equality of the laws. [53]

[Footnote 53: Leges, rem surdam, inexorabilem esse. T. Liv. ii. 3.]

Amidst the general joy, the sullen and angry countenance of the Praetorian guards betrayed their inward dissatisfaction. They had reluctantly submitted to Pertinax; they dreaded the strictness of the ancient discipline, which he was preparing to restore; and they regretted the license of the former reign. Their discontents were secretly fomented by Laetus, their praefect, who found, when it was too late, that his new emperor would reward a servant, but would not be ruled by a favorite. On the third day of his reign, the soldiers seized on a noble senator, with a design to carry him to the camp, and to invest him with the Imperial purple. Instead of being dazzled by the dangerous honor, the affrighted victim escaped from their violence, and took refuge at the feet of Pertinax. A short time afterwards, Sosius Falco, one of the consuls of the year, a rash youth, [54] but of an ancient and opulent family, listened to the voice of ambition; and a conspiracy was formed during a short absence of Pertinax, which was crushed by his sudden return to Rome, and his resolute behavior. Falco was on the point of being justly condemned to death as a public enemy had he not been saved by the earnest and sincere entreaties of the injured emperor, who conjured the senate, that the purity of his reign might not be stained by the blood even of a guilty senator.

[Footnote 54: If we credit Capitolinus, (which is rather difficult,) Falco behaved with the most petulant indecency to Pertinax, on the day of his accession. The wise emperor only admonished him of his youth and in experience. Hist. August. p. 55.]

These disappointments served only to irritate the rage of the Praetorian guards. On the twenty-eighth of March, eighty-six days only after the death of Commodus, a general sedition broke out in the camp, which the officers wanted either power or inclination to suppress. Two or three hundred of the most desperate soldiers marched at noonday, with arms in their hands and fury in their looks, towards the Imperial palace. The gates were thrown open by their companions upon guard, and by the domestics of the old court, who had already formed a secret conspiracy against the life of the too virtuous emperor. On the news of their approach, Pertinax, disdaining either flight or concealment, advanced to meet his assassins; and recalled to their minds his own innocence, and the sanctity of their recent oath. For a few moments they stood in silent suspense, ashamed of their atrocious design, and awed by the venerable aspect and majestic firmness of their sovereign, till at length, the despair of pardon reviving their fury, a barbarian of the country of Tongress [55] levelled the first blow against Pertinax, who was instantly despatched with a multitude of wounds. His head, separated from his body, and placed on a lance, was carried in triumph to the Praetorian camp, in the sight of a mournful and indignant people, who lamented the unworthy fate of that excellent prince, and the transient blessings of a reign, the memory of which could serve only to aggravate their approaching misfortunes. [56]

[Footnote 55: The modern bishopric of Liege. This soldier probably belonged to the Batavian horse-guards, who were mostly raised in the duchy of Gueldres and the neighborhood, and were distinguished by their valor, and by the boldness with which they swam their horses across the broadest and most rapid rivers. Tacit. Hist. iv. 12 Dion, l. lv p. 797 Lipsius de magnitudine Romana, l. i. c. 4.]

[Footnote 56: Dion, l. lxxiii. p. 1232. Herodian, l. ii. p. 60. Hist. August. p. 58. Victor in Epitom. et in Caesarib. Eutropius, viii. 16.]

CHAPTER V

SALE OF THE EMPIRE TO DIDIUS JULIANUS

PART I

PUBLIC SALE OF THE EMPIRE TO DIDIUS JULIANUS BY THE PRAETORIAN GUARDS—CLODIUS ALBINUS IN BRITAIN, PESCENNIUS NIGER IN SYRIA, AND SEPTIMUS SEVERUS IN PANNONIA, DECLARE AGAINST THE MURDERERS OF PERTINAX—CIVIL WARS AND VICTORY OF SEVERUS OVER HIS THREE RIVALS—RELAXATION OF DISCIPLINE—NEW MAXIMS OF GOVERNMENT

The power of the sword is more sensibly felt in an extensive monarchy, than in a small community. It has been calculated by the ablest politicians, that no state, without being soon exhausted, can maintain above the hundredth part of its members in arms and idleness. But although this relative proportion may be uniform, the influence of the army over the rest of the society will vary according to the degree of its positive strength. The advantages of military science and discipline cannot be exerted, unless a proper number of soldiers are united into one body, and actuated by one soul. With a handful of men, such a union would be ineffectual; with an unwieldy host, it would be impracticable; and the powers of the machine would be alike destroyed by the extreme minuteness or the excessive weight of its springs. To illustrate this observation, we need only reflect, that there is no superiority of natural strength, artificial weapons, or acquired skill, which could enable one man to keep in constant subjection one hundred of his fellow-creatures: the tyrant of a single town, or a small district, would soon discover that a hundred armed followers were a weak defence against ten thousand peasants or citizens; but a hundred thousand well-disciplined soldiers will command, with despotic sway, ten millions of subjects; and a body of ten or fifteen thousand guards will strike terror into the most numerous populace that ever crowded the streets of an immense capital. The Praetorian bands, whose licentious fury was the first symptom and cause of the decline of the Roman empire, scarcely amounted to the last-mentioned number [1] They derived their institution from Augustus. That crafty tyrant, sensible that laws might color, but that arms alone could maintain, his usurped dominion, had gradually formed this powerful body of guards, in constant readiness to protect his person, to awe the senate, and either to prevent or to crush the first motions of rebellion. He distinguished these favored troops by a double pay and superior privileges; but, as their formidable aspect would at once have alarmed and irritated the Roman people, three cohorts only were stationed in the capital, whilst the remainder was dispersed in the adjacent towns of Italy. [2] But after fifty years of peace and servitude, Tiberius ventured on a decisive measure, which forever rivetted the fetters of his country. Under the fair pretences of relieving Italy from the heavy burden of military quarters, and of introducing a stricter discipline among the guards, he assembled them at Rome, in a permanent camp, [3] which was fortified with skilful care, [4] and placed on a commanding situation. [5]

[Footnote 1: They were originally nine or ten thousand men, (for Tacitus and son are not agreed upon the subject,) divided into as many cohorts. Vitellius increased them to sixteen thousand, and as far as we can learn from inscriptions, they never afterwards sunk much below that number. See Lipsius de magnitudine Romana, i. 4.]

[Footnote 2: Sueton. in August. c. 49.]

[Footnote 3: Tacit. Annal. iv. 2. Sueton. in Tiber. c. 37. Dion Cassius, l. lvii. p. 867.]

[Footnote 4: In the civil war between Vitellius and Vespasian, the Praetorian camp was attacked and defended with all the machines used in the siege of the best fortified cities. Tacit. Hist. iii. 84.]

[Footnote 5: Close to the walls of the city, on the broad summit of the Quirinal and Viminal hills. See Nardini Roma Antica, p. 174. Donatus de Roma Antiqua, p. 46. Note: Not on both these hills: neither Donatus nor Nardini justify this position. (Whitaker's Review. p. 13.) At the northern extremity of this hill (the Viminal) are some considerable remains of a walled enclosure which bears all the appearance of a Roman camp, and therefore is generally thought to correspond with the Castra Praetoria. Cramer's Italy 390.—M.]

Such formidable servants are always necessary, but often fatal to the throne of despotism. By thus introducing the Praetorian guards as it were into the palace and the senate, the emperors taught them to perceive their own strength, and the weakness of the civil government; to view the vices of their masters with familiar contempt, and to lay aside that reverential awe, which distance only, and mystery, can preserve towards an imaginary power. In the luxurious idleness of an opulent city, their pride was nourished by the sense of their irresistible weight; nor was it possible to conceal from them, that the person of the sovereign, the authority of the senate, the public treasure, and the seat of empire, were all in their hands. To divert the Praetorian bands from these dangerous reflections, the firmest and best established princes were obliged to mix blandishments with commands, rewards with punishments, to flatter their pride, indulge their pleasures, connive at their irregularities, and to purchase their precarious faith by a liberal donative; which, since the elevation of Claudius, was enacted as a legal claim, on the accession of every new emperor. [6]

[Footnote 6: Claudius, raised by the soldiers to the empire, was the first who gave a donative. He gave quina dena, 120l. (Sueton. in Claud. c. 10:) when Marcus, with his colleague Lucius Versus, took quiet possession of the throne, he gave vicena, 160l. to each of the guards. Hist. August. p. 25, (Dion, l. lxxiii. p. 1231.) We may form some idea of the amount of these sums, by Hadrian's complaint that the promotion of a Caesar had cost him ter millies, two millions and a half sterling.]

The advocate of the guards endeavored to justify by arguments the power which they asserted by arms; and to maintain that, according to the purest principles of the constitution, their consent was essentially necessary in the appointment of an emperor. The election of consuls, of generals, and of magistrates, however it had been recently usurped by the senate, was the ancient and undoubted right of the Roman people. [7] But where was the Roman people to be found? Not surely amongst the mixed multitude of slaves and strangers that filled the streets of Rome; a servile populace, as devoid of spirit as destitute of property. The defenders of the state, selected from the flower of the Italian youth, [8] and trained in the exercise of arms and virtue, were the genuine representatives of the people, and the best entitled to elect the military chief of the republic. These assertions, however defective in reason, became unanswerable when the fierce Praetorians increased their weight, by throwing, like the barbarian conqueror of Rome, their swords into the scale. [9]

[Footnote 7: Cicero de Legibus, iii. 3. The first book of Livy, and the second of Dionysius of Halicarnassus, show the authority of the people, even in the election of the kings.]

[Footnote 8: They were originally recruited in Latium, Etruria, and the old colonies, (Tacit. Annal. iv. 5.) The emperor Otho compliments their vanity with the flattering titles of Italiae, Alumni, Romana were juventus. Tacit. Hist. i. 84.]

[Footnote 9: In the siege of Rome by the Gauls. See Livy, v. 48. Plutarch. in Camill. p. 143.]

The Praetorians had violated the sanctity of the throne by the atrocious murder of Pertinax; they dishonored the majesty of it by their subsequent conduct. The camp was without a leader, for even the praefect Laetus, who had excited the tempest, prudently declined the public indignation. Amidst the wild disorder, Sulpicianus, the emperor's father-in-law, and governor of the city, who had been sent to the camp on the first alarm of mutiny, was endeavoring to calm the fury of the multitude, when he was silenced by the clamorous return of the murderers, bearing on a lance the head of Pertinax. Though history has accustomed us to observe every principle and every passion yielding to the imperious dictates of ambition, it is scarcely credible that, in these moments of horror, Sulpicianus should have aspired to ascend a throne polluted with the recent blood of so near a relation and so excellent a prince. He had already begun to use the only effectual argument, and to treat for the Imperial dignity; but the more prudent of the Praetorians, apprehensive that, in this private contract, they should not obtain a just price for so valuable a commodity, ran out upon the ramparts; and, with a loud voice, proclaimed that the Roman world was to be disposed of to the best bidder by public auction. [10]

[Footnote 10: Dion, L. lxxiii. p. 1234. Herodian, l. ii. p. 63. Hist. August p. 60. Though the three historians agree that it was in fact an auction, Herodian alone affirms that it was proclaimed as such by the soldiers.]

This infamous offer, the most insolent excess of military license, diffused a universal grief, shame, and indignation throughout the city. It reached at length the ears of Didius Julianus, a wealthy senator, who, regardless of the public calamities, was indulging himself in the luxury of the table. [11] His wife and his daughter, his freedmen and his parasites, easily convinced him that he deserved the throne, and earnestly conjured him to embrace so fortunate an opportunity. The vain old man hastened to the Praetorian camp, where Sulpicianus was still in treaty with the guards, and began to bid against him from the foot of the rampart. The unworthy negotiation was transacted by faithful emissaries, who passed alternately from one candidate to the other, and acquainted each of them with the offers of his rival. Sulpicianus had already promised a donative of five thousand drachms (above one hundred and sixty pounds) to each soldier; when Julian, eager for the prize, rose at once to the sum of six thousand two hundred and fifty drachms, or upwards of two hundred pounds sterling. The gates of the camp were instantly thrown open to the purchaser; he was declared emperor, and received an oath of allegiance from the soldiers, who retained humanity enough to stipulate that he should pardon and forget the competition of Sulpicianus. [11/1]

[Footnote 11: Spartianus softens the most odious parts of the character and elevation of Julian.]

[Footnote 11/1: One of the principal causes of the preference of Julianus by the soldiers, was the dexterty dexterity with which he reminded them that Sulpicianus would not fail to revenge on them the death of his son-in-law. (See Dion, p. 1234, 1234. c. 11. Herod. ii. 6.)—W.]

It was now incumbent on the Praetorians to fulfil the conditions of the sale. They placed their new sovereign, whom they served and despised, in the centre of their ranks, surrounded him on every side with their shields, and conducted him in close order of battle through the deserted streets of the city. The senate was commanded to assemble; and those who had been the distinguished friends of Pertinax, or the personal enemies of Julian, found it necessary to affect a more than common share of satisfaction at this happy revolution. [12] After Julian had filled the senate house with armed soldiers, he expatiated on the freedom of his election, his own eminent virtues, and his full assurance of the affections of the senate. The obsequious assembly congratulated their own and the public felicity; engaged their allegiance, and conferred on him all the several branches of the Imperial power. [13] From the senate Julian was conducted, by the same military procession, to take possession of the palace. The first objects that struck his eyes, were the abandoned trunk of Pertinax, and the frugal entertainment prepared for his supper. The one he viewed with indifference, the other with contempt. A magnificent feast was prepared by his order, and he amused himself, till a very late hour, with dice, and the performances of Pylades, a celebrated dancer. Yet it was observed, that after the crowd of flatterers dispersed, and left him to darkness, solitude, and terrible reflection, he passed a sleepless night; revolving most probably in his mind his own rash folly, the fate of his virtuous predecessor, and the doubtful and dangerous tenure of an empire which had not been acquired by merit, but purchased by money. [14]

[Footnote 12: Dion Cassius, at that time praetor, had been a personal enemy to Julian, i. lxxiii. p. 1235.]

[Footnote 13: Hist. August. p. 61. We learn from thence one curious circumstance, that the new emperor, whatever had been his birth, was immediately aggregated to the number of patrician families. Note: A new fragment of Dion shows some shrewdness in the character of Julian. When the senate voted him a golden statue, he preferred one of brass, as more lasting. He "had always observed," he said, "that the statues of former emperors were soon destroyed. Those of brass alone remained." The indignant historian adds that he was wrong. The virtue of sovereigns alone preserves their images: the brazen statue of Julian was broken to pieces at his death. Mai. Fragm. Vatican. p. 226.—M.]

[Footnote 14: Dion, l. lxxiii. p. 1235. Hist. August. p. 61. I have endeavored to blend into one consistent story the seeming contradictions of the two writers. Note: The contradiction as M. Guizot observed, is irreconcilable. He quotes both passages: in one Julianus is represented as a miser, in the other as a voluptuary. In the one he refuses to eat till the body of Pertinax has been buried; in the other he gluts himself with every luxury almost in the sight of his headless remains.—M.]

He had reason to tremble. On the throne of the world he found himself without a friend, and even without an adherent. The guards themselves were ashamed of the prince whom their avarice had persuaded them to accept; nor was there a citizen who did not consider his elevation with horror, as the last insult on the Roman name. The nobility, whose conspicuous station, and ample possessions, exacted the strictest caution, dissembled their sentiments, and met the affected civility of the emperor with smiles of complacency and professions of duty. But the people, secure in their numbers and obscurity, gave a free vent to their passions. The streets and public places of Rome resounded with clamors and imprecations. The enraged multitude affronted the person of Julian, rejected his liberality, and, conscious of the impotence of their own resentment, they called aloud on the legions of the frontiers to assert the violated majesty of the Roman empire. The public discontent was soon diffused from the centre to the frontiers of the empire. The armies of Britain, of Syria, and of Illyricum, lamented the death of Pertinax, in whose company, or under whose command, they had so often fought and conquered. They received with surprise, with indignation, and perhaps with envy, the extraordinary intelligence, that the Praetorians had disposed of the empire by public auction; and they sternly refused to ratify the ignominious bargain. Their immediate and unanimous revolt was fatal to Julian, but it was fatal at the same time to the public peace, as the generals of the respective armies, Clodius Albinus, Pescennius Niger, and Septimius Severus, were still more anxious to succeed than to revenge the murdered Pertinax. Their forces were exactly balanced. Each of them was at the head of three legions, [15] with a numerous train of auxiliaries; and however different in their characters, they were all soldiers of experience and capacity.

[Footnote 15: Dion, l. lxxiii. p. 1235.]

Clodius Albinus, governor of Britain, surpassed both his competitors in the nobility of his extraction, which he derived from some of the most illustrious names of the old republic. [16] But the branch from which he claimed his descent was sunk into mean circumstances, and transplanted into a remote province. It is difficult to form a just idea of his true character. Under the philosophic cloak of austerity, he stands accused of concealing most of the vices which degrade human nature. [17] But his accusers are those venal writers who adored the fortune of Severus, and trampled on the ashes of an unsuccessful rival. Virtue, or the appearances of virtue, recommended Albinus to the confidence and good opinion of Marcus; and his preserving with the son the same interest which he had acquired with the father, is a proof at least that he was possessed of a very flexible disposition. The favor of a tyrant does not always suppose a want of merit in the object of it; he may, without intending it, reward a man of worth and ability, or he may find such a man useful to his own service. It does not appear that Albinus served the son of Marcus, either as the minister of his cruelties, or even as the associate of his pleasures. He was employed in a distant honorable command, when he received a confidential letter from the emperor, acquainting him of the treasonable designs of some discontented generals, and authorizing him to declare himself the guardian and successor of the throne, by assuming the title and ensigns of Caesar. [18] The governor of Britain wisely declined the dangerous honor, which would have marked him for the jealousy, or involved him in the approaching ruin, of Commodus. He courted power by nobler, or, at least, by more specious arts. On a premature report of the death of the emperor, he assembled his troops; and, in an eloquent discourse, deplored the inevitable mischiefs of despotism, described the happiness and glory which their ancestors had enjoyed under the consular government, and declared his firm resolution to reinstate the senate and people in their legal authority. This popular harangue was answered by the loud acclamations of the British legions, and received at Rome with a secret murmur of applause. Safe in the possession of his little world, and in the command of an army less distinguished indeed for discipline than for numbers and valor, [19] Albinus braved the menaces of Commodus, maintained towards Pertinax a stately ambiguous reserve, and instantly declared against the usurpation of Julian. The convulsions of the capital added new weight to his sentiments, or rather to his professions of patriotism. A regard to decency induced him to decline the lofty titles of Augustus and Emperor; and he imitated perhaps the example of Galba, who, on a similar occasion, had styled himself the Lieutenant of the senate and people. [20]

[Footnote 16: The Posthumian and the Ce'onian; the former of whom was raised to the consulship in the fifth year after its institution.]

[Footnote 17: Spartianus, in his undigested collections, mixes up all the virtues and all the vices that enter into the human composition, and bestows them on the same object. Such, indeed are many of the characters in the Augustan History.]

[Footnote 18: Hist. August. p. 80, 84.]

[Footnote 19: Pertinax, who governed Britain a few years before, had been left for dead, in a mutiny of the soldiers. Hist. August. p 54. Yet they loved and regretted him; admirantibus eam virtutem cui irascebantur.]

[Footnote 20: Sueton. in Galb. c. 10.]

Personal merit alone had raised Pescennius Niger, from an obscure birth and station, to the government of Syria; a lucrative and important command, which in times of civil confusion gave him a near prospect of the throne. Yet his parts seem to have been better suited to the second than to the first rank; he was an unequal rival, though he might have approved himself an excellent lieutenant, to Severus, who afterwards displayed the greatness of his mind by adopting several useful institutions from a vanquished enemy. [21] In his government Niger acquired the esteem of the soldiers and the love of the provincials. His rigid discipline fortified the valor and confirmed the obedience of the former, whilst the voluptuous Syrians were less delighted with the mild firmness of his administration, than with the affability of his manners, and the apparent pleasure with which he attended their frequent and pompous festivals. [22] As soon as the intelligence of the atrocious murder of Pertinax had reached Antioch, the wishes of Asia invited Niger to assume the Imperial purple and revenge his death. The legions of the eastern frontier embraced his cause; the opulent but unarmed provinces, from the frontiers of Aethiopia [23] to the Hadriatic, cheerfully submitted to his power; and the kings beyond the Tigris and the Euphrates congratulated his election, and offered him their homage and services. The mind of Niger was not capable of receiving this sudden tide of fortune: he flattered himself that his accession would be undisturbed by competition and unstained by civil blood; and whilst he enjoyed the vain pomp of triumph, he neglected to secure the means of victory. Instead of entering into an effectual negotiation with the powerful armies of the West, whose resolution might decide, or at least must balance, the mighty contest; instead of advancing without delay towards Rome and Italy, where his presence was impatiently expected, [24] Niger trifled away in the luxury of Antioch those irretrievable moments which were diligently improved by the decisive activity of Severus. [25]

[Footnote 21: Hist. August. p. 76.]

[Footnote 22: Herod. l. ii. p. 68. The Chronicle of John Malala, of Antioch, shows the zealous attachment of his countrymen to these festivals, which at once gratified their superstition, and their love of pleasure.]

[Footnote 23: A king of Thebes, in Egypt, is mentioned, in the Augustan History, as an ally, and, indeed, as a personal friend of Niger. If Spartianus is not, as I strongly suspect, mistaken, he has brought to light a dynasty of tributary princes totally unknown to history.]

[Footnote 24: Dion, l. lxxiii. p. 1238. Herod. l. ii. p. 67. A verse in every one's mouth at that time, seems to express the general opinion of the three rivals; Optimus est Niger, [Fuscus, which preserves the quantity.—M.] bonus After, pessimus Albus. Hist. August. p. 75.]

[Footnote 25: Herodian, l. ii. p. 71.]

The country of Pannonia and Dalmatia, which occupied the space between the Danube and the Hadriatic, was one of the last and most difficult conquests of the Romans. In the defence of national freedom, two hundred thousand of these barbarians had once appeared in the field, alarmed the declining age of Augustus, and exercised the vigilant prudence of Tiberius at the head of the collected force of the empire. [26] The Pannonians yielded at length to the arms and institutions of Rome. Their recent subjection, however, the neighborhood, and even the mixture, of the unconquered tribes, and perhaps the climate, adapted, as it has been observed, to the production of great bodies and slow minds, [27] all contributed to preserve some remains of their original ferocity, and under the tame and uniform countenance of Roman provincials, the hardy features of the natives were still to be discerned. Their warlike youth afforded an inexhaustible supply of recruits to the legions stationed on the banks of the Danube, and which, from a perpetual warfare against the Germans and Sarmazans, were deservedly esteemed the best troops in the service.

[Footnote 26: See an account of that memorable war in Velleius Paterculus, is 110, &c., who served in the army of Tiberius.]

[Footnote 27: Such is the reflection of Herodian, l. ii. p. 74. Will the modern Austrians allow the influence?]

The Pannonian army was at this time commanded by Septimius Severus, a native of Africa, who, in the gradual ascent of private honors, had concealed his daring ambition, which was never diverted from its steady course by the allurements of pleasure, the apprehension of danger, or the feelings of humanity. [28] On the first news of the murder of Pertinax, he assembled his troops, painted in the most lively colors the crime, the insolence, and the weakness of the Praetorian guards, and animated the legions to arms and to revenge. He concluded (and the peroration was thought extremely eloquent) with promising every soldier about four hundred pounds; an honorable donative, double in value to the infamous bribe with which Julian had purchased the empire. [29] The acclamations of the army immediately saluted Severus with the names of Augustus, Pertinax, and Emperor; and he thus attained the lofty station to which he was invited, by conscious merit and a long train of dreams and omens, the fruitful offsprings either of his superstition or policy. [30]

[Footnote 28: In the letter to Albinus, already mentioned, Commodus accuses Severus, as one of the ambitious generals who censured his conduct, and wished to occupy his place. Hist. August. p. 80.]

[Footnote 29: Pannonia was too poor to supply such a sum. It was probably promised in the camp, and paid at Rome, after the victory. In fixing the sum, I have adopted the conjecture of Casaubon. See Hist. August. p. 66. Comment. p. 115.]

[Footnote 30: Herodian, l. ii. p. 78. Severus was declared emperor on the banks of the Danube, either at Carnuntum, according to Spartianus, (Hist. August. p. 65,) or else at Sabaria, according to Victor. Mr. Hume, in supposing that the birth and dignity of Severus were too much inferior to the Imperial crown, and that he marched into Italy as general only, has not considered this transaction with his usual accuracy, (Essay on the original contract.) Note: Carnuntum, opposite to the mouth of the Morava: its position is doubtful, either Petronel or Haimburg. A little intermediate village seems to indicate by its name (Altenburg) the site of an old town. D'Anville Geogr. Anc. Sabaria, now Sarvar.—G. Compare note 37.—M.]

The new candidate for empire saw and improved the peculiar advantage of his situation. His province extended to the Julian Alps, which gave an easy access into Italy; and he remembered the saying of Augustus, That a Pannonian army might in ten days appear in sight of Rome. [31] By a celerity proportioned to the greatness of the occasion, he might reasonably hope to revenge Pertinax, punish Julian, and receive the homage of the senate and people, as their lawful emperor, before his competitors, separated from Italy by an immense tract of sea and land, were apprised of his success, or even of his election. During the whole expedition, he scarcely allowed himself any moments for sleep or food; marching on foot, and in complete armor, at the head of his columns, he insinuated himself into the confidence and affection of his troops, pressed their diligence, revived their spirits, animated their hopes, and was well satisfied to share the hardships of the meanest soldier, whilst he kept in view the infinite superiority of his reward.

[Footnote 31: Velleius Paterculus, l. ii. c. 3. We must reckon the march from the nearest verge of Pannonia, and extend the sight of the city as far as two hundred miles.]

The wretched Julian had expected, and thought himself prepared, to dispute the empire with the governor of Syria; but in the invincible and rapid approach of the Pannonian legions, he saw his inevitable ruin. The hasty arrival of every messenger increased his just apprehensions. He was successively informed, that Severus had passed the Alps; that the Italian cities, unwilling or unable to oppose his progress, had received him with the warmest professions of joy and duty; that the important place of Ravenna had surrendered without resistance, and that the Hadriatic fleet was in the hands of the conqueror. The enemy was now within two hundred and fifty miles of Rome; and every moment diminished the narrow span of life and empire allotted to Julian.

He attempted, however, to prevent, or at least to protract, his ruin. He implored the venal faith of the Praetorians, filled the city with unavailing preparations for war, drew lines round the suburbs, and even strengthened the fortifications of the palace; as if those last intrenchments could be defended, without hope of relief, against a victorious invader. Fear and shame prevented the guards from deserting his standard; but they trembled at the name of the Pannonian legions, commanded by an experienced general, and accustomed to vanquish the barbarians on the frozen Danube. [32] They quitted, with a sigh, the pleasures of the baths and theatres, to put on arms, whose use they had almost forgotten, and beneath the weight of which they were oppressed. The unpractised elephants, whose uncouth appearance, it was hoped, would strike terror into the army of the north, threw their unskilful riders; and the awkward evolutions of the marines, drawn from the fleet of Misenum, were an object of ridicule to the populace; whilst the senate enjoyed, with secret pleasure, the distress and weakness of the usurper. [33]

[Footnote 32: This is not a puerile figure of rhetoric, but an allusion to a real fact recorded by Dion, l. lxxi. p. 1181. It probably happened more than once.]

[Footnote 33: Dion, l. lxxiii. p. 1233. Herodian, l. ii. p. 81. There is no surer proof of the military skill of the Romans, than their first surmounting the idle terror, and afterwards disdaining the dangerous use, of elephants in war. Note: These elephants were kept for processions, perhaps for the games. Se Herod. in loc.—M.]

Every motion of Julian betrayed his trembling perplexity. He insisted that Severus should be declared a public enemy by the senate. He entreated that the Pannonian general might be associated to the empire. He sent public ambassadors of consular rank to negotiate with his rival; he despatched private assassins to take away his life. He designed that the Vestal virgins, and all the colleges of priests, in their sacerdotal habits, and bearing before them the sacred pledges of the Roman religion, should advance in solemn procession to meet the Pannonian legions; and, at the same time, he vainly tried to interrogate, or to appease, the fates, by magic ceremonies and unlawful sacrifices. [34]

[Footnote 34: Hist. August. p. 62, 63. Note: Quae ad speculum dicunt fieri in quo pueri praeligatis oculis, incantate..., respicere dicuntur. Tuncque puer vidisse dicitur et adventun Severi et Juliani decessionem. This seems to have been a practice somewhat similar to that of which our recent Egyptian travellers relate such extraordinary circumstances. See also Apulius, Orat. de Magia.—M.]

PART II

Severus, who dreaded neither his arms nor his enchantments, guarded himself from the only danger of secret conspiracy, by the faithful attendance of six hundred chosen men, who never quitted his person or their cuirasses, either by night or by day, during the whole march. Advancing with a steady and rapid course, he passed, without difficulty, the defiles of the Apennine, received into his party the troops and ambassadors sent to retard his progress, and made a short halt at Interamnia, about seventy miles from Rome. His victory was already secure, but the despair of the Praetorians might have rendered it bloody; and Severus had the laudable ambition of ascending the throne without drawing the sword. [35] His emissaries, dispersed in the capital, assured the guards, that provided they would abandon their worthless prince, and the perpetrators of the murder of Pertinax, to the justice of the conqueror, he would no longer consider that melancholy event as the act of the whole body. The faithless Praetorians, whose resistance was supported only by sullen obstinacy, gladly complied with the easy conditions, seized the greatest part of the assassins, and signified to the senate, that they no longer defended the cause of Julian. That assembly, convoked by the consul, unanimously acknowledged Severus as lawful emperor, decreed divine honors to Pertinax, and pronounced a sentence of deposition and death against his unfortunate successor. Julian was conducted into a private apartment of the baths of the palace, and beheaded as a common criminal, after having purchased, with an immense treasure, an anxious and precarious reign of only sixty-six days. [36] The almost incredible expedition of Severus, who, in so short a space of time, conducted a numerous army from the banks of the Danube to those of the Tyber, proves at once the plenty of provisions produced by agriculture and commerce, the goodness of the roads, the discipline of the legions, and the indolent, subdued temper of the provinces. [37]

[Footnote 35: Victor and Eutropius, viii. 17, mention a combat near the Milvian bridge, the Ponte Molle, unknown to the better and more ancient writers.]

[Footnote 36: Dion, l. lxxiii. p. 1240. Herodian, l. ii. p. 83. Hist. August. p. 63.]

[Footnote 37: From these sixty-six days, we must first deduct sixteen, as Pertinax was murdered on the 28th of March, and Severus most probably elected on the 13th of April, (see Hist. August. p. 65, and Tillemont, Hist. des Empereurs, tom. iii. p. 393, note 7.) We cannot allow less than ten days after his election, to put a numerous army in motion. Forty days remain for this rapid march; and as we may compute about eight hundred miles from Rome to the neighborhood of Vienna, the army of Severus marched twenty miles every day, without halt or intermission.]

The first cares of Severus were bestowed on two measures the one dictated by policy, the other by decency; the revenge, and the honors, due to the memory of Pertinax. Before the new emperor entered Rome, he issued his commands to the Praetorian guards, directing them to wait his arrival on a large plain near the city, without arms, but in the habits of ceremony, in which they were accustomed to attend their sovereign. He was obeyed by those haughty troops, whose contrition was the effect of their just terrors. A chosen part of the Illyrian army encompassed them with levelled spears. Incapable of flight or resistance, they expected their fate in silent consternation. Severus mounted the tribunal, sternly reproached them with perfidy and cowardice, dismissed them with ignominy from the trust which they had betrayed, despoiled them of their splendid ornaments, and banished them, on pain of death, to the distance of a hundred miles from the capital. During the transaction, another detachment had been sent to seize their arms, occupy their camp, and prevent the hasty consequences of their despair. [38]

[Footnote 38: Dion, l. lxxiv. p. 1241. Herodian, l. ii. p. 84.] The funeral and consecration of Pertinax was next solemnized with every circumstance of sad magnificence. [39] The senate, with a melancholy pleasure, performed the last rites to that excellent prince, whom they had loved, and still regretted. The concern of his successor was probably less sincere; he esteemed the virtues of Pertinax, but those virtues would forever have confined his ambition to a private station. Severus pronounced his funeral oration with studied eloquence, inward satisfaction, and well-acted sorrow; and by this pious regard to his memory, convinced the credulous multitude, that he alone was worthy to supply his place. Sensible, however, that arms, not ceremonies, must assert his claim to the empire, he left Rome at the end of thirty days, and without suffering himself to be elated by this easy victory, prepared to encounter his more formidable rivals.

[Footnote 39: Dion, (l. lxxiv. p. 1244,) who assisted at the ceremony as a senator, gives a most pompous description of it.]

The uncommon abilities and fortune of Severus have induced an elegant historian to compare him with the first and greatest of the Caesars. [40] The parallel is, at least, imperfect. Where shall we find, in the character of Severus, the commanding superiority of soul, the generous clemency, and the various genius, which could reconcile and unite the love of pleasure, the thirst of knowledge, and the fire of ambition? [41] In one instance only, they may be compared, with some degree of propriety, in the celerity of their motions, and their civil victories. In less than four years, [42] Severus subdued the riches of the East, and the valor of the West. He vanquished two competitors of reputation and ability, and defeated numerous armies, provided with weapons and discipline equal to his own. In that age, the art of fortification, and the principles of tactics, were well understood by all the Roman generals; and the constant superiority of Severus was that of an artist, who uses the same instruments with more skill and industry than his rivals. I shall not, however, enter into a minute narrative of these military operations; but as the two civil wars against Niger and against Albinus were almost the same in their conduct, event, and consequences, I shall collect into one point of view the most striking circumstances, tending to develop the character of the conqueror and the state of the empire.

[Footnote 40: Herodian, l. iii. p. 112]

[Footnote 41: Though it is not, most assuredly, the intention of Lucan to exalt the character of Caesar, yet the idea he gives of that hero, in the tenth book of the Pharsalia, where he describes him, at the same time, making love to Cleopatra, sustaining a siege against the power of Egypt, and conversing with the sages of the country, is, in reality, the noblest panegyric. Note: Lord Byron wrote, no doubt, from a reminiscence of that passage—"It is possible to be a very great man, and to be still very inferior to Julius Caesar, the most complete character, so Lord Bacon thought, of all antiquity. Nature seems incapable of such extraordinary combinations as composed his versatile capacity, which was the wonder even of the Romans themselves. The first general; the only triumphant politician; inferior to none in point of eloquence; comparable to any in the attainments of wisdom, in an age made up of the greatest commanders, statesmen, orators, and philosophers, that ever appeared in the world; an author who composed a perfect specimen of military annals in his travelling carriage; at one time in a controversy with Cato, at another writing a treatise on punuing, and collecting a set of good sayings; fighting and making love at the same moment, and willing to abandon both his empire and his mistress for a sight of the fountains of the Nile. Such did Julius Caesar appear to his contemporaries, and to those of the subsequent ages who were the most inclined to deplore and execrate his fatal genius." Note 47 to Canto iv. of Childe Harold.—M.]

[Footnote 42: Reckoning from his election, April 13, 193, to the death of Albinus, February 19, 197. See Tillemont's Chronology.]

Falsehood and insincerity, unsuitable as they seem to the dignity of public transactions, offend us with a less degrading idea of meanness, than when they are found in the intercourse of private life. In the latter, they discover a want of courage; in the other, only a defect of power: and, as it is impossible for the most able statesmen to subdue millions of followers and enemies by their own personal strength, the world, under the name of policy, seems to have granted them a very liberal indulgence of craft and dissimulation. Yet the arts of Severus cannot be justified by the most ample privileges of state reason. He promised only to betray, he flattered only to ruin; and however he might occasionally bind himself by oaths and treaties, his conscience, obsequious to his interest, always released him from the inconvenient obligation. [43]

[Footnote 43: Herodian, l. ii. p. 85.]

If his two competitors, reconciled by their common danger, had advanced upon him without delay, perhaps Severus would have sunk under their united effort. Had they even attacked him, at the same time, with separate views and separate armies, the contest might have been long and doubtful. But they fell, singly and successively, an easy prey to the arts as well as arms of their subtle enemy, lulled into security by the moderation of his professions, and overwhelmed by the rapidity of his action. He first marched against Niger, whose reputation and power he the most dreaded: but he declined any hostile declarations, suppressed the name of his antagonist, and only signified to the senate and people his intention of regulating the eastern provinces. In private, he spoke of Niger, his old friend and intended successor, [44] with the most affectionate regard, and highly applauded his generous design of revenging the murder of Pertinax. To punish the vile usurper of the throne, was the duty of every Roman general. To persevere in arms, and to resist a lawful emperor, acknowledged by the senate, would alone render him criminal. [45] The sons of Niger had fallen into his hands among the children of the provincial governors, detained at Rome as pledges for the loyalty of their parents. [46] As long as the power of Niger inspired terror, or even respect, they were educated with the most tender care, with the children of Severus himself; but they were soon involved in their father's ruin, and removed first by exile, and afterwards by death, from the eye of public compassion. [47]

[Footnote 44: Whilst Severus was very dangerously ill, it was industriously given out, that he intended to appoint Niger and Albinus his successors. As he could not be sincere with respect to both, he might not be so with regard to either. Yet Severus carried his hypocrisy so far, as to profess that intention in the memoirs of his own life.]

[Footnote 45: Hist. August. p. 65.]

[Footnote 46: This practice, invented by Commodus, proved very useful to Severus. He found at Rome the children of many of the principal adherents of his rivals; and he employed them more than once to intimidate, or seduce, the parents.]

[Footnote 47: Herodian, l. iii. p. 95. Hist. August. p. 67, 68.]

Whilst Severus was engaged in his eastern war, he had reason to apprehend that the governor of Britain might pass the sea and the Alps, occupy the vacant seat of empire, and oppose his return with the authority of the senate and the forces of the West. The ambiguous conduct of Albinus, in not assuming the Imperial title, left room for negotiation. Forgetting, at once, his professions of patriotism, and the jealousy of sovereign power, he accepted the precarious rank of Caesar, as a reward for his fatal neutrality. Till the first contest was decided, Severus treated the man, whom he had doomed to destruction, with every mark of esteem and regard. Even in the letter, in which he announced his victory over Niger, he styles Albinus the brother of his soul and empire, sends him the affectionate salutations of his wife Julia, and his young family, and entreats him to preserve the armies and the republic faithful to their common interest. The messengers charged with this letter were instructed to accost the Caesar with respect, to desire a private audience, and to plunge their daggers into his heart. [48] The conspiracy was discovered, and the too credulous Albinus, at length, passed over to the continent, and prepared for an unequal contest with his rival, who rushed upon him at the head of a veteran and victorious army.

[Footnote 48: Hist. August. p. 84. Spartianus has inserted this curious letter at full length.]

The military labors of Severus seem inadequate to the importance of his conquests. Two engagements, [48/1] the one near the Hellespont, the other in the narrow defiles of Cilicia, decided the fate of his Syrian competitor; and the troops of Europe asserted their usual ascendant over the effeminate natives of Asia. [49] The battle of Lyons, where one hundred and fifty thousand Romans [50] were engaged, was equally fatal to Albinus. The valor of the British army maintained, indeed, a sharp and doubtful contest, with the hardy discipline of the Illyrian legions. The fame and person of Severus appeared, during a few moments, irrecoverably lost, till that warlike prince rallied his fainting troops, and led them on to a decisive victory. [51] The war was finished by that memorable day. [51/1]

[Footnote 48/1: There were three actions; one near Cyzicus, on the Hellespont, one near Nice, in Bithynia, the third near the Issus, in Cilicia, where Alexander conquered Darius. (Dion, lxiv. c. 6. Herodian, iii. 2, 4.)—W Herodian represents the second battle as of less importance than Dion—M.]

[Footnote 49: Consult the third book of Herodian, and the seventy-fourth book of Dion Cassius.]

[Footnote 50: Dion, l. lxxv. p. 1260.]

[Footnote 51: Dion, l. lxxv. p. 1261. Herodian, l. iii. p. 110. Hist. August. p. 68. The battle was fought in the plain of Trevoux, three or four leagues from Lyons. See Tillemont, tom. iii. p. 406, note 18.]

[Footnote 51/1: According to Herodian, it was his lieutenant Laetus who led back the troops to the battle, and gained the day, which Severus had almost lost. Dion also attributes to Laetus a great share in the victory. Severus afterwards put him to death, either from fear or jealousy.—W. and G. Wenck and M. Guizot have not given the real statement of Herodian or of Dion. According to the former, Laetus appeared with his own army entire, which he was suspected of having designedly kept disengaged when the battle was still doudtful, or rather after the rout of severus. Dion says that he did not move till Severus had won the victory.—M.]

The civil wars of modern Europe have been distinguished, not only by the fierce animosity, but likewise by the obstinate perseverance, of the contending factions. They have generally been justified by some principle, or, at least, colored by some pretext, of religion, freedom, or loyalty. The leaders were nobles of independent property and hereditary influence. The troops fought like men interested in the decision of the quarrel; and as military spirit and party zeal were strongly diffused throughout the whole community, a vanquished chief was immediately supplied with new adherents, eager to shed their blood in the same cause. But the Romans, after the fall of the republic, combated only for the choice of masters. Under the standard of a popular candidate for empire, a few enlisted from affection, some from fear, many from interest, none from principle. The legions, uninflamed by party zeal, were allured into civil war by liberal donatives, and still more liberal promises. A defeat, by disabling the chief from the performance of his engagements, dissolved the mercenary allegiance of his followers, and left them to consult their own safety by a timely desertion of an unsuccessful cause. It was of little moment to the provinces, under whose name they were oppressed or governed; they were driven by the impulsion of the present power, and as soon as that power yielded to a superior force, they hastened to implore the clemency of the conqueror, who, as he had an immense debt to discharge, was obliged to sacrifice the most guilty countries to the avarice of his soldiers. In the vast extent of the Roman empire, there were few fortified cities capable of protecting a routed army; nor was there any person, or family, or order of men, whose natural interest, unsupported by the powers of government, was capable of restoring the cause of a sinking party. [52]

[Footnote 52: Montesquieu, Considerations sur la Grandeur et la Decadence des Romains, c. xiii.]

Yet, in the contest between Niger and Severus, a single city deserves an honorable exception. As Byzantium was one of the greatest passages from Europe into Asia, it had been provided with a strong garrison, and a fleet of five hundred vessels was anchored in the harbor. [53] The impetuosity of Severus disappointed this prudent scheme of defence; he left to his generals the siege of Byzantium, forced the less guarded passage of the Hellespont, and, impatient of a meaner enemy, pressed forward to encounter his rival. Byzantium, attacked by a numerous and increasing army, and afterwards by the whole naval power of the empire, sustained a siege of three years, and remained faithful to the name and memory of Niger. The citizens and soldiers (we know not from what cause) were animated with equal fury; several of the principal officers of Niger, who despaired of, or who disdained, a pardon, had thrown themselves into this last refuge: the fortifications were esteemed impregnable, and, in the defence of the place, a celebrated engineer displayed all the mechanic powers known to the ancients. [54] Byzantium, at length, surrendered to famine. The magistrates and soldiers were put to the sword, the walls demolished, the privileges suppressed, and the destined capital of the East subsisted only as an open village, subject to the insulting jurisdiction of Perinthus. The historian Dion, who had admired the flourishing, and lamented the desolate, state of Byzantium, accused the revenge of Severus, for depriving the Roman people of the strongest bulwark against the barbarians of Pontus and Asia [55] The truth of this observation was but too well justified in the succeeding age, when the Gothic fleets covered the Euxine, and passed through the undefined Bosphorus into the centre of the Mediterranean.

[Footnote 53: Most of these, as may be supposed, were small open vessels; some, however, were galleys of two, and a few of three ranks of oars.]

[Footnote 54: The engineer's name was Priscus. His skill saved his life, and he was taken into the service of the conqueror. For the particular facts of the siege, consult Dion Cassius (l. lxxv. p. 1251) and Herodian, (l. iii. p. 95;) for the theory of it, the fanciful chevalier de Folard may be looked into. See Polybe, tom. i. p. 76.]

[Footnote 55: Notwithstanding the authority of Spartianus, and some modern Greeks, we may be assured, from Dion and Herodian, that Byzantium, many years after the death of Severus, lay in ruins. There is no contradiction between the relation of Dion and that of Spartianus and the modern Greeks. Dion does not say that Severus destroyed Byzantium, but that he deprived it of its franchises and privileges, stripped the inhabitants of their property, razed the fortifications, and subjected the city to the jurisdiction of Perinthus. Therefore, when Spartian, Suidas, Cedrenus, say that Severus and his son Antoninus restored to Byzantium its rights and franchises, ordered temples to be built, &c., this is easily reconciled with the relation of Dion. Perhaps the latter mentioned it in some of the fragments of his history which have been lost. As to Herodian, his expressions are evidently exaggerated, and he has been guilty of so many inaccuracies in the history of Severus, that we have a right to suppose one in this passage.—G. from W Wenck and M. Guizot have omitted to cite Zosimus, who mentions a particular portico built by Severus, and called, apparently, by his name. Zosim. Hist. ii. c. xxx. p. 151, 153, edit Heyne.—M.]

Both Niger and Albinus were discovered and put to death in their flight from the field of battle. Their fate excited neither surprise nor compassion. They had staked their lives against the chance of empire, and suffered what they would have inflicted; nor did Severus claim the arrogant superiority of suffering his rivals to live in a private station. But his unforgiving temper, stimulated by avarice, indulged a spirit of revenge, where there was no room for apprehension. The most considerable of the provincials, who, without any dislike to the fortunate candidate, had obeyed the governor under whose authority they were accidentally placed, were punished by death, exile, and especially by the confiscation of their estates. Many cities of the East were stripped of their ancient honors, and obliged to pay, into the treasury of Severus, four times the amount of the sums contributed by them for the service of Niger. [56]

[Footnote 56: Dion, l. lxxiv. p. 1250.]

Till the final decision of the war, the cruelty of Severus was, in some measure, restrained by the uncertainty of the event, and his pretended reverence for the senate. The head of Albinus, accompanied with a menacing letter, announced to the Romans that he was resolved to spare none of the adherents of his unfortunate competitors. He was irritated by the just auspicion that he had never possessed the affections of the senate, and he concealed his old malevolence under the recent discovery of some treasonable correspondences. Thirty-five senators, however, accused of having favored the party of Albinus, he freely pardoned, and, by his subsequent behavior, endeavored to convince them, that he had forgotten, as well as forgiven, their supposed offences. But, at the same time, he condemned forty-one [57] other senators, whose names history has recorded; their wives, children, and clients attended them in death, [57/1] and the noblest provincials of Spain and Gaul were involved in the same ruin. [57/2] Such rigid justice—for so he termed it—was, in the opinion of Severus, the only conduct capable of insuring peace to the people or stability to the prince; and he condescended slightly to lament, that to be mild, it was necessary that he should first be cruel. [58]

[Footnote 57: Dion, (l. lxxv. p. 1264;) only twenty-nine senators are mentioned by him, but forty-one are named in the Augustan History, p. 69, among whom were six of the name of Pescennius. Herodian (l. iii. p. 115) speaks in general of the cruelties of Severus.]

[Footnote 57/1: Wenck denies that there is any authority for this massacre of the wives of the senators. He adds, that only the children and relatives of Niger and Albinus were put to death. This is true of the family of Albinus, whose bodies were thrown into the Rhone; those of Niger, according to Lampridius, were sent into exile, but afterwards put to death. Among the partisans of Albinus who were put to death were many women of rank, multae foeminae illustres. Lamprid. in Sever.—M.]

[Footnote 57/2: A new fragment of Dion describes the state of Rome during this contest. All pretended to be on the side of Severus; but their secret sentiments were often betrayed by a change of countenance on the arrival of some sudden report. Some were detected by overacting their loyalty, Mai. Fragm. Vatican. p. 227 Severus told the senate he would rather have their hearts than their votes.—Ibid.—M.]

[Footnote 58: Aurelius Victor.]

The true interest of an absolute monarch generally coincides with that of his people. Their numbers, their wealth, their order, and their security, are the best and only foundations of his real greatness; and were he totally devoid of virtue, prudence might supply its place, and would dictate the same rule of conduct. Severus considered the Roman empire as his property, and had no sooner secured the possession, than he bestowed his care on the cultivation and improvement of so valuable an acquisition. Salutary laws, executed with inflexible firmness, soon corrected most of the abuses with which, since the death of Marcus, every part of the government had been infected. In the administration of justice, the judgments of the emperor were characterized by attention, discernment, and impartiality; and whenever he deviated from the strict line of equity, it was generally in favor of the poor and oppressed; not so much indeed from any sense of humanity, as from the natural propensity of a despot to humble the pride of greatness, and to sink all his subjects to the same common level of absolute dependence. His expensive taste for building, magnificent shows, and above all a constant and liberal distribution of corn and provisions, were the surest means of captivating the affection of the Roman people. [59] The misfortunes of civil discord were obliterated. The calm of peace and prosperity was once more experienced in the provinces; and many cities, restored by the munificence of Severus, assumed the title of his colonies, and attested by public monuments their gratitude and felicity. [60] The fame of the Roman arms was revived by that warlike and successful emperor, [61] and he boasted, with a just pride, that, having received the empire oppressed with foreign and domestic wars, he left it established in profound, universal, and honorable peace. [62]

[Footnote 59: Dion, l. lxxvi. p. 1272. Hist. August. p. 67. Severus celebrated the secular games with extraordinary magnificence, and he left in the public granaries a provision of corn for seven years, at the rate of 75,000 modii, or about 2500 quarters per day. I am persuaded that the granaries of Severus were supplied for a long term, but I am not less persuaded, that policy on one hand, and admiration on the other, magnified the hoard far beyond its true contents.]

[Footnote 60: See Spanheim's treatise of ancient medals, the inscriptions, and our learned travellers Spon and Wheeler, Shaw, Pocock, &c, who, in Africa, Greece, and Asia, have found more monuments of Severus than of any other Roman emperor whatsoever.]

[Footnote 61: He carried his victorious arms to Seleucia and Ctesiphon, the capitals of the Parthian monarchy. I shall have occasion to mention this war in its proper place.]

[Footnote 62: Etiam in Britannis, was his own just and emphatic expression Hist. August. 73.]

Although the wounds of civil war appeared completely healed, its mortal poison still lurked in the vitals of the constitution.

Severus possessed a considerable share of vigor and ability; but the daring soul of the first Caesar, or the deep policy of Augustus, were scarcely equal to the task of curbing the insolence of the victorious legions. By gratitude, by misguided policy, by seeming necessity, Severus was reduced to relax the nerves of discipline. [63] The vanity of his soldiers was flattered with the honor of wearing gold rings their ease was indulged in the permission of living with their wives in the idleness of quarters. He increased their pay beyond the example of former times, and taught them to expect, and soon to claim, extraordinary donatives on every public occasion of danger or festivity. Elated by success, enervated by luxury, and raised above the level of subjects by their dangerous privileges, [64] they soon became incapable of military fatigue, oppressive to the country, and impatient of a just subordination. Their officers asserted the superiority of rank by a more profuse and elegant luxury. There is still extant a letter of Severus, lamenting the licentious stage of the army, [64/1] and exhorting one of his generals to begin the necessary reformation from the tribunes themselves; since, as he justly observes, the officer who has forfeited the esteem, will never command the obedience, of his soldiers. [65] Had the emperor pursued the train of reflection, he would have discovered, that the primary cause of this general corruption might be ascribed, not indeed to the example, but to the pernicious indulgence, however, of the commander-in-chief.

[Footnote 63: Herodian, l. iii. p. 115. Hist. August. p. 68.]

[Footnote 64: Upon the insolence and privileges of the soldier, the 16th satire, falsely ascribed to Juvenal, may be consulted; the style and circumstances of it would induce me to believe, that it was composed under the reign of Severus, or that of his son.]

[Footnote 64/1: Not of the army, but of the troops in Gaul. The contents of this letter seem to prove that Severus was really anxious to restore discipline Herodian is the only historian who accuses him of being the first cause of its relaxation.—G. from W Spartian mentions his increase of the pays.—M.]

[Footnote 65: Hist. August. p. 73.]

The Praetorians, who murdered their emperor and sold the empire, had received the just punishment of their treason; but the necessary, though dangerous, institution of guards was soon restored on a new model by Severus, and increased to four times the ancient number. [66] Formerly these troops had been recruited in Italy; and as the adjacent provinces gradually imbibed the softer manners of Rome, the levies were extended to Macedonia, Noricum, and Spain. In the room of these elegant troops, better adapted to the pomp of courts than to the uses of war, it was established by Severus, that from all the legions of the frontiers, the soldiers most distinguished for strength, valor, and fidelity, should be occasionally draughted; and promoted, as an honor and reward, into the more eligible service of the guards. [67] By this new institution, the Italian youth were diverted from the exercise of arms, and the capital was terrified by the strange aspect and manners of a multitude of barbarians. But Severus flattered himself, that the legions would consider these chosen Praetorians as the representatives of the whole military order; and that the present aid of fifty thousand men, superior in arms and appointments to any force that could be brought into the field against them, would forever crush the hopes of rebellion, and secure the empire to himself and his posterity.

[Footnote 66: Herodian, l. iii. p. 131.]

[Footnote 67: Dion, l. lxxiv. p. 1243.]

The command of these favored and formidable troops soon became the first office of the empire. As the government degenerated into military despotism, the Praetorian Praefect, who in his origin had been a simple captain of the guards, [67/1] was placed not only at the head of the army, but of the finances, and even of the law. In every department of administration, he represented the person, and exercised the authority, of the emperor. The first praefect who enjoyed and abused this immense power was Plautianus, the favorite minister of Severus. His reign lasted above ten years, till the marriage of his daughter with the eldest son of the emperor, which seemed to assure his fortune, proved the occasion of his ruin. [68] The animosities of the palace, by irritating the ambition and alarming the fears of Plautianus, [68/1] threatened to produce a revolution, and obliged the emperor, who still loved him, to consent with reluctance to his death. [69] After the fall of Plautianus, an eminent lawyer, the celebrated Papinian, was appointed to execute the motley office of Praetorian Praefect.

[Footnote 67/1: The Praetorian Praefect had never been a simple captain of the guards; from the first creation of this office, under Augustus, it possessed great power. That emperor, therefore, decreed that there should be always two Praetorian Praefects, who could only be taken from the equestrian order Tiberius first departed from the former clause of this edict; Alexander Severus violated the second by naming senators praefects. It appears that it was under Commodus that the Praetorian Praefects obtained the province of civil jurisdiction. It extended only to Italy, with the exception of Rome and its district, which was governed by the Praefectus urbi. As to the control of the finances, and the levying of taxes, it was not intrusted to them till after the great change that Constantine I. made in the organization of the empire at least, I know no passage which assigns it to them before that time; and Drakenborch, who has treated this question in his Dissertation de official praefectorum praetorio, vi., does not quote one.—W.]

[Footnote 68: One of his most daring and wanton acts of power, was the castration of a hundred free Romans, some of them married men, and even fathers of families; merely that his daughter, on her marriage with the young emperor, might be attended by a train of eunuchs worthy of an eastern queen. Dion, l. lxxvi. p. 1271.]

[Footnote 68/1: Plautianus was compatriot, relative, and the old friend, of Severus; he had so completely shut up all access to the emperor, that the latter was ignorant how far he abused his powers: at length, being informed of it, he began to limit his authority. The marriage of Plautilla with Caracalla was unfortunate; and the prince who had been forced to consent to it, menaced the father and the daughter with death when he should come to the throne. It was feared, after that, that Plautianus would avail himself of the power which he still possessed, against the Imperial family; and Severus caused him to be assassinated in his presence, upon the pretext of a conspiracy, which Dion considers fictitious.—W. This *note is not, perhaps, very necessary and does not contain the whole facts. Dion considers the conspiracy the invention of Caracalla, by whose command, almost by whose hand, Plautianus was slain in the presence of Severus.—M.]*

[Footnote 69: Dion, l. lxxvi. p. 1274. Herodian, l. iii. p. 122, 129. The grammarian of Alexander seems, as is not unusual, much better acquainted with this mysterious transaction, and more assured of the guilt of Plautianus than the Roman senator ventures to be.]

Till the reign of Severus, the virtue and even the good sense of the emperors had been distinguished by their zeal or affected reverence for the senate, and by a tender regard to the nice frame of civil policy instituted by Augustus. But the youth of Severus had been trained in the implicit obedience of camps, and his riper years spent in the despotism of military command. His haughty and inflexible spirit could not discover, or would not acknowledge, the advantage of preserving an intermediate power, however imaginary, between the emperor and the army. He disdained to profess himself the servant of an assembly that detested his person and trembled at his frown; he issued his commands, where his requests would have proved as effectual; assumed the conduct and style of a sovereign and a conqueror, and exercised, without disguise, the whole legislative, as well as the executive power.

The victory over the senate was easy and inglorious. Every eye and every passion were directed to the supreme magistrate, who possessed the arms and treasure of the state; whilst the senate, neither elected by the people, nor guarded by military force, nor animated by public spirit, rested its declining authority on the frail and crumbling basis of ancient opinion. The fine theory of a republic insensibly vanished, and made way for the more natural and substantial feelings of monarchy. As the freedom and honors of Rome were successively communicated to the provinces, in which the old government had been either unknown, or was remembered with abhorrence, the tradition of republican maxims was gradually obliterated. The Greek historians of the age of the Antonines [70] observe, with a malicious pleasure, that although the sovereign of Rome, in compliance with an obsolete prejudice, abstained from the name of king, he possessed the full measure of regal power. In the reign of Severus, the senate was filled with polished and eloquent slaves from the eastern provinces, who justified personal flattery by speculative principles of servitude. These new advocates of prerogative were heard with pleasure by the court, and with patience by the people, when they inculcated the duty of passive obedience, and descanted on the inevitable mischiefs of freedom. The lawyers and historians concurred in teaching, that the Imperial authority was held, not by the delegated commission, but by the irrevocable resignation of the senate; that the emperor was freed from the restraint of civil laws, could command by his arbitrary will the lives and fortunes of his subjects, and might dispose of the empire as of his private patrimony. [71] The most eminent of the civil lawyers, and particularly Papinian, Paulus, and Ulpian, flourished under the house of Severus; and the Roman jurisprudence, having closely united itself with the system of monarchy, was supposed to have attained its full majority and perfection.

[Footnote 70: Appian in Prooem.]

[Footnote 71: Dion Cassius seems to have written with no other view than to form these opinions into an historical system. The Pandea's will how how assiduously the lawyers, on their side, laboree in the cause of prerogative.]

The contemporaries of Severus in the enjoyment of the peace and glory of his reign, forgave the cruelties by which it had been introduced. Posterity, who experienced the fatal effects of his maxims and example, justly considered him as the principal author of the decline of the Roman empire.

CHAPTER VI

THE DEATH OF SEVERUS, TYRANNY OF CARACALLA, USURPATION OF MARCINUS

PART I

THE DEATH OF SEVERUS—TYRANNY OF CARACALLA—USURPATION OF MARCINUS—FOLLIES OF ELAGABALUS—VIRTUES OF ALEXANDER SEVERUS—LICENTIOUSNESS OF THE ARMY—GENERAL STATE OF THE ROMAN FINANCES

The ascent to greatness, however steep and dangerous, may entertain an active spirit with the consciousness and exercise of its own powers: but the possession of a throne could never yet afford a lasting satisfaction to an ambitious mind. This melancholy truth was felt and acknowledged by Severus. Fortune and merit had, from an humble station, elevated him to the first place among mankind. "He had been all things," as he said himself, "and all was of little value." [1] Distracted with the care, not of acquiring, but of preserving an empire, oppressed with age and infirmities, careless of fame, [2] and satiated with power, all his prospects of life were closed. The desire of perpetuating the greatness of his family was the only remaining wish of his ambition and paternal tenderness.

[Footnote 1: Hist. August. p. 71. "Omnia fui, et nihil expedit."]

[Footnote 2: Dion Cassius, l. lxxvi. p. 1284.]

Like most of the Africans, Severus was passionately addicted to the vain studies of magic and divination, deeply versed in the interpretation of dreams and omens, and perfectly acquainted with the science of judicial astrology; which, in almost every age except the present, has maintained its dominion over the mind of man. He had lost his first wife, while he was governor of the Lionnese Gaul. [3] In the choice of a second, he sought only to connect himself with some favorite of fortune; and as soon as he had discovered that the young lady of Emesa in Syria had a royal nativity, he solicited and obtained her hand. [4] Julia Domna (for that was her name) deserved all that the stars could promise her.

She possessed, even in advanced age, the attractions of beauty, [5] and united to a lively imagination a firmness of mind, and strength of judgment, seldom bestowed on her sex. Her amiable qualities never made any deep impression on the dark and jealous temper of her husband; but in her son's reign, she administered the principal affairs of the empire, with a prudence that supported his authority, and with a moderation that sometimes corrected his wild extravagances. [6] Julia applied herself to letters and philosophy, with some success, and with the most splendid reputation. She was the patroness of every art, and the friend of every man of genius. [7] The grateful flattery of the learned has celebrated her virtues; but, if we may credit the scandal of ancient history, chastity was very far from being the most conspicuous virtue of the empress Julia. [8]

[Footnote 3: About the year 186. M. de Tillemont is miserably embarrassed with a passage of Dion, in which the empress Faustina, who died in the year 175, is introduced as having contributed to the marriage of Severus and Julia, (l. lxxiv. p. 1243.) The learned compiler forgot that Dion is relating not a real fact, but a dream of Severus; and dreams are circumscribed to no limits of time or space. Did M. de

Tillemont imagine that marriages were consummated in the temple of Venus at Rome? Hist. des Empereurs, tom. iii. p. 389. Note 6.]

[Footnote 4: Hist. August. p. 65.]

[Footnote 5: Hist. August. p. 5.]

[Footnote 6: Dion Cassius, l. lxxvii. p. 1304, 1314.]

[Footnote 7: See a dissertation of Menage, at the end of his edition of Diogenes Laertius, de Foeminis Philosophis.]

[Footnote 8: Dion, l. lxxvi. p. 1285. Aurelius Victor.]

Two sons, Caracalla [9] and Geta, were the fruit of this marriage, and the destined heirs of the empire. The fond hopes of the father, and of the Roman world, were soon disappointed by these vain youths, who displayed the indolent security of hereditary princes; and a presumption that fortune would supply the place of merit and application. Without any emulation of virtue or talents, they discovered, almost from their infancy, a fixed and implacable antipathy for each other.

[Footnote 9: Bassianus was his first name, as it had been that of his maternal grandfather. During his reign, he assumed the appellation of Antoninus, which is employed by lawyers and ancient historians. After his death, the public indignation loaded him with the nicknames of Tarantus and Caracalla. The first was borrowed from a celebrated Gladiator, the second from a long Gallic gown which he distributed to the people of Rome.]

Their aversion, confirmed by years, and fomented by the arts of their interested favorites, broke out in childish, and gradually in more serious competitions; and, at length, divided the theatre, the circus, and the court, into two factions, actuated by the hopes and fears of their respective leaders. The prudent emperor endeavored, by every expedient of advice and authority, to allay this growing animosity. The unhappy discord of his sons clouded all his prospects, and threatened to overturn a throne raised with so much labor, cemented with so much blood, and guarded with every defence of arms and treasure. With an impartial hand he maintained between them an exact balance of favor, conferred on both the rank of Augustus, with the revered name of Antoninus; and for the first time the Roman world beheld three emperors. [10] Yet even this equal conduct served only to inflame the contest, whilst the fierce Caracalla asserted the right of primogeniture, and the milder Geta courted the affections of the people and the soldiers. In the anguish of a disappointed father, Severus foretold that the weaker of his sons would fall a sacrifice to the stronger; who, in his turn, would be ruined by his own vices. [11]

[Footnote 10: The elevation of Caracalla is fixed by the accurate M. de Tillemont to the year 198; the association of Geta to the year 208.]

[Footnote 11: Herodian, l. iii. p. 130. The lives of Caracalla and Geta, in the Augustan History.]

In these circumstances the intelligence of a war in Britain, and of an invasion of the province by the barbarians of the North, was received with pleasure by Severus. Though the vigilance of his lieutenants might have been sufficient to repel the distant enemy, he resolved to embrace the honorable pretext of withdrawing his sons from the luxury of Rome, which enervated their minds and irritated their passions;

and of inuring their youth to the toils of war and government. Notwithstanding his advanced age, (for he was above threescore,) and his gout, which obliged him to be carried in a litter, he transported himself in person into that remote island, attended by his two sons, his whole court, and a formidable army. He immediately passed the walls of Hadrian and Antoninus, and entered the enemy's country, with a design of completing the long attempted conquest of Britain. He penetrated to the northern extremity of the island, without meeting an enemy. But the concealed ambuscades of the Caledonians, who hung unseen on the rear and flanks of his army, the coldness of the climate and the severity of a winter march across the hills and morasses of Scotland, are reported to have cost the Romans above fifty thousand men. The Caledonians at length yielded to the powerful and obstinate attack, sued for peace, and surrendered a part of their arms, and a large tract of territory. But their apparent submission lasted no longer than the present terror. As soon as the Roman legions had retired, they resumed their hostile independence. Their restless spirit provoked Severus to send a new army into Caledonia, with the most bloody orders, not to subdue, but to extirpate the natives. They were saved by the death of their haughty enemy. [12]

[Footnote 12: Dion, l. lxxvi. p. 1280, &c. Herodian, l. iii. p. 132, &c.]

This Caledonian war, neither marked by decisive events, nor attended with any important consequences, would ill deserve our attention; but it is supposed, not without a considerable degree of probability, that the invasion of Severus is connected with the most shining period of the British history or fable. Fingal, whose fame, with that of his heroes and bards, has been revived in our language by a recent publication, is said to have commanded the Caledonians in that memorable juncture, to have eluded the power of Severus, and to have obtained a signal victory on the banks of the Carun, in which the son of the King of the World, Caracul, fled from his arms along the fields of his pride. [13] Something of a doubtful mist still hangs over these Highland traditions; nor can it be entirely dispelled by the most ingenious researches of modern criticism; [14] but if we could, with safety, indulge the pleasing supposition, that Fingal lived, and that Ossian sung, the striking contrast of the situation and manners of the contending nations might amuse a philosophic mind.

The parallel would be little to the advantage of the more civilized people, if we compared the unrelenting revenge of Severus with the generous clemency of Fingal; the timid and brutal cruelty of Caracalla with the bravery, the tenderness, the elegant genius of Ossian; the mercenary chiefs, who, from motives of fear or interest, served under the imperial standard, with the free-born warriors who started to arms at the voice of the king of Morven; if, in a word, we contemplated the untutored Caledonians, glowing with the warm virtues of nature, and the degenerate Romans, polluted with the mean vices of wealth and slavery.

[Footnote 13: Ossian's Poems, vol. i. p. 175.]

[Footnote 14: That the Caracul of Ossian is the Caracalla of the Roman History, is, perhaps, the only point of British antiquity in which Mr. Macpherson and Mr. Whitaker are of the same opinion; and yet the opinion is not without difficulty. In the Caledonian war, the son of Severus was known only by the appellation of Antoninus, and it may seem strange that the Highland bard should describe him by a nickname, invented four years afterwards, scarcely used by the Romans till after the death of that emperor, and seldom employed by the most ancient historians. See Dion, l. lxxvii. p. 1317. Hist. August. p. 89 Aurel. Victor. Euseb. in Chron. ad ann. 214. Note: The historical authority of Macpherson's Ossian has not increased since Gibbon wrote. We may, indeed, consider it exploded. Mr. Whitaker, in a letter to Gibbon (Misc. Works, vol. ii. p. 100,) attempts, not very successfully, to weaken this objection of the historian.—M.]

The declining health and last illness of Severus inflamed the wild ambition and black passions of Caracalla's soul. Impatient of any delay or division of empire, he attempted, more than once, to shorten the small remainder of his father's days, and endeavored, but without success, to excite a mutiny among the troops. [15] The old emperor had often censured the misguided lenity of Marcus, who, by a single act of justice, might have saved the Romans from the tyranny of his worthless son. Placed in the same situation, he experienced how easily the rigor of a judge dissolves away in the tenderness of a parent. He deliberated, he threatened, but he could not punish; and this last and only instance of mercy was more fatal to the empire than a long series of cruelty. [16] The disorder of his mind irritated the pains of his body; he wished impatiently for death, and hastened the instant of it by his impatience. He expired at York in the sixty-fifth year of his life, and in the eighteenth of a glorious and successful reign. In his last moments he recommended concord to his sons, and his sons to the army. The salutary advice never reached the heart, or even the understanding, of the impetuous youths; but the more obedient troops, mindful of their oath of allegiance, and of the authority of their deceased master, resisted the solicitations of Caracalla, and proclaimed both brothers emperors of Rome. The new princes soon left the Caledonians in peace, returned to the capital, celebrated their father's funeral with divine honors, and were cheerfully acknowledged as lawful sovereigns, by the senate, the people, and the provinces. Some preeminence of rank seems to have been allowed to the elder brother; but they both administered the empire with equal and independent power. [17]

[Footnote 15: Dion, l. lxxvi. p. 1282. Hist. August. p. 71. Aurel. Victor.]

[Footnote 16: Dion, l. lxxvi. p. 1283. Hist. August. p. 89]

[Footnote 17: Dion, l. lxxvi. p. 1284. Herodian, l. iii. p. 135.]

Such a divided form of government would have proved a source of discord between the most affectionate brothers. It was impossible that it could long subsist between two implacable enemies, who neither desired nor could trust a reconciliation. It was visible that one only could reign, and that the other must fall; and each of them, judging of his rival's designs by his own, guarded his life with the most jealous vigilance from the repeated attacks of poison or the sword. Their rapid journey through Gaul and Italy, during which they never ate at the same table, or slept in the same house, displayed to the provinces the odious spectacle of fraternal discord. On their arrival at Rome, they immediately divided the vast extent of the imperial palace. [18] No communication was allowed between their apartments; the doors and passages were diligently fortified, and guards posted and relieved with the same strictness as in a besieged place. The emperors met only in public, in the presence of their afflicted mother; and each surrounded by a numerous train of armed followers. Even on these occasions of ceremony, the dissimulation of courts could ill disguise the rancor of their hearts. [19]

[Footnote 18: Mr. Hume is justly surprised at a passage of Herodian, (l. iv. p. 139,) who, on this occasion, represents the Imperial palace as equal in extent to the rest of Rome. The whole region of the Palatine Mount, on which it was built, occupied, at most, a circumference of eleven or twelve thousand feet, (see the Notitia and Victor, in Nardini's Roma Antica.) But we should recollect that the opulent senators had almost surrounded the city with their extensive gardens and suburb palaces, the greatest part of which had been gradually confiscated by the emperors. If Geta resided in the gardens that bore his name on the Janiculum, and if Caracalla inhabited the gardens of Maecenas on the Esquiline, the rival brothers were separated from each other by the distance of several miles; and yet the intermediate space was filled by the Imperial gardens of Sallust, of Lucullus, of Agrippa, of Domitian, of Caius, &c., all skirting *round the city, and all connected with each other, and with the palace, by bridges thrown over the Tiber and the streets. But this explanation of Herodian would require, though it ill deserves, a particular dissertation, illustrated by a map of ancient Rome. (Hume, Essay on Populousness of Ancient Nations.— M.)]*

[Footnote 19: Herodian, l. iv. p. 139]

This latent civil war already distracted the whole government, when a scheme was suggested that seemed of mutual benefit to the hostile brothers. It was proposed, that since it was impossible to reconcile their minds, they should separate their interest, and divide the empire between them. The conditions of the treaty were already drawn with some accuracy. It was agreed that Caracalla, as the elder brother should remain in possession of Europe and the western Africa; and that he should relinquish the sovereignty of Asia and Egypt to Geta, who might fix his residence at Alexandria or Antioch, cities little inferior to Rome itself in wealth and greatness; that numerous armies should be constantly encamped on either side of the Thracian Bosphorus, to guard the frontiers of the rival monarchies; and that the senators of European extraction should acknowledge the sovereign of Rome, whilst the natives of Asia followed the emperor of the East. The tears of the empress Julia interrupted the negotiation, the first idea of which had filled every Roman breast with surprise and indignation. The mighty mass of conquest was so intimately united by the hand of time and policy, that it required the most forcible violence to rend it asunder. The Romans had reason to dread, that the disjointed members would soon be reduced by a civil war under the dominion of one master; but if the separation was permanent, the division of the provinces must terminate in the dissolution of an empire whose unity had hitherto remained inviolate. [20]

[Footnote 20: Herodian, l. iv. p. 144.]

Had the treaty been carried into execution, the sovereign of Europe might soon have been the conqueror of Asia; but Caracalla obtained an easier, though a more guilty, victory. He artfully listened to his mother's entreaties, and consented to meet his brother in her apartment, on terms of peace and reconciliation. In the midst of their conversation, some centurions, who had contrived to conceal themselves, rushed with drawn swords upon the unfortunate Geta. His distracted mother strove to protect him in her arms; but, in the unavailing struggle, she was wounded in the hand, and covered with the blood of her younger son, while she saw the elder animating and assisting [21] the fury of the assassins. As soon as the deed was perpetrated, Caracalla, with hasty steps, and horror in his countenance, ran towards the Praetorian camp, as his only refuge, and threw himself on the ground before the statues of the tutelar deities. [22] The soldiers attempted to raise and comfort him. In broken and disordered words he informed them of his imminent danger, and fortunate escape; insinuating that he had prevented the designs of his enemy, and declared his resolution to live and die with his faithful troops. Geta had been the favorite of the soldiers; but complaint was useless, revenge was dangerous, and they still reverenced the son of Severus. Their discontent died away in idle murmurs, and Caracalla soon convinced them of the justice of his cause, by distributing in one lavish donative the accumulated treasures of his father's reign. [23] The real sentiments of the soldiers alone were of importance to his power or safety. Their declaration in his favor commanded the dutiful professions of the senate. The obsequious assembly was always prepared to ratify the decision of fortune; [23/1] but as Caracalla wished to assuage the first emotions of public indignation, the name of Geta was mentioned with decency, and he received the funeral honors of a Roman emperor. [24] Posterity, in pity to his misfortune, has cast a veil over his vices. We consider that young prince as the innocent victim of his brother's ambition, without recollecting that he himself wanted power, rather than inclination, to consummate the same attempts of revenge and murder. [24/1]

[Footnote 21: Caracalla consecrated, in the temple of Serapis, the sword with which, as he boasted, he had slain his brother Geta. Dion, l. lxxvii p. 1307.]

[Footnote 22: Herodian, l. iv. p. 147. In every Roman camp there was a small chapel near the headquarters, in which the statues of the tutelar deities were preserved and adored; and we may remark that the eagles, and other military ensigns, were in the first rank of these deities; an excellent institution, which confirmed discipline by the sanction of religion. See Lipsius de Militia Romana, iv. 5, v. 2.]

[Footnote 23: Herodian, l. iv. p. 148. Dion, l. lxxvii. p. 1289.]

[Footnote 23/1: The account of this transaction, in a new passage of Dion, varies in some degree from this statement. It adds that the next morning, in the senate, Antoninus requested their indulgence, not because he had killed his brother, but because he was hoarse, and could not address them. Mai. Fragm. p. 228.—M.]

[Footnote 24: Geta was placed among the gods. Sit divus, dum non sit vivus said his brother. Hist. August. p. 91. Some marks of Geta's consecration are still found upon medals.]

[Footnote 24/1: The favorable judgment which history has given of Geta is not founded solely on a feeling of pity; it is supported by the testimony of contemporary historians: he was too fond of the pleasures of the table, and showed great mistrust of his brother; but he was humane, well instructed; he often endeavored to mitigate the rigorous decrees of Severus and Caracalla. Herod iv. 3. Spartian in Geta.—W.]

The crime went not unpunished. Neither business, nor pleasure, nor flattery, could defend Caracalla from the stings of a guilty conscience; and he confessed, in the anguish of a tortured mind, that his disordered fancy often beheld the angry forms of his father and his brother rising into life, to threaten and upbraid him. [25] The consciousness of his crime should have induced him to convince mankind, by the virtues of his reign, that the bloody deed had been the involuntary effect of fatal necessity. But the repentance of Caracalla only prompted him to remove from the world whatever could remind him of his guilt, or recall the memory of his murdered brother. On his return from the senate to the palace, he found his mother in the company of several noble matrons, weeping over the untimely fate of her younger son. The jealous emperor threatened them with instant death; the sentence was executed against Fadilla, the last remaining daughter of the emperor Marcus; [25/1] and even the afflicted Julia was obliged to silence her lamentations, to suppress her sighs, and to receive the assassin with smiles of joy and approbation. It was computed that, under the vague appellation of the friends of Geta, above twenty thousand persons of both sexes suffered death. His guards and freedmen, the ministers of his serious business, and the companions of his looser hours, those who by his interest had been promoted to any commands in the army or provinces, with the long connected chain of their dependants, were included in the proscription; which endeavored to reach every one who had maintained the smallest correspondence with Geta, who lamented his death, or who even mentioned his name. [26] Helvius Pertinax, son to the prince of that name, lost his life by an unseasonable witticism. [27] It was a sufficient crime of Thrasea Priscus to be descended from a family in which the love of liberty seemed an hereditary quality. [28] The particular causes of calumny and suspicion were at length exhausted; and when a senator was accused of being a secret enemy to the government, the emperor was satisfied with the general proof that he was a man of property and virtue. From this well-grounded principle he frequently drew the most bloody inferences. [28/1]

[Footnote 25: Dion, l. lxxvii. p. 1307]

[Footnote 25/1: The most valuable paragraph of dion, which the industry of M. Manas recovered, relates to this daughter of Marcus, executed by Caracalla. Her name, as appears from Fronto, as well as from Dion, was Cornificia. When commanded to choose the kind of death she was to suffer, she burst into womanish tears; but remembering her father Marcus, she thus spoke:—"O my hapless soul, (... animula,) now imprisoned in the body, burst forth! be free! show them, however reluctant to believe it, that thou art the daughter of Marcus." She then laid aside all her ornaments, and preparing herself for death, ordered her veins to be opened. Mai. Fragm. Vatican ii p. 220.—M.]

[Footnote 26: Dion, l. lxxvii. p. 1290. Herodian, l. iv. p. 150. Dion (p. 2298) says, that the comic poets no longer durst employ the name of Geta in their plays, and that the estates of those who mentioned it in their testaments were confiscated.]

[Footnote 27: Caracalla had assumed the names of several conquered nations; Pertinax observed, that the name of Geticus (he had obtained some advantage over the Goths, or Getae) would be a proper addition to Parthieus, Alemannicus, &c. Hist. August. p. 89.]

[Footnote 28: Dion, l. lxxvii. p. 1291. He was probably descended from Helvidius Priscus, and Thrasea Paetus, those patriots, whose firm, but useless and unseasonable, virtue has been immortalized by Tacitus. Note: M. Guizot is indignant at this "cold" observation of Gibbon on the noble character of Thrasea; but he admits that his virtue was useless to the public, and unseasonable amidst the vices of his age.—M.]

[Footnote 28/1: Caracalla reproached all those who demanded no favors of him. "It is clear that if you make me no requests, you do not trust me; if you do not trust me, you suspect me; if you suspect me, you fear me; if you fear me, you hate me." And forthwith he condemned them as conspirators, a good specimen of the sorites in a tyrant's logic. See Fragm. Vatican p.—M.]

PART II

The execution of so many innocent citizens was bewailed by the secret tears of their friends and families. The death of Papinian, the Praetorian Praefect, was lamented as a public calamity. [28/2] During the last seven years of Severus, he had exercised the most important offices of the state, and, by his salutary influence, guided the emperor's steps in the paths of justice and moderation. In full assurance of his virtue and abilities, Severus, on his death-bed, had conjured him to watch over the prosperity and union of the Imperial family. [29] The honest labors of Papinian served only to inflame the hatred which Caracalla had already conceived against his father's minister. After the murder of Geta, the Praefect was commanded to exert the powers of his skill and eloquence in a studied apology for that atrocious deed. The philosophic Seneca had condescended to compose a similar epistle to the senate, in the name of the son and assassin of Agrippina. [30] "That it was easier to commit than to justify a parricide," was the glorious reply of Papinian; [31] who did not hesitate between the loss of life and that of honor. Such intrepid virtue, which had escaped pure and unsullied from the intrigues courts, the habits of business, and the arts of his profession, reflects more lustre on the memory of Papinian, than all his great employments, his numerous writings, and the superior reputation as a lawyer, which he has preserved through every age of the Roman jurisprudence. [32]

[Footnote 28/2: Papinian was no longer Praetorian Praefect. Caracalla had deprived him of that office immediately after the death of Severus. Such is the statement of Dion; and the testimony of Spartian, who gives Papinian the Praetorian praefecture till his death, is of little weight opposed to that of a senator then living at Rome.—W.]

[Footnote 29: It is said that Papinian was himself a relation of the empress Julia.]

[Footnote 30: Tacit. Annal. xiv. 2.]

[Footnote 31: Hist. August. p. 88.]

[Footnote 32: With regard to Papinian, see Heineccius's Historia Juris Roma ni, l. 330, &c.]

It had hitherto been the peculiar felicity of the Romans, and in the worst of times the consolation, that the virtue of the emperors was active, and their vice indolent. Augustus, Trajan, Hadrian, and Marcus visited their extensive dominions in person, and their progress was marked by acts of wisdom and beneficence. The tyranny of Tiberius, Nero, and Domitian, who resided almost constantly at Rome, or in the adjacent was confined to the senatorial and equestrian orders. [33] But Caracalla was the common enemy of mankind. He left capital (and he never returned to it) about a year after the murder of Geta. The rest of his reign was spent in the several provinces of the empire, particularly those of the East, and province was by turns the scene of his rapine and cruelty. The senators, compelled by fear to attend his capricious motions,were obliged to provide daily entertainments at an immense expense, which he abandoned with contempt to his guards; and to erect, in every city, magnificent palaces and theatres, which he either disdained to visit, or ordered immediately thrown down. The most wealthy families ruined by partial fines and confiscations, and the great body of his subjects oppressed by ingenious and aggravated taxes. [34] In the midst of peace, and upon the slightest provocation, he issued his commands, at Alexandria, in Egypt for a general massacre. From a secure post in the temple of Serapis, he viewed and directed the slaughter of many thousand citizens, as well as strangers, without distinguishing the number or the crime of the sufferers; since as he coolly informed the senate, all the Alexandrians, those who perished, and those who had escaped, were alike guilty. [35]

[Footnote 33: Tiberius and Domitian never moved from the neighborhood of Rome. Nero made a short journey into Greece. "Et laudatorum Principum usus ex aequo, quamvis procul agentibus. Saevi proximis ingruunt." Tacit. Hist. iv. 74.]

[Footnote 34: Dion, l. lxxvii. p. 1294.]

[Footnote 35: Dion, l. lxxvii. p. 1307. Herodian, l. iv. p. 158. The former represents it as a cruel massacre, the latter as a perfidious one too. It seems probable that the Alexandrians has irritated the tyrant by their railleries, and perhaps by their tumults. Note: After these massacres, Caracalla also deprived the Alexandrians of their spectacles and public feasts; he divided the city into two parts by a wall with towers at intervals, to prevent the peaceful communications of the citizens. Thus was treated the unhappy Alexandria, says Dion, by the savage beast of Ausonia. This, in fact, was the epithet which the oracle had applied to him; it is said, indeed, that he was much pleased with the name and often boasted of it. Dion, lxxvii. p. 1307.—G.]

The wise instructions of Severus never made any lasting impression on the mind of his son, who, although not destitute of imagination and eloquence, was equally devoid of judgment and humanity. [36] One dangerous maxim, worthy of a tyrant, was remembered and abused by Caracalla. "To secure the affections of the army, and to esteem the rest of his subjects as of little moment." [37] But the liberality of the father had been restrained by prudence, and his indulgence to the troops was tempered by firmness and authority. The careless profusion of the son was the policy of one reign, and the inevitable ruin both of the army and of the empire. The vigor of the soldiers, instead of being confirmed by the severe discipline of camps, melted away in the luxury of cities. The excessive increase of their pay and donatives [38] exhausted the state to enrich the military order, whose modesty in peace, and service in war, is best secured by an honorable poverty. The demeanor of Caracalla was haughty and full of pride; but with the troops he forgot even the proper dignity of his rank, encouraged their insolent familiarity, and, neglecting the essential duties of a general, affected to imitate the dress and manners of a common soldier.

[Footnote 36: Dion, l. lxxvii. p. 1296.]

[Footnote 37: Dion, l. lxxvi. p. 1284. Mr. Wotton (Hist. of Rome, p. 330) suspects that this maxim was invented by Caracalla himself, and attributed to his father.]

[Footnote 38: Dion (l. lxxviii. p. 1343) informs us that the extraordinary gifts of Caracalla to the army amounted annually to seventy millions of drachmae (about two millions three hundred and fifty thousand pounds.) There is another passage in Dion, concerning the military pay, infinitely curious, were it not obscure, imperfect, and probably corrupt. The best sense seems to be, that the Praetorian guards received twelve hundred and fifty drachmae, (forty pounds a year) (Dion, l. lxxvii. p. 1307.) Under the reign of Augustus, they were paid at the rate of two drachmae, or denarii, per day, 720 a year, (Tacit. Annal. i. 17.) Domitian, who increased the soldiers' pay one fourth, must have raised the Praetorians to 960 drachmae, (Gronoviue de Pecunia Veteri, l. iii. c. 2.) These successive augmentations ruined the empire; for, with the soldiers' pay, their numbers too were increased. We have seen the Praetorians alone increased from 10,000 to 50,000 men. Note: Valois and Reimar have explained in a very simple and probable manner this passage of Dion, which Gibbon seems to me not to have understood. He ordered that the soldiers should receive, as the reward of their services the Praetorians 1250 drachms, the other 5000 drachms. Valois thinks that the numbers have been transposed, and that Caracalla added 5000 drachms to the donations made to the Praetorians, 1250 to those of the legionaries. The Praetorians, in fact, always received more than the others. The error of Gibbon arose from his considering that this referred to the annual pay of the soldiers, while it relates to the sum they received as a reward for their services on their discharge: donatives means recompense for service. Augustus had settled that the Praetorians, after sixteen campaigns, should receive 5000 drachms: the legionaries received only 3000 after twenty years. Caracalla added 5000 drachms to the donative of the Praetorians, 1250 to that of the legionaries. Gibbon appears to have been mistaken both in confounding this donative on discharge with the annual pay, and in not paying attention to the remark of Valois on the transposition of the numbers in the text.—G]

It was impossible that such a character, and such conduct as that of Caracalla, could inspire either love or esteem; but as long as his vices were beneficial to the armies, he was secure from the danger of rebellion. A secret conspiracy, provoked by his own jealousy, was fatal to the tyrant. The Praetorian praefecture was divided between two ministers. The military department was intrusted to Adventus, an experienced rather than able soldier; and the civil affairs were transacted by Opilius Macrinus, who, by his dexterity in business, had raised himself, with a fair character, to that high office. But his favor varied with the caprice of the emperor, and his life might depend on the slightest suspicion, or the most casual circumstance. Malice or fanaticism had suggested to an African, deeply skilled in the knowledge of futurity, a very dangerous prediction, that Macrinus and his son were destined to reign over the empire. The report was soon diffused through the province; and when the man was sent in chains to Rome, he still asserted, in the presence of the praefect of the city, the faith of his prophecy. That magistrate, who had received the most pressing instructions to inform himself of the successors of Caracalla, immediately communicated the examination of the African to the Imperial court, which at that time resided in Syria. But, notwithstanding the diligence of the public messengers, a friend of Macrinus found means to apprise him of the approaching danger. The emperor received the letters from Rome; and as he was then engaged in the conduct of a chariot race, he delivered them unopened to the Praetorian Praefect, directing him to despatch the ordinary affairs, and to report the more important business that might be contained in them. Macrinus read his fate, and resolved to prevent it. He inflamed the discontents of some inferior officers, and employed the hand of Martialis, a desperate soldier, who had been refused the rank of centurion. The devotion of Caracalla prompted him to make a pilgrimage from Edessa to the celebrated temple of the Moon at Carrhae. [381] He was attended by a body of cavalry: but having stopped on the road for some necessary occasion, his guards preserved a respectful distance, and Martialis, approaching his person under a presence of duty, stabbed him with a dagger. The bold assassin was instantly killed by a Scythian archer of the Imperial guard. Such was the end of a monster whose life disgraced human nature, and whose reign accused the patience of the Romans. [39] The grateful soldiers forgot his vices, remembered only his partial liberality, and obliged the senate to prostitute their own dignity and that of religion, by granting him a place among the gods. Whilst he was upon earth, Alexander the Great was the only hero whom this god deemed worthy his admiration. He assumed the name and ensigns of Alexander, formed a Macedonian phalanx of guards, persecuted the disciples of Aristotle, and displayed, with a puerile enthusiasm, the only sentiment by which he discovered any regard for virtue or glory. We can easily conceive, that after the battle of Narva, and the conquest of Poland, Charles XII. (though he still wanted the more elegant accomplishments of the son of Philip) might boast of having rivalled his valor and magnanimity; but in no one action of his life did Caracalla express the faintest resemblance of the Macedonian hero, except in the murder of a great number of his own and of his father's friends. [40]

[Footnote 381: Carrhae, now Harran, between Edessan and Nisibis, famous for the defeat of Crassus—the Haran from whence Abraham set out for the land of Canaan. This city has always been remarkable for its attachment to Sabaism—G]

[Footnote 39: Dion, l. lxxviii. p. 1312. Herodian, l. iv. p. 168.]

[Footnote 40: The fondness of Caracalla for the name and ensigns of Alexander is still preserved on the medals of that emperor. See Spanheim, de Usu Numismatum, Dissertat. xii. Herodian (l. iv. p. 154) had seen very ridiculous pictures, in which a figure was drawn with one side of the face like Alexander, and the other like Caracalla.]

After the extinction of the house of Severus, the Roman world remained three days without a master. The choice of the army (for the authority of a distant and feeble senate was little regarded) hung in anxious suspense, as no candidate presented himself whose distinguished birth and merit could engage their attachment and unite their suffrages. The decisive weight of the Praetorian guards elevated the hopes of their praefects, and these powerful ministers began to assert their legal claim to fill the vacancy of the Imperial throne. Adventus, however, the senior praefect, conscious of his age and infirmities, of his small reputation, and his smaller abilities, resigned the dangerous honor to the crafty ambition of his colleague Macrinus, whose well-dissembled grief removed all suspicion of his being accessary to his master's death. [41] The troops neither loved nor esteemed his character. They cast their eyes around in search of a competitor, and at last yielded with reluctance to his promises of unbounded liberality and indulgence. A short time after his accession, he conferred on his son Diadumenianus, at the age of only ten years, the Imperial title, and the popular name of Antoninus. The beautiful figure of the youth, assisted by an additional donative, for which the ceremony furnished a pretext, might attract, it was hoped, the favor of the army, and secure the doubtful throne of Macrinus.

[Footnote 41: Herodian, l. iv. p. 169. Hist. August. p. 94.]

The authority of the new sovereign had been ratified by the cheerful submission of the senate and provinces. They exulted in their unexpected deliverance from a hated tyrant, and it seemed of little consequence to examine into the virtues of the successor of Caracalla. But as soon as the first transports of joy and surprise had subsided, they began to scrutinize the merits of Macrinus with a critical severity, and to arraign the nasty choice of the army. It had hitherto been considered as a fundamental maxim of the constitution, that the emperor must be always chosen in the senate, and the sovereign power, no longer exercised by the whole body, was always delegated to one of its members. But Macrinus was not a senator. [42] The sudden elevation of the Praetorian praefects betrayed the meanness of their origin; and the equestrian order was still in possession of that great office, which commanded with arbitrary sway the lives and fortunes of the senate. A murmur of indignation was heard, that a man, whose obscure [43] extraction had never been illustrated by any signal service, should dare to invest himself with the purple, instead of bestowing it on some distinguished senator, equal in birth and dignity to the splendor of the Imperial station. As soon as the character of Macrinus was surveyed by the sharp eye of discontent, some vices, and many defects, were easily discovered. The choice of his ministers was in many instances justly censured, and the dissastified dissatisfied people, with their usual candor, accused at once his indolent tameness and his excessive severity. [44]

[Footnote 42: Dion, l. lxxxviii. p. 1350. Elagabalus reproached his predecessor with daring to seat himself on the throne; though, as Praetorian praefect, he could not have been admitted into the senate after the voice of the crier had cleared the house. The personal favor of Plautianus and Sejanus had broke through the established rule. They rose, indeed, from the equestrian order; but they preserved the praefecture, with the rank of senator and even with the annulship.]

[Footnote 43: He was a native of Caesarea, in Numidia, and began his fortune by serving in the household of Plautian, from whose ruin he narrowly escaped. His enemies asserted that he was born a slave, and had exercised, among other infamous professions, that of Gladiator. The fashion of aspersing the birth and condition of an adversary seems to have lasted from the time of the Greek orators to the learned grammarians of the last age.]

[Footnote 44: Both Dion and Herodian speak of the virtues and vices of Macrinus with candor and impartiality; but the author of his life, in the Augustan History, seems to have implicitly copied some of the venal writers, employed by Elagabalus, to blacken the memory of his predecessor.]

His rash ambition had climbed a height where it was difficult to stand with firmness, and impossible to fall without instant destruction. Trained in the arts of courts and the forms of civil business, he trembled in the presence of the fierce and undisciplined multitude, over whom he had assumed the command; his military talents were despised, and his personal courage suspected; a whisper that circulated in the camp, disclosed the fatal secret of the conspiracy against the late emperor, aggravated the guilt of murder by the baseness of hypocrisy, and heightened contempt by detestation. To alienate the soldiers, and to provoke inevitable ruin, the character of a reformer was only wanting; and such was the peculiar hardship of his fate, that Macrinus was compelled to exercise that invidious office. The prodigality of Caracalla had left behind it a long train of ruin and disorder; and if that worthless tyrant had been capable of reflecting on the sure consequences of his own conduct, he would perhaps have enjoyed the dark prospect of the distress and calamities which he bequeathed to his successors.

In the management of this necessary reformation, Macrinus proceeded with a cautious prudence, which would have restored health and vigor to the Roman army in an easy and almost imperceptible manner. To the soldiers already engaged in the service, he was constrained to leave the dangerous privileges and extravagant pay given by Caracalla; but the new recruits were received on the more moderate though liberal establishment of Severus, and gradually formed to modesty and obedience. [45] One fatal error destroyed the salutary effects of this judicious plan. The numerous army, assembled in the East by the late emperor, instead of being immediately dispersed by Macrinus through the several provinces, was suffered to remain united in Syria, during the winter that followed his elevation. In the luxurious idleness of their quarters, the troops viewed their strength and numbers, communicated their complaints, and revolved in their minds the advantages of another revolution. The veterans, instead of being flattered by the advantageous distinction, were alarmed by the first steps of the emperor, which they considered as the presage of his future intentions. The recruits, with sullen reluctance, entered on a service, whose labors were increased while its rewards were diminished by a covetous and unwarlike sovereign. The murmurs of the army swelled with impunity into seditious clamors; and the partial mutinies betrayed a spirit of discontent and disaffection that waited only for the slightest occasion to break out on every side into a general rebellion. To minds thus disposed, the occasion soon presented itself.

[Footnote 45: Dion, l. lxxxiii. p. 1336. The sense of the author is as the intention of the emperor; but Mr. Wotton has mistaken both, by understanding the distinction, not of veterans and recruits, but of old and new legions. History of Rome, p. 347.]

The empress Julia had experienced all the vicissitudes of fortune. From an humble station she had been raised to greatness, only to taste the superior bitterness of an exalted rank. She was doomed to weep over the death of one of her sons, and over the life of the other. The cruel fate of Caracalla, though her good sense must have long taught her to expect it, awakened the feelings of a mother and of an empress. Notwithstanding the respectful civility expressed by the usurper towards the widow of Severus, she descended with a painful struggle into the condition of a subject, and soon withdrew herself, by a voluntary death, from the anxious and humiliating dependence. [46] [46/1] Julia Maesa, her sister, was ordered to leave the court and Antioch. She retired to Emesa with an immense fortune, the fruit of twenty years' favor accompanied by her two daughters, Soaemias and Mamae, each of whom was a widow, and each had an only son. Bassianus, [46/2] for that was the name of the son of Soaemias, was consecrated to the honorable ministry of high priest of the Sun; and this holy vocation, embraced either from prudence or superstition, contributed to raise the Syrian youth to the empire of Rome. A numerous body of troops was stationed at Emesa; and as the severe discipline of Macrinus had constrained them to pass the winter encamped, they were eager to revenge the cruelty of such unaccustomed hardships. The soldiers, who resorted in crowds to the temple of the Sun, beheld with veneration and delight the elegant dress and figure of the young pontiff; they recognized, or they thought that they recognized, the features of Caracalla, whose memory they now adored. The artful Maesa saw and cherished their rising partiality, and readily sacrificing her daughter's reputation to the fortune of her grandson, she insinuated that Bassianus was the natural son of their murdered sovereign. The sums distributed by her emissaries with a lavish hand silenced every objection, and the profusion sufficiently proved the affinity, or at least the resemblance, of Bassianus with the great original. The young Antoninus (for he had assumed and polluted that respectable name) was declared emperor by the troops of Emesa, asserted his hereditary right, and called aloud on the armies to follow the standard of a young and liberal prince, who had taken up arms to revenge his father's death and the oppression of the military order. [47]

[Footnote 46: Dion, l. lxxviii. p. 1330. The abridgment of Xiphilin, though less particular, is in this place clearer than the original.]

[Footnote 46/1: As soon as this princess heard of the death of Caracalla, she wished to starve herself to death: the respect shown to her by Macrinus, in making no change in her attendants or her court, induced her to prolong her life. But it appears, as far as the mutilated text of Dion and the imperfect epitome of Xiphilin permit us to judge, that she conceived projects of ambition, and endeavored to raise herself to the empire. She wished to tread in the steps of Semiramis and Nitocris, whose country bordered on her own. Macrinus sent her an order immediately to leave Antioch, and to retire wherever she chose. She returned to her former purpose, and starved herself to death.—G.]

[Footnote 462: He inherited this name from his great-grandfather of the mother's side, Bassianus, father of Julia Maesa, his grandmother, and of Julia Domna, wife of Severus. Victor (in his epitome) is perhaps the only historian who has given the key to this genealogy, when speaking of Caracalla. His Bassianus ex avi materni nomine dictus. Caracalla, Elagabalus, and Alexander Seyerus, bore successively this name.—G.]

[Footnote 47: According to Lampridius, (Hist. August. p. 135,) Alexander Severus lived twenty-nine years three months and seven days. As he was killed March 19, 235, he was born December 12, 205 and was consequently about this time thirteen years old, as his elder cousin might be about seventeen. This computation suits much better the history of the young princes than that of Herodian, (l. v. p. 181,) who represents them as three years younger; whilst, by an opposite error of chronology, he lengthens the reign of Elagabalus two years beyond its real duration. For the particulars of the conspiracy, see Dion, l. lxxviii. p. 1339. Herodian, l. v. p. 184.]

Whilst a conspiracy of women and eunuchs was concerted with prudence, and conducted with rapid vigor, Macrinus, who, by a decisive motion, might have crushed his infant enemy, floated between the opposite extremes of terror and security, which alike fixed him inactive at Antioch. A spirit of rebellion diffused itself through all the camps and garrisons of Syria, successive detachments murdered their officers, [48] and joined the party of the rebels; and the tardy restitution of military pay and privileges was imputed to the acknowledged weakness of Macrinus. At length he marched out of Antioch, to meet the increasing and zealous army of the young pretender. His own troops seemed to take the field with faintness and reluctance; but, in the heat of the battle, [49] the Praetorian guards, almost by an involuntary impulse, asserted the superiority of their valor and discipline. The rebel ranks were broken; when the mother and grandmother of the Syrian prince, who, according to their eastern custom, had attended the army, threw themselves from their covered chariots, and, by exciting the compassion of the soldiers, endeavored to animate their drooping courage. Antoninus himself, who, in the rest of his life, never acted like a man, in this important crisis of his fate, approved himself a hero, mounted his horse, and, at the head of his rallied troops, charged sword in hand among the thickest of the enemy; whilst the eunuch Gannys, [49/1] whose occupations had been confined to female cares and the soft luxury of Asia, displayed the talents of an able and experienced general. The battle still raged with doubtful violence, and Macrinus might have obtained the victory, had he not betrayed his own cause by a shameful and precipitate flight. His cowardice served only to protract his life a few days, and to stamp deserved ignominy on his misfortunes. It is scarcely necessary to add, that his son Diadumenianus was involved in the same fate.

As soon as the stubborn Praetorians could be convinced that they fought for a prince who had basely deserted them, they surrendered to the conqueror: the contending parties of the Roman army, mingling tears of joy and tenderness, united under the banners of the imagined son of Caracalla, and the East acknowledged with pleasure the first emperor of Asiatic extraction.

[Footnote 48: By a most dangerous proclamation of the pretended Antoninus, every soldier who brought in his officer's head became entitled to his private estate, as well as to his military commission.]

[Footnote 49: Dion, l. lxxviii. p. 1345. Herodian, l. v. p. 186. The battle was fought near the village of Immae, about two-and-twenty miles from Antioch.]

[Footnote 49/1: Gannys was not a eunuch. Dion, p. 1355.—W]

The letters of Macrinus had condescended to inform the senate of the slight disturbance occasioned by an impostor in Syria, and a decree immediately passed, declaring the rebel and his family public enemies; with a promise of pardon, however, to such of his deluded adherents as should merit it by an immediate return to their duty. During the twenty days that elapsed from the declaration of the victory of Antoninus, (for in so short an interval was the fate of the Roman world decided,) the capital and the provinces, more especially those of the East, were distracted with hopes and fears, agitated with tumult, and stained with a useless effusion of civil blood, since whosoever of the rivals prevailed in Syria must reign over the empire. The specious letters in which the young conqueror announced his victory to the obedient senate were filled with professions of virtue and moderation; the shining examples of Marcus and Augustus, he should ever consider as the great rule of his administration; and he affected to dwell with pride on the striking resemblance of his own age and fortunes with those of Augustus, who in the earliest youth had revenged, by a successful war, the murder of his father. By adopting the style of Marcus Aurelius Antoninus, son of Antoninus and grandson of Severus, he tacitly asserted his hereditary claim to the empire; but, by assuming the tribunitian and proconsular powers before they had been conferred on him by a decree of the senate, he offended the delicacy of Roman prejudice. This new and injudicious violation of the constitution was probably dictated either by the ignorance of his Syrian courtiers, or the fierce disdain of his military followers. [50]

[Footnote 50: Dion, l. lxxix. p. 1353.]

As the attention of the new emperor was diverted by the most trifling amusements, he wasted many months in his luxurious progress from Syria to Italy, passed at Nicomedia his first winter after his victory, and deferred till the ensuing summer his triumphal entry into the capital. A faithful picture, however, which preceded his arrival, and was placed by his immediate order over the altar of Victory in the senate house, conveyed to the Romans the just but unworthy resemblance of his person and manners. He was drawn in his sacerdotal robes of silk and gold, after the loose flowing fashion of the Medes and Phoenicians; his head was covered with a lofty tiara, his numerous collars and bracelets were adorned with gems of an inestimable value. His eyebrows were tinged with black, and his cheeks painted with an artificial red and white. [51] The grave senators confessed with a sigh, that, after having long experienced the stern tyranny of their own countrymen, Rome was at length humbled beneath the effeminate luxury of Oriental despotism.

[Footnote 51: Dion, l. lxxix. p. 1363. Herodian, l. v. p. 189.]

The Sun was worshipped at Emesa, under the name of Elagabalus, [52] and under the form of a black conical stone, which, as it was universally believed, had fallen from heaven on that sacred place. To this protecting deity, Antoninus, not without some reason, ascribed his elevation to the throne. The display of superstitious gratitude was the only serious business of his reign. The triumph of the god of Emesa over all the religions of the earth, was the great object of his zeal and vanity; and the appellation of Elagabalus (for he presumed as pontiff and favorite to adopt that sacred name) was dearer to him than all the titles of Imperial greatness. In a solemn procession through the streets of Rome, the way was strewed with gold dust; the black stone, set in precious gems, was placed on a chariot drawn by six milk-white horses richly caparisoned. The pious emperor held the reins, and, supported by his ministers, moved slowly backwards, that he might perpetually enjoy the felicity of the divine presence. In a magnificent temple raised on the Palatine Mount, the sacrifices of the god Elagabalus were celebrated with every circumstance of cost and solemnity. The richest wines, the most extraordinary victims, and the rarest aromatics, were profusely consumed on his altar. Around the altar, a chorus of Syrian damsels performed their lascivious dances to the sound of barbarian music, whilst the gravest personages of the state and army, clothed in long Phoenician tunics, officiated in the meanest functions, with affected zeal and secret indignation. [53]

[Footnote 52: This name is derived by the learned from two Syrian words, Ela a God, and Gabal, to form, the forming or plastic god, a proper, and even happy epithet for the sun. Wotton's History of Rome, p. 378 Note: The name of Elagabalus has been disfigured in various ways. Herodian calls him; Lampridius, and the more modern writers, make him Heliogabalus. Dion calls him Elegabalus; but Elegabalus was the true name, as it appears on the medals. (Eckhel. de Doct. num. vet. t. vii. p. 250.) As to its etymology, that which Gibbon adduces is given by Bochart, Chan. ii. 5; but Salmasius, on better grounds. (not. in Lamprid. in Elagab.,) derives the name of Elagabalus from the idol of that god, represented by Herodian and the medals in the form of a mountain, (gibel in Hebrew,) or great stone cut to a point, with marks which represent the sun. As it was not permitted, at Hierapolis, in Syria, to make statues of the sun and moon, because, it was said, they are themselves sufficiently visible, the sun was represented at Emesa in the form of a great stone, which, as it appeared, had fallen from heaven. Spanheim, Caesar. notes, p. 46.—G. The name of Elagabalus, in "nummis rarius legetur." Rasche, Lex. Univ. Ref. Numm. Rasche quotes two.—M]

[Footnote 53: Herodian, l. v. p. 190.]

PART III

To this temple, as to the common centre of religious worship, the Imperial fanatic attempted to remove the Ancilia, the Palladium, [54] and all the sacred pledges of the faith of Numa. A crowd of inferior deities attended in various stations the majesty of the god of Emesa; but his court was still imperfect, till a female of distinguished rank was admitted to his bed. Pallas had been first chosen for his consort; but as it was dreaded lest her warlike terrors might affright the soft delicacy of a Syrian deity, the Moon, adorned by the Africans under the name of Astarte, was deemed a more suitable companion for the Sun. Her image, with the rich offerings of her temple as a marriage portion, was transported with solemn pomp from Carthage to Rome, and the day of these mystic nuptials was a general festival in the capital and throughout the empire. [55]

[Footnote 54: He broke into the sanctuary of Vesta, and carried away a statue, which he supposed to be the palladium; but the vestals boasted that, by a pious fraud, they had imposed a counterfeit image on the profane intruder. Hist. August., p. 103.]

[Footnote 55: Dion, l. lxxix. p. 1360. Herodian, l. v. p. 193. The subjects of the empire were obliged to make liberal presents to the new married couple; and whatever they had promised during the life of Elagabalus was carefully exacted under the administration of Mamaea.]

A rational voluptuary adheres with invariable respect to the temperate dictates of nature, and improves the gratifications of sense by social intercourse, endearing connections, and the soft coloring of taste and the imagination. But Elagabalus, (I speak of the emperor of that name,) corrupted by his youth, his country, and his fortune, abandoned himself to the grossest pleasures with ungoverned fury, and soon found disgust and satiety in the midst of his enjoyments. The inflammatory powers of art were summoned to his aid: the confused multitude of women, of wines, and of dishes, and the studied variety of attitude and sauces, served to revive his languid appetites. New terms and new inventions in these sciences, the only ones cultivated and patronized by the monarch, [56] signalized his reign, and transmitted his infamy to succeeding times. A capricious prodigality supplied the want of taste and elegance; and whilst Elagabalus lavished away the treasures of his people in the wildest extravagance, his own voice and that of his flatterers applauded a spirit of magnificence unknown to the tameness of his predecessors. To confound the order of seasons and climates, [57] to sport with the passions and prejudices of his subjects, and to subvert every law of nature and decency, were in the number of his most delicious amusements. A long train of concubines, and a rapid succession of wives, among whom was a vestal virgin, ravished by force from her sacred asylum, [58] were insufficient to satisfy the impotence of his passions. The master of the Roman world affected to copy the dress and manners of the female sex, preferred the distaff to the sceptre, and dishonored the principal dignities of the empire by distributing them among his numerous lovers; one of whom was publicly invested with the title and authority of the emperor's, or, as he more properly styled himself, of the empress's husband. [59]

[Footnote 56: The invention of a new sauce was liberally rewarded; but if it was not relished, the inventor was confined to eat of nothing else till he had discoveredanother more agreeable to the Imperial palate Hist. August. p. 111.]

[Footnote 57: He never would eat sea-fish except at a great distance from the sea; he then would distribute vast quantities of the rarest sorts, brought at an immense expense, to the peasants of the inland country. Hist. August. p. 109.]

[Footnote 58: Dion, l. lxxix. p. 1358. Herodian, l. v. p. 192.]

[Footnote 59: Hierocles enjoyed that honor; but he would have been supplanted by one Zoticus, had he not contrived, by a potion, to enervate the powers of his rival, who, being found on trial unequal to his reputation, was driven with ignominy from the palace. Dion, l. lxxix. p. 1363, 1364. A dancer was made praefect of the city, a charioteer praefect of the watch, a barber praefect of the provisions. These three *ministers, with many inferior officers, were all recommended enormitate membrorum. Hist. August. p. 105.]*

It may seem probable, the vices and follies of Elagabalus have been adorned by fancy, and blackened by prejudice. [60] Yet, confining ourselves to the public scenes displayed before the Roman people, and attested by grave and contemporary historians, their inexpressible infamy surpasses that of any other age or country. The license of an eastern monarch is secluded from the eye of curiosity by the inaccessible walls of his seraglio. The sentiments of honor and gallantry have introduced a refinement of pleasure, a regard for decency, and a respect for the public opinion, into the modern courts of Europe; [60/1] but the corrupt and opulent nobles of Rome gratified every vice that could be collected from the mighty conflux of nations and manners. Secure of impunity, careless of censure, they lived without restraint in the patient and humble society of their slaves and parasites. The emperor, in his turn, viewing every rank of his subjects with the same contemptuous indifference, asserted without control his sovereign privilege of lust and luxury.

[Footnote 60: Even the credulous compiler of his life, in the Augustan History (p. 111) is inclined to suspect that his vices may have been exaggerated.]

[Footnote 60/1: Wenck has justly observed that Gibbon should have reckoned the influence of Christianity in this great change. In the most savage times, and the most corrupt courts, since the introduction of Christianity there have been no Neros or Domitians, no Commodus or Elagabalus.—M.]

The most worthless of mankind are not afraid to condemn in others the same disorders which they allow in themselves; and can readily discover some nice difference of age, character, or station, to justify the partial distinction. The licentious soldiers, who had raised to the throne the dissolute son of Caracalla, blushed at their ignominious choice, and turned with disgust from that monster, to contemplate with pleasure the opening virtues of his cousin Alexander, the son of Mamaea. The crafty Maesa, sensible that her grandson Elagabalus must inevitably destroy himself by his own vices, had provided another and surer support of her family. Embracing a favorable moment of fondness and devotion, she had persuaded the young emperor to adopt Alexander, and to invest him with the title of Caesar, that his own divine occupations might be no longer interrupted by the care of the earth. In the second rank that amiable prince soon acquired the affections of the public, and excited the tyrant's jealousy, who resolved to terminate the dangerous competition, either by corrupting the manners, or by taking away the life, of his rival. His arts proved unsuccessful; his vain designs were constantly discovered by his own loquacious folly, and disappointed by those virtuous and faithful servants whom the prudence of Mamaea had placed about the person of her son. In a hasty sally of passion, Elagabalus resolved to execute by force what he had been unable to compass by fraud, and by a despotic sentence degraded his cousin from the rank and honors of Caesar. The message was received in the senate with silence, and in the camp with fury. The Praetorian guards swore to protect Alexander, and to revenge the dishonored majesty of the throne. The tears and promises of the trembling Elagabalus, who only begged them to spare his life, and to leave him in the possession of his beloved Hierocles, diverted their just indignation; and they contented themselves with empowering their praefects to watch over the safety of Alexander, and the conduct of the emperor. [61]

[Footnote 61: Dion, l. lxxix. p. 1365. Herodian, l. v. p. 195—201. Hist. August. p. 105. The last of the three historians seems to have followed the best authors in his account of the revolution.]

It was impossible that such a reconciliation should last, or that even the mean soul of Elagabalus could hold an empire on such humiliating terms of dependence. He soon attempted, by a dangerous experiment, to try the temper of the soldiers. The report of the death of Alexander, and the natural suspicion that he had been murdered, inflamed their passions into fury, and the tempest of the camp could only be appeased by the presence and authority of the popular youth. Provoked at this new instance of their affection for his cousin, and their contempt for his person, the emperor ventured to punish some of the leaders of the mutiny. His unseasonable severity proved instantly fatal to his minions, his mother, and himself. Elagabalus was massacred by the indignant Praetorians, his mutilated corpse dragged through the streets of the city, and thrown into the Tiber. His memory was branded with eternal infamy by the senate; the justice of whose decree has been ratified by posterity. [62]

[See Island In The Tiber: Elagabalus was thrown into the Tiber]

[Footnote 62: The aera of the death of Elagabalus, and of the accession of Alexander, has employed the learning and ingenuity of Pagi, Tillemont, Valsecchi, Vignoli, and Torre, bishop of Adria. The question is most assuredly intricate; but I still adhere to the authority of Dion, the truth of whose calculations is undeniable, and the purity of whose text is justified by the agreement of Xiphilin, Zonaras, and Cedrenus. Elagabalus reigned three years nine months and four days, from his victory over Macrinus, and was killed March 10, 222. But what shall we reply to the medals, undoubtedly genuine, which reckon the fifth year of his tribunitian power? We shall reply, with the learned Valsecchi, that the usurpation of Macrinus was annihilated, and that the son of Caracalla dated his reign from his father's death? After resolving this great difficulty, the smaller knots of this question may be easily untied, or cut asunder. Note: This opinion of Valsecchi has been triumphantly contested by Eckhel, who has shown the impossibility of reconciling it with the medals of Elagabalus, and has given the most satisfactory explanation of the five tribunates of that emperor. He ascended the throne and received the tribunitian power the 16th of May, in the year of Rome 971; and on the 1st January of the next year, 972, he began a new tribunate, according to the custom established by preceding emperors. During the years 972, 973, 974, he enjoyed the tribunate, and commenced his fifth in the year 975, during which he was killed on the 10th March. Eckhel de Doct. Num. viii. 430 &c.—G.]

In the room of Elagabalus, his cousin Alexander was raised to the throne by the Praetorian guards. His relation to the family of Severus, whose name he assumed, was the same as that of his predecessor; his virtue and his danger had already endeared him to the Romans, and the eager liberality of the senate conferred upon him, in one day, the various titles and powers of the Imperial dignity. [63] But as Alexander was a modest and dutiful youth, of only seventeen years of age, the reins of government were in the hands of two women, of his mother, Mamaea, and of Maesa, his grandmother. After the death of the latter, who survived but a short time the elevation of Alexander, Mamaea remained the sole regent of her son and of the empire.

[Footnote 63: Hist. August. p. 114. By this unusual precipitation, the senate meant to confound the hopes of pretenders, and prevent the factions of the armies.]

In every age and country, the wiser, or at least the stronger, of the two sexes, has usurped the powers of the state, and confined the other to the cares and pleasures of domestic life. In hereditary monarchies, however, and especially in those of modern Europe, the gallant spirit of chivalry, and the law of succession, have accustomed us to allow a singular exception; and a woman is often acknowledged the absolute sovereign of a great kingdom, in which she would be deemed incapable of exercising the smallest employment, civil or military. But as the Roman emperors were still considered as the generals and magistrates of the republic, their wives and mothers, although distinguished by the name of Augusta were never associated to their personal honors; and a female reign would have appeared an inexpiable prodigy in the eyes of those primitive Romans, who married without love, or loved without delicacy and respect. [64] The haughty Agripina aspired, indeed, to share the honors of the empire which she had conferred on her son; but her mad ambition, detested by every citizen who felt for the dignity of Rome, was disappointed by the artful firmness of Seneca and Burrhus. [65] The good sense, or the indifference, of succeeding princes, restrained them from offending the prejudices of their subjects; and it was reserved for the profligate Elagabalus to discharge the acts of the senate with the name of his mother Soaemias, who was placed by the side of the consuls, and subscribed, as a regular member, the decrees of the legislative assembly. Her more prudent sister, Mamaea, declined the useless and odious prerogative, and a solemn law was enacted, excluding women forever from the senate, and devoting to the infernal gods the head of the wretch by whom this sanction should be violated. [66] The substance, not the pageantry, of power. was the object of Mamaea's manly ambition. She maintained an absolute and lasting empire over the mind of her son, and in his affection the mother could not brook a rival. Alexander, with her consent, married the daughter of a patrician; but his respect for his father-in-law, and love for the empress, were inconsistent with the tenderness of interest of Mamaea. The patrician was executed on the ready accusation of treason, and the wife of Alexander driven with ignominy from the palace, and banished into Africa. [67]

[Footnote 64: Metellus Numidicus, the censor, acknowledged to the Roman people, in a public oration, that had kind nature allowed us to exist without the help of women, we should be delivered from a very troublesome companion; and he could recommend matrimony only as the sacrifice of private pleasure to public duty. Aulus Gellius, i. 6.]

[Footnote 65: Tacit. Annal. xiii. 5.]

[Footnote 66: Hist. August. p. 102, 107.]

[Footnote 67: Dion, l. lxxx. p. 1369. Herodian, l. vi. p. 206. Hist. August. p. 131. Herodian represents the patrician as innocent. The Augustian History, on the authority of Dexippus, condemns him, as guilty of a conspiracy against the life of Alexander. It is impossible to pronounce between them; but Dion is an irreproachable witness of the jealousy and cruelty of Mamaea towards the young empress, whose hard fate Alexander lamented, but durst not oppose.]

Notwithstanding this act of jealous cruelty, as well as some instances of avarice, with which Mamaea is charged, the general tenor of her administration was equally for the benefit of her son and of the empire. With the approbation of the senate, she chose sixteen of the wisest and most virtuous senators as a perpetual council of state, before whom every public business of moment was debated and determined. The celebrated Ulpian, equally distinguished by his knowledge of, and his respect for, the laws of Rome, was at their head; and the prudent firmness of this aristocracy restored order and authority to the government. As soon as they had purged the city from foreign superstition and luxury, the remains of the capricious tyranny of Elagabalus, they applied themselves to remove his worthless creatures from every department of the public administration, and to supply their places with men of virtue and ability. Learning, and the love of justice, became the only recommendations for civil offices; valor, and the love of discipline, the only qualifications for military employments. [68]

[Footnote 68: Herodian, l. vi. p. 203. Hist. August. p. 119. The latter insinuates, that when any law was to be passed, the council was assisted by a number of able lawyers and experienced senators, whose opinions were separately given, and taken down in writing.]

But the most important care of Mamaea and her wise counsellors, was to form the character of the young emperor, on whose personal qualities the happiness or misery of the Roman world must ultimately depend. The fortunate soil assisted, and even prevented, the hand of cultivation. An excellent understanding soon convinced Alexander of the advantages of virtue, the pleasure of knowledge, and the necessity of labor. A natural mildness and moderation of temper preserved him from the assaults of passion, and the allurements of vice. His unalterable regard for his mother, and his esteem for the wise Ulpian, guarded his unexperienced youth from the poison of flattery. [68/1]

[Footnote 68/1: Alexander received into his chapel all the religions which prevailed in the empire; he admitted Jesus Christ, Abraham, Orpheus, Apollonius of Tyana, &c. It was almost certain that his mother Mamaea had instructed him in the morality of Christianity. Historians in general agree in calling her a Christian; there is reason to believe that she had begun to have a taste for the principles of Christianity. (See Tillemont, Alexander Severus) Gibbon has not noticed this circumstance; he appears to have wished to lower the character of this empress; he has throughout followed the narrative of Herodian, who, by the acknowledgment of Capitolinus himself, detested Alexander. Without believing the exaggerated praises of Lampridius, he ought not to have followed the unjust severity of Herodian, and, above all, not to have forgotten to say that the virtuous Alexander Severus had insured to the Jews the preservation of their privileges, and permitted the exercise of Christianity. Hist. Aug. p. 121. The Christians had established their worship in a public place, of which the victuallers (cauponarii) claimed, not the property, but possession by custom. Alexander answered, that it was better that the place should be used for the service of God, in any form, than for victuallers.—G. I have scrupled to omit this note, as it contains some points worthy of notice; but it is very unjust to Gibbon, who mentions almost all the circumstances, which he is accused of omitting, in another, and, according to his plan, a better place, and, perhaps, in stronger terms than M. Guizot. See Chap. xvi.— M.]

The simple journal of his ordinary occupations exhibits a pleasing picture of an accomplished emperor, [69] and, with some allowance for the difference of manners, might well deserve the imitation of modern princes. Alexander rose early: the first moments of the day were consecrated to private devotion, and his domestic chapel was filled with the images of those heroes, who, by improving or reforming human life, had deserved the grateful reverence of posterity. But as he deemed the service of mankind the most acceptable worship of the gods, the greatest part of his morning hours was employed in his council, where he discussed public affairs, and determined private causes, with a patience and discretion above his years. The dryness of business was relieved by the charms of literature; and a portion of time was always set apart for his favorite studies of poetry, history, and philosophy. The works of Virgil and Horace, the republics of Plato and Cicero, formed his taste, enlarged his understanding, and gave him the noblest ideas of man and government. The exercises of the body succeeded to those of the mind; and Alexander, who was tall, active, and robust, surpassed most of his equals in the gymnastic arts. Refreshed by the use of the bath and a slight dinner, he resumed, with new vigor, the business of the day; and, till the hour of supper, the principal meal of the Romans, he was attended by his secretaries, with whom he read and answered the multitude of letters, memorials, and petitions, that must have been addressed to the master of the greatest part of the world. His table was served with the most frugal simplicity, and whenever he was at liberty to consult his own inclination, the company consisted of a few select friends, men of learning and virtue, amongst whom Ulpian was constantly invited. Their conversation was familiar and instructive; and the pauses were occasionally enlivened by the recital of some pleasing composition, which supplied the place of the dancers, comedians, and even gladiators, so frequently summoned to the tables of the rich and luxurious Romans. [70] The dress of Alexander was plain and modest, his demeanor courteous and affable: at the proper hours his palace was open to all his subjects, but the voice of a crier was heard, as in the Eleusinian mysteries, pronouncing the same salutary admonition: "Let none enter these holy walls, unless he is conscious of a pure and innocent mind." [71]

[Footnote 69: See his life in the Augustan History. The undistinguishing compiler has buried these interesting anecdotes under a load of trivial unmeaning circumstances.]

[Footnote 70: See the 13th Satire of Juvenal.]

[Footnote 71: Hist. August. p. 119.]

Such a uniform tenor of life, which left not a moment for vice or folly, is a better proof of the wisdom and justice of Alexander's government, than all the trifling details preserved in the compilation of Lampridius. Since the accession of Commodus, the Roman world had experienced, during the term of forty years, the successive and various vices of four tyrants. From the death of Elagabalus, it enjoyed an auspicious calm of thirteen years. [71/1] The provinces, relieved from the oppressive taxes invented by Caracalla and his pretended son, flourished in peace and prosperity, under the administration of magistrates, who were convinced by experience that to deserve the love of the subjects, was their best and only method of obtaining the favor of their sovereign. While some gentle restraints were imposed on the innocent luxury of the Roman people, the price of provisions and the interest of money, were reduced by the paternal care of Alexander, whose prudent liberality, without distressing the industrious, supplied the wants and amusements of the populace. The dignity, the freedom, the authority of the senate was restored; and every virtuous senator might approach the person of the emperor without a fear and without a blush.

[Footnote 71/1: Wenck observes that Gibbon, enchanted with the virtue of Alexander has heightened, particularly in this sentence, its effect on the state of the world. His own account, which follows, of the insurrections and foreign wars, is not in harmony with this beautiful picture.—M.]

The name of Antoninus, ennobled by the virtues of Pius and Marcus, had been communicated by adoption to the dissolute Verus, and by descent to the cruel Commodus. It became the honorable appellation of the sons of Severus, was bestowed on young Diadumenianus, and at length prostituted to the infamy of the high priest of Emesa. Alexander, though pressed by the studied, and, perhaps, sincere importunity of the senate, nobly refused the borrowed lustre of a name; whilst in his whole conduct he labored to restore the glories and felicity of the age of the genuine Antonines. [72]

[Footnote 72: See, in the Hist. August. p. 116, 117, the whole contest between Alexander and the senate, extracted from the journals of that assembly. It happened on the sixth of March, probably of the year 223, when the Romans had enjoyed, almost a twelvemonth, the blessings of his reign. Before the appellation of Antoninus was offered him as a title of honor, the senate waited to see whether Alexander would not assume it as a family name.]

In the civil administration of Alexander, wisdom was enforced by power, and the people, sensible of the public felicity, repaid their benefactor with their love and gratitude. There still remained a greater, a more necessary, but a more difficult enterprise; the reformation of the military order, whose interest and temper, confirmed by long impunity, rendered them impatient of the restraints of discipline, and careless of the blessings of public tranquillity. In the execution of his design, the emperor affected to display his love, and to conceal his fear of the army. The most rigid economy in every other branch of the administration supplied a fund of gold and silver for the ordinary pay and the extraordinary rewards of the troops. In their marches he relaxed the severe obligation of carrying seventeen days' provision on their shoulders. Ample magazines were formed along the public roads, and as soon as they entered the enemy's country, a numerous train of mules and camels waited on their haughty laziness. As Alexander despaired of correcting the luxury of his soldiers, he attempted, at least, to direct it to objects of martial pomp and ornament, fine horses, splendid armor, and shields enriched with silver and gold. He shared whatever fatigues he was obliged to impose, visited, in person, the sick and wounded, preserved an exact register of their services and his own gratitude, and expressed on every occasion, the warmest regard for a body of men, whose welfare, as he affected to declare, was so closely connected with that of the state. [73] By the most gentle arts he labored to inspire the fierce multitude with a sense of duty, and to restore at least a faint image of that discipline to which the Romans owed their empire over so many other nations, as warlike and more powerful than themselves. But his prudence was vain, his courage fatal, and the attempt towards a reformation served only to inflame the ills it was meant to cure.

[Footnote 73: It was a favorite saying of the emperor's Se milites magis servare, quam seipsum, quod salus publica in his esset. Hist. Aug. p. 130.]

The Praetorian guards were attached to the youth of Alexander. They loved him as a tender pupil, whom they had saved from a tyrant's fury, and placed on the Imperial throne. That amiable prince was sensible of the obligation; but as his gratitude was restrained within the limits of reason and justice, they soon were more dissatisfied with the virtues of Alexander, than they had ever been with the vices of Elagabalus. Their praefect, the wise Ulpian, was the friend of the laws and of the people; he was considered as the enemy of the soldiers, and to his pernicious counsels every scheme of reformation was imputed. Some trifling accident blew up their discontent into a furious mutiny; and the civil war raged, during three days, in Rome, whilst the life of that excellent minister was defended by the grateful people. Terrified, at length, by the sight of some houses in flames, and by the threats of a general conflagration, the people yielded with a sigh, and left the virtuous but unfortunate Ulpian to his fate. He was pursued into the Imperial palace, and massacred at the feet of his master, who vainly strove to cover him with the purple, and to obtain his pardon from the inexorable soldiers. [73/1] Such was the deplorable weakness of government, that the emperor was unable to revenge his murdered friend and his insulted dignity, without stooping to the arts of patience and dissimulation. Epagathus, the principal leader of the mutiny, was removed from Rome, by the honorable employment of praefect of Egypt: from that high rank he was gently degraded to the government of Crete; and when at length, his popularity among the guards was effaced by time and absence, Alexander ventured to inflict the tardy but deserved punishment of his crimes. [74] Under the reign of a just and virtuous prince, the tyranny of the army threatened with instant death his most faithful ministers, who were suspected of an intention to correct their intolerable disorders. The historian Dion Cassius had commanded the Pannonian legions with the spirit of ancient discipline. Their brethren of Rome, embracing the common cause of military license, demanded the head of the reformer. Alexander, however, instead of yielding to their seditious clamors, showed a just sense of his merit and services, by appointing him his colleague in the consulship, and defraying from his own treasury the expense of that vain dignity: but as was justly apprehended, that if the soldiers beheld him with the ensigns of his office, they would revenge the insult in his blood, the nominal first magistrate of the state retired, by the emperor's advice, from the city, and spent the greatest part of his consulship at his villas in Campania. [75] [75/1]

[Footnote 73/1: Gibbon has confounded two events altogether different— the quarrel of the people with the Praetorians, which lasted three days, and the assassination of Ulpian by the latter. Dion relates first the death of Ulpian, afterwards, reverting back according to a manner which is usual with him, he says that during the life of Ulpian, there had been a war of three days between the Praetorians and the people. But Ulpian was not the cause. Dion says, on the contrary, that it was occasioned by some unimportant circumstance; whilst he assigns a weighty reason for the murder of Ulpian, the judgment by which that Praetorian praefect had condemned his predecessors, Chrestus and Flavian, to death, whom the soldiers wished to revenge. Zosimus (l. 1, c. xi.) attributes this sentence to Mamaera; but, even then, the troops might have imputed it to Ulpian, who had reaped all the advantage and was otherwise odious to them.—W.]

[Footnote 74: Though the author of the life of Alexander (Hist. August. p. 182) mentions the sedition raised against Ulpian by the soldiers, he conceals the catastrophe, as it might discover a weakness in the administration of his hero. From this designed omission, we may judge of the weight and candor of that author.]

[Footnote 75: For an account of Ulpian's fate and his own danger, see the mutilated conclusion of Dion's History, l. lxxx. p. 1371.]

[Footnote 75/1: Dion possessed no estates in Campania, and was not rich. He only says that the emperor advised him to reside, during his consulate, in some place out of Rome; that he returned to Rome after the end of his consulate, and had an interview with the emperor in Campania. He asked and obtained leave to pass the rest of his life in his native city, (Nice, in Bithynia:) it was there that he finished his history, which closes with his second consulship.—W.]

PART IV

The lenity of the emperor confirmed the insolence of the troops; the legions imitated the example of the guards, and defended their prerogative of licentiousness with the same furious obstinacy. The administration of Alexander was an unavailing struggle against the corruption of his age. In Ilyricum, in Mauritania, in Armenia, in Mesopotamia, in Germany, fresh mutinies perpetually broke out; his officers were murdered, his authority was insulted, and his life at last sacrificed to the fierce discontents of the army. [76] One particular fact well deserves to be recorded, as it illustrates the manners of the troops, and exhibits a singular instance of their return to a sense of duty and obedience. Whilst the emperor lay at Antioch, in his Persian expedition, the particulars of which we shall hereafter relate, the punishment of some soldiers, who had been discovered in the baths of women, excited a sedition in the legion to which they belonged. Alexander ascended his tribunal, and with a modest firmness represented to the armed multitude the absolute necessity, as well as his inflexible resolution, of correcting the vices introduced by his impure predecessor, and of maintaining the discipline, which could not be relaxed without the ruin of the Roman name and empire. Their clamors interrupted his mild expostulation. "Reserve your shout," said the undaunted emperor, "till you take the field against the Persians, the Germans, and the Sarmatians. Be silent in the presence of your sovereign and benefactor, who bestows upon you the corn, the clothing, and the money of the provinces. Be silent, or I shall no longer style you solders, but citizens, [77] if those indeed who disclaim the laws of Rome deserve to be ranked among the meanest of the people." His menaces inflamed the fury of the legion, and their brandished arms already threatened his person. "Your courage," resumed the intrepid Alexander, "would be more nobly displayed in the field of battle; me you may destroy, you cannot intimidate; and the severe justice of the republic would punish your crime and revenge my death." The legion still persisted in clamorous sedition, when the emperor pronounced, with a loud voice, the decisive sentence, "Citizens! lay down your arms, and depart in peace to your respective habitations." The tempest was instantly appeased: the soldiers, filled with grief and shame, silently confessed the justice of their punishment, and the power of discipline, yielded up their arms and military ensigns, and retired in confusion, not to their camp, but to the several inns of the city. Alexander enjoyed, during thirty days, the edifying spectacle of their repentance; nor did he restore them to their former rank in the army, till he had punished with death those tribunes whose connivance had occasioned the mutiny. The grateful legion served the emperor whilst living, and revenged him when dead. [78]

[Footnote 76: Annot. Reimar. ad Dion Cassius, l. lxxx. p. 1369.]

[Footnote 77: Julius Caesar had appeased a sedition with the same word, Quirites; which, thus opposed to soldiers, was used in a sense of contempt, and reduced the offenders to the less honorable condition of mere citizens. Tacit. Annal. i. 43.]

[Footnote 78: Hist. August. p. 132.]

The resolutions of the multitude generally depend on a moment; and the caprice of passion might equally determine the seditious legion to lay down their arms at the emperor's feet, or to plunge them into his breast. Perhaps, if this singular transaction had been investigated by the penetration of a philosopher, we should discover the secret causes which on that occasion authorized the boldness of the prince, and commanded the obedience of the troops; and perhaps, if it had been related by a judicious historian, we should find this action, worthy of Caesar himself, reduced nearer to the level of probability and the common standard of the character of Alexander Severus. The abilities of that amiable prince seem to have been inadequate to the difficulties of his situation, the firmness of his conduct inferior to the purity of his intentions. His virtues, as well as the vices of Elagabalus, contracted a tincture of weakness and effeminacy from the soft climate of Syria, of which he was a native; though he blushed at his foreign origin, and listened with a vain complacency to the flattering genealogists, who derived his race from the ancient stock of Roman nobility. [79] The pride and avarice of his mother cast a shade on the glories of his reign; an by exacting from his riper years the same dutiful obedience which she had justly claimed from his unexperienced youth, Mamaea exposed to public ridicule both her son's character and her own. [80] The fatigues of the Persian war irritated the military discontent; the unsuccessful event [80/1] degraded the reputation of the emperor as a general, and even as a soldier. Every cause prepared, and every circumstance hastened, a revolution, which distracted the Roman empire with a long series of intestine calamities.

[Footnote 79: From the Metelli. Hist. August. p. 119. The choice was judicious. In one short period of twelve years, the Metelli could reckon seven consulships and five triumphs. See Velleius Paterculus, ii. 11, and the Fasti.]

[Footnote 80: The life of Alexander, in the Augustan History, is the mere idea of a perfect prince, an awkward imitation of the Cyropaedia. The account of his reign, as given by Herodian, is rational and moderate, consistent with the general history of the age; and, in some of the most invidious particulars, confirmed by the decisive fragments of Dion. Yet from a very paltry prejudice, the greater number of our modern writers abuse Herodian, and copy the Augustan History. See Mess de Tillemont and Wotton.

From the opposite prejudice, the emperor Julian (in Caesarib. p. 315) dwells with a visible satisfaction on the effeminate weakness of the Syrian, and the ridiculous avarice of his mother.]

[Footnote 80/1: Historians are divided as to the success of the campaign against the Persians; Herodian alone speaks of defeat. Lampridius, Eutropius, Victor, and others, say that it was very glorious to Alexander; that he beat Artaxerxes in a great battle, and repelled him from the frontiers of the empire. This much is certain, that Alexander, on his return to Rome, (Lamp. Hist. Aug. c. 56, 133, 134,) received the honors of a triumph, and that he said, in his oration to the people. Quirites, vicimus Persas, milites divites reduximus, vobis congiarium pollicemur, cras ludos circenses Persicos donabimus. Alexander, says Eckhel, had too much modesty and wisdom to permit himself to receive honors which ought only to be the reward of victory, if he had not deserved them; he would have contented himself with dissembling his losses. Eckhel, Doct. Num. vet. vii. 276. The medals represent him as in triumph; one, among others, displays him crowned by Victory between two rivers, the Euphrates and the Tigris. P. M. TR. P. xii. Cos. iii. PP. Imperator paludatus D. hastam. S. parazonium, stat inter duos fluvios humi jacentes, et ab accedente retro Victoria coronatur. Ae. max. mod. (Mus. Reg. Gall.) Although Gibbon treats this question more in detail when he speaks of the Persian monarchy, I have thought fit to place here what contradicts his opinion.—G]

The dissolute tyranny of Commodus, the civil wars occasioned by his death, and the new maxims of policy introduced by the house of Severus, had all contributed to increase the dangerous power of the army, and to obliterate the faint image of laws and liberty that was still impressed on the minds of the Romans. The internal change, which undermined the foundations of the empire, we have endeavored to explain with some degree of order and perspicuity. The personal characters of the emperors, their victories, laws, follies, and fortunes, can interest us no farther than as they are connected with the general history of the Decline and Fall of the monarchy. Our constant attention to that great object will not suffer us to overlook a most important edict of Antoninus Caracalla, which communicated to all the free inhabitants of the empire the name and privileges of Roman citizens. His unbounded liberality flowed not, however, from the sentiments of a generous mind; it was the sordid result of avarice, and will naturally be illustrated by some observations on the finances of that state, from the victorious ages of the commonwealth to the reign of Alexander Severus. The siege of Veii in Tuscany, the first considerable enterprise of the Romans, was protracted to the tenth year, much less by the strength of the place than by the unskillfulness of the besiegers. The unaccustomed hardships of so many winter campaigns, at the distance of near twenty miles from home, [81] required more than common encouragements; and the senate wisely prevented the clamors of the people, by the institution of a regular pay for the soldiers, which was levied by a general tribute, assessed according to an equitable proportion on the property of the citizens. [82] During more than two hundred years after the conquest of Veii, the victories of the republic added less to the wealth than to the power of Rome. The states of Italy paid their tribute in military service only, and the vast force, both by sea and land, which was exerted in the Punic wars, was maintained at the expense of the Romans themselves. That high-spirited people (such is often the generous enthusiasm of freedom) cheerfully submitted to the most excessive but voluntary burdens, in the just confidence that they should speedily enjoy the rich harvest of their labors. Their expectations were not disappointed. In the course of a few years, the riches of Syracuse, of Carthage, of Macedonia, and of Asia, were brought in triumph to Rome. The treasures of Perseus alone amounted to near two millions sterling, and the Roman people, the sovereign of so many nations, was forever delivered from the weight of taxes. [83] The increasing revenue of the provinces was found sufficient to defray the ordinary establishment of war and government, and the superfluous mass of gold and silver was deposited in the temple of Saturn, and reserved for any unforeseen emergency of the state. [84]

[Footnote 81: According to the more accurate Dionysius, the city itself was only a hundred stadia, or twelve miles and a half, from Rome, though some out-posts might be advanced farther on the side of Etruria. Nardini, in a professed treatise, has combated the popular opinion and the authority of two popes, and has removed Veii from Civita Castellana, to a little spot called Isola, in the midway between Rome and the Lake Bracianno. Note: See the interesting account of the site and ruins of Veii in Sir W Gell's topography of Rome and its Vicinity. v. ii. p. 303.—M.]

[Footnote 82: See the 4th and 5th books of Livy. In the Roman census, property, power, and taxation were commensurate with each other.]

[Footnote 83: Plin. Hist. Natur. l. xxxiii. c. 3. Cicero de Offic. ii. 22. Plutarch, P. Aemil. p. 275.]

[Footnote 84: See a fine description of this accumulated wealth of ages in Phars. l. iii. v. 155, &c.]

History has never, perhaps, suffered a greater or more irreparable injury than in the loss of the curious register [84/1] bequeathed by Augustus to the senate, in which that experienced prince so accurately balanced the revenues and expenses of the Roman empire. [85] Deprived of this clear and comprehensive estimate, we are reduced to collect a few imperfect hints from such of the ancients as have accidentally turned aside from the splendid to the more useful parts of history. We are informed that, by the conquests of Pompey, the tributes of Asia were raised from fifty to one hundred and thirty-five millions of drachms; or about four millions and a half sterling. [86] [86/1] Under the last and most indolent of the Ptolemies, the revenue of Egypt is said to have amounted to twelve thousand five hundred talents; a sum equivalent to more than two millions and a half of our money, but which was afterwards considerably improved by the more exact economy of the Romans, and the increase of the trade of Aethiopia and India. [87] Gaul was enriched by rapine, as Egypt was by commerce, and the tributes of those two great provinces have been compared as nearly equal to each other in value. [88] The ten thousand Euboic or Phoenician talents, about four millions sterling, [89] which vanquished Carthage was condemned to pay within the term of fifty years, were a slight acknowledgment of the superiority of Rome, [90] and cannot bear the least proportion with the taxes afterwards raised both on the lands and on the persons of the inhabitants, when the fertile coast of Africa was reduced into a province. [91]

[Footnote 84/1: See Rationarium imperii. Compare besides Tacitus, Suet. Aug. c. ult. Dion, p. 832. Other emperors kept and published similar registers. See a dissertation of Dr. Wolle, de Rationario imperii Rom. Leipsig, 1773. The last book of Appian also contained the statistics of the Roman empire, but it is lost.—W.]

[Footnote 85: Tacit. in Annal. i. ll. It seems to have existed in the time of Appian.]

[Footnote 86: Plutarch, in Pompeio, p. 642.]

[Footnote 86/1: Wenck contests the accuracy of Gibbon's version of Plutarch, and supposes that Pompey only raised the revenue from 50,000,000 to 85,000,000 of drachms; but the text of Plutarch seems clearly to mean that his conquests added 85,000,000 to the ordinary revenue. Wenck adds, "Plutarch says in another part, that Antony made Asia pay, at one time, 200,000 talents, that is to say, 38,875,000 L. sterling." But Appian explains this by saying that it was the revenue of ten years, which brings the annual revenue, at the time of Antony, to 3,875,000 L. sterling.—M.]

[Footnote 87: Strabo, l. xvii. p. 798.]

[Footnote 88: Velleius Paterculus, l. ii. c. 39. He seems to give the preference to the revenue of Gaul.]

[Footnote 89: The Euboic, the Phoenician, and the Alexandrian talents were double in weight to the Attic. See Hooper on ancient weights and measures, p. iv. c. 5. It is very probable that the same talent was carried from Tyre to Carthage.]

[Footnote 90: Polyb. l. xv. c. 2.]

[Footnote 91: Appian in Punicis, p. 84.]

Spain, by a very singular fatality, was the Peru and Mexico of the old world. The discovery of the rich western continent by the Phoenicians, and the oppression of the simple natives, who were compelled to labor in their own mines for the benefit of strangers, form an exact type of the more recent history of Spanish America. [92] The Phoenicians were acquainted only with the sea-coast of Spain; avarice, as well as ambition, carried the arms of Rome and Carthage into the heart of the country, and almost every part of the soil was found pregnant with copper, silver, and gold. [92/1] Mention is made of a mine near Carthagena which yielded every day twenty-five thousand drachmns of silver, or about three hundred thousand pounds a year. [93] Twenty thousand pound weight of gold was annually received from the provinces of Asturia, Gallicia, and Lusitania. [94]

[Footnote 92: Diodorus Siculus, l. 5. Oadiz was built by the Phoenicians a little more than a thousand years before Christ. See Vell. Pa ter. i.2.]

[Footnote 92/1: Compare Heeren's Researches vol. i. part ii. p.]

[Footnote 93: Strabo, l. iii. p. 148.]

[Footnote 94: Plin. Hist. Natur. l. xxxiii. c. 3. He mentions likewise a silver mine in Dalmatia, that yielded every day fifty pounds to the state.]

We want both leisure and materials to pursue this curious inquiry through the many potent states that were annihilated in the Roman empire. Some notion, however, may be formed of the revenue of the provinces where considerable wealth had been deposited by nature, or collected by man, if we observe the severe attention that was directed to the abodes of solitude and sterility. Augustus once received a petition from the inhabitants of Gyarus, humbly praying that they might be relieved from one third of their excessive impositions. Their whole tax amounted indeed to no more than one hundred and fifty drachms, or about five pounds: but Gyarus was a little island, or rather a rock, of the Aegean Sea, destitute of fresh water and every necessary of life, and inhabited only by a few wretched fishermen. [95]

[Footnote 95: Strabo, l. x. p. 485. Tacit. Annal. iu. 69, and iv. 30. See Tournefort (Voyages au Levant, Lettre viii.) a very lively picture of the actual misery of Gyarus.]

From the faint glimmerings of such doubtful and scattered lights, we should be inclined to believe, 1st, That (with every fair allowance for the differences of times and circumstances) the general income of the Roman provinces could seldom amount to less than fifteen or twenty millions of our money; [96] and, 2dly, That so ample a revenue must have been fully adequate to all the expenses of the moderate government instituted by Augustus, whose court was the modest family of a private senator, and whose military establishment was calculated for the defence of the frontiers, without any aspiring views of conquest, or any serious apprehension of a foreign invasion.

[Footnote 96: Lipsius de magnitudine Romana (l. ii. c. 3) computes the revenue at one hundred and fifty millions of gold crowns; but his whole book, though learned and ingenious, betrays a very heated imagination. Note: If Justus Lipsius has exaggerated the revenue of the Roman empire Gibbon, on the other hand, has underrated it. He fixes it at fifteen or twenty millions of our money. But if we take only, on a moderate calculation, the taxes in the provinces which he has already cited, they will amount, considering the augmentations made by Augustus, to nearly that sum. There remain also the provinces of Italy, of Rhaetia, of Noricum, Pannonia, and Greece, &c., &c. Let us pay attention, besides, to the prodigious expenditure of some emperors, (Suet. Vesp. 16;) we shall see that such a revenue could not be sufficient. The authors of the Universal History, part xii., assign forty millions sterling as the sum to about which the public revenue might amount.—G. from W.]

Notwithstanding the seeming probability of both these conclusions, the latter of them at least is positively disowned by the language and conduct of Augustus. It is not easy to determine whether, on this occasion, he acted as the common father of the Roman world, or as the oppressor of liberty; whether he wished to relieve the provinces, or to impoverish the senate and the equestrian order. But no sooner had he assumed the reins of government, than he frequently intimated the insufficiency of the tributes, and the necessity of throwing an equitable proportion of the public burden upon Rome and Italy. [96/1] In the prosecution of this unpopular design, he advanced, however, by cautious and well-weighed steps. The introduction of customs was followed by the establishment of an excise, and the scheme of taxation was completed by an artful assessment on the real and personal property of the Roman citizens, who had been exempted from any kind of contribution above a century and a half.

[Footnote 96/1: It is not astonishing that Augustus held this language. The senate declared also under Nero, that the state could not exist without the imposts as well augmented as founded by Augustus. Tac. Ann. xiii. 50. After the abolition of the different tributes paid by Italy, an abolition which took place A. U. 646, 694, and 695, the state derived no revenues from that great country, but the twentieth part of the manumissions, (vicesima manumissionum,) and Ciero laments this in many places, particularly in his epistles to ii. 15.—G. from W.]

I. In a great empire like that of Rome, a natural balance of money must have gradually established itself. It has been already observed, that as the wealth of the provinces was attracted to the capital by the strong hand of conquest and power, so a considerable part of it was restored to the industrious provinces by the gentle influence of commerce and arts. In the reign of Augustus and his successors, duties were imposed on every kind of merchandise, which through a thousand channels flowed to the great centre of opulence and luxury; and in whatsoever manner the law was expressed, it was the Roman purchaser, and not the provincial merchant, who paid the tax. [97] The rate of the customs varied from the eighth to the fortieth part of the value of the commodity; and we have a right to suppose that the variation was directed by the unalterable maxims of policy; that a higher duty was fixed on the articles of luxury than on those of necessity, and that the productions raised or manufactured by the labor of the subjects of the empire were treated with more indulgence than was shown to the pernicious, or at least the unpopular commerce of Arabia and India. [98] There is still extant a long but imperfect catalogue of eastern commodities, which about the time of Alexander

Severus were subject to the payment of duties; cinnamon, myrrh, pepper, ginger, and the whole tribe of aromatics a great variety of precious stones, among which the diamond was the most remarkable for its price, and the emerald for its beauty; [99] Parthian and Babylonian leather, cottons, silks, both raw and manufactured, ebony ivory, and eunuchs. [100] We may observe that the use and value of those effeminate slaves gradually rose with the decline of the empire.

[Footnote 97: Tacit. Annal. xiii. 31. Note: The customs (portoria) existed in the times of the ancient kings of Rome. They were suppressed in Italy, A. U. 694, by the Praetor, Cecilius Matellus Nepos. Augustus only reestablished them. See note above.—W.]

[Footnote 98: See Pliny, (Hist. Natur. l. vi. c. 23, lxii. c. 18.) His observation that the Indian commodities were sold at Rome at a hundred times their original price, may give us some notion of the produce of the customs, since that original price amounted to more than eight hundred thousand pounds.]

[Footnote 99: The ancients were unacquainted with the art of cutting diamonds.]

[Footnote 100: M. Bouchaud, in his treatise de l'Impot chez les Romains, has transcribed this catalogue from the Digest, and attempts to illustrate it by a very prolix commentary. Note: In the Pandects, l. 39, t. 14, de Publican. Compare Cicero in Verrem. c. 72—74.—W.]

II. The excise, introduced by Augustus after the civil wars, was extremely moderate, but it was general. It seldom exceeded one per cent.; but it comprehended whatever was sold in the markets or by public auction, from the most considerable purchases of lands and houses, to those minute objects which can only derive a value from their infinite multitude and daily consumption. Such a tax, as it affects the body of the people, has ever been the occasion of clamor and discontent. An emperor well acquainted with the wants and resources of the state was obliged to declare, by a public edict, that the support of the army depended in a great measure on the produce of the excise. [101]

[Footnote 101: Tacit. Annal. i. 78. Two years afterwards, the reduction of the poor kingdom of Cappadocia gave Tiberius a pretence for diminishing the excise of one half, but the relief was of very short duration.]

III. When Augustus resolved to establish a permanent military force for the defence of his government against foreign and domestic enemies, he instituted a peculiar treasury for the pay of the soldiers, the rewards of the veterans, and the extra-ordinary expenses of war. The ample revenue of the excise, though peculiarly appropriated to those uses, was found inadequate. To supply the deficiency, the emperor suggested a new tax of five per cent. on all legacies and inheritances. But the nobles of Rome were more tenacious of property than of freedom. Their indignant murmurs were received by Augustus with his usual temper. He candidly referred the whole business to the senate, and exhorted them to provide for the public service by some other expedient of a less odious nature. They were divided and perplexed. He insinuated to them, that their obstinacy would oblige him to propose a general land tax and capitation. They acquiesced in silence. [102]. The new imposition on legacies and inheritances was, however, mitigated by some restrictions. It did not take place unless the object was of a certain value, most probably of fifty or a hundred pieces of gold; [103] nor could it be exacted from the nearest of kin on the father's side. [104] When the rights of nature and poverty were thus secured, it seemed reasonable, that a stranger, or a distant relation, who acquired an unexpected accession of fortune, should cheerfully resign a twentieth part of it, for the benefit of the state. [105]

[Footnote 102: Dion Cassius, l. lv. p. 794, l. lvi. p. 825. Note: Dion neither mentions this proposition nor the capitation. He only says that the emperor imposed a tax upon landed property, and sent every where men employed to make a survey, without fixing how much, and for how much each was to pay. The senators then preferred giving the tax on legacies and inheritances.—W.]

[Footnote 103: The sum is only fixed by conjecture.]

[Footnote 104: As the Roman law subsisted for many ages, the Cognati, or relations on the mother's side, were not called to the succession. This harsh institution was gradually undermined by humanity, and finally abolished by Justinian.]

[Footnote 105: Plin. Panegyric. c. 37.]

Such a tax, plentiful as it must prove in every wealthy community, was most happily suited to the situation of the Romans, who could frame their arbitrary wills, according to the dictates of reason or caprice, without any restraint from the modern fetters of entails and settlements. From various causes, the partiality of paternal affection often lost its influence over the stern patriots of the commonwealth, and the dissolute nobles of the empire; and if the father bequeathed to his son the fourth part of his estate, he removed all ground of legal complaint. [106] But a rich childish old man was a domestic tyrant, and his power increased with his years and infirmities. A servile crowd, in which he frequently reckoned praetors and consuls, courted his smiles, pampered his avarice, applauded his follies, served his passions, and waited with impatience for his death. The arts of attendance and flattery were formed into a most lucrative science; those who professed it acquired a peculiar appellation; and the whole city, according to the lively descriptions of satire, was divided between two parties, the hunters and their game. [107] Yet, while so many unjust and extravagant wills were every day dictated by cunning and subscribed by folly, a few were the result of rational esteem and virtuous gratitude. Cicero, who had so often defended the lives and fortunes of his fellow-citizens, was rewarded with legacies to the amount of a hundred and seventy thousand pounds; [108] nor do the friends of the younger Pliny seem to have been less generous to that amiable orator. [109] Whatever was the motive of the testator, the treasury claimed, without distinction, the twentieth part of his estate: and in the course of two or three generations, the whole property of the subject must have gradually passed through the coffers of the state.

[Footnote 106: See Heineccius in the Antiquit. Juris Romani, l. ii.]

[Footnote 107: Horat. l. ii. Sat. v. Potron. c. 116, &c. Plin. l. ii. Epist. 20.]

[Footnote 108: Cicero in Philip. ii. c. 16.]

[Footnote 109: See his epistles. Every such will gave him an occasion of displaying his reverence to the dead, and his justice to the living. He reconciled both in his behavior to a son who had been disinherited by his mother, (v.l.)]

In the first and golden years of the reign of Nero, that prince, from a desire of popularity, and perhaps from a blind impulse of benevolence, conceived a wish of abolishing the oppression of the customs and excise. The wisest senators applauded his magnanimity: but they diverted him from the execution of a design which would have dissolved the strength and resources of the republic. [110] Had it indeed been possible to realize this dream of fancy, such princes as Trajan and the Antonines would surely have embraced with ardor the glorious opportunity of conferring so signal an obligation on mankind. Satisfied, however, with alleviating the public burden, they attempted not to remove it. The mildness and precision of their laws ascertained the rule and measure of taxation, and protected the subject of every rank against arbitrary interpretations, antiquated claims, and the insolent vexation of the farmers of the revenue. [111] For it is somewhat singular, that, in every age, the best and wisest of the Roman governors persevered in this pernicious method of collecting the principal branches at least of the excise and customs. [112]

[Footnote 110: Tacit. Annal. xiii. 50. Esprit des Loix, l. xii. c. 19.]

[Footnote 111: See Pliny's Panegyric, the Augustan History, and Burman de Vectigal. passim.]

[Footnote 112: The tributes (properly so called) were not farmed; since the good princes often remitted many millions of arrears.]

The sentiments, and, indeed, the situation, of Caracalla were very different from those of the Antonines. Inattentive, or rather averse, to the welfare of his people, he found himself under the necessity of gratifying the insatiate avarice which he had excited in the army. Of the several impositions introduced by Augustus, the twentieth on inheritances and legacies was the most fruitful, as well as the most comprehensive. As its influence was not confined to Rome or Italy, the produce continually increased with the gradual extension of the Roman City. The new citizens, though charged, on equal terms, [113] with the payment of new taxes, which had not affected them as subjects, derived an ample compensation from the rank they obtained, the privileges they acquired, and the fair prospect of honors and fortune that was thrown open to their ambition. But the favor which implied a distinction was lost in the prodigality of Caracalla, and the reluctant provincials were compelled to assume the vain title, and the real obligations, of Roman citizens. [113/1] Nor was the rapacious son of Severus contented with such a measure of taxation as had appeared sufficient to his moderate predecessors. Instead of a twentieth, he exacted a tenth of all legacies and inheritances; and during his reign (for the ancient proportion was restored after his death) he crushed alike every part of the empire under the weight of his iron sceptre. [114]

[Footnote 113: The situation of the new citizens is minutely described by Pliny, (Panegyric, c. 37, 38, 39). Trajan published a law very much in their favor.]

[Footnote 113/1: Gibbon has adopted the opinion of Spanheim and of Burman, which attributes to Caracalla this edict, which gave the right of the city to all the inhabitants of the provinces. This opinion may be disputed. Several passages of Spartianus, of Aurelius Victor, and of Aristides, attribute this edict to Marc. Aurelius. See a learned essay, entitled Joh. P. Mahneri Comm. de Marc. Aur. Antonino Constitutionis de Civitate Universo Orbi Romano data auctore. Halae, 1772, 8vo. It appears that Marc. Aurelius made some modifications of this edict, which released the provincials from some of the charges imposed by the right of the city, and deprived them of some of the advantages which it conferred. Caracalla annulled these modifications.—W.]

[Footnote 114: Dion, l. lxxvii. p. 1295.]

When all the provincials became liable to the peculiar impositions of Roman citizens, they seemed to acquire a legal exemption from the tributes which they had paid in their former condition of subjects. Such were not the maxims of government adopted by Caracalla and his pretended son. The old as well as the new taxes were, at the same time, levied in the provinces. It was reserved for the virtue of Alexander to relieve them in a great measure from this intolerable grievance, by reducing the tributes to a thirteenth part of the sum exacted at the time of his accession. [115] It is impossible to conjecture the motive that engaged him to spare so trifling a remnant of the public evil; but the noxious weed, which had not been totally eradicated, again sprang up with the most luxuriant growth, and in the succeeding age darkened the Roman world with its deadly shade. In the course of this history, we shall be too often summoned to explain the land tax, the capitation, and the heavy contributions of corn, wine, oil, and meat, which were exacted from the provinces for the use of the court, the army, and the capital.

[Footnote 115: He who paid ten aurei, the usual tribute, was charged with no more than the third part of an aureus, and proportional pieces of gold were coined by Alexander's order. Hist. August. p. 127, with the commentary of Salmasius.]

As long as Rome and Italy were respected as the centre of government, a national spirit was preserved by the ancient, and insensibly imbibed by the adopted, citizens. The principal commands of the army were filled by men who had received a liberal education, were well instructed in the advantages of laws and letters, and who had risen, by equal steps, through the regular succession of civil and military honors. [116] To their influence and example we may partly ascribe the modest obedience of the legions during the two first centuries of the Imperial history.

[Footnote 116: See the lives of Agricola, Vespasian, Trajan, Severus, and his three competitors; and indeed of all the eminent men of those times. But when the last enclosure of the Roman constitution was trampled down by Caracalla, the separation of professions gradually succeeded to the distinction of ranks. The more polished citizens of the internal provinces were alone qualified to act as lawyers and magistrates. The rougher trade of arms was abandoned to the peasants and barbarians of the frontiers, who knew no country but their camp, no science but that of war no civil laws, and scarcely those of military discipline. With bloody hands, savage manners, and desperate resolutions, they sometimes guarded, but much oftener subverted, the throne of the emperors.]

CHAPTER VII

TYRANNY OF MAXIMIN, REBELLION, CIVIL WARS, DEATH OF MAXIMIN

PART I

THE ELEVATION AND TYRANNY OF MAXIMIN—REBELLION IN AFRICA AND ITALY, UNDER THE AUTHORITY OF THE SENATE—CIVIL WARS AND SEDITION—VIOLENT DEATHS OF MAXIMIN AND HIS SON, OF MAXIMUS AND BALBINUS, AND OF THE THREE GORDIAN—USURPATION AND SECULAR GAMES OF PHILIP

Of the various forms of government which have prevailed in the world, an hereditary monarchy seems to present the fairest scope for ridicule. Is it possible to relate without an indignant smile, that, on the father's decease, the property of a nation, like that of a drove of oxen, descends to his infant son, as yet unknown to mankind and to himself; and that the bravest warriors and the wisest statesmen, relinquishing their natural right to empire, approach the royal cradle with bended knees and protestations of inviolable fidelity? Satire and declamation may paint these obvious topics in the most dazzling colors, but our more serious thoughts will respect a useful prejudice, that establishes a rule of succession, independent of the passions of mankind; and we shall cheerfully acquiesce in any expedient which deprives the multitude of the dangerous, and indeed the ideal, power of giving themselves a master.

In the cool shade of retirement, we may easily devise imaginary forms of government, in which the sceptre shall be constantly bestowed on the most worthy, by the free and incorrupt suffrage of the whole community. Experience overturns these airy fabrics, and teaches us, that in a large society, the election of a monarch can never devolve to the wisest, or to the most numerous part of the people. The army is the only order of men sufficiently united to concur in the same sentiments, and powerful enough to impose them on the rest of their fellow-citizens; but the temper of soldiers, habituated at once to violence and to slavery, renders them very unfit guardians of a legal, or even a civil constitution. Justice, humanity, or political wisdom, are qualities they are too little acquainted with in themselves, to appreciate them in others. Valor will acquire their esteem, and liberality will purchase their suffrage; but the first of these merits is often lodged in the most savage breasts; the latter can only exert itself at the expense of the public; and both may be turned against the possessor of the throne, by the ambition of a daring rival.

The superior prerogative of birth, when it has obtained the sanction of time and popular opinion, is the plainest and least invidious of all distinctions among mankind. The acknowledged right extinguishes the hopes of faction, and the conscious security disarms the cruelty of the monarch. To the firm establishment of this idea we owe the peaceful succession and mild administration of European monarchies. To the defect of it we must attribute the frequent civil wars, through which an Asiatic despot is obliged to cut his way to the throne of his fathers. Yet, even in the East, the sphere of contention is usually limited to the princes of the reigning house, and as soon as the more fortunate competitor has removed his brethren by the sword and the bowstring, he no longer entertains any jealousy of his meaner subjects. But the Roman empire, after the authority of the senate had sunk into contempt, was a vast scene of confusion. The royal, and even noble, families of the provinces had long since been led in triumph before the car of the haughty republicans. The ancient families of Rome had successively fallen beneath the tyranny of the Caesars; and whilst those princes were shackled by the forms of a commonwealth, and disappointed by the repeated failure of their posterity, [1] it was impossible that any idea of hereditary succession should have taken root in the minds of their subjects. The right to the throne, which none could claim from birth, every one assumed from merit. The daring hopes of ambition were set loose from the salutary restraints of law and prejudice; and the meanest of mankind might, without folly, entertain a hope of being raised by valor and fortune to a rank in the army, in which a single crime would enable him to wrest the sceptre of the world from his feeble and unpopular master. After the murder of Alexander Severus, and the elevation of Maximin, no emperor could think himself safe upon the throne, and every barbarian peasant of the frontier might aspire to that august, but dangerous station.

[Footnote 1: There had been no example of three successive generations on the throne; only three instances of sons who succeeded their fathers. The marriages of the Caesars (notwithstanding the permission, and the frequent practice of divorces) were generally unfruitful.]

About thirty-two years before that event, the emperor Severus, returning from an eastern expedition, halted in Thrace, to celebrate, with military games, the birthday of his younger son, Geta. The country flocked in crowds to behold their sovereign, and a young barbarian of gigantic stature earnestly solicited, in his rude dialect, that he might be allowed to contend for the prize of wrestling. As the pride of discipline would have been disgraced in the overthrow of a Roman soldier by a Thracian peasant, he was matched with the stoutest followers of the camp, sixteen of whom he successively laid on the ground. His victory was rewarded by some trifling gifts, and a permission to enlist in the troops. The next day, the happy barbarian was distinguished above a crowd of recruits, dancing and exulting after the fashion of his country. As soon as he perceived that he had attracted the emperor's notice, he instantly ran up to his horse, and followed him on foot, without the least appearance of fatigue, in a long and rapid career. "Thracian," said Severus with astonishment, "art thou disposed to wrestle after thy race?" "Most willingly, sir," replied the unwearied youth; and, almost in a breath, overthrew seven of the strongest soldiers in the army. A gold collar was the prize of his matchless vigor and activity, and he was immediately appointed to serve in the horseguards who always attended on the person of the sovereign. [2]

[Footnote 2: Hist. August p. 138.]

Maximin, for that was his name, though born on the territories of the empire, descended from a mixed race of barbarians. His father was a Goth, and his mother of the nation of the Alani. He displayed on every occasion a valor equal to his strength; and his native fierceness was soon tempered or disguised by the knowledge of the world. Under the reign of Severus and his son, he obtained the rank of centurion, with the favor and esteem of both those princes, the former of whom was an excellent judge of merit. Gratitude forbade Maximin to serve under the assassin of Caracalla. Honor taught him to decline the effeminate insults of Elagabalus. On the accession of Alexander he returned to court, and was placed by that prince in a station useful to the service, and honorable to himself. The fourth legion, to which he was appointed tribune, soon became, under his care, the best disciplined of the whole army. With the general applause of the soldiers, who bestowed on their favorite hero the names of Ajax and Hercules, he was successively promoted to the first military command; [3] and had not he still retained too much of his savage origin, the emperor might perhaps have given his own sister in marriage to the son of Maximin. [4]

[Footnote 3: Hist. August. p. 140. Herodian, l. vi. p. 223. Aurelius Victor. By comparing these authors, it should seem that Maximin had the particular command of the Tribellian horse, with the general commission of disciplining the recruits of the whole army. His biographer ought to have marked, with more care, his exploits, and the successive steps of his military promotions.]

[Footnote 4: See the original letter of Alexander Severus, Hist. August. p. 149.]

Instead of securing his fidelity, these favors served only to inflame the ambition of the Thracian peasant, who deemed his fortune inadequate to his merit, as long as he was constrained to acknowledge a superior. Though a stranger to real wisdom, he was not devoid of a selfish cunning, which showed him that the emperor had lost the affection of the army, and taught him to improve their discontent to his own advantage. It is easy for faction and calumny to shed their poison on the administration of the best of princes, and to accuse even their virtues by artfully confounding them with those vices to which they bear the nearest affinity. The troops listened with pleasure to the emissaries of Maximin. They blushed at their own ignominious patience, which, during thirteen years, had supported the vexatious discipline imposed by an effeminate Syrian, the timid slave of his mother and of the senate. It was time, they cried, to cast away that useless phantom of the civil power, and to elect for their prince and general a real soldier, educated in camps, exercised in war, who would assert the glory, and distribute among his companions the treasures, of the empire. A great army was at that time assembled on the banks of the Rhine, under the command of the emperor himself, who, almost immediately after his return from the

Persian war, had been obliged to march against the barbarians of Germany. The important care of training and reviewing the new levies was intrusted to Maximin. One day, as he entered the field of exercise, the troops either from a sudden impulse, or a formed conspiracy, saluted him emperor, silenced by their loud acclamations his obstinate refusal, and hastened to consummate their rebellion by the murder of Alexander Severus.

The circumstances of his death are variously related. The writers, who suppose that he died in ignorance of the ingratitude and ambition of Maximin, affirm, that, after taking a frugal repast in the sight of the army, he retired to sleep, and that, about the seventh hour of the day, a part of his own guards broke into the imperial tent, and, with many wounds, assassinated their virtuous and unsuspecting prince. [5] If we credit another, and indeed a more probable account, Maximin was invested with the purple by a numerous detachment, at the distance of several miles from the head-quarters; and he trusted for success rather to the secret wishes than to the public declarations of the great army. Alexander had sufficient time to awaken a faint sense of loyalty among the troops; but their reluctant professions of fidelity quickly vanished on the appearance of Maximin, who declared himself the friend and advocate of the military order, and was unanimously acknowledged emperor of the Romans by the applauding legions. The son of Mamaea, betrayed and deserted, withdrew into his tent, desirous at least to conceal his approaching fate from the insults of the multitude. He was soon followed by a tribune and some centurions, the ministers of death; but instead of receiving with manly resolution the inevitable stroke, his unavailing cries and entreaties disgraced the last moments of his life, and converted into contempt some portion of the just pity which his innocence and misfortunes must inspire. His mother, Mamaea, whose pride and avarice he loudly accused as the cause of his ruin, perished with her son. The most faithful of his friends were sacrificed to the first fury of the soldiers. Others were reserved for the more deliberate cruelty of the usurper; and those who experienced the mildest treatment, were stripped of their employments, and ignominiously driven from the court and army. [6]

[Footnote 5: Hist. August. p. 135. I have softened some of the most improbable circumstances of this wretched biographer. From his ill-worded narration, it should seem that the prince's buffoon having accidentally entered the tent, and awakened the slumbering monarch, the fear of punishment urged him to persuade the disaffected soldiers to commit the murder.]

[Footnote 6: Herodian, l. vi. 223-227.]

The former tyrants, Caligula and Nero, Commodus, and Caracalla, were all dissolute and unexperienced youths, [7] educated in the purple, and corrupted by the pride of empire, the luxury of Rome, and the perfidious voice of flattery. The cruelty of Maximin was derived from a different source, the fear of contempt. Though he depended on the attachment of the soldiers, who loved him for virtues like their own, he was conscious that his mean and barbarian origin, his savage appearance, and his total ignorance of the arts and institutions of civil life, [8] formed a very unfavorable contrast with the amiable manners of the unhappy Alexander. He remembered, that, in his humbler fortune, he had often waited before the door of the haughty nobles of Rome, and had been denied admittance by the insolence of their slaves. He recollected too the friendship of a few who had relieved his poverty, and assisted his rising hopes. But those who had spurned, and those who had protected, the Thracian, were guilty of the same crime, the knowledge of his original obscurity. For this crime many were put to death; and by the execution of several of his benefactors, Maximin published, in characters of blood, the indelible history of his baseness and ingratitude. [9]

[Footnote 7: Caligula, the eldest of the four, was only twenty-five years of age when he ascended the throne; Caracalla was twenty-three, Commodus nineteen, and Nero no more than seventeen.]

[Footnote 8: It appears that he was totally ignorant of the Greek language; which, from its universal use in conversation and letters, was an essential part of every liberal education.]

[Footnote 9: Hist. August. p. 141. Herodian, l. vii. p. 237. The latter of these historians has been most unjustly censured for sparing the vices of Maximin.]

The dark and sanguinary soul of the tyrant was open to every suspicion against those among his subjects who were the most distinguished by their birth or merit. Whenever he was alarmed with the sound of treason, his cruelty was unbounded and unrelenting. A conspiracy against his life was either discovered or imagined, and Magnus, a consular senator, was named as the principal author of it. Without a witness, without a trial, and without an opportunity of defence, Magnus, with four thousand of his supposed accomplices, was put to death. Italy and the whole empire were infested with innumerable spies and informers. On the slightest accusation, the first of the Roman nobles, who had governed provinces, commanded armies, and been adorned with the consular and triumphal ornaments, were chained on the public carriages, and hurried away to the emperor's presence. Confiscation, exile, or simple death, were esteemed uncommon instances of his lenity. Some of the unfortunate sufferers he ordered to be sewed up in the hides of slaughtered animals, others to be exposed to wild beasts, others again to be beaten to death with clubs. During the three years of his reign, he disdained to visit either Rome or Italy. His camp, occasionally removed from the banks of the Rhine to those of the Danube, was the seat of his stern despotism, which trampled on every principle of law and justice, and was supported by the avowed power of the sword. [10] No man of noble birth, elegant accomplishments, or knowledge of civil business, was suffered near his person; and the court of a Roman emperor revived the idea of those ancient chiefs of slaves and gladiators, whose savage power had left a deep impression of terror and detestation. [11]

[Footnote 10: The wife of Maximin, by insinuating wise counsels with female gentleness, sometimes brought back the tyrant to the way of truth and humanity. See Ammianus Marcellinus, l. xiv. c. l, where he alludes to the fact which he had more fully related under the reign of the Gordians. We may collect from the medals, that Paullina was the name of this benevolent empress; and from the title of Diva, that she died before Maximin. (Valesius ad loc. cit. Ammian.) Spanheim de U. et P. N. tom. ii. p. 300. Note: If we may believe Syrcellus and Zonaras, in was Maximin himself who ordered her death—G]

[Footnote 11: He was compared to Spartacus and Athenio. Hist. August p. 141.]

As long as the cruelty of Maximin was confined to the illustrious senators, or even to the bold adventurers, who in the court or army expose themselves to the caprice of fortune, the body of the people viewed their sufferings with indifference, or perhaps with pleasure. But the tyrant's avarice, stimulated by the insatiate desires of the soldiers, at length attacked the public property. Every city of the empire was possessed of an independent revenue, destined to purchase corn for the multitude, and to supply the expenses of the games and entertainments. By a single act of authority, the whole mass of wealth was at once confiscated for the use of the Imperial treasury. The temples were stripped of their most valuable offerings of gold and silver, and the statues of gods, heroes, and emperors, were melted down and coined into money. These impious orders could not be executed without tumults and massacres, as in many places the people chose rather to die in the defence of their altars, than to behold in the midst of peace their cities exposed to the rapine and cruelty of war. The soldiers themselves, among whom this sacrilegious plunder was distributed, received it with a blush; and hardened as they were in acts of violence, they dreaded the just reproaches of their friends and relations. Throughout the Roman world a general cry of indignation was heard, imploring vengeance on the common enemy of human kind; and at length, by an act of private oppression, a peaceful and unarmed province was driven into rebellion against him. [12]

[Footnote 12: Herodian, l. vii. p. 238. Zosim. l. i. p. 15.]

The procurator of Africa was a servant worthy of such a master, who considered the fines and confiscations of the rich as one of the most fruitful branches of the Imperial revenue. An iniquitous sentence had been pronounced against some opulent youths of that country, the execution of which would have stripped them of far the greater part of their patrimony. In this extremity, a resolution that must either complete or prevent their ruin, was dictated by despair. A respite of three days, obtained with difficulty from the rapacious treasurer, was employed in collecting from their estates a great number of slaves and peasants blindly devoted to the commands of their lords, and armed with the rustic weapons of clubs and axes. The leaders of the conspiracy, as they were admitted to the audience of the procurator, stabbed him with the daggers concealed under their garments, and, by the assistance of their tumultuary train, seized on the little town of Thysdrus, [13] and erected the standard of rebellion against the sovereign of the Roman empire. They rested their hopes on the hatred of mankind against Maximin, and they judiciously resolved to oppose to that detested tyrant an emperor whose mild virtues had already acquired the love and esteem of the Romans, and whose authority over the province would give weight and stability to the enterprise. Gordianus, their proconsul, and the object of their choice, refused, with unfeigned reluctance, the dangerous honor, and begged with tears, that they would suffer him to terminate in peace a long and innocent life, without staining his feeble age with civil blood. Their menaces compelled him to accept the Imperial purple, his only refuge, indeed, against the jealous cruelty of Maximin; since, according to the reasoning of tyrants, those who have been esteemed worthy of the throne deserve death, and those who deliberate have already rebelled. [14]

[Footnote 13: In the fertile territory of Byzacium, one hundred and fifty miles to the south of Carthage. This city was decorated, probably by the Gordians, with the title of colony, and with a fine amphitheatre, which is still in a very perfect state. See Intinerar. Wesseling, p. 59; and Shaw's Travels, p. 117.]

[Footnote 14: Herodian, l. vii. p. 239. Hist. August. p. 153.]

The family of Gordianus was one of the most illustrious of the Roman senate. On the father's side he was descended from the Gracchi; on his mother's, from the emperor Trajan. A great estate enabled him to support the dignity of his birth, and in the enjoyment of it, he displayed an elegant taste and beneficent disposition. The palace in Rome, formerly inhabited by the great Pompey, had been, during several generations, in the possession of Gordian's family. [15] It was distinguished by ancient trophies of naval victories, and decorated with the works of modern painting. His villa on the road to Praeneste was celebrated for baths of singular beauty and extent, for three stately rooms of a hundred feet in length, and for a magnificent portico, supported by two hundred columns of the four most curious and costly sorts of marble. [16] The public shows exhibited at his expense, and in which the people were entertained with many hundreds of wild beasts and gladiators, [17] seem to surpass the fortune of a subject; and whilst the liberality of other magistrates was confined to a few solemn festivals at Rome, the magnificence of Gordian was repeated, when he was aedile, every month in the year, and extended, during his consulship, to the principal cities of Italy. He was twice elevated to the last-mentioned dignity, by Caracalla and by Alexander; for he possessed the uncommon talent of acquiring the esteem of virtuous princes, without alarming the jealousy of tyrants. His long life was innocently spent in the study of letters and the peaceful honors of Rome; and, till he was named proconsul of Africa by the voice of the senate and the approbation of Alexander, [18] he appears prudently to have declined the command of armies and the government of provinces. [181] As long as that emperor lived, Africa was happy under the administration of his worthy representative: after the barbarous Maximin had usurped the throne, Gordianus alleviated the miseries which he was unable to prevent. When he reluctantly accepted the purple, he was above fourscore years old; a last and valuable remains of the happy age of the Antonines, whose virtues he revived in his own conduct, and celebrated in an elegant poem of thirty books. With the venerable proconsul, his son, who had accompanied him into Africa as his lieutenant, was likewise declared emperor. His manners were less pure, but his character was equally amiable with that of his father. Twenty-two acknowledged concubines, and a library of sixty-two thousand volumes, attested the variety of his inclinations; and from the productions which he left behind him, it appears that the former as well as the latter were designed for use rather than for ostentation. [19] The Roman people acknowledged in the features of the younger Gordian the resemblance of Scipio Africanus, [19/1] recollected with pleasure that his mother was the granddaughter of Antoninus Pius, and rested the public hope on those latent virtues which had hitherto, as they fondly imagined, lain concealed in the luxurious indolence of private life.

[Footnote 15: Hist. Aug. p. 152. The celebrated house of Pompey in carinis was usurped by Marc Antony, and consequently became, after the Triumvir's death, a part of the Imperial domain. The emperor Trajan allowed, and even encouraged, the rich senators to purchase those magnificent and useless places, (Plin. Panegyric. c. 50;) and it may seem probable, that, on this occasion, Pompey's house came into the possession of Gordian's great-grandfather.]

[Footnote 16: The Claudian, the Numidian, the Carystian, and the Synnadian. The colors of Roman marbles have been faintly described and imperfectly distinguished. It appears, however, that the Carystian was a sea-green, and that the marble of Synnada was white mixed with oval spots of purple. See Salmasius ad Hist. August. p. 164.]

[Footnote 17: Hist. August. p. 151, 152. He sometimes gave five hundred pair of gladiators, never less than one hundred and fifty. He once gave for the use of the circus one hundred Sicilian, and as many Cappaecian Cappadecian horses. The animals designed for hunting were chiefly bears, boars, bulls, stags, elks, wild asses, &c. Elephants and lions seem to have been appropriated to Imperial magnificence.]

[Footnote 18: See the original letter, in the Augustan History, p. 152, which at once shows Alexander's respect for the authority of the senate, and his esteem for the proconsul appointed by that assembly.]

[Footnote 181: Herodian expressly says that he had administered many provinces, lib. vii. 10.—W.]

[Footnote 19: By each of his concubines, the younger Gordian left three or four children. His literary productions, though less numerous, were by no means contemptible.]

[Footnote 19/1: Not the personal likeness, but the family descent from the Scipiod.—W.]

As soon as the Gordians had appeased the first tumult of a popular election, they removed their court to Carthage. They were received with the acclamations of the Africans, who honored their virtues, and who, since the visit of Hadrian, had never beheld the majesty of a Roman emperor. But these vain acclamations neither strengthened nor confirmed the title of the Gordians. They were induced by principle, as well as interest, to solicit the approbation of the senate; and a deputation of the noblest provincials was sent, without delay, to Rome, to relate and justify the conduct of their countrymen, who, having long suffered with patience, were at length resolved to act with vigor. The letters of the new princes were modest and respectful, excusing the necessity which had obliged them to accept the Imperial title; but submitting their election and their fate to the supreme judgment of the senate. [20]

[Footnote 20: Herodian, l. vii. p. 243. Hist. August. p. 144.]

The inclinations of the senate were neither doubtful nor divided. The birth and noble alliances of the Gordians had intimately connected them with the most illustrious houses of Rome. Their fortune had created many dependants in that assembly, their merit had acquired many friends. Their mild administration opened the flattering prospect of the restoration, not only of the civil but even of the republican government. The terror of military violence, which had first obliged the senate to forget the murder of Alexander, and to ratify the election of a barbarian peasant, [21] now produced a contrary effect, and provoked them to assert the injured rights of freedom and humanity. The hatred of Maximin towards the senate was declared and implacable; the tamest submission had not appeased his fury, the most cautious innocence would not remove his suspicions; and even the care of their own safety urged them to share the fortune of an enterprise, of which (if unsuccessful) they were sure to be the first victims. These considerations, and perhaps others of a more private nature, were debated in a previous conference of the consuls and the magistrates. As soon as their resolution was decided, they convoked in the temple of Castor the whole body of the senate, according to an ancient form of secrecy, [22] calculated to awaken their attention, and to conceal their decrees. "Conscript fathers," said the consul Syllanus, "the two Gordians, both of consular dignity, the one your proconsul, the other your lieutenant, have been declared emperors by the general consent of Africa. Let us return thanks," he boldly continued, "to the youth of Thysdrus; let us return thanks to the faithful people of Carthage, our generous deliverers from a horrid monster—Why do you hear me thus coolly, thus timidly? Why do you cast those anxious looks on each other? Why hesitate? Maximin is a public enemy! may his enmity soon expire with him, and may we long enjoy the prudence and felicity of Gordian the father, the valor and constancy of Gordian the son!" [23] The noble ardor of the consul revived the languid spirit of the senate. By a unanimous decree, the election of the Gordians was ratified, Maximin, his son, and his adherents, were pronounced enemies of their country, and liberal rewards were offered to whomsoever had the courage and good fortune to destroy them. [See Temple Of Castor and Pollux]

[Footnote 21: Quod. tamen patres dum periculosum existimant; inermes armato esistere approbaverunt.—Aurelius Victor.]

[Footnote 22: Even the servants of the house, the scribes, &c., were excluded, and their office was filled by the senators themselves. We are obliged to the Augustan History. p. 159, for preserving this curious example of the old discipline of the commonwealth.]

[Footnote 23: This spirited speech, translated from the Augustan historian, p. 156, seems transcribed by him from the origina registers of the senate]

During the emperor's absence, a detachment of the Praetorian guards remained at Rome, to protect, or rather to command, the capital. The praefect Vitalianus had signalized his fidelity to Maximin, by the alacrity with which he had obeyed, and even prevented the cruel mandates of the tyrant. His death alone could rescue the authority of the senate, and the lives of the senators from a state of danger and suspense. Before their resolves had transpired, a quaestor and some tribunes were commissioned to take his devoted life. They executed the order with equal boldness and success; and, with their bloody daggers in their hands, ran through the streets, proclaiming to the people and the soldiers the news of the happy revolution. The enthusiasm of liberty was seconded by the promise of a large donative, in lands and money; the statues of Maximin were thrown down; the capital of the empire acknowledged, with transport, the authority of the two Gordians and the senate; [24] and the example of Rome was followed by the rest of Italy.

[Footnote 24: Herodian, l. vii. p. 244]

A new spirit had arisen in that assembly, whose long patience had been insulted by wanton despotism and military license. The senate assumed the reins of government, and, with a calm intrepidity, prepared to vindicate by arms the cause of freedom. Among the consular senators recommended by their merit and services to the favor of the emperor Alexander, it was easy to select twenty, not unequal to the command of an army, and the conduct of a war. To these was the defence of Italy intrusted. Each was appointed to act in his respective department, authorized to enroll and discipline the Italian youth; and instructed to fortify the ports and highways, against the impending invasion of Maximin. A number of deputies, chosen from the most illustrious of the senatorian and equestrian orders, were despatched at the same time to the governors of the several provinces, earnestly conjuring them to fly to the assistance of their country, and to remind the nations of their ancient ties of friendship with the Roman senate and people. The general respect with which these deputies were received, and the zeal of Italy and the provinces in favor of the senate, sufficiently prove that the subjects of Maximin were reduced to that uncommon distress, in which the body of the people has more to fear from oppression than from resistance. The consciousness of that melancholy truth, inspires a degree of persevering fury, seldom to be found in those civil wars which are artificially supported for the benefit of a few factious and designing leaders. [25]

[Footnote 25: Herodian, l. vii. p. 247, l. viii. p. 277. Hist. August. p 156-158.]

For while the cause of the Gordians was embraced with such diffusive ardor, the Gordians themselves were no more. The feeble court of Carthage was alarmed by the rapid approach of Capelianus, governor of Mauritania, who, with a small band of veterans, and a fierce host of barbarians, attacked a faithful, but unwarlike province. The younger Gordian sallied out to meet the enemy at the head of a few guards, and a numerous undisciplined multitude, educated in the peaceful luxury of Carthage. His useless valor served only to procure him an honorable death on the field of battle. His aged father, whose reign had not exceeded thirty-six days, put an end to his life on the first news of the defeat. Carthage, destitute of defence, opened her gates to the conqueror, and Africa was exposed to the rapacious cruelty of a slave, obliged to satisfy his unrelenting master with a large account of blood and treasure. [26]

[Footnote 26: Herodian, l. vii. p. 254. Hist. August. p. 150-160. We may observe, that one month and six days, for the reign of Gordian, is a just correction of Casaubon and Panvinius, instead of the absurd reading of one year and six months. See Commentar. p. 193. Zosimus relates, l. i. p. 17, that the two Gordians perished by a tempest in the midst of their navigation. A strange ignorance of history, or a strange abuse of metaphors!]

The fate of the Gordians filled Rome with just but unexpected terror. The senate, convoked in the temple of Concord, affected to transact the common business of the day; and seemed to decline, with trembling anxiety, the consideration of their own and the public danger. A silent consternation prevailed in the assembly, till a senator, of the name and family of Trajan, awakened his brethren from their fatal lethargy. He represented to them that the choice of cautious, dilatory measures had been long since out of their power; that Maximin, implacable by nature, and exasperated by injuries, was advancing towards Italy, at the head of the military force of the empire; and that their only remaining alternative was either to meet him bravely in the field, or tamely to expect the tortures and ignominious death reserved for unsuccessful rebellion. "We have lost," continued he, "two excellent princes; but unless we desert ourselves, the hopes of the republic have not perished with the Gordians. Many are the senators whose virtues have deserved, and whose abilities would sustain, the Imperial dignity. Let us elect two emperors, one of whom may conduct the war against the public enemy, whilst his colleague remains at Rome to direct the civil administration. I cheerfully expose myself to the danger and envy of the nomination, and give my vote in favor of Maximus and Balbinus. Ratify my choice, conscript fathers, or appoint in their place, others more worthy of the empire." The general apprehension silenced the whispers of jealousy; the merit of the candidates was universally acknowledged; and the house resounded with the sincere acclamations of "Long life and victory to the emperors Maximus and Balbinus. You are happy in the judgment of the senate; may the republic be happy under your administration!" [27]

[Footnote 27: See the Augustan History, p. 166, from the registers of the senate; the date is confessedly faulty but the coincidence of the Apollinatian games enables us to correct it.]

PART II

The virtues and the reputation of the new emperors justified the most sanguine hopes of the Romans. The various nature of their talents seemed to appropriate to each his peculiar department of peace and war, without leaving room for jealous emulation. Balbinus was an admired orator, a poet of distinguished fame, and a wise magistrate, who had exercised with innocence and applause the civil jurisdiction in almost all the interior provinces of the empire. His birth was noble, [28] his fortune affluent, his manners liberal and affable. In him the love of pleasure was corrected by a sense of dignity, nor had the habits of ease deprived him of a capacity for business. The mind of Maximus was formed in a rougher mould. By his valor and abilities he had raised himself from the meanest origin to the first employments of the state and army. His victories over the Sarmatians and the Germans, the austerity of his life, and the rigid impartiality of his justice, while he was a Praefect of the city, commanded the esteem of a people whose affections were engaged in favor of the more amiable Balbinus. The two colleagues had both been consuls, (Balbinus had twice enjoyed that honorable office,) both had been named among the twenty lieutenants of the senate; and since the one was sixty and the other seventy-four years old, [29] they had both attained the full maturity of age and experience.

[Footnote 28: He was descended from Cornelius Balbus, a noble Spaniard, and the adopted son of Theophanes, the Greek historian. Balbus obtained the freedom of Rome by the favor of Pompey, and preserved it by the eloquence of Cicero. (See Orat. pro Cornel. Balbo.) The friendship of Caesar, (to whom he rendered the most important secret services in the civil war) raised him to the consulship and the pontificate, honors never yet possessed by a stranger. The nephew of this Balbus triumphed over the Garamantes. See Dictionnaire de Bayle, au mot Balbus, where he distinguishes the several persons of that name, and rectifies, with his usual accuracy, the mistakes of former writers concerning them.]

[Footnote 29: Zonaras, l. xii. p. 622. But little dependence is to be had on the authority of a modern Greek, so grossly ignorant of the history of the third century, that he creates several imaginary emperors, and confounds those who really existed.]

After the senate had conferred on Maximus and Balbinus an equal portion of the consular and tribunitian powers, the title of Fathers of their country, and the joint office of Supreme Pontiff, they ascended to the Capitol to return thanks to the gods, protectors of Rome. [30] The solemn rites of sacrifice were disturbed by a sedition of the people. The licentious multitude neither loved the rigid Maximus, nor did they sufficiently fear the mild and humane Balbinus. Their increasing numbers surrounded the temple of Jupiter; with obstinate clamors they asserted their inherent right of consenting to the election of their sovereign; and demanded, with an apparent moderation, that, besides the two emperors, chosen by the senate, a third should be added of the family of the Gordians, as a just return of gratitude to those princes who had sacrificed their lives for the republic. At the head of the city-guards, and the youth of the equestrian order, Maximus and Balbinus attempted to cut their way through the seditious multitude. The multitude, armed with sticks and stones, drove them back into the Capitol. It is prudent to yield when the contest, whatever may be the issue of it, must be fatal to both parties. A boy, only thirteen years of age, the grandson of the elder, and nephew [30/1] of the younger Gordian, was produced to the people, invested with the ornaments and title of Caesar. The tumult was appeased by this easy condescension; and the two emperors, as soon as they had been peaceably acknowledged in Rome, prepared to defend Italy against the common enemy.

[Footnote 30: Herodian, l. vii. p. 256, supposes that the senate was at first convoked in the Capitol, and is very eloquent on the occasion. The Augustar History p. 116, seems much more authentic.]

[Footnote 30/1: According to some, the son.—G.]

Whilst in Rome and Africa, revolutions succeeded each other with such amazing rapidity, that the mind of Maximin was agitated by the most furious passions. He is said to have received the news of the rebellion of the Gordians, and of the decree of the senate against him, not with the temper of a man, but the rage of a wild beast; which, as it could not discharge itself on the distant senate, threatened the life of his son, of his friends, and of all who ventured to approach his person. The grateful intelligence of the death of the Gordians was quickly followed by the assurance that the senate, laying aside all hopes of pardon or accommodation, had substituted in their room two emperors, with whose merit he could not be unacquainted. Revenge was the only consolation left to Maximin, and revenge could only be obtained by arms. The strength of the legions had been assembled by Alexander from all parts of the empire. Three successful campaigns against the Germans and the Sarmatians, had raised their fame, confirmed their discipline, and even increased their numbers, by filling the ranks with the flower of the barbarian youth. The life of Maximin had been spent in war, and the candid severity of history cannot refuse him the valor of a soldier, or even the abilities of an experienced general. [31] It might naturally be expected, that a prince of such a character, instead of suffering the rebellion to gain stability by delay, should immediately have marched from the banks of the Danube to those of the Tyber, and that his victorious army, instigated by contempt for the senate, and eager to gather the spoils of Italy, should have burned with impatience to finish the easy and lucrative conquest. Yet as far as we can trust to the obscure chronology of that period, [32] it appears that the operations of some foreign war deferred the Italian expedition till the ensuing spring. From the prudent conduct of Maximin, we may learn that the savage features of his character have been exaggerated by the pencil of party, that his passions, however impetuous, submitted to the force of reason, and that the barbarian possessed something of the generous spirit of Sylla, who subdued the enemies of Rome before he suffered himself to revenge his private injuries. [33]

[Footnote 31: *In Herodian, l. vii. p. 249, and in the Augustan History, we have three several orations of Maximin to his army, on the rebellion of Africa and Rome: M. de Tillemont has very justly observed that they neither agree with each other nor with truth. Histoire des Empereurs, tom. iii. p. 799.*]

[Footnote 32: *The carelessness of the writers of that age, leaves us in a singular perplexity. 1. We know that Maximus and Balbinus were killed during the Capitoline games. Herodian, l. viii. p. 285. The authority of Censorinus (de Die Natali, c. 18) enables us to fix those games with certainty to the year 238, but leaves us in ignorance of the month or day. 2. The election of Gordian by the senate is fixed with equal certainty to the 27th of May; but we are at a loss to discover whether it was in the same or the preceding year. Tillemont and Muratori, who maintain the two opposite opinions, bring into the field a desultory troop of authorities, conjectures and probabilities. The one seems to draw out, the other to contract the series of events between those periods, more than can be well reconciled to reason and history. Yet it is necessary to choose between them. Note: Eckhel has more recently treated these chronological questions with a perspicuity which gives great probability to his conclusions. Setting aside all the historians, whose contradictions are irreconcilable, he has only consulted the medals, and has arranged the events before us in the following order:— Maximin, A. U. 990, after having conquered the Germans, reenters Pannonia, establishes his winter quarters at Sirmium, and prepares himself to make war against the people of the North. In the year 991, in the cal ends of January, commences his fourth tribunate. The Gordians are chosen emperors in Africa, probably at the beginning of the month of March. The senate confirms this election with joy, and declares Maximin the enemy of Rome. Five days after he had heard of this revolt, Maximin sets out from Sirmium on his march to Italy. These events took place about the beginning of April; a little after, the Gordians are slain in Africa by Capellianus, procurator of Mauritania. The senate, in its alarm, names as emperors Balbus and Maximus Pupianus, and intrusts the latter with the war against Maximin. Maximin is stopped on his road near Aquileia, by the want of provisions, and by the melting of the snows: he begins the siege of Aquileia at the end of April. Pupianus assembles his army at Ravenna. Maximin and his son are assassinated by the soldiers enraged at the resistance of Aquileia: and this was probably in the middle of May. Pupianus returns to Rome, and assumes the government with Balbinus; they are assassinated towards the end of July Gordian the younger ascends the throne. Eckhel de Doct. Vol vii 295.—G.*]

[Footnote 33: *Velleius Paterculus, l. ii. c. 24. The president de Montesquieu (in his dialogue between Sylla and Eucrates) expresses the sentiments of the dictator in a spirited, and even a sublime manner.*]

When the troops of Maximin, advancing in excellent order, arrived at the foot of the Julian Alps, they were terrified by the silence and desolation that reigned on the frontiers of Italy. The villages and open towns had been abandoned on their approach by the inhabitants, the cattle was driven away, the provisions removed or destroyed, the bridges broken down, nor was any thing left which could afford either shelter or subsistence to an invader. Such had been the wise orders of the generals of the senate: whose design was to protract the war, to ruin the army of Maximin by the slow operation of famine, and to consume his strength in the sieges of the principal cities of Italy, which they had plentifully stored with men and provisions from the deserted country. Aquileia received and withstood the first shock of the invasion. The streams that issue from the head of the Hadriatic Gulf, swelled by the melting of the winter snows, [34] opposed an unexpected obstacle to the arms of Maximin. At length, on a singular bridge, constructed with art and difficulty, of large hogsheads, he transported his army to the opposite bank, rooted up the beautiful vineyards in the neighborhood of Aquileia, demolished the suburbs, and employed the timber of the buildings in the engines and towers, with which on every side he attacked the city. The walls, fallen to decay during the security of a long peace, had been hastily repaired on this sudden emergency: but the firmest defence of Aquileia consisted in the constancy of the citizens; all ranks of whom, instead of being dismayed, were animated by the extreme danger, and their knowledge of the tyrant's unrelenting temper. Their courage was supported and directed by Crispinus and Menophilus, two of the twenty lieutenants of the senate, who, with a small body of regular troops, had thrown themselves into the besieged place. The army of Maximin was repulsed in repeated attacks, his machines destroyed by showers of artificial fire; and the generous enthusiasm of the Aquileians was exalted into a confidence of success, by the opinion that Belenus, their tutelar deity, combated in person in the defence of his distressed worshippers. [35]

[Footnote 34: Muratori (Annali d' Italia, tom. ii. p. 294) thinks the melting of the snows suits better with the months of June or July, than with those of February. The opinion of a man who passed his life between the Alps and the Apennines, is undoubtedly of great weight; yet I observe, 1. That the long winter, of which Muratori takes advantage, is to be found only in the Latin version, and not in the Greek text of Herodian. 2. That the vicissitudes of suns and rains, to which the soldiers of Maximin were exposed, (Herodian, l. viii. p. 277,) denote the spring rather than the summer. We may observe, likewise, that these several streams, as they melted into one, composed the Timavus, so poetically (in every sense of the word) described by Virgil. They are about twelve miles to the east of Aquileia. See Cluver. Italia Antiqua, tom. i. p. 189, &c.]

[Footnote 35: Herodian, l. viii. p. 272. The Celtic deity was supposed to be Apollo, and received under that name the thanks of the senate. A temple was likewise built to Venus the Bald, in honor of the women of Aquileia, who had given up their hair to make ropes for the military engines.]

The emperor Maximus, who had advanced as far as Ravenna, to secure that important place, and to hasten the military preparations, beheld the event of the war in the more faithful mirror of reason and policy. He was too sensible, that a single town could not resist the persevering efforts of a great army; and he dreaded, lest the enemy, tired with the obstinate resistance of Aquileia, should on a sudden relinquish the fruitless siege, and march directly towards Rome. The fate of the empire and the cause of freedom must then be committed to the chance of a battle; and what arms could he oppose to the veteran legions of the Rhine and Danube? Some troops newly levied among the generous but enervated youth of Italy; and a body of German auxiliaries, on whose firmness, in the hour of trial, it was dangerous to depend. In the midst of these just alarms, the stroke of domestic conspiracy punished the crimes of Maximin, and delivered Rome and the senate from the calamities that would surely have attended the victory of an enraged barbarian.

The people of Aquileia had scarcely experienced any of the common miseries of a siege; their magazines were plentifully supplied, and several fountains within the walls assured them of an inexhaustible resource of fresh water. The soldiers of Maximin were, on the contrary, exposed to the inclemency of the season, the contagion of disease, and the horrors of famine. The open country was ruined, the rivers filled with the slain, and polluted with blood. A spirit of despair and disaffection began to diffuse itself among the troops; and as they were cut off from all intelligence, they easily believed that the whole empire had embraced the cause of the senate, and that they were left as devoted victims to perish under the impregnable walls of Aquileia. The fierce temper of the tyrant was exasperated by disappointments, which he imputed to the cowardice of his army; and his wanton and ill-timed cruelty, instead of striking terror, inspired hatred, and a just desire of revenge. A party of Praetorian guards, who trembled for their wives and children in the camp of Alba, near Rome, executed the sentence of the senate.

Maximin, abandoned by his guards, was slain in his tent, with his son, (whom he had associated to the honors of the purple,) Anulinus the praefect, and the principal ministers of his tyranny. [36] The sight of their heads, borne on the point of spears, convinced the citizens of Aquileia that the siege was at an end; the gates of the city were thrown open, a liberal market was provided for the hungry troops of Maximin, and the whole army joined in solemn protestations of fidelity to the senate and the people of Rome, and to their lawful emperors Maximus and Balbinus. Such was the deserved fate of a brutal savage, destitute, as he has generally been represented, of every sentiment that distinguishes a civilized, or even a human being. The body was suited to the soul. The stature of Maximin exceeded the measure of eight feet, and circumstances almost incredible are related of his matchless strength and appetite. [37] Had he lived in a less enlightened age, tradition and poetry might well have described him as one of those monstrous giants, whose supernatural power was constantly exerted for the destruction of mankind.

[Footnote 36: Herodian, l. viii. p. 279. Hist. August. p. 146. The duration of Maximin's reign has not been defined with much accuracy, except by Eutropius, who allows him three years and a few days, (l. ix. 1;) we may depend on the integrity of the text, as the Latin original is checked by the Greek version of Paeanius.]

[Footnote 37: Eight Roman feet and one third, which are equal to above eight English feet, as the two measures are to each other in the proportion of 967 to 1000. See Graves's discourse on the Roman foot. We are told that Maximin could drink in a day an amphora (or about seven gallons) of wine, and eat thirty or forty pounds of meat. He could move a loaded wagon, break a horse's leg with his fist, crumble stones in his hand, and tear up small trees by the roots. See his life in the Augustan History.]

It is easier to conceive than to describe the universal joy of the Roman world on the fall of the tyrant, the news of which is said to have been carried in four days from Aquileia to Rome. The return of Maximus was a triumphal procession; his colleague and young Gordian went out to meet him, and the three princes made their entry into the capital, attended by the ambassadors of almost all the cities of Italy, saluted with the splendid offerings of gratitude and superstition, and received with the unfeigned acclamations of the senate and people, who persuaded themselves that a golden age would succeed to an age of iron. [38] The conduct of the two emperors corresponded with these expectations. They administered justice in person; and the rigor of the one was tempered by the other's clemency. The oppressive taxes with which Maximin had loaded the rights of inheritance and succession, were repealed, or at least moderated. Discipline was revived, and with the advice of the senate many wise laws were enacted by their imperial ministers, who endeavored to restore a civil constitution on the ruins of military tyranny. "What reward may we expect for delivering Rome from a monster?" was the question asked by Maximus, in a moment of freedom and confidence.

Balbinus answered it without hesitation—"The love of the senate, of the people, and of all mankind." "Alas!" replied his more penetrating colleague—"alas! I dread the hatred of the soldiers, and the fatal effects of their resentment." [39] His apprehensions were but too well justified by the event.

[Footnote 38: See the congratulatory letter of Claudius Julianus, the consul to the two emperors, in the Augustan History.]

[Footnote 39: Hist. August. p. 171.]

Whilst Maximus was preparing to defend Italy against the common foe, Balbinus, who remained at Rome, had been engaged in scenes of blood and intestine discord. Distrust and jealousy reigned in the senate; and even in the temples where they assembled, every senator carried either open or concealed arms. In the midst of their deliberations, two veterans of the guards, actuated either by curiosity or a sinister motive, audaciously thrust themselves into the house, and advanced by degrees beyond the altar of Victory. Gallicanus, a consular, and Maecenas, a Praetorian senator, viewed with indignation their insolent intrusion: drawing their daggers, they laid the spies (for such they deemed them) dead at the foot of the altar, and then, advancing to the door of the senate, imprudently exhorted the multitude to massacre the Praetorians, as the secret adherents of the tyrant. Those who escaped the first fury of the tumult took refuge in the camp, which they defended with superior advantage against the reiterated attacks of the people, assisted by the numerous bands of gladiators, the property of opulent nobles. The civil war lasted many days, with infinite loss and confusion on both sides. When the pipes were broken that supplied the camp with water, the Praetorians were reduced to intolerable distress; but in their turn they made desperate sallies into the city, set fire to a great number of houses, and filled the streets with the blood of the inhabitants. The emperor Balbinus attempted, by ineffectual edicts and precarious truces, to reconcile the factions at Rome. But their animosity, though smothered for a while, burnt with redoubled violence. The soldiers, detesting the senate and the people, despised the weakness of a prince, who wanted either the spirit or the power to command the obedience of his subjects. [40]

[Footnote 40: Herodian, l. viii. p. 258.]

After the tyrant's death, his formidable army had acknowledged, from necessity rather than from choice, the authority of Maximus, who transported himself without delay to the camp before Aquileia. As soon as he had received their oath of fidelity, he addressed them in terms full of mildness and moderation; lamented, rather than arraigned the wild disorders of the times, and assured the soldiers, that of all their past conduct the senate would remember only their generous desertion of the tyrant, and their voluntary return to their duty. Maximus enforced his exhortations by a liberal donative, purified the camp by a solemn sacrifice of expiation, and then dismissed the legions to their several provinces, impressed, as he hoped, with a lively sense of gratitude and obedience. [41] But nothing could reconcile the haughty spirit of the Praetorians. They attended the emperors on the memorable day of their public entry into Rome; but amidst the general acclamations, the sullen, dejected countenance of the guards sufficiently declared that they considered themselves as the object, rather than the partners, of the triumph. When the whole body was united in their camp, those who had served under Maximin, and those who had remained at Rome, insensibly communicated to each other their complaints and apprehensions. The emperors chosen by the army had perished with ignominy; those elected by the senate were seated on the throne. [42] The long discord between the civil and military powers was decided by a war, in which the former had obtained a complete victory. The soldiers must now learn a new doctrine of submission to the senate; and whatever clemency was affected by that politic assembly, they dreaded a slow revenge, colored by the name of discipline, and justified by fair pretences of the public good. But their fate was still in their own hands; and if they had courage to despise the vain terrors of an impotent republic, it was easy to convince the world, that those who were masters of the arms, were masters of the authority, of the state.

[Footnote 41: Herodian, l. viii. p. 213.]

[Footnote 42: The observation had been made imprudently enough in the acclamations of the senate, and with regard to the soldiers it carried the appearance of a wanton insult. Hist. August. p. 170.]

When the senate elected two princes, it is probable that, besides the declared reason of providing for the various emergencies of peace and war, they were actuated by the secret desire of weakening by division the despotism of the supreme magistrate. Their policy was effectual, but it proved fatal both to their emperors and to themselves. The jealousy of power was soon exasperated by the difference of character. Maximus despised Balbinus as a luxurious noble, and was in his turn disdained by his colleague as an obscure soldier. Their silent discord was understood rather than seen; [43] but the mutual consciousness prevented them from uniting in any vigorous measures of defence against their common enemies of the Praetorian camp. The whole city was employed in the Capitoline games, and the emperors were left almost alone in the palace. On a sudden, they were alarmed by the approach of a troop of desperate assassins. Ignorant of each other's situation or designs, (for they already occupied very distant apartments,) afraid to give or to receive assistance, they wasted the important moments in idle debates and fruitless recriminations. The arrival of the guards put an end to the vain strife. They seized on these emperors of the senate, for such they called them with malicious contempt, stripped them of their garments, and dragged them in insolent triumph through the streets of Rome, with the design of inflicting a slow and cruel death on these unfortunate princes. The fear of a rescue from the faithful Germans of the Imperial guards, shortened their tortures; and their bodies, mangled with a thousand wounds, were left exposed to the insults or to the pity of the populace. [44]

[Footnote 43: Discordiae tacitae, et quae intelligerentur potius quam viderentur. Hist. August. p. 170. This well-chosen expression is probably stolen from some better writer.]

[Footnote 44: Herodian, l. viii. p. 287, 288.]

In the space of a few months, six princes had been cut off by the sword. Gordian, who had already received the title of Caesar, was the only person that occurred to the soldiers as proper to fill the vacant throne. [45] They carried him to the camp, and unanimously saluted him Augustus and Emperor. His name was dear to the senate and people; his tender age promised a long impunity of military license; and the submission of Rome and the provinces to the choice of the Praetorian guards, saved the republic, at the expense indeed of its freedom and dignity, from the horrors of a new civil war in the heart of the capital. [46]

[Footnote 45: Quia non alius erat in praesenti, is the expression of the Augustan History.]

[Footnote 46: Quintus Curtius (l. x. c. 9,) pays an elegant compliment to the emperor of the day, for having, by his happy accession, extinguished so many firebrands, sheathed so many swords, and put an end to the evils of a divided government. After weighing with attention every word of the passage, I am of opinion, that it suits better with the elevation of Gordian, than with any other period of the Roman history. In that case, it may serve to decide the age of Quintus Curtius. Those who place him under the first Caesars, argue from the purity of his style but are embarrassed by the silence of Quintilian, in his accurate list of Roman historians. Note: This conjecture of Gibbon is without foundation. Many passages in the work of Quintus Curtius clearly place him at an earlier period. Thus, in speaking of the Parthians, he says, Hinc in Parthicum perventum est, tunc ignobilem gentem: nunc caput omnium qui post Euphratem et Tigrim amnes siti Rubro mari terminantur. The Parthian empire had this extent only in the first age of the vulgar aera: to that age, therefore, must be assigned the date of Quintus Curtius. Although the critics (says M. de Sainte Croix) have multiplied conjectures on this subject, most of them have ended by adopting the opinion which places Quintus Curtius under the reign of Claudius. See Just. Lips. ad Ann. Tac. ii. 20. Michel le Tellier Praef. in Curt. Tillemont Hist. des Emp. i. p. 251. Du Bos Reflections sur la Poesie, 2d Partie. Tiraboschi Storia della, Lett. Ital. ii. 149. Examen. crit. des Historiens d'Alexandre, 2d ed. p. 104, 849, 850.—G. —This interminable question seems as much perplexed as ever. The first argument of M. Guizot is a strong one, except that Parthian is often used by later writers for Persian. Cunzius, in his preface to an edition published at Helmstadt, (1802,) maintains the opinion of Bagnolo, which assigns Q. Curtius to the time of Constantine the Great. Schmieder, in his edit. Gotting. 1803, sums up in this sentence, aetatem Curtii ignorari pala mest.—M.]

As the third Gordian was only nineteen years of age at the time of his death, the history of his life, were it known to us with greater accuracy than it really is, would contain little more than the account of his education, and the conduct of the ministers, who by turns abused or guided the simplicity of his unexperienced youth. Immediately after his accession, he fell into the hands of his mother's eunuchs, that pernicious vermin of the East, who, since the days of Elagabalus, had infested the Roman palace. By the artful conspiracy of these wretches, an impenetrable veil was drawn between an innocent prince and his oppressed subjects, the virtuous disposition of Gordian was deceived, and the honors of the empire sold without his knowledge, though in a very public manner, to the most worthless of mankind. We are ignorant by what fortunate accident the emperor escaped from this ignominious slavery, and devolved his confidence on a minister, whose wise counsels had no object except the glory of his sovereign and the happiness of the people. It should seem that love and learning introduced Misitheus to the favor of Gordian. The young prince married the daughter of his master of rhetoric, and promoted his father-in-law to the first offices of the empire. Two admirable letters that passed between them are still extant. The minister, with the conscious dignity of virtue, congratulates Gordian that he is delivered from the tyranny of the eunuchs, [47] and still more that he is sensible of his deliverance. The emperor acknowledges, with an amiable confusion, the errors of his past conduct; and laments, with singular propriety, the misfortune of a monarch, from whom a venal tribe of courtiers perpetually labor to conceal the truth. [48]

[Footnote 47: Hist. August. p. 161. From some hints in the two letters, I should expect that the eunuchs were not expelled the palace without some degree of gentle violence, and that the young Gordian rather approved of, than consented to, their disgrace.]

[Footnote 48: Duxit uxorem filiam Misithei, quem causa eloquentiae dignum parentela sua putavit; et praefectum statim fecit; post quod, non puerile jam et contemptibile videbatur imperium.]

The life of Misitheus had been spent in the profession of letters, not of arms; yet such was the versatile genius of that great man, that, when he was appointed Praetorian Praefect, he discharged the military duties of his place with vigor and ability. The Persians had invaded Mesopotamia, and threatened Antioch. By the persuasion of his father-in-law, the young emperor quitted the luxury of Rome, opened, for the last time recorded in history, the temple of Janus, and marched in person into the East. On his approach, with a great army, the Persians withdrew their garrisons from the cities which they had already taken, and retired from the Euphrates to the Tigris. Gordian enjoyed the pleasure of announcing to the senate the first success of his arms, which he ascribed, with a becoming modesty and gratitude, to the wisdom of his father and Praefect. During the whole expedition, Misitheus watched over the safety and discipline of the army; whilst he prevented their dangerous murmurs by maintaining a regular plenty in the camp, and by establishing ample magazines of vinegar, bacon, straw, barley, and wheat in all the cities of the frontier. [49] But the prosperity of Gordian expired with Misitheus, who died of a flux, not with out very strong suspicions of poison. Philip, his successor in the praefecture, was an Arab by birth, and consequently, in the earlier part of his life, a robber by profession. His rise from so obscure a station to the first dignities of the empire, seems to prove that he was a bold and able leader. But his boldness prompted him to aspire to the throne, and his abilities were employed to supplant, not to serve, his indulgent master. The minds of the soldiers were irritated by an artificial scarcity, created by his contrivance in the camp; and the distress of the army was attributed to the youth and incapacity of the prince. It is not in our power to trace the successive steps of the secret conspiracy and open sedition, which were at length fatal to Gordian. A sepulchral monument was erected to his memory on the spot [50] where he was killed, near the conflux of the Euphrates with the little river Aboras. [51] The fortunate Philip, raised to the empire by the votes of the soldiers, found a ready obedience from the senate and the provinces. [52]

[Footnote 49: Hist. August. p. 162. Aurelius Victor. Porphyrius in Vit Plotin. ap. Fabricium, Biblioth. Graec. l. iv. c. 36. The philosopher Plotinus accompanied the army, prompted by the love of knowledge, and by the hope of penetrating as far as India.]

[Footnote 50: About twenty miles from the little town of Circesium, on the frontier of the two empires. Note: Now Kerkesia; placed in the angle formed by the juncture of the Chaboras, or al Khabour, with the Euphrates. This situation appeared advantageous to Diocletian, that he raised fortifications to make it the but wark of the empire on the side of Mesopotamia. D'Anville. Geog. Anc. ii. 196.—G. It is the Carchemish of the Old Testament, 2 Chron. xxxv. 20. Ier. xlvi. 2.—M.]

[Footnote 51: The inscription (which contained a very singular pun) was erased by the order of Licinius, who claimed some degree of relationship to Philip, (Hist. August. p. 166;) but the tumulus, or mound of earth which formed the sepulchre, still subsisted in the time of Julian. See Ammian Marcellin. xxiii. 5.]

[Footnote 52: Aurelius Victor. Eutrop. ix. 2. Orosius, vii. 20. Ammianus Marcellinus, xxiii. 5. Zosimus, l. i. p. 19. Philip, who was a native of Bostra, was about forty years of age. Note: Now Bosra. It was once the metropolis of a province named Arabia, and the chief city of Auranitis, of which the name is preserved in Beled Hauran, the limits of which meet the desert. D'Anville. Geog. Anc. ii. 188. According to Victor, (in Caesar.,) Philip was a native of Tracbonitis another province of Arabia.—G.]

We cannot forbear transcribing the ingenious, though somewhat fanciful description, which a celebrated writer of our own times has traced of the military government of the Roman empire. What in that age was called the Roman empire, was only an irregular republic, not unlike the aristocracy [53] of Algiers, [54] where the militia, possessed of the sovereignty, creates and deposes a magistrate, who is styled a Dey. Perhaps, indeed, it may be laid down as a general rule, that a military government is, in some respects, more republican than monarchical. Nor can it be said that the soldiers only partook of the government by their disobedience and rebellions. The speeches made to them by the emperors, were they not at length of the same nature as those formerly pronounced to the people by the consuls and the tribunes? And although the armies had no regular place or forms of assembly; though their debates were short, their action sudden, and their resolves seldom the result of cool reflection, did they not dispose, with absolute sway, of the public fortune? What was the emperor, except the minister of a violent government, elected for the private benefit of the soldiers?

[Footnote 53: Can the epithet of Aristocracy be applied, with any propriety, to the government of Algiers? Every military government floats between two extremes of absolute monarchy and wild democracy.]

[Footnote 54: The military republic of the Mamelukes in Egypt would have afforded M. de Montesquieu (see Considerations sur la Grandeur et la Decadence des Romains, c. 16) a juster and more noble parallel.]

"When the army had elected Philip, who was Praetorian praefect to the third Gordian, the latter demanded that he might remain sole emperor; he was unable to obtain it. He requested that the power might be equally divided between them; the army would not listen to his speech. He consented to be degraded to the rank of Caesar; the favor was refused him. He desired, at least, he might be appointed Praetorian praefect; his prayer was rejected. Finally, he pleaded for his life. The army, in these several judgments, exercised the supreme magistracy." According to the historian, whose doubtful narrative the President De Montesquieu has adopted, Philip, who, during the whole transaction, had preserved a sullen silence, was inclined to spare the innocent life of his benefactor; till, recollecting that his innocence might excite a dangerous compassion in the Roman world, he commanded, without regard to his suppliant cries, that he should be seized, stripped, and led away to instant death. After a moment's pause, the inhuman sentence was executed. [55]

[Footnote 55: The Augustan History (p. 163, 164) cannot, in this instance, be reconciled with itself or with probability. How could Philip condemn his predecessor, and yet consecrate his memory? How could he order his public execution, and yet, in his letters to the senate, exculpate himself from the guilt of his death? Philip, though an ambitious usurper, was by no means a mad tyrant. Some chronological difficulties have likewise been discovered by the nice eyes of Tillemont and Muratori, in this supposed association of Philip to the empire. Note: Wenck endeavors to reconcile these discrepancies. He supposes that Gordian was led away, and died a natural death in prison. This is directly contrary to the statement of Capitolinus and of Zosimus, whom he adduces in support of his theory. He is more successful in his precedents of usurpers deifying the victims of their ambition. Sit divus, dummodo non sit vivus.—M.]

PART III

On his return from the East to Rome, Philip, desirous of obliterating the memory of his crimes, and of captivating the affections of the people, solemnized the secular games with infinite pomp and magnificence. Since their institution or revival by Augustus, [56] they had been celebrated by Claudius, by Domitian, and by Severus, and were now renewed the fifth time, on the accomplishment of the full period of a thousand years from the foundation of Rome. Every circumstance of the secular games was skillfully adapted to inspire the superstitious mind with deep and solemn reverence. The long interval between them [57] exceeded the term of human life; and as none of the spectators had already seen them, none could flatter themselves with the expectation of beholding them a second time. The mystic sacrifices were performed, during three nights, on the banks of the Tyber; and the Campus Martius resounded with music and dances, and was illuminated with innumerable lamps and torches. Slaves and strangers were excluded from any participation in these national ceremonies. A chorus of twenty-seven youths, and as many virgins, of noble families, and whose parents were both alive, implored the propitious gods in favor of the present, and for the hope of the rising generation; requesting, in religious hymns, that according to the faith of their ancient oracles, they would still maintain the virtue, the felicity, and the empire of the Roman people. [58] The magnificence of Philip's shows and entertainments dazzled the eyes of the multitude. The devout were employed in the rites of superstition, whilst the reflecting few revolved in their anxious minds the past history and the future fate of the empire.[58]

[Footnote 56: The account of the last supposed celebration, though in an enlightened period of history, was so very doubtful and obscure, that the alternative seems not doubtful. When the popish jubilees, the copy of the secular games, were invented by Boniface VII., the crafty pope pretended that he only revived an ancient institution. See M. le Chais, Lettres sur les Jubiles.]

[Footnote 57: Either of a hundred or a hundred and ten years. Varro and Livy adopted the former opinion, but the infallible authority of the Sybil consecrated the latter, (Censorinus de Die Natal. c. 17.) The emperors Claudius and Philip, however, did not treat the oracle with implicit respect.]

[Footnote 58: The idea of the secular games is best understood from the poem of Horace, and the description of Zosimus, 1. l. ii. p. 167, &c.]

Since Romulus, with a small band of shepherds and outlaws, fortified himself on the hills near the Tyber, ten centuries had already elapsed. [59] During the four first ages, the Romans, in the laborious school of poverty, had acquired the virtues of war and government: by the vigorous exertion of those virtues, and by the assistance of fortune, they had obtained, in the course of the three succeeding centuries, an absolute empire over many countries of Europe, Asia, and Africa. The last three hundred years had been consumed in apparent prosperity and internal decline. The nation of soldiers, magistrates, and legislators, who composed the thirty-five tribes of the Roman people, were dissolved into the common mass of mankind, and confounded with the millions of servile provincials, who had received the name, without adopting the spirit, of Romans. A mercenary army, levied among the subjects and barbarians of the frontier, was the only order of men who preserved and abused their independence. By their tumultuary election, a Syrian, a Goth, or an Arab, was exalted to the throne of Rome, and invested with despotic power over the conquests and over the country of the Scipios.

[Footnote 59: The received calculation of Varro assigns to the foundation of Rome an aera that corresponds with the 754th year before Christ. But so little is the chronology of Rome to be depended on, in the more early ages, that Sir Isaac Newton has brought the same event as low as the year 627 (Compare Niebuhr vol. i. p. 271.—M.)]

The limits of the Roman empire still extended from the Western Ocean to the Tigris, and from Mount Atlas to the Rhine and the Danube. To the undiscerning eye of the vulgar, Philip appeared a monarch no less powerful than Hadrian or Augustus had formerly been. The form was still the same, but the animating health and vigor were fled. The industry of the people was discouraged and exhausted by a long series of oppression. The discipline of the legions, which alone, after the extinction of every other virtue, had propped the greatness of the state, was corrupted by the ambition, or relaxed by the weakness, of the emperors. The strength of the frontiers, which had always consisted in arms rather than in fortifications, was insensibly undermined; and the fairest provinces were left exposed to the rapaciousness or ambition of the barbarians, who soon discovered the decline of the Roman empire.

CHAPTER VIII

STATE OF PERSIA AND RESTORATION OF THE MONARCHY

PART I

OF THE STATE OF PERSIA AFTER THE RESTORATION OF THE MONARCHY BY ARTAXERXES

Whenever Tacitus indulges himself in those beautiful episodes, in which he relates some domestic transaction of the Germans or of the Parthians, his principal object is to relieve the attention of the reader from a uniform scene of vice and misery. From the reign of Augustus to the time of Alexander Severus, the enemies of Rome were in her bosom—the tyrants and the soldiers; and her prosperity had a very distant and feeble interest in the revolutions that might happen beyond the Rhine and the Euphrates. But when the military order had levelled, in wild anarchy, the power of the prince, the laws of the senate, and even the discipline of the camp, the barbarians of the North and of the East, who had long hovered on the frontier, boldly attacked the provinces of a declining monarchy. Their vexatious inroads were changed into formidable irruptions, and, after a long vicissitude of mutual calamities, many tribes of the victorious invaders established themselves in the provinces of the Roman Empire. To obtain a clearer knowledge of these great events, we shall endeavor to form a previous idea of the character, forces, and designs of those nations who avenged the cause of Hannibal and Mithridates.

In the more early ages of the world, whilst the forest that covered Europe afforded a retreat to a few wandering savages, the inhabitants of Asia were already collected into populous cities, and reduced under extensive empires, the seat of the arts, of luxury, and of despotism. The Assyrians reigned over the East, [1] till the sceptre of Ninus and Semiramis dropped from the hands of their enervated successors. The Medes and the Babylonians divided their power, and were themselves swallowed up in the monarchy of the Persians, whose arms could not be confined within the narrow limits of Asia. Followed, as it is said, by two millions of men, Xerxes, the descendant of Cyrus, invaded Greece.

Thirty thousand soldiers, under the command of Alexander, the son of Philip, who was intrusted by the Greeks with their glory and revenge, were sufficient to subdue Persia. The princes of the house of Seleucus usurped and lost the Macedonian command over the East. About the same time, that, by an ignominious treaty, they resigned to the Romans the country on this side Mount Tarus, they were driven by the Parthians, [100/1] an obscure horde of Scythian origin, from all the provinces of Upper Asia. The formidable power of the Parthians, which spread from India to the frontiers of Syria, was in its turn subverted by Ardshir, or Artaxerxes; the founder of a new dynasty, which, under the name of Sassanides, governed Persia till the invasion of the Arabs. This great revolution, whose fatal influence was soon experienced by the Romans, happened in the fourth year of Alexander Severus, two hundred and twenty-six years after the Christian era. [2] [2/1]

[Footnote 1: An ancient chronologist, quoted by Valleius Paterculus, (l. i. c. 6,) observes, that the Assyrians, the Medes, the Persians, and the Macedonians, reigned over Asia one thousand nine hundred and ninety-five years, from the accession of Ninus to the defeat of Antiochus by the Romans. As the latter of these great events happened 289 years before Christ, the former may be placed 2184 years before the same aera. The Astronomical Observations, found at Babylon, by Alexander, went fifty years higher.]

[Footnote 100/1: The Parthians were a tribe of the Indo-Germanic branch which dwelt on the south-east of the Caspian, and belonged to the same race as the Getae, the Massagetae, and other nations, confounded by the ancients under the vague denomination of Scythians. Klaproth, Tableaux Hist. d l'Asie, p. 40. Strabo (p. 747) calls the Parthians Carduchi, i.e., the inhabitants of Curdistan.—M.]

[Footnote 2: In the five hundred and thirty-eighth year of the aera of Seleucus. See Agathias, l. ii. p. 63. This great event (such is the carelessness of the Orientals) is placed by Eutychius as high as the tenth year of Commodus, and by Moses of Chorene as low as the reign of Philip. Ammianus Marcellinus has so servilely copied (xxiii. 6) his ancient materials, which are indeed very good, that he describes the family of the Arsacides as still seated on the Persian throne in the middle of the fourth century.]

[Footnote 2/1: The Persian History, if the poetry of the Shah Nameh, the Book of Kings, may deserve that name mentions four dynasties from the earliest ages to the invasion of the Saracens. The Shah Nameh was composed with the view of perpetuating the remains of the original Persian records or traditions which had survived the Saracenic invasion. The task was undertaken by the poet Dukiki, and afterwards, under the patronage of Mahmood of Ghazni, completed by Ferdusi. The first of these dynasties is that of Kaiomors, as Sir W. Jones observes, the dark and fabulous period; the second, that of the Kaianian, the heroic and poetical, in which the earned have discovered some curious, and imagined some fanciful, analogies with the Jewish, the Greek, and the Roman accounts of the eastern world. See, on the Shah Nameh, Translation by Goerres, with Von Hammer's Review, Vienna Jahrbuch von Lit. 17, 75, 77. Malcolm's Persia, 8vo. ed. i. 503. Macan's Preface to his Critical Edition of the Shah Nameh. On the early Persian History, a very sensible abstract of various opinions in Malcolm's Hist. of Persian.—M.]

Artaxerxes had served with great reputation in the armies of Artaban, the last king of the Parthians, and it appears that he was driven into exile and rebellion by royal ingratitude, the customary reward for superior merit. His birth was obscure, and the obscurity equally gave room to the aspersions of his enemies, and the flattery of his adherents. If we credit the scandal of the former, Artaxerxes sprang from the illegitimate commerce of a tanner's wife with a common soldier. [3] The latter represent him as descended from a branch of the ancient kings of Persian, though time and misfortune had gradually reduced his ancestors to the humble station of private citizens. [4] As the lineal heir of the monarchy, he asserted his right to the throne, and challenged the noble task of delivering the Persians from the oppression under which they groaned above five centuries since the death of Darius. The Parthians were defeated in three great battles. [4/1] In the last of these their king Artaban was slain, and the spirit of the nation was forever broken. [5] The authority of Artaxerxes was solemnly acknowledged in a great assembly held at Balch in Khorasan. [5/1] Two younger branches of the royal house of Arsaces were confounded among the prostrate satraps. A third, more mindful of ancient grandeur than of present necessity, attempted to retire, with a numerous train of vessels, towards their kinsman, the king of Armenia; but this little army of deserters was intercepted, and cut off, by the vigilance of the conqueror, [6] who boldly assumed the double diadem, and the title of King of Kings, which had been enjoyed by his predecessor. But these pompous titles, instead of gratifying the vanity of the Persian, served only to admonish him of his duty, and to inflame in his soul and should the ambition of restoring in their full splendor, the religion and empire of Cyrus.

[Footnote 3: The tanner's name was Babec; the soldier's, Sassan: from the former Artaxerxes obtained the surname of Babegan, from the latter all his descendants have been styled Sassanides.]

[Footnote 4: D'Herbelot, Bibliotheque Orientale, Ardshir.]

[Footnote 4/1: In the plain of Hoormuz, the son of Babek was hailed in the field with the proud title of Shahan Shah, king of kings—a name ever since assumed by the sovereigns of Persia. Malcolm, i. 71.—M.]

[Footnote 5: Dion Cassius, l. lxxx. Herodian, l. vi. p. 207. Abulpharagins Dynast. p. 80.]

[Footnote 5/1: See the Persian account of the rise of Ardeschir Babegan in Malcolm I 69.—M.]

[Footnote 6: See Moses Chorenensis, l. ii. c. 65—71.]

I. During the long servitude of Persia under the Macedonian and the Parthian yoke, the nations of Europe and Asia had mutually adopted and corrupted each other's superstitions. The Arsacides, indeed, practised the worship of the Magi; but they disgraced and polluted it with a various mixture of foreign idolatry. [6/1] The memory of Zoroaster, the ancient prophet and philosopher of the Persians, [7] was still revered in the East; but the obsolete and mysterious language, in which the Zendavesta was composed, [8] opened a field of dispute to seventy sects, who variously explained the fundamental doctrines of their religion, and were all indifferently devided by a crowd of infidels, who rejected the divine mission and miracles of the prophet. To suppress the idolaters, reunite the schismatics, and confute the unbelievers, by the infallible decision of a general council, the pious Artaxerxes summoned the Magi from all parts of his dominions. These priests, who had so long sighed in contempt and obscurity obeyed the welcome summons; and, on the appointed day, appeared, to the number of about eighty thousand. But as the debates of so tumultuous an assembly could not have been directed by the authority of reason, or influenced by the art of policy, the Persian synod was reduced, by successive operations, to forty thousand, to four thousand, to four hundred, to forty, and at last to seven Magi, the most respected for their learning and piety. One of these, Erdaviraph, a young but holy prelate, received from the hands of his brethren three cups of soporiferous wine. He drank them off, and instantly fell into a long and profound sleep. As soon as he waked, he related to the king and to the believing multitude, his journey to heaven, and his intimate conferences with the Deity. Every doubt was silenced by this supernatural evidence; and the articles of the faith of Zoroaster were fixed with equal authority and precision. [9] A short delineation of that celebrated system will be found useful, not only to display the character of the Persian nation, but to illustrate many of their most important transactions, both in peace and war, with the Roman empire. [10]

[Footnote 6/1: Silvestre de Sacy (Antiquites de la Perse) had proved the neglect of the Zoroastrian religion under the Parthian kings.—M.]

[Footnote 7: Hyde and Prideaux, working up the Persian legends and their own conjectures into a very agreeable story, represent Zoroaster as a contemporary of Darius Hystaspes. But it is sufficient to observe, that the Greek writers, who lived almost in the age of Darius, agree in placing the aera of Zoroaster many hundred, or even thousand, years before their own time. The judicious criticisms of Mr. Moyle perceived, and maintained against his uncle, Dr. Prideaux, the antiquity of the Persian prophet. See his work, vol. ii. Note: There are three leading theories concerning the age of Zoroaster: 1. That which assigns him to an age of great and almost indefinite antiquity—it is that of Moyle, adopted by Gibbon, Volney, Recherches sur l'Histoire, ii. 2. Rhode, also, (die Heilige Sage, &c.,) in a very ingenious and ably-developed theory, throws the Bactrian prophet far back into antiquity 2. Foucher, (Mem. de l'Acad. xxvii. 253,) Tychsen, (in Com. Soc. Gott. ii. 112), Heeren, (Ideen. i. 459,) and recently Holty, identify the Gushtasp of the Persian mythological history with Cyaxares the First, the king of the Medes, and consider the religion to be Median in its origin. M. Guizot considers this opinion most probable, note in loc. 3. Hyde, Prideaux, Anquetil du Perron, Kleuker, Herder, Goerres, (Mythen-Geschichte,) Von Hammer. (Wien. Jahrbuch, vol. ix.,) Malcolm, (i. 528,) De Guigniaut, (Relig. de l'Antiq. 2d part, vol. iii.,) Klaproth, (Tableaux de l'Asie, p. 21,) make Gushtasp Darius Hystaspes, and Zoroaster his contemporary. The silence of Herodotus appears the great objection to this theory. Some writers, as M. Foucher (resting, as

M. Guizot observes, on the doubtful authority of Pliny,) make more than one Zoroaster, and so attempt to reconcile the conflicting theories.— M.]

[Footnote 8: That ancient idiom was called the Zend. The language of the commentary, the Pehlvi, though much more modern, has ceased many ages ago to be a living tongue. This fact alone (if it is allowed as authentic) sufficiently warrants the antiquity of those writings which M d'Anquetil has brought into Europe, and translated into French. Note: Zend signifies life, living. The word means, either the collection of the canonical books of the followers of Zoroaster, or the language itself in which they are written. They are the books that contain the word of life whether the language was originally called Zend, or whether it was so called from the contents of the books. Avesta means word, oracle, revelation: this term is not the title of a particular work, but of the collection of the books of Zoroaster, as the revelation of Ormuzd. This collection is sometimes called Zendavesta, sometimes briefly Zend. The Zend was the ancient language of Media, as is proved by its affinity with the dialects of Armenia and Georgia; it was already a dead language under the Arsacides in the country which was the scene of the events recorded in the Zendavesta. Some critics, among others Richardson and Sir W. Jones, have called in question the antiquity of these books. The former pretended that Zend had never been a written or spoken language, but had been invented in the later times by the Magi, for the purposes of their art; but Kleuker, in the dissertations which he added to those of Anquetil and the Abbe Foucher, has proved that the Zend was a living and spoken language.—G. Sir W. Jones appears to have abandoned his doubts, on discovering the affinity between the Zend and the Sanskrit. Since the time of Kleuker, this question has been investigated by many learned scholars. Sir W. Jones, Leyden, (Asiat. Research. x. 283,) and Mr. Erskine, (Bombay Trans. ii. 299,) consider it a derivative from the Sanskrit. The antiquity of the Zendavesta has likewise been asserted by Rask, the great Danish linguist, who, according to Malcolm, brought back from the East fresh transcripts and additions to those published by Anquetil. According to Rask, the Zend and Sanskrit are sister dialects; the one the parent of the Persian, the other of the Indian family of languages.—G. and M.—But the subject is more satisfactorily illustrated in Bopp's comparative Grammar of the Sanscrit, Zend, Greek, Latin, Lithuanian, Gothic, and German languages. Berlin. 1833-5. According to Bopp, the Zend is, in some respects, of a more remarkable structure than the Sanskrit. Parts of the Zendavesta have been published in the original, by M. Bournouf, at Paris, and M. Ol. shausen, in Hamburg.—M.—The Pehlvi was the language of the countries bordering on Assyria, and probably of Assyria itself. Pehlvi signifies valor, heroism; the Pehlvi, therefore, was the language of the ancient heroes and kings of Persia, the valiant. (Mr. Erskine prefers the derivation from Pehla, a border.—M.) It contains a number of Aramaic roots. Anquetil considered it formed from the Zend. Kleuker does not adopt this opinion. The Pehlvi, he says, is much more flowing, and less overcharged with vowels, than the Zend. The books of Zoroaster, first written in Zend, were afterwards translated into Pehlvi and Parsi. The Pehlvi had fallen into disuse under the dynasty of the Sassanides, but the learned still wrote it. The Parsi, the dialect of Pars or Farristan, was then prevailing dialect. Kleuker, Anhang zum Zend Avesta, 2, ii. part i. p. 158, part ii. 31.—G.—Mr. Erskine (Bombay Transactions) considers the existing Zendavesta to have been compiled in the time of Ardeschir Babegan.—M.]

[Footnote 9: Hyde de Religione veterum Pers. c. 21.]

[Footnote 10: I have principally drawn this account from the Zendavesta of M. d'Anquetil, and the Sadder, subjoined to Dr. Hyde's treatise. It must, however, be confessed, that the studied obscurity of a prophet, the figurative style of the East, and the deceitful medium of a French or Latin version may have betrayed us into error and heresy, in this abridgment of Persian theology. Note: It is to be regretted that Gibbon followed the post-Mahometan Sadder of Hyde.—M.]

The great and fundamental article of the system, was the celebrated doctrine of the two principles; a bold and injudicious attempt of Eastern philosophy to reconcile the existence of moral and physical evil with the attributes of a beneficent Creator and Governor of the world. The first and original Being, in whom, or by whom, the universe exists, is denominated in the writings of Zoroaster, Time without bounds; [10/1] but it must be confessed, that this infinite substance seems rather a metaphysical, abstraction of the mind, than a real object endowed with self-consciousness, or possessed of moral perfections. From either the blind or the intelligent operation of this infinite Time, which bears but too near an affinity with the chaos of the Greeks, the two secondary but active principles of the universe, were from all eternity produced, Ormusd and Ahriman, each of them possessed of the powers of creation, but each disposed, by his invariable nature, to exercise them with different designs. [10/2] The principle of good is eternally aborbed in light; the principle of evil eternally buried in darkness. The wise benevolence of Ormusd formed man capable of virtue, and abundantly provided his fair habitation with the materials of happiness. By his vigilant providence, the motion of the planets, the order of the seasons, and the temperate mixture of the elements, are preserved. But the malice of Ahriman has long since pierced Ormusd's egg; or, in other words, has violated the harmony of his works. Since that fatal eruption, the most minute articles of good and evil are intimately intermingled and agitated together; the rankest poisons spring up amidst the most salutary plants; deluges, earthquakes, and conflagrations attest the conflict of Nature, and the little world of man is perpetually shaken by vice and misfortune. Whilst the rest of human kind are led away captives in the chains of their infernal enemy, the faithful Persian alone reserves his religious adoration for his friend and protector Ormusd, and fights under his banner of light, in the full confidence that he shall, in the last day, share the glory of his triumph. At that decisive period, the enlightened wisdom of goodness will render the power of Ormusd superior to the furious malice of his rival. Ahriman and his followers, disarmed and subdued, will sink into their native darkness; and virtue will maintain the eternal peace and harmony of the universe. [11] [11/1]

[Footnote 10/1: Zeruane Akerene, so translated by Anquetil and Kleuker. There is a dissertation of Foucher on this subject, Mem. de l'Acad. des Inscr. t. xxix. According to Bohlen (das alte Indien) it is the Sanskrit Sarvan Akaranam, the Uncreated Whole; or, according to Fred. Schlegel, Sarvan Akharyam the Uncreate Indivisible.—M.]

[Footnote 10/2: This is an error. Ahriman was not forced by his invariable nature to do evil; the Zendavesta expressly recognizes (see the Izeschne) that he was born good, that in his origin he was light; envy rendered him evil; he became jealous of the power and attributes of Ormuzd; then light was changed into darkness, and Ahriman was precipitated into the abyss. See the Abridgment of the Doctrine of the Ancient Persians, by Anquetil, c. ii Section 2.—G.]

[Footnote 11: The modern Parsees (and in some degree the Sadder) exalt Ormusd into the first and omnipotent cause, whilst they degrade Ahriman into an inferior but rebellious spirit. Their desire of pleasing the Mahometans may have contributed to refine their theological systems.]

[Footnote 11/1: According to the Zendavesta, Ahriman will not be annihilated or precipitated forever into darkness: at the resurrection of the dead he will be entirely defeated by Ormuzd, his power will be destroyed, his kingdom overthrown to its foundations, he will himself be purified in torrents of melting metal; he will change his heart and his will, become holy, heavenly establish in his dominions the law and word of Ormuzd, unite himself with him in everlasting friendship, and both will sing hymns in honor of the Great Eternal. See Anquetil's Abridgment. Kleuker, Anhang part iii. p 85, 36; and the Izeschne, one of the books of the Zendavesta. According to the Sadder Bun-Dehesch, a more modern work, Ahriman is to be annihilated: but this is contrary to the text itself of the Zendavesta, and to the idea its author gives of the kingdom of Eternity, after the twelve thousand years assigned to the contest between Good and Evil.—G.]

PART II

The theology of Zoroaster was darkly comprehended by foreigners, and even by the far greater number of his disciples; but the most careless observers were struck with the philosophic simplicity of the Persian worship. "That people," said Herodotus, [12] "rejects the use of temples, of altars, and of statues, and smiles at the folly of those nations who imagine that the gods are sprung from, or bear any affinity with, the human nature. The tops of the highest mountains are the places chosen for sacrifices. Hymns and prayers are the principal worship; the Supreme God, who fills the wide circle of heaven, is the object to whom they are addressed." Yet, at the same time, in the true spirit of a polytheist, he accuseth them of adoring Earth, Water, Fire, the Winds, and the Sun and Moon. But the Persians of every age have denied the charge, and explained the equivocal conduct, which might appear to give a color to it. The elements, and more particularly Fire, Light, and the Sun, whom they called Mithra, [12/1] were the objects of their religious reverence, because they considered them as the purest symbols, the noblest productions, and the most powerful agents of the Divine Power and Nature. [13]

[Footnote 12: Herodotus, l. i. c. 131. But Dr. Prideaux thinks, with reason, that the use of temples was afterwards permitted in the Magian religion. Note: The Pyraea, or fire temples of the Zoroastrians, (observes Kleuker, Persica, p. 16,) were only to be found in Media or Aderbidjan, provinces into which Herodotus did not penetrate.—M.]

[Footnote 12/1: Among the Persians Mithra is not the Sun: Anquetil has contested and triumphantly refuted the opinion of those who confound them, and it is evidently contrary to the text of the Zendavesta. Mithra is the first of the genii, or jzeds, created by Ormuzd; it is he who watches over all nature. Hence arose the misapprehension of some of the Greeks, who have said that Mithra was the summus deus of the Persians: he has a thousand ears and ten thousand eyes. The Chaldeans appear to have assigned him a higher rank than the Persians. It is he who bestows upon the earth the light of the sun. The sun. named Khor, (brightness,) is thus an inferior genius, who, with many other genii, bears a part in the functions of Mithra. These assistant genii to another genius are called his kamkars; but in the Zendavesta they are never confounded. On the days sacred to a particular genius, the Persian ought to recite, not only the prayers addressed to him, but those also which are addressed to his kamkars; thus the hymn or iescht of Mithra is recited on the day of the sun, (Khor,) and vice versa. It is probably this which has sometimes caused them to be confounded; but Anquetil had himself exposed this error, which Kleuker, and all who have studied the Zendavesta, have noticed. See viii. Diss. of Anquetil. Kleuker's Anhang, part iii. p. 132.—G. M. Guizot is unquestionably right, according to the pure and original doctrine of the Zend. The Mithriac worship, which was so extensively propagated in the West, and in which Mithra and the sun were perpetually confounded, seems to have been formed from a fusion of Zoroastrianism and Chaldaism, or the Syrian worship of the sun. An excellent abstract of the question, with references to the works of the chief modern writers on his curious subject, De Sacy, Kleuker, Von Hammer, &c., may be found in De Guigniaut's translation of Kreuzer. Relig. d'Antiquite, notes viii. ix. to book ii. vol. i. 2d part, page 728.—M.]

[Footnote 13: Hyde de Relig. Pers. c. 8. Notwithstanding all their distinctions and protestations, which seem sincere enough, their tyrants, the Mahometans, have constantly stigmatized them as idolatrous worshippers of the fire.]

Every mode of religion, to make a deep and lasting impression on the human mind, must exercise our obedience, by enjoining practices of devotion, for which we can assign no reason; and must acquire our esteem, by inculcating moral duties analogous to the dictates of our own hearts. The religion of Zoroaster was abundantly provided with the former and possessed a sufficient portion of the latter. At the age of puberty, the faithful Persian was invested with a mysterious girdle, the badge of the divine protection; and from that moment all the actions of his life, even the most indifferent, or the most necessary, were sanctified by their peculiar prayers, ejaculations, or genuflections; the omission of which, under any circumstances, was a grievous sin, not inferior in guilt to the violation of the moral duties. The moral duties, however, of justice, mercy, liberality, &c., were in their turn required of the disciple of Zoroaster, who wished to escape the persecution of Ahriman, and to live with Ormusd in a blissful eternity, where the degree of felicity will be exactly proportioned to the degree of virtue and piety. [14]

[Footnote 14: See the Sadder, the smallest part of which consists of moral precepts. The ceremonies enjoined are infinite and trifling. Fifteen genuflections, prayers, &c., were required whenever the devout Persian cut his nails or made water; or as often as he put on the sacred girdle Sadder, Art. 14, 50, 60. Note: Zoroaster exacted much less ceremonial observance, than at a later period, the priests of his doctrines. This is the progress of all religions the worship, simple in its origin, is gradually overloaded with minute superstitions. The maxim of the Zendavesta, on the relative merit of sowing the earth and of prayers, quoted below by Gibbon, proves that Zoroaster did not attach too much importance to these observances. Thus it is not from the Zendavesta that Gibbon derives the proof of his allegation, but from the Sadder, a much later work.—G]

But there are some remarkable instances in which Zoroaster lays aside the prophet, assumes the legislator, and discovers a liberal concern for private and public happiness, seldom to be found among the grovelling or visionary schemes of superstition. Fasting and celibacy, the common means of purchasing the divine favor, he condemns with abhorrence, as a criminal rejection of the best gifts of Providence. The saint, in the Magian religion, is obliged to beget children, to plant useful trees, to destroy noxious animals, to convey water to the dry lands of Persia, and to work out his salvation by pursuing all the labors of agriculture. [14/1] We may quote from the Zendavesta a wise and benevolent maxim, which compensates for many an absurdity. "He who sows the ground with care and diligence acquires a greater stock of religious merit than he could gain by the repetition of ten thousand prayers." [15] In the spring of every year a festival was celebrated, destined to represent the primitive equality, and the present connection, of mankind. The stately kings of Persia, exchanging their vain pomp for more genuine greatness, freely mingled with the humblest but most useful of their subjects. On that day the husbandmen were admitted, without distinction, to the table of the king and his satraps. The monarch accepted their petitions, inquired into their grievances, and conversed with them on the most equal terms. "From your labors," was he accustomed to say, (and to say with truth, if not with sincerity,) "from your labors we receive our subsistence; you derive your tranquillity from our vigilance: since, therefore, we are mutually necessary to each other, let us live together like brothers in concord and love." [16] Such a festival must indeed have degenerated, in a wealthy and despotic empire, into a theatrical representation; but it was at least a comedy well worthy of a royal audience, and which might sometimes imprint a salutary lesson on the mind of a young prince.

[Footnote 14/1: See, on Zoroaster's encouragement of agriculture, the ingenious remarks of Heeren, Ideen, vol. i. p. 449, &c., and Rhode, Heilige Sage, p. 517—M.]

[Footnote 15: Zendavesta, tom. i. p. 224, and Precis du Systeme de Zoroastre, tom. iii.]

[Footnote 16: Hyde de Religione Persarum, c. 19.]

Had Zoroaster, in all his institutions, invariably supported this exalted character, his name would deserve a place with those of Numa and Confucius, and his system would be justly entitled to all the applause, which it has pleased some of our divines, and even some of our philosophers, to bestow on it. But in that motley composition, dictated by reason and passion, by enthusiasm and by selfish motives, some useful and sublime truths were disgraced by a mixture of the most abject and dangerous superstition. The Magi, or sacerdotal order, were extremely numerous, since, as we have already seen, fourscore thousand of them were convened in a general council. Their forces were multiplied by discipline. A regular hierarchy was diffused through all the provinces of Persia; and the Archimagus, who resided at Balch, was respected as the visible head of the church, and the lawful successor of Zoroaster. [17] The property of the Magi was very considerable. Besides the less invidious possession of a large tract of the most fertile lands of Media, [18] they levied a general tax on the fortunes and the industry of the Persians. [19] "Though your good works," says the interested prophet, "exceed in number the leaves of the trees, the drops of rain, the stars in the heaven, or the sands on the sea-shore, they will all be unprofitable to you, unless they are accepted by the destour, or priest. To obtain the acceptation of this guide to salvation, you must faithfully pay him tithes of all you possess, of your goods, of your lands, and of your money. If the destour be satisfied, your soul will escape hell tortures; you will secure praise in this world and happiness in the next. For the destours are the teachers of religion; they know all things, and they deliver all men." [20] [20/1]

[Footnote 17: Hyde de Religione Persarum, c. 28. Both Hyde and Prideaux affect to apply to the Magian the terms consecrated to the Christian hierarchy.]

[Footnote 18: Ammian. Marcellin. xxiii. 6. He informs us (as far as we may credit him) of two curious particulars: 1. That the Magi derived some of their most secret doctrines from the Indian Brachmans; and 2. That they were a tribe, or family, as well as order.]

[Footnote 19: The divine institution of tithes exhibits a singular instance of conformity between the law of Zoroaster and that of Moses. Those who cannot otherwise account for it, may suppose, if they please that the Magi of the latter times inserted so useful an interpolation into the writings of their prophet.]

[Footnote 20: Sadder, Art. viii.]

[Footnote 20/1: The passage quoted by Gibbon is not taken from the writings of Zoroaster, but from the Sadder, a work, as has been before said, much later than the books which form the Zendavesta. and written by a Magus for popular use; what it contains, therefore, cannot be attributed to Zoroaster. It is remarkable that Gibbon should fall into this error, for Hyde himself does not ascribe the Sadder to Zoroaster; he remarks that it is written inverse, while Zoroaster always wrote in prose. Hyde, i. p. 27. Whatever may be the case as to the latter assertion, for which there appears little foundation, it is unquestionable that the Sadder is of much later date. The Abbe Foucher does not even believe it to be an extract from the works of Zoroaster. See his Diss. before quoted. Mem. de l'Acad. des Ins. t. xxvii.—G. Perhaps it is rash to speak of any part of the Zendavesta as the writing of Zoroaster, though it may be a *genuine representation of his. As to the Sadder, Hyde (in Praef.) considered it not above 200 years old. It is manifestly post-Mahometan. See Art. xxv. on fasting.—M.]*

These convenient maxims of reverence and implicit were doubtless imprinted with care on the tender minds of youth; since the Magi were the masters of education in Persia, and to their hands the children even of the royal family were intrusted. [21] The Persian priests, who were of a speculative genius, preserved and investigated the secrets of Oriental philosophy; and acquired, either by superior knowledge, or superior art, the reputation of being well versed in some occult sciences, which have derived their appellation from the Magi. [22] Those of more active dispositions mixed with the world in courts and cities; and it is observed, that the administration of Artaxerxes was in a great measure directed by the counsels of the sacerdotal order, whose dignity, either from policy or devotion, that prince restored to its ancient splendor. [23]

[Footnote 21: Plato in Alcibiad.]

[Footnote 22: Pliny (Hist. Natur. l. xxx. c. 1) observes, that magic held mankind by the triple chain of religion, of physic, and of astronomy.]

[Footnote 23: Agathias, l. iv. p. 134.]

The first counsel of the Magi was agreeable to the unsociable genius of their faith, [24] to the practice of ancient kings, [25] and even to the example of their legislator, who had a victim to a religious war, excited by his own intolerant zeal. [26] By an edict of Artaxerxes, the exercise of every worship, except that of Zoroaster, was severely prohibited. The temples of the Parthians, and the statues of their deified monarchs, were thrown down with ignominy. [27] The sword of Aristotle (such was the name given by the Orientals to the polytheism and philosophy of the Greeks) was easily broken; [28] the flames of persecution soon reached the more stubborn Jews and Christians; [29] nor did they spare the heretics of their own nation and religion. The majesty of Ormusd, who was jealous of a rival, was seconded by the despotism of Artaxerxes, who could not suffer a rebel; and the schismatics within his vast empire were soon reduced to the inconsiderable number of eighty thousand. [30] [30/1] This spirit of persecution reflects dishonor on the religion of Zoroaster; but as it was not productive of any civil commotion, it served to strengthen the new monarchy, by uniting all the various inhabitants of Persia in the bands of religious zeal. [30/2]

[Footnote 24: Mr. Hume, in the Natural History of Religion, sagaciously remarks, that the most refined and philosophic sects are constantly the most intolerant. Note: Hume's comparison is rather between theism and polytheism. In India, in Greece, and in modern Europe, philosophic religion has looked down with contemptuous toleration on the superstitions of the vulgar.—M.]

[Footnote 25: Cicero de Legibus, ii. 10. Xerxes, by the advice of the Magi, destroyed the temples of Greece.]

[Footnote 26: Hyde de Relig. Persar. c. 23, 24. D'Herbelot, Bibliotheque Orientale, Zurdusht. Life of Zoroaster in tom. ii. of the Zendavesta.]

[Footnote 27: Compare Moses of Chorene, l. ii. c. 74, with Ammian. Marcel lin. xxiii. 6. Hereafter I shall make use of these passages.]

[Footnote 28: Rabbi Abraham, in the Tarikh Schickard, p. 108, 109.]

[Footnote 29: Basnage, Histoire des Juifs, l. viii. c. 3. Sozomen, l. ii. c. 1 Manes, who suffered an ignominious death, may be deemed a Magian as well as a Christian heretic.]

[Footnote 30: Hyde de Religione Persar. c. 21.]

[Footnote 30/1: It is incorrect to attribute these persecutions to Artaxerxes. The Jews were held in honor by him, and their schools flourished during his reign. Compare Jost, Geschichte der Israeliter, b. xv. 5, with Basnage. Sapor was forced by the people to temporary severities; but their real persecution did not begin till the reigns of Yezdigerd and Kobad. Hist. of Jews, iii. 236. According to Sozomen, i. viii., Sapor first persecuted the Christians. Manes was put to death by Varanes the First, A. D. 277. Beausobre, Hist. de Man. i. 209.—M.]

[Footnote 30/2: In the testament of Ardischer in Ferdusi, the poet assigns these sentiments to the dying king, as he addresses his son: Never forget that as a king, you are at once the protector of religion and of your country. Consider the altar and the throne as inseparable; they must always sustain each other. Malcolm's Persia. i. 74—M]

II. Artaxerxes, by his valor and conduct, had wrested the sceptre of the East from the ancient royal family of Parthia. There still remained the more difficult task of establishing, throughout the vast extent of Persia, a uniform and vigorous administration. The weak indulgence of the Arsacides had resigned to their sons and brothers the principal provinces, and the greatest offices of the kingdom in the nature of hereditary possessions. The vitaxoe, or eighteen most powerful satraps, were permitted to assume the regal title; and the vain pride of the monarch was delighted with a nominal dominion over so many vassal kings. Even tribes of barbarians in their mountains, and the Greek cities of Upper Asia, [31] within their walls, scarcely acknowledged, or seldom obeyed. any superior; and the Parthian empire exhibited, under other names, a lively image of the feudal system [32] which has since prevailed in Europe. But the active victor, at the head of a numerous and disciplined army, visited in person every province of Persia. The defeat of the boldest rebels, and the reduction of the strongest fortifications, [33] diffused the terror of his arms, and prepared the way for the peaceful reception of his authority. An obstinate resistance was fatal to the chiefs; but their followers were treated with lenity. [34] A cheerful submission was rewarded with honors and riches, but the prudent Artaxerxes suffering no person except himself to assume the title of king, abolished every intermediate power between the throne and the people. His kingdom, nearly equal in extent to modern Persia, was, on every side, bounded by the sea, or by great rivers; by the Euphrates, the Tigris, the Araxes, the Oxus, and the Indus, by the Caspian Sea, the Gulf of Persia. [35] That country was computed to contain, in the last century, five hundred and fifty-four cities, sixty thousand villages, and about forty millions of souls. [36] If we compare the administration of the house of Sassan with that of the house of Sefi, the political influence of the Magian with that of the Mahometan religion, we shall probably infer, that the kingdom of Artaxerxes contained at least as great a number of cities, villages, and inhabitants. But it must likewise be confessed, that in every age the want of harbors on the sea-coast, and the scarcity of fresh water in the inland provinces, have been very unfavorable to the commerce and agriculture of the Persians; who, in the calculation of their numbers, seem to have indulged one of the nearest, though most common, artifices of national vanity.

[Footnote 31: These colonies were extremely numerous. Seleucus Nicator founded thirty-nine cities, all named from himself, or some of his relations, (see Appian in Syriac. p. 124.) The aera of Seleucus (still in

use among the eastern Christians) appears as late as the year 508, of Christ 196, on the medals of the Greek cities within the Parthian empire. See Moyle's works, vol. i. p. 273, &c., and M. Freret, Mem. de l'Academie, tom. xix.]

[Footnote 32: The modern Persians distinguish that period as the dynasty of the kings of the nations. See Plin. Hist. Nat. vi. 25.]

[Footnote 33: Eutychius (tom. i. p. 367, 371, 375) relates the siege of the island of Mesene in the Tigris, with some circumstances not unlike the story of Nysus and Scylla.]

[Footnote 34: Agathias, ii. 64, [and iv. p. 260.] The princes of Segestan de fended their independence during many years. As romances generally transport to an ancient period the events of their own time, it is not impossible that the fabulous exploits of Rustan, Prince of Segestan, many have been grafted on this real history.]

[Footnote 35: We can scarcely attribute to the Persian monarchy the sea-coast of Gedrosia or Macran, which extends along the Indian Ocean from Cape Jask (the promontory Capella) to Cape Goadel. In the time of Alexander, and probably many ages afterwards, it was thinly inhabited by a savage people of Icthyophagi, or Fishermen, who knew no arts, who acknowledged no master, and who were divided by in-hospitable deserts from the rest of the world. (See Arrian de Reb. Indicis.) In the twelfth century, the little town of Taiz (supposed by M. d'Anville to be the Teza of Ptolemy) was peopled and enriched by the resort of the Arabian merchants. (See Geographia Nubiens, p. 58, and d'Anville, Geographie Ancienne, tom. ii. p. 283.) In the last age, the whole country was divided between three princes, one Mahometan and two Idolaters, who maintained their independence against the successors of Shah Abbas. (Voyages de Tavernier, part i. l. v. p. 635.)]

[Footnote 36: Chardin, tom. iii c 1 2, 3.]

As soon as the ambitious mind of Artaxerxes had triumphed ever the resistance of his vassals, he began to threaten the neighboring states, who, during the long slumber of his predecessors, had insulted Persia with impunity. He obtained some easy victories over the wild Scythians and the effeminate Indians; but the Romans were an enemy, who, by their past injuries and present power, deserved the utmost efforts of his arms. A forty years' tranquillity, the fruit of valor and moderation, had succeeded the victories of Trajan. During the period that elapsed from the accession of Marcus to the reign of Alexander, the Roman and the Parthian empires were twice engaged in war; and although the whole strength of the Arsacides contended with a part only of the forces of Rome, the event was most commonly in favor of the latter. Macrinus, indeed, prompted by his precarious situation and pusillanimous temper, purchased a peace at the expense of near two millions of our money; [37] but the generals of Marcus, the emperor Severus, and his son, erected many trophies in Armenia, Mesopotamia, and Assyria. Among their exploits, the imperfect relation of which would have unseasonably interrupted the more important series of domestic revolutions, we shall only mention the repeated calamities of the two great cities of Seleucia and Ctesiphon.

[Footnote 37: Dion, l. xxviii. p. 1335.]

Seleucia, on the western bank of the Tigris, about forty-five miles to the north of ancient Babylon, was the capital of the Macedonian conquests in Upper Asia. [38] Many ages after the fall of their empire, Seleucia retained the genuine characters of a Grecian colony, arts, military virtue, and the love of freedom. The independent republic was governed by a senate of three hundred nobles; the people consisted of six hundred thousand citizens; the walls were strong, and as long as concord prevailed among the several orders of the state, they viewed with contempt the power of the Parthian: but the madness of faction was sometimes provoked to implore the dangerous aid of the common enemy, who was posted almost at the gates of the colony. [39] The Parthian monarchs, like the Mogul sovereigns of Hindostan, delighted in the pastoral life of their Scythian ancestors; and the Imperial camp was frequently pitched in the plain of Ctesiphon, on the eastern bank of the Tigris, at the distance of only three miles from Seleucia. [40] The innumerable attendants on luxury and despotism resorted to the court, and the little village of Ctesiphon insensibly swelled into a great city. [41] Under the reign of Marcus, the Roman generals penetrated as far as Ctesiphon and Seleucia. They were received as friends by the Greek colony; they attacked as enemies the seat of the Parthian kings; yet both cities experienced the same treatment. The sack and conflagration of Seleucia, with the massacre of three hundred thousand of the inhabitants, tarnished the glory of the Roman triumph. [42] Seleucia, already exhausted by the neighborhood of a too powerful rival, sunk under the fatal blow; but Ctesiphon, in about thirty-three years, had sufficiently recovered its strength to maintain an obstinate siege against the emperor Severus. The city was, however, taken by assault; the king, who defended it in person, escaped with precipitation; a hundred thousand captives, and a rich booty, rewarded the fatigues of the Roman soldiers. [43] Notwithstanding these misfortunes, Ctesiphon succeeded to Babylon and to Seleucia, as one of the great capitals of the East. In summer, the monarch of Persia enjoyed at Ecbatana the cool breezes of the mountains of Media; but the mildness of the climate engaged him to prefer Ctesiphon for his winter residence.

[Footnote 38: For the precise situation of Babylon, Seleucia, Ctesiphon, Moiain, and Bagdad, cities often confounded with each other, see an excellent Geographical Tract of M. d'Anville, in Mem. de l'Academie, tom. xxx.]

[Footnote 39: Tacit. Annal. xi. 42. Plin. Hist. Nat. vi. 26.]

[Footnote 40: This may be inferred from Strabo, l. xvi. p. 743.]

[Footnote 41: That most curious traveller, Bernier, who followed the camp of Aurengzebe from Delhi to Cashmir, describes with great accuracy the immense moving city. The guard of cavalry consisted of 35,000 men, that of infantry of 10,000. It was computed that the camp contained 150,000 horses, mules, and elephants; 50,000 camels, 50,000 oxen, and between 300,000 and 400,000 persons. Almost all Delhi followed the court, whose magnificence supported its industry.]

[Footnote 42: Dion, l. lxxi. p. 1178. Hist. August. p. 38. Eutrop. viii. 10 Euseb. in Chronic. Quadratus (quoted in the Augustan History) attempted to vindicate the Romans by alleging that the citizens of Seleucia had first violated their faith.]

[Footnote 43: Dion, l. lxxv. p. 1263. Herodian, l. iii. p. 120. Hist. August. p. 70.]

From these successful inroads the Romans derived no real or lasting benefit; nor did they attempt to preserve such distant conquests, separated from the provinces of the empire by a large tract of intermediate desert. The reduction of the kingdom of Osrhoene was an acquisition of less splendor indeed, but of a far more solid advantage. That little state occupied the northern and most fertile part of Mesopotamia, between the Euphrates and the Tigris. Edessa, its capital, was situated about twenty miles beyond the former of those rivers; and the inhabitants, since the time of Alexander, were a mixed race of Greeks, Arabs, Syrians, and Armenians. [44] The feeble sovereigns of Osrhoene, placed on the dangerous verge of two contending empires, were attached from inclination to the Parthian cause; but the superior power of Rome exacted from them a reluctant homage, which is still attested by their medals. After the conclusion of the Parthian war under Marcus, it was judged prudent to secure some substantia, pledges of their doubtful fidelity. Forts were constructed in several parts of the country, and a Roman garrison was fixed in the strong town of Nisibis. During the troubles that followed the death of Commodus, the princes of Osrhoene attempted to shake off the yoke; but the stern policy of Severus confirmed their dependence, [45] and the perfidy of Caracalla completed the easy conquest. Abgarus, the last king of Edessa, was sent in chains to Rome, his dominions reduced into a province, and his capital dignified with the rank of colony; and thus the Romans, about ten years before the fall of the Parthian monarchy, obtained a firm and permanent establishment beyond the Euphrates. [46]

[Footnote 44: The polished citizens of Antioch called those of Edessa mixed barbarians. It was, however, some praise, that of the three dialects of the Syriac, the purest and most elegant (the Aramaean) was spoken at Edessa. This remark M. Bayer (Hist. Edess. p 5) has borrowed from George of Malatia, a Syrian writer.]

[Footnote 45: Dion, l. lxxv. p. 1248, 1249, 1250. M. Bayer has neglected to use this most important passage.]

[Footnote 46: This kingdom, from Osrhoes, who gave a new name to the country, to the last Abgarus, had lasted 353 years. See the learned work of M. Bayer, Historia Osrhoena et Edessena.]

Prudence as well as glory might have justified a war on the side of Artaxerxes, had his views been confined to the defence or acquisition of a useful frontier. but the ambitious Persian openly avowed a far more extensive design of conquest; and he thought himself able to support his lofty pretensions by the arms of reason as well as by those of power. Cyrus, he alleged, had first subdued, and his successors had for a long time possessed, the whole extent of Asia, as far as the Propontis and the Aegean Sea; the provinces of Caria and Ionia, under their empire, had been governed by Persian satraps, and all Egypt, to the confines of Aethiopia, had acknowledged their sovereignty. [47] Their rights had been suspended, but not destroyed, by a long usurpation; and as soon as he received the Persian diadem, which birth and successful valor had placed upon his head, the first great duty of his station called upon him to restore the ancient limits and splendor of the monarchy. The Great King, therefore, (such was the haughty style of his embassies to the emperor Alexander,) commanded the Romans instantly to depart from all the provinces of his ancestors, and, yielding to the Persians the empire of Asia, to content themselves with the undisturbed possession of Europe. This haughty mandate was delivered by four hundred of the tallest and most beautiful of the Persians; who, by their fine horses, splendid arms, and rich apparel, displayed the pride and greatness of their master. [48] Such an embassy was much less an offer of negotiation than a declaration of war. Both Alexander Severus and Artaxerxes, collecting the military force of the Roman and Persian monarchies, resolved in this important contest to lead their armies in person.

[Footnote 47: Xenophon, in the preface to the Cyropaedia, gives a clear and magnificent idea of the extent of the empire of Cyrus. Herodotus (l. iii. c. 79, &c.) enters into a curious and particular description of the twenty great Satrapies into which the Persian empire was divided by Darius Hystaspes.]

[Footnote 48: Herodian, vi. 209, 212.]

If we credit what should seem the most authentic of all records, an oration, still extant, and delivered by the emperor himself to the senate, we must allow that the victory of Alexander Severus was not inferior to any of those formerly obtained over the Persians by the son of Philip. The army of the Great King consisted of one hundred and twenty thousand horse, clothed in complete armor of steel; of seven hundred elephants, with towers filled with archers on their backs, and of eighteen hundred chariots armed with scythes. This formidable host, the like of which is not to be found in eastern history, and has scarcely been imagined in eastern romance, [49] was discomfited in a great battle, in which the Roman Alexander proved himself an intrepid soldier and a skilful general. The Great King fled before his valor; an immense booty, and the conquest of Mesopotamia, were the immediate fruits of this signal victory. Such are the circumstances of this ostentatious and improbable relation, dictated, as it too plainly appears, by the vanity of the monarch, adorned by the unblushing servility of his flatterers, and received without contradiction by a distant and obsequious senate. [50] Far from being inclined to believe that the arms of Alexander obtained any memorable advantage over the Persians, we are induced to suspect that all this blaze of imaginary glory was designed to conceal some real disgrace.

[Footnote 49: There were two hundred scythed chariots at the battle of Arbela, in the host of Darius. In the vast army of Tigranes, which was vanquished by Lucullus, seventeen thousand horse only were completely armed. Antiochus brought fifty-four elephants into the field against the Romans: by his frequent wars and negotiations with the princes of India, he had once collected a hundred and fifty of those great animals; but it may be questioned whether the most powerful monarch of Hindostan evci formed a line of battle of seven hundred elephants. Instead of three or four thousand elephants, which the Great Mogul was supposed to possess, Tavernier (Voyages, part ii. l. i. p. 198) discovered, by a more accurate inquiry, that he had only five hundred for his baggage, and eighty or ninety for the service of war. The Greeks have varied with regard to the number which Porus brought into the field; but Quintus Curtius, (viii. 13,) in this instance judicious and moderate, is contented with eighty-five elephants, distinguished by their size and strength. In Siam, where these animals are the most numerous and the most esteemed, eighteen elephants are allowed as a sufficient proportion for each of the nine brigades into which a just army is divided. The whole number, of one hundred and sixty-two elephants of war, may sometimes be doubled. Hist. des Voyages, tom. ix. p. 260. Note: Compare Gibbon's note 10 to ch. lvii—M.]

[Footnote 50: Hist. August. p. 133. Note: See M. Guizot's note, p. 267. According to the Persian authorities Ardeschir extended his conquests to the Euphrates. Malcolm i. 71.—M.]

Our suspicious are confirmed by the authority of a contemporary historian, who mentions the virtues of Alexander with respect, and his faults with candor. He describes the judicious plan which had been formed for the conduct of the war. Three Roman armies were destined to invade Persia at the same time, and by different roads. But the operations of the campaign, though wisely concerted, were not executed either with ability or success. The first of these armies, as soon as it had entered the marshy plains of Babylon, towards the artificial conflux of the Euphrates and the Tigris, [51] was encompassed by the superior numbers, and destroyed by the arrows of the enemy. The alliance of Chosroes, king of Armenia, [52] and the long tract of mountainous country, in which the Persian cavalry was of little service, opened a secure entrance into the heart of Media, to the second of the Roman armies. These brave troops laid waste the adjacent provinces, and by several successful actions against Artaxerxes, gave a faint color to the emperor's vanity. But the retreat of this victorious army was imprudent, or at least unfortunate. In repassing the mountains, great numbers of soldiers perished by the badness of the roads, and the severity of the winter season. It had been resolved, that whilst these two great detachments penetrated into the opposite extremes of the Persian dominions, the main body, under the command of Alexander himself, should support their attack, by invading the centre of the kingdom. But the unexperienced youth, influenced by his mother's counsels, and perhaps by his own fears, deserted the bravest troops, and the fairest prospect of victory; and after consuming in Mesopotamia an inactive and inglorious summer, he led back to Antioch an army diminished by sickness, and provoked by disappointment. The behavior of Artaxerxes had been very different. Flying with rapidity from the hills of Media to the marshes of the Euphrates, he had everywhere opposed the invaders in person; and in either fortune had united with the ablest conduct the most undaunted resolution. But in several obstinate engagements against the veteran legions of Rome, the Persian monarch had lost the flower of his troops. Even his victories had weakened his power. The favorable opportunities of the absence of Alexander, and of the confusions that followed that emperor's death, presented themselves in vain to his ambition. Instead of expelling the Romans, as he pretended, from the continent of Asia, he found himself unable to wrest from their hands the little province of Mesopotamia. [53]

[Footnote 51: M. de Tillemont has already observed, that Herodian's geography is somewhat confused.]

[Footnote 52: Moses of Chorene (Hist. Armen. l. ii. c. 71) illustrates this invasion of Media, by asserting that Chosroes, king of Armenia, defeated Artaxerxes, and pursued him to the confines of India. The exploits of Chosroes have been magnified; and he acted as a dependent ally to the Romans.]

[Footnote 53: For the account of this war, see Herodian, l. vi. p. 209, 212. The old abbreviators and modern compilers have blindly followed the Augustan History.]

The reign of Artaxerxes, which, from the last defeat of the Parthians, lasted only fourteen years, forms a memorable aera in the history of the East, and even in that of Rome. His character seems to have been marked by those bold and commanding features, that generally distinguish the princes who conquer, from those who inherit an empire. Till the last period of the Persian monarchy, his code of laws was respected as the groundwork of their civil and religious policy. [54] Several of his sayings are preserved. One of them in particular discovers a deep insight into the constitution of government. "The authority of the prince," said Artaxerxes, "must be defended by a military force; that force can only be maintained by taxes; all taxes must, at last, fall upon agriculture; and agriculture can never flourish except under the protection of justice and moderation." [55] Artaxerxes bequeathed his new empire, and his ambitious designs against the Romans, to Sapor, a son not unworthy of his great father; but those designs were too extensive for the power of Persia, and served only to involve both nations in a long series of destructive wars and reciprocal calamities.

[Footnote 54: Eutychius, tom. ii. p. 180, vers. Pocock. The great Chosroes Noushirwan sent the code of Artaxerxes to all his satraps, as the invariable rule of their conduct.]

[Footnote 55: D'Herbelot, Bibliotheque Orientale, au mot Ardshir. We may observe, that after an ancient period of fables, and a long interval of darkness, the modern histories of Persia begin to assume an air of truth with the dynasty of Sassanides. Compare Malcolm, i. 79.—M.]

The Persians, long since civilized and corrupted, were very far from possessing the martial independence, and the intrepid hardiness, both of mind and body, which have rendered the northern barbarians masters of the world. The science of war, that constituted the more rational force of Greece and Rome, as it now does of Europe, never made any considerable progress in the East. Those disciplined evolutions which harmonize and animate a confused multitude, were unknown to the Persians. They were equally unskilled in the arts of constructing, besieging, or defending regular fortifications. They trusted more to their numbers than to their courage; more to their courage than to their discipline. The infantry was a half-armed, spiritless crowd of peasants, levied in haste by the allurements of plunder, and as easily dispersed by a victory as by a defeat. The monarch and his nobles transported into the camp the pride and luxury of the seraglio. Their military operations were impeded by a useless train of women, eunuchs, horses, and camels; and in the midst of a successful campaign, the Persian host was often separated or destroyed by an unexpected famine. [56]

[Footnote 56: Herodian, l. vi. p. 214. Ammianus Marcellinus, l. xxiii. c. 6. Some differences may be observed between the two historians, the natural effects of the changes produced by a century and a half.]

But the nobles of Persia, in the bosom of luxury and despotism, preserved a strong sense of personal gallantry and national honor. From the age of seven years they were taught to speak truth, to shoot with the bow, and to ride; and it was universally confessed, that in the two last of these arts, they had made a more than common proficiency. [57] The most distinguished youth were educated under the monarch's eye, practised their exercises in the gate of his palace, and were severely trained up to the habits of temperance and obedience, in their long and laborious parties of hunting. In every province, the satrap maintained a like school of military virtue. The Persian nobles (so natural is the idea of feudal tenures) received from the king's bounty lands and houses, on the condition of their service in war. They were ready on the first summons to mount on horseback, with a martial and splendid train of followers, and to join the numerous bodies of guards, who were carefully selected from among the most robust slaves, and the bravest adventures of Asia. These armies, both of light and of heavy cavalry, equally formidable by the impetuosity of their charge and the rapidity of their motions, threatened, as an impending cloud, the eastern provinces of the declining empire of Rome. [58]

[Footnote 57: The Persians are still the most skilful horsemen, and their horses the finest in the East.]

[Footnote 58: From Herodotus, Xenophon, Herodian, Ammianus, Chardin, &c., I have extracted such probable accounts of the Persian nobility, as seem either common to every age, or particular to that of the Sassanides.]

CHAPTER IX

STATE OF GERMANY UNTIL THE BARBARIANS

PART I

THE STATE OF GERMANY TILL THE INVASION OF THE BARBARIANS IN THE TIME OF THE EMPEROR DECIUS

The government and religion of Persia have deserved some notice, from their connection with the decline and fall of the Roman empire. We shall occasionally mention the Scythian or Sarmatian tribes, [1001] which, with their arms and horses, their flocks and herds, their wives and families, wandered over the immense plains which spread themselves from the Caspian Sea to the Vistula, from the confines of Persia to those of Germany. But the warlike Germans, who first resisted, then invaded, and at length overturned the Western monarchy of Rome, will occupy a much more important place in this history, and possess a stronger, and, if we may use the expression, a more domestic, claim to our attention and regard. The most civilized nations of modern Europe issued from the woods of Germany; and in the rude institutions of those barbarians we may still distinguish the original principles of our present laws and manners. In their primitive state of simplicity and independence, the Germans were surveyed by the discerning eye, and delineated by the masterly pencil, of Tacitus, [1002] the first of historians who applied the science of philosophy to the study of facts. The expressive conciseness of his descriptions has served to exercise the diligence of innumerable antiquarians, and to excite the genius and penetration of the philosophic historians of our own times. The subject, however various and important, has already been so frequently, so ably, and so successfully discussed, that it is now grown familiar to the reader, and difficult to the writer. We shall therefore content ourselves with observing, and indeed with repeating, some of the most important circumstances of climate, of manners, and of institutions, which rendered the wild barbarians of Germany such formidable enemies to the Roman power.

[Footnote 1001: The Scythians, even according to the ancients, are not Sarmatians. It may be doubted whether Gibbon intended to confound them.—M. —The Greeks, after having divided the world into Greeks and barbarians. divided the barbarians into four great classes, the Celts, the Scythians, the Indians, and the Ethiopians. They called Celts all the inhabitants of Gaul. Scythia extended from the Baltic Sea to the Lake Aral: the people enclosed in the angle to the north-east, between Celtica and Scythia, were called Celto-Scythians, and the Sarmatians were placed in the southern part of that angle. But these names of Celts, of Scythians, of Celto-Scythians, and Sarmatians, were invented, says Schlozer, by the profound cosmographical ignorance of the Greeks, and have no real ground; they are purely geographical divisions, without any relation to the true affiliation of the different races. Thus all the inhabitants of Gaul are called Celts by most of the ancient writers; yet Gaul contained three totally distinct nations, the Belgae, the Aquitani, and the Gauls, properly so called. Hi omnes lingua institutis, legibusque inter se differunt. Caesar. Com. c. i. It is thus the Turks call all Europeans Franks. Schlozer, Allgemeine Nordische Geschichte, p. 289. 1771. Bayer (de Origine et priscis Sedibus Scytharum, in Opusc. p. 64) says, Primus eorum, de quibus constat, Ephorus, in quarto historiarum libro, orbem terrarum inter Scythas, Indos, Aethiopas et Celtas divisit. Fragmentum ejus loci Cosmas Indicopleustes in topographia Christiana, f. 148, conservavit. Video igitur Ephorum, cum locorum positus per certa capita distribuere et explicare constitueret, insigniorum nomina gentium vastioribus spatiis adhibuisse, nulla mala fraude et successu infelici. Nam Ephoro quoquomodo dicta pro exploratis habebant Graeci plerique et Romani: ita gliscebat error posteritate. Igitur tot tamque diversae stirpis gentes non modo intra communem quandam regionem definitae, unum omnes Scytharum nomen his auctoribus subierunt, sed etiam ab illa regionis adpellatione in eandem nationem sunt conflatae. Sic Cimmeriorum res cum Scythicis, Scytharum cum Sarmaticis, Russicis, Hunnicis, Tataricis commiscentur.—G.]

[Footnote 1002: The Germania of Tacitus has been a fruitful source of hypothesis to the ingenuity of modern writers, who have endeavored to account for the form of the work and the views of the author. According to Luden, (Geschichte des T. V. i. 432, and note,) it contains the unfinished and disarranged for a larger work. An anonymous writer, supposed by Luden to be M. Becker, conceives that it was intended as an episode in his larger history. According to M. Guizot, "Tacite a peint les Germains comme Montaigne et Rousseau les sauvages, dans un acces d'humeur contre sa patrie: son livre est une satire des moeurs Romaines, l'eloquente boutade d'un patriote philosophe qui veut voir la vertu la, ou il ne rencontre pas la mollesse honteuse et la depravation savante d'une vielle societe." Hist. de la Civilisation Moderne, i. 258.—M.]

Ancient Germany, excluding from its independent limits the province westward of the Rhine, which had submitted to the Roman yoke, extended itself over a third part of Europe. [1] Almost the whole of modern Germany, Denmark, Norway, Sweden, Finland, Livonia, Prussia, and the greater part of Poland, were peopled by the various tribes of one great nation, whose complexion, manners, and language denoted a common origin, and preserved a striking resemblance. On the west, ancient Germany was divided by the Rhine from the Gallic, and on the south, by the Danube, from the Illyrian, provinces of the empire. A ridge of hills, rising from the Danube, and called the Carpathian Mountains, covered Germany on the side of Dacia or Hungary. The eastern frontier was faintly marked by the mutual fears of the Germans and the Sarmatians, and was often confounded by the mixture of warring and confederating tribes of the two nations. In the remote darkness of the north, the ancients imperfectly descried a frozen ocean that lay beyond the Baltic Sea, and beyond the Peninsula, or islands [1001] of Scandinavia.

[Footnote 1: Germany was not of such vast extent. It is from Caesar, and more particularly from Ptolemy, (says Gatterer,) that we can know what was the state of ancient Germany before the wars with the Romans had changed the positions of the tribes. Germany, as changed by these wars, has been described by Strabo, Pliny, and Tacitus. Germany, properly so called, was bounded on the west by the Rhine, on the east by the Vistula, on the north by the southern point of Norway, by Sweden, and Esthonia. On the south, the Maine and the mountains to the north of Bohemia formed the limits. Before the time of Caesar, the country between the Maine and the Danube was partly occupied by the Helvetians and other Gauls, partly by the Hercynian forest but, from the time of Caesar to the great migration, these boundaries were advanced as far as the Danube, or, what is the same thing, to the Suabian Alps, although the Hercynian forest still occupied, from north to south, a space of nine days' journey on both banks of the Danube. "Gatterer, Versuch einer all-gemeinen Welt-Geschichte," p. 424, edit. de 1792. This vast country was far from being inhabited by a single nation divided into different tribes of the same origin. We may reckon three principal races, very distinct in their language, their origin, and their customs. 1. To the east, the Slaves or Vandals. 2. To the west, the Cimmerians or Cimbri. 3. Between the Slaves and Cimbrians, the Germans, properly so called, the Suevi of Tacitus. The South was inhabited, before Julius Caesar, by nations of Gaulish origin, afterwards by the Suevi.—G. On the position of these nations, the German antiquaries differ. I. The Slaves, or Sclavonians, or Wendish tribes, according to Schlozer, were originally settled in parts of Germany unknown to the Romans, Mecklenburgh, Pomerania, Brandenburgh, Upper Saxony; and Lusatia. According to Gatterer, they remained to the east of the Theiss, the Niemen, and the Vistula, till the third century. The Slaves, according to Procopius and Jornandes, formed three great divisions. 1. The Venedi or Vandals, who took the latter name, (the Wenden,) having expelled the Vandals, properly so called, (a Suevian race, the conquerors of Africa,) from the country between the Memel and the Vistula. 2. The Antes, who inhabited between the Dneister and the Dnieper. 3. The Sclavonians, properly so called, in the north of Dacia. During the great migration, these races advanced into Germany as far as the Saal and the Elbe. The Sclavonian language is the stem from which have issued the Russian, the Polish, the Bohemian, and the dialects of Lusatia, of some parts of the duchy of Luneburgh, of Carniola, Carinthia, and Styria, &c.; those of Croatia, Bosnia, and Bulgaria. Schlozer, Nordische Geschichte, p. 323, 335. II. The Cimbric race. Adelung calls by this name all who were not Suevi. This race had passed the Rhine, before the time of Caesar, occupied Belgium, and are the Belgae of Caesar and Pliny. The Cimbrians also occupied the Isle of Jutland. The Cymri of Wales and of Britain are of this race. Many tribes on the right bank of the Rhine, the Guthini in Jutland, the Usipeti in Westphalia, the Sigambri in the duchy of Berg, were German Cimbrians. III. The Suevi, known in very early times by the Romans, for they are mentioned by L. Corn. Sisenna, who lived 123 years before Christ, (Nonius v. Lancea.) This race, the real Germans, extended to the Vistula, and from the Baltic to the Hercynian forest. The name of Suevi was sometimes confined to a single tribe, as by Caesar to the Catti. The name of the Suevi has been preserved in Suabia. These three were the principal races which inhabited Germany; they moved from east to west, and are the parent stem of the modern natives. But northern Europe, according to Schlozer, was not peopled by them alone; other races, of different origin, and speaking different languages, have inhabited and left descendants in these countries. The German tribes called themselves, from very remote times, by the generic name of Teutons, (Teuten, Deutschen,) which Tacitus derives from that of one of their gods, Tuisco. It appears more probable that it means merely men, people. Many savage nations have given themselves no other name. Thus the Laplanders call themselves Almag, people; the Samoiedes Nilletz, Nissetsch, men, &c. As to the name of Germans, (Germani,) Caesar found it in use in Gaul, and adopted it as a word already known to the Romans. Many of the learned (from a passage of Tacitus, de Mor Germ. c. 2) have supposed that it was only applied to the Teutons after Caesar's time; but Adelung has triumphantly refuted this opinion. The name of Germans is found in the Fasti Capitolini. See Gruter, Iscrip. 2899, in which the consul Marcellus, in the year of Rome 531, is said to have defeated the Gauls, the Insubrians, and the Germans, commanded by Virdomar. See Adelung, Aelt. Geschichte der Deutsch, p. 102.—Compressed from G.]

[Footnote 1001: The modern philosophers of Sweden seem agreed that the waters of the Baltic gradually sink in a regular proportion, which they have ventured to estimate at half an inch every year. Twenty centuries ago the flat country of Scandinavia must have been covered by the sea; while the high lands rose above the waters, as so many islands of various forms and dimensions. Such, indeed, is the notion given us by Mela, Pliny, and Tacitus, of the vast countries round the Baltic. See in the Bibliotheque Raisonnee, tom. xl. and xlv. a large abstract of Dalin's History of Sweden, composed in the Swedish language. Note: Modern geologists have rejected this theory of the depression of the Baltic, as inconsistent with recent observation. The considerable changes which have taken place on its shores, Mr. Lyell, from actual observation now decidedly attributes to the regular and uniform elevation of the land.—Lyell's Geology, b. ii. c. 17—M.]

Some ingenious writers [2] have suspected that Europe was much colder formerly than it is at present; and the most ancient descriptions of the climate of Germany tend exceedingly to confirm their theory. The general complaints of intense frost and eternal winter, are perhaps little to be regarded, since we have no method of reducing to the accurate standard of the thermometer, the feelings, or the expressions, of an orator born in the happier regions of Greece or Asia. But I shall select two remarkable circumstances of a less equivocal nature. 1. The great rivers which covered the Roman provinces, the Rhine and the Danube, were frequently frozen over, and capable of supporting the most enormous weights. The barbarians, who often chose that severe season for their inroads, transported, without apprehension or danger, their numerous armies, their cavalry, and their heavy wagons, over a vast and solid bridge of ice. [3] Modern ages have not presented an instance of a like phenomenon. 2. The reindeer, that useful animal, from whom the savage of the North derives the best comforts of his dreary life, is of a constitution that supports, and even requires, the most intense cold. He is found on the rock of Spitzberg, within ten degrees of the Pole; he seems to delight in the snows of Lapland and Siberia: but at present he cannot subsist, much less multiply, in any country to the south of the Baltic. [4] In the time of Caesar the reindeer, as well as the elk and the wild bull, was a native of the Hercynian forest, which then overshadowed a great part of Germany and Poland. [5] The modern improvements sufficiently explain the causes of the diminution of the cold. These immense woods have been gradually cleared, which intercepted from the earth the rays of the sun. [6] The morasses have been drained, and, in proportion as the soil has been cultivated, the air has become more temperate. Canada, at this day, is an exact picture of ancient Germany. Although situated in the same parallel with the finest provinces of France and England, that country experiences the most rigorous cold. The reindeer are very numerous, the ground is covered with deep and lasting snow, and the great river of St. Lawrence is regularly frozen, in a season when the waters of the Seine and the Thames are usually free from ice. [7]

[Footnote 2: In particular, Mr. Hume, the Abbe du Bos, and M. Pelloutier. Hist. des Celtes, tom. i.]

[Footnote 3: Diodorus Siculus, l. v. p. 340, edit. Wessel. Herodian, l. vi. p. 221. Jornandes, c. 55. On the banks of the Danube, the wine, when brought to table, was frequently frozen into great lumps, frusta vini. Ovid. Epist. ex Ponto, l. iv. 7, 9, 10. Virgil. Georgic. l. iii. 355. The fact is confirmed by a soldier and a philosopher, who had experienced the intense cold of Thrace. See Xenophon, Anabasis, l. vii. p. 560, edit. Hutchinson. Note: The Danube is constantly frozen over. At Pesth the bridge is usually taken up, and the traffic and communication between the two banks carried on over the ice. The Rhine is likewise in many parts passable at least two years out of five. Winter campaigns are so unusual, in modern warfare, that I recollect but one instance of an army crossing either river on the ice. In the thirty years' war, (1635,) Jan van Werth, an Imperialist partisan, crossed the Rhine from Heidelberg on the ice with 5000 men, and surprised Spiers. Pichegru's memorable campaign, (1794-5,) when the freezing of the Meuse and Waal opened Holland to his conquests, and his cavalry and artillery attacked the ships frozen in, on the Zuyder Zee, was in a winter of unprecedented severity.—M. 1845.]

[Footnote 4: Buffon, Histoire Naturelle, tom. xii. p. 79, 116.]

[Footnote 5: Caesar de Bell. Gallic. vi. 23, &c. The most inquisitive of the Germans were ignorant of its utmost limits, although some of them had travelled in it more than sixty days' journey. Note: The passage of Caesar, "parvis renonum tegumentis utuntur," is obscure, observes Luden, (Geschichte des Teutschen Volkes,) and insufficient to prove the reindeer to have existed in Germany. It is supported however, by a fragment of Sallust. Germani intectum rhenonibus corpus tegunt.—M. It has been suggested to me that Caesar (as old Gesner supposed) meant the reindeer in the following description. Est bos cervi figura cujus a media fronte inter aures unum cornu existit, excelsius magisque directum (divaricatum, qu?) his quae nobis nota sunt cornibus. At ejus summo, sicut palmae, rami quam late diffunduntur. Bell. vi.—M. 1845.]

[Footnote 6: Cluverius (Germania Antiqua, l. iii. c. 47) investigates the small and scattered remains of the Hercynian wood.]

[Footnote 7: Charlevoix, Histoire du Canada.]

It is difficult to ascertain, and easy to exaggerate, the influence of the climate of ancient Germany over the minds and bodies of the natives. Many writers have supposed, and most have allowed, though, as it should seem, without any adequate proof, that the rigorous cold of the North was favorable to long life and generative vigor, that the women were more fruitful, and the human species more prolific, than in warmer or more temperate climates. [8] We may assert, with greater confidence, that the keen air of Germany formed the large and masculine limbs of the natives, who were, in general, of a more lofty stature than the people of the South, [9] gave them a kind of strength better adapted to violent exertions than to patient labor, and inspired them with constitutional bravery, which is the result of nerves and spirits. The severity of a winter campaign, that chilled the courage of the Roman troops, was scarcely felt by these hardy children of the North, [10] who, in their turn, were unable to resist the summer heats, and dissolved away in languor and sickness under the beams of an Italian sun. [11]

[Footnote 8: Olaus Rudbeck asserts that the Swedish women often bear ten or twelve children, and not uncommonly twenty or thirty; but the authority of Rudbeck is much to be suspected.]

[Footnote 9: In hos artus, in haec corpora, quae miramur, excrescunt. Taeit Germania, 3, 20. Cluver. l. i. c. 14.]

[Footnote 10: Plutarch. in Mario. The Cimbri, by way of amusement, often did down mountains of snow on their broad shields.]

[Footnote 11: The Romans made war in all climates, and by their excellent discipline were in a great measure preserved in health and vigor. It may be remarked, that man is the only animal which can live and multiply in every country from the equator to the poles. The hog seems to approach the nearest to our species in that privilege.]

PART II

There is not any where upon the globe a large tract of country, which we have discovered destitute of inhabitants, or whose first population can be fixed with any degree of historical certainty. And yet, as the most philosophic minds can seldom refrain from investigating the infancy of great nations, our curiosity consumes itself in toilsome and disappointed efforts. When Tacitus considered the purity of the German blood, and the forbidding aspect of the country, he was disposed to pronounce those barbarians Indigene, or natives of the soil. We may allow with safety, and perhaps with truth, that ancient Germany was not originally peopled by any foreign colonies already formed into a political society; [12] but that the name and nation received their existence from the gradual union of some wandering savages of the Hercynian woods. To assert those savages to have been the spontaneous production of the earth which they inhabited would be a rash inference, condemned by religion, and unwarranted by reason.

[Footnote 12: Facit. Germ. c. 3. The emigration of the Gauls followed the course of the Danube, and discharged itself on Greece and Asia. Tacitus could discover only one inconsiderable tribe that retained any traces of a Gallic origin. Note: The Gothini, who must not be confounded with the Gothi, a Suevian tribe. In the time of Caesar many other tribes of Gaulish origin dwelt along the course of the Danube, who could not long resist the attacks of the Suevi. The Helvetians, who dwelt on the borders of the Black Forest, between the Maine and the Danube, had been expelled long before the time of Caesar. He mentions also the Volci Tectosagi, who came from Languedoc and settled round the Black Forest. The Boii, who had penetrated into that forest, and also have left traces of their name in Bohemia, were subdued in the first century by the Marcomanni. The Boii settled in Noricum, were mingled afterwards with the Lombards, and received the name of Boio Arii (Bavaria) or Boiovarii: var, in some German dialects, appearing to mean remains, descendants. Compare Malte B-m, Geography, vol. i. p. 410, edit 1832—M.]

Such rational doubt is but ill suited with the genius of popular vanity. Among the nations who have adopted the Mosaic history of the world, the ark of Noah has been of the same use, as was formerly to the Greeks and Romans the siege of Troy. On a narrow basis of acknowledged truth, an immense but rude superstructure of fable has been erected; and the wild Irishman, [13] as well as the wild Tartar, [14] could point out the individual son of Japhet, from whose loins his ancestors were lineally descended. The last century abounded with antiquarians of profound learning and easy faith, who, by the dim light of legends and traditions, of conjectures and etymologies, conducted the great grandchildren of Noah from the Tower of Babel to the extremities of the globe. Of these judicious critics, one of the most entertaining was Oaus Rudbeck, professor in the university of Upsal. [15] Whatever is celebrated either in history or fable, this zealous patriot ascribes to his country. From Sweden (which formed so considerable a part of ancient Germany) the Greeks themselves derived their alphabetical characters, their astronomy, and their religion. Of that delightful region (for such it appeared to the eyes of a native) the Atlantis of Plato, the country of the Hyperboreans, the gardens of the Hesperides, the Fortunate Islands, and even the Elysian Fields, were all but faint and imperfect transcripts. A clime so profusely favored by Nature could not long remain desert after the flood. The learned Rudbeck allows the family of Noah a few years to multiply from eight to about twenty thousand persons. He then disperses them into small colonies to replenish the earth, and to propagate the human species. The German or Swedish detachment (which marched, if I am not mistaken, under the command of Askenaz, the son of Gomer, the son of Japhet) distinguished itself by a more than common diligence in the prosecution of this great work. The northern hive cast its swarms over the greatest part of Europe, Africa, and Asia; and (to use the author's metaphor) the blood circulated from the extremities to the heart.

[Footnote 13: According to Dr. Keating, (History of Ireland, p. 13, 14,) the giant Portholanus, who was the son of Seara, the son of Esra, the son of Sru, the son of Framant, the son of Fathaclan, the son of Magog, the son of Japhet, the son of Noah, landed on the coast of Munster the 14th day of May, in the year of the world one thousand nine hundred and seventy-eight. Though he succeeded in his great enterprise, the loose behavior of his wife rendered his domestic life very unhappy, and provoked him to such a degree, that he killed—her favorite greyhound. This, as the learned historian very properly observes, was the first instance of female falsehood and infidelity ever known in Ireland.]

[Footnote 14: Genealogical History of the Tartars, by Abulghazi Bahadur Khan.]

[Footnote 15: His work, entitled Atlantica, is uncommonly scarce. Bayle has given two most curious extracts from it. Republique des Lettres Janvier et Fevrier, 1685.]

But all this well-labored system of German antiquities is annihilated by a single fact, too well attested to admit of any doubt, and of too decisive a nature to leave room for any reply. The Germans, in the age of Tacitus, were unacquainted with the use of letters; [16] and the use of letters is the principal circumstance that distinguishes a civilized people from a herd of savages incapable of knowledge or reflection. Without that artificial help, the human memory soon dissipates or corrupts the ideas intrusted to her charge; and the nobler faculties of the mind, no longer supplied with models or with materials, gradually forget their powers; the judgment becomes feeble and lethargic, the imagination languid or irregular. Fully to apprehend this important truth, let us attempt, in an improved society, to calculate the immense distance between the man of learning and the illiterate peasant. The former, by reading and reflection, multiplies his own experience, and lives in distant ages and remote countries; whilst the latter, rooted to a single spot, and confined to a few years of existence, surpasses but very little his fellow-laborer, the ox, in the exercise of his mental faculties. The same, and even a greater, difference will be found between nations than between individuals; and we may safely pronounce, that without some species of writing, no people has ever preserved the faithful annals of their history, ever made any considerable progress in the abstract sciences, or ever possessed, in any tolerable degree of perfection, the useful and agreeable arts of life.

[Footnote 16: Tacit. Germ. ii. 19. Literarum secreta viri pariter ac foeminae ignorant. We may rest contented with this decisive authority, without entering into the obscure disputes concerning the antiquity of the Runic characters. The learned Celsius, a Swede, a scholar, and a philosopher, was of opinion, that they were nothing more than the Roman letters, with the curves changed into straight lines *for the ease of engraving. See Pelloutier, Histoire des Celtes, l. ii. c. 11. Dictionnaire Diplomatique, tom. i. p. 223. We may add, that the oldest Runic inscriptions are supposed to be of the third century, and the most ancient writer who mentions the Runic characters is Venan tius Frotunatus, (Carm. vii. 18,) who lived towards the end of the sixth century. Barbara fraxineis pingatur Runa tabellis. Note: The obscure subject of the Runic characters has exercised the industry and ingenuity of the modern scholars of the north. There are three distinct theories; one, maintained by Schlozer, (Nordische Geschichte, p. 481, &c.,) who considers their sixteen letters to be a corruption of the Roman alphabet, post-Christian in their date, and Schlozer would attribute their introduction into the north to the Alemanni. The second, that of Frederick Schlegel, (Vorlesungen uber alte und neue Literatur,) supposes that these characters were left on the coasts of the Mediterranean and Northern Seas by the Phoenicians, preserved by the priestly castes, and employed for purposes of magic. Their common origin from the Phoenician would account for heir similarity to the Roman letters. The last, to which we incline, claims much higher and more venerable antiquity for the Runic, and supposes them to have been the original characters of the Indo-Teutonic tribes, brought from the East, and preserved among the different races of that stock. See Ueber Deutsche Runen von W. C. Grimm, 1821. A Memoir by Dr. Legis. Fundgruben des alten Nordens. Foreign Quarterly Review vol. ix. p. 438.—M.]*

Of these arts, the ancient Germans were wretchedly destitute. [16/1] They passed their lives in a state of ignorance and poverty, which it has pleased some declaimers to dignify with the appellation of virtuous simplicity. Modern Germany is said to contain about two thousand three hundred walled towns. [17] In a much wider extent of country, the geographer Ptolemy could discover no more than ninety places which he decorates with the name of cities; [18] though, according to our ideas, they would but ill deserve that splendid title. We can only suppose them to have been rude fortifications, constructed in the centre of the woods, and designed to secure the women, children, and cattle, whilst the warriors of the tribe marched out to repel a sudden invasion. [19] But Tacitus asserts, as a well-known fact, that the Germans, in his time, had no cities; [20] and that they affected to despise the works of Roman industry, as places of confinement rather than of security. [21] Their edifices were not even contiguous, or formed into regular villas; [22] each barbarian fixed his independent dwelling on the spot to which a plain, a wood, or a stream of fresh water, had induced him to give the preference. Neither stone, nor brick, nor tiles, were employed in these slight habitations. [23] They were indeed no more than low huts, of a circular figure, built of rough timber, thatched with straw, and pierced at the top to leave a free passage for the smoke. In the most inclement winter, the hardy German was satisfied with a scanty garment made of the skin of some animal. The nations who dwelt towards the North clothed themselves in furs; and the women manufactured for their own use a coarse kind of linen. [24] The game of various sorts, with which the forests of Germany were plentifully stocked, supplied its inhabitants with food and exercise. [25] Their monstrous herds of cattle, less remarkable indeed for their beauty than for their utility, [26] formed the principal object of their wealth. A small quantity of corn was the only produce exacted from the earth; the use of orchards or artificial meadows was unknown to the Germans; nor can we expect any improvements in agriculture from a people, whose prosperity every year experienced a general change by a new division of the arable lands, and who, in that strange operation, avoided disputes, by suffering a great part of their territory to lie waste and without tillage. [27]

[Footnote 16/1: Luden (the author of the Geschichte des Teutschen Volkes) has surpassed most writers in his patriotic enthusiasm for the virtues and noble manners of his ancestors. Even the cold of the climate, and the want of vines and fruit trees, as well as the barbarism of the inhabitants, are calumnies of the luxurious Italians. M. Guizot, on the other side, (in his Histoire de la Civilisation, vol. i. p. 272, &c.,) has drawn a curious parallel between the Germans of Tacitus and the North American Indians.—M.]

[Footnote 17: Recherches Philosophiques sur les Americains, tom. iii. p. 228. The author of that very curious work is, if I am not misinformed, a German by birth. (De Pauw.)]

[Footnote 18: The Alexandrian Geographer is often criticized by the accurate Cluverius.]

[Footnote 19: See Caesar, and the learned Mr. Whitaker in his History of Manchester, vol. i.]

[Footnote 20: Tacit. Germ. 15.]

[Footnote 21: When the Germans commanded the Ubii of Cologne to cast off the Roman yoke, and with their new freedom to resume their ancient manners, they insisted on the immediate demolition of the walls of the colony. "Postulamus a vobis, muros coloniae, munimenta servitii, detrahatis; etiam fera animalia, si clausa teneas, virtutis obliviscuntur." Tacit. Hist. iv. 64.]

[Footnote 22: The straggling villages of Silesia are several miles in length. See Cluver. l. i. c. 13.]

[Footnote 23: One hundred and forty years after Tacitus, a few more regular structures were erected near the Rhine and Danube. Herodian, l. vii. p. 234.]

[Footnote 24: Tacit. Germ. 17.]

[Footnote 25: Tacit. Germ. 5.]

[Footnote 26: Caesar de Bell. Gall. vi. 21.]

[Footnote 27: Tacit. Germ. 26. Caesar, vi. 22.]

Gold, silver, and iron, were extremely scarce in Germany. Its barbarous inhabitants wanted both skill and patience to investigate those rich veins of silver, which have so liberally rewarded the attention of the princes of Brunswick and Saxony. Sweden, which now supplies Europe with iron, was equally ignorant of its own riches; and the appearance of the arms of the Germans furnished a sufficient proof how little iron they were able to bestow on what they must have deemed the noblest use of that metal. The various transactions of peace and war had introduced some Roman coins (chiefly silver) among the borderers of the Rhine and Danube; but the more distant tribes were absolutely unacquainted with the use of money, carried on their confined traffic by the exchange of commodities, and prized their rude earthen vessels as of equal value with the silver vases, the presents of Rome to their princes and ambassadors. [28] To a mind capable of reflection, such leading facts convey more instruction, than a tedious detail of subordinate circumstances. The value of money has been settled by general consent to express our wants and our property, as letters were invented to express our ideas; and both these institutions, by giving a more active energy to the powers and passions of human nature, have contributed to multiply the objects they were designed to represent. The use of gold and silver is in a great measure factitious; but it would be impossible to enumerate the important and various services which agriculture, and all the arts, have received from iron, when tempered and fashioned by the operation of fire, and the dexterous hand of man. Money, in a word, is the most universal incitement, iron the most powerful instrument, of human industry; and it is very difficult to conceive by what means a people, neither actuated by the one, nor seconded by the other, could emerge from the grossest barbarism. [29]

[Footnote 28: Tacit. Germ. 6.]

[Footnote 29: It is said that the Mexicans and Peruvians, without the use of either money or iron, had made a very great progress in the arts. Those arts, and the monuments they produced, have been strangely magnified. See Recherches sur les Americains, tom. ii. p. 153, &c]

If we contemplate a savage nation in any part of the globe, a supine indolence and a carelessness of futurity will be found to constitute their general character. In a civilized state, every faculty of man is expanded and exercised; and the great chain of mutual dependence connects and embraces the several members of society. The most numerous portion of it is employed in constant and useful labor. The select few, placed by fortune above that necessity, can, however, fill up their time by the pursuits of interest or glory, by the improvement of their estate or of their understanding, by the duties, the pleasures, and even the follies of social life. The Germans were not possessed of these varied resources. The care of the house and family, the management of the land and cattle, were delegated to the old and the infirm, to women and slaves. The lazy warrior, destitute of every art that might employ his leisure hours, consumed his days and nights in the animal gratifications of sleep and food. And yet, by a wonderful diversity of nature, (according to the remark of a writer who had pierced into its darkest recesses,) the same barbarians are by turns the most indolent and the most restless of mankind. They delight in sloth, they detest tranquility. [30] The languid soul, oppressed with its own weight, anxiously required some new and powerful sensation; and war and danger were the only amusements adequate to its fierce temper. The sound that summoned the German to arms was grateful to his ear. It roused him from his uncomfortable lethargy, gave him an active pursuit, and, by strong exercise of the body, and violent emotions of the mind, restored him to a more lively sense of his existence. In the dull intervals of peace, these barbarians were immoderately addicted to deep gaming and excessive drinking; both of which, by different means, the one by inflaming their passions, the other by extinguishing their reason, alike relieved them from the pain of thinking. They gloried in passing whole days and nights at table; and the blood of friends and relations often stained their numerous and drunken assemblies. [31] Their debts of honor (for in that light they have transmitted to us those of play) they discharged with the most romantic fidelity. The desperate gamester, who had staked his person and liberty on a last throw of the dice, patiently submitted to the decision of fortune, and suffered himself to be bound, chastised, and sold into remote slavery, by his weaker but more lucky antagonist. [32]

[Footnote 30: Tacit. Germ. 15.]

[Footnote 31: Tacit. Germ. 22, 23.]

[Footnote 32: Id. 24. The Germans might borrow the arts of play from the Romans, but the passion is wonderfully inherent in the human species.]

Strong beer, a liquor extracted with very little art from wheat or barley, and corrupted (as it is strongly expressed by Tacitus) into a certain semblance of wine, was sufficient for the gross purposes of German debauchery. But those who had tasted the rich wines of Italy, and afterwards of Gaul, sighed for that more delicious species of intoxication. They attempted not, however, (as has since been executed with so much success,) to naturalize the vine on the banks of the Rhine and Danube; nor did they endeavor to procure by industry the materials of an advantageous commerce. To solicit by labor what might be ravished by arms, was esteemed unworthy of the German spirit. [33] The intemperate thirst of strong liquors often urged the barbarians to invade the provinces on which art or nature had bestowed those much envied presents. The Tuscan who betrayed his country to the Celtic nations, attracted them into Italy by the prospect of the rich fruits and delicious wines, the productions of a happier climate. [34] And in the same manner the German auxiliaries, invited into France during the civil wars of the sixteenth century, were allured by the promise of plenteous quarters in the provinces of Champaigne and Burgundy. [35] Drunkenness, the most illiberal, but not the most dangerous of our vices, was sometimes capable, in a less civilized state of mankind, of occasioning a battle, a war, or a revolution.

[Footnote 33: Tacit. Germ. 14.]

[Footnote 34: Plutarch. in Camillo. T. Liv. v. 33.]

[Footnote 35: Dubos. Hist. de la Monarchie Francoise, tom. i. p. 193.]

The climate of ancient Germany has been modified, and the soil fertilized, by the labor of ten centuries from the time of Charlemagne. The same extent of ground which at present maintains, in ease and plenty, a million of husbandmen and artificers, was unable to supply a hundred thousand lazy warriors with the simple necessaries of life. [36] The Germans abandoned their immense forests to the exercise of hunting, employed in pasturage the most considerable part of their lands, bestowed on the small remainder a rude and careless cultivation, and then accused the scantiness and sterility of a country that refused to maintain the multitude of its inhabitants. When the return of famine severely admonished them of the importance of the arts, the national distress was sometimes alleviated by the emigration of a third, perhaps, or a fourth part of their youth. [37] The possession and the enjoyment of property are the pledges which bind a civilized people to an improved country. But the Germans, who carried with them what they most valued, their arms, their cattle, and their women, cheerfully abandoned the vast silence of their woods for the unbounded hopes of plunder and conquest. The innumerable swarms that issued, or seemed to issue, from the great storehouse of nations, were multiplied by the fears of the vanquished, and by the credulity of succeeding ages. And from facts thus exaggerated, an opinion was gradually established, and has been supported by writers of distinguished reputation, that, in the age of Caesar and Tacitus, the inhabitants of the North were far more numerous than they are in our days. [38] A more serious inquiry into the causes of population seems to have convinced modern philosophers of the falsehood, and indeed the impossibility, of the supposition. To the names of Mariana and of Machiavel, [39] we can oppose the equal names of Robertson and Hume. [40]

[Footnote 36: The Helvetian nation, which issued from a country called Switzerland, contained, of every age and sex, 368,000 persons, (Caesar de Bell. Gal. i. 29.) At present, the number of people in the Pays de Vaud (a small district on the banks of the Leman Lake, much more distinguished for politeness than for industry) amounts to 112,591. See an excellent tract of M. Muret, in the Memoires de la Societe de Born.]

[Footnote 37: Paul Diaconus, c. 1, 2, 3. Machiavel, Davila, and the rest of Paul's followers, represent these emigrations too much as regular and concerted measures.]

[Footnote 38: Sir William Temple and Montesquieu have indulged, on this subject, the usual liveliness of their fancy.]

[Footnote 39: Machiavel, Hist. di Firenze, l. i. Mariana, Hist. Hispan. l. v. c. 1]

[Footnote 40: Robertson's Charles V. Hume's Political Essays. Note: It is a wise observation of Malthus, that these nations "were not populous in proportion to the land they occupied, but to the food they produced." They were prolific from their pure morals and constitutions, but their institutions were not calculated to produce food for those whom they brought into being.—M—1845.]

A warlike nation like the Germans, without either cities, letters, arts, or money, found some compensation for this savage state in the enjoyment of liberty. Their poverty secured their freedom, since our desires and our possessions are the strongest fetters of despotism. "Among the Suiones (says Tacitus) riches are held in honor. They are therefore subject to an absolute monarch, who, instead of intrusting his people with the free use of arms, as is practised in the rest of Germany, commits them to the safe custody, not of a citizen, or even of a freedman, but of a slave. The neighbors of the Suiones, the Sitones, are sunk even below servitude; they obey a woman." [41] In the mention of these exceptions, the great historian sufficiently acknowledges the general theory of government. We are only at a loss to conceive by what means riches and despotism could penetrate into a remote corner of the North, and extinguish the generous flame that blazed with such fierceness on the frontier of the Roman provinces, or how the ancestors of those Danes and Norwegians, so distinguished in latter ages by their unconquered spirit, could thus tamely resign the great character of German liberty. [42] Some tribes, however, on the coast of the Baltic, acknowledged the authority of kings, though without relinquishing the rights of men, [43] but in the far greater part of Germany, the form of government was a democracy, tempered, indeed, and controlled, not so much by general and positive laws, as by the occasional ascendant of birth or valor, of eloquence or superstition. [44]

[Footnote 41: Tacit. German. 44, 45. Freinshemius (who dedicated his supplement to Livy to Christina of Sweden) thinks proper to be very angry with the Roman who expressed so very little reverence for Northern queens. Note: The Suiones and the Sitones are the ancient inhabitants of Scandinavia, their name may be traced in that of Sweden; they did not belong to the race of the Suevi, but that of the non-Suevi or Cimbri, whom the Suevi, in very remote times, drove back part to the west, part to the north; they were afterwards mingled with Suevian tribes, among others the Goths, who have traces of their name and power in the isle of Gothland.—G]

[Footnote 42: May we not suspect that superstition was the parent of despotism? The descendants of Odin, (whose race was not extinct till the year 1060) are said to have reigned in Sweden above a thousand years. The temple of Upsal was the ancient seat of religion and empire. In the year 1153 I find a singular law, prohibiting the use and profession of arms to any except the king's guards. Is it not probable that it was colored by the pretence of reviving an old institution? See Dalin's History of Sweden in the Bibliotheque Raisonneo tom. xl. and xlv.]

[Footnote 43: Tacit. Germ. c. 43.]

[Footnote 44: Id. c. 11, 12, 13, & c.]

Civil governments, in their first institution, are voluntary associations for mutual defence. To obtain the desired end, it is absolutely necessary that each individual should conceive himself obliged to submit his private opinions and actions to the judgment of the greater number of his associates. The German tribes were contented with this rude but liberal outline of political society. As soon as a youth, born of free parents, had attained the age of manhood, he was introduced into the general council of his countrymen, solemnly invested with a shield and spear, and adopted as an equal and worthy member of the military commonwealth. The assembly of the warriors of the tribe was convened at stated seasons, or on sudden emergencies. The trial of public offences, the election of magistrates, and the great business of peace and war, were determined by its independent voice. Sometimes indeed, these important questions were previously considered and prepared in a more select council of the principal chieftains. [45] The magistrates might deliberate and persuade, the people only could resolve and execute; and the resolutions of the Germans were for the most part hasty and violent. Barbarians accustomed to place their freedom in gratifying the present passion, and their courage in overlooking all future consequences, turned away with indignant contempt from the remonstrances of justice and policy, and it was the practice to signify by a hollow murmur their dislike of such timid counsels. But whenever a more popular orator proposed to vindicate the meanest citizen from either foreign or domestic injury, whenever he called upon his fellow-countrymen to assert the national honor, or to pursue some enterprise full of danger and glory, a loud clashing of shields and spears expressed the eager applause of the assembly. For the Germans always met in arms, and it was constantly to be dreaded, lest an irregular multitude, inflamed with faction and strong liquors, should use those arms to enforce, as well as to declare, their furious resolves. We may recollect how often the diets of Poland have been polluted with blood, and the more numerous party has been compelled to yield to the more violent and seditious. [46]

[Footnote 45: Grotius changes an expression of Tacitus, pertractantur into Proetractantur. The correction is equally just and ingenious.]

[Footnote 46: Even in our ancient parliament, the barons often carried a question, not so much by the number of votes, as by that of their armed followers.]

A general of the tribe was elected on occasions of danger; and, if the danger was pressing and extensive, several tribes concurred in the choice of the same general. The bravest warrior was named to lead his countrymen into the field, by his example rather than by his commands. But this power, however limited, was still invidious. It expired with the war, and in time of peace the German tribes acknowledged not any supreme chief. [47] Princes were, however, appointed, in the general assembly, to administer justice, or rather to compose differences, [48] in their respective districts. In the choice of these magistrates, as much regard was shown to birth as to merit. [49] To each was assigned, by the public, a guard, and a council of a hundred persons, and the first of the princes appears to have enjoyed a preeminence of rank and honor which sometimes tempted the Romans to compliment him with the regal title. [50]

[Footnote 47: Caesar de Bell. Gal. vi. 23.]

[Footnote 48: Minuunt controversias, is a very happy expression of Caesar's.]

[Footnote 49: Reges ex nobilitate, duces ex virtute sumunt. Tacit Germ. 7]

[Footnote 50: Cluver. Germ. Ant. l. i. c. 38.]

The comparative view of the powers of the magistrates, in two remarkable instances, is alone sufficient to represent the whole system of German manners. The disposal of the landed property within their district was absolutely vested in their hands, and they distributed it every year according to a new division. [51] At the same time they were not authorized to punish with death, to imprison, or even to strike a private citizen. [52] A people thus jealous of their persons, and careless of their possessions, must have been totally destitute of industry and the arts, but animated with a high sense of honor and independence.

[Footnote 51: Caesar, vi. 22. Tacit Germ. 26.]

[Footnote 52: Tacit. Germ. 7.]

PART III

The Germans respected only those duties which they imposed on themselves. The most obscure soldier resisted with disdain the authority of the magistrates. The noblest youths blushed not to be numbered among the faithful companions of some renowned chief, to whom they devoted their arms and service. A noble emulation prevailed among the companions, to obtain the first place in the esteem of their chief; amongst the chiefs, to acquire the greatest number of valiant companions. To be ever surrounded by a band of select youths was the pride and strength of the chiefs, their ornament in peace, their defence in war. The glory of such distinguished heroes diffused itself beyond the narrow limits of their own tribe. Presents and embassies solicited their friendship, and the fame of their arms often insured victory to the party which they espoused. In the hour of danger it was shameful for the chief to be surpassed in valor by his companions; shameful for the companions not to equal the valor of their chief. To survive his fall in battle, was indelible infamy. To protect his person, and to adorn his glory with the trophies of their own exploits, were the most sacred of their duties. The chiefs combated for victory, the companions for the chief. The noblest warriors, whenever their native country was sunk into the laziness of peace, maintained their numerous bands in some distant scene of action, to exercise their restless spirit, and to acquire renown by voluntary dangers. Gifts worthy of soldiers—the warlike steed, the bloody and even victorious lance—were the rewards which the companions claimed from the liberality of their chief. The rude plenty of his hospitable board was the only pay that he could bestow, or they would accept. War, rapine, and the free-will offerings of his friends, supplied the materials of this munificence. [53] This institution, however it might accidentally weaken the several republics, invigorated the general character of the Germans, and even ripened amongst them all the virtues of which barbarians are susceptible; the faith and valor, the hospitality and the courtesy, so conspicuous long afterwards in the ages of chivalry.

The honorable gifts, bestowed by the chief on his brave companions, have been supposed, by an ingenious writer, to contain the first rudiments of the fiefs, distributed after the conquest of the Roman provinces, by the barbarian lords among their vassals, with a similar duty of homage and military service. [54] These conditions are, however, very repugnant to the maxims of the ancient Germans, who delighted in mutual presents; but without either imposing, or accepting, the weight of obligations. [55]

[Footnote 53: Tacit. Germ. 13, 14.]

[Footnote 54: Esprit des Loix, l. xxx. c. 3. The brilliant imagination of Montesquieu is corrected, however, by the dry, cold reason of the Abbe de Mably. Observations sur l'Histoire de France, tom. i. p. 356.]

[Footnote 55: Gaudent muneribus, sed nec data imputant, nec acceptis obligautur. Tacit. Germ. c. 21.]

"In the days of chivalry, or more properly of romance, all the men were brave, and all the women were chaste;" and notwithstanding the latter of these virtues is acquired and preserved with much more difficulty than the former, it is ascribed, almost without exception, to the wives of the ancient Germans. Polygamy was not in use, except among the princes, and among them only for the sake of multiplying their alliances. Divorces were prohibited by manners rather than by laws. Adulteries were punished as rare and inexpiable crimes; nor was seduction justified by example and fashion. [56] We may easily discover that Tacitus indulges an honest pleasure in the contrast of barbarian virtue with the dissolute conduct of the Roman ladies; yet there are some striking circumstances that give an air of truth, or at least probability, to the conjugal faith and chastity of the Germans.

[Footnote 56: The adulteress was whipped through the village. Neither wealth nor beauty could inspire compassion, or procure her a second husband. 18, 19.]

Although the progress of civilization has undoubtedly contributed to assuage the fiercer passions of human nature, it seems to have been less favorable to the virtue of chastity, whose most dangerous enemy is the softness of the mind. The refinements of life corrupt while they polish the intercourse of the sexes. The gross appetite of love becomes most dangerous when it is elevated, or rather, indeed, disguised by sentimental passion. The elegance of dress, of motion, and of manners, gives a lustre to beauty, and inflames the senses through the imagination. Luxurious entertainments, midnight dances, and licentious spectacles, present at once temptation and opportunity to female frailty. [57] From such dangers the unpolished wives of the barbarians were secured by poverty, solitude, and the painful cares of a domestic life. The German huts, open, on every side, to the eye of indiscretion or jealousy, were a better safeguard of conjugal fidelity, than the walls, the bolts, and the eunuchs of a Persian haram. To this reason another may be added, of a more honorable nature. The Germans treated their women with esteem and confidence, consulted them on every occasion of importance, and fondly believed, that in their breasts resided a sanctity and wisdom more than human. Some of the interpreters of fate, such as Velleda, in the Batavian war, governed, in the name of the deity, the fiercest nations of Germany. [58] The rest of the sex, without being adored as goddesses, were respected as the free and equal companions of soldiers; associated even by the marriage ceremony to a life of toil, of danger, and of glory. [59] In their great invasions, the camps of the barbarians were filled with a multitude of women, who remained firm and undaunted amidst the sound of arms, the various forms of destruction, and the honorable wounds of their sons and husbands. [60] Fainting armies of Germans have, more than once, been driven back upon the enemy, by the generous despair of the women, who dreaded death much less than servitude. If the day was irrecoverably lost, they well knew how to deliver themselves and their children, with their own hands, from an insulting victor. [61] Heroines of such a cast may claim our admiration; but they were most assuredly neither lovely, nor very susceptible of love. Whilst they affected to emulate the stern virtues of man, they must have resigned that attractive softness, in which principally consist the charm and weakness of woman. Conscious pride taught the German females to suppress every tender emotion that stood in competition with honor, and the first honor of the sex has ever been that of chastity. The sentiments and conduct of these high-spirited matrons may, at once, be considered as a cause, as an effect, and as a proof of the general character of the nation. Female courage, however it may be raised by fanaticism, or confirmed by habit, can be only a faint and imperfect imitation of the manly valor that distinguishes the age or country in which it may be found.

[Footnote 57: Ovid employs two hundred lines in the research of places the most favorable to love. Above all, he considers the theatre as the best adapted to collect the beauties of Rome, and to melt them into tenderness and sensuality,]

[Footnote 58: Tacit. Germ. iv. 61, 65.]

[Footnote 59: The marriage present was a yoke of oxen, horses, and arms. See Germ. c. 18. Tacitus is somewhat too florid on the subject.]

[Footnote 60: The change of exigere into exugere is a most excellent correction.]

[Footnote 61: Tacit. Germ. c. 7. Plutarch in Mario. Before the wives of the Teutones destroyed themselves and their children, they had offered to surrender, on condition that they should be received as the slaves of the vestal virgins.]

The religious system of the Germans (if the wild opinions of savages can deserve that name) was dictated by their wants, their fears, and their ignorance. [62] They adored the great visible objects and agents of nature, the Sun and the Moon, the Fire and the Earth; together with those imaginary deities, who were supposed to preside over the most important occupations of human life. They were persuaded, that, by some ridiculous arts of divination, they could discover the will of the superior beings, and that human sacrifices were the most precious and acceptable offering to their altars. Some applause has been hastily bestowed on the sublime notion, entertained by that people, of the Deity, whom they neither confined within the walls of the temple, nor represented by any human figure; but when we recollect, that the Germans were unskilled in architecture, and totally unacquainted with the art of sculpture, we shall readily assign the true reason of a scruple, which arose not so much from a superiority of reason, as from a want of ingenuity. The only temples in Germany were dark and ancient groves, consecrated by the reverence of succeeding generations. Their secret gloom, the imagined residence of an invisible power, by presenting no distinct object of fear or worship, impressed the mind with a still deeper sense of religious horror; [63] and the priests, rude and illiterate as they were, had been taught by experience the use of every artifice that could preserve and fortify impressions so well suited to their own interest.

[Footnote 62: Tacitus has employed a few lines, and Cluverius one hundred and twenty-four pages, on this obscure subject. The former discovers in Germany the gods of Greece and Rome. The latter is positive, that, under the emblems of the sun, the moon, and the fire, his pious ancestors worshipped the Trinity in unity]

[Footnote 63: The sacred wood, described with such sublime horror by Lucan, was in the neighborhood of Marseilles; but there were many of the same kind in Germany. Note: The ancient Germans had shapeless idols, and, when they began to build more settled habitations, they raised also temples, such as that to the goddess Teufana, who presided over divination. See Adelung, Hist. of Ane Germans, p 296—G]

The same ignorance, which renders barbarians incapable of conceiving or embracing the useful restraints of laws, exposes them naked and unarmed to the blind terrors of superstition. The German priests, improving this favorable temper of their countrymen, had assumed a jurisdiction even in temporal concerns, which the magistrate could not venture to exercise; and the haughty warrior patiently submitted to the lash of correction, when it was inflicted, not by any human power, but by the immediate order of the god of war. [64] The defects of civil policy were sometimes supplied by the interposition of ecclesiastical authority. The latter was constantly exerted to maintain silence and decency in the popular assemblies; and was sometimes extended to a more enlarged concern for the national welfare. A solemn procession was occasionally celebrated in the present countries of

Mecklenburgh and Pomerania. The unknown symbol of the Earth, covered with a thick veil, was placed on a carriage drawn by cows; and in this manner the goddess, whose common residence was in the Isles of Rugen, visited several adjacent tribes of her worshippers. During her progress the sound of war was hushed, quarrels were suspended, arms laid aside, and the restless Germans had an opportunity of tasting the blessings of peace and harmony. [65] The truce of God, so often and so ineffectually proclaimed by the clergy of the eleventh century, was an obvious imitation of this ancient custom. [66]

[Footnote 64: Tacit. Germania, c. 7.]

[Footnote 65: Tacit. Germania, c. 40.]

[Footnote 66: See Dr. Robertson's History of Charles V. vol. i. note 10.]

But the influence of religion was far more powerful to inflame, than to moderate, the fierce passions of the Germans. Interest and fanaticism often prompted its ministers to sanctify the most daring and the most unjust enterprises, by the approbation of Heaven, and full assurances of success. The consecrated standards, long revered in the groves of superstition, were placed in the front of the battle; [67] and the hostile army was devoted with dire execrations to the gods of war and of thunder. [68] In the faith of soldiers (and such were the Germans) cowardice is the most unpardonable of sins. A brave man was the worthy favorite of their martial deities; the wretch who had lost his shield was alike banished from the religious and civil assemblies of his countrymen. Some tribes of the north seem to have embraced the doctrine of transmigration, [69] others imagined a gross paradise of immortal drunkenness. [70] All agreed, that a life spent in arms, and a glorious death in battle, were the best preparations for a happy futurity, either in this or in another world.

[Footnote 67: Tacit. Germania, c. 7. These standards were only the heads of wild beasts.]

[Footnote 68: See an instance of this custom, Tacit. Annal. xiii. 57.]

[Footnote 69: Caesar Diodorus, and Lucan, seem to ascribe this doctrine to the Gauls, but M. Pelloutier (Histoire des Celtes, l. iii. c. 18) labors to reduce their expressions to a more orthodox sense.]

[Footnote 70: Concerning this gross but alluring doctrine of the Edda, see Fable xx. in the curious version of that book, published by M. Mallet, in his Introduction to the History of Denmark.]

The immortality so vainly promised by the priests, was, in some degree, conferred by the bards. That singular order of men has most deservedly attracted the notice of all who have attempted to investigate the antiquities of the Celts, the Scandinavians, and the Germans. Their genius and character, as well as the reverence paid to that important office, have been sufficiently illustrated. But we cannot so easily express, or even conceive, the enthusiasm of arms and glory which they kindled in the breast of their audience. Among a polished people, a taste for poetry is rather an amusement of the fancy, than a passion of the soul. And yet, when in calm retirement we peruse the combats described by Homer or Tasso, we are insensibly seduced by the fiction, and feel a momentary glow of martial ardor. But how faint, how cold is the sensation which a peaceful mind can receive from solitary study! It was in the hour of battle, or in the feast of victory, that the bards celebrated the glory of the heroes of ancient days, the ancestors of those warlike chieftains, who listened with transport to their artless but animated strains. The view of arms and of danger heightened the effect of the military song; and the passions which it tended to excite, the desire of fame, and the contempt of death, were the habitual sentiments of a German mind. [71] [71/1]

[Footnote 71: See Tacit. Germ. c. 3. Diod. Sicul. l. v. Strabo, l. iv. p. 197. The classical reader may remember the rank of Demodocus in the Phaeacian court, and the ardor infused by Tyrtaeus into the fainting Spartans. Yet there is little probability that the Greeks and the Germans were the same people. Much learned trifling might be spared, if our antiquarians would condescend to reflect, that similar manners will naturally be produced by similar situations.]

[Footnote 71/1: Besides these battle songs, the Germans sang at their festival banquets, (Tac. Ann. i. 65,) and around the bodies of their slain heroes. King Theodoric, of the tribe of the Goths, killed in a battle against Attila, was honored by songs while he was borne from the field of battle. Jornandes, c. 41. The same honor was paid to the remains of Attila. Ibid. c. 49. According to some historians, the Germans had songs also at their weddings; but this appears to me inconsistent with their customs, in which marriage was no more than the purchase of a wife. Besides, there is but one instance of this, that of the Gothic king, Ataulph, who sang himself the nuptial hymn when he espoused Placidia, sister of the emperors Arcadius and Honorius, (Olympiodor. p. 8.) But this marriage was celebrated according to the Roman rites, of which the nuptial songs formed a part. Adelung, p. 382.—G. Charlemagne is said to have collected the national songs of the ancient Germans. Eginhard, Vit. Car. Mag.—M.]

Such was the situation, and such were the manners of the ancient Germans. Their climate, their want of learning, of arts, and of laws, their notions of honor, of gallantry, and of religion, their sense of freedom, impatience of peace, and thirst of enterprise, all contributed to form a people of military heroes. And yet we find, that during more than two hundred and fifty years that elapsed from the defeat of Varus to the reign of Decius, these formidable barbarians made few considerable attempts, and not any material impression on the luxurious and enslaved provinces of the empire. Their progress was checked by their want of arms and discipline, and their fury was diverted by the intestine divisions of ancient Germany. I. It has been observed, with ingenuity, and not without truth, that the command of iron soon gives a nation the command of gold. But the rude tribes of Germany, alike destitute of both those valuable metals, were reduced slowly to acquire, by their unassisted strength, the possession of the one as well as the other. The face of a German army displayed their poverty of iron. Swords, and the longer kind of lances, they could seldom use. Their frameoe (as they called them in their own language) were long spears headed with a sharp but narrow iron point, and which, as occasion required, they either darted from a distance, or pushed in close onset. With this spear, and with a shield, their cavalry was contented. A multitude of darts, scattered [72] with incredible force, were an additional resource of the infantry. Their military dress, when they wore any, was nothing more than a loose mantle. A variety of colors was the only ornament of their wooden or osier shields. Few of the chiefs were distinguished by cuirasses, scarcely any by helmets. Though the horses of Germany were neither beautiful, swift, nor practised in the skilful evolutions of the Roman manege, several of the nations obtained renown by their cavalry; but, in general, the principal strength of the Germans consisted in their infantry, [73] which was drawn up in several deep columns, according to the distinction of tribes and families. Impatient of fatigue and delay, these half-armed warriors rushed to battle with dissonant shouts and disordered ranks; and sometimes, by the effort of native valor, prevailed over the constrained and more artificial bravery of the Roman mercenaries. But as the barbarians poured forth their whole souls on the first onset, they knew not how to rally or to retire. A repulse was a sure defeat; and a defeat was most commonly total destruction. When we recollect the complete armor of the Roman soldiers, their discipline, exercises, evolutions, fortified camps, and military engines, it appears a just matter of surprise, how the naked and unassisted valor of the barbarians could dare to encounter, in the field, the strength of the legions, and the various troops of the auxiliaries, which seconded their operations. The contest was too unequal, till the introduction of luxury had enervated the vigor, and a spirit of disobedience and sedition had relaxed the discipline, of the Roman armies. The introduction of barbarian auxiliaries into those armies, was a measure attended with very obvious dangers, as it might gradually instruct the Germans in the arts of war and of policy. Although they were admitted in small numbers and with the strictest precaution, the example of Civilis was proper to convince the Romans, that the danger was not imaginary, and that their precautions were not always sufficient. [74] During the civil wars that followed the death of Nero, that artful and intrepid Batavian, whom his enemies condescended to compare with Hannibal and Sertorius, [75] formed a great design of freedom and ambition. Eight Batavian cohorts renowned in the wars of Britain and Italy, repaired to his standard. He introduced an army of Germans into Gaul, prevailed on the powerful cities of Treves and Langres to embrace his cause, defeated the legions, destroyed their fortified camps, and employed against the Romans the military knowledge which he had acquired in their service. When at length, after an obstinate struggle, he yielded to the power of the empire, Civilis secured himself and his country by an honorable treaty. The Batavians still continued to occupy the islands of the Rhine, [76] the allies, not the servants, of the Roman monarchy.

[Footnote 72: Missilia spargunt, Tacit. Germ. c. 6. Either that historian used a vague expression, or he meant that they were thrown at random.]

[Footnote 73: It was their principal distinction from the Sarmatians, who generally fought on horseback.]

[Footnote 74: The relation of this enterprise occupies a great part of the fourth and fifth books of the History of Tacitus, and is more remarkable for its eloquence than perspicuity. Sir Henry Saville has observed several inaccuracies.]

[Footnote 75: Tacit. Hist. iv. 13. Like them he had lost an eye.]

[Footnote 76: It was contained between the two branches of the old Rhine, as they subsisted before the face of the country was changed by art and nature. See Cluver German. Antiq. l. iii. c. 30, 37.]

II. The strength of ancient Germany appears formidable, when we consider the effects that might have been produced by its united effort. The wide extent of country might very possibly contain a million of warriors, as all who were of age to bear arms were of a temper to use them. But this fierce multitude, incapable of concerting or executing any plan of national greatness, was agitated by various and often hostile intentions. Germany was divided into more than forty independent states; and, even in each state, the union of the several tribes was extremely loose and precarious. The barbarians were easily provoked; they knew not how to forgive an injury, much less an insult; their resentments were bloody and implacable. The casual disputes that so frequently happened in their tumultuous parties of hunting or drinking, were sufficient to inflame the minds of whole nations; the private feuds of any considerable chieftains diffused itself among their followers and allies. To chastise the insolent, or to plunder the defenceless, were alike causes of war. The most formidable states of Germany affected to encompass their territories with a wide frontier of solitude and devastation. The awful distance preserved by their neighbors attested the terror of their arms, and in some measure defended them from the danger of unexpected incursions. [77]

[Footnote 77: Caesar de Bell. Gal. l. vi. 23.]

"The Bructeri [77/1] (it is Tacitus who now speaks) were totally exterminated by the neighboring tribes, [78] provoked by their insolence, allured by the hopes of spoil, and perhaps inspired by the tutelar deities of the empire. Above sixty thousand barbarians were destroyed; not by the Roman arms, but in our sight, and for our entertainment. May the nations, enemies of Rome, ever preserve this enmity to each other! We have now attained the utmost verge of prosperity, [79] and have nothing left to demand of fortune, except the discord of the barbarians." [80]—These sentiments, less worthy of the humanity than of the patriotism of Tacitus, express the invariable maxims of the policy of his countrymen. They deemed it a much safer expedient to divide than to combat the barbarians, from whose defeat they could derive neither honor nor advantage. The money and negotiations of Rome insinuated themselves into the heart of Germany; and every art of seduction was used with dignity, to conciliate those nations whom their proximity to the Rhine or Danube might render the most useful friends as well as the most troublesome enemies. Chiefs of renown and power were flattered by the most trifling presents, which they received either as marks of distinction, or as the instruments of luxury. In civil dissensions the weaker faction endeavored to strengthen its interest by entering into secret connections with the governors of the frontier provinces. Every quarrel among the Germans was fomented by the intrigues of Rome; and every plan of union and public good was defeated by the stronger bias of private jealousy and interest. [81]

[Footnote 77/1: The Bructeri were a non-Suevian tribe, who dwelt below the duchies of Oldenburgh, and Lauenburgh, on the borders of the Lippe, and in the Hartz Mountains. It was among them that the priestess Velleda obtained her renown.—G.]

[Footnote 78: They are mentioned, however, in the ivth and vth centuries by Nazarius, Ammianus, Claudian, &c., as a tribe of Franks. See Cluver. Germ. Antiq. l. iii. c. 13.]

[Footnote 79: Urgentibus is the common reading; but good sense, Lipsius, and some Mss. declare for Vergentibus.]

[Footnote 80: Tacit Germania, c. 33. The pious Abbe de la Bleterie is very angry with Tacitus, talks of the devil, who was a murderer from the beginning, &c., &c.]

[Footnote 81: Many traces of this policy may be discovered in Tacitus and Dion: and many more may be inferred from the principles of human nature.]

The general conspiracy which terrified the Romans under the reign of Marcus Antoninus, comprehended almost all the nations of Germany, and even Sarmatia, from the mouth of the Rhine to that of the Danube. [82] It is impossible for us to determine whether this hasty confederation was formed by necessity, by reason, or by passion; but we may rest assured, that the barbarians were neither allured by the indolence, nor provoked by the ambition, of the Roman monarch. This dangerous invasion required all the firmness and vigilance of Marcus. He fixed generals of ability in the several stations of attack, and assumed in person the conduct of the most important province on the Upper Danube. After a long and doubtful conflict, the spirit of the barbarians was subdued. The Quadi and the Marcomanni, [83] who had taken the lead in the war, were the most severely punished in its catastrophe. They were commanded to retire five miles [84] from their own banks of the Danube, and to deliver up the flower of the youth, who were immediately sent into Britain, a remote island, where they might be secure as hostages, and useful as soldiers. [85] On the frequent rebellions of the Quadi and Marcomanni, the irritated emperor resolved to reduce their country into the form of a province. His designs were disappointed by death. This formidable league, however, the only one that appears in the two first centuries of the Imperial history, was entirely dissipated, without leaving any traces behind in Germany.

[Footnote 82: Hist. Aug. p. 31. Ammian. Marcellin. l. xxxi. c. 5. Aurel. Victor. The emperor Marcus was reduced to sell the rich furniture of the palace, and to enlist slaves and robbers.]

[Footnote 83: The Marcomanni, a colony, who, from the banks of the Rhine occupied Bohemia and Moravia, had once erected a great and formidable monarchy under their king Maroboduus. See Strabo, l. vii. [p. 290.] Vell. Pat. ii. 108. Tacit. Annal. ii. 63. Note: The Mark-manaen, the March-men or borderers. There seems little doubt that this was an appellation, rather than a proper name of a part of the great Suevian or Teutonic race.—M.]

[Footnote 84: Mr. Wotton (History of Rome, p. 166) increases the prohibition to ten times the distance. His reasoning is specious, but not conclusive. Five miles were sufficient for a fortified barrier.]

[Footnote 85: Dion, l. lxxi. and lxxii.]

In the course of this introductory chapter, we have confined ourselves to the general outlines of the manners of Germany, without attempting to describe or to distinguish the various tribes which filled that great country in the time of Caesar, of Tacitus, or of Ptolemy. As the ancient, or as new tribes successively present themselves in the series of this history, we shall concisely mention their origin, their situation, and their particular character. Modern nations are fixed and permanent societies, connected among themselves by laws and government, bound to their native soil by arts and agriculture. The German tribes were voluntary and fluctuating associations of soldiers, almost of savages. The same territory often changed its inhabitants in the tide of conquest and emigration. The same communities, uniting in a plan of defence or invasion, bestowed a new title on their new confederacy. The dissolution of an ancient confederacy restored to the independent tribes their peculiar but long-forgotten appellation. A victorious state often communicated its own name to a vanquished people. Sometimes crowds of volunteers flocked from all parts to the standard of a favorite leader; his camp became their country, and some circumstance of the enterprise soon gave a common denomination to the mixed multitude. The distinctions of the ferocious invaders were perpetually varied by themselves, and confounded by the astonished subjects of the Roman empire. [86]

[Footnote 86: See an excellent dissertation on the origin and migrations of nations, in the Memoires de l'Academie des Inscriptions, tom. xviii. p. 48—71. It is seldom that the antiquarian and the philosopher are so happily blended.]

Wars, and the administration of public affairs, are the principal subjects of history; but the number of persons interested in these busy scenes is very different, according to the different condition of mankind. In great monarchies, millions of obedient subjects pursue their useful occupations in peace and obscurity. The attention of the writer, as well as of the reader, is solely confined to a court, a capital, a regular army, and the districts which happen to be the occasional scene of military operations. But a state of freedom and barbarism, the season of civil commotions, or the situation of petty republics, [87] raises almost every member of the community into action, and consequently into notice. The irregular divisions, and the restless motions, of the people of Germany, dazzle our imagination, and seem to multiply their numbers. The profuse enumeration of kings, of warriors, of armies and nations, inclines us to forget that the same objects are continually repeated under a variety of appellations, and that the most splendid appellations have been frequently lavished on the most inconsiderable objects.

[Footnote 87: Should we suspect that Athens contained only 21,000 citizens, and Sparta no more than 39,000? See Hume and Wallace on the number of mankind in ancient and modern times. Note: This number, though too positively stated, is probably not far wrong, as an average estimate. On the subject of Athenian population, see St. Croix, Acad. des Inscrip. xlviii. Boeckh, Public Economy of Athens, i. 47. Eng Trans, Fynes Clinton, Fasti Hellenici, vol. i. p. 381. The latter author estimates the citizens of Sparta at 33,000—M.]

CHAPTER X

EMPERORS DECIUS, GALLUS, AEMILIANUS, VALERIAN AND GALLIENUS

PART I

THE EMPERORS DECIUS, GALLUS, AEMILIANUS, VALERIAN AND GALLIENUS—THE GENERAL IRRUPTION OF THE BARBARIANS—THE THIRTY TYRANTS

From the great secular games celebrated by Philip, to the death of the emperor Gallienus, there elapsed twenty years of shame and misfortune. During that calamitous period, every instant of time was marked, every province of the Roman world was afflicted, by barbarous invaders, and military tyrants, and the ruined empire seemed to approach the last and fatal moment of its dissolution. The confusion of the times, and the scarcity of authentic memorials, oppose equal difficulties to the historian, who attempts to preserve a clear and unbroken thread of narration. Surrounded with imperfect fragments, always concise, often obscure, and sometimes contradictory, he is reduced to collect, to compare, and to conjecture: and though he ought never to place his conjectures in the rank of facts, yet the knowledge of human nature, and of the sure operation of its fierce and unrestrained passions, might, on some occasions, supply the want of historical materials.

There is not, for instance, any difficulty in conceiving, that the successive murders of so many emperors had loosened all the ties of allegiance between the prince and people; that all the generals of Philip were disposed to imitate the example of their master; and that the caprice of armies, long since habituated to frequent and violent revolutions, might every day raise to the throne the most obscure of their fellow-soldiers. History can only add, that the rebellion against the emperor Philip broke out in the summer of the year two hundred and forty-nine, among the legions of Maesia; and that a subaltern officer, [1] named Marinus, was the object of their seditious choice. Philip was alarmed. He dreaded lest the treason of the Maesian army should prove the first spark of a general conflagration. Distracted with the consciousness of his guilt and of his danger, he communicated the intelligence to the senate. A gloomy silence prevailed, the effect of fear, and perhaps of disaffection; till at length Decius, one of the assembly, assuming a spirit worthy of his noble extraction, ventured to discover more intrepidity than the emperor seemed to possess. He treated the whole business with contempt, as a hasty and inconsiderate tumult, and Philip's rival as a phantom of royalty, who in a very few days would be destroyed by the same inconstancy that had created him. The speedy completion of the prophecy inspired Philip with a just esteem for so able a counsellor; and Decius appeared to him the only person capable of restoring peace and discipline to an army whose tumultuous spirit did not immediately subside after the murder of Marinus. Decius, [2] who long resisted his own nomination, seems to have insinuated the danger of presenting a leader of merit to the angry and apprehensive minds of the soldiers; and his prediction was again confirmed by the event. The legions of Maesia forced their judge to become their accomplice. They left him only the alternative of death or the purple. His subsequent conduct, after that decisive measure, was unavoidable. He conducted, or followed, his army to the confines of Italy, whither Philip, collecting all his force to repel the formidable competitor whom he had raised up, advanced to meet him. The Imperial troops were superior in number; but the rebels formed an army of veterans, commanded by an able and experienced leader. Philip was either killed in the battle, or put to death a few days afterwards at Verona. His son and associate in the empire was massacred at Rome by the Praetorian guards; and the victorious Decius, with more favorable circumstances than the ambition of that age can usually plead, was universally acknowledged by the senate and provinces. It is reported, that, immediately after his reluctant acceptance of the title of Augustus, he had assured Philip, by a private message, of his innocence and loyalty, solemnly protesting, that, on his arrival on Italy, he would resign the Imperial ornaments, and return to the condition of an obedient subject. His professions might be sincere; but in the situation where fortune had placed him, it was scarcely possible that he could either forgive or be forgiven. [3]

[Footnote 1: The expression used by Zosimus and Zonaras may signify that Marinus commanded a century, a cohort, or a legion.]

[Footnote 2: His birth at Bubalia, a little village in Pannonia, (Eutrop. ix. Victor. in Caesarib. et Epitom.,) seems to contradict, unless it was merely accidental, his supposed descent from the Decii. Six hundred years had bestowed nobility on the Decii: but at the commencement of that period, they were only plebeians of merit, and among the first who shared the consulship with the haughty patricians. Plebeine Deciorum animae, &c. Juvenal, Sat. viii. 254. See the spirited speech of Decius, in Livy. x. 9, 10.]

[Footnote 3: Zosimus, l. i. p. 20, c. 22. Zonaras, l. xii. p. 624, edit. Louvre.]

The emperor Decius had employed a few months in the works of peace and the administration of justice, when he was summoned to the banks of the Danube by the invasion of the Goths. This is the first considerable occasion in which history mentions that great people, who afterwards broke the Roman power, sacked the Capitol, and reigned in Gaul, Spain, and Italy. So memorable was the part which they acted in the subversion of the Western empire, that the name of Goths is frequently but improperly used as a general appellation of rude and warlike barbarism.

In the beginning of the sixth century, and after the conquest of Italy, the Goths, in possession of present greatness, very naturally indulged themselves in the prospect of past and of future glory. They wished to preserve the memory of their ancestors, and to transmit to posterity their own achievements. The principal minister of the court of Ravenna, the learned Cassiodorus, gratified the inclination of the conquerors in a Gothic history, which consisted of twelve books, now reduced to the imperfect abridgment of Jornandes. [4] These writers passed with the most artful conciseness over the misfortunes of the nation, celebrated its successful valor, and adorned the triumph with many Asiatic trophies, that more properly belonged to the people of Scythia. On the faith of ancient songs, the uncertain, but the only memorials of barbarians, they deduced the first origin of the Goths from the vast island, or peninsula, of Scandinavia. [5] [5/1] That extreme country of the North was not unknown to the conquerors of Italy: the ties of ancient consanguinity had been strengthened by recent offices of friendship; and a Scandinavian king had cheerfully abdicated his savage greatness, that he might pass the remainder of his days in the peaceful and polished court of Ravenna. [6] Many vestiges, which cannot be ascribed to the arts of popular vanity, attest the ancient residence of the Goths in the countries beyond the Rhine. From the time of the geographer Ptolemy, the southern part of Sweden seems to have continued in the possession of the less enterprising remnant of the nation, and a large territory is even at present divided into east and west Gothland. During the middle ages, (from the ninth to the twelfth century,) whilst Christianity was advancing with a slow progress into the North, the Goths and the Swedes composed two distinct and sometimes hostile members of the same monarchy. [7] The latter of these two names has prevailed without extinguishing the former. The Swedes, who might well be satisfied with their own fame in arms, have, in every age, claimed the kindred glory of the Goths. In a moment of discontent against the court of Rome, Charles the Twelfth insinuated, that his victorious troops were not degenerated from their brave ancestors, who had already subdued the mistress of the world. [8]

[Footnote 4: See the prefaces of Cassiodorus and Jornandes; it is surprising that the latter should be omitted in the excellent edition, published by Grotius, of the Gothic writers.]

[Footnote 5: On the authority of Ablavius, Jornandes quotes some old Gothic chronicles in verse. De Reb. Geticis, c. 4.]

[Footnote 5/1: The Goths have inhabited Scandinavia, but it was not their original habitation. This great nation was anciently of the Suevian race; it occupied, in the time of Tacitus, and long before, Mecklenburgh, Pomerania Southern Prussia and the north-west of Poland. A little before the birth of J. C., and in the first years of that century, they belonged to the kingdom of Marbod, king of the Marcomanni: but Cotwalda, a young Gothic prince, delivered them from that tyranny, and established his own power over the kingdom of the Marcomanni, already much weakened by the victories of Tiberius. The power of the Goths at that time must have been great: it was probably from them that the Sinus Codanus (the Baltic) took this name, as it was afterwards called Mare Suevicum, and Mare Venedicum, during the superiority of the proper Suevi and the Venedi. The epoch in which the Goths passed into Scandinavia is unknown. See Adelung, Hist. of Anc. Germany, p. 200. Gatterer, Hist. Univ. 458.—G. —M. St. Martin observes, that the Scandinavian descent of the Goths rests on the authority of Jornandes, who professed to derive it from the traditions of the Goths. He is supported by Procopius and Paulus Diaconus. Yet the Goths are unquestionably the same with the Getae of the earlier historians. St. Martin, note on Le Beau, Hist. du bas Empire, iii. 324. The identity of the Getae and Goths is by no means generally admitted. On the whole, they seem to be one vast branch of the Indo-Teutonic race, who spread irregularly towards the north of Europe, and at different periods, and in different regions, came in contact with the more civilized nations of the south. At this period, there seems to have been a reflux of these Gothic tribes from the North. Malte Brun considers that there are strong grounds for receiving the Islandic traditions commented by the Danish Varro, M. Suhm. From these, and the voyage of Pytheas, which Malte Brun considers genuine, the Goths were in possession of Scandinavia, Ey-Gothland, 250 years before J. C., and of a tract on the continent (Reid-Gothland) between the mouths of the Vistula and the Oder. In their southern migration, they followed the course of the Vistula; afterwards, of the Dnieper. Malte Brun, Geogr. i. p. 387, edit. 1832. Geijer, the historian of Sweden, ably maintains the Scandinavian origin of the Goths. The Gothic language, according to Bopp, is the link between the Sanscrit and the modern Teutonic dialects: "I think that I am reading Sanscrit when I am reading Olphilas." Bopp, Conjugations System der Sanscrit Sprache, preface, p. x—M.]

[Footnote 6: Jornandes, c. 3.]

[Footnote 7: See in the Prolegomena of Grotius some large extracts from Adam of Bremen, and Saxo-Grammaticus. The former wrote in the year 1077, the latter flourished about the year 1200.]

[Footnote 8: Voltaire, Histoire de Charles XII. l. iii. When the Austrians desired the aid of the court of Rome against Gustavus Adolphus, they always represented that conqueror as the lineal successor of Alaric. Harte's History of Gustavus, vol. ii. p. 123.]

Till the end of the eleventh century, a celebrated temple subsisted at Upsal, the most considerable town of the Swedes and Goths. It was enriched with the gold which the Scandinavians had acquired in their piratical adventures, and sanctified by the uncouth representations of the three principal deities, the god of war, the goddess of generation, and the god of thunder. In the general festival, that was solemnized every ninth year, nine animals of every species (without excepting the human) were sacrificed, and their bleeding bodies suspended in the sacred grove adjacent to the temple. [9] The only traces that now subsist of this barbaric superstition are contained in the Edda, [9/1] a system of mythology, compiled in Iceland about the thirteenth century, and studied by the learned of Denmark and Sweden, as the most valuable remains of their ancient traditions.

[Footnote 9: See Adam of Bremen in Grotii Prolegomenis, p. 105. The temple of Upsal was destroyed by Ingo, king of Sweden, who began his reign in the year 1075, and about fourscore years afterwards, a Christian cathedral was erected on its ruins. See Dalin's History of Sweden, in the Bibliotheque Raisonee.]

[Footnote 9/1: The Eddas have at length been made accessible to European scholars by the completion of the publication of the Saemundine Edda by the Arna Magnaean Commission, in 3 vols. 4to., with a copious lexicon of northern mythology.—M.]

Notwithstanding the mysterious obscurity of the Edda, we can easily distinguish two persons confounded under the name of Odin; the god of war, and the great legislator of Scandinavia. The latter, the Mahomet of the North, instituted a religion adapted to the climate and to the people. Numerous tribes on either side of the Baltic were subdued by the invincible valor of Odin, by his persuasive eloquence, and by the fame which he acquired of a most skilful magician. The faith that he had propagated, during a long and prosperous life, he confirmed by a voluntary death. Apprehensive of the ignominious approach of disease and infirmity, he resolved to expire as became a warrior. In a solemn assembly of the Swedes and Goths, he wounded himself in nine mortal places, hastening away (as he asserted with his dying voice) to prepare the feast of heroes in the palace of the God of war. [10]

[Footnote 10: Mallet, Introduction a l'Histoire du Dannemarc.]

The native and proper habitation of Odin is distinguished by the appellation of As-gard. The happy resemblance of that name with As-burg, or As-of, [11] words of a similar signification, has given rise to an historical system of so pleasing a contexture, that we could almost wish to persuade ourselves of its truth. It is supposed that Odin was the chief of a tribe of barbarians which dwelt on the banks of the Lake Maeotis, till the fall of Mithridates and the arms of Pompey menaced the North with servitude. That Odin, yielding with indignant fury to a power which he was unable to resist, conducted his tribe from the frontiers of the Asiatic Sarmatia into Sweden, with the great design of forming, in that inaccessible retreat of freedom, a religion and a people, which, in some remote age, might be subservient to his immortal revenge; when his invincible Goths, armed with martial fanaticism, should issue in numerous swarms from the neighborhood of the Polar circle, to chastise the oppressors of mankind. [12]

[Footnote 11: Mallet, c. iv. p. 55, has collected from Strabo, Pliny, Ptolemy, and Stephanus Byzantinus, the vestiges of such a city and people.]

[Footnote 12: This wonderful expedition of Odin, which, by deducting the enmity of the Goths and Romans from so memorable a cause, might supply the noble groundwork of an epic poem, cannot safely be received as authentic history. According to the obvious sense of the Edda, and the interpretation of the most skilful critics, As-gard, instead of denoting a real city of the Asiatic Sarmatia, is the fictitious appellation of the mystic abode of the gods, the Olympus of Scandinavia; from whence the prophet was supposed to descend, when he announced his new religion to the Gothic nations, who were already seated in the southern parts of Sweden. Note: A curious letter may be consulted on this subject from the Swede, Ihre counsellor in the Chancery of Upsal, printed at Upsal by Edman, in 1772 and translated into German by M. Schlozer. Gottingen, printed for Dietericht, 1779.—G. —Gibbon, at a later period of his work, recanted his opinion of the truth of this expedition of Odin. The Asiatic origin of the Goths is almost certain from the affinity of their language to the Sanscrit and Persian; but their northern writers, when all mythology was reduced to hero worship.—M.]

If so many successive generations of Goths were capable of preserving a faint tradition of their Scandinavian origin, we must not expect, from such unlettered barbarians, any distinct account of the time and circumstances of their emigration. To cross the Baltic was an easy and natural attempt. The inhabitants of Sweden were masters of a sufficient number of large vessels, with oars, [13] and the distance is little more than one hundred miles from Carlscroon to the nearest ports of Pomerania and Prussia. Here, at length, we land on firm and historic ground. At least as early as the Christian aera, [14] and as late as the age of the Antonines, [15] the Goths were established towards the mouth of the Vistula, and in that fertile province where the commercial cities of Thorn, Elbing, Koningsberg, and Dantzick, were long afterwards founded. [16] Westward of the Goths, the numerous tribes of the Vandals were spread along the banks of the Oder, and the sea-coast of Pomerania and Mecklenburgh. A striking resemblance of manners, complexion, religion, and language, seemed to indicate that the Vandals and the Goths were originally one great people. [17] The latter appear to have been subdivided into Ostrogoths, Visigoths, and Gepidae. [18] The distinction among the Vandals was more strongly marked by the independent names of Heruli, Burgundians, Lombards, and a variety of other petty states, many of which, in a future age, expanded themselves into powerful monarchies. [18/1]

[Footnote 13: Tacit. Germania, c. 44.]

[Footnote 14: Tacit. Annal. ii. 62. If we could yield a firm assent to the navigations of Pytheas of Marseilles, we must allow that the Goths had passed the Baltic at least three hundred years before Christ.]

[Footnote 15: Ptolemy, l. ii.]

[Footnote 16: By the German colonies who followed the arms of the Teutonic knights. The conquest and conversion of Prussia were completed by those adventurers in the thirteenth century.]

[Footnote 17: Pliny (Hist. Natur. iv. 14) and Procopius (in Bell. Vandal. l. i. c. l) agree in this opinion. They lived in distant ages, and possessed different means of investigating the truth.]

[Footnote 18: The Ostro and Visi, the eastern and western Goths, obtained those denominations from their original seats in Scandinavia. In all their future marches and settlements they preserved, with their names, the same relative situation. When they first departed from Sweden, the infant colony was contained in three vessels. The third, being a heavy sailer, lagged behind, and the crew, which afterwards swelled into a nation, received from that circumstance the appellation of Gepidae or Loiterers. Jornandes, c. 17. Note: It was not in Scandinavia that the Goths were divided into Ostrogoths and Visigoths; that division took place after their irruption into Dacia in the third century: those who came from Mecklenburgh and Pomerania were called Visigoths; those who came from the south of Prussia, and the northwest of Poland, called themselves Ostrogoths. Adelung, Hist. All. p. 202 Gatterer, Hist. Univ. 431.—G.]

[Footnote 18/1: This opinion is by no means probable. The Vandals and the Goths equally belonged to the great division of the Suevi, but the two tribes were very different. Those who have treated on this part of history, appear to me to have neglected to remark that the ancients almost always gave the name of the dominant and conquering people to all the weaker and conquered races. So Pliny calls Vindeli, Vandals, all the people of the north-east of Europe, because at that epoch the Vandals were doubtless the conquering tribe. Caesar, on the contrary, ranges under the name of Suevi, many of the tribes whom Pliny reckons as Vandals, because the Suevi, properly so called, were then the most powerful tribe in Germany. When the Goths, become in their turn conquerors, had subjugated the nations whom they encountered on their way, these nations lost their name with their liberty, and became of Gothic origin. The Vandals themselves were then considered as Goths; the Heruli, the Gepidae, &c., suffered the same fate. A common origin was thus attributed to tribes who had only been united by the conquests of some dominant nation, and this confusion has given rise to a number of historical errors.—G. —M. St. Martin has a learned note (to Le Beau, v. 261) on the origin of the Vandals. The difficulty appears to be in rejecting the close analogy of the name with the Vend or Wendish race, who were of Sclavonian, not of Suevian or German, origin. M. St. Martin supposes that the different races spread from the head of the Adriatic to the Baltic, and even the Veneti, on the shores of the Adriatic, the Vindelici, the tribes which gave their name to Vindobena, Vindoduna, Vindonissa, were branches of the same stock with the Sclavonian Venedi, who at one time gave their name to the Baltic; that they all spoke dialects of the Wendish language, which still prevails in Carinthia, Carniola, part of Bohemia, and Lusatia, and is hardly extinct in Mecklenburgh and Pomerania. The Vandal race, once so fearfully celebrated in the annals of mankind, has so utterly perished from the face of the earth, that we are not aware that any vestiges of their language can be traced, so as to throw light on the disputed question of their German, their Sclavonian, or independent origin. The weight of ancient authority seems against M. St. Martin's opinion. Compare, on the Vandals, Malte Brun. 394. Also Gibbon's note, c. xli. n. 38.—M.]

In the age of the Antonines, the Goths were still seated in Prussia. About the reign of Alexander Severus, the Roman province of Dacia had already experienced their proximity by frequent and destructive inroads. [19] In this interval, therefore, of about seventy years, we must place the second migration of the Goths from the Baltic to the Euxine; but the cause that produced it lies concealed among the various motives which actuate the conduct of unsettled barbarians. Either a pestilence or a famine, a victory or a defeat, an oracle of the gods or the eloquence of a daring leader, were sufficient to impel the Gothic arms on the milder climates of the south. Besides the influence of a martial religion, the numbers and spirit of the Goths were equal to the most dangerous adventures. The use of round bucklers and short swords rendered them formidable in a close engagement; the manly obedience which they yielded to hereditary kings, gave uncommon union and stability to their councils; [20] and the renowned Amala, the hero of that age, and the tenth ancestor of Theodoric, king of Italy, enforced, by the ascendant of personal merit, the prerogative of his birth, which he derived from the Anses, or demi gods of the Gothic nation. [21]

[Footnote 19: See a fragment of Peter Patricius in the Excerpta Legationum and with regard to its probable date, see Tillemont, Hist, des Empereurs, tom. iii. p. 346.]

[Footnote 20: Omnium harum gentium insigne, rotunda scuta, breves gladii, et erga rages obsequium. Tacit. Germania, c. 43. The Goths probably acquired their iron by the commerce of amber.]

[Footnote 21: Jornandes, c. 13, 14.]

The fame of a great enterprise excited the bravest warriors from all the Vandalic states of Germany, many of whom are seen a few years afterwards combating under the common standard of the Goths. [22] The first motions of the emigrants carried them to the banks of the Prypec, a river universally conceived by the ancients to be the southern branch of the Borysthenes. [23] The windings of that great stream through the plains of Poland and Russia gave a direction to their line of march, and a constant supply of fresh water and pasturage to their numerous herds of cattle. They followed the unknown course of the river, confident in their valor, and careless of whatever power might oppose their progress. The Bastarnae and the Venedi were the first who presented themselves; and the flower of their youth, either from choice or compulsion, increased the Gothic army. The Bastarnae dwelt on the northern side of the Carpathian Mountains: the immense tract of land that separated the Bastarnae from the savages of Finland was possessed, or rather wasted, by the Venedi; [24] we have some reason to believe that the first of these nations, which distinguished itself in the Macedonian war, [25] and was afterwards divided into the formidable tribes of the Peucini, the Borani, the Carpi, &c., derived its origin from the Germans. [25/1] With better authority, a Sarmatian extraction may be assigned to the Venedi, who rendered themselves so famous in the middle ages. [26] But the confusion of blood and manners on that doubtful frontier often perplexed the most accurate observers. [27] As the Goths advanced near the Euxine Sea, they encountered a purer race of Sarmatians, the Jazyges, the Alani, [27/1] and the Roxolani; and they were probably the first Germans who saw the mouths of the Borysthenes, and of the Tanais. If we inquire into the characteristic marks of the people of Germany and of Sarmatia, we shall discover that those two great portions of human kind were principally distinguished by fixed huts or movable tents, by a close dress or flowing garments, by the marriage of one or of several wives, by a military force, consisting, for the most part, either of infantry or cavalry; and above all, by the use of the Teutonic, or of the Sclavonian language; the last of which has been diffused by conquest, from the confines of Italy to the neighborhood of Japan.

[Footnote 22: The Heruli, and the Uregundi or Burgundi, are particularly mentioned. See Mascou's History of the Germans, l. v. A passage in the Augustan History, p. 28, seems to allude to this great emigration. The Marcomannic war was partly occasioned by the pressure of barbarous tribes, who fled before the arms of more northern barbarians.]

[Footnote 23: D'Anville, Geographie Ancienne, and the third part of his incomparable map of Europe.]

[Footnote 24: Tacit. Germania, c. 46.]

[Footnote 25: Cluver. Germ. Antiqua, l. iii. c. 43.]

[Footnote 25/1: The Bastarnae cannot be considered original inhabitants of Germany Strabo and Tacitus appear to doubt it; Pliny alone calls them Germans: Ptolemy and Dion treat them as Scythians, a vague appellation at this period of history; Livy, Plutarch, and Diodorus Siculus, call them Gauls, and this is the most probable opinion. They descended from the Gauls who entered Germany under Signoesus. They are

always found associated with other Gaulish tribes, such as the Boll, the Taurisci, &c., and not to the German tribes. The names of their chiefs or princes, Chlonix, Chlondicus. Deldon, are not German names. Those who were settled in the island of Peuce in the Danube, took the name of Peucini. The Carpi appear in 237 as a Suevian tribe who had made an irruption into Maesia. Afterwards they reappear under the Ostrogoths, with whom they were probably blended. Adelung, p. 236, 278.—G.]

[Footnote 26: The Venedi, the Slavi, and the Antes, were the three great tribes of the same people. Jornandes, 24. Note Dagger: They formed the great Sclavonian nation.—G.]

[Footnote 27: Tacitus most assuredly deserves that title, and even his cautious suspense is a proof of his diligent inquiries.]

[Footnote 27/1: Jac. Reineggs supposed that he had found, in the mountains of Caucasus, some descendants of the Alani. The Tartars call them Edeki-Alan: they speak a peculiar dialect of the ancient language of the Tartars of Caucasus. See J. Reineggs' Descr. of Caucasus, p. 11, 13.—G. According to Klaproth, they are the Ossetes of the present day in Mount Caucasus and were the same with the Albanians of antiquity. Klaproth, Hist. de l'Asie, p. 180.—M.]

PART II

The Goths were now in possession of the Ukraine, a country of considerable extent and uncommon fertility, intersected with navigable rivers, which, from either side, discharge themselves into the Borysthenes; and interspersed with large and leafy forests of oaks. The plenty of game and fish, the innumerable bee-hives deposited in the hollow of old trees, and in the cavities of rocks, and forming, even in that rude age, a valuable branch of commerce, the size of the cattle, the temperature of the air, the aptness of the soil for every species of grain, and the luxuriancy of the vegetation, all displayed the liberality of Nature, and tempted the industry of man. [28] But the Goths withstood all these temptations, and still adhered to a life of idleness, of poverty, and of rapine.

[Footnote 28: Genealogical History of the Tartars, p. 593. Mr. Bell (vol. ii. p 379) traversed the Ukraine, in his journey from Petersburgh to Constantinople. The modern face of the country is a just representation of the ancient, since, in the hands of the Cossacks, it still remains in a state of nature.]

The Scythian hordes, which, towards the east, bordered on the new settlements of the Goths, presented nothing to their arms, except the doubtful chance of an unprofitable victory. But the prospect of the Roman territories was far more alluring; and the fields of Dacia were covered with rich harvests, sown by the hands of an industrious, and exposed to be gathered by those of a warlike, people. It is probable that the conquests of Trajan, maintained by his successors, less for any real advantage than for ideal dignity, had contributed to weaken the empire on that side. The new and unsettled province of Dacia was neither strong enough to resist, nor rich enough to satiate, the rapaciousness of the barbarians. As long as the remote banks of the Niester were considered as the boundary of the Roman power, the fortifications of the Lower Danube were more carelessly guarded, and the inhabitants of Maesia lived in supine security, fondly conceiving themselves at an inaccessible distance from any barbarian invaders. The irruptions of the Goths, under the reign of Philip, fatally convinced them of their mistake. The king, or leader, of that fierce nation, traversed with contempt the province of Dacia, and passed both the Niester and the Danube without encountering any opposition capable of retarding his progress. The relaxed discipline of the Roman troops betrayed the most important posts, where they were stationed, and the fear of deserved punishment induced great numbers of them to enlist under the Gothic standard. The various multitude of barbarians appeared, at length, under the walls of Marcianopolis, a city built by Trajan in honor of his sister, and at that time the capital of the second Maesia. [29] The inhabitants consented to ransom their lives and property by the payment of a large sum of money, and the invaders retreated back into their deserts, animated, rather than satisfied, with the first success of their arms against an opulent but feeble country. Intelligence was soon transmitted to the emperor Decius, that Cniva, king of the Goths, had passed the Danube a second time, with more considerable forces; that his numerous detachments scattered devastation over the province of Maesia, whilst the main body of the army, consisting of seventy thousand Germans and Sarmatians, a force equal to the most daring achievements, required the presence of the Roman monarch, and the exertion of his military power.

[Footnote 29: In the sixteenth chapter of Jornandes, instead of secundo Maesiam we may venture to substitute secundam, the second Maesia, of which Marcianopolis was certainly the capital. (See Hierocles de Provinciis, and Wesseling ad locum, p. 636. Itinerar.) It is surprising how this palpable error of the scribe should escape the judicious correction of Grotius. Note: Luden has observed that Jornandes mentions two passages over the Danube; this relates to the second irruption into Maesia. Geschichte des T V. ii. p. 448.—M.]

Decius found the Goths engaged before Nicopolis, one of the many monuments of Trajan's victories. [30] On his approach they raised the siege, but with a design only of marching away to a conquest of greater importance, the siege of Philippopolis, a city of Thrace, founded by the father of Alexander, near the foot of Mount Haemus. [31] Decius followed them through a difficult country, and by forced marches; but when he imagined himself at a considerable distance from the rear of the Goths, Cniva turned with rapid fury on his pursuers. The camp of the Romans was surprised and pillaged, and, for the first time, their emperor fled in disorder before a troop of half-armed barbarians. After a long resistance, Philoppopolis, destitute of succor, was taken by storm. A hundred thousand persons are reported to have been massacred in the sack of that great city. [32] Many prisoners of consequence became a valuable accession to the spoil; and Priscus, a brother of the late emperor Philip, blushed not to assume the purple, under the protection of the barbarous enemies of Rome. [33] The time, however, consumed in that tedious siege, enabled Decius to revive the courage, restore the discipline, and recruit the numbers of his troops. He intercepted several parties of Carpi, and other Germans, who were hastening to share the victory of their countrymen, [34] intrusted the passes of the mountains to officers of approved valor and fidelity, [35] repaired and strengthened the fortifications of the Danube, and exerted his utmost vigilance to oppose either the progress or the retreat of the Goths. Encouraged by the return of fortune, he anxiously waited for an opportunity to retrieve, by a great and decisive blow, his own glory, and that of the Roman arms. [36]

[Footnote 30: The place is still called Nicop. D'Anville, Geographie Ancienne, tom. i. p. 307. The little stream, on whose banks it stood, falls into the Danube.]

[Footnote 31: Stephan. Byzant. de Urbibus, p. 740. Wesseling, Itinerar. p. 136. Zonaras, by an odd mistake, ascribes the foundation of Philippopolis to the immediate predecessor of Decius. Note: Now Philippopolis or Philiba; its situation among the hills caused it to be also called Trimontium. D'Anville, Geog. Anc. i. 295.—G.]

[Footnote 32: Ammian. xxxi. 5.]

[Footnote 33: Aurel. Victor. c. 29.]

[Footnote 34: Victorioe Carpicoe, on some medals of Decius, insinuate these advantages.]

[Footnote 35: Claudius (who afterwards reigned with so much glory) was posted in the pass of Thermopylae with 200 Dardanians, 100 heavy and 160 light horse, 60 Cretan archers, and 1000 well-armed recruits. See an original letter from the emperor to his officer, in the Augustan History, p. 200.]

[Footnote 36: Jornandes, c. 16—18. Zosimus, l. i. p. 22. In the general account of this war, it is easy to discover the opposite prejudices of the Gothic and the Grecian writer. In carelessness alone they are alike.]

At the same time when Decius was struggling with the violence of the tempest, his mind, calm and deliberate amidst the tumult of war, investigated the more general causes, that, since the age of the Antonines, had so impetuously urged the decline of the Roman greatness. He soon discovered that it was impossible to replace that greatness on a permanent basis, without restoring public virtue, ancient principles and manners, and the oppressed majesty of the laws. To execute this noble but arduous design, he first resolved to revive the obsolete office of censor; an office which, as long as it had subsisted in its pristine integrity, had so much contributed to the perpetuity of the state, [37] till it was usurped and gradually neglected by the Caesars. [38] Conscious that the favor of the sovereign may confer power, but that the esteem of the people can alone bestow authority, he submitted the choice of the censor to the unbiased voice of the senate. By their unanimous votes, or rather acclamations, Valerian, who was afterwards emperor, and who then served with distinction in the army of Decius, was declared the most worthy of that exalted honor. As soon as the decree of the senate was transmitted to the emperor, he assembled a great council in his camp, and before the investiture of the censor elect, he apprised him of the difficulty and importance of his great office. "Happy Valerian," said the prince to his distinguished subject, "happy in the general approbation of the senate and of the Roman republic! Accept the censorship of mankind; and judge of our manners. You will select those who deserve to continue members of the senate; you will restore the equestrian order to its ancient splendor; you will improve the revenue, yet moderate the public burdens. You will distinguish into regular classes the various and infinite multitude of citizens, and accurately view the military strength, the wealth, the virtue, and the resources of Rome. Your decisions shall obtain the force of laws. The army, the palace, the ministers of justice, and the great officers of the empire, are all subject to your tribunal. None are exempted, excepting only the ordinary consuls, [39] the praefect of the city, the king of the sacrifices, and (as long as she preserves her chastity inviolate) the eldest of the vestal virgins. Even these few, who may not dread the severity, will anxiously solicit the esteem, of the Roman censor." [40]

[Footnote 37: Montesquieu, Grandeur et Decadence des Romains, c. viii. He illustrates the nature and use of the censorship with his usual ingenuity, and with uncommon precision.]

[Footnote 38: Vespasian and Titus were the last censors, (Pliny, Hist. Natur vii. 49. Censorinus de Die Natali.) The modesty of Trajan refused an honor which he deserved, and his example became a law to the Antonines. See Pliny's Panegyric, c. 45 and 60.]

[Footnote 39: Yet in spite of his exemption, Pompey appeared before that tribunal during his consulship. The occasion, indeed, was equally singular and honorable. Plutarch in Pomp. p. 630.]

[Footnote 40: See the original speech in the Augustan Hist. p. 173-174.]

A magistrate, invested with such extensive powers, would have appeared not so much the minister, as the colleague of his sovereign. [41] Valerian justly dreaded an elevation so full of envy and of suspicion. He modestly argued the alarming greatness of the trust, his own insufficiency, and the incurable corruption of the times. He artfully insinuated, that the office of censor was inseparable from the Imperial dignity, and that the feeble hands of a subject were unequal to the support of such an immense weight of cares and of power. [42] The approaching event of war soon put an end to the prosecution of a project so specious, but so impracticable; and whilst it preserved Valerian from the danger, saved the emperor Decius from the disappointment, which would most probably have attended it. A censor may maintain, he can never restore, the morals of a state. It is impossible for such a magistrate to exert his authority with benefit, or even with effect, unless he is supported by a quick sense of honor and virtue in the minds of the people, by a decent reverence for the public opinion, and by a train of useful prejudices combating on the side of national manners. In a period when these principles are annihilated, the censorial jurisdiction must either sink into empty pageantry, or be converted into a partial instrument of vexatious oppression. [43] It was easier to vanquish the Goths than to eradicate the public vices; yet even in the first of these enterprises, Decius lost his army and his life.

[Footnote 41: This transaction might deceive Zonaras, who supposes that Valerian was actually declared the colleague of Decius, l. xii. p. 625.]

[Footnote 42: Hist. August. p. 174. The emperor's reply is omitted.]

[Footnote 43: Such as the attempts of Augustus towards a reformation of manness. Tacit. Annal. iii. 24.]

The Goths were now, on every side, surrounded and pursued by the Roman arms. The flower of their troops had perished in the long siege of Philippopolis, and the exhausted country could no longer afford subsistence for the remaining multitude of licentious barbarians. Reduced to this extremity, the Goths would gladly have purchased, by the surrender of all their booty and prisoners, the permission of an undisturbed retreat. But the emperor, confident of victory, and resolving, by the chastisement of these invaders, to strike a salutary terror into the nations of the North, refused to listen to any terms of accommodation. The high-spirited barbarians preferred death to slavery. An obscure town of Maesia, called Forum Terebronii, [44] was the scene of the battle. The Gothic army was drawn up in three lines, and either from choice or accident, the front of the third line was covered by a morass. In the beginning of the action, the son of Decius, a youth of the fairest hopes, and already associated to the honors of the purple, was slain by an arrow, in the sight of his afflicted father; who, summoning all his fortitude, admonished the dismayed troops, that the loss of a single soldier was of little importance to the republic. [45] The conflict was terrible; it was the combat of despair against grief and rage. The first line of the Goths at length gave way in disorder; the second, advancing to sustain it, shared its fate; and the third only remained entire, prepared to dispute the passage of the morass, which was imprudently attempted by the presumption of the enemy. "Here the fortune of the day turned, and all things became adverse to the Romans; the place deep with ooze, sinking under those who stood, slippery to such as advanced; their armor heavy, the waters deep; nor could they wield, in that uneasy situation, their weighty javelins. The barbarians, on the contrary, were inured to encounter in the bogs, their persons tall, their spears long, such as could wound at a distance." [46] In this morass the Roman army, after an ineffectual struggle, was irrecoverably lost; nor could the body of the emperor ever be found. [47] Such was the fate of Decius, in the fiftieth year of his age; an accomplished prince, active in war and affable in peace; [48] who, together with his son, has deserved to be compared, both in life and death, with the brightest examples of ancient virtue. [49]

[Footnote 44: Tillemont, Histoire des Empereurs, tom. iii. p. 598. As Zosimus and some of his followers mistake the Danube for the Tanais, they place the field of battle in the plains of Scythia.]

[Footnote 45: Aurelius Victor allows two distinct actions for the deaths of the two Decii; but I have preferred the account of Jornandes.]

[Footnote 46: I have ventured to copy from Tacitus (Annal. i. 64) the picture of a similar engagement between a Roman army and a German tribe.]

[Footnote 47: Jornandes, c. 18. Zosimus, l. i. p. 22, [c. 23.] Zonaras, l. xii. p. 627. Aurelius Victor.]

[Footnote 48: The Decii were killed before the end of the year two hundred and fifty-one, since the new princes took possession of the consulship on the ensuing calends of January.]

[Footnote 49: Hist. August. p. 223, gives them a very honorable place among the small number of good emperors who reigned between Augustus and Diocletian.]

This fatal blow humbled, for a very little time, she insolence of the legions. They appeared to have patiently expected, and submissively obeyed, the decree of the senate which regulated the succession to the throne. From a just regard for the memory of Decius, the Imperial title was conferred on Hostilianus, his only surviving son; but an equal rank, with more effectual power, was granted to Gallus, whose experience and ability seemed equal to the great trust of guardian to the young prince and the distressed empire. [50] The first care of the new emperor was to deliver the Illyrian provinces from the intolerable weight of the victorious Goths. He consented to leave in their hands the rich fruits of their invasion, an immense booty, and what was still more disgraceful, a great number of prisoners of the highest merit and quality. He plentifully supplied their camp with every conveniency that could assuage their angry spirits or facilitate their so much wished-for departure; and he even promised to pay them annually a large sum of gold, on condition they should never afterwards infest the Roman territories by their incursions. [51]

[Footnote 50: Haec ubi Patres comperere.. .. decernunt. Victor in Caesaribus.]

[Footnote 51: Zonaras, l. xii. p. 628.]

In the age of the Scipios, the most opulent kings of the earth, who courted the protection of the victorious commonwealth, were gratified with such trifling presents as could only derive a value from the hand that bestowed them; an ivory chair, a coarse garment of purple, an inconsiderable piece of plate, or a quantity of copper coin. [52] After the wealth of nations had centred in Rome, the emperors displayed their greatness, and even their policy, by the regular exercise of a steady and moderate liberality towards the allies of the state. They relieved the poverty of the barbarians, honored their merit, and recompensed their fidelity. These voluntary marks of bounty were understood to flow, not from the fears, but merely from the generosity or the gratitude of the Romans; and whilst presents and subsidies were liberally distributed among friends and suppliants, they were sternly refused to such as claimed them as a debt. [53] But this stipulation, of an annual payment to a victorious enemy, appeared without disguise in the light of an ignominious tribute; the minds of the Romans were not yet accustomed to accept such unequal laws from a tribe of barbarians; and the prince, who by a necessary concession had probably saved his country, became the object of the general contempt and aversion. The death of Hostiliamus, though it happened in the midst of a raging pestilence, was interpreted as the personal crime of Gallus; [54] and even the defeat of the later emperor was ascribed by the voice of suspicion to the perfidious counsels of his hated successor. [55] The tranquillity which the empire enjoyed during the first year of his administration, [56] served rather to inflame than to appease the public discontent; and as soon as the apprehensions of war were removed, the infamy of the peace was more deeply and more sensibly felt.

[Footnote 52: A Sella, a Toga, and a golden Patera of five pounds weight, were accepted with joy and gratitude by the wealthy king of Egypt. (Livy, xxvii. 4.) Quina millia Aeris, a weight of copper, in value about eighteen pounds sterling, was the usual present made to foreign are ambassadors. (Livy, xxxi. 9.)]

[Footnote 53: See the firmness of a Roman general so late as the time of Alexander Severus, in the Excerpta Legationum, p. 25, edit. Louvre.]

[Footnote 54: For the plague, see Jornandes, c. 19, and Victor in Caesaribus.]

[Footnote 55: These improbable accusations are alleged by Zosimus, l. i. p. 28, 24.]

[Footnote 56: Jornandes, c. 19. The Gothic writer at least observed the peace which his victorious countrymen had sworn to Gallus.]

But the Romans were irritated to a still higher degree, when they discovered that they had not even secured their repose, though at the expense of their honor. The dangerous secret of the wealth and weakness of the empire had been revealed to the world. New swarms of barbarians, encouraged by the success, and not conceiving themselves bound by the obligation of their brethren, spread devastation though the Illyrian provinces, and terror as far as the gates of Rome. The defence of the monarchy, which seemed abandoned by the pusillanimous emperor, was assumed by Aemilianus, governor of Pannonia and Maesia; who rallied the scattered forces, and revived the fainting spirits of the troops. The barbarians were unexpectedly attacked, routed, chased, and pursued beyond the Danube. The victorious leader distributed as a donative the money collected for the tribute, and the acclamations of the soldiers proclaimed him emperor on the field of battle. [57] Gallus, who, careless of the general welfare, indulged himself in the pleasures of Italy, was almost in the same instant informed of the success, of the revolt, and of the rapid approach of his aspiring lieutenant. He advanced to meet him as far as the plains of Spoleto. When the armies came in sight of each other, the soldiers of Gallus compared the ignominious conduct of their sovereign with the glory of his rival. They admired the valor of Aemilianus; they were attracted by his liberality, for he offered a considerable increase of pay to all deserters. [58] The murder of Gallus, and of his son Volusianus, put an end to the civil war; and the senate gave a legal sanction to the rights of conquest. The letters of Aemilianus to that assembly displayed a mixture of moderation and vanity. He assured them, that he should resign to their wisdom the civil administration; and, contenting himself with the quality of their general, would in a short time assert the glory of Rome, and deliver the empire from all the barbarians both of the North and of the East. [59] His pride was flattered by the applause of the senate; and medals are still extant, representing him with the name and attributes of Hercules the Victor, and Mars the Avenger. [60]

[Footnote 57: Zosimus, l. i. p. 25, 26.]

[Footnote 58: Victor in Caesaribus.]

[Footnote 59: Zonaras, l. xii. p. 628.]

[Footnote 60: Banduri Numismata, p. 94.]

If the new monarch possessed the abilities, he wanted the time, necessary to fulfil these splendid promises. Less than four months intervened between his victory and his fall. [61] He had vanquished Gallus: he sunk under the weight of a competitor more formidable than Gallus. That unfortunate prince had sent Valerian, already distinguished by the honorable title of censor, to bring the legions of Gaul and Germany [62] to his aid. Valerian executed that commission with zeal and fidelity; and as he arrived too late to save his sovereign, he resolved to revenge him. The troops of Aemilianus, who still lay encamped in the plains of Spoleto, were awed by the sanctity of his character, but much more by the superior strength of his army; and as they were now become as incapable of personal attachment as they had always been of constitutional principle, they readily imbrued their hands in the blood of a prince who so lately had been the object of their partial choice. The guilt was theirs, [62/1] but the advantage of it was Valerian's; who obtained the possession of the throne by the means indeed of a civil war, but with a degree of innocence singular in that age of revolutions; since he owed neither gratitude nor allegiance to his predecessor, whom he dethroned.

[Footnote 61: Eutropius, l. ix. c. 6, says tertio mense. Eusebio this emperor.]

[Footnote 62: Zosimus, l. i. p. 28. Eutropius and Victor station Valerian's army in Rhaetia.]

[Footnote 62/1: Aurelius Victor says that Aemilianus died of a natural disorder. Tropius, in speaking of his death, does not say that he was assassinated—G.]

Valerian was about sixty years of age [63] when he was invested with the purple, not by the caprice of the populace, or the clamors of the army, but by the unanimous voice of the Roman world. In his gradual ascent through the honors of the state, he had deserved the favor of virtuous princes, and had declared himself the enemy of tyrants. [64] His noble birth, his mild but unblemished manners, his learning, prudence, and experience, were revered by the senate and people; and if mankind (according to the observation of an ancient writer) had been left at liberty to choose a master, their choice would most assuredly have fallen on Valerian. [65] Perhaps the merit of this emperor was inadequate to his reputation; perhaps his abilities, or at least his spirit, were affected by the languor and coldness of old age. The consciousness of his decline engaged him to share the throne with a younger and more active associate; [66] the emergency of the times demanded a general no less than a prince; and the experience of the Roman censor might have directed him where to bestow the Imperial purple, as the reward of military merit. But instead of making a judicious choice, which would have confirmed his reign and endeared his memory, Valerian, consulting only the dictates of affection or vanity, immediately invested with the supreme honors his son Gallienus, a youth whose effeminate vices had been hitherto concealed by the obscurity of a private station. The joint government of the father and the son subsisted about seven, and the sole administration of Gallien continued about eight, years. But the whole period was one uninterrupted series of confusion and calamity. As the Roman empire was at the same time, and on every side, attacked by the blind fury of foreign invaders, and the wild ambition of domestic usurpers, we shall consult order and perspicuity, by pursuing, not so much the doubtful arrangement of dates, as the more natural distribution of subjects. The most dangerous enemies of Rome, during the reigns of Valerian and Gallienus, were, 1. The Franks; 2. The Alemanni; 3. The Goths; and, 4. The

Persians. Under these general appellations, we may comprehend the adventures of less considerable tribes, whose obscure and uncouth names would only serve to oppress the memory and perplex the attention of the reader.

[Footnote 63: He was about seventy at the time of his accession, or, as it is more probable, of his death. Hist. August. p. 173. Tillemont, Hist. des Empereurs, tom. iii. p. 893, note 1.]

[Footnote 64: Inimicus tyrannorum. Hist. August. p. 173. In the glorious struggle of the senate against Maximin, Valerian acted a very spirited part. Hist. August. p. 156.]

[Footnote 65: According to the distinction of Victor, he seems to have received the title of Imperator from the army, and that of Augustus from the senate.]

[Footnote 66: From Victor and from the medals, Tillemont (tom. iii. p. 710) very justly infers, that Gallienus was associated to the empire about the month of August of the year 253.]

I. As the posterity of the Franks compose one of the greatest and most enlightened nations of Europe, the powers of learning and ingenuity have been exhausted in the discovery of their unlettered ancestors. To the tales of credulity have succeeded the systems of fancy. Every passage has been sifted, every spot has been surveyed, that might possibly reveal some faint traces of their origin. It has been supposed that Pannonia, [67] that Gaul, that the northern parts of Germany, [68] gave birth to that celebrated colony of warriors. At length the most rational critics, rejecting the fictitious emigrations of ideal conquerors, have acquiesced in a sentiment whose simplicity persuades us of its truth. [69] They suppose, that about the year two hundred and forty, [70] a new confederacy was formed under the name of Franks, by the old inhabitants of the Lower Rhine and the Weser. [70/1] The present circle of Westphalia, the Landgraviate of Hesse, and the duchies of Brunswick and Luneburg, were the ancient of the Chauci who, in their inaccessible morasses, defied the Roman arms; [71] of the Cherusci, proud of the fame of Arminius; of the Catti, formidable by their firm and intrepid infantry; and of several other tribes of inferior power and renown. [72] The love of liberty was the ruling passion of these Germans; the enjoyment of it their best treasure; the word that expressed that enjoyment, the most pleasing to their ear. They deserved, they assumed, they maintained the honorable appellation of Franks, or Freemen; which concealed, though it did not extinguish, the peculiar names of the several states of the confederacy. [73] Tacit consent, and mutual advantage, dictated the first laws of the union; it was gradually cemented by habit and experience. The league of the Franks may admit of some comparison with the Helvetic body; in which every canton, retaining its independent sovereignty, consults with its brethren in the common cause, without acknowledging the authority of any supreme head, or representative assembly. [74] But the principle of the two confederacies was extremely different. A peace of two hundred years has rewarded the wise and honest policy of the Swiss. An inconstant spirit, the thirst of rapine, and a disregard to the most solemn treaties, disgraced the character of the Franks.

[Footnote 67: Various systems have been formed to explain a difficult passage in Gregory of Tours, l. ii. c. 9.]

[Footnote 68: The Geographer of Ravenna, i. 11, by mentioning Mauringania, on the confines of Denmark, as the ancient seat of the Franks, gave birth to an ingenious system of Leibritz.]

[Footnote 69: See Cluver. Germania Antiqua, l. iii. c. 20. M. Freret, in the Memoires de l'Academie des Inscriptions, tom. xviii.]

[Footnote 70: Most probably under the reign of Gordian, from an accidental circumstance fully canvassed by Tillemont, tom. iii. p. 710, 1181.]

[Footnote 70/1: The confederation of the Franks appears to have been formed, 1. Of the Chauci. 2. Of the Sicambri, the inhabitants of the duchy of Berg. 3. Of the Attuarii, to the north of the Sicambri, in the principality of Waldeck, between the Dimel and the Eder. 4. Of the Bructeri, on the banks of the Lippe, and in the Hartz. 5. Of the Chamavii, the Gambrivii of Tacitua, who were established, at the time of the Frankish confederation, in the country of the Bructeri. 6. Of the Catti, in Hessia.—G. The Salii and Cherasci are added. Greenwood's Hist. of Germans, i 193.—M.]

[Footnote 71: Plin. Hist. Natur. xvi. l. The Panegyrists frequently allude to the morasses of the Franks.]

[Footnote 72: Tacit. Germania, c. 30, 37.]

[Footnote 73: In a subsequent period, most of those old names are occasionally mentioned. See some vestiges of them in Cluver. Germ. Antiq. l. iii.]

[Footnote 74: Simler de Republica Helvet. cum notis Fuselin.]

PART III

The Romans had long experienced the daring valor of the people of Lower Germany. The union of their strength threatened Gaul with a more formidable invasion, and required the presence of Gallienus, the heir and colleague of Imperial power. [75] Whilst that prince, and his infant son Salonius, displayed, in the court of Treves, the majesty of the empire its armies were ably conducted by their general, Posthumus, who, though he afterwards betrayed the family of Valerian, was ever faithful to the great interests of the monarchy. The treacherous language of panegyrics and medals darkly announces a long series of victories. Trophies and titles attest (if such evidence can attest) the fame of Posthumus, who is repeatedly styled the Conqueror of the Germans, and the Savior of Gaul. [76]

[Footnote 75: Zosimus, l. i. p. 27.]

[Footnote 76: M. de Brequigny (in the Memoires de l'Academie, tom. xxx.) has given us a very curious life of Posthumus. A series of the Augustan History from Medals and Inscriptions has been more than once planned, and is still much wanted. Note: M. Eckhel, Keeper of the Cabinet of Medals, and Professor of Antiquities at Vienna, lately deceased, has supplied this want by his excellent work, Doctrina veterum Nummorum, conscripta a Jos. Eckhel, 8 vol. in 4to Vindobona, 1797.—G. Captain Smyth has likewise printed (privately) a valuable Descriptive Catologue of a series of Large Brass Medals of this period Bedford, 1834.—M. 1845.]

But a single fact, the only one indeed of which we have any distinct knowledge, erases, in a great measure, these monuments of vanity and adulation. The Rhine, though dignified with the title of Safeguard of the provinces, was an imperfect barrier against the daring spirit of enterprise with which the Franks were actuated. Their rapid devastations stretched from the river to the foot of the Pyrenees; nor were they stopped by those mountains. Spain, which had never dreaded, was unable to resist, the inroads of the Germans. During twelve years, the greatest part of the reign of Gallie nus, that opulent country was the theatre of unequal and destructive hostilities. Tarragona, the flourishing capital of a peaceful province, was sacked and almost destroyed; [77] and so late as the days of Orosius, who wrote in the fifth century, wretched cottages, scattered amidst the ruins of magnificent cities, still recorded the rage of the barbarians. [78] When the exhausted country no longer supplied a variety of plunder, the Franks seized on some vessels in the ports of Spain, [79] and transported themselves into Mauritania. The distant province was astonished with the fury of these barbarians, who seemed to fall from a new world, as their name, manners, and complexion, were equally unknown on the coast of Africa. [80]

[Footnote 77: Aurel. Victor, c. 33. Instead of Poene direpto, both the sense and the expression require deleto; though indeed, for different reasons, it is alike difficult to correct the text of the best, and of the worst, writers.]

[Footnote 78: In the time of Ausonius (the end of the fourth century) Ilerda or Lerida was in a very ruinous state, (Auson. Epist. xxv. 58,) which probably was the consequence of this invasion.]

[Footnote 79: Valesius is therefore mistaken in supposing that the Franks had invaded Spain by sea.]

[Footnote 80: Aurel. Victor. Eutrop. ix. 6.]

II. In that part of Upper Saxony, beyond the Elbe, which is at present called the Marquisate of Lusace, there existed, in ancient times, a sacred wood, the awful seat of the superstition of the Suevi. None were permitted to enter the holy precincts, without confessing, by their servile bonds and suppliant posture, the immediate presence of the sovereign Deity. [81] Patriotism contributed, as well as devotion, to consecrate the Sonnenwald, or wood of the Semnones. [82] It was universally believed, that the nation had received its first existence on that sacred spot. At stated periods, the numerous tribes who gloried in the Suevic blood, resorted thither by their ambassadors; and the memory of their common extraction was perpetuated by barbaric rites and human sacrifices. The wide-extended name of Suevi filled the interior countries of Germany, from the banks of the Oder to those of the Danube. They were distinguished from the other Germans by their peculiar mode of dressing their long hair, which they gathered into a rude knot on the crown of the head; and they delighted in an ornament that showed their ranks more lofty and terrible in the eyes of the enemy. [83] Jealous as the Germans were of military renown, they all confessed the superior valor of the Suevi; and the tribes of the Usipetes and Tencteri, who, with a vast army, encountered the dictator Caesar, declared that they esteemed it not a disgrace to have fled before a people to whose arms the immortal gods themselves were unequal. [84]

[Footnote 81: Tacit.Germania, 38.]

[Footnote 82: Cluver. Germ. Antiq. iii. 25.]

[Footnote 83: Sic Suevi a ceteris Germanis, sic Suerorum ingenui a servis separantur. A proud separation!]

[Footnote 84: Caesar in Bello Gallico, iv. 7.]

In the reign of the emperor Caracalla, an innumerable swarm of Suevi appeared on the banks of the Mein, and in the neighborhood of the Roman provinces, in quest either of food, of plunder, or of glory. [85] The hasty army of volunteers gradually coalesced into a great and permanent nation, and as it was composed from so many different tribes, assumed the name of Alemanni, [85/1] or Allmen; to denote at once their various lineage and their common bravery. [86] The latter was soon felt by the Romans in many a hostile inroad. The Alemanni fought chiefly on horseback; but their cavalry was rendered still more formidable by a mixture of light infantry, selected from the bravest and most active of the youth, whom frequent exercise had inured to accompany the horsemen in the longest march, the most rapid charge, or the most precipitate retreat. [87]

[Footnote 85: Victor in Caracal. Dion Cassius, lxvii. p. 1350.]

[Footnote 85/1: The nation of the Alemanni was not originally formed by the Suavi properly so called; these have always preserved their own name. Shortly afterwards they made (A. D. 357) an irruption into Rhaetia, and it was not long after that they were reunited with the Alemanni. Still they have always been a distinct people; at the present day, the people who inhabit the north-west of the Black Forest call themselves Schwaben, Suabians, Sueves, while those who inhabit near the Rhine, in Ortenau, the Brisgaw, the Margraviate of Baden, do not consider themselves Suabians, and are by origin Alemanni. The Teucteri and the Usipetae, inhabitants of the interior and of the north of Westphalia, formed, says Gatterer, the nucleus of the Alemannic nation; they occupied the country where the name of the Alemanni first appears, as conquered in 213, by Caracalla. They were well trained to fight on horseback, (according to Tacitus, Germ. c. 32;) and Aurelius Victor gives the same praise to the Alemanni: finally, they never made part of the Frankish league. The Alemanni became subsequently a centre round which gathered a multitude of German tribes, See Eumen. Panegyr. c. 2. Amm. Marc. xviii. 2, xxix. 4.—G. —The question whether the Suevi was a generic name comprehending the clans which peopled central Germany, is rather hastily decided by M. Guizot Mr. Greenwood, who has studied the modern German writers on their own origin, supposes the Suevi, Alemanni, and Marcomanni, one people, under different appellations. History of Germany, vol i.—M.]

[Footnote 86: This etymology (far different from those which amuse the fancy of the learned) is preserved by Asinius Quadratus, an original historian, quoted by Agathias, i. c. 5.]

[Footnote 87: The Suevi engaged Caesar in this manner, and the manoeuvre deserved the approbation of the conqueror, (in Bello Gallico, i. 48.)]

This warlike people of Germans had been astonished by the immense preparations of Alexander Severus; they were dismayed by the arms of his successor, a barbarian equal in valor and fierceness to themselves. But still hovering on the frontiers of the empire, they increased the general disorder that ensued after the death of Decius. They inflicted severe wounds on the rich provinces of Gaul; they were the first who removed the veil that covered the feeble majesty of Italy. A numerous body of the Alemanni penetrated across the Danube and through the Rhaetian Alps into the plains of Lombardy, advanced as far as Ravenna, and displayed the victorious banners of barbarians almost in sight of Rome. [88]

[Footnote 88: Hist. August. p. 215, 216. Dexippus in the Excerpts. Legationam, p. 8. Hieronym. Chron. Orosius, vii. 22.]

The insult and the danger rekindled in the senate some sparks of their ancient virtue. Both the emperors were engaged in far distant wars, Valerian in the East, and Gallienus on the Rhine. All the hopes and resources of the Romans were in themselves. In this emergency, the senators resumed the defence of the republic, drew out the Praetorian guards, who had been left to garrison the capital, and filled up their numbers, by enlisting into the public service the stoutest and most willing of the Plebeians. The Alemanni, astonished with the sudden appearance of an army more numerous than their own, retired into Germany, laden with spoil; and their retreat was esteemed as a victory by the unwarlike Romans. [89]

[Footnote 89: Zosimus, l. i. p. 34.]

When Gallienus received the intelligence that his capital was delivered from the barbarians, he was much less delighted than alarmed with the courage of the senate, since it might one day prompt them to rescue the public from domestic tyranny as well as from foreign invasion. His timid ingratitude was published to his subjects, in an edict which prohibited the senators from exercising any military employment, and even from approaching the camps of the legions. But his fears were groundless. The rich and luxurious nobles, sinking into their natural character, accepted, as a favor, this disgraceful exemption from military service; and as long as they were indulged in the enjoyment of their baths, their theatres, and their villas, they cheerfully resigned the more dangerous cares of empire to the rough hands of peasants and soldiers. [90]

[Footnote 90: Aurel. Victor, in Gallieno et Probo. His complaints breathe as uncommon spirit of freedom.]

Another invasion of the Alemanni, of a more formidable aspect, but more glorious event, is mentioned by a writer of the lower empire. Three hundred thousand are said to have been vanquished, in a battle near Milan, by Gallienus in person, at the head of only ten thousand Romans. [91] We may, however, with great probability, ascribe this incredible victory either to the credulity of the historian, or to some exaggerated exploits of one of the emperor's lieutenants. It was by arms of a very different nature, that Gallienus endeavored to protect Italy from the fury of the Germans. He espoused Pipa, the daughter of a king of the Marcomanni, a Suevic tribe, which was often confounded with the Alemanni in their wars and conquests. [92] To the father, as the price of his alliance, he granted an ample settlement in Pannonia. The native charms of unpolished beauty seem to have fixed the daughter in the affections of the inconstant emperor, and the bands of policy were more firmly connected by those of love. But the haughty prejudice of Rome still refused the name of marriage to the profane mixture of a citizen and a barbarian; and has stigmatized the German princess with the opprobrious title of concubine of Gallienus. [93]

[Footnote 91: Zonaras, l. xii. p. 631.]

[Footnote 92: One of the Victors calls him king of the Marcomanni; the other of the Germans.]

[Footnote 93: See Tillemont, Hist. des Empereurs, tom. iii. p. 398, &c.]

III. We have already traced the emigration of the Goths from Scandinavia, or at least from Prussia, to the mouth of the Borysthenes, and have followed their victorious arms from the Borysthenes to the Danube. Under the reigns of Valerian and Gallienus, the frontier of the last-mentioned river was perpetually infested by the inroads of Germans and Sarmatians; but it was defended by the Romans with more than usual firmness and success. The provinces that were the seat of war, recruited the armies of Rome with an inexhaustible supply of hardy soldiers; and more than one of these Illyrian peasants attained the station, and displayed the abilities, of a general. Though flying parties of the barbarians, who incessantly hovered on the banks of the Danube, penetrated sometimes to the confines of Italy and Macedonia, their progress was commonly checked, or their return intercepted, by the

Imperial lieutenants. [94] But the great stream of the Gothic hostilities was diverted into a very different channel. The Goths, in their new settlement of the Ukraine, soon became masters of the northern coast of the Euxine: to the south of that inland sea were situated the soft and wealthy provinces of Asia Minor, which possessed all that could attract, and nothing that could resist, a barbarian conqueror.

[Footnote 94: See the lives of Claudius, Aurelian, and Probus, in the Augustan History.]

The banks of the Borysthenes are only sixty miles distant from the narrow entrance [95] of the peninsula of Crim Tartary, known to the ancients under the name of Chersonesus Taurica. [96] On that inhospitable shore, Euripides, embellishing with exquisite art the tales of antiquity, has placed the scene of one of his most affecting tragedies. [97] The bloody sacrifices of Diana, the arrival of Orestes and Pylades, and the triumph of virtue and religion over savage fierceness, serve to represent an historical truth, that the Tauri, the original inhabitants of the peninsula, were, in some degree, reclaimed from their brutal manners by a gradual intercourse with the Grecian colonies, which settled along the maritime coast. The little kingdom of Bosphorus, whose capital was situated on the Straits, through which the Maeotis communicates itself to the Euxine, was composed of degenerate Greeks and half-civilized barbarians. It subsisted, as an independent state, from the time of the Peloponnesian war, [98] was at last swallowed up by the ambition of Mithridates, [99] and, with the rest of his dominions, sunk under the weight of the Roman arms. From the reign of Augustus, [100] the kings of Bosphorus were the humble, but not useless, allies of the empire. By presents, by arms, and by a slight fortification drawn across the Isthmus, they effectually guarded against the roving plunderers of Sarmatia, the access of a country, which, from its peculiar situation and convenient harbors, commanded the Euxine Sea and Asia Minor. [101] As long as the sceptre was possessed by a lineal succession of kings, they acquitted themselves of their important charge with vigilance and success. Domestic factions, and the fears, or private interest, of obscure usurpers, who seized on the vacant throne, admitted the Goths into the heart of Bosphorus. With the acquisition of a superfluous waste of fertile soil, the conquerors obtained the command of a naval force, sufficient to transport their armies to the coast of Asia. [102] These ships used in the navigation of the Euxine were of a very singular construction. They were slight flat-bottomed barks framed of timber only, without the least mixture of iron, and occasionally covered with a shelving roof, on the appearance of a tempest. [103] In these floating houses, the Goths carelessly trusted themselves to the mercy of an unknown sea, under the conduct of sailors pressed into the service, and whose skill and fidelity were equally suspicious. But the hopes of plunder had banished every idea of danger, and a natural fearlessness of temper supplied in their minds the more rational confidence, which is the just result of knowledge and experience. Warriors of such a daring spirit must have often murmured against the cowardice of their guides, who required the strongest assurances of a settled calm before they would venture to embark; and would scarcely ever be tempted to lose sight of the land. Such, at least, is the practice of the modern Turks; [104] and they are probably not inferior, in the art of navigation, to the ancient inhabitants of Bosphorus.

[Footnote 95: It is about half a league in breadth. Genealogical History of the Tartars, p 598.]

[Footnote 96: M. de Peyssonel, who had been French Consul at Caffa, in his Observations sur les Peuples Barbares, que ont habite les bords du Danube]

[Footnote 97: Eeripides in Iphigenia in Taurid.]

[Footnote 98: Strabo, l. vii. p. 309. The first kings of Bosphorus were the allies of Athens.]

[Footnote 99: Appian in Mithridat.]

[Footnote 100: It was reduced by the arms of Agrippa. Orosius, vi. 21. Eu tropius, vii. 9. The Romans once advanced within three days' march of the Tanais. Tacit. Annal. xii. 17.]

[Footnote 101: See the Toxaris of Lucian, if we credit the sincerity and the virtues of the Scythian, who relates a great war of his nation against the kings of Bosphorus.]

[Footnote 102: Zosimus, l. i. p. 28.]

[Footnote 103: Strabo, l. xi. Tacit. Hist. iii. 47. They were called Camaroe.]

[Footnote 104: See a very natural picture of the Euxine navigation, in the xvith letter of Tournefort.]

The fleet of the Goths, leaving the coast of Circassia on the left hand, first appeared before Pityus, [105] the utmost limits of the Roman provinces; a city provided with a convenient port, and fortified with a strong wall. Here they met with a resistance more obstinate than they had reason to expect from the feeble garrison of a distant fortress. They were repulsed; and their disappointment seemed to diminish the terror of the Gothic name. As long as Successianus, an officer of superior rank and merit, defended that frontier, all their efforts were ineffectual; but as soon as he was removed by Valerian to a more honorable but less important station, they resumed the attack of Pityus; and by the destruction of that city, obliterated the memory of their former disgrace. [106]

[Footnote 105: Arrian places the frontier garrison at Dioscurias, or Sebastopolis, forty-four miles to the east of Pityus. The garrison of Phasis consisted in his time of only four hundred foot. See the Periplus of the Euxine. Note: Pityus is Pitchinda, according to D'Anville, ii. 115.—G. Rather Boukoun.—M. Dioscurias is Iskuriah.—G.]

[Footnote 106: Zosimus, l. i. p. 30.]

Circling round the eastern extremity of the Euxine Sea, the navigation from Pityus to Trebizond is about three hundred miles. [107] The course of the Goths carried them in sight of the country of Colchis, so famous by the expedition of the Argonauts; and they even attempted, though without success, to pillage a rich temple at the mouth of the River Phasis. Trebizond, celebrated in the retreat of the ten thousand as an ancient colony of Greeks, [108] derived its wealth and splendor from the magnificence of the emperor Hadrian, who had constructed an artificial port on a coast left destitute by nature of secure harbors. [109] The city was large and populous; a double enclosure of walls seemed to defy the fury of the Goths, and the usual garrison had been strengthened by a reenforcement of ten thousand men. But there are not any advantages capable of supplying the absence of discipline and vigilance. The numerous garrison of Trebizond, dissolved in riot and luxury, disdained to guard their impregnable fortifications. The Goths soon discovered the supine negligence of the besieged, erected a lofty pile of fascines, ascended the walls in the silence of the night, and entered the defenceless city sword in hand. A general massacre of the people ensued, whilst the affrighted soldiers escaped through the opposite gates of the town. The most holy temples, and the most splendid edifices, were involved in a common destruction. The booty that fell into the hands of the Goths was immense: the wealth of the adjacent countries had been deposited in Trebizond, as in a secure place of refuge. The number of captives was incredible, as the victorious barbarians ranged without opposition through the extensive province of Pontus. [110] The rich spoils of Trebizond filled a great fleet of ships that had been found in the port.

The robust youth of the sea-coast were chained to the oar; and the Goths, satisfied with the success of their first naval expedition, returned in triumph to their new establishment in the kingdom of Bosphorus. [111]

[Footnote 107: Arrian (in Periplo Maris Euxine, p. 130) calls the distance 2610 stadia.]

[Footnote 108: Xenophon, Anabasis, l. iv. p. 348, edit. Hutchinson. Note: Fallmerayer (Geschichte des Kaiserthums von Trapezunt, p. 6, &c) assigns a very ancient date to the first (Pelasgic) foundation of Trapezun (Trebizond)—M.]

[Footnote 109: Arrian, p. 129. The general observation is Tournefort's.]

[Footnote 110: See an epistle of Gregory Thaumaturgus, bishop of Neo-Caeoarea, quoted by Mascou, v. 37.]

[Footnote 111: Zosimus, l. i. p. 32, 33.]

The second expedition of the Goths was undertaken with greater powers of men and ships; but they steered a different course, and, disdaining the exhausted provinces of Pontus, followed the western coast of the Euxine, passed before the wide mouths of the Borysthenes, the Niester, and the Danube, and increasing their fleet by the capture of a great number of fishing barks, they approached the narrow outlet through which the Euxine Sea pours its waters into the Mediterranean, and divides the continents of Europe and Asia. The garrison of Chalcedon was encamped near the temple of Jupiter Urius, on a promontory that commanded the entrance of the Strait; and so inconsiderable were the dreaded invasions of the barbarians that this body of troops surpassed in number the Gothic army. But it was in numbers alone that they surpassed it. They deserted with precipitation their advantageous post, and abandoned the town of Chalcedon, most plentifully stored with arms and money, to the discretion of the conquerors. Whilst they hesitated whether they should prefer the sea or land Europe or Asia, for the scene of their hostilities, a perfidious fugitive pointed out Nicomedia, [111/1] once the capital of the kings of Bithynia, as a rich and easy conquest. He guided the march which was only sixty miles from the camp of Chalcedon, [112] directed the resistless attack, and partook of the booty; for the Goths had learned sufficient policy to reward the traitor whom they detested. Nice, Prusa, Apamaea, Cius, [112/1] cities that had sometimes rivalled, or imitated, the splendor of Nicomedia, were involved in the same calamity, which, in a few weeks, raged without control through the whole province of Bithynia. Three hundred years of peace, enjoyed by the soft inhabitants of Asia, had abolished the exercise of arms, and removed the apprehension of danger. The ancient walls were suffered to moulder away, and all the revenue of the most opulent cities was reserved for the construction of baths, temples, and theatres. [113]

[Footnote 111/1: It has preserved its name, joined to the preposition of place in that of Nikmid. D'Anv. Geog. Anc. ii. 28.—G.]

[Footnote 112: Itiner. Hierosolym. p. 572. Wesseling.]

[Footnote 112/1: Now Isnik, Bursa, Mondania Ghio or Kemlik D'Anv. ii. 23.—G.]

[Footnote 113: Zosimus, l.. p. 32, 33.]

When the city of Cyzicus withstood the utmost effort of Mithridates, [114] it was distinguished by wise laws, a naval power of two hundred galleys, and three arsenals, of arms, of military engines, and of corn. [115] It was still the seat of wealth and luxury; but of its ancient strength, nothing remained except the situation, in a little island of the Propontis, connected with the continent of Asia only by two bridges. From the recent sack of Prusa, the Goths advanced within eighteen miles. [116] of the city, which they had devoted to destruction; but the ruin of Cyzicus was delayed by a fortunate accident. The season was rainy, and the Lake Apolloniates, the reservoir of all the springs of Mount Olympus, rose to an uncommon height. The little river of Rhyndacus, which issues from the lake, swelled into a broad and rapid stream, and stopped the progress of the Goths. Their retreat to the maritime city of Heraclea, where the fleet had probably been stationed, was attended by a long train of wagons, laden with the spoils of Bithynia, and was marked by the flames of Nico and Nicomedia, which they wantonly burnt. [117] Some obscure hints are mentioned of a doubtful combat that secured their retreat. [118] But even a complete victory would have been of little moment, as the approach of the autumnal equinox summoned them to hasten their return. To navigate the Euxine before the month of May, or after that of September, is esteemed by the modern Turks the most unquestionable instance of rashness and folly. [119]

[Footnote 114: He besieged the place with 400 galleys, 150,000 foot, and a numerous cavalry. See Plutarch in Lucul. Appian in Mithridat Cicero pro Lege Manilia, c. 8.]

[Footnote 115: Strabo, l. xii. p. 573.]

[Footnote 116: Pocock's Description of the East, l. ii. c. 23, 24.]

[Footnote 117: Zosimus, l. i. p. 33.]

[Footnote 118: Syncellus tells an unintelligible story of Prince Odenathus, who defeated the Goths, and who was killed by Prince Odenathus.]

[Footnote 119: Voyages de Chardin, tom. i. p. 45. He sailed with the Turks from Constantinople to Caffa.]

When we are informed that the third fleet, equipped by the Goths in the ports of Bosphorus, consisted of five hundred sails of ships, [120] our ready imagination instantly computes and multiplies the formidable armament; but, as we are assured by the judicious Strabo, [121] that the piratical vessels used by the barbarians of Pontus and the Lesser Scythia, were not capable of containing more than twenty-five or thirty men we may safely affirm, that fifteen thousand warriors, at the most, embarked in this great expedition. Impatient of the limits of the Euxine, they steered their destructive course from the Cimmerian to the Thracian Bosphorus. When they had almost gained the middle of the Straits, they were suddenly driven back to the entrance of them; till a favorable wind, springing up the next day, carried them in a few hours into the placid sea, or rather lake, of the Propontis. Their landing on the little island of Cyzicus was attended with the ruin of that ancient and noble city. From thence issuing again through the narrow passage of the Hellespont, they pursued their winding navigation amidst the numerous islands scattered over the Archipelago, or the Aegean Sea. The assistance of captives and deserters must have been very necessary to pilot their vessels, and to direct their various incursions, as well on the coast of Greece as on that of Asia. At length the Gothic fleet anchored in the port of Piraeus, five miles distant from Athens, [122] which had attempted to make some preparations for a vigorous defence. Cleodamus, one of the engineers employed by the emperor's orders to fortify the maritime cities against the Goths, had already begun to repair the ancient walls, fallen to decay since the time of

Scylla. The efforts of his skill were ineffectual, and the barbarians became masters of the native seat of the muses and the arts. But while the conquerors abandoned themselves to the license of plunder and intemperance, their fleet, that lay with a slender guard in the harbor of Piraeus, was unexpectedly attacked by the brave Dexippus, who, flying with the engineer Cleodamus from the sack of Athens, collected a hasty band of volunteers, peasants as well as soldiers, and in some measure avenged the calamities of his country. [123]

[Footnote 120: Syncellus (p. 382) speaks of this expedition, as undertaken by the Heruli.]

[Footnote 121: Strabo, l. xi. p. 495.]

[Footnote 122: Plin. Hist. Natur. iii. 7.]

[Footnote 123: Hist. August. p. 181. Victor, c. 33. Orosius, vii. 42. Zosimus, l. i. p. 35. Zonaras, l. xii. 635. Syncellus, p. 382. It is not without some attention, that we can explain and conciliate their imperfect hints. We can still discover some traces of the partiality of Dexippus, in the relation of his own and his countrymen's exploits. Note: According to a new fragment of Dexippus, published by Mai, the 2000 men took up a strong position in a mountainous and woods district, and kept up a harassing warfare. He expresses a hope of being speedily joined by the Imperial fleet. Dexippus in rov. Byzantinorum Collect a Niebuhr, p. 26, 8—M.]

But this exploit, whatever lustre it might shed on the declining age of Athens, served rather to irritate than to subdue the undaunted spirit of the northern invaders. A general conflagration blazed out at the same time in every district of Greece. Thebes and Argos, Corinth and Sparta, which had formerly waged such memorable wars against each other, were now unable to bring an army into the field, or even to defend their ruined fortifications. The rage of war, both by land and by sea, spread from the eastern point of Sunium to the western coast of Epirus. The Goths had already advanced within sight of Italy, when the approach of such imminent danger awakened the indolent Gallienus from his dream of pleasure. The emperor appeared in arms; and his presence seems to have checked the ardor, and to have divided the strength, of the enemy. Naulobatus, a chief of the Heruli, accepted an honorable capitulation, entered with a large body of his countrymen into the service of Rome, and was invested with the ornaments of the consular dignity, which had never before been profaned by the hands of a barbarian. [124] Great numbers of the Goths, disgusted with the perils and hardships of a tedious voyage, broke into Maesia, with a design of forcing their way over the Danube to their settlements in the Ukraine. The wild attempt would have proved inevitable destruction, if the discord of the Roman generals had not opened to the barbarians the means of an escape. [125] The small remainder of this destroying host returned on board their vessels; and measuring back their way through the Hellespont and the Bosphorus, ravaged in their passage the shores of Troy, whose fame, immortalized by Homer, will probably survive the memory of the Gothic conquests. As soon as they found themselves in safety within the basin of the Euxine, they landed at Anchialus in Thrace, near the foot of Mount Haemus; and, after all their toils, indulged themselves in the use of those pleasant and salutary hot baths. What remained of the voyage was a short and easy navigation. [126] Such was the various fate of this third and greatest of their naval enterprises. It may seem difficult to conceive how the original body of fifteen thousand warriors could sustain the losses and divisions of so bold an adventure. But as their numbers were gradually wasted by the sword, by shipwrecks, and by the influence of a warm climate, they were perpetually renewed by troops of banditti and deserters, who flocked to the standard of plunder, and by a crowd of fugitive slaves, often of German or Sarmatian extraction, who eagerly seized the glorious opportunity of freedom and revenge. In these expeditions, the Gothic nation claimed a superior share of honor and danger; but the tribes that fought under the Gothic banners are sometimes distinguished and sometimes confounded in the imperfect histories of that age; and as the barbarian fleets seemed to issue from the mouth of the Tanais, the vague but familiar appellation of Scythians was frequently bestowed on the mixed multitude. [127]

[Footnote 124: Syncellus, p. 382. This body of Heruli was for a long time faithful and famous.]

[Footnote 125: Claudius, who commanded on the Danube, thought with propriety and acted with spirit. His colleague was jealous of his fame Hist. August. p. 181.]

[Footnote 126: Jornandes, c. 20.]

[Footnote 127: Zosimus and the Greeks (as the author of the Philopatris) give the name of Scythians to those whom Jornandes, and the Latin writers, constantly represent as Goths.]

PART IV

In the general calamities of mankind, the death of an individual, however exalted, the ruin of an edifice, however famous, are passed over with careless inattention. Yet we cannot forget that the temple of Diana at Ephesus, after having risen with increasing splendor from seven repeated misfortunes, [128] was finally burnt by the Goths in their third naval invasion. The arts of Greece, and the wealth of Asia, had conspired to erect that sacred and magnificent structure. It was supported by a hundred and twenty-seven marble columns of the Ionic order. They were the gifts of devout monarchs, and each was sixty feet high. The altar was adorned with the masterly sculptures of Praxiteles, who had, perhaps, selected from the favorite legends of the place the birth of the divine children of Latona, the concealment of Apollo after the slaughter of the Cyclops, and the clemency of Bacchus to the vanquished Amazons. [129] Yet the length of the temple of Ephesus was only four hundred and twenty-five feet, about two thirds of the measure of the church of St. Peter's at Rome. [130] In the other dimensions, it was still more inferior to that sublime production of modern architecture. The spreading arms of a Christian cross require a much greater breadth than the oblong temples of the Pagans; and the boldest artists of antiquity would have been startled at the proposal of raising in the air a dome of the size and proportions of the Pantheon. The temple of Diana was, however, admired as one of the wonders of the world. Successive empires, the Persian, the Macedonian, and the Roman, had revered its sanctity and enriched its splendor. [131] But the rude savages of the Baltic were destitute of a taste for the elegant arts, and they despised the ideal terrors of a foreign superstition. [132]

[Footnote 128: Hist. Aug. p. 178. Jornandes, c. 20.]

[Footnote 129: Strabo, l. xiv. p. 640. Vitruvius, l. i. c. i. praefat l vii. Tacit Annal. iii. 61. Plin. Hist. Nat. xxxvi. 14.]

[Footnote 130: The length of St. Peter's is 840 Roman palms; each palm is very little short of nine English inches. See Greaves's Miscellanies vol. i. p. 233; on the Roman Foot. Note: St. Paul's Cathedral is 500 feet. Dallaway on Architecture—M.]

[Footnote 131: The policy, however, of the Romans induced them to abridge the extent of the sanctuary or asylum, which by successive privileges had spread itself two stadia round the temple. Strabo, l. xiv. p. 641. Tacit. Annal. iii. 60, &c.]

[Footnote 132: They offered no sacrifices to the Grecian gods. See Epistol Gregor. Thaumat.]

Another circumstance is related of these invasions, which might deserve our notice, were it not justly to be suspected as the fanciful conceit of a recent sophist. We are told, that in the sack of Athens the Goths had collected all the libraries, and were on the point of setting fire to this funeral pile of Grecian learning, had not one of their chiefs, of more refined policy than his brethren, dissuaded them from the design; by the profound observation, that as long as the Greeks were addicted to the study of books, they would never apply themselves to the exercise of arms. [133] The sagacious counsellor (should the truth of the fact be admitted) reasoned like an ignorant barbarian. In the most polite and powerful nations, genius of every kind has displayed itself about the same period; and the age of science has generally been the age of military virtue and success.

[Footnote 133: Zonaras, l. xii. p. 635. Such an anecdote was perfectly suited to the taste of Montaigne. He makes use of it in his agreeable Essay on Pedantry, l. i. c. 24.]

IV. The new sovereign of Persia, Artaxerxes and his son Sapor, had triumphed (as we have already seen) over the house of Arsaces. Of the many princes of that ancient race, Chosroes, king of Armenia, had alone preserved both his life and his independence. He defended himself by the natural strength of his country; by the perpetual resort of fugitives and malecontents; by the alliance of the Romans, and above all, by his own courage.

Invincible in arms, during a thirty years' war, he was at length assassinated by the emissaries of Sapor, king of Persia. The patriotic satraps of Armenia, who asserted the freedom and dignity of the crown, implored the protection of Rome in favor of Tiridates, the lawful heir. But the son of Chosroes was an infant, the allies were at a distance, and the Persian monarch advanced towards the frontier at the head of an irresistible force. Young Tiridates, the future hope of his country, was saved by the fidelity of a servant, and Armenia continued above twenty-seven years a reluctant province of the great monarchy of Persia. [134] Elated with this easy conquest, and presuming on the distresses or the degeneracy of the Romans, Sapor obliged the strong garrisons of Carrhae and Nisibis [1341] to surrender, and spread devastation and terror on either side of the Euphrates.

[Footnote 134: Moses Chorenensis, l. ii. c. 71, 73, 74. Zonaras, l. xii. p. 628. The anthentic relation of the Armenian historian serves to rectify the confused account of the Greek. The latter talks of the children of Tiridates, who at that time was himself an infant. (Compare St Martin Memoires sur l'Armenie, i. p. 301.—M.)]

[Footnote 134/1: Nisibis, according to Persian authors, was taken by a miracle, the wall fell, in compliance with the prayers of the army. Malcolm's Persia, l. 76.—M]

The loss of an important frontier, the ruin of a faithful and natural ally, and the rapid success of Sapor's ambition, affected Rome with a deep sense of the insult as well as of the danger. Valerian flattered himself, that the vigilance of his lieutenants would sufficiently provide for the safety of the Rhine and of the Danube; but he resolved, notwithstanding his advanced age, to march in person to the defence of the Euphrates.

During his progress through Asia Minor, the naval enterprises of the Goths were suspended, and the afflicted province enjoyed a transient and fallacious calm. He passed the Euphrates, encountered the Persian monarch near the walls of Edessa, was vanquished, and taken prisoner by Sapor. The particulars of this great event are darkly and imperfectly represented; yet, by the glimmering light which is afforded us, we may discover a long series of imprudence, of error, and of deserved misfortunes on the side of the Roman emperor. He reposed an implicit confidence in Macrianus, his Praetorian praefect. [135] That worthless minister rendered his master formidable only to the oppressed subjects, and contemptible to the enemies of Rome. [136] By his weak or wicked counsels, the Imperial army was betrayed into a situation where valor and military skill were equally unavailing. [137] The vigorous attempt of the Romans to cut their way through the Persian host was repulsed with great slaughter; [138] and Sapor, who encompassed the camp with superior numbers, patiently waited till the increasing rage of famine and pestilence had insured his victory. The licentious murmurs of the legions soon accused Valerian as the cause of their calamities; their seditious clamors demanded an instant capitulation. An immense sum of gold was offered to purchase the permission of a disgraceful retreat. But the Persian, conscious of his superiority, refused the money with disdain; and detaining the deputies, advanced in order of battle to the foot of the Roman rampart, and insisted on a personal conference with the emperor. Valerian was reduced to the necessity of intrusting his life and dignity to the faith of an enemy. The interview ended as it was natural to expect. The emperor was made a prisoner, and his astonished troops laid down their arms. [139] In such a moment of triumph, the pride and policy of Sapor prompted him to fill the vacant throne with a successor entirely dependent on his pleasure. Cyriades, an obscure fugitive of Antioch, stained with every vice, was chosen to dishonor the Roman purple; and the will of the Persian victor could not fail of being ratified by the acclamations, however reluctant, of the captive army. [140]

[Footnote 135: Hist. Aug. p. 191. As Macrianus was an enemy to the Christians, they charged him with being a magician.]

[Footnote 136: Zosimus, l. i. p. 33.]

[Footnote 137: Hist. Aug. p. 174.]

[Footnote 138: Victor in Caesar. Eutropius, ix. 7.]

[Footnote 139: Zosimus, l. i. p. 33. Zonaras, l. xii. p. 630. Peter Patricius, in the Excerpta Legat. p. 29.]

[Footnote 140: Hist. August. p. 185. The reign of Cyriades appears in that collection prior to the death of Valerian; but I have preferred a probable series of events to the doubtful chronology of a most inaccurate writer]

The Imperial slave was eager to secure the favor of his master by an act of treason to his native country. He conducted Sapor over the Euphrates, and, by the way of Chalcis, to the metropolis of the East. So rapid were the motions of the Persian cavalry, that, if we may credit a very judicious historian, [141] the city of Antioch was surprised when the idle multitude was fondly gazing on the amusements of the theatre. The splendid buildings of Antioch, private as well as public, were either pillaged or destroyed; and the numerous inhabitants were put to the sword, or led away into captivity. [142] The tide of devastation was stopped for a moment by the resolution of the high priest of Emesa. Arrayed in his sacerdotal robes, he appeared at the head of a great body of fanatic peasants, armed only with slings, and defended his god and his property from the sacrilegious hands of the followers of Zoroaster. [143] But the ruin of Tarsus, and of many other cities, furnishes a melancholy proof that, except in this singular instance, the conquest of Syria and Cilicia scarcely interrupted the progress of the Persian arms. The advantages of the narrow passes of Mount Taurus were abandoned, in which an invader, whose principal force consisted in his cavalry, would have been engaged in a very unequal combat: and Sapor was permitted to form the siege of Caesarea, the capital of Cappadocia; a city, though of the second rank, which was supposed to contain four hundred thousand inhabitants. Demosthenes commanded in the place, not so much by the commission of the emperor, as in the voluntary defence of his country. For a long time he deferred its fate; and when at last Caesarea was betrayed by the perfidy of a physician, he cut his way through the Persians, who had been ordered to exert their utmost diligence to take him alive. This heroic chief escaped the power of a foe who might either have honored or punished his obstinate valor; but many thousands of his fellow-citizens were involved in a general massacre, and Sapor is accused of treating his prisoners with wanton and unrelenting cruelty. [144] Much should undoubtedly be allowed for national animosity, much for humbled pride and impotent revenge; yet, upon the whole, it is certain, that the same prince, who, in Armenia, had displayed the mild aspect of a legislator, showed himself to the Romans under the stern features of a conqueror. He despaired of making any permanent establishment in the empire, and sought only to leave behind him a wasted desert, whilst he transported into Persia the people and the treasures of the provinces. [145]

[Footnote 141: The sack of Antioch, anticipated by some historians, is assigned, by the decisive testimony of Ammianus Marcellinus, to the reign of Gallienus, xxiii. 5. Note: Heyne, in his note on Zosimus, contests this opinion of Gibbon and observes, that the testimony of Ammianus is in fact by no means clear, decisive. Gallienus and Valerian reigned together. Zosimus, in a passage, l. iiii. 32, 8, distinctly places this event before the capture of Valerian. —M.]

[Footnote 142: Zosimus, l. i. p. 35.]

[Footnote 143: John Malala, tom. i. p. 391. He corrupts this probable event by some fabulous circumstances.]

[Footnote 144: Zonaras, l. xii. p. 630. Deep valleys were filled up with the slain. Crowds of prisoners were driven to water like beasts, and many perished for want of food.]

[Footnote 145: Zosimus, l. i. p. 25 asserts, that Sapor, had he not preferred spoil to conquest, might have remained master of Asia.]

At the time when the East trembled at the name of Sapor, he received a present not unworthy of the greatest kings; a long train of camels, laden with the most rare and valuable merchandises. The rich offering was accompanied with an epistle, respectful, but not servile, from Odenathus, one of the noblest and most opulent senators of Palmyra. "Who is this Odenathus," (said the haughty victor, and he commanded that the present should be cast into the Euphrates,) "that he thus insolently presumes to write to his lord? If he entertains a hope of mitigating his punishment, let him fall prostrate before the foot of our throne, with his hands bound behind his back. Should he hesitate, swift destruction shall be poured on his head, on his whole race, and on his country." [146] The desperate extremity to which the Palmyrenian was reduced, called into action all the latent powers of his soul. He met Sapor; but he met him in arms.

Infusing his own spirit into a little army collected from the villages of Syria [147] and the tents of the desert, [148] he hovered round the Persian host, harassed their retreat, carried off part of the treasure, and, what was dearer than any treasure, several of the women of the great king; who was at last obliged to repass the Euphrates with some marks of haste and confusion. [149] By this exploit, Odenathus laid the foundations of his future fame and fortunes. The majesty of Rome, oppressed by a Persian, was protected by a Syrian or Arab of Palmyra.

[Footnote 146: Peter Patricius in Excerpt. Leg. p. 29.]

[Footnote 147: Syrorum agrestium manu. Sextus Rufus, c. 23. Rufus Victor the Augustan History, (p. 192,) and several inscriptions, agree in making Odenathus a citizen of Palmyra.]

[Footnote 148: He possessed so powerful an interest among the wandering tribes, that Procopius (Bell. Persic. l. ii. c. 5) and John Malala, (tom. i. p. 391) style him Prince of the Saracens.]

[Footnote 149: Peter Patricius, p. 25.]

The voice of history, which is often little more than the organ of hatred or flattery, reproaches Sapor with a proud abuse of the rights of conquest. We are told that Valerian, in chains, but invested with the Imperial purple, was exposed to the multitude, a constant spectacle of fallen greatness; and that whenever the Persian monarch mounted on horseback, he placed his foot on the neck of a Roman emperor. Notwithstanding all the remonstrances of his allies, who repeatedly advised him to remember the vicissitudes of fortune, to dread the returning power of Rome, and to make his illustrious captive the pledge of peace, not the object of insult, Sapor still remained inflexible. When Valerian sunk under the weight of shame and grief, his skin, stuffed with straw, and formed into the likeness of a human figure, was preserved for ages in the most celebrated temple of Persia; a more real monument of triumph, than the fancied trophies of brass and marble so often erected by Roman vanity. [150] The tale is moral and pathetic, but the truth [150/1] of it may very fairly be called in question. The letters still extant from the princes of the East to Sapor are manifest forgeries; [151] nor is it natural to suppose that a jealous monarch should, even in the person of a rival, thus publicly degrade the majesty of kings. Whatever treatment the unfortunate Valerian might experience in Persia, it is at least certain that the only emperor of Rome who had ever fallen into the hands of the enemy, languished away his life in hopeless captivity.

[Footnote 150: The Pagan writers lament, the Christian insult, the misfortunes of Valerian. Their various testimonies are accurately collected by Tillemont, tom. iii. p. 739, &c. So little has been preserved of eastern history before Mahomet, that the modern Persians are totally ignorant of the victory Sapor, an event so glorious to their nation. See Bibliotheque Orientale. Note: Malcolm appears to write from Persian authorities, i. 76.—M.]

[Footnote 150/1: Yet Gibbon himself records a speech of the emperor Galerius, which alludes to the cruelties exercised against the living, and the indignities to which they exposed the dead Valerian, vol. ii. ch. 13. Respect for the kingly character would by no means prevent an eastern monarch from ratifying his pride and his vengeance on a fallen foe.—M.]

[Footnote 151: One of these epistles is from Artavasdes, king of Armenia; since Armenia was then a province of Persia, the king, the kingdom, and the epistle must be fictitious.]

The emperor Gallienus, who had long supported with impatience the censorial severity of his father and colleague, received the intelligence of his misfortunes with secret pleasure and avowed indifference. "I knew that my father was a mortal," said he; "and since he has acted as it becomes a brave man, I am satisfied." Whilst Rome lamented the fate of her sovereign, the savage coldness of his son was extolled by the servile courtiers as the perfect firmness of a hero and a stoic. [152] It is difficult to paint the light, the various, the inconstant character of Gallienus, which he displayed without constraint, as soon as he became sole possessor of the empire. In every art that he attempted, his lively genius enabled him to succeed; and as his genius was destitute of judgment, he attempted every art, except the important ones of war and government. He was a master of several curious, but useless sciences, a ready orator, an elegant poet, [153] a skilful gardener, an excellent cook, and most contemptible prince. When the great emergencies of the state required his presence and attention, he was engaged in conversation with the philosopher Plotinus, [154] wasting his time in trifling or licentious pleasures, preparing his initiation to the Grecian mysteries, or soliciting a place in the Arcopagus of Athens. His profuse magnificence insulted the general poverty; the solemn ridicule of his triumphs impressed a deeper sense of the public disgrace. [155] The repeated intelligence of invasions, defeats, and rebellions, he received with a careless smile; and singling out, with affected contempt, some particular production of the lost province, he carelessly asked, whether Rome must be ruined, unless it was supplied with linen from Egypt, and arras cloth from Gaul. There were, however, a few short moments in the life of Gallienus, when, exasperated by some recent injury, he suddenly appeared the intrepid soldier and the cruel tyrant; till, satiated with blood, or fatigued by resistance, he insensibly sunk into the natural mildness and indolence of his character. [156]

[Footnote 152: See his life in the Augustan History.]

[Footnote 153: There is still extant a very pretty Epithalamium, composed by Gallienus for the nuptials of his nephews:—"Ite ait, O juvenes, pariter sudate medullis Omnibus, inter vos: non murmura vestra columbae, Brachia non hederae, non vincant oscula conchae."]

[Footnote 154: He was on the point of giving Plotinus a ruined city of Campania to try the experiment of realizing Plato's Republic. See the Life of Plotinus, by Porphyry, in Fabricius's Biblioth. Graec. l. iv.]

[Footnote 155: A medal which bears the head of Gallienus has perplexed the antiquarians by its legend and reverse; the former Gallienoe Augustoe, the latter Ubique Pax. M. Spanheim supposes that the coin was struck by some of the enemies of Gallienus, and was designed as a severe satire on that effeminate prince. But as the use of irony may seem unworthy of the gravity of the Roman mint, M. de Vallemont has deduced from a passage of Trebellius Pollio (Hist. Aug. p. 198) an ingenious and natural solution. Galliena was first cousin to the emperor. By delivering Africa from the usurper Celsus, she deserved the title of Augusta. On a medal in the French king's collection, we read a similar inscription of Faustina Augusta round the head of Marcus Aurelius. With regard to the Ubique Pax, it is easily explained by the vanity of Gallienus, who seized, perhaps, the occasion of some momentary calm. See Nouvelles de la Republique des Lettres, Janvier, 1700, p. 21—34.]

[Footnote 156: This singular character has, I believe, been fairly transmitted to us. The reign of his immediate successor was short and busy; and the historians who wrote before the elevation of the family of Constantine could not have the most remote interest to misrepresent the character of Gallienus.]

At the time when the reins of government were held with so loose a hand, it is not surprising, that a crowd of usurpers should start up in every province of the empire against the son of Valerian. It was probably some ingenious fancy, of comparing the thirty tyrants of Rome with the thirty tyrants of Athens, that induced the writers of the Augustan History to select that celebrated number, which has been gradually received into a popular appellation. [157] But in every light the parallel is idle and defective. What resemblance can we discover between a council of thirty persons, the united oppressors of a single city, and an uncertain list of independent rivals, who rose and fell in irregular succession through the extent of a vast empire? Nor can the number of thirty be completed, unless we include in the account the women and children who were honored with the Imperial title. The reign of Gallienus, distracted as it was, produced only nineteen pretenders to the throne: Cyriades, Macrianus, Balista, Odenathus, and Zenobia, in the East; in Gaul, and the western provinces, Posthumus, Lollianus, Victorinus, and his mother Victoria, Marius, and Tetricus; in Illyricum and the confines of the Danube, Ingenuus, Regillianus, and Aureolus; in Pontus, [158] Saturninus; in Isauria, Trebellianus; Piso in Thessaly; Valens in Achaia; Aemilianus in Egypt; and Celsus in Africa. [1581] To illustrate the obscure monuments of the life and death of each individual, would prove a laborious task, alike barren of instruction and of amusement. We may content ourselves with investigating some general characters, that most strongly mark the condition of the times, and the manners of the men, their pretensions, their motives, their fate, and their destructive consequences of their usurpation. [159]

[Footnote 157: Pollio expresses the most minute anxiety to complete the number. Note: Compare a dissertation of Manso on the thirty tyrants at the end of his Leben Constantius des Grossen. Breslau, 1817.—M.]

[Footnote 158: The place of his reign is somewhat doubtful; but there was a tyrant in Pontus, and we are acquainted with the seat of all the others.]

[Footnote 1581: Captain Smyth, in his "Catalogue of Medals," p. 307, substitutes two new names to make up the number of nineteen, for those of Odenathus and Zenobia. He subjoins this list:—1. 2. 3. Of those whose coins Those whose coins Those of whom no are undoubtedly true. are suspected. coins are known. Posthumus. Cyriades. Valens. Laelianus, (Lollianus, G.) Ingenuus. Balista Victorinus Celsus. Saturninus. Marius. Piso Frugi. Trebellianus. Tetricus. —M. 1815 Macrianus. Quietus. Regalianus (Regillianus, G.) Alex. Aemilianus. Aureolus. Sulpicius Antoninus]

[Footnote 159: Tillemont, tom. iii. p. 1163, reckons them somewhat differently.]

It is sufficiently known, that the odious appellation of Tyrant was often employed by the ancients to express the illegal seizure of supreme power, without any reference to the abuse of it. Several of the pretenders, who raised the standard of rebellion against the emperor Gallienus, were shining models of virtue, and almost all possessed a considerable share of vigor and ability. Their merit had recommended them to the favor of Valerian, and gradually promoted them to the most important commands of the empire. The generals, who assumed the title of Augustus, were either respected by their troops for their able conduct and severe discipline, or admired for valor and success in war, or beloved for frankness and generosity. The field of victory was often the scene of their election; and even the armorer Marius, the most contemptible of all the candidates for the purple, was distinguished, however by intrepid courage, matchless strength, and blunt honesty. [160] His mean and recent trade cast, indeed, an air of ridicule on his elevation; [1601] but his birth could not be more obscure than was that of the greater part of his rivals, who were born of peasants, and enlisted in the army as private soldiers. In times of confusion, every active genius finds the place assigned him by nature: in a general state of war, military merit is the road to glory and to greatness. Of the nineteen tyrants Tetricus only was a senator; Piso alone was a noble. The blood of Numa, through twenty-eight successive generations, ran in the veins of Calphurnius

Piso, [161] who, by female alliances, claimed a right of exhibiting, in his house, the images of Crassus and of the great Pompey. [162] His ancestors had been repeatedly dignified with all the honors which the commonwealth could bestow; and of all the ancient families of Rome, the Calphurnian alone had survived the tyranny of the Caesars. The personal qualities of Piso added new lustre to his race. The usurper Valens, by whose order he was killed, confessed, with deep remorse, that even an enemy ought to have respected the sanctity of Piso; and although he died in arms against Gallienus, the senate, with the emperor's generous permission, decreed the triumphal ornaments to the memory of so virtuous a rebel. [163] [See Roman Coins: From The British Museum. Number four depicts Crassus.]

[Footnote 160: See the speech of Marius in the Augustan History, p. 197. The accidental identity of names was the only circumstance that could tempt Pollio to imitate Sallust.]

[Footnote 1601: Marius was killed by a soldier, who had formerly served as a workman in his shop, and who exclaimed, as he struck, "Behold the sword which thyself hast forged." Trob vita.—G.]

[Footnote 161: "Vos, O Pompilius sanguis!" is Horace's address to the Pisos See Art. Poet. v. 292, with Dacier's and Sanadon's notes.]

[Footnote 162: Tacit. Annal. xv. 48. Hist. i. 15. In the former of these passages we may venture to change paterna into materna. In every generation from Augustus to Alexander Severus, one or more Pisos appear as consuls. A Piso was deemed worthy of the throne by Augustus, (Tacit. Annal. i. 13;) a second headed a formidable conspiracy against Nero; and a third was adopted, and declared Caesar, by Galba.]

[Footnote 163: Hist. August. p. 195. The senate, in a moment of enthusiasm, seems to have presumed on the approbation of Gallienus.]

The lieutenants of Valerian were grateful to the father, whom they esteemed. They disdained to serve the luxurious indolence of his unworthy son. The throne of the Roman world was unsupported by any principle of loyalty; and treason against such a prince might easily be considered as patriotism to the state. Yet if we examine with candor the conduct of these usurpers, it will appear, that they were much oftener driven into rebellion by their fears, than urged to it by their ambition. They dreaded the cruel suspicions of Gallienus; they equally dreaded the capricious violence of their troops. If the dangerous favor of the army had imprudently declared them deserving of the purple, they were marked for sure destruction; and even prudence would counsel them to secure a short enjoyment of empire, and rather to try the fortune of war than to expect the hand of an executioner.

When the clamor of the soldiers invested the reluctant victims with the ensigns of sovereign authority, they sometimes mourned in secret their approaching fate. "You have lost," said Saturninus, on the day of his elevation, "you have lost a useful commander, and you have made a very wretched emperor." [164]

[Footnote 164: Hist. August p. 196.]

The apprehensions of Saturninus were justified by the repeated experience of revolutions. Of the nineteen tyrants who started up under the reign of Gallienus, there was not one who enjoyed a life of peace, or a natural death. As soon as they were invested with the bloody purple, they inspired their adherents with the same fears and ambition which had occasioned their own revolt. Encompassed with domestic conspiracy, military sedition, and civil war, they trembled on the edge of precipices, in which, after a longer or shorter term of anxiety, they were inevitably lost. These precarious monarchs received, however, such honors as the flattery of their respective armies and provinces could bestow; but their claim, founded on rebellion, could never obtain the sanction of law or history. Italy, Rome, and the senate, constantly adhered to the cause of Gallienus, and he alone was considered as the sovereign of the empire. That prince condescended, indeed, to acknowledge the victorious arms of Odenathus, who deserved the honorable distinction, by the respectful conduct which he always maintained towards the son of Valerian. With the general applause of the Romans, and the consent of Gallienus, the senate conferred the title of Augustus on the brave Palmyrenian; and seemed to intrust him with the government of the East, which he already possessed, in so independent a manner, that, like a private succession, he bequeathed it to his illustrious widow, Zenobia. [165]

[Footnote 165: The association of the brave Palmyrenian was the most popular act of the whole reign of Gallienus. Hist. August. p. 180.]

The rapid and perpetual transitions from the cottage to the throne, and from the throne to the grave, might have amused an indifferent philosopher; were it possible for a philosopher to remain indifferent amidst the general calamities of human kind. The election of these precarious emperors, their power and their death, were equally destructive to their subjects and adherents. The price of their fatal elevation was instantly discharged to the troops by an immense donative, drawn from the bowels of the exhausted people. However virtuous was their character, however pure their intentions, they found themselves reduced to the hard necessity of supporting their usurpation by frequent acts of rapine and cruelty. When they fell, they involved armies and provinces in their fall. There is still extant a most savage mandate from Gallienus to one of his ministers, after the suppression of Ingenuus, who had assumed the purple in Illyricum.

"It is not enough," says that soft but inhuman prince, "that you exterminate such as have appeared in arms; the chance of battle might have served me as effectually. The male sex of every age must be extirpated; provided that, in the execution of the children and old men, you can contrive means to save our reputation. Let every one die who has dropped an expression, who has entertained a thought against me, against me, the son of Valerian, the father and brother of so many princes. [166] Remember that Ingenuus was made emperor: tear, kill, hew in pieces. I write to you with my own hand, and would inspire you with my own feelings." [167] Whilst the public forces of the state were dissipated in private quarrels, the defenceless provinces lay exposed to every invader. The bravest usurpers were compelled, by the perplexity of their situation, to conclude ignominious treaties with the common enemy, to purchase with oppressive tributes the neutrality or services of the Barbarians, and to introduce hostile and independent nations into the heart of the Roman monarchy. [168]

[Footnote 166: Gallienus had given the titles of Caesar and Augustus to his son Saloninus, slain at Cologne by the usurper Posthumus. A second son of Gallienus succeeded to the name and rank of his elder brother Valerian, the brother of Gallienus, was also associated to the empire: several other brothers, sisters, nephews, and nieces of the emperor formed a very numerous royal family. See Tillemont, tom iii, and M. de Brequigny in the Memoires de l'Academie, tom xxxii p. 262.]

[Footnote 167: Hist. August. p. 188.]

[Footnote 168: Regillianus had some bands of Roxolani in his service; Posthumus a body of Franks. It was, perhaps, in the character of auxiliaries that the latter introduced themselves into Spain.]

Such were the barbarians, and such the tyrants, who, under the reigns of Valerian and Gallienus, dismembered the provinces, and reduced the empire to the lowest pitch of disgrace and ruin, from whence it seemed impossible that it should ever emerge. As far as the barrenness of materials would permit, we have attempted to trace, with order and perspicuity, the general events of that calamitous period. There still remain some particular facts; I. The disorders of Sicily; II. The tumults of Alexandria; and, III. The rebellion of the Isaurians, which may serve to reflect a strong light on the horrid picture.

I. Whenever numerous troops of banditti, multiplied by success and impunity, publicly defy, instead of eluding the justice of their country, we may safely infer, that the excessive weakness of the government is felt and abused by the lowest ranks of the community. The situation of Sicily preserved it from the Barbarians; nor could the disarmed province have supported a usurper. The sufferings of that once flourishing and still fertile island were inflicted by baser hands. A licentious crowd of slaves and peasants reigned for a while over the plundered country, and renewed the memory of the servile wars of more ancient times. [169] Devastations, of which the husbandman was either the victim or the accomplice, must have ruined the agriculture of Sicily; and as the principal estates were the property of the opulent senators of Rome, who often enclosed within a farm the territory of an old republic, it is not improbable, that this private injury might affect the capital more deeply, than all the conquests of the Goths or the Persians.

[Footnote 169: The Augustan History, p. 177. See Diodor. Sicul. l. xxxiv.]

II. The foundation of Alexandria was a noble design, at once conceived and executed by the son of Philip. The beautiful and regular form of that great city, second only to Rome itself, comprehended a circumference of fifteen miles; [170] it was peopled by three hundred thousand free inhabitants, besides at least an equal number of slaves. [171] The lucrative trade of Arabia and India flowed through the port of Alexandria, to the capital and provinces of the empire. [1711] Idleness was unknown. Some were employed in blowing of glass, others in weaving of linen, others again manufacturing the papyrus. Either sex, and every age, was engaged in the pursuits of industry, nor did even the blind or the lame want occupations suited to their condition. [172] But the people of Alexandria, a various mixture of nations, united the vanity and inconstancy of the Greeks with the superstition and obstinacy of the Egyptians. The most trifling occasion, a transient scarcity of flesh or lentils, the neglect of an accustomed salutation, a mistake of precedency in the public baths, or even a religious dispute, [173] were at any time sufficient to kindle a sedition among that vast multitude, whose resentments were furious and implacable. [174] After the captivity of Valerian and the insolence of his son had relaxed the authority of the laws, the Alexandrians abandoned themselves to the ungoverned rage of their passions, and their unhappy country was the theatre of a civil war, which continued (with a few short and suspicious truces) above twelve years. [175] All intercourse was cut off between the several quarters of the afflicted city, every street was polluted with blood, every building of strength converted into a citadel; nor did the tumults subside till a considerable part of Alexandria was irretrievably ruined. The spacious and magnificent district of Bruchion, [1751] with its palaces and musaeum, the residence of the kings and philosophers of Egypt, is described above a century afterwards, as already reduced to its present state of dreary solitude. [176]

[Footnote 170: Plin. Hist. Natur. v. 10.]

[Footnote 171: Diodor. Sicul. l. xvii. p. 590, edit. Wesseling.]

[Footnote 1711: Berenice, or Myos-Hormos, on the Red Sea, received the eastern commodities. From thence they were transported to the Nile, and down the Nile to Alexandria.—M.]

[Footnote 172: See a very curious letter of Hadrian, in the Augustan History, p. 245.]

[Footnote 173: Such as the sacrilegious murder of a divine cat. See Diodor. Sicul. l. i. Note: The hostility between the Jewish and Grecian part of the population afterwards between the two former and the Christian, were unfailing causes of tumult, sedition, and massacre. In no place were the religious disputes, after the establishment of Christianity, more frequent or more sanguinary. See Philo. de Legat. Hist. of Jews, ii. 171, iii. 111, 198. Gibbon, iii c. xxi. viii. c. xlvii.—M.]

[Footnote 174: Hist. August. p. 195. This long and terrible sedition was first occasioned by a dispute between a soldier and a townsman about a pair of shoes.]

[Footnote 175: Dionysius apud. Euses. Hist. Eccles. vii. p. 21. Ammian xxii. 16.]

[Footnote 1751: The Bruchion was a quarter of Alexandria which extended along the largest of the two ports, and contained many palaces, inhabited by the Ptolemies. D'Anv. Geogr. Anc. iii. 10.—G.]

[Footnote 176: Scaliger. Animadver. ad Euseb. Chron. p. 258. Three dissertations of M. Bonamy, in the Mem. de l'Academie, tom. ix.]

III. The obscure rebellion of Trebellianus, who assumed the purple in Isauria, a petty province of Asia Minor, was attended with strange and memorable consequences. The pageant of royalty was soon destroyed by an officer of Gallienus; but his followers, despairing of mercy, resolved to shake off their allegiance, not only to the emperor, but to the empire, and suddenly returned to the savage manners from which they had never perfectly been reclaimed. Their craggy rocks, a branch of the wide-extended Taurus, protected their inaccessible retreat. The tillage of some fertile valleys [177] supplied them with necessaries, and a habit of rapine with the luxuries of life. In the heart of the Roman monarchy, the Isaurians long continued a nation of wild barbarians. Succeeding princes, unable to reduce them to obedience, either by arms or policy, were compelled to acknowledge their weakness, by surrounding the hostile and independent spot with a strong chain of fortifications, [178] which often proved insufficient to restrain the incursions of these domestic foes. The Isaurians, gradually extending their territory to the sea-coast, subdued the western and mountainous part of Cilicia, formerly the nest of those daring pirates, against whom the republic had once been obliged to exert its utmost force, under the conduct of the great Pompey. [179]

[Footnote 177: Strabo, l. xiii. p. 569.]

[Footnote 178: Hist. August. p. 197.]

[Footnote 179: See Cellarius, Geogr Antiq. tom. ii. p. 137, upon the limits of Isauria.]

Our habits of thinking so fondly connect the order of the universe with the fate of man, that this gloomy period of history has been decorated with inundations, earthquakes, uncommon meteors, preternatural darkness, and a crowd of prodigies fictitious or exaggerated. [180] But a long and general famine was a calamity of a more serious kind. It was the inevitable consequence of rapine and oppression, which extirpated the produce of the present, and the hope of future harvests. Famine is almost always followed by epidemical diseases, the effect of scanty and unwholesome food. Other causes must, however, have contributed to the furious plague, which, from the year two hundred and fifty to the year two hundred and sixty-five, raged without interruption in every province, every city, and almost every family, of the Roman empire. During some time five thousand persons died daily in Rome; and many towns, that had escaped the hands of the Barbarians, were entirely depopulated. [181]

[Footnote 180: Hist August p 177.]

[Footnote 181: Hist. August. p. 177. Zosimus, l. i. p. 24. Zonaras, l. xii. p. 623. Euseb. Chronicon. Victor in Epitom. Victor in Caesar. Eutropius, ix. 5. Orosius, vii. 21.]

We have the knowledge of a very curious circumstance, of some use perhaps in the melancholy calculation of human calamities. An exact register was kept at Alexandria of all the citizens entitled to receive the distribution of corn. It was found, that the ancient number of those comprised between the ages of forty and seventy, had been equal to the whole sum of claimants, from fourteen to fourscore years of age, who remained alive after the reign of Gallienus. [182] Applying this authentic fact to the most correct tables of mortality, it evidently proves, that above half the people of Alexandria had perished; and could we venture to extend the analogy to the other provinces, we might suspect, that war, pestilence, and famine, had consumed, in a few years, the moiety of the human species. [183]

[Footnote 182: Euseb. Hist. Eccles. vii. 21. The fact is taken from the Letters of Dionysius, who, in the time of those troubles, was bishop of Alexandria.]

[Footnote 183: In a great number of parishes, 11,000 persons were found between fourteen and eighty; 5365 between forty and seventy. See Buffon, Histoire Naturelle, tom. ii. p. 590.]

CHAPTER XI

REIGN OF CLAUDIUS, DEFEAT OF THE GOTHS

PART I

REIGN OF CLAUDIUS—DEFEAT OF THE GOTHS—VICTORIES, TRIUMPH, AND DEATH OF AURELIAN

Under the deplorable reigns of Valerian and Gallienus, the empire was oppressed and almost destroyed by the soldiers, the tyrants, and the barbarians. It was saved by a series of great princes, who derived their obscure origin from the martial provinces of Illyricum. Within a period of about thirty years, Claudius, Aurelian, Probus, Diocletian and his colleagues, triumphed over the foreign and domestic enemies of the state, reestablished, with the military discipline, the strength of the frontiers, and deserved the glorious title of Restorers of the Roman world.

The removal of an effeminate tyrant made way for a succession of heroes. The indignation of the people imputed all their calamities to Gallienus, and the far greater part were indeed, the consequence of his dissolute manners and careless administration. He was even destitute of a sense of honor, which so frequently supplies the absence of public virtue; and as long as he was permitted to enjoy the possession of Italy, a victory of the barbarians, the loss of a province, or the rebellion of a general, seldom disturbed the tranquil course of his pleasures. At length, a considerable army, stationed on the Upper Danube, invested with the Imperial purple their leader Aureolus; who, disdaining a confined and barren reign over the mountains of Rhaetia, passed the Alps, occupied Milan, threatened Rome, and challenged Gallienus to dispute in the field the sovereignty of Italy. The emperor, provoked by the insult, and alarmed by the instant danger, suddenly exerted that latent vigor which sometimes broke through the indolence of his temper. Forcing himself from the luxury of the palace, he appeared in arms at the head of his legions, and advanced beyond the Po to encounter his competitor. The corrupted name of Pontirolo [1] still preserves the memory of a bridge over the Adda, which, during the action, must have proved an object of the utmost importance to both armies. The Rhaetian usurper, after receiving a total defeat and a dangerous wound, retired into Milan. The siege of that great city was immediately formed; the walls were battered with every engine in use among the ancients; and Aureolus, doubtful of his internal strength, and hopeless of foreign succors already anticipated the fatal consequences of unsuccessful rebellion.

[Footnote 1: Pons Aureoli, thirteen miles from Bergamo, and thirty-two from Milan. See Cluver. Italia, Antiq. tom. i. p. 245. Near this place, in the year 1703, the obstinate battle of Cassano was fought between the French and Austrians. The excellent relation of the Chevalier de Folard, who was present, gives a very distinct idea of the ground. See Polybe de Folard, tom. iii. p. 233-248.]

His last resource was an attempt to seduce the loyalty of the besiegers. He scattered libels through the camp, inviting the troops to desert an unworthy master, who sacrificed the public happiness to his luxury, and the lives of his most valuable subjects to the slightest suspicions. The arts of Aureolus diffused fears and discontent among the principal officers of his rival. A conspiracy was formed by Heraclianus the Praetorian praefect, by Marcian, a general of rank and reputation, and by Cecrops, who commanded a numerous body of Dalmatian guards. The death of Gallienus was resolved; and notwithstanding their desire of first terminating the siege of Milan, the extreme danger which accompanied every moment's delay obliged them to hasten the execution of their daring purpose. At a late hour of the night, but while the emperor still protracted the pleasures of the table, an alarm was suddenly given, that Aureolus, at the head of all his forces, had made a desperate sally from the town; Gallienus, who was never deficient in personal bravery, started from his silken couch, and without allowing himself time either to put on his armor, or to assemble his guards, he mounted on horseback, and rode full speed towards the supposed place of the attack. Encompassed by his declared or concealed enemies, he soon, amidst the nocturnal tumult, received a mortal dart from an uncertain hand. Before he expired, a patriotic sentiment using in the mind of Gallienus, induced him to name a deserving successor; and it was his last request, that the Imperial ornaments should be delivered to Claudius, who then commanded a detached army in the neighborhood of Pavia. The report at least was diligently propagated, and the order cheerfully obeyed by the conspirators, who had already agreed to place Claudius on the throne. On the first news of the emperor's death, the troops expressed some suspicion and resentment, till the one was removed, and the other assuaged, by a donative of twenty pieces of gold to each soldier. They then ratified the election, and acknowledged the merit of their new sovereign. [2]

[Footnote 2: On the death of Gallienus, see Trebellius Pollio in Hist. August. p. 181. Zosimus, l. i. p. 37. Zonaras, l. xii. p. 634. Eutrop. ix. ll. Aurelius Victor in Epitom. Victor in Caesar. I have compared and blended them all, but have chiefly followed Aurelius Victor, who seems to have had the best memoirs.]

The obscurity which covered the origin of Claudius, though it was afterwards embellished by some flattering fictions, [3] sufficiently betrays the meanness of his birth. We can only discover that he was a native of one of the provinces bordering on the Danube; that his youth was spent in arms, and that his modest valor attracted the favor and confidence of Decius. The senate and people already considered him as an excellent officer, equal to the most important trusts; and censured the inattention of Valerian, who suffered him to remain in the subordinate station of a tribune. But it was not long before that emperor distinguished the merit of Claudius, by declaring him general and chief of the Illyrian frontier, with the command of all the troops in Thrace, Maesia, Dacia, Pannonia, and Dalmatia, the appointments of the praefect of Egypt, the establishment of the proconsul of Africa, and the sure prospect of the consulship. By his victories over the Goths, he deserved from the senate the honor of a statue, and excited the jealous apprehensions of Gallienus. It was impossible that a soldier could esteem so dissolute a sovereign, nor is it easy to conceal a just contempt. Some unguarded expressions which dropped from Claudius were officiously transmitted to the royal ear. The emperor's answer to an officer of confidence describes in very lively colors his own character, and that of the times. "There is not any thing capable of giving me more serious concern, than the intelligence contained in your last despatch; [4] that some malicious suggestions have indisposed towards us the mind of our friend and parent Claudius. As you regard your allegiance, use every means to appease his resentment, but conduct your negotiation with secrecy; let it not reach the knowledge of the Dacian troops; they are already provoked, and it might inflame their fury. I myself have sent him some presents: be it your care that he accept them with pleasure. Above all, let him not suspect that I am made acquainted with his imprudence. The fear of my anger might urge him to desperate counsels." [5] The presents which accompanied this humble epistle, in which the monarch solicited a reconciliation with his discontented subject, consisted of a considerable sum of money, a splendid wardrobe, and a valuable service of silver and gold plate. By such arts Gallienus softened the indignation and dispelled the fears of his Illyrian general; and during the remainder of that reign, the formidable sword of Claudius was always drawn in the cause of a master whom he despised. At last, indeed, he received from the conspirators the bloody purple of Gallienus: but he had been absent from their camp and counsels; and however he might applaud the deed, we may candidly presume that he was innocent of the knowledge of it. [6] When Claudius ascended the throne, he was about fifty-four years of age.

[Footnote 3: Some supposed him, oddly enough, to be a bastard of the younger Gordian. Others took advantage of the province of Dardania, to deduce his origin from Dardanus, and the ancient kings of Troy.]

[Footnote 4: Notoria, a periodical and official despatch which the emperor received from the frumentarii, or agents dispersed through the provinces. Of these we may speak hereafter.]

[Footnote 5: Hist. August. p. 208. Gallienus describes the plate, vestments, etc., like a man who loved and understood those splendid trifles.]

[Footnote 6: Julian (Orat. i. p. 6) affirms that Claudius acquired the empire in a just and even holy manner. But we may distrust the partiality of a kinsman.]

The siege of Milan was still continued, and Aureolus soon discovered that the success of his artifices had only raised up a more determined adversary. He attempted to negotiate with Claudius a treaty of alliance and partition. "Tell him," replied the intrepid emperor, "that such proposals should have been made to Gallienus; he, perhaps, might have listened to them with patience, and accepted a colleague as despicable as himself." [7] This stern refusal, and a last unsuccessful effort, obliged Aureolus to yield the city and himself to the discretion of the conqueror. The judgment of the army pronounced him worthy of death; and Claudius, after a feeble resistance, consented to the execution of the sentence. Nor was the zeal of the senate less ardent in the cause of their new sovereign. They ratified, perhaps with a sincere transport of zeal, the election of Claudius; and, as his predecessor had shown himself the personal enemy of their order, they exercised, under the name of justice, a severe revenge against his friends and family. The senate was permitted to discharge the ungrateful office of punishment, and the emperor reserved for himself the pleasure and merit of obtaining by his intercession a general act of indemnity. [8]

[Footnote 7: Hist. August. p. 203. There are some trifling differences concerning the circumstances of the last defeat and death of Aureolus]

[Footnote 8: Aurelius Victor in Gallien. The people loudly prayed for the damnation of Gallienus. The senate decreed that his relations and servants should be thrown down headlong from the Gemonian stairs. An obnoxious officer of the revenue had his eyes torn out whilst under examination. Note: The expression is curious, "terram matrem deosque inferos impias uti Gallieno darent."—M.]

Such ostentatious clemency discovers less of the real character of Claudius, than a trifling circumstance in which he seems to have consulted only the dictates of his heart. The frequent rebellions of the provinces had involved almost every person in the guilt of treason, almost every estate in the case of confiscation; and Gallienus often displayed his liberality by distributing among his officers the property of his subjects. On the accession of Claudius, an old woman threw herself at his feet, and complained that a general of the late emperor had obtained an arbitrary grant of her patrimony. This general was Claudius himself, who had not entirely escaped the contagion of the times. The emperor blushed at the reproach, but deserved the confidence which she had reposed in his equity. The confession of his fault was accompanied with immediate and ample restitution. [9]

[Footnote 9: Zonaras, l. xii. p. 137.]

In the arduous task which Claudius had undertaken, of restoring the empire to its ancient splendor, it was first necessary to revive among his troops a sense of order and obedience. With the authority of a veteran commander, he represented to them that the relaxation of discipline had introduced a long train of disorders, the effects of which were at length experienced by the soldiers themselves; that a people ruined by oppression, and indolent from despair, could no longer supply a numerous army with the means of luxury, or even of subsistence; that the danger of each individual had increased with the despotism of the military order, since princes who tremble on the throne will guard their safety by the instant sacrifice of every obnoxious subject. The emperor expiated on the mischiefs of a lawless caprice, which the soldiers could only gratify at the expense of their own blood; as their seditious elections had so frequently been followed by civil wars, which consumed the flower of the legions either in the field of battle, or in the cruel abuse of victory. He painted in the most lively colors the exhausted state of the treasury, the desolation of the provinces, the disgrace of the Roman name, and the insolent triumph of rapacious barbarians. It was against those barbarians, he declared, that he intended to point the first effort of their arms. Tetricus might reign for a while over the West, and even Zenobia might preserve the dominion of the East. [10] These usurpers were his personal adversaries; nor could he think of indulging any private resentment till he had saved an empire, whose impending ruin would, unless it was timely prevented, crush both the army and the people.

[Footnote 10: Zonaras on this occasion mentions Posthumus but the registers of the senate (Hist. August. p. 203) prove that Tetricus was already emperor of the western provinces.]

The various nations of Germany and Sarmatia, who fought under the Gothic standard, had already collected an armament more formidable than any which had yet issued from the Euxine. On the banks of the Niester, one of the great rivers that discharge themselves into that sea, they constructed a fleet of two thousand, or even of six thousand vessels; [11] numbers which, however incredible they may seem, would have been insufficient to transport their pretended army of three hundred and twenty thousand barbarians. Whatever might be the real strength of the Goths, the vigor and success of the expedition were not adequate to the greatness of the preparations. In their passage through the Bosphorus, the unskilful pilots were overpowered by the violence of the current; and while the multitude of their ships were crowded in a narrow channel, many were dashed against each other, or against the shore. The barbarians made several descents on the coasts both of Europe and Asia; but the open country was already plundered, and they were repulsed with shame and loss from the fortified cities which they assaulted. A spirit of discouragement and division arose in the fleet, and some of their chiefs sailed away towards the islands of Crete and Cyprus; but the main body, pursuing a more steady course, anchored at length near the foot of Mount Athos, and assaulted the city of Thessalonica, the wealthy capital of all the Macedonian provinces. Their attacks, in which they displayed a fierce but artless bravery, were soon interrupted by the rapid approach of Claudius, hastening to a scene of action that deserved the presence of a warlike prince at the head of the remaining powers of the empire. Impatient for battle, the Goths immediately broke up their camp, relinquished the siege of Thessalonica, left their navy at the foot of Mount Athos, traversed the hills of Macedonia, and pressed forwards to engage the last defence of Italy.

[Footnote 11: The Augustan History mentions the smaller, Zonaras the larger number; the lively fancy of Montesquieu induced him to prefer the latter.]

We still posses an original letter addressed by Claudius to the senate and people on this memorable occasion. "Conscript fathers," says the emperor, "know that three hundred and twenty thousand Goths have invaded the Roman territory. If I vanquish them, your gratitude will reward my services. Should I fall, remember that I am the successor of Gallienus. The whole republic is fatigued and exhausted. We shall fight after Valerian, after Ingenuus, Regillianus, Lollianus, Posthumus, Celsus, and a thousand others, whom a just contempt for Gallienus provoked into rebellion. We are in want of darts, of spears, and of shields. The strength of the empire, Gaul, and Spain, are usurped by Tetricus, and we blush to acknowledge that the archers of the East serve under the banners of Zenobia. Whatever we shall perform will be sufficiently great." [12] The melancholy firmness of this epistle announces a hero careless of his fate, conscious of his danger, but still deriving a well-grounded hope from the resources of his own mind.

[Footnote 12: Trebell. Pollio in Hist. August. p. 204.]

The event surpassed his own expectations and those of the world. By the most signal victories he delivered the empire from this host of barbarians, and was distinguished by posterity under the glorious appellation of the Gothic Claudius. The imperfect historians of an irregular war [13] do not enable as to describe the order and circumstances of his exploits; but, if we could be indulged in the allusion, we might distribute into three acts this memorable tragedy. I. The decisive battle was fought near Naissus, a city of Dardania. The legions at first gave way, oppressed by numbers, and dismayed by misfortunes. Their ruin was inevitable, had not the abilities of their emperor prepared a seasonable relief. A large detachment, rising out of the secret and difficult passes of the mountains, which, by his order, they had occupied, suddenly assailed the rear of the victorious Goths.

The favorable instant was improved by the activity of Claudius. He revived the courage of his troops, restored their ranks, and pressed the barbarians on every side. Fifty thousand men are reported to have been slain in the battle of Naissus. Several large bodies of barbarians, covering their retreat with a movable fortification of wagons, retired, or rather escaped, from the field of slaughter.

II. We may presume that some insurmountable difficulty, the fatigue, perhaps, or the disobedience, of the conquerors, prevented Claudius from completing in one day the destruction of the Goths. The war was diffused over the province of Maesia, Thrace, and Macedonia, and its operations drawn out into a variety of marches, surprises, and tumultuary engagements, as well by sea as by land. When the Romans suffered any loss, it was commonly occasioned by their own cowardice or rashness; but the superior talents of the emperor, his perfect knowledge of the country, and his judicious choice of measures as well as officers, assured on most occasions the success of his arms. The immense booty, the fruit of so many victories, consisted for the greater part of cattle and slaves. A select body of the Gothic youth was received among the Imperial troops; the remainder was sold into servitude; and so considerable was the number of female captives, that every soldier obtained to his share two or three women. A circumstance from which we may conclude, that the invaders entertained some designs of settlement as well as of plunder; since even in a naval expedition, they were accompanied by their families.

III. The loss of their fleet, which was either taken or sunk, had intercepted the retreat of the Goths. A vast circle of Roman posts, distributed with skill, supported with firmness, and gradually closing towards a common centre, forced the barbarians into the most inaccessible parts of Mount Haemus, where they found a safe refuge, but a very scanty subsistence. During the course of a rigorous winter in which they were besieged by the emperor's troops, famine and pestilence, desertion and the sword, continually diminished the imprisoned multitude. On the return of spring, nothing appeared in arms except a hardy and desperate band, the remnant of that mighty host which had embarked at the mouth of the Niester.

[Footnote 13: Hist. August. in Claud. Aurelian. et Prob. Zosimus, l. i. p. 38-42. Zonaras, l. xii. p. 638. Aurel. Victor in Epitom. Victor Junior in Caesar. Eutrop. ix ll. Euseb. in Chron.]

The pestilence which swept away such numbers of the barbarians, at length proved fatal to their conqueror. After a short but glorious reign of two years, Claudius expired at Sirmium, amidst the tears and acclamations of his subjects. In his last illness, he convened the principal officers of the state and army, and in their presence recommended Aurelian, [14] one of his generals, as the most deserving of the throne, and the best qualified to execute the great design which he himself had been permitted only to undertake. The virtues of Claudius, his valor, affability, justice, and temperance, his love of fame and of his country, place him in that short list of emperors who added lustre to the Roman purple. Those virtues, however, were celebrated with peculiar zeal and complacency by the courtly writers of the age of Constantine, who was the great grandson of Crispus, the elder brother of Claudius. The voice of flattery was soon taught to repeat, that gods, who so hastily had snatched Claudius from the earth, rewarded his merit and piety by the perpetual establishment of the empire in his family. [15]

[Footnote 14: According to Zonaras, (l. xii. p. 638,) Claudius, before his death, invested him with the purple; but this singular fact is rather contradicted than confirmed by other writers.]

[Footnote 15: See the Life of Claudius by Pollio, and the Orations of Mamertinus, Eumenius, and Julian. See likewise the Caesars of Julian p. 318. In Julian it was not adulation, but superstition and vanity.]

Notwithstanding these oracles, the greatness of the Flavian family (a name which it had pleased them to assume) was deferred above twenty years, and the elevation of Claudius occasioned the immediate ruin of his brother Quintilius, who possessed not sufficient moderation or courage to descend into the private station to which the patriotism of the late emperor had condemned him. Without delay or reflection, he assumed the purple at Aquileia, where he commanded a considerable force; and though his reign lasted only seventeen days, [15/1] he had time to obtain the sanction of the senate, and to experience a mutiny of the troops.

As soon as he was informed that the great army of the Danube had invested the well-known valor of Aurelian with Imperial power, he sunk under the fame and merit of his rival; and ordering his veins to be opened, prudently withdrew himself from the unequal contest. [16]

[Footnote 15/1: Such is the narrative of the greater part of the older historians; but the number and the variety of his medals seem to require more time, and give probability to the report of Zosimus, who makes him reign some months.—G.]

[Footnote 16: Zosimus, l. i. p. 42. Pollio (Hist. August. p. 107) allows him virtues, and says, that, like Pertinax, he was killed by the licentious soldiers. According to Dexippus, he died of a disease.]

The general design of this work will not permit us minutely to relate the actions of every emperor after he ascended the throne, much less to deduce the various fortunes of his private life. We shall only observe, that the father of Aurelian was a peasant of the territory of Sirmium, who occupied a small farm, the property of Aurelius, a rich senator. His warlike son enlisted in the troops as a common soldier, successively rose to the rank of a centurion, a tribune, the praefect of a legion, the inspector of the camp, the general, or, as it was then called, the duke, of a frontier; and at length, during the Gothic war, exercised the important office of commander-in-chief of the cavalry. In every station he distinguished himself by matchless valor, [17] rigid discipline, and successful conduct. He was invested with the consulship by the emperor Valerian, who styles him, in the pompous language of that age, the deliverer of Illyricum, the restorer of Gaul, and the rival of the Scipios. At the recommendation of Valerian, a senator of the highest rank and merit, Ulpius Crinitus, whose blood was derived from the same source as that of Trajan, adopted the Pannonian peasant, gave him his daughter in marriage, and relieved with his ample fortune the honorable poverty which Aurelian had preserved inviolate. [18]

[Footnote 17: Theoclius (as quoted in the Augustan History, p. 211) affirms that in one day he killed with his own hand forty-eight Sarmatians, and in several subsequent engagements nine hundred and fifty. This heroic valor was admired by the soldiers, and celebrated in their rude songs, the burden of which was, mille, mile, mille, occidit.]

[Footnote 18: Acholius (ap. Hist. August. p. 213) describes the ceremony of the adoption, as it was performed at Byzantium, in the presence of the emperor and his great officers.]

The reign of Aurelian lasted only four years and about nine months; but every instant of that short period was filled by some memorable achievement. He put an end to the Gothic war, chastised the Germans who invaded Italy, recovered Gaul, Spain, and Britain out of the hands of Tetricus, and destroyed the proud monarchy which Zenobia had erected in the East on the ruins of the afflicted empire.

It was the rigid attention of Aurelian, even to the minutest articles of discipline, which bestowed such uninterrupted success on his arms. His military regulations are contained in a very concise epistle to one of his inferior officers, who is commanded to enforce them, as he wishes to become a tribune, or as he is desirous to live. Gaming, drinking, and the arts of divination, were severely prohibited. Aurelian expected that his soldiers should be modest, frugal, and laborous; that their armor should be constantly kept bright, their weapons sharp, their clothing and horses ready for immediate service; that they should live in their quarters with chastity and sobriety, without damaging the cornfields, without stealing even a sheep, a fowl, or a bunch of grapes, without exacting from their landlords, either salt, or oil, or wood. "The public allowance," continues the emperor, "is sufficient for their support; their wealth should be collected from the spoils of the enemy, not from the tears of the provincials." [19] A single instance will serve to display the rigor, and even cruelty, of Aurelian. One of the soldiers had seduced the wife of his host. The guilty wretch was fastened to two trees forcibly drawn towards each other, and his limbs were torn asunder by their sudden separation. A few such examples impressed a salutary consternation. The punishments of Aurelian were terrible; but he had seldom occasion to punish more than once the same offence. His own conduct gave a sanction to his laws, and the seditious legions dreaded a chief who had learned to obey, and who was worthy to command.

[Footnote 19: Hist. August, p. 211 This laconic epistle is truly the work of a soldier; it abounds with military phrases and words, some of which cannot be understood without difficulty. Ferramenta samiata is well explained by Salmasius. The former of the words means all weapons of offence, and is contrasted with Arma, defensive armor The latter signifies keen and well sharpened.]

PART II

The death of Claudius had revived the fainting spirit of the Goths. The troops which guarded the passes of Mount Haemus, and the banks of the Danube, had been drawn away by the apprehension of a civil war; and it seems probable that the remaining body of the Gothic and Vandalic tribes embraced the favorable opportunity, abandoned their settlements of the Ukraine, traversed the rivers, and swelled with new multitudes the destroying host of their countrymen. Their united numbers were at length encountered by Aurelian, and the bloody and doubtful conflict ended only with the approach of night. [20] Exhausted by so many calamities, which they had mutually endured and inflicted during a twenty years' war, the Goths and the Romans consented to a lasting and beneficial treaty. It was earnestly solicited by the barbarians, and cheerfully ratified by the legions, to whose suffrage the prudence of Aurelian referred the decision of that important question. The Gothic nation engaged to supply the armies of Rome with a body of two thousand auxiliaries, consisting entirely of cavalry, and stipulated in return an undisturbed retreat, with a regular market as far as the Danube, provided by the emperor's care, but at their own expense. The treaty was observed with such religious fidelity, that when a party of five hundred men straggled from the camp in quest of plunder, the king or general of the barbarians commanded that the guilty leader should be apprehended and shot to death with darts, as a victim devoted to the sanctity of their engagements. [201] It is, however, not unlikely, that the precaution of Aurelian, who had exacted as hostages the sons and daughters of the Gothic chiefs, contributed something to this pacific temper. The youths he trained in the exercise of arms, and near his own person: to the damsels he gave a liberal and Roman education, and by bestowing them in marriage on some of his principal officers, gradually introduced between the two nations the closest and most endearing connections. [21]

[Footnote 20: Zosimus, l. i. p. 45.]

[Footnote 201: The five hundred stragglers were all slain.—M.]

[Footnote 21: Dexipphus (ap. Excerpta Legat. p. 12) relates the whole transaction under the name of Vandals. Aurelian married one of the Gothic ladies to his general Bonosus, who was able to drink with the Goths and discover their secrets. Hist. August. p. 247.]

But the most important condition of peace was understood rather than expressed in the treaty. Aurelian withdrew the Roman forces from Dacia, and tacitly relinquished that great province to the Goths and Vandals. [22] His manly judgment convinced him of the solid advantages, and taught him to despise the seeming disgrace, of thus contracting the frontiers of the monarchy. The Dacian subjects, removed from those distant possessions which they were unable to cultivate or defend, added strength and populousness to the southern side of the Danube. A fertile territory, which the repetition of barbarous inroads had changed into a desert, was yielded to their industry, and a new province of Dacia still preserved the memory of Trajan's conquests. The old country of that name detained, however, a considerable number of its inhabitants, who dreaded exile more than a Gothic master. [23] These degenerate Romans continued to serve the empire, whose allegiance they had renounced, by introducing among their conquerors the first notions of agriculture, the useful arts, and the conveniences of civilized life. An intercourse of commerce and language was gradually established between the opposite banks of the Danube; and after Dacia became an independent state, it often proved the firmest barrier of the empire against the invasions of the savages of the North. A sense of interest attached these more settled barbarians to the alliance of Rome, and a permanent interest very frequently ripens into sincere and useful friendship. This various colony, which filled the ancient province, and was insensibly blended into one great people, still acknowledged the superior renown and authority of the Gothic tribe, and claimed the fancied honor of a Scandinavian origin. At the same time, the lucky though accidental resemblance of the name of Getae, [231] infused among the credulous Goths a vain persuasion, that in a remote age, their own ancestors, already seated in the Dacian provinces, had received the instructions of Zamolxis, and checked the victorious arms of Sesostris and Darius. [24]

[Footnote 22: Hist. August. p. 222. Eutrop. ix. 15. Sextus Rufus, c. 9. de Mortibus Persecutorum, c. 9.]

[Footnote 23: The Walachians still preserve many traces of the Latin language and have boasted, in every age, of their Roman descent. They are surrounded by, but not mixed with, the barbarians. See a Memoir of M. d'Anville on ancient Dacia, in the Academy of Inscriptions, tom. xxx.]

[Footnote 231: The connection between the Getae and the Goths is still in my opinion incorrectly maintained by some learned writers—M.]

[Footnote 24: See the first chapter of Jornandes. The Vandals, however, (c. 22,) maintained a short independence between the Rivers Marisia and Crissia, (Maros and Keres,) which fell into the Teiss.]

While the vigorous and moderate conduct of Aurelian restored the Illyrian frontier, the nation of the Alemanni [25] violated the conditions of peace, which either Gallienus had purchased, or Claudius had imposed, and, inflamed by their impatient youth, suddenly flew to arms. Forty thousand horse appeared in the field, [26] and the numbers of the infantry doubled those of the cavalry. [27] The first objects of their avarice were a few cities of the Rhaetian frontier; but their hopes soon rising with success, the rapid march of the Alemanni traced a line of devastation from the Danube to the Po. [28]

[Footnote 25: Dexippus, p. 7—12. Zosimus, l. i. p. 43. Vopiscus in Aurelian in Hist. August. However these historians differ in names, (Alemanni Juthungi, and Marcomanni,) it is evident that they mean the same people, and the same war; but it requires some care to conciliate and explain them.]

[Footnote 26: Cantoclarus, with his usual accuracy, chooses to translate three hundred thousand: his version is equally repugnant to sense and to grammar.]

[Footnote 27: We may remark, as an instance of bad taste, that Dexippus applies to the light infantry of the Alemanni the technical terms proper only to the Grecian phalanx.]

[Footnote 28: In Dexippus, we at present read Rhodanus: M. de Valois very judiciously alters the word to Eridanus.]

The emperor was almost at the same time informed of the irruption, and of the retreat, of the barbarians. Collecting an active body of troops, he marched with silence and celerity along the skirts of the Hercynian forest; and the Alemanni, laden with the spoils of Italy, arrived at the Danube, without suspecting, that on the opposite bank, and in an advantageous post, a Roman army lay concealed and prepared to intercept their return. Aurelian indulged the fatal security of the barbarians, and permitted about half their forces to pass the river without disturbance and without precaution. Their situation and astonishment gave him an easy victory; his skilful conduct improved the advantage. Disposing the legions in a semicircular form, he advanced the two horns of the crescent across the Danube, and wheeling them on a sudden towards the centre, enclosed the rear of the German host. The dismayed barbarians, on whatsoever side they cast their eyes, beheld, with despair, a wasted country, a deep and rapid stream, a victorious and implacable enemy.

Reduced to this distressed condition, the Alemanni no longer disdained to sue for peace. Aurelian received their ambassadors at the head of his camp, and with every circumstance of martial pomp that could display the greatness and discipline of Rome. The legions stood to their arms in well-ordered ranks and awful silence. The principal commanders, distinguished by the ensigns of their rank, appeared on horseback on either side of the Imperial throne. Behind the throne the consecrated images of the emperor, and his predecessors, [29] the golden eagles, and the various titles of the legions, engraved in letters of gold, were exalted in the air on lofty pikes covered with silver. When Aurelian assumed his seat, his manly grace and majestic figure [30] taught the barbarians to revere the person as well as the purple of their conqueror. The ambassadors fell prostrate on the ground in silence. They were commanded to rise, and permitted to speak. By the assistance of interpreters they extenuated their perfidy, magnified their exploits, expatiated on the vicissitudes of fortune and the advantages of peace, and, with an ill-timed confidence, demanded a large subsidy, as the price of the alliance which they offered to the Romans. The answer of the emperor was stern and imperious. He treated their offer with contempt, and their demand with indignation, reproached the barbarians, that they were as ignorant of the arts of war as of the laws of peace, and finally dismissed them with the choice only of submitting to this unconditional mercy, or awaiting the utmost severity of his resentment. [31] Aurelian had resigned a distant province to the Goths; but it was dangerous to trust or to pardon these perfidious barbarians, whose formidable power kept Italy itself in perpetual alarms.

[Footnote 29: The emperor Claudius was certainly of the number; but we are ignorant how far this mark of respect was extended; if to Caesar and Augustus, it must have produced a very awful spectacle; a long line of the masters of the world.]

[Footnote 30: Vopiscus in Hist. August. p. 210.]

[Footnote 31: Dexippus gives them a subtle and prolix oration, worthy of a Grecian sophist.]

Immediately after this conference, it should seem that some unexpected emergency required the emperor's presence in Pannonia.

He devolved on his lieutenants the care of finishing the destruction of the Alemanni, either by the sword, or by the surer operation of famine. But an active despair has often triumphed over the indolent assurance of success. The barbarians, finding it impossible to traverse the Danube and the Roman camp, broke through the posts in their rear, which were more feebly or less carefully guarded; and with incredible diligence, but by a different road, returned towards the mountains of Italy. [32] Aurelian, who considered the war as totally extinguished, received the mortifying intelligence of the escape of the Alemanni, and of the ravage which they already committed in the territory of Milan. The legions were commanded to follow, with as much expedition as those heavy bodies were capable of exerting, the rapid flight of an enemy whose infantry and cavalry moved with almost equal swiftness. A few days afterwards, the emperor himself marched to the relief of Italy, at the head of a chosen body of auxiliaries, (among whom were the hostages and cavalry of the Vandals,) and of all the Praetorian guards who had served in the wars on the Danube. [33]

[Footnote 32: Hist. August. p. 215.]

[Footnote 33: Dexippus, p. 12.]

As the light troops of the Alemanni had spread themselves from the Alps to the Apennine, the incessant vigilance of Aurelian and his officers was exercised in the discovery, the attack, and the pursuit of the numerous detachments. Notwithstanding this desultory war, three considerable battles are mentioned, in which the principal force of both armies was obstinately engaged. [34] The success was various. In the first, fought near Placentia, the Romans received so severe a blow, that, according to the expression of a writer extremely partial to Aurelian, the immediate dissolution of the empire was apprehended. [35] The crafty barbarians, who had lined the woods, suddenly attacked the legions in the dusk of the evening, and, it is most probable, after the fatigue and disorder of a long march.

The fury of their charge was irresistible; but, at length, after a dreadful slaughter, the patient firmness of the emperor rallied his troops, and restored, in some degree, the honor of his arms. The second battle was fought near Fano in Umbria; on the spot which, five hundred years before, had been fatal to the brother of Hannibal. [36] Thus far the successful Germans had advanced along the Aemilian and Flaminian way, with a design of sacking the defenceless mistress of the world. But Aurelian, who, watchful for the safety of Rome, still hung on their rear, found in this place the decisive moment of giving them a total and irretrievable defeat. [37] The flying remnant of their host was exterminated in a third and last battle near Pavia; and Italy was delivered from the inroads of the Alemanni.

[Footnote 34: Victor Junior in Aurelian.]

[Footnote 35: Vopiscus in Hist. August. p. 216.]

[Footnote 36: The little river, or rather torrent, of, Metaurus, near Fano, has been immortalized, by finding such an historian as Livy, and such a poet as Horace.]

[Footnote 37: It is recorded by an inscription found at Pesaro. See Gruter cclxxvi. 3.]

Fear has been the original parent of superstition, and every new calamity urges trembling mortals to deprecate the wrath of their invisible enemies. Though the best hope of the republic was in the valor and conduct of Aurelian, yet such was the public consternation, when the barbarians were hourly expected at the gates of Rome, that, by a decree of the senate the Sibylline books were consulted. Even the emperor himself from a motive either of religion or of policy, recommended this salutary measure, chided the tardiness of the senate, [38] and offered to supply whatever expense, whatever animals, whatever captives of any nation, the gods should require. Notwithstanding this liberal offer, it does not appear, that any human victims expiated with their blood the sins of the Roman people. The Sibylline books enjoined ceremonies of a more harmless nature, processions of priests in white robes, attended by a chorus of youths and virgins; lustrations of the city and adjacent country; and sacrifices, whose powerful influence disabled the barbarians from passing the mystic ground on which they had been celebrated. However puerile in themselves, these superstitious arts were subservient to the success of the war; and if, in the decisive battle of Fano, the Alemanni fancied they saw an army of spectres combating on the side of Aurelian, he received a real and effectual aid from this imaginary reenforcement. [39]

[Footnote 38: One should imagine, he said, that you were assembled in a Christian church, not in the temple of all the gods.]

[Footnote 39: Vopiscus, in Hist. August. p. 215, 216, gives a long account of these ceremonies from the Registers of the senate.]

But whatever confidence might be placed in ideal ramparts, the experience of the past, and the dread of the future, induced the Romans to construct fortifications of a grosser and more substantial kind. The seven hills of Rome had been surrounded, by the successors of Romulus, with an ancient wall of more than thirteen miles. [40] The vast enclosure may seem disproportioned to the strength and numbers of the infant state. But it was necessary to secure an ample extent of pasture and arable land, against the frequent and sudden incursions of the tribes of Latium, the perpetual enemies of the republic. With the progress of Roman greatness, the city and its inhabitants gradually increased, filled up the vacant space, pierced through the useless walls, covered the field of Mars, and, on every side, followed the public highways in long and beautiful suburbs. [41] The extent of the new walls, erected by Aurelian, and finished in the reign of Probus, was magnified by popular estimation to near fifty, [42] but is reduced by accurate measurement to about twenty-one miles. [43] It was a great but a melancholy labor, since the defence of the capital betrayed the decline of the monarchy. The Romans of a more prosperous age, who trusted to the arms of the legions the safety of the frontier camps, [44] were very far from entertaining a suspicion, that it would ever become necessary to fortify the seat of empire against the inroads of the barbarians. [45]

[Footnote 40: Plin. Hist. Natur. iii. 5. To confirm our idea, we may observe, that for a long time Mount Caelius was a grove of oaks, and Mount Viminal was overrun with osiers; that, in the fourth century, the Aventine was a vacant and solitary retirement; that, till the time of Augustus, the Esquiline was an

unwholesome burying-ground; and that the numerous inequalities, remarked by the ancients in the Quirinal, sufficiently prove that it was not covered with buildings. Of the seven hills, the Capitoline and Palatine only, with the adjacent valleys, were the primitive habitations of the Roman people. But this subject would require a dissertation.]

[Footnote 41: Exspatiantia tecta multas addidere urbes, is the expression of Pliny.]

[Footnote 42: Hist. August. p. 222. Both Lipsius and Isaac Vossius have eagerly embraced this measure.]

[Footnote 43: See Nardini, Roman Antica, l. i. c. 8. Note: But compare Gibbon, ch. xli. note 77.—M.]

[Footnote 44: Tacit. Hist. iv. 23.]

[Footnote 45: For Aurelian's walls, see Vopiscus in Hist. August. p. 216, 222. Zosimus, l. i. p. 43. Eutropius, ix. 15. Aurel. Victor in Aurelian Victor Junior in Aurelian. Euseb. Hieronym. et Idatius in Chronic]

The victory of Claudius over the Goths, and the success of Aurelian against the Alemanni, had already restored to the arms of Rome their ancient superiority over the barbarous nations of the North. To chastise domestic tyrants, and to reunite the dismembered parts of the empire, was a task reserved for the second of those warlike emperors. Though he was acknowledged by the senate and people, the frontiers of Italy, Africa, Illyricum, and Thrace, confined the limits of his reign. Gaul, Spain, and Britain, Egypt, Syria, and Asia Minor, were still possessed by two rebels, who alone, out of so numerous a list, had hitherto escaped the dangers of their situation; and to complete the ignominy of Rome, these rival thrones had been usurped by women.

A rapid succession of monarchs had arisen and fallen in the provinces of Gaul. The rigid virtues of Posthumus served only to hasten his destruction. After suppressing a competitor, who had assumed the purple at Mentz, he refused to gratify his troops with the plunder of the rebellious city; and in the seventh year of his reign, became the victim of their disappointed avarice. [46] The death of Victorinus, his friend and associate, was occasioned by a less worthy cause. The shining accomplishments [47] of that prince were stained by a licentious passion, which he indulged in acts of violence, with too little regard to the laws of society, or even to those of love. [48] He was slain at Cologne, by a conspiracy of jealous husbands, whose revenge would have appeared more justifiable, had they spared the innocence of his son. After the murder of so many valiant princes, it is somewhat remarkable, that a female for a long time controlled the fierce legions of Gaul, and still more singular, that she was the mother of the unfortunate Victorinus. The arts and treasures of Victoria enabled her successively to place Marius and Tetricus on the throne, and to reign with a manly vigor under the name of those dependent emperors. Money of copper, of silver, and of gold, was coined in her name; she assumed the titles of Augusta and Mother of the Camps: her power ended only with her life; but her life was perhaps shortened by the ingratitude of Tetricus. [49]

[Footnote 46: His competitor was Lollianus, or Aelianus, if, indeed, these names mean the same person. See Tillemont, tom. iii. p. 1177. Note: The medals which bear the name of Lollianus are considered forgeries except one in the museum of the Prince of Waldeck there are many extent bearing the name of Laelianus, which appears to have been that of the competitor of Posthumus. Eckhel. Doct. Num. t. vi. 149—G.]

[Footnote 47: The character of this prince by Julius Aterianus (ap. Hist. August. p. 187) is worth transcribing, as it seems fair and impartial Victorino qui Post Junium Posthumium Gallias rexit neminem existemo praeferendum; non in virtute Trajanum; non Antoninum in clementia; non in gravitate Nervam; non in gubernando aerario Vespasianum; non in Censura totius vitae ac severitate militari Pertinacem vel Severum. Sed omnia haec libido et cupiditas voluptatis mulierriae sic perdidit, ut nemo audeat virtutes ejus in literas mittere quem constat omnium judicio meruisse puniri.]

[Footnote 48: He ravished the wife of Attitianus, an actuary, or army agent, Hist. August. p. 186. Aurel. Victor in Aurelian.]

[Footnote 49: Pollio assigns her an article among the thirty tyrants. Hist. August. p. 200.]

When, at the instigation of his ambitious patroness, Tetricus assumed the ensigns of royalty, he was governor of the peaceful province of Aquitaine, an employment suited to his character and education. He reigned four or five years over Gaul, Spain, and Britain, the slave and sovereign of a licentious army, whom he dreaded, and by whom he was despised. The valor and fortune of Aurelian at length opened the prospect of a deliverance. He ventured to disclose his melancholy situation, and conjured the emperor to hasten to the relief of his unhappy rival. Had this secret correspondence reached the ears of the soldiers, it would most probably have cost Tetricus his life; nor could he resign the sceptre of the West without committing an act of treason against himself. He affected the appearances of a civil war, led his forces into the field, against Aurelian, posted them in the most disadvantageous manner, betrayed his own counsels to his enemy, and with a few chosen friends deserted in the beginning of the action. The rebel legions, though disordered and dismayed by the unexpected treachery of their chief, defended themselves with desperate valor, till they were cut in pieces almost to a man, in this bloody and memorable battle, which was fought near Chalons in Champagne. [50] The retreat of the irregular auxiliaries, Franks and Batavians, [51] whom the conqueror soon compelled or persuaded to repass the Rhine, restored the general tranquillity, and the power of Aurelian was acknowledged from the wall of Antoninus to the columns of Hercules.

[Footnote 50: Pollio in Hist. August. p. 196. Vopiscus in Hist. August. p. 220. The two Victors, in the lives of Gallienus and Aurelian. Eutrop. ix. 13. Euseb. in Chron. Of all these writers, only the two last (but with strong probability) place the fall of Tetricus before that of Zenobia. M. de Boze (in the Academy of Inscriptions, tom. xxx.) does not wish, and Tillemont (tom. iii. p. 1189) does not dare to follow them. I have been fairer than the one, and bolder than the other.]

[Footnote 51: Victor Junior in Aurelian. Eumenius mentions Batavicoe; some critics, without any reason, would fain alter the word to Bagandicoe.] As early as the reign of Claudius, the city of Autun, alone and unassisted, had ventured to declare against the legions of Gaul. After a siege of seven months, they stormed and plundered that unfortunate city, already wasted by famine. [52] Lyons, on the contrary, had resisted with obstinate disaffection the arms of Aurelian. We read of the punishment of Lyons, [53] but there is not any mention of the rewards of Autun. Such, indeed, is the policy of civil war; severely to remember injuries, and to forget the most important services. Revenge is profitable, gratitude is expensive.

[Footnote 52: Eumen. in Vet. Panegyr. iv. 8.]

[Footnote 53: Vopiscus in Hist. August. p. 246. Autun was not restored till the reign of Diocletian. See Eumenius de restaurandis scholis.]

Aurelian had no sooner secured the person and provinces of Tetricus, than he turned his arms against Zenobia, the celebrated queen of Palmyra and the East. Modern Europe has produced several illustrious women who have sustained with glory the weight of empire; nor is our own age destitute of such distinguished characters. But if we except the doubtful achievements of Semiramis, Zenobia is perhaps the only female whose superior genius broke through the servile indolence imposed on her sex by the climate and manners of Asia. [54] She claimed her descent from the Macedonian kings of Egypt, [541] equalled in beauty her ancestor Cleopatra, and far surpassed that princess in chastity [55] and valor. Zenobia was esteemed the most lovely as well as the most heroic of her sex. She was of a dark complexion, (for in speaking of a lady these trifles become important.) Her teeth were of a pearly whiteness, and her large black eyes sparkled with uncommon fire, tempered by the most attractive sweetness. Her voice was strong and harmonious. Her manly understanding was strengthened and adorned by study. She was not ignorant of the Latin tongue, but possessed in equal perfection the Greek, the Syriac, and the Egyptian languages. She had drawn up for her own use an epitome of oriental history, and familiarly compared the beauties of Homer and Plato under the tuition of the sublime Longinus.

[Footnote 54: Almost everything that is said of the manners of Odenathus and Zenobia is taken from their lives in the Augustan History, by Trebeljus Pollio; see p. 192, 198.]

[Footnote 541: According to some Christian writers, Zenobia was a Jewess. (Jost Geschichte der Israel. iv. 16. Hist. of Jews, iii. 175.)—M.]

[Footnote 55: She never admitted her husband's embraces but for the sake of posterity. If her hopes were baffled, in the ensuing month she reiterated the experiment.]

This accomplished woman gave her hand to Odenathus, [551] who, from a private station, raised himself to the dominion of the East. She soon became the friend and companion of a hero. In the intervals of war, Odenathus passionately delighted in the exercise of hunting; he pursued with ardor the wild beasts of the desert, lions, panthers, and bears; and the ardor of Zenobia in that dangerous amusement was not inferior to his own. She had inured her constitution to fatigue, disdained the use of a covered carriage, generally appeared on horseback in a military habit, and sometimes marched several miles on foot at the head of the troops. The success of Odenathus was in a great measure ascribed to her incomparable prudence and fortitude. Their splendid victories over the Great King, whom they twice pursued as far as the gates of Ctesiphon, laid the foundations of their united fame and power. The armies which they commanded, and the provinces which they had saved, acknowledged not any other sovereigns than their invincible chiefs. The senate and people of Rome revered a stranger who had avenged their captive emperor, and even the insensible son of Valerian accepted Odenathus for his legitimate colleague.

[Footnote 551: According to Zosimus, Odenathus was of a noble family in Palmyra and according to Procopius, he was prince of the Saracens, who inhabit the ranks of the Euphrates. Echhel. Doct. Num. vii. 489.—G.]

PART III

After a successful expedition against the Gothic plunderers of Asia, the Palmyrenian prince returned to the city of Emesa in Syria. Invincible in war, he was there cut off by domestic treason, and his favorite amusement of hunting was the cause, or at least the occasion, of his death. [56] His nephew Maeonius presumed to dart his javelin before that of his uncle; and though admonished of his error, repeated the same insolence. As a monarch, and as a sportsman, Odenathus was provoked, took away his horse, a mark of ignominy among the barbarians, and chastised the rash youth by a short confinement. The offence was soon forgot, but the punishment was remembered; and Maeonius, with a few daring associates, assassinated his uncle in the midst of a great entertainment. Herod, the son of Odenathus, though not of Zenobia, a young man of a soft and effeminate temper, [57] was killed with his father. But Maeonius obtained only the pleasure of revenge by this bloody deed. He had scarcely time to assume the title of Augustus, before he was sacrificed by Zenobia to the memory of her husband. [58]

[Footnote 56: Hist. August. p. 192, 193. Zosimus, l. i. p. 36. Zonaras, l. xii p. 633. The last is clear and probable, the others confused and inconsistent. The text of Syncellus, if not corrupt, is absolute nonsense.]

[Footnote 57: Odenathus and Zenobia often sent him, from the spoils of the enemy, presents of gems and toys, which he received with infinite delight.]

[Footnote 58: Some very unjust suspicions have been cast on Zenobia, as if she was accessory to her husband's death.]

With the assistance of his most faithful friends, she immediately filled the vacant throne, and governed with manly counsels Palmyra, Syria, and the East, above five years. By the death of Odenathus, that authority was at an end which the senate had granted him only as a personal distinction; but his martial widow, disdaining both the senate and Gallienus, obliged one of the Roman generals, who was sent against her, to retreat into Europe, with the loss of his army and his reputation. [59] Instead of the little passions which so frequently perplex a female reign, the steady administration of Zenobia was guided by the most judicious maxims of policy. If it was expedient to pardon, she could calm her resentment; if it was necessary to punish, she could impose silence on the voice of pity. Her strict economy was accused of avarice; yet on every proper occasion she appeared magnificent and liberal. The neighboring states of Arabia, Armenia, and Persia, dreaded her enmity, and solicited her alliance. To the dominions of Odenathus, which extended from the Euphrates to the frontiers of Bithynia, his widow added the inheritance of her ancestors, the populous and fertile kingdom of Egypt. [60] [60/1] The emperor Claudius acknowledged her merit, and was content, that, while he pursued the Gothic war, she should assert the dignity of the empire in the East. [61] The conduct, however, of Zenobia, was attended with some ambiguity; not is it unlikely that she had conceived the design of erecting an independent and hostile monarchy. She blended with the popular manners of Roman princes the stately pomp of the courts of Asia, and exacted from her subjects the same adoration that was paid to the successor of Cyrus. She bestowed on her three sons [61] a Latin education, and often showed them to the troops adorned with the Imperial purple. For herself she reserved the diadem, with the splendid but doubtful title of Queen of the East.

[Footnote 59: Hist. August. p. 180, 181.]

[Footnote 60: See, in Hist. August. p. 198, Aurelian's testimony to her merit; and for the conquest of Egypt, Zosimus, l. i. p. 39, 40.]

[Footnote 60/1: This seems very doubtful. Claudius, during all his reign, is represented as emperor on the medals of Alexandria, which are very numerous. If Zenobia possessed any power in Egypt, it could only have been at the beginning of the reign of Aurelian. The same circumstance throws great improbability on her conquests in Galatia. Perhaps Zenobia administered Egypt in the name of Claudius, and emboldened by the death of that prince, subjected it to her own power.—G.]

[Footnote 61: Timolaus, Herennianus, and Vaballathus. It is supposed that the two former were already dead before the war. On the last, Aurelian bestowed a small province of Armenia, with the title of King; several of his medals are still extant. See Tillemont, tom. 3, p. 1190.]

When Aurelian passed over into Asia, against an adversary whose sex alone could render her an object of contempt, his presence restored obedience to the province of Bithynia, already shaken by the arms and intrigues of Zenobia. [62] Advancing at the head of his legions, he accepted the submission of Ancyra, and was admitted into Tyana, after an obstinate siege, by the help of a perfidious citizen. The generous though fierce temper of Aurelian abandoned the traitor to the rage of the soldiers; a superstitious reverence induced him to treat with lenity the countrymen of Apollonius the philosopher. [63] Antioch was deserted on his approach, till the emperor, by his salutary edicts, recalled the fugitives, and granted a general pardon to all, who, from necessity rather than choice, had been engaged in the service of the Palmyrenian Queen. The unexpected mildness of such a conduct reconciled the minds of the Syrians, and as far as the gates of Emesa, the wishes of the people seconded the terror of his arms. [64]

[Footnote 62: Zosimus, l. i. p. 44.]

[Footnote 63: Vopiscus (in Hist. August. p. 217) gives us an authentic letter and a doubtful vision, of Aurelian. Apollonius of Tyana was born about the same time as Jesus Christ. His life (that of the former) is related in so fabulous a manner by his disciples, that we are at a loss to discover whether he was a sage, an impostor, or a fanatic.]

[Footnote 64: Zosimus, l. i. p. 46.]

Zenobia would have ill deserved her reputation, had she indolently permitted the emperor of the West to approach within a hundred miles of her capital. The fate of the East was decided in two great battles; so similar in almost every circumstance, that we can scarcely distinguish them from each other, except by observing that the first was fought near Antioch, [65] and the second near Emesa. [66] In both the queen of Palmyra animated the armies by her presence, and devolved the execution of her orders on Zabdas, who had already signalized his military talents by the conquest of Egypt. The numerous forces of Zenobia consisted for the most part of light archers, and of heavy cavalry clothed in complete steel. The Moorish and Illyrian horse of Aurelian were unable to sustain the ponderous charge of their antagonists. They fled in real or affected disorder, engaged the Palmyrenians in a laborious pursuit, harassed them by a desultory combat, and at length discomfited this impenetrable but unwieldy body of cavalry. The light infantry, in the mean time, when they had exhausted their quivers, remaining without protection against a closer onset, exposed their naked sides to the swords of the legions. Aurelian had chosen these veteran troops, who were usually stationed on the Upper Danube, and whose valor had been severely tried in the Alemannic war. [67] After the defeat of Emesa, Zenobia found it impossible to collect a third army. As far as the frontier of Egypt, the nations subject to her empire had joined the standard of the conqueror, who detached Probus, the bravest of his generals, to possess himself of the Egyptian provinces. Palmyra was the last resource of the widow of Odenathus. She retired within the walls of her capital, made every preparation for a vigorous resistance, and declared, with the intrepidity of a heroine, that the last moment of her reign and of her life should be the same.

[Footnote 65: At a place called Immae. Eutropius, Sextus Rufus, and Jerome, mention only this first battle.]

[Footnote 66: Vopiscus (in Hist. August. p. 217) mentions only the second.]

[Footnote 67: Zosimus, l. i. p. 44—48. His account of the two battles is clear and circumstantial.]

Amid the barren deserts of Arabia, a few cultivated spots rise like islands out of the sandy ocean. Even the name of Tadmor, or Palmyra, by its signification in the Syriac as well as in the Latin language, denoted the multitude of palm-trees which afforded shade and verdure to that temperate region. The air was pure, and the soil, watered by some invaluable springs, was capable of producing fruits as well as corn. A place possessed of such singular advantages, and situated at a convenient distance [68] between the Gulf of Persia and the Mediterranean, was soon frequented by the caravans which conveyed to the nations of Europe a considerable part of the rich commodities of India. Palmyra insensibly increased into an opulent and independent city, and connecting the Roman and the Parthian monarchies by the mutual benefits of commerce, was suffered to observe an humble neutrality, till at length, after the victories of Trajan, the little republic sunk into the bosom of Rome, and flourished more than one hundred and fifty years in the subordinate though honorable rank of a colony. It was during that peaceful period, if we may judge from a few remaining inscriptions, that the wealthy Palmyrenians constructed those temples, palaces, and porticos of Grecian architecture, whose ruins, scattered over an extent of several miles, have deserved the curiosity of our travellers. The elevation of Odenathus and Zenobia appeared to reflect new splendor on their country, and Palmyra, for a while, stood forth the rival of Rome: but the competition was fatal, and ages of prosperity were sacrificed to a moment of glory. [69]

[Footnote 68: It was five hundred and thirty-seven miles from Seleucia, and two hundred and three from the nearest coast of Syria, according to the reckoning of Pliny, who, in a few words, (Hist. Natur. v. 21,) gives an excellent description of Palmyra. Note: Talmor, or Palmyra, was probably at a very early period the connecting link between the commerce of Tyre and Babylon. Heeren, Ideen, v. i. p. ii. p. 125. Tadmor was probably built by Solomon as a commercial station. Hist. of Jews, v. p. 271—M.]

[Footnote 69: Some English travellers from Aleppo discovered the ruins of Palmyra about the end of the last century. Our curiosity has since been gratified in a more splendid manner by Messieurs Wood and Dawkins. For the history of Palmyra, we may consult the masterly dissertation of Dr. Halley in the Philosophical Transactions: Lowthorp's Abridgment, vol. iii. p. 518.]

In his march over the sandy desert between Emesa and Palmyra, the emperor Aurelian was perpetually harassed by the Arabs; nor could he always defend his army, and especially his baggage, from those flying troops of active and daring robbers, who watched the moment of surprise, and eluded the slow pursuit of the legions. The siege of Palmyra was an object far more difficult and important, and the emperor, who, with incessant vigor, pressed the attacks in person, was himself wounded with a dart. "The Roman people," says Aurelian, in an original letter, "speak with contempt of the war which I am waging against a woman. They are ignorant both of the character and of the power of Zenobia. It is impossible to enumerate her warlike preparations, of stones, of arrows, and of every species of missile weapons. Every part of the walls is provided with two or three balistoe and artificial fires are thrown from her military engines. The fear of punishment has armed her with a desperate courage. Yet still I trust in the protecting deities of Rome, who have hitherto been favorable to all my undertakings." [70] Doubtful, however, of the protection of the gods, and of the event of the siege, Aurelian judged it more prudent to offer terms of an advantageous capitulation; to the queen, a splendid retreat; to the citizens, their ancient privileges. His proposals were obstinately rejected, and the refusal was accompanied with insult.

[Footnote 70: Vopiscus in Hist. August. p. 218.]

The firmness of Zenobia was supported by the hope, that in a very short time famine would compel the Roman army to repass the desert; and by the reasonable expectation that the kings of the East, and particularly the Persian monarch, would arm in the defence of their most natural ally. But fortune, and the perseverance of Aurelian, overcame every obstacle. The death of Sapor, which happened about this time, [71] distracted the councils of Persia, and the inconsiderable succors that attempted to relieve Palmyra, were easily intercepted either by the arms or the liberality of the emperor. From every part of Syria, a regular succession of convoys safely arrived in the camp, which was increased by the return of Probus with his victorious troops from the conquest of Egypt. It was then that Zenobia resolved to fly. She mounted the fleetest of her dromedaries, [72] and had already reached the banks of the Euphrates, about sixty miles from Palmyra, when she was overtaken by the pursuit of Aurelian's light horse, seized, and brought back a captive to the feet of the emperor. Her capital soon afterwards surrendered, and was treated with unexpected lenity. The arms, horses, and camels, with an immense treasure of gold, silver, silk, and precious stones, were all delivered to the conqueror, who, leaving only a garrison of six hundred archers, returned to Emesa, and employed some time in the distribution of rewards and punishments at the end of so memorable a war, which restored to the obedience of Rome those provinces that had renounced their allegiance since the captivity of Valerian.

[Footnote 71: From a very doubtful chronology I have endeavored to extract the most probable date.]

[Footnote 72: Hist. August. p. 218. Zosimus, l. i. p. 50. Though the camel is a heavy beast of burden, the dromedary, which is either of the same or of a kindred species, is used by the natives of Asia and Africa on all occasions which require celerity. The Arabs affirm, that he will run over as much ground in one day as their fleetest horses can perform in eight or ten. See Buffon, Hist. Naturelle, tom. xi. p. 222, and Shaw's Travels p. 167]

When the Syrian queen was brought into the presence of Aurelian, he sternly asked her, How she had presumed to rise in arms against the emperors of Rome! The answer of Zenobia was a prudent mixture of respect and firmness. "Because I disdained to consider as Roman emperors an Aureolus or a Gallienus. You alone I acknowledge as my conqueror and my sovereign." [73] But as female fortitude is commonly artificial, so it is seldom steady or consistent. The courage of Zenobia deserted her in the hour of trial; she trembled at the angry clamors of the soldiers, who called aloud for her immediate execution, forgot the generous despair of Cleopatra, which she had proposed as her model, and ignominiously purchased life by the sacrifice of her fame and her friends. It was to their counsels, which governed the weakness of her sex, that she imputed the guilt of her obstinate resistance; it was on their heads that she directed the vengeance of the cruel Aurelian. The fame of Longinus, who was included among the numerous and perhaps innocent victims of her fear, will survive that of the queen who betrayed, or the tyrant who condemned him. Genius and learning were incapable of moving a fierce unlettered soldier, but they had served to elevate and harmonize the soul of Longinus. Without uttering a complaint, he calmly followed the executioner, pitying his unhappy mistress, and bestowing comfort on his afflicted friends. [74]

[Footnote 73: Pollio in Hist. August. p. 199.]

[Footnote 74: Vopiscus in Hist. August. p. 219. Zosimus, l. i. p. 51.]

Returning from the conquest of the East, Aurelian had already crossed the Straits which divided Europe from Asia, when he was provoked by the intelligence that the Palmyrenians had massacred the governor and garrison which he had left among them, and again erected the standard of revolt. Without a moment's deliberation, he once more turned his face towards Syria. Antioch was alarmed by his rapid approach, and the helpless city of Palmyra felt the irresistible weight of his resentment. We have a letter of Aurelian himself, in which he acknowledges, [75] that old men, women, children, and peasants, had been involved in that dreadful execution, which should have been confined to armed rebellion; and although his principal concern seems directed to the reestablishment of a temple of the Sun, he discovers some pity for the remnant of the Palmyrenians, to whom he grants the permission of rebuilding and inhabiting their city. But it is easier to destroy than to restore. The seat of commerce, of arts, and of Zenobia, gradually sunk into an obscure town, a trifling fortress, and at length a miserable village. The present citizens of Palmyra, consisting of thirty or forty families, have erected their mud cottages within the spacious court of a magnificent temple.

[Footnote 75: Hist. August. p. 219.]

Another and a last labor still awaited the indefatigable Aurelian; to suppress a dangerous though obscure rebel, who, during the revolt of Palmyra, had arisen on the banks of the Nile. Firmus, the friend and ally, as he proudly styled himself, of Odenathus and Zenobia, was no more than a wealthy merchant of Egypt. In the course of his trade to India, he had formed very intimate connections with the Saracens and the Blemmyes, whose situation on either coast of the Red Sea gave them an easy introduction into the Upper Egypt. The Egyptians he inflamed with the hope of freedom, and, at the head of their furious multitude, broke into the city of Alexandria, where he assumed the Imperial purple, coined money, published edicts, and raised an army, which, as he vainly boasted, he was capable of maintaining from the sole profits of his paper trade. Such troops were a feeble defence against the approach of Aurelian; and it seems almost unnecessary to relate, that Firmus was routed, taken, tortured, and put to death. [76] Aurelian might now congratulate the senate, the people, and himself, that in little more than three years, he had restored universal peace and order to the Roman world.

[Footnote 76: See Vopiscus in Hist. August. p. 220, 242. As an instance of luxury, it is observed, that he had glass windows. He was remarkable for his strength and appetite, his courage and dexterity. From the letter of Aurelian, we may justly infer, that Firmus was the last of the rebels, and consequently that Tetricus was already suppressed.]

Since the foundation of Rome, no general had more nobly deserved a triumph than Aurelian; nor was a triumph ever celebrated with superior pride and magnificence. [77] The pomp was opened by twenty elephants, four royal tigers, and above two hundred of the most curious animals from every climate of the North, the East, and the South. They were followed by sixteen hundred gladiators, devoted to the cruel amusement of the amphitheatre. The wealth of Asia, the arms and ensigns of so many conquered nations, and the magnificent plate and wardrobe of the Syrian queen, were disposed in exact symmetry or artful disorder. The ambassadors of the most remote parts of the earth, of Aethiopia, Arabia, Persia, Bactriana, India, and China, all remarkable by their rich or singular dresses, displayed the fame and power of the Roman emperor, who exposed likewise to the public view the presents that he had received, and particularly a great number of crowns of gold, the offerings of grateful cities.

The victories of Aurelian were attested by the long train of captives who reluctantly attended his triumph, Goths, Vandals, Sarmatians, Alemanni, Franks, Gauls, Syrians, and Egyptians. Each people was distinguished by its peculiar inscription, and the title of Amazons was bestowed on ten martial heroines of the Gothic nation who had been taken in arms. [78] But every eye, disregarding the crowd of captives, was fixed on the emperor Tetricus and the queen of the East. The former, as well as his son, whom he had created Augustus, was dressed in Gallic trousers, [79] a saffron tunic, and a robe of purple. The beauteous figure of Zenobia was confined by fetters of gold; a slave supported the gold chain which encircled her neck, and she almost fainted under the intolerable weight of jewels. She preceded on foot the magnificent chariot, in which she once hoped to enter the gates of Rome. It was followed by two other chariots, still more sumptuous, of Odenathus and of the Persian monarch. The triumphal car of Aurelian (it had formerly been used by a Gothic king) was drawn, on this memorable occasion, either by four stags or by four elephants. [80] The most illustrious of the senate, the people, and the army closed the solemn procession. Unfeigned joy, wonder, and gratitude, swelled the acclamations of the multitude; but the satisfaction of the senate was clouded by the appearance of Tetricus; nor could they suppress a rising murmur, that the haughty emperor should thus expose to public ignominy the person of a Roman and a magistrate. [81]

[Footnote 77: See the triumph of Aurelian, described by Vopiscus. He relates the particulars with his usual minuteness; and, on this occasion, they happen to be interesting. Hist. August. p. 220.]

[Footnote 78: Among barbarous nations, women have often combated by the side of their husbands. But it is almost impossible that a society of Amazons should ever have existed either in the old or new world. Note: Klaproth's theory on the origin of such traditions is at least recommended by its ingenuity. The males of a tribe having gone out on a marauding expedition, and having been cut off to a man, the females may have endeavored, for a time, to maintain their independence in their camp village, till their children grew up. Travels, ch. xxx. Eng. Trans—M.]

[Footnote 79: The use of braccoe, breeches, or trousers, was still considered in Italy as a Gallic and barbarian fashion. The Romans, however, had made great advances towards it. To encircle the legs and thighs with fascioe, or bands, was understood, in the time of Pompey and Horace, to be a proof of ill health or effeminacy. In the age of Trajan, the custom was confined to the rich and luxurious. It gradually was adopted by the meanest of the people. See a very curious note of Casaubon, ad Sueton. in August. c. 82.]

[Footnote 80: Most probably the former; the latter seen on the medals of Aurelian, only denote (according to the learned Cardinal Norris) an oriental victory.]

[Footnote 81: The expression of Calphurnius, (Eclog. i. 50) Nullos decet captiva triumphos, as applied to Rome, contains a very manifest allusion and censure.]

But however, in the treatment of his unfortunate rivals, Aurelian might indulge his pride, he behaved towards them with a generous clemency, which was seldom exercised by the ancient conquerors. Princes who, without success, had defended their throne or freedom, were frequently strangled in prison, as soon as the triumphal pomp ascended the Capitol. These usurpers, whom their defeat had convicted of the crime of treason, were permitted to spend their lives in affluence and honorable repose.

The emperor presented Zenobia with an elegant villa at Tibur, or Tivoli, about twenty miles from the capital; the Syrian queen insensibly sunk into a Roman matron, her daughters married into noble families, and her race was not yet extinct in the fifth century. [82] Tetricus and his son were reinstated in their rank and fortunes. They erected on the Caelian hill a magnificent palace, and as soon as it was finished, invited Aurelian to supper. On his entrance, he was agreeably surprised with a picture which represented their singular history. They were delineated offering to the emperor a civic crown and the sceptre of Gaul, and again receiving at his hands the ornaments of the senatorial dignity. The father was afterwards invested with the government of Lucania, [83] and Aurelian, who soon admitted the abdicated monarch to his friendship and conversation, familiarly asked him, Whether it were not more desirable to administer a province of Italy, than to reign beyond the Alps. The son long continued a respectable member of the senate; nor was there any one of the Roman nobility more esteemed by Aurelian, as well as by his successors. [84]

[Footnote 82: Vopiscus in Hist. August. p. 199. Hieronym. in Chron. Prosper in Chron. Baronius supposes that Zenobius, bishop of Florence in the time of St. Ambrose, was of her family.]

[Footnote 83: Vopisc. in Hist. August. p. 222. Eutropius, ix. 13. Victor Junior. But Pollio, in Hist. August. p. 196, says, that Tetricus was made corrector of all Italy.]

[Footnote 84: Hist. August. p. 197.]

So long and so various was the pomp of Aurelian's triumph, that although it opened with the dawn of day, the slow majesty of the procession ascended not the Capitol before the ninth hour; and it was already dark when the emperor returned to the palace. The festival was protracted by theatrical representations, the games of the circus, the hunting of wild beasts, combats of gladiators, and naval engagements. Liberal donatives were distributed to the army and people, and several institutions, agreeable or beneficial to the city, contributed to perpetuate the glory of Aurelian. A considerable portion of his oriental spoils was consecrated to the gods of Rome; the Capitol, and every other temple, glittered with the offerings of his ostentatious piety; and the temple of the Sun alone received above fifteen thousand pounds of gold. [85] This last was a magnificent structure, erected by the emperor on the side of the Quirinal hill, and dedicated, soon after the triumph, to that deity whom Aurelian adored as the parent of his life and fortunes. His mother had been an inferior priestess in a chapel of the Sun; a peculiar devotion to the god of Light was a sentiment which the fortunate peasant imbibed in his infancy; and every step of his elevation, every victory of his reign, fortified superstition by gratitude. [86]

[Footnote 85: Vopiscus in Hist. August. 222. Zosimus, l. i. p. 56. He placed in it the images of Belus and of the Sun, which he had brought from Palmyra. It was dedicated in the fourth year of his reign, (Euseb in Chron.,) but was most assuredly begun immediately on his accession.]

[Footnote 86: See, in the Augustan History, p. 210, the omens of his fortune. His devotion to the Sun appears in his letters, on his medals, and is mentioned in the Caesars of Julian. Commentaire de Spanheim, p. 109.]

The arms of Aurelian had vanquished the foreign and domestic foes of the republic. We are assured, that, by his salutary rigor, crimes and factions, mischievous arts and pernicious connivance, the luxurious growth of a feeble and oppressive government, were eradicated throughout the Roman world. [87] But if we attentively reflect how much swifter is the progress of corruption than its cure, and if we remember that the years abandoned to public disorders exceeded the months allotted to the martial reign of Aurelian, we must confess that a few short intervals of peace were insufficient for the arduous work of reformation. Even his attempt to restore the integrity of the coin was opposed by a formidable insurrection. The emperor's vexation breaks out in one of his private letters. "Surely," says he, "the gods have decreed that my life should be a perpetual warfare. A sedition within the walls has just now given birth to a very serious civil war. The workmen of the mint, at the instigation of Felicissimus, a slave to whom I had intrusted an employment in the finances, have risen in rebellion. They are at length suppressed; but seven thousand of my soldiers have been slain in the contest, of those troops whose ordinary station is in Dacia, and the camps along the Danube." [88] Other writers, who confirm the same fact, add likewise, that it happened soon after Aurelian's triumph; that the decisive engagement was fought on the Caelian hill; that the workmen of the mint had adulterated the coin; and that the emperor restored the public credit, by delivering out good money in exchange for the bad, which the people was commanded to bring into the treasury. [89]

[Footnote 87: Vopiscus in Hist. August. p. 221.]

[Footnote 88: Hist. August. p. 222. Aurelian calls these soldiers Hiberi Riporiences Castriani, and Dacisci.]

[Footnote 89: Zosimus, l. i. p. 56. Eutropius, ix. 14. Aurel Victor.]

We might content ourselves with relating this extraordinary transaction, but we cannot dissemble how much in its present form it appears to us inconsistent and incredible. The debasement of the coin is indeed well suited to the administration of Gallienus; nor is it unlikely that the instruments of the corruption might dread the inflexible justice of Aurelian. But the guilt, as well as the profit, must have been confined to a very few; nor is it easy to conceive by what arts they could arm a people whom they had injured, against a monarch whom they had betrayed. We might naturally expect that such miscreants should have shared the public detestation with the informers and the other ministers of oppression; and that the reformation of the coin should have been an action equally popular with the destruction of those obsolete accounts, which by the emperor's order were burnt in the forum of Trajan. [90] In an age when the principles of commerce were so imperfectly understood, the most desirable end might perhaps be effected by harsh and injudicious means; but a temporary grievance of such a nature can scarcely excite and support a serious civil war. The repetition of intolerable taxes, imposed either on the land or on the necessaries of life, may at last provoke those who will not, or who cannot, relinquish their country. But the case is far otherwise in every operation which, by whatsoever expedients, restores the just value of money. The transient evil is soon obliterated by the permanent benefit, the loss is divided among multitudes; and if a few wealthy individuals experience a sensible diminution of treasure, with their riches, they at the same time lose the degree of weight and importance which they derived from the possession of them. However Aurelian might choose to disguise the real cause of the insurrection, his reformation of the coin could furnish only a faint pretence to a party already powerful and discontented. Rome, though deprived of freedom, was distracted by faction. The people, towards whom the emperor, himself a plebeian, always expressed a peculiar fondness, lived in perpetual dissension with the senate, the equestrian order, and the Praetorian guards. [91] Nothing less than the firm though secret conspiracy of those orders, of the authority of the first, the wealth of the second, and the arms of the third, could have displayed a strength capable of contending in battle with the veteran legions of the Danube, which, under the conduct of a martial sovereign, had achieved the conquest of the West and of the East.

[Footnote 90: Hist. August. p. 222. Aurel Victor.]

[Footnote 91: It already raged before Aurelian's return from Egypt. See Vipiscus, who quotes an original letter. Hist. August. p. 244.]

Whatever was the cause or the object of this rebellion, imputed with so little probability to the workmen of the mint, Aurelian used his victory with unrelenting rigor. [92] He was naturally of a severe disposition. A peasant and a soldier, his nerves yielded not easily to the impressions of sympathy, and he could sustain without emotion the sight of tortures and death. Trained from his earliest youth in the exercise of arms, he set too small a value on the life of a citizen, chastised by military execution the slightest offences, and transferred the stern discipline of the camp into the civil administration of the laws. His love of justice often became a blind and furious passion and whenever he deemed his own or the public safety endangered, he disregarded the rules of evidence, and the proportion of punishments. The unprovoked rebellion with which the Romans rewarded his services, exasperated his haughty spirit. The noblest families of the capital were involved in the guilt or suspicion of this dark conspiracy. A nasty spirit of revenge urged the bloody prosecution, and it proved fatal to one of the nephews of the emperor. The executioners (if we may use the expression of a contemporary poet) were fatigued, the prisons were crowded, and the unhappy senate lamented the death or absence of its most illustrious members. [93] Nor was the pride of Aurelian less offensive to that assembly than his cruelty. Ignorant or impatient of the restraints of civil institutions, he disdained to hold his power by any other title than that of the sword, and governed by right of conquest an empire which he had saved and subdued. [94]

[Footnote 92: Vopiscus in Hist. August p. 222. The two Victors. Eutropius ix. 14. Zosimus (l. i. p. 43) mentions only three senators, and placed their death before the eastern war.]

[Footnote 93: Nulla catenati feralis pompa senatus Carnificum lassabit opus; nec carcere pleno Infelix raros numerabit curia Patres. Calphurn. Eclog. i. 60.]

[Footnote 94: According to the younger Victor, he sometimes wore the diadem, Deus and Dominus appear on his medals.]

It was observed by one of the most sagacious of the Roman princes, that the talents of his predecessor Aurelian were better suited to the command of an army, than to the government of an empire. [95] Conscious of the character in which nature and experience had enabled him to excel, he again took the field a few months after his triumph. It was expedient to exercise the restless temper of the legions in some foreign war, and the Persian monarch, exulting in the shame of Valerian, still braved with impunity the offended majesty of Rome. At the head of an army, less formidable by its numbers than by its discipline and valor, the emperor advanced as far as the Straits which divide Europe from Asia. He there experienced that the most absolute power is a weak defence against the effects of despair. He had threatened one of his secretaries who was accused of extortion; and it was known that he seldom threatened in vain. The last hope which remained for the criminal, was to involve some of the principal officers of the army in his danger, or at least in his fears. Artfully counterfeiting his master's hand, he showed them, in a long and bloody list, their own names devoted to death. Without suspecting or examining the fraud, they resolved to secure their lives by the murder of the emperor. On his march, between Byzantium and Heraclea, Aurelian was suddenly attacked by the conspirators, whose stations gave them a right to surround his person, and after a short resistance, fell by the hand of Mucapor, a general whom he had always loved and trusted. He died regretted by the army, detested by the senate, but universally acknowledged as a warlike and fortunate prince, the useful, though severe reformer of a degenerate state. [96]

[Footnote 95: It was the observation of Dioclatian. See Vopiscus in Hist. August. p. 224.]

[Footnote 96: Vopiscus in Hist. August. p. 221. Zosimus, l. i. p. 57. Eutrop ix. 15. The two Victors.]

CHAPTER XII

REIGN OF TACTUS, PROBUS, CARUS AND HIS SONS

PART I

CONDUCT OF THE ARMY AND SENATE AFTER THE DEATH OF AURELIAN—REIGN OF TACTUS, PROBUS, CARUS AND HIS SONS

Such was the unhappy condition of the Roman emperors, that, whatever might be their conduct, their fate was commonly the same. A life of pleasure or virtue, of severity or mildness, of indolence or glory, alike led to an untimely grave; and almost every reign is closed by the same disgusting repetition of treason and murder. The death of Aurelian, however, is remarkable by its extraordinary consequences. The legions admired, lamented, and revenged their victorious chief. The artifice of his perfidious secretary was discovered and punished.

The deluded conspirators attended the funeral of their injured sovereign, with sincere or well-feigned contrition, and submitted to the unanimous resolution of the military order, which was signified by the following epistle: "The brave and fortunate armies to the senate and people of Rome.—The crime of one man, and the error of many, have deprived us of the late emperor Aurelian. May it please you, venerable lords and fathers! to place him in the number of the gods, and to appoint a successor whom your judgment shall declare worthy of the Imperial purple! None of those whose guilt or misfortune have contributed to our loss, shall ever reign over us." [1] The Roman senators heard, without surprise, that another emperor had been assassinated in his camp; they secretly rejoiced in the fall of Aurelian; and, besides the recent notoriety of the facts, constantly draws his materials from the Journals of the Senate, and the but the modest and dutiful address of the legions, when it was communicated in full assembly by the consul, diffused the most pleasing astonishment. Such honors as fear and perhaps esteem could extort, they liberally poured forth on the memory of their deceased sovereign. Such acknowledgments as gratitude could inspire, they returned to the faithful armies of the republic, who entertained so just a sense of the legal authority of the senate in the choice of an emperor. Yet, notwithstanding this flattering appeal, the most prudent of the assembly declined exposing their safety and dignity to the caprice of an armed multitude. The strength of the legions was, indeed, a pledge of their sincerity, since those who may command are seldom reduced to the necessity of dissembling; but could it naturally be expected, that a hasty repentance would correct the inveterate habits of fourscore years? Should the soldiers relapse into their accustomed seditions, their insolence might disgrace the majesty of the senate, and prove fatal to the object of its choice. Motives like these dictated a decree, by which the election of a new emperor was referred to the suffrage of the military order.

[Footnote 1: Vopiscus in Hist. August. p. 222. Aurelius Victor mentions a formal deputation from the troops to the senate.]

The contention that ensued is one of the best attested, but most improbable events in the history of mankind. [2] The troops, as if satiated with the exercise of power, again conjured the senate to invest one of its own body with the Imperial purple. The senate still persisted in its refusal; the army in its request. The reciprocal offer was pressed and rejected at least three times, and, whilst the obstinate modesty of either party was resolved to receive a master from the hands of the other, eight months insensibly elapsed; an amazing period of tranquil anarchy, during which the Roman world remained without a sovereign, without a usurper, and without a sedition. [2/1] The generals and magistrates appointed by Aurelian continued to execute their ordinary functions; and it is observed, that a proconsul of Asia was the only considerable person removed from his office in the whole course of the interregnum.

[Footnote 2: Vopiscus, our principal authority, wrote at Rome, sixteen years only after the death of Aurelian; and, besides the recent notoriety of the facts, constantly draws his materials from the Journals of the Senate, and the original papers of the Ulpian library. Zosimus and Zonaras appear as ignorant of this transaction as they were in general of the Roman constitution.]

[Footnote 2/1: The interregnum could not be more than seven months; Aurelian was assassinated in the middle of March, the year of Rome 1028. Tacitus was elected the 25th September in the same year.—G.]

An event somewhat similar, but much less authentic, is supposed to have happened after the death of Romulus, who, in his life and character, bore some affinity with Aurelian. The throne was vacant during twelve months, till the election of a Sabine philosopher, and the public peace was guarded in the same manner, by the union of the several orders of the state. But, in the time of Numa and Romulus, the arms of the people were controlled by the authority of the Patricians; and the balance of freedom was easily preserved in a small and virtuous community. [3] The decline of the Roman state, far different from its infancy, was attended with every circumstance that could banish from an interregnum the prospect of obedience and harmony: an immense and tumultuous capital, a wide extent of empire, the servile equality of despotism, an army of four hundred thousand mercenaries, and the experience of frequent revolutions. Yet, notwithstanding all these temptations, the discipline and memory of Aurelian still restrained the seditious temper of the troops, as well as the fatal ambition of their leaders. The flower of the legions maintained their stations on the banks of the Bosphorus, and the Imperial standard awed the less powerful camps of Rome and of the provinces. A generous though transient enthusiasm seemed to animate the military order; and we may hope that a few real patriots cultivated the returning friendship of the army and the senate, as the only expedient capable of restoring the republic to its ancient beauty and vigor.

[Footnote 3: Liv. i. 17 Dionys. Halicarn. l. ii. p. 115. Plutarch in Numa, p. 60. The first of these writers relates the story like an orator, the second like a lawyer, and the third like a moralist, and none of them probably without some intermixture of fable.]

On the twenty-fifth of September, near eight months after the murder of Aurelian, the consul convoked an assembly of the senate, and reported the doubtful and dangerous situation of the empire. He slightly insinuated, that the precarious loyalty of the soldiers depended on the chance of every hour, and of every accident; but he represented, with the most convincing eloquence, the various dangers that might attend any further delay in the choice of an emperor. Intelligence, he said, was already received, that the Germans had passed the Rhine, and occupied some of the strongest and most opulent cities of Gaul. The ambition of the Persian king kept the East in perpetual alarms; Egypt, Africa, and Illyricum, were exposed to foreign and domestic arms, and the levity of Syria would prefer even a female sceptre to the sanctity of the Roman laws. The consul, then addressing himself to Tacitus, the first of the senators, [4] required his opinion on the important subject of a proper candidate for the vacant throne.

[Footnote 4: Vopiscus (in Hist. August p. 227) calls him "primae sententia consularis;" and soon afterwards Princeps senatus. It is natural to suppose, that the monarchs of Rome, disdaining that humble title, resigned it to the most ancient of the senators.]

If we can prefer personal merit to accidental greatness, we shall esteem the birth of Tacitus more truly noble than that of kings. He claimed his descent from the philosophic historian, whose writings will instruct the last generations of mankind. [5] The senator Tacitus was then seventy-five years of age. [6] The long period of his innocent life was adorned with wealth and honors. He had twice been invested with the consular dignity, [7] and enjoyed with elegance and sobriety his ample patrimony of between two and three millions sterling. [8] The experience of so many princes, whom he had esteemed or endured, from the vain follies of Elagabalus to the useful rigor of Aurelian, taught him to form a just estimate of the duties, the dangers, and the temptations of their sublime station. From the assiduous study of his immortal ancestor, he derived the knowledge of the Roman constitution, and of human nature. [9] The voice of the people had already named Tacitus as the citizen the most worthy of empire. The ungrateful rumor reached his ears, and induced him to seek the retirement of one of his villas in Campania. He had passed two months in the delightful privacy of Baiae, when he reluctantly obeyed the summons of the consul to resume his honorable place in the senate, and to assist the republic with his counsels on this important occasion.

[Footnote 5: The only objection to this genealogy is, that the historian was named Cornelius, the emperor, Claudius. But under the lower empire, surnames were extremely various and uncertain.]

[Footnote 6: Zonaras, l. xii. p. 637. The Alexandrian Chronicle, by an obvious mistake, transfers that age to Aurelian.]

[Footnote 7: In the year 273, he was ordinary consul. But he must have been Suffectus many years before, and most probably under Valerian.]

[Footnote 8: Bis millies octingenties. Vopiscus in Hist. August p. 229. This sum, according to the old standard, was equivalent to eight hundred and forty thousand Roman pounds of silver, each of the value of three pounds sterling. But in the age of Tacitus, the coin had lost much of its weight and purity.]

[Footnote 9: After his accession, he gave orders that ten copies of the historian should be annually transcribed and placed in the public libraries. The Roman libraries have long since perished, and the most valuable part of Tacitus was preserved in a single Ms., and discovered in a monastery of Westphalia. See Bayle, Dictionnaire, Art. Tacite, and Lipsius ad Annal. ii. 9.]

He arose to speak, when from every quarter of the house, he was saluted with the names of Augustus and emperor. "Tacitus Augustus, the gods preserve thee! we choose thee for our sovereign; to thy care we intrust the republic and the world. Accept the empire from the authority of the senate. It is due to thy rank, to thy conduct, to thy manners." As soon as the tumult of acclamations subsided, Tacitus attempted to decline the dangerous honor, and to express his wonder, that they should elect his age and infirmities to succeed the martial vigor of Aurelian. "Are these limbs, conscript fathers! fitted to sustain the weight of armor, or to practise the exercises of the camp? The variety of climates, and the hardships of a military life, would soon oppress a feeble constitution, which subsists only by the most tender management. My exhausted strength scarcely enables me to discharge the duty of a senator; how insufficient would it prove to the arduous labors of war and government! Can you hope, that the legions will respect a weak old man, whose days have been spent in the shade of peace and retirement? Can you desire that I should ever find reason to regret the favorable opinion of the senate?" [10]

[Footnote 10: Vopiscus in Hist. August. p. 227.]

The reluctance of Tacitus (and it might possibly be sincere) was encountered by the affectionate obstinacy of the senate. Five hundred voices repeated at once, in eloquent confusion, that the greatest of the Roman princes, Numa, Trajan, Hadrian, and the Antonines, had ascended the throne in a very advanced season of life; that the mind, not the body, a sovereign, not a soldier, was the object of their choice; and that they expected from him no more than to guide by his wisdom the valor of the legions. These pressing though tumultuary instances were seconded by a more regular oration of Metius Falconius, the next on the consular bench to Tacitus himself. He reminded the assembly of the evils which Rome had endured from the vices of headstrong and capricious youths, congratulated them on the election of a virtuous and experienced senator, and, with a manly, though perhaps a selfish, freedom, exhorted Tacitus to remember the reasons of his elevation, and to seek a successor, not in his own family, but in the republic. The speech of Falconius was enforced by a general acclamation. The emperor elect submitted to the authority of his country, and received the voluntary homage of his equals. The judgment of the senate was confirmed by the consent of the Roman people, and of the Praetorian guards. [11]

[Footnote 11: Hist. August. p. 228. Tacitus addressed the Praetorians by the appellation of sanctissimi milites, and the people by that of sacratissim. Quirites.]

The administration of Tacitus was not unworthy of his life and principles. A grateful servant of the senate, he considered that national council as the author, and himself as the subject, of the laws. [12] He studied to heal the wounds which Imperial pride, civil discord, and military violence, had inflicted on the constitution, and to restore, at least, the image of the ancient republic, as it had been preserved by the policy of Augustus, and the virtues of Trajan and the Antonines. It may not be useless to recapitulate some of the most important prerogatives which the senate appeared to have regained by the election of Tacitus. [13] 1. To invest one of their body, under the title of emperor, with the general command of the armies, and the government of the frontier provinces. 2. To determine the list, or, as it was then styled, the College of Consuls. They were twelve in number, who, in successive pairs, each, during the space of two months, filled the year, and represented the dignity of that ancient office. The authority of the senate, in the nomination of the consuls, was exercised with such independent freedom, that no regard was paid to an irregular request of the emperor in favor of his brother Florianus. "The senate," exclaimed Tacitus, with the honest transport of a patriot, "understand the character of a prince whom they have chosen." 3. To appoint the proconsuls and presidents of the provinces, and to confer on all the magistrates their civil jurisdiction. 4. To receive appeals through the intermediate office of the praefect of the city from all the tribunals of the empire. 5. To give force and validity, by their decrees, to such as they should approve of the emperor's edicts. 6. To these several branches of authority we may add some inspection over the finances, since, even in the stern reign of Aurelian, it was in their power to divert a part of the revenue from the public service. [14]

[Footnote 12: In his manumissions he never exceeded the number of a hundred, as limited by the Caninian law, which was enacted under Augustus, and at length repealed by Justinian. See Casaubon ad locum Vopisci.]

[Footnote 13: See the lives of Tacitus, Florianus, and Probus, in the Augustan History; we may be well assured, that whatever the soldier gave the senator had already given.]

[Footnote 14: Vopiscus in Hist. August. p. 216. The passage is perfectly clear, both Casaubon and Salmasius wish to correct it.]

Circular epistles were sent, without delay, to all the principal cities of the empire, Treves, Milan, Aquileia, Thessalo nica, Corinth, Athens, Antioch, Alexandria, and Carthage, to claim their obedience, and to inform them of the happy revolution, which had restored the Roman senate to its ancient dignity. Two of these epistles are still extant. We likewise possess two very singular fragments of the private correspondence of the senators on this occasion. They discover the most excessive joy, and the most unbounded hopes. "Cast away your indolence," it is thus that one of the senators addresses his friend, "emerge from your retirements of Baiae and Puteoli. Give yourself to the city, to the senate. Rome flourishes, the whole republic flourishes. Thanks to the Roman army, to an army truly Roman; at length we have recovered our just authority, the end of all our desires. We hear appeals, we appoint proconsuls, we create emperors; perhaps too we may restrain them—to the wise a word is sufficient." [15] These lofty expectations were, however, soon disappointed; nor, indeed, was it possible that the armies and the provinces should long obey the luxurious and unwarlike nobles of Rome. On the slightest touch, the unsupported fabric of their pride and power fell to the ground. The expiring senate displayed a sudden lustre, blazed for a moment and was extinguished forever.

[Footnote 15: Vopiscus in Hist. August. p. 230, 232, 233. The senators celebrated the happy restoration with hecatombs and public rejoicings.]

All that had yet passed at Rome was no more than a theatrical representation, unless it was ratified by the more substantial power of the legions. Leaving the senators to enjoy their dream of freedom and ambition, Tacitus proceeded to the Thracian camp, and was there, by the Praetorian praefect, presented to the assembled troops, as the prince whom they themselves had demanded, and whom the senate had bestowed. As soon as the praefect was silent, the emperor addressed himself to the soldiers with eloquence and propriety. He gratified their avarice by a liberal distribution of treasure, under the names of pay and donative. He engaged their esteem by a spirited declaration, that although his age might disable him from the performance of military exploits, his counsels should never be unworthy of a Roman general, the successor of the brave Aurelian. [16]

[Footnote 16: Hist. August. p. 228.]

Whilst the deceased emperor was making preparations for a second expedition into the East, he had negotiated with the Alani, [16/1] a Scythian people, who pitched their tents in the neighborhood of the Lake Moeotis. Those barbarians, allured by presents and subsidies, had promised to invade Persia with a numerous body of light cavalry. They were faithful to their engagements; but when they arrived on the Roman frontier, Aurelian was already dead, the design of the Persian war was at least suspended, and the generals, who, during the interregnum, exercised a doubtful authority, were unprepared either to receive or to oppose them. Provoked by such treatment, which they considered as trifling and perfidious, the Alani had recourse to their own valor for their payment and revenge; and as they moved with the usual swiftness of Tartars, they had soon spread themselves over the provinces of Pontus, Cappadocia, Cilicia, and Galatia. The legions, who from the opposite shores of the Bosphorus could almost distinguish the flames of the cities and villages, impatiently urged their general to lead them against the invaders. The conduct of Tacitus was suitable to his age and station. He convinced the barbarians of the faith, as well as the power, of the empire. Great numbers of the Alani, appeased by the punctual discharge of the engagements which Aurelian had contracted with them, relinquished their booty and captives, and quietly retreated to their own deserts, beyond the Phasis. Against the remainder, who refused peace, the Roman emperor waged, in person, a successful war. Seconded by an army of brave and experienced veterans, in a few weeks he delivered the provinces of Asia from the terror of the Scythian invasion. [17]

[Footnote 16/1: On the Alani, see ch. xxvi. note 55.—M.]

[Footnote 17: Vopiscus in Hist. August. p. 230. Zosimus, l. i. p. 57. Zonaras, l. xii. p. 637. Two passages in the life of Probus (p. 236, 238) convince me, that these Scythian invaders of Pontus were Alani. If we may believe Zosimus, (l. i. p. 58,) Florianus pursued them as far as the Cimmerian Bosphorus. But he had scarcely time for so long and difficult an expedition.]

But the glory and life of Tacitus were of short duration. Transported, in the depth of winter, from the soft retirement of Campania to the foot of Mount Caucasus, he sunk under the unaccustomed hardships of a military life. The fatigues of the body were aggravated by the cares of the mind. For a while, the angry and selfish passions of the soldiers had been suspended by the enthusiasm of public virtue. They soon broke out with redoubled violence, and raged in the camp, and even in the tent of the aged emperor. His mild and amiable character served only to inspire contempt, and he was incessantly tormented with factions which he could not assuage, and by demands which it was impossible to satisfy. Whatever flattering expectations he had conceived of reconciling the public disorders, Tacitus soon was convinced that the licentiousness of the army disdained the feeble restraint of laws, and his last hour was hastened by anguish and disappointment. It may be doubtful whether the soldiers imbrued their hands in the blood of this innocent prince. [18] It is certain that their insolences was the cause of his death. He expired at Tyana in Cappadocia, after a reign of only six months and about twenty days. [19]

[Footnote 18: Eutropius and Aurelius Victor only say that he died; Victor Junior adds, that it was of a fever. Zosimus and Zonaras affirm, that he was killed by the soldiers. Vopiscus mentions both accounts, and seems to hesitate. Yet surely these jarring opinions are easily reconciled.]

[Footnote 19: According to the two Victors, he reigned exactly two hundred days.]

The eyes of Tacitus were scarcely closed, before his brother Florianus showed himself unworthy to reign, by the hasty usurpation of the purple, without expecting the approbation of the senate. The reverence for the Roman constitution, which yet influenced the camp and the provinces, was sufficiently strong to dispose them to censure, but not to provoke them to oppose, the precipitate ambition of Florianus. The discontent would have evaporated in idle murmurs, had not the general of the East, the heroic Probus, boldly declared himself the avenger of the senate.

The contest, however, was still unequal; nor could the most able leader, at the head of the effeminate troops of Egypt and Syria, encounter, with any hopes of victory, the legions of Europe, whose irresistible strength appeared to support the brother of Tacitus. But the fortune and activity of Probus triumphed over every obstacle. The hardy veterans of his rival, accustomed to cold climates, sickened and consumed away in the sultry heats of Cilicia, where the summer proved remarkably unwholesome. Their numbers were diminished by frequent desertion; the passes of the mountains were feebly defended; Tarsus opened its gates; and the soldiers of Florianus, when they had permitted him to enjoy the Imperial title about three months, delivered the empire from civil war by the easy sacrifice of a prince whom they despised. [20]

[Footnote 20: Hist. August, p. 231. Zosimus, l. i. p. 58, 59. Zonaras, l. xii. p. 637. Aurelius Victor says, that Probus assumed the empire in Illyricum; an opinion which (though adopted by a very learned man) would throw that period of history into inextricable confusion.]

The perpetual revolutions of the throne had so perfectly erased every notion of hereditary title, that the family of an unfortunate emperor was incapable of exciting the jealousy of his successors. The children of Tacitus and Florianus were permitted to descend into a private station, and to mingle with the general mass of the people. Their poverty indeed became an additional safeguard to their innocence. When Tacitus was elected by the senate, he resigned his ample patrimony to the public service; [21] an act of generosity specious in appearance, but which evidently disclosed his intention of transmitting the empire to his descendants. The only consolation of their fallen state was the remembrance of transient greatness, and a distant hope, the child of a flattering prophecy, that at the end of a thousand years, a monarch of the race of Tacitus should arise, the protector of the senate, the restorer of Rome, and the conqueror of the whole earth. [22]

[Footnote 21: Hist. August. p. 229]

[Footnote 22: He was to send judges to the Parthians, Persians, and Sarmatians, a president to Taprobani, and a proconsul to the Roman island, (supposed by Casaubon and Salmasius to mean Britain.) Such a history as mine (says Vopiscus with proper modesty) will not subsist a thousand years, to expose or justify the prediction.]

The peasants of Illyricum, who had already given Claudius and Aurelian to the sinking empire, had an equal right to glory in the elevation of Probus. [23] Above twenty years before, the emperor Valerian, with his usual penetration, had discovered the rising merit of the young soldier, on whom he conferred the rank of tribune, long before the age prescribed by the military regulations. The tribune soon justified his choice, by a victory over a great body of Sarmatians, in which he saved the life of a near relation of Valerian; and deserved to receive from the emperor's hand the collars, bracelets, spears, and banners, the mural and the civic crown, and all the honorable rewards reserved by ancient Rome for successful valor. The third, and afterwards the tenth, legion were intrusted to the command of Probus, who, in every step of his promotion, showed himself superior to the station which he filled. Africa and Pontus, the Rhine, the Danube, the Euphrates, and the Nile, by turns afforded him the most splendid occasions of displaying his personal prowess and his conduct in war. Aurelian was indebted for the honest courage with which he often checked the cruelty of his master. Tacitus, who desired by the abilities of his generals to supply his own deficiency of military talents, named him commander-in-chief of all the eastern provinces, with five times the usual salary, the promise of the consulship, and the hope of a triumph. When Probus ascended the Imperial throne, he was about forty-four years of age; [24] in the full possession of his fame, of the love of the army, and of a mature vigor of mind and body.

[Footnote 23: For the private life of Probus, see Vopiscus in Hist. August p. 234—237]

[Footnote 24: According to the Alexandrian chronicle, he was fifty at the time of his death.]

His acknowledge merit, and the success of his arms against Florianus, left him without an enemy or a competitor. Yet, if we may credit his own professions, very far from being desirous of the empire, he had accepted it with the most sincere reluctance. "But it is no longer in my power," says Probus, in a private letter, "to lay down a title so full of envy and of danger. I must continue to personate the character which the soldiers have imposed upon me." [25] His dutiful address to the senate displayed the sentiments, or at least the language, of a Roman patriot: "When you elected one of your order, conscript fathers! to succeed the emperor Aurelian, you acted in a manner suitable to your justice and wisdom. For you are the legal sovereigns of the world, and the power which you derive from your ancestors will descend to your posterity. Happy would it have been, if Florianus, instead of usurping the purple of his brother, like a private inheritance, had expected what your majesty might determine, either in his favor, or in that of other person. The prudent soldiers have punished his rashness. To me they have offered the title of Augustus. But I submit to your clemency my pretensions and my merits." [26] When this respectful epistle was read by the consul, the senators were unable to disguise their satisfaction, that Probus should condescend thus numbly to solicit a sceptre which he already possessed. They celebrated with the warmest gratitude his virtues, his exploits, and above all his moderation. A decree immediately passed, without a dissenting voice, to ratify the election of the eastern armies, and to confer on their chief all the several branches of the Imperial dignity: the names of Caesar and Augustus, the title of Father of his country, the right of making in the same day three motions in the senate, [27] the office of Pontifex, Maximus, the tribunitian power, and the proconsular command; a mode of investiture, which, though it seemed to multiply the authority of the emperor, expressed the constitution of the ancient republic. The reign of Probus corresponded with this fair beginning. The senate was permitted to direct the civil administration of the empire. Their faithful general asserted the honor of the Roman arms, and often laid at their feet crowns of gold and barbaric trophies, the fruits of his numerous victories. [28] Yet, whilst he gratified their vanity, he must secretly have despised their indolence and weakness. Though it was every moment in their power to repeal the disgraceful edict of Gallienus, the proud successors of the Scipios patiently acquiesced in their exclusion from all military employments. They soon experienced, that those who refuse the sword must renounce the sceptre.

[Footnote 25: This letter was addressed to the Praetorian praefect, whom (on condition of his good behavior) he promised to continue in his great office. See Hist. August. p. 237.]

[Footnote 26: Vopiscus in Hist. August. p. 237. The date of the letter is assuredly faulty. Instead of Nen. Februar. we may read Non August.]

[Footnote 27: Hist. August. p. 238. It is odd that the senate should treat Probus less favorably than Marcus Antoninus. That prince had received, even before the death of Pius, Jus quintoe relationis. See Capitolin. in Hist. August. p. 24.]

[Footnote 28: See the dutiful letter of Probus to the senate, after his German victories. Hist. August. p. 239.]

PART II

The strength of Aurelian had crushed on every side the enemies of Rome. After his death they seemed to revive with an increase of fury and of numbers. They were again vanquished by the active vigor of Probus, who, in a short reign of about six years, [29] equalled the fame of ancient heroes, and restored peace and order to every province of the Roman world. The dangerous frontier of Rhaetia he so firmly secured, that he left it without the suspicion of an enemy. He broke the wandering power of the Sarmatian tribes, and by the terror of his arms compelled those barbarians to relinquish their spoil. The Gothic nation courted the alliance of so warlike an emperor. [30] He attacked the Isaurians in their mountains, besieged and took several of their strongest castles, [31] and flattered himself that he had forever suppressed a domestic foe, whose independence so deeply wounded the majesty of the empire. The troubles excited by the usurper Firmus in the Upper Egypt had never been perfectly appeased, and the cities of Ptolemais and Coptos, fortified by the alliance of the Blemmyes, still maintained an obscure rebellion. The chastisement of those cities, and of their auxiliaries the savages of the South, is said to have alarmed the court of Persia, [32] and the Great King sued in vain for the friendship of Probus. Most of the exploits which distinguished his reign were achieved by the personal valor and conduct of the emperor, insomuch that the writer of his life expresses some amazement how, in so short a time, a single man could be present in so many distant wars. The remaining actions he intrusted to the care of his lieutenants, the judicious choice of whom forms no inconsiderable part of his glory. Carus, Diocletian, Maximian, Constantius, Galerius, Asclepiodatus, Annibalianus, and a crowd of other chiefs, who afterwards ascended or supported the throne, were trained to arms in the severe school of Aurelian and Probus. [33]

[Footnote 29: The date and duration of the reign of Probus are very correctly ascertained by Cardinal Noris in his learned work, De Epochis Syro-Macedonum, p. 96—105. A passage of Eusebius connects the second year of Probus with the aeras of several of the Syrian cities.]

[Footnote 30: Vopiscus in Hist. August. p. 239.]

[Footnote 31: Zosimus (l. i. p. 62—65) tells us a very long and trifling story of Lycius, the Isaurian robber.]

[Footnote 32: Zosim. l. i. p. 65. Vopiscus in Hist. August. p. 239, 240. But it seems incredible that the defeat of the savages of Aethiopia could affect the Persian monarch.]

[Footnote 33: Besides these well-known chiefs, several others are named by Vopiscus, (Hist. August. p. 241,) whose actions have not reached knowledge.]

But the most important service which Probus rendered to the republic was the deliverance of Gaul, and the recovery of seventy flourishing cities oppressed by the barbarians of Germany, who, since the death of Aurelian, had ravaged that great province with impunity. [34] Among the various multitude of those fierce invaders we may distinguish, with some degree of clearness, three great armies, or rather nations, successively vanquished by the valor of Probus. He drove back the Franks into their morasses; a descriptive circumstance from whence we may infer, that the confederacy known by the manly appellation of Free, already occupied the flat maritime country, intersected and almost overflown by the stagnating waters of the Rhine, and that several tribes of the Frisians and Batavians had acceded to their alliance. He vanquished the Burgundians, a considerable people of the Vandalic race. [34/1] They had wandered in quest of booty from the banks of the Oder to those of the Seine. They esteemed themselves sufficiently fortunate to purchase, by the restitution of all their booty, the permission of an undisturbed retreat. They attempted to elude that article of the treaty. Their punishment was immediate and terrible. [35] But of all the invaders of Gaul, the most formidable were the Lygians, a distant people, who reigned over a wide domain on the frontiers of Poland and Silesia. [36] In the Lygian nation, the Arii held the first rank by their numbers and fierceness. "The Arii" (it is thus that they are described by the energy of Tacitus) "study to improve by art and circumstances the innate terrors of their barbarism. Their shields are black, their bodies are painted black. They choose for the combat the darkest hour of the night. Their host advances, covered as it were with a funeral shade; [37] nor do they often find an enemy capable of sustaining so strange and infernal an aspect. Of all our senses, the eyes are the first vanquished in battle." [38] Yet the arms and discipline of the Romans easily discomfited these horrid phantoms. The Lygii were defeated in a general engagement, and Semno, the most renowned of their chiefs, fell alive into the hands of Probus. That prudent emperor, unwilling to reduce a brave people to despair, granted them an honorable capitulation, and permitted them to return in safety to their native country. But the losses which they suffered in the march, the battle, and the retreat, broke the power of the nation: nor is the Lygian name ever repeated in the history either of Germany or of the empire. The deliverance of Gaul is reported to have cost the lives of four hundred thousand of the invaders; a work of labor to the Romans, and of expense to the emperor, who gave a piece of gold for the head of every barbarian. [39] But as the fame of warriors is built on the destruction of human kind, we may naturally suspect, that the sanguinary account was multiplied by the avarice of the soldiers, and accepted without any very severe examination by the liberal vanity of Probus.

[Footnote 34: See the Caesars of Julian, and Hist. August. p. 238, 240, 241.]

[Footnote 34/1: It was only under the emperors Diocletian and Maximian, that the Burgundians, in concert with the Alemanni, invaded the interior of Gaul; under the reign of Probus, they did no more than pass the river which separated them from the Roman Empire: they were repelled. Gatterer presumes that this river was the Danube; a passage in Zosimus appears to me rather to indicate the Rhine. Zos. l. i. p. 37, edit H. Etienne, 1581.—G. On the origin of the Burgundians may be consulted Malte Brun, Geogr vi. p. 396, (edit. 1831,) who observes that all the remains of the Burgundian language indicate that they spoke a Gothic dialect.—M.]

[Footnote 35: Zosimus, l. i. p. 62. Hist. August. p. 240. But the latter supposes the punishment inflicted with the consent of their kings: if so, it was partial, like the offence.]

[Footnote 36: See Cluver. Germania Antiqua, l. iii. Ptolemy places in their country the city of Calisia, probably Calish in Silesia. Note: Luden (vol ii. 501) supposes that these have been erroneously identified with the Lygii of Tacitus. Perhaps one fertile source of mistakes has been, that the Romans have turned appellations into national names. Malte Brun observes of the Lygii, "that their name appears Sclavonian, and signifies 'inhabitants of plains;' they are probably the Lieches of the middle ages, and the ancestors of the Poles. We find among the Arii the worship of the two twin gods known in the Sclavian mythology." Malte Brun, vol. i. p. 278, (edit. 1831.)—M. But compare Schafarik, Slawische Alterthumer, 1, p. 406. They were of German or Keltish descent, occupying the Wendish (or Slavian) district, Luhy.—M. 1845.]

[Footnote 37: Feralis umbra, is the expression of Tacitus: it is surely a very bold one.]

[Footnote 38: Tacit. Germania, (c. 43.)]

[Footnote 39: Vopiscus in Hist. August. p. 238]

Since the expedition of Maximin, the Roman generals had confined their ambition to a defensive war against the nations of Germany, who perpetually pressed on the frontiers of the empire. The more daring Probus pursued his Gallic victories, passed the Rhine, and displayed his invincible eagles on the banks of the Elbe and the Necker. He was fully convinced that nothing could reconcile the minds of the barbarians to peace, unless they experienced, in their own country, the calamities of war. Germany, exhausted by the ill success of the last emigration, was astonished by his presence. Nine of the most considerable princes repaired to his camp, and fell prostrate at his feet. Such a treaty was humbly received by the Germans, as it pleased the conqueror to dictate. He exacted a strict restitution of the effects and captives which they had carried away from the provinces; and obliged their own magistrates to punish the more obstinate robbers who presumed to detain any part of the spoil. A considerable tribute of corn, cattle, and horses, the only wealth of barbarians, was reserved for the use of the garrisons which Probus established on the limits of their territory. He even entertained some thoughts of compelling the Germans to relinquish the exercise of arms, and to trust their differences to the justice, their safety to the power, of Rome. To accomplish these salutary ends, the constant residence of an Imperial governor, supported by a numerous army, was indispensably requisite. Probus therefore judged it more expedient to defer the execution of so great a design; which was indeed rather of specious than solid utility. [40] Had Germany been reduced into the state of a province, the Romans, with immense labor and expense, would have acquired only a more extensive boundary to defend against the fiercer and more active barbarians of Scythia.

[Footnote 40: *Hist. August. 238, 239. Vopiscus quotes a letter from the emperor to the senate, in which he mentions his design of reducing Germany into a province.*]

Instead of reducing the warlike natives of Germany to the condition of subjects, Probus contented himself with the humble expedient of raising a bulwark against their inroads. The country which now forms the circle of Swabia had been left desert in the age of Augustus by the emigration of its ancient inhabitants. [41] The fertility of the soil soon attracted a new colony from the adjacent provinces of Gaul. Crowds of adventurers, of a roving temper and of desperate fortunes, occupied the doubtful possession, and acknowledged, by the payment of tithes the majesty of the empire. [42] To protect these new subjects, a line of frontier garrisons was gradually extended from the Rhine to the Danube. About the reign of Hadrian, when that mode of defence began to be practised, these garrisons were connected and covered by a strong intrenchment of trees and palisades. In the place of so rude a bulwark, the emperor Probus constructed a stone wall of a considerable height, and strengthened it by towers at convenient distances. From the neighborhood of Newstadt and Ratisbon on the Danube, it stretched across hills, valleys, rivers, and morasses, as far as Wimpfen on the Necker, and at length terminated on the banks of the Rhine, after a winding course of near two hundred miles. [43] This important barrier, uniting the two mighty streams that protected the provinces of Europe, seemed to fill up the vacant space through which the barbarians, and particularly the Alemanni, could penetrate with the greatest facility into the heart of the empire. But the experience of the world, from China to Britain, has exposed the vain attempt of fortifying any extensive tract of country. [44] An active enemy, who can select and vary his points of attack, must, in the end, discover some feeble spot, on some unguarded moment. The strength, as well as the attention, of the defenders is divided; and such are the blind effects of terror on the firmest troops, that a line broken in a single place is almost instantly deserted. The fate of the wall which Probus erected may confirm the general observation. Within a few years after his death, it was overthrown by the Alemanni. Its scattered ruins, universally ascribed to the power of the Daemon, now serve only to excite the wonder of the Swabian peasant.

[Footnote 41: *Strabo, l. vii. According to Valleius Paterculus, (ii. 108,) Maroboduus led his Marcomanni into Bohemia; Cluverius (German. Antiq. iii. 8) proves that it was from Swabia.*]

[Footnote 42: These settlers, from the payment of tithes, were denominated Decunates. Tacit. Germania, c. 29]

[Footnote 43: See notes de l'Abbe de la Bleterie a la Germanie de Tacite, p. 183. His account of the wall is chiefly borrowed (as he says himself) from the Alsatia Illustrata of Schoepflin.]

[Footnote 44: See Recherches sur les Chinois et les Egyptiens, tom. ii. p. 81—102. The anonymous author is well acquainted with the globe in general, and with Germany in particular: with regard to the latter, he quotes a work of M. Hanselman; but he seems to confound the wall of Probus, designed against the Alemanni, with the fortification of the Mattiaci, constructed in the neighborhood of Frankfort against the Catti. Note: De Pauw is well known to have been the author of this work, as of the Recherches sur les Americains before quoted. The judgment of M. Remusat on this writer is in a very different, I fear a juster tone. Quand au lieu de rechercher, d'examiner, d'etudier, on se borne, comme cet ecrivain, a juger a prononcer, a decider, sans connoitre ni l'histoire. ni les langues, sans recourir aux sources, sans meme se douter de leur existence, on peut en imposer pendant quelque temps a des lecteurs prevenus ou peu instruits; mais le mepris qui ne manque guere de succeder a cet engouement fait bientot justice de ces assertions hazardees, et elles retombent dans l'oubli d'autant plus promptement, qu'elles ont ete posees avec plus de confiance. Sur les l angues Tartares, p. 231.—M.]

Among the useful conditions of peace imposed by Probus on the vanquished nations of Germany, was the obligation of supplying the Roman army with sixteen thousand recruits, the bravest and most robust of their youth. The emperor dispersed them through all the provinces, and distributed this dangerous reenforcement, in small bands of fifty or sixty each, among the national troops; judiciously observing, that the aid which the republic derived from the barbarians should be felt but not seen. [45] Their aid was now become necessary. The feeble elegance of Italy and the internal provinces could no longer support the weight of arms. The hardy frontiers of the Rhine and Danube still produced minds and bodies equal to the labors of the camp; but a perpetual series of wars had gradually diminished their numbers. The infrequency of marriage, and the ruin of agriculture, affected the principles of population, and not only destroyed the strength of the present, but intercepted the hope of future, generations. The wisdom of Probus embraced a great and beneficial plan of replenishing the exhausted frontiers, by new colonies of captive or fugitive barbarians, on whom he bestowed lands, cattle, instruments of husbandry, and every encouragement that might engage them to educate a race of soldiers for the service of the republic. Into Britain, and most probably into Cambridgeshire, [46] he transported a considerable body of Vandals. The impossibility of an escape reconciled them to their situation, and in the subsequent troubles of that island, they approved themselves the most faithful servants of the state. [47] Great numbers of Franks and Gepidae were settled on the banks of the Danube and the Rhine. A hundred thousand Bastarnae, expelled from their own country, cheerfully accepted an establishment in Thrace, and soon imbibed the manners and sentiments of Roman subjects. [48] But the expectations of Probus were too often disappointed. The impatience and idleness of the barbarians could ill brook the slow labors of agriculture. Their unconquerable love of freedom, rising against despotism, provoked them into hasty rebellions, alike fatal to themselves and to the provinces; [49] nor could these artificial supplies, however repeated by succeeding emperors, restore the important limit of Gaul and Illyricum to its ancient and native vigor.

[Footnote 45: He distributed about fifty or sixty barbarians to a Numerus, as it was then called, a corps with whose established number we are not exactly acquainted.]

[Footnote 46: Camden's Britannia, Introduction, p. 136; but he speaks from a very doubtful conjecture.]

[Footnote 47: Zosimus, l. i. p. 62. According to Vopiscus, another body of Vandals was less faithful.]

[Footnote 48: Hist. August. p. 240. They were probably expelled by the Goths. Zosim. l. i. p. 66.]

[Footnote 49: Hist. August. p. 240.]

Of all the barbarians who abandoned their new settlements, and disturbed the public tranquillity, a very small number returned to their own country. For a short season they might wander in arms through the empire; but in the end they were surely destroyed by the power of a warlike emperor. The successful rashness of a party of Franks was attended, however, with such memorable consequences, that it ought not to be passed unnoticed. They had been established by Probus, on the sea-coast of Pontus, with a view of strengthening the frontier against the inroads of the Alani. A fleet stationed in one of the harbors of the Euxine fell into the hands of the Franks; and they resolved, through unknown seas, to explore their way from the mouth of the Phasis to that of the Rhine. They easily escaped through the Bosphorus and the Hellespont, and cruising along the Mediterranean, indulged their appetite for revenge and plunder by frequent descents on the unsuspecting shores of Asia, Greece, and Africa. The opulent city of Syracuse, in whose port the natives of Athens and Carthage had formerly been sunk, was sacked by a handful of barbarians, who massacred the greatest part of the trembling inhabitants. From the Island of Sicily, the Franks proceeded to the columns of Hercules, trusted themselves to the ocean, coasted round Spain and Gaul, and steering their triumphant course through the British Channel, at length finished their surprising voyage, by landing in safety on the Batavian or Frisian shores. [50] The example of their success, instructing their countrymen to conceive the advantages and to despise the dangers of the sea, pointed out to their enterprising spirit a new road to wealth and glory.

[Footnote 50: Panegyr. Vet. v. 18. Zosimus, l. i. p. 66.]

Notwithstanding the vigilance and activity of Probus, it was almost impossible that he could at once contain in obedience every part of his wide-extended dominions. The barbarians, who broke their chains, had seized the favorable opportunity of a domestic war. When the emperor marched to the relief of Gaul, he devolved the command of the East on Saturninus. That general, a man of merit and experience, was driven into rebellion by the absence of his sovereign, the levity of the Alexandrian people, the pressing instances of his friends, and his own fears; but from the moment of his elevation, he never entertained a hope of empire, or even of life. "Alas!" he said, "the republic has lost a useful servant, and the rashness of an hour has destroyed the services of many years. You know not," continued he, "the misery of sovereign power; a sword is perpetually suspended over our head. We dread our very guards, we distrust our companions. The choice of action or of repose is no longer in our disposition, nor is there any age, or character, or conduct, that can protect us from the censure of envy. In thus exalting me to the throne, you have doomed me to a life of cares, and to an untimely fate. The only consolation which remains is, the assurance that I shall not fall alone." [51] But as the former part of his prediction was verified by the victory, so the latter was disappointed by the clemency of Probus. That amiable prince attempted even to save the unhappy Saturninus from the fury of the soldiers. He had more than once solicited the usurper himself to place some confidence in the mercy of a sovereign who so highly esteemed his character, that he had punished, as a malicious informer, the first who related the improbable news of his disaffection. [52] Saturninus might, perhaps, have embraced the generous offer, had he not been restrained by the obstinate distrust of his adherents. Their guilt was deeper, and their hopes more sanguine, than those of their experienced leader.

[Footnote 51: Vopiscus in Hist. August. p. 245, 246. The unfortunate orator had studied rhetoric at Carthage; and was therefore more probably a Moor (Zosim. l. i. p. 60) than a Gaul, as Vopiscus calls him.]

[Footnote 52: Zonaras, l. xii. p. 638.]

The revolt of Saturninus was scarcely extinguished in the East, before new troubles were excited in the West, by the rebellion of Bonosus and Proculus, in Gaul. The most distinguished merit of those two officers was their respective prowess, of the one in the combats of Bacchus, of the other in those of Venus, [53] yet neither of them was destitute of courage and capacity, and both sustained, with honor, the august character which the fear of punishment had engaged them to assume, till they sunk at length beneath the superior genius of Probus. He used the victory with his accustomed moderation, and spared the fortune, as well as the lives of their innocent families. [54]

[Footnote 53: A very surprising instance is recorded of the prowess of Procufus. He had taken one hundred Sarmatian virgins. The rest of the story he must relate in his own language: "Ex his una necte decem inivi; omnes tamen, quod in me erat, mulieres intra dies quindecim reddidi." Vopiscus in Hist. August. p. 246.]

[Footnote 54: Proculus, who was a native of Albengue, on the Genoese coast armed two thousand of his own slaves. His riches were great, but they were acquired by robbery. It was afterwards a saying of his family, sibi non placere esse vel principes vel latrones. Vopiscus in Hist. August. p. 247.]

The arms of Probus had now suppressed all the foreign and domestic enemies of the state. His mild but steady administration confirmed the reestablishment of the public tranquillity; nor was there left in the provinces a hostile barbarian, a tyrant, or even a robber, to revive the memory of past disorders. It was time that the emperor should revisit Rome, and celebrate his own glory and the general happiness. The triumph due to the valor of Probus was conducted with a magnificence suitable to his fortune, and the people who had so lately admired the trophies of Aurelian, gazed with equal pleasure on those of his heroic successor. [55] We cannot, on this occasion, forget the desperate courage of about fourscore gladiators, reserved, with near six hundred others, for the inhuman sports of the amphitheatre. Disdaining to shed their blood for the amusement of the populace, they killed their keepers, broke from the place of their confinement, and filled the streets of Rome with blood and confusion. After an obstinate resistance, they were overpowered and cut in pieces by the regular forces; but they obtained at least an honorable death, and the satisfaction of a just revenge. [56]

[Footnote 55: Hist. August. p. 240.]

[Footnote 56: Zosim. l. i. p. 66.]

The military discipline which reigned in the camps of Probus was less cruel than that of Aurelian, but it was equally rigid and exact. The latter had punished the irregularities of the soldiers with unrelenting severity, the former prevented them by employing the legions in constant and useful labors. When Probus commanded in Egypt, he executed many considerable works for the splendor and benefit of that rich country. The navigation of the Nile, so important to Rome itself, was improved; and temples, buildings, porticos, and palaces were constructed by the hands of the soldiers, who acted by turns as architects, as engineers, and as husbandmen. [57] It was reported of Hannibal, that in order to preserve his troops from the dangerous temptations of idleness, he had obliged them to form large plantations of olive-trees along the coast of Africa. [58] From a similar principle, Probus exercised his legions in covering with rich vineyards the hills of Gaul and Pannonia, and two considerable spots are described, which were entirely dug and planted by military labor. [59] One of these, known under the name of Mount Almo, was situated near Sirmium, the country where Probus was born, for which he ever retained a partial affection, and whose gratitude he endeavored to secure, by converting into tillage a large and unhealthy tract of marshy ground. An army thus employed constituted perhaps the most useful, as well as the bravest, portion of Roman subjects.

[Footnote 57: Hist. August. p. 236.]

[Footnote 58: Aurel. Victor. in Prob. But the policy of Hannibal, unnoticed by any more ancient writer, is irreconcilable with the history of his life. He left Africa when he was nine years old, returned to it when he was forty-five, and immediately lost his army in the decisive battle of Zama. Livilus, xxx. 37.]

[Footnote 59: Hist. August. p. 240. Eutrop. ix. 17. Aurel. Victor. in Prob. Victor Junior. He revoked the prohibition of Domitian, and granted a general permission of planting vines to the Gauls, the Britons, and the Pannonians.]

But in the prosecution of a favorite scheme, the best of men, satisfied with the rectitude of their intentions, are subject to forget the bounds of moderation; nor did Probus himself sufficiently consult the patience and disposition of his fierce legionaries. [60] The dangers of the military profession seem only to be compensated by a life of pleasure and idleness; but if the duties of the soldier are incessantly aggravated by the labors of the peasant, he will at last sink under the intolerable burden, or shake it off with indignation. The imprudence of Probus is said to have inflamed the discontent of his troops. More attentive to the interests of mankind than to those of the army, he expressed the vain hope, that, by the establishment of universal peace, he should soon abolish the necessity of a standing and mercenary force. [61] The unguarded expression proved fatal to him. In one of the hottest days of summer, as he severely urged the unwholesome labor of draining the marshes of Sirmium, the soldiers, impatient of fatigue, on a sudden threw down their tools, grasped their arms, and broke out into a furious mutiny. The emperor, conscious of his danger, took refuge in a lofty tower, constructed for the purpose of surveying the progress of the work. [62] The tower was instantly forced, and a thousand swords were plunged at once into the bosom of the unfortunate Probus. The rage of the troops subsided as soon as it had been gratified. They then lamented their fatal rashness, forgot the severity of the emperor, whom they had massacred, and hastened to perpetuate, by an honorable monument, the memory of his virtues and victories. [63]

[Footnote 60: Julian bestows a severe, and indeed excessive, censure on the rigor of Probus, who, as he thinks, almost deserved his fate.]

[Footnote 61: Vopiscus in Hist. August. p. 241. He lavishes on this idle hope a large stock of very foolish eloquence.]

[Footnote 62: Turris ferrata. It seems to have been a movable tower, and cased with iron.]

[Footnote 63: Probus, et vere probus situs est; Victor omnium gentium Barbararum; victor etiam tyrannorum.]

When the legions had indulged their grief and repentance for the death of Probus, their unanimous consent declared Carus, his Praetorian praefect, the most deserving of the Imperial throne. Every circumstance that relates to this prince appears of a mixed and doubtful nature. He gloried in the title of Roman Citizen; and affected to compare the purity of his blood with the foreign and even barbarous origin of the preceding emperors; yet the most inquisitive of his contemporaries, very far from admitting his claim, have variously deduced his own birth, or that of his parents, from Illyricum, from Gaul, or from Africa. [64] Though a soldier, he had received a learned education; though a senator, he was invested with the first dignity of the army; and in an age when the civil and military professions began to be irrecoverably separated from each other, they were united in the person of Carus. Notwithstanding the severe justice which he exercised against the assassins of Probus, to whose favor and esteem he was highly indebted, he could not escape the suspicion of being accessory to a deed from whence he derived the principal advantage. He enjoyed, at least, before his elevation, an acknowledged character of virtue and abilities; [65] but his austere temper insensibly degenerated into moroseness and cruelty; and the imperfect writers of his life almost hesitate whether they shall not rank him in the number of Roman tyrants. [66] When Carus assumed the purple, he was about sixty years of age, and his two sons, Carinus and Numerian had already attained the season of manhood. [67]

[Footnote 64: Yet all this may be conciliated. He was born at Narbonne in Illyricum, confounded by Eutropius with the more famous city of that name in Gaul. His father might be an African, and his mother a noble Roman. Carus himself was educated in the capital. See Scaliger Animadversion. ad Euseb. Chron. p. 241.]

[Footnote 65: Probus had requested of the senate an equestrian statue and a marble palace, at the public expense, as a just recompense of the singular merit of Carus. Vopiscus in Hist. August. p. 249.]

[Footnote 66: Vopiscus in Hist. August. p. 242, 249. Julian excludes the emperor Carus and both his sons from the banquet of the Caesars.]

[Footnote 67: John Malala, tom. i. p. 401. But the authority of that ignorant Greek is very slight. He ridiculously derives from Carus the city of Carrhae, and the province of Caria, the latter of which is mentioned by Homer.]

The authority of the senate expired with Probus; nor was the repentance of the soldiers displayed by the same dutiful regard for the civil power, which they had testified after the unfortunate death of Aurelian. The election of Carus was decided without expecting the approbation of the senate, and the new emperor contented himself with announcing, in a cold and stately epistle, that he had ascended the vacant throne. [68] A behavior so very opposite to that of his amiable predecessor afforded no favorable presage of the new reign: and the Romans, deprived of power and freedom, asserted their privilege of licentious murmurs. [69] The voice of congratulation and flattery was not, however, silent; and we may still peruse, with pleasure and contempt, an eclogue, which was composed on the accession of the emperor Carus. Two shepherds, avoiding the noontide heat, retire into the cave of Faunus. On a spreading beech they discover some recent characters. The rural deity had described, in prophetic verses, the felicity promised to the empire under the reign of so great a prince. Faunus hails the approach of that hero, who, receiving on his shoulders the sinking weight of the Roman world, shall extinguish war and faction, and once again restore the innocence and security of the golden age. [70]

[Footnote 68: Hist. August. p. 249. Carus congratulated the senate, that one of their own order was made emperor.]

[Footnote 69: Hist. August. p. 242.]

[Footnote 70: See the first eclogue of Calphurnius. The design of it is preferes by Fontenelle to that of Virgil's Pollio. See tom. iii. p. 148.]

It is more than probable, that these elegant trifles never reached the ears of a veteran general, who, with the consent of the legions, was preparing to execute the long-suspended design of the Persian war. Before his departure for this distant expedition, Carus conferred on his two sons, Carinus and Numerian, the title of Caesar, and investing the former with almost an equal share of the Imperial power, directed the young prince, first to suppress some troubles which had arisen in Gaul, and afterwards to fix the seat of his residence at Rome, and to assume the government of the Western provinces. [71] The safety of Illyricum was confirmed by a memorable defeat of the Sarmatians; sixteen thousand of those barbarians remained on the field of battle, and the number of captives amounted to twenty thousand. The old emperor, animated with the fame and prospect of victory, pursued his march, in the midst of winter, through the countries of Thrace and Asia Minor, and at length, with his younger son, Numerian, arrived on the confines of the Persian monarchy. There, encamping on the summit of a lofty mountain, he pointed out to his troops the opulence and luxury of the enemy whom they were about to invade.

[Footnote 71: Hist. August. p. 353. Eutropius, ix. 18. Pagi. Annal.]

The successor of Artaxerxes, [71/1] Varanes, or Bahram, though he had subdued the Segestans, one of the most warlike nations of Upper Asia, [72] was alarmed at the approach of the Romans, and endeavored to retard their progress by a negotiation of peace. [72/1]

His ambassadors entered the camp about sunset, at the time when the troops were satisfying their hunger with a frugal repast. The Persians expressed their desire of being introduced to the presence of the Roman emperor. They were at length conducted to a soldier, who was seated on the grass. A piece of stale bacon and a few hard peas composed his supper. A coarse woollen garment of purple was the only circumstance that announced his dignity. The conference was conducted with the same disregard of courtly elegance. Carus, taking off a cap which he wore to conceal his baldness, assured the ambassadors, that, unless their master acknowledged the superiority of Rome, he would speedily render Persia as naked of trees as his own head was destitute of hair. [73] Notwithstanding some traces of art and preparation, we may discover in this scene the manners of Carus, and the severe simplicity which the martial princes, who succeeded Gallienus, had already restored in the Roman camps. The ministers of the Great King trembled and retired.

[Footnote 71/1: Three monarchs had intervened, Sapor, (Shahpour,) Hormisdas, (Hormooz,) Varanes; Baharam the First.—M.]

[Footnote 72: Agathias, l. iv. p. 135. We find one of his sayings in the Bibliotheque Orientale of M. d'Herbelot. "The definition of humanity includes all other virtues."]

[Footnote 72/1: The manner in which his life was saved by the Chief Pontiff from a conspiracy of his nobles, is as remarkable as his saying. "By the advice (of the Pontiff) all the nobles absented themselves from court. The king wandered through his palace alone. He saw no one; all was silence around. He became alarmed and distressed. At last the Chief Pontiff appeared, and bowed his head in apparent misery, but spoke not a word. The king entreated him to declare what had happened. The virtuous man boldly related all that had passed, and conjured Bahram, in the name of his glorious ancestors, to change his conduct and save himself from destruction. The king was much moved, professed himself most penitent, and said he was resolved his future life should prove his sincerity. The overjoyed High Priest, delighted at this success, made a signal, at which all the nobles and attendants were in an instant, as if by magic, in their usual places. The monarch now perceived that only one opinion prevailed on his past conduct. He repeated therefore to his nobles all he had said to the Chief Pontiff, and his future reign was unstained by cruelty or oppression." Malcolm's Persia,—M.]

[Footnote 73: Synesius tells this story of Carinus; and it is much more natural to understand it of Carus, than (as Petavius and Tillemont choose to do) of Probus.]

The threats of Carus were not without effect. He ravaged Mesopotamia, cut in pieces whatever opposed his passage, made himself master of the great cities of Seleucia and Ctesiphon, (which seemed to have surrendered without resistance,) and carried his victorious arms beyond the Tigris. [74] He had seized the favorable moment for an invasion. The Persian councils were distracted by domestic factions, and the greater part of their forces were detained on the frontiers of India. Rome and the East received with transports the news of such important advantages. Flattery and hope painted, in the most lively colors, the fall of Persia, the conquest of Arabia, the submission of Egypt, and a lasting deliverance from the inroads of the Scythian nations. [75] But the reign of Carus was destined to expose the vanity of predictions. They were scarcely uttered before they were contradicted by his death; an event attended with such ambiguous circumstances, that it may be related in a letter from his own secretary to the praefect of the city. "Carus," says he, "our dearest emperor, was confined by sickness to his bed, when a furious tempest arose in the camp. The darkness which overspread the sky was so thick, that we could no longer distinguish each other; and the incessant flashes of lightning took from us the knowledge of all that passed in the general confusion. Immediately after the most violent clap of thunder, we heard a sudden cry that the emperor was dead; and it soon appeared, that his chamberlains, in a rage of grief, had set fire to the royal pavilion; a circumstance which gave rise to the report that Carus was killed by lightning. But, as far as we have been able to investigate the truth, his death was the natural effect of his disorder." [76]

[Footnote 74: Vopiscus in Hist. August. p. 250. Eutropius, ix. 18. The two Victors.]

[Footnote 75: To the Persian victory of Carus I refer the dialogue of the Philopatris, which has so long been an object of dispute among the learned. But to explain and justify my opinion, would require a dissertation. Note: Niebuhr, in the new edition of the Byzantine Historians, (vol. x.) has boldly assigned the Philopatris to the tenth century, and to the reign of Nicephorus Phocas. An opinion so decisively pronounced by Niebuhr and favorably received by Hase, the learned editor of Leo Diaconus, commands respectful consideration. But the whole tone of the work appears to me altogether inconsistent with any period in which philosophy did not stand, as it were, on some ground of equality with Christianity. The doctrine of the Trinity is sarcastically introduced rather as the strange doctrine of a new religion, than the established tenet of a faith universally prevalent. The argument, adopted from Solanus, concerning the formula of the procession of the Holy Ghost, is utterly worthless, as it is a mere quotation in the words of the Gospel of St. John, xv. 26. The only argument of any value is the historic one, from the allusion to the recent violation of many virgins in the Island of Crete. But neither is the language of Niebuhr quite accurate, nor his reference to the Acroases of Theodosius satisfactory. When, then, could this occurrence take place? Why not in the devastation of the island by the Gothic pirates, during the reign of Claudius. Hist. Aug. in Claud. p. 814. edit. Var. Lugd. Bat 1661.—M.]

[Footnote 76: Hist. August. p. 250. Yet Eutropius, Festus, Rufus, the two Victors, Jerome, Sidonius Apollinaris, Syncellus, and Zonaras, all ascribe the death of Carus to lightning.]

PART III

The vacancy of the throne was not productive of any disturbance. The ambition of the aspiring generals was checked by their natural fears, and young Numerian, with his absent brother Carinus, were unanimously acknowledged as Roman emperors.

The public expected that the successor of Carus would pursue his father's footsteps, and, without allowing the Persians to recover from their consternation, would advance sword in hand to the palaces of Susa and Ecbatana. [77] But the legions, however strong in numbers and discipline, were dismayed by the most abject superstition. Notwithstanding all the arts that were practised to disguise the manner of the late emperor's death, it was found impossible to remove the opinion of the multitude, and the power of opinion is irresistible. Places or persons struck with lightning were considered by the ancients with pious horror, as singularly devoted to the wrath of Heaven. [78] An oracle was remembered, which marked the River Tigris as the fatal boundary of the Roman arms. The troops, terrified with the fate of Carus and with their own danger, called aloud on young Numerian to obey the will of the gods, and to lead them away from this inauspicious scene of war. The feeble emperor was unable to subdue their obstinate prejudice, and the Persians wondered at the unexpected retreat of a victorious enemy. [79]

[Footnote 77: See Nemesian. Cynegeticon, v. 71, &c.]

[Footnote 78: See Festus and his commentators on the word Scribonianum. Places struck by lightning were surrounded with a wall; things were buried with mysterious ceremony.]

[Footnote 79: Vopiscus in Hist. August. p. 250. Aurelius Victor seems to believe the prediction, and to approve the retreat.]

The intelligence of the mysterious fate of the late emperor was soon carried from the frontiers of Persia to Rome; and the senate, as well as the provinces, congratulated the accession of the sons of Carus. These fortunate youths were strangers, however, to that conscious superiority, either of birth or of merit, which can alone render the possession of a throne easy, and as it were natural. Born and educated in a private station, the election of their father raised them at once to the rank of princes; and his death, which happened about sixteen months afterwards, left them the unexpected legacy of a vast empire. To sustain with temper this rapid elevation, an uncommon share of virtue and prudence was requisite; and Carinus, the elder of the brothers, was more than commonly deficient in those qualities. In the Gallic war he discovered some degree of personal courage; [80] but from the moment of his arrival at Rome, he abandoned himself to the luxury of the capital, and to the abuse of his fortune. He was soft, yet cruel; devoted to pleasure, but destitute of taste; and though exquisitely susceptible of vanity, indifferent to the public esteem. In the course of a few months, he successively married and divorced nine wives, most of whom he left pregnant; and notwithstanding this legal inconstancy, found time to indulge such a variety of irregular appetites, as brought dishonor on himself and on the noblest houses of Rome. He beheld with inveterate hatred all those who might remember his former obscurity, or censure his present conduct. He banished, or put to death, the friends and counsellors whom his father had placed about him, to guide his inexperienced youth; and he persecuted with the meanest revenge his school-fellows and companions who had not sufficiently respected the latent majesty of the emperor.

With the senators, Carinus affected a lofty and regal demeanor, frequently declaring, that he designed to distribute their estates among the populace of Rome. From the dregs of that populace he selected his favorites, and even his ministers. The palace, and even the Imperial table, were filled with singers, dancers, prostitutes, and all the various retinue of vice and folly. One of his doorkeepers [81] he intrusted with the government of the city. In the room of the Praetorian praefect, whom he put to death, Carinus substituted one of the ministers of his looser pleasures. Another, who possessed the same, or even a more infamous, title to favor, was invested with the consulship. A confidential secretary, who had acquired uncommon skill in the art of forgery, delivered the indolent emperor, with his own consent from the irksome duty of signing his name.

[Footnote 80: Nemesian. Cynegeticon, v 69. He was a contemporary, but a poet.]

[Footnote 81: Cancellarius. This word, so humble in its origin, has, by a singular fortune, risen into the title of the first great office of state in the monarchies of Europe. See Casaubon and Salmasius, ad Hist. August, p. 253.]

When the emperor Carus undertook the Persian war, he was induced, by motives of affection as well as policy, to secure the fortunes of his family, by leaving in the hands of his eldest son the armies and provinces of the West. The intelligence which he soon received of the conduct of Carinus filled him with shame and regret; nor had he concealed his resolution of satisfying the republic by a severe act of justice, and of adopting, in the place of an unworthy son, the brave and virtuous Constantius, who at that time was governor of Dalmatia. But the elevation of Constantius was for a while deferred; and as soon as the father's death had released Carinus from the control of fear or decency, he displayed to the Romans the extravagancies of Elagabalus, aggravated by the cruelty of Domitian. [82]

[Footnote 82: Vopiscus in Hist. August. p. 253, 254. Eutropius, x. 19. Vic to Junior. The reign of Diocletian indeed was so long and prosperous, that it must have been very unfavorable to the reputation of Carinus.]

The only merit of the administration of Carinus that history could record, or poetry celebrate, was the uncommon splendor with which, in his own and his brother's name, he exhibited the Roman games of the theatre, the circus, and the amphitheatre. More than twenty years afterwards, when the courtiers of Diocletian represented to their frugal sovereign the fame and popularity of his munificent predecessor, he acknowledged that the reign of Carinus had indeed been a reign of pleasure. [83] But this vain prodigality, which the prudence of Diocletian might justly despise, was enjoyed with surprise and transport by the Roman people. The oldest of the citizens, recollecting the spectacles of former days, the triumphal pomp of Probus or Aurelian, and the secular games of the emperor Philip, acknowledged that they were all surpassed by the superior magnificence of Carinus. [84]

[Footnote 83: Vopiscus in Hist. August. p. 254. He calls him Carus, but the sense is sufficiently obvious, and the words were often confounded.]

[Footnote 84: See Calphurnius, Eclog. vii. 43. We may observe, that the spectacles of Probus were still recent, and that the poet is seconded by the historian.]

The spectacles of Carinus may therefore be best illustrated by the observation of some particulars, which history has condescended to relate concerning those of his predecessors. If we confine ourselves solely to the hunting of wild beasts, however we may censure the vanity of the design or the cruelty of the execution, we are obliged to confess that neither before nor since the time of the Romans so much art and expense have ever been lavished for the amusement of the people. [85] By the order of Probus, a great quantity of large trees, torn up by the roots, were transplanted into the midst of the circus. The spacious and shady forest was immediately filled with a thousand ostriches, a thousand stags, a thousand fallow deer, and a thousand wild boars; and all this variety of game was abandoned to the riotous impetuosity of the multitude. The tragedy of the succeeding day consisted in the massacre of a hundred lions, an equal number of lionesses, two hundred leopards, and three hundred bears. [86] The collection prepared by the younger Gordian for his triumph, and which his successor exhibited in the secular games, was less remarkable by the number than by the singularity of the animals. Twenty zebras displayed their elegant forms and variegated beauty to the eyes of the Roman people. [87] Ten elks, and as many camelopards, the loftiest and most harmless creatures that wander over the plains of Sarmatia and Aethiopia, were contrasted with thirty African hyaenas and ten Indian tigers, the most implacable savages of the torrid zone. The unoffending strength with which Nature has endowed the greater quadrupeds was admired in the rhinoceros, the hippopotamus of the Nile, [88] and a majestic troop of thirty-two elephants. [89] While the populace gazed with stupid wonder on the splendid show, the naturalist might indeed observe the figure and properties of so many different species, transported from every part of the ancient world into the amphitheatre of Rome. But this accidental benefit, which science might derive from folly, is surely insufficient to justify such a wanton abuse of the public riches. There occurs, however, a single instance in the first Punic war, in which the senate wisely connected this amusement of the multitude with the interest of the state. A considerable number of elephants, taken in the defeat of the Carthaginian army, were driven through the circus by a few slaves, armed only with blunt javelins. [90] The useful spectacle served to impress the Roman soldier with a just contempt for those unwieldy animals; and he no longer dreaded to encounter them in the ranks of war.

[Footnote 85: *The philosopher Montaigne (Essais, l. iii. 6) gives a very just and lively view of Roman magnificence in these spectacles.*]

[Footnote 86: *Vopiscus in Hist. August. p. 240.*]

[Footnote 87: *They are called Onagri; but the number is too inconsiderable for mere wild asses. Cuper (de Elephantis Exercitat. ii. 7) has proved from Oppian, Dion, and an anonymous Greek, that zebras had been seen at Rome. They were brought from some island of the ocean, perhaps Madagascar.*]

[Footnote 88: *Carinus gave a hippopotamus, (see Calphurn. Eclog. vi. 66.) In the latter spectacles, I do not recollect any crocodiles, of which Augustus once exhibited thirty-six. Dion Cassius, l. lv. p. 781.*]

[Footnote 89: *Capitolin. in Hist. August. p. 164, 165. We are not acquainted with the animals which he calls archeleontes; some read argoleontes others agrioleontes: both corrections are very nugatory*]

[Footnote 90: *Plin. Hist. Natur. viii. 6, from the annals of Piso.*]

The hunting or exhibition of wild beasts was conducted with a magnificence suitable to a people who styled themselves the masters of the world; nor was the edifice appropriated to that entertainment less expressive of Roman greatness. Posterity admires, and will long admire, the awful remains of the amphitheatre of Titus, which so well deserved the epithet of Colossal. [91] It was a building of an elliptic figure, five hundred and sixty-four feet in length, and four hundred and sixty-seven in breadth, founded on fourscore arches, and rising, with four successive orders of architecture, to the height of one hundred and forty feet. [92] The outside of the edifice was encrusted with marble, and decorated with statues. The slopes of the vast concave, which formed the inside, were filled and surrounded with sixty or eighty rows of seats of marble likewise, covered with cushions, and capable of receiving with ease about fourscore thousand spectators. [93] Sixty-four vomitories (for by that name the doors were very aptly distinguished) poured forth the immense multitude; and the entrances, passages, and staircases were contrived with such exquisite skill, that each person, whether of the senatorial, the equestrian, or the plebeian order, arrived at his destined place without trouble or confusion. [94] Nothing was omitted, which, in any respect, could be subservient to the convenience and pleasure of the spectators.

They were protected from the sun and rain by an ample canopy, occasionally drawn over their heads. The air was continally refreshed by the playing of fountains, and profusely impregnated by the grateful scent of aromatics. In the centre of the edifice, the arena, or stage, was strewed with the finest sand, and successively assumed the most different forms. At one moment it seemed to rise out of the earth, like the garden of the Hesperides, and was afterwards broken into the rocks and caverns of Thrace. The subterraneous pipes conveyed an inexhaustible supply of water; and what had just before appeared a level plain, might be suddenly converted into a wide lake, covered with armed vessels, and replenished with the monsters of the deep. [95] In the decoration of these scenes, the Roman emperors displayed their wealth and liberality; and we read on various occasions that the whole furniture of the amphitheatre consisted either of silver, or of gold, or of amber. [96] The poet who describes the games of Carinus, in the character of a shepherd, attracted to the capital by the fame of their magnificence, affirms that the nets designed as a defence against the wild beasts, were of gold wire; that the porticos were gilded; and that the belt or circle which divided the several ranks of spectators from each other was studded with a precious mosaic of beautiful stones. [97]

[Footnote 91: See Maffei, Verona Illustrata, p. iv. l. i. c. 2.]

[Footnote 92: Maffei, l. ii. c. 2. The height was very much exaggerated by the ancients. It reached almost to the heavens, according to Calphurnius, (Eclog. vii. 23,) and surpassed the ken of human sight, according to Ammianus Marcellinus (xvi. 10.) Yet how trifling to the great pyramid of Egypt, which rises 500 feet perpendicular]

[Footnote 93: According to different copies of Victor, we read 77,000, or 87,000 spectators; but Maffei (l. ii. c. 12) finds room on the open seats for no more than 34,000. The remainder were contained in the upper covered galleries.]

[Footnote 94: See Maffei, l. ii. c. 5—12. He treats the very difficult subject with all possible clearness, and like an architect, as well as an antiquarian.]

[Footnote 95: Calphurn. Eclog vii. 64, 73. These lines are curious, and the whole eclogue has been of infinite use to Maffei. Calphurnius, as well as Martial, (see his first book,) was a poet; but when they described the amphitheatre, they both wrote from their own senses, and to those of the Romans.]

[Footnote 96: Consult Plin. Hist. Natur. xxxiii. 16, xxxvii. 11.]

[Footnote 97: Balteus en gemmis, en inlita porticus auro Certatim radiant, &c. Calphurn. vii.]

In the midst of this glittering pageantry, the emperor Carinus, secure of his fortune, enjoyed the acclamations of the people, the flattery of his courtiers, and the songs of the poets, who, for want of a more essential merit, were reduced to celebrate the divine graces of his person. [98] In the same hour, but at the distance of nine hundred miles from Rome, his brother expired; and a sudden revolution transferred into the hands of a stranger the sceptre of the house of Carus. [99]

[Footnote 98: Et Martis vultus et Apollinis esse putavi, says Calphurnius; but John Malala, who had perhaps seen pictures of Carinus, describes him as thick, short, and white, tom. i. p. 403.]

[Footnote 99: With regard to the time when these Roman games were celebrated, Scaliger, Salmasius, and Cuper have given themselves a great deal of trouble to perplex a very clear subject.]

The sons of Carus never saw each other after their father's death. The arrangements which their new situation required were probably deferred till the return of the younger brother to Rome, where a triumph was decreed to the young emperors for the glorious success of the Persian war. [100] It is uncertain whether they intended to divide between them the administration, or the provinces, of the empire; but it is very unlikely that their union would have proved of any long duration. The jealousy of power must have been inflamed by the opposition of characters. In the most corrupt of times, Carinus was unworthy to live: Numerian deserved to reign in a happier period. His affable manners and gentle virtues secured him, as soon as they became known, the regard and affections of the public. He possessed the elegant accomplishments of a poet and orator, which dignify as well as adorn the humblest and the most exalted station. His eloquence, however it was applauded by the senate, was formed not so much on the model of Cicero, as on that of the modern declaimers; but in an age very far from being destitute of poetical merit, he contended for the prize with the most celebrated of his contemporaries, and still remained the friend of his rivals; a circumstance which evinces either the goodness of his heart, or the superiority of his genius. [101] But the talents of Numerian were rather of the contemplative than of the active kind. When his father's elevation reluctantly forced him from the shade of retirement, neither his temper nor his pursuits had qualified him for the command of armies. His constitution was destroyed by the hardships of the Persian war; and he had contracted, from the heat of the climate, [102] such a weakness in his eyes, as obliged him, in the course of a long retreat, to confine himself to the solitude and darkness of a tent or litter.

The administration of all affairs, civil as well as military, was devolved on Arrius Aper, the Praetorian praefect, who to the power of his important office added the honor of being father-in-law to Numerian. The Imperial pavilion was strictly guarded by his most trusty adherents; and during many days, Aper delivered to the army the supposed mandates of their invisible sovereign. [103]

[Footnote 100: Nemesianus (in the Cynegeticon) seems to anticipate in his fancy that auspicious day.]

[Footnote 101: He won all the crowns from Nemesianus, with whom he vied in didactic poetry. The senate erected a statue to the son of Carus, with a very ambiguous inscription, "To the most powerful of orators." See Vopiscus in Hist. August. p. 251.]

[Footnote 102: A more natural cause, at least, than that assigned by Vopiscus, (Hist. August. p. 251,) incessantly weeping for his father's death.]

[Footnote 103: In the Persian war, Aper was suspected of a design to betray Carus. Hist. August. p. 250.]

It was not till eight months after the death of Carus, that the Roman army, returning by slow marches from the banks of the Tigris, arrived on those of the Thracian Bosphorus. The legions halted at

Chalcedon in Asia, while the court passed over to Heraclea, on the European side of the Propontis. [104] But a report soon circulated through the camp, at first in secret whispers, and at length in loud clamors, of the emperor's death, and of the presumption of his ambitious minister, who still exercised the sovereign power in the name of a prince who was no more. The impatience of the soldiers could not long support a state of suspense. With rude curiosity they broke into the Imperial tent, and discovered only the corpse of Numerian. [105] The gradual decline of his health might have induced them to believe that his death was natural; but the concealment was interpreted as an evidence of guilt, and the measures which Aper had taken to secure his election became the immediate occasion of his ruin Yet, even in the transport of their rage and grief, the troops observed a regular proceeding, which proves how firmly discipline had been reestablished by the martial successors of Gallienus. A general assembly of the army was appointed to be held at Chalcedon, whither Aper was transported in chains, as a prisoner and a criminal. A vacant tribunal was erected in the midst of the camp, and the generals and tribunes formed a great military council. They soon announced to the multitude that their choice had fallen on Diocletian, commander of the domestics or body-guards, as the person the most capable of revenging and succeeding their beloved emperor. The future fortunes of the candidate depended on the chance or conduct of the present hour. Conscious that the station which he had filled exposed him to some suspicions, Diocletian ascended the tribunal, and raising his eyes towards the Sun, made a solemn profession of his own innocence, in the presence of that all-seeing Deity. [106] Then, assuming the tone of a sovereign and a judge, he commanded that Aper should be brought in chains to the foot of the tribunal. "This man," said he, "is the murderer of Numerian;" and without giving him time to enter on a dangerous justification, drew his sword, and buried it in the breast of the unfortunate praefect. A charge supported by such decisive proof was admitted without contradiction, and the legions, with repeated acclamations, acknowledged the justice and authority of the emperor Diocletian. [107]

[Footnote 104: We are obliged to the Alexandrian Chronicle, p. 274, for the knowledge of the time and place where Diocletian was elected emperor.]

[Footnote 105: Hist. August. p. 251. Eutrop. ix. 88. Hieronym. in Chron. According to these judicious writers, the death of Numerian was discovered by the stench of his dead body. Could no aromatics be found in the Imperial household?]

[Footnote 106: Aurel. Victor. Eutropius, ix. 20. Hieronym. in Chron.]

[Footnote 107: Vopiscus in Hist. August. p. 252. The reason why Diocletian killed Aper, (a wild boar,) was founded on a prophecy and a pun, as foolish as they are well known.]

Before we enter upon the memorable reign of that prince, it will be proper to punish and dismiss the unworthy brother of Numerian. Carinus possessed arms and treasures sufficient to support his legal title to the empire. But his personal vices overbalanced every advantage of birth and situation. The most faithful servants of the father despised the incapacity, and dreaded the cruel arrogance, of the son. The hearts of the people were engaged in favor of his rival, and even the senate was inclined to prefer a usurper to a tyrant. The arts of Diocletian inflamed the general discontent; and the winter was employed in secret intrigues, and open preparations for a civil war. In the spring, the forces of the East and of the West encountered each other in the plains of Margus, a small city of Maesia, in the neighborhood of the Danube. [108] The troops, so lately returned from the Persian war, had acquired their glory at the expense of health and numbers; nor were they in a condition to contend with the unexhausted strength of the legions of Europe. Their ranks were broken, and, for a moment, Diocletian despaired of the purple and of life. But the advantage which Carinus had obtained by the valor of his soldiers, he quickly lost by the infidelity of his officers. A tribune, whose wife he had seduced, seized the opportunity of revenge, and, by a single blow, extinguished civil discord in the blood of the adulterer. [109]

[Footnote 108: Eutropius marks its situation very accurately; it was between the Mons Aureus and Viminiacum. M. d'Anville (Geographic Ancienne, tom. i. p. 304) places Margus at Kastolatz in Servia, a little below Belgrade and Semendria. Note: Kullieza—Eton Atlas—M.]

[Footnote 109: Hist. August. p. 254. Eutropius, ix. 20. Aurelius Victor et Epitome]

CHAPTER XIII

REIGN OF DIOCLETIAN AND HIS THREE ASSOCIATES

PART I

THE REIGN OF DIOCLETIAN AND HIS THREE ASSOCIATES, MAXIMIAN, GALERIUS, AND CONSTANTIUS—GENERAL RE-ESTABLISHMENT OF ORDER AND TRANQUILITY—THE PERSIAN WAR, VICTORY, AND TRIUMPH—THE NEW FORM OF ADMINISTRATION—ABDICATION AND RETIREMENT OF DIOCLETIAN AND MAXIMIAN

As the reign of Diocletian was more illustrious than that of any of his predecessors, so was his birth more abject and obscure. The strong claims of merit and of violence had frequently superseded the ideal prerogatives of nobility; but a distinct line of separation was hitherto preserved between the free and the servile part of mankind. The parents of Diocletian had been slaves in the house of Anulinus, a Roman senator; nor was he himself distinguished by any other name than that which he derived from a small town in Dalmatia, from whence his mother deduced her origin. [1] It is, however, probable that his father obtained the freedom of the family, and that he soon acquired an office of scribe, which was commonly exercised by persons of his condition. [2] Favorable oracles, or rather the consciousness of superior merit, prompted his aspiring son to pursue the profession of arms and the hopes of fortune; and it would be extremely curious to observe the gradation of arts and accidents which enabled him in the end to fulfil those oracles, and to display that merit to the world. Diocletian was successively promoted to the government of Maesia, the honors of the consulship, and the important command of the guards of the palace. He distinguished his abilities in the Persian war; and after the death of Numerian, the slave, by the confession and judgment of his rivals, was declared the most worthy of the Imperial throne. The malice of religious zeal, whilst it arraigns the savage fierceness of his colleague Maximian, has affected to cast suspicions on the personal courage of the emperor Diocletian. [3] It would not be easy to persuade us of the cowardice of a soldier of fortune, who acquired and preserved the esteem of the legions as well as the favor of so many warlike princes. Yet even calumny is sagacious enough to discover and to attack the most vulnerable part. The valor of Diocletian was never found inadequate to his duty, or to the occasion; but he appears not to have possessed the daring and generous spirit of a hero, who courts danger and fame, disdains artifice, and boldly challenges the allegiance of his equals. His abilities were useful rather than splendid; a vigorous mind, improved by the experience and study of mankind; dexterity and application in business; a judicious mixture of liberality and economy, of mildness and rigor; profound dissimulation, under the disguise of military frankness; steadiness to pursue his ends; flexibility to vary his means; and, above all, the great art of submitting his own passions, as well as those of others, to the interest of his ambition, and of coloring his ambition with the most specious pretences of justice and public utility. Like Augustus, Diocletian may be considered as the founder of a new empire. Like the adopted son of Caesar, he was distinguished as a statesman rather than as a warrior; nor did either of those princes employ force, whenever their purpose could be effected by policy.

[Footnote 1: Eutrop. ix. 19. Victor in Epitome. The town seems to have been properly called Doclia, from a small tribe of Illyrians, (see Cellarius, Geograph. Antiqua, tom. i. p. 393;) and the original name of the fortunate slave was probably Docles; he first lengthened it to the Grecian harmony of Diocles, and at length to the Roman majesty of Diocletianus. He likewise assumed the Patrician name of Valerius and it is usually given him by Aurelius Victor.]

[Footnote 2: See Dacier on the sixth satire of the second book of Horace Cornel. Nepos, 'n Vit. Eumen. c. l.]

[Footnote 3: Lactantius (or whoever was the author of the little treatise De Mortibus Persecutorum) accuses Diocletian of timidity in two places, c. 7. 8. In chap. 9 he says of him, "erat in omni tumultu meticulosu et animi disjectus."]

The victory of Diocletian was remarkable for its singular mildness. A people accustomed to applaud the clemency of the conqueror, if the usual punishments of death, exile, and confiscation, were inflicted with any degree of temper and equity, beheld, with the most pleasing astonishment, a civil war, the flames of which were extinguished in the field of battle. Diocletian received into his confidence Aristobulus, the principal minister of the house of Carus, respected the lives, the fortunes, and the dignity, of his adversaries, and even continued in their respective stations the greater number of the servants of Carinus. [4] It is not improbable that motives of prudence might assist the humanity of the artful Dalmatian; of these servants, many had purchased his favor by secret treachery; in others, he esteemed their grateful fidelity to an unfortunate master. The discerning judgment of Aurelian, of Probus, and of Carus, had filled the several departments of the state and army with officers of approved merit, whose removal would have injured the public service, without promoting the interest of his successor. Such a conduct, however, displayed to the Roman world the fairest prospect of the new reign, and the emperor affected to confirm this favorable prepossession, by declaring, that, among all the virtues of his predecessors, he was the most ambitious of imitating the humane philosophy of Marcus Antoninus. [5]

[Footnote 4: In this encomium, Aurelius Victor seems to convey a just, though indirect, censure of the cruelty of Constantius. It appears from the Fasti, that Aristobulus remained praefect of the city, and that he ended with Diocletian the consulship which he had commenced with Carinus.]

[Footnote 5: Aurelius Victor styles Diocletian, "Parentum potius quam Dominum." See Hist. August. p. 30.]

The first considerable action of his reign seemed to evince his sincerity as well as his moderation. After the example of Marcus, he gave himself a colleague in the person of Maximian, on whom he bestowed at first the title of Caesar, and afterwards that of Augustus. [6] But the motives of his conduct, as well as the object of his choice, were of a very different nature from those of his admired predecessor. By investing a luxurious youth with the honors of the purple, Marcus had discharged a debt of private gratitude, at the expense, indeed, of the happiness of the state. By associating a friend and a fellow-soldier to the labors of government, Diocletian, in a time of public danger, provided for the defence both of the East and of the West. Maximian was born a peasant, and, like Aurelian, in the territory of Sirmium. Ignorant of letters, [7] careless of laws, the rusticity of his appearance and manners still betrayed in the most elevated fortune the meanness of his extraction. War was the only art which he professed. In a long course of service, he had distinguished himself on every frontier of the empire; and though his military talents were formed to obey rather than to command, though, perhaps, he never attained the skill of a consummate general, he was capable, by his valor, constancy, and experience, of executing the most arduous undertakings. Nor were the vices of Maximian less useful to his benefactor. Insensible to pity, and fearless of consequences, he was the ready instrument of every act of cruelty which the policy of that artful prince might at once suggest and disclaim. As soon as a bloody sacrifice had been offered to prudence or to revenge, Diocletian, by his seasonable intercession, saved the remaining few whom he had never designed to punish, gently censured the severity of his stern colleague, and enjoyed the comparison of a golden and an iron age, which was universally applied to their opposite maxims of government. Notwithstanding the difference of their characters, the two emperors maintained, on the throne, that friendship which they had contracted in a private station. The haughty, turbulent spirit of Maximian, so fatal, afterwards, to himself and to the public peace, was accustomed to respect the genius of Diocletian, and confessed the ascendant of reason over brutal violence. [8] From a motive either of pride or superstition, the two emperors assumed the titles, the one of Jovius, the other of Herculius. Whilst the motion of the world (such was the language of their venal orators) was maintained by the all-seeing wisdom of Jupiter, the invincible arm of Hercules purged the earth from monsters and tyrants. [9]

[Footnote 6: The question of the time when Maximian received the honors of Caesar and Augustus has divided modern critics, and given occasion to a great deal of learned wrangling. I have followed M. de Tillemont, (Histoire des Empereurs, tom. iv. p. 500-505,) who has weighed the several reasons and difficulties with his scrupulous accuracy.   Note: Eckbel concurs in this view, viii p. 15.—M.]

[Footnote 7: In an oration delivered before him, (Panegyr. Vet. ii. 8,) Mamertinus expresses a doubt, whether his hero, in imitating the conduct of Hannibal and Scipio, had ever heard of their names. From thence we may fairly infer, that Maximian was more desirous of being considered as a soldier than as a man of letters; and it is in this manner that we can often translate the language of flattery into that of truth.]

[Footnote 8: Lactantius de M. P. c. 8. Aurelius Victor. As among the Panegyrics, we find orations pronounced in praise of Maximian, and others which flatter his adversaries at his expense, we derive some knowledge from the contrast.]

[Footnote 9: See the second and third Panegyrics, particularly iii. 3, 10, 14 but it would be tedious to copy the diffuse and affected expressions of their false eloquence. With regard to the titles, consult Aurel. Victor Lactantius de M. P. c. 52. Spanheim de Usu Numismatum, &c. xii 8.]

But even the omnipotence of Jovius and Herculius was insufficient to sustain the weight of the public administration. The prudence of Diocletian discovered that the empire, assailed on every side by the barbarians, required on every side the presence of a great army, and of an emperor. With this view, he resolved once more to divide his unwieldy power, and with the inferior title of Caesars, [9/1] to confer on two generals of approved merit an unequal share of the sovereign authority. [10] Galerius, surnamed Armentarius, from his original profession of a herdsman, and Constantius, who from his pale complexion had acquired the denomination of Chlorus, [11] were the two persons invested with the second honors of the Imperial purple. In describing the country, extraction, and manners of Herculius, we have already delineated those of Galerius, who was often, and not improperly, styled the younger Maximian, though, in many instances both of virtue and ability, he appears to have possessed a manifest superiority over the elder. The birth of Constantius was less obscure than that of his colleagues. Eutropius, his father, was one of the most considerable nobles of Dardania, and his mother was the niece of the emperor Claudius. [12] Although the youth of Constantius had been spent in arms, he was endowed with a mild and amiable disposition, and the popular voice had long since acknowledged him worthy of the rank which he at last attained. To strengthen the bonds of political, by those of domestic, union, each of the emperors assumed the character of a father to one of the Caesars, Diocletian to Galerius, and Maximian to Constantius; and each, obliging them to repudiate their former wives, bestowed his daughter in marriage or his adopted son. [13] These four princes distributed among themselves the wide extent of the Roman empire. The defence of Gaul, Spain, [14] and Britain, was intrusted to Constantius: Galerius was stationed on the banks of the Danube, as the safeguard of the Illyrian provinces. Italy and Africa were considered as the department of Maximian; and for his peculiar portion, Diocletian reserved Thrace, Egypt, and the rich countries of Asia. Every one was sovereign with his own jurisdiction; but their united authority extended over the whole monarchy, and each of them was prepared to assist his colleagues with his counsels or presence. The Caesars, in their exalted rank, revered the majesty of the emperors, and the three younger princes invariably acknowledged, by their gratitude and obedience, the common parent of their fortunes. The suspicious jealousy of power found not any place among them; and the singular happiness of their union has been compared to a chorus of music, whose harmony was regulated and maintained by the skilful hand of the first artist. [15]

[Footnote 9/1: On the relative power of the Augusti and the Caesars, consult a dissertation at the end of Manso's Leben Constantius des Grossen—M.]

[Footnote 10: Aurelius Victor. Victor in Epitome. Eutrop. ix. 22. Lactant de M. P. c. 8. Hieronym. in Chron.]

[Footnote 11: It is only among the modern Greeks that Tillemont can discover his appellation of Chlorus. Any remarkable degree of paleness seems inconsistent with the rubor mentioned in Panegyric, v. 19.]

[Footnote 12: Julian, the grandson of Constantius, boasts that his family was derived from the warlike Maesians. Misopogon, p. 348. The Dardanians dwelt on the edge of Maesia.]

[Footnote 13: Galerius married Valeria, the daughter of Diocletian; if we speak with strictness, Theodora, the wife of Constantius, was daughter only to the wife of Maximian. Spanheim, Dissertat, xi. 2.]

[Footnote 14: This division agrees with that of the four praefectures; yet there is some reason to doubt whether Spain was not a province of Maximian. See Tillemont, tom. iv. p. 517. Note: According to Aurelius Victor and other authorities, Thrace belonged to the division of Galerius. See Tillemont, iv. 36. But the laws of Diocletian are in general dated in Illyria or Thrace.—M.]

[Footnote 15: Julian in Caesarib. p. 315. Spanheim's notes to the French translation, p. 122.]

This important measure was not carried into execution till about six years after the association of Maximian, and that interval of time had not been destitute of memorable incidents. But we have preferred, for the sake of perspicuity, first to describe the more perfect form of Diocletian's government, and afterwards to relate the actions of his reign, following rather the natural order of the events, than the dates of a very doubtful chronology.

The first exploit of Maximian, though it is mentioned in a few words by our imperfect writers, deserves, from its singularity, to be recorded in a history of human manners. He suppressed the peasants of Gaul, who, under the appellation of Bagaudae, [16] had risen in a general insurrection; very similar to those which in the fourteenth century successively afflicted both France and England. [17] It should seem that very many of those institutions, referred by an easy solution to the feudal system, are derived from the Celtic barbarians. When Caesar subdued the Gauls, that great nation was already divided into three orders of men; the clergy, the nobility, and the common people. The first governed by superstition, the second by arms, but the third and last was not of any weight or account in their public councils. It was very natural for the plebeians, oppressed by debt, or apprehensive of injuries, to implore the protection of some powerful chief, who acquired over their persons and property the same absolute right as, among the Greeks and Romans, a master exercised over his slaves. [18] The greatest part of the nation was gradually reduced into a state of servitude; compelled to perpetual labor on the estates of the Gallic nobles, and confined to the soil, either by the real weight of fetters, or by the no less cruel and forcible restraints of the laws. During the long series of troubles which agitated Gaul, from the reign of Gallienus to that of Diocletian, the condition of these servile peasants was peculiarly miserable; and they experienced at once the complicated tyranny of their masters, of the barbarians, of the soldiers, and of the officers of the revenue. [19]

[Footnote 16: The general name of Bagaudoe (in the signification of rebels) continued till the fifth century in Gaul. Some critics derive it from a Celtic word Bagad, a tumultuous assembly. Scaliger ad Euseb. Du Cange Glossar. (Compare S. Turner, Anglo-Sax. History, i. 214.—M.)]

[Footnote 17: Chronique de Froissart, vol. i. c. 182, ii. 73, 79. The naivete of his story is lost in our best modern writers.]

[Footnote 18: Caesar de Bell. Gallic. vi. 13. Orgetorix, the Helvetian, could arm for his defence a body of ten thousand slaves.]

[Footnote 19: Their oppression and misery are acknowledged by Eumenius (Panegyr. vi. 8,) Gallias efferatas injuriis.]

Their patience was at last provoked into despair. On every side they rose in multitudes, armed with rustic weapons, and with irresistible fury. The ploughman became a foot soldier, the shepherd mounted on horseback, the deserted villages and open towns were abandoned to the flames, and the ravages of the peasants equalled those of the fiercest barbarians. [20] They asserted the natural rights of men, but they asserted those rights with the most savage cruelty. The Gallic nobles, justly dreading their revenge, either took refuge in the fortified cities, or fled from the wild scene of anarchy. The peasants reigned without control; and two of their most daring leaders had the folly and rashness to assume the Imperial ornaments. [21] Their power soon expired at the approach of the legions. The strength of union and discipline obtained an easy victory over a licentious and divided multitude. [22] A severe retaliation was inflicted on the peasants who were found in arms; the affrighted remnant returned to their respective habitations, and their unsuccessful effort for freedom served only to confirm their slavery. So strong and uniform is the current of popular passions, that we might almost venture, from very scanty materials, to relate the particulars of this war; but we are not disposed to believe that the principal leaders, Aelianus and Amandus, were Christians, [23] or to insinuate, that the rebellion, as it happened in the time of Luther, was occasioned by the abuse of those benevolent principles of Christianity, which inculcate the natural freedom of mankind.

[Footnote 20: Panegyr. Vet. ii. 4. Aurelius Victor.]

[Footnote 21: Aelianus and Amandus. We have medals coined by them Goltzius in Thes. R. A. p. 117, 121.]

[Footnote 22: Levibus proeliis domuit. Eutrop. ix. 20.]

[Footnote 23: The fact rests indeed on very slight authority, a life of St. Babolinus, which is probably of the seventh century. See Duchesne Scriptores Rer. Francicar. tom. i. p. 662.]

Maximian had no sooner recovered Gaul from the hands of the peasants, than he lost Britain by the usurpation of Carausius. Ever since the rash but successful enterprise of the Franks under the reign of Probus, their daring countrymen had constructed squadrons of light brigantines, in which they incessantly ravaged the provinces adjacent to the ocean. [24] To repel their desultory incursions, it was found necessary to create a naval power; and the judicious measure was prosecuted with prudence and vigor. Gessoriacum, or Boulogne, in the straits of the British Channel, was chosen by the emperor for the station of the Roman fleet; and the command of it was intrusted to Carausius, a Menapian of the meanest origin, [25] but who had long signalized his skill as a pilot, and his valor as a soldier. The integrity of the new admiral corresponded not with his abilities. When the German pirates sailed from their own harbors, he connived at their passage, but he diligently intercepted their return, and appropriated to his own use an ample share of the spoil which they had acquired. The wealth of Carausius was, on this occasion, very justly considered as an evidence of his guilt; and Maximian had already given orders for his death. But the crafty Menapian foresaw and prevented the severity of the emperor. By his liberality he had attached to his fortunes the fleet which he commanded, and secured the barbarians in his interest. From the port of Boulogne he sailed over to Britain, persuaded the legion, and the auxiliaries which guarded that island, to embrace his party, and boldly assuming, with the Imperial purple, the title of Augustus defied the justice and the arms of his injured sovereign. [26]

[Footnote 24: Aurelius Victor calls them Germans. Eutropius (ix. 21) gives them the name of Saxons. But Eutropius lived in the ensuing century, and seems to use the language of his own times.]

[Footnote 25: The three expressions of Eutropius, Aurelius Victor, and Eumenius, "vilissime natus," "Bataviae alumnus," and "Menapiae civis," give us a very doubtful account of the birth of Carausius. Dr. Stukely, however, (Hist. of Carausius, p. 62,) chooses to make him a native of St. David's and a prince of the blood royal of Britain. The former idea he had found in Richard of Cirencester, p. 44. Note: The Menapians were settled between the Scheldt and the Meuse, is the northern part of Brabant. D'Anville, Geogr. Anc. i. 93.—G.]

[Footnote 26: Panegyr. v. 12. Britain at this time was secure, and slightly guarded.]

When Britain was thus dismembered from the empire, its importance was sensibly felt, and its loss sincerely lamented. The Romans celebrated, and perhaps magnified, the extent of that noble island, provided on every side with convenient harbors; the temperature of the climate, and the fertility of the soil, alike adapted for the production of corn or of vines; the valuable minerals with which it abounded; its rich pastures covered with innumerable flocks, and its woods free from wild beasts or venomous serpents. Above all, they regretted the large amount of the revenue of Britain, whilst they confessed, that such a province well deserved to become the seat of an independent monarchy. [27] During the space of seven years it was possessed by Carausius; and fortune continued propitious to a rebellion supported with courage and ability. The British emperor defended the frontiers of his dominions against the Caledonians of the North, invited, from the continent, a great number of skilful artists, and displayed, on a variety of coins that are still extant, his taste and opulence. Born on the confines of the Franks, he courted the friendship of that formidable people, by the flattering imitation of their dress and manners. The bravest of their youth he enlisted among his land or sea forces; and, in return for their useful alliance, he communicated to the barbarians the dangerous knowledge of military and naval arts. Carausius still preserved the possession of Boulogne and the adjacent country. His fleets rode triumphant in the channel, commanded the mouths of the Seine and of the Rhine, ravaged the coasts of the ocean, and diffused beyond the columns of Hercules the terror of his name. Under his command, Britain, destined in a future age to obtain the empire of the sea, already assumed its natural and respectable station of a maritime power. [28]

[Footnote 27: Panegyr. Vet v 11, vii. 9. The orator Eumenius wished to exalt the glory of the hero (Constantius) with the importance of the conquest. Notwithstanding our laudable partiality for our native country, it is difficult to conceive, that, in the beginning of the fourth century England deserved all these commendations. A century and a half before, it hardly paid its own establishment.]

[Footnote 28: As a great number of medals of Carausius are still preserved, he is become a very favorite object of antiquarian curiosity, and every circumstance of his life and actions has been investigated with sagacious accuracy. Dr. Stukely, in particular, has devoted a large volume to the British emperor. I have used his materials, and rejected most of his fanciful conjectures.]

By seizing the fleet of Boulogne, Carausius had deprived his master of the means of pursuit and revenge. And when, after a vast expense of time and labor, a new armament was launched into the water, [29] the Imperial troops, unaccustomed to that element, were easily baffled and defeated by the veteran sailors of the usurper. This disappointed effort was soon productive of a treaty of peace. Diocletian and his colleague, who justly dreaded the enterprising spirit of Carausius, resigned to him the sovereignty of Britain, and reluctantly admitted their perfidious servant to a participation of the Imperial honors. [30] But the adoption of the two Caesars restored new vigor to the Romans arms; and while the Rhine was guarded by the presence of Maximian, his brave associate Constantius assumed the conduct of the British war. His first enterprise was against the important place of Boulogne. A stupendous mole, raised across the entrance of the harbor, intercepted all hopes of relief. The town surrendered after an obstinate defence; and a considerable part of the naval strength of Carausius fell into the hands of the besiegers. During the three years which Constantius employed in preparing a fleet adequate to the conquest of Britain, he secured the coast of Gaul, invaded the country of the Franks, and deprived the usurper of the assistance of those powerful allies.

[Footnote 29: When Mamertinus pronounced his first panegyric, the naval preparations of Maximian were completed; and the orator presaged an assured victory. His silence in the second panegyric might alone inform us that the expedition had not succeeded.]

[Footnote 30: Aurelius Victor, Eutropius, and the medals, (Pax Augg.) inform us of this temporary reconciliation; though I will not presume (as Dr. Stukely has done, Medallic History of Carausius, p. 86, &c) to insert the identical articles of the treaty.]

Before the preparations were finished, Constantius received the intelligence of the tyrant's death, and it was considered as a sure presage of the approaching victory. The servants of Carausius imitated the example of treason which he had given. He was murdered by his first minister, Allectus, and the assassin succeeded to his power and to his danger. But he possessed not equal abilities either to exercise the one or to repel the other.

He beheld, with anxious terror, the opposite shores of the continent already filled with arms, with troops, and with vessels; for Constantius had very prudently divided his forces, that he might likewise divide the attention and resistance of the enemy. The attack was at length made by the principal squadron, which, under the command of the praefect Asclepiodatus, an officer of distinguished merit, had been assembled in the north of the Seine. So imperfect in those times was the art of navigation, that orators have celebrated the daring courage of the Romans, who ventured to set sail with a side-wind, and on a stormy day. The weather proved favorable to their enterprise. Under the cover of a thick fog, they escaped the fleet of Allectus, which had been stationed off the Isle of Wight to receive them, landed in safety on some part of the western coast, and convinced the Britons, that a superiority of naval strength will not always protect their country from a foreign invasion. Asclepiodatus had no sooner disembarked the imperial troops, then he set fire to his ships; and, as the expedition proved fortunate, his heroic conduct was universally admired. The usurper had posted himself near London, to expect the formidable attack of Constantius, who commanded in person the fleet of Boulogne; but the descent of a new enemy required his immediate presence in the West. He performed this long march in so precipitate a manner, that he encountered the whole force of the praefect with a small body of harassed and disheartened troops. The engagement was soon terminated by the total defeat and death of Allectus; a single battle, as it has often happened, decided the fate of this great island; and when Constantius landed on the shores of Kent, he found them covered with obedient subjects. Their acclamations were loud and unanimous; and the virtues of the conqueror may induce us to believe, that they sincerely rejoiced in a revolution, which, after a separation of ten years, restored Britain to the body of the Roman empire. [31]

[Footnote 31: With regard to the recovery of Britain, we obtain a few hints from Aurelius Victor and Eutropius.]

PART II

Britain had none but domestic enemies to dread; and as long as the governors preserved their fidelity, and the troops their discipline, the incursions of the naked savages of Scotland or Ireland could never materially affect the safety of the province.

The peace of the continent, and the defence of the principal rivers which bounded the empire, were objects of far greater difficulty and importance. The policy of Diocletian, which inspired the councils of his associates, provided for the public tranquility, by encouraging a spirit of dissension among the barbarians, and by strengthening the fortifications of the Roman limit. In the East he fixed a line of camps from Egypt to the Persian dominions, and for every camp, he instituted an adequate number of stationary troops, commanded by their respective officers, and supplied with every kind of arms, from the new arsenals which he had formed at Antioch, Emesa, and Damascus. [32] Nor was the precaution of the emperor less watchful against the well-known valor of the barbarians of Europe. From the mouth of the Rhine to that of the Danube, the ancient camps, towns, and citidels, were diligently reestablished, and, in the most exposed places, new ones were skilfully constructed: the strictest vigilance was introduced among the garrisons of the frontier, and every expedient was practised that could render the long chain of fortifications firm and impenetrable. [33] A barrier so respectable was seldom violated, and the barbarians often turned against each other their disappointed rage. The Goths, the Vandals, the Gepidae, the Burgundians, the Alemanni, wasted each other's strength by destructive hostilities: and whosoever vanquished, they vanquished the enemies of Rome. The subjects of Diocletian enjoyed the bloody spectacle, and congratulated each other, that the mischiefs of civil war were now experienced only by the barbarians. [34]

[Footnote 32: John Malala, in Chron, Antiochen. tom. i. p. 408, 409.]

[Footnote 33: Zosim. l. i. p. 3. That partial historian seems to celebrate the vigilance of Diocletian with a design of exposing the negligence of Constantine; we may, however, listen to an orator: "Nam quid ego alarum et cohortium castra percenseam, toto Rheni et Istri et Euphraus limite restituta." Panegyr. Vet. iv. 18.]

[Footnote 34: Ruunt omnes in sanguinem suum populi, quibus ron contigilesse Romanis, obstinataeque feritatis poenas nunc sponte persolvunt. Panegyr. Vet. iii. 16. Mamertinus illustrates the fact by the example of almost all the nations in the world.]

Notwithstanding the policy of Diocletian, it was impossible to maintain an equal and undisturbed tranquillity during a reign of twenty years, and along a frontier of many hundred miles. Sometimes the barbarians suspended their domestic animosities, and the relaxed vigilance of the garrisons sometimes gave a passage to their strength or dexterity. Whenever the provinces were invaded, Diocletian conducted himself with that calm dignity which he always affected or possessed; reserved his presence for such occasions as were worthy of his interposition, never exposed his person or reputation to any unnecessary danger, insured his success by every means that prudence could suggest, and displayed, with ostentation, the consequences of his victory. In wars of a more difficult nature, and more doubtful event, he employed the rough valor of Maximian; and that faithful soldier was content to ascribe his own victories to the wise counsels and auspicious influence of his benefactor. But after the adoption of the two Caesars, the emperors themselves, retiring to a less laborious scene of action, devolved on their adopted sons the defence of the Danube and of the Rhine. The vigilant Galerius was never reduced to the necessity of vanquishing an army of barbarians on the Roman territory. [35] The brave and active Contsantius delivered Gaul from a very furious inroad of the Alemanni; and his victories of Langres and Vindonissa appear to have been actions of considerable danger and merit. As he traversed the open country with a feeble guard, he was encompassed on a sudden by the superior multitude of the enemy. He retreated with difficulty towards Langres; but, in the general consternation, the citizens refused to open their gates, and the wounded prince was drawn up the wall by the means of a rope. But, on the news of his distress, the Roman troops hastened from all sides to his relief, and before the evening he had satisfied his honor and revenge by the slaughter of six thousand Alemanni. [36] From the monuments of those times, the obscure traces of several other victories over the barbarians of Sarmatia and Germany might possibly be collected; but the tedious search would not be rewarded either with amusement or with instruction.

[Footnote 35: He complained, though not with the strictest truth, "Jam fluxisse annos quindecim in quibus, in Illyrico, ad ripam Danubii relegatus cum gentibus barbaris luctaret." Lactant. de M. P. c. 18.]

[Footnote 36: In the Greek text of Eusebius, we read six thousand, a number which I have preferred to the sixty thousand of Jerome, Orosius Eutropius, and his Greek translator Paeanius.]

The conduct which the emperor Probus had adopted in the disposal of the vanquished, was imitated by Diocletian and his associates. The captive barbarians, exchanging death for slavery, were distributed among the provincials, and assigned to those districts (in Gaul, the territories of Amiens, Beauvais, Cambray, Treves, Langres, and Troyes, are particularly specified [37] which had been depopulated by the calamities of war. They were usefully employed as shepherds and husbandmen, but were denied the exercise of arms, except when it was found expedient to enroll them in the military service. Nor did the emperors refuse the property of lands, with a less servile tenure, to such of the barbarians as solicited the protection of Rome. They granted a settlement to several colonies of the Carpi, the Bastarnae, and the Sarmatians; and, by a dangerous indulgence, permitted them in some measure to retain their national manners and independence. [38] Among the provincials, it was a subject of flattering exultation, that the barbarian, so lately an object of terror, now cultivated their lands, drove their cattle to the neighboring fair, and contributed by his labor to the public plenty. They congratulated their masters on the powerful accession of subjects and soldiers; but they forgot to observe, that multitudes of secret enemies, insolent from favor, or desperate from oppression, were introduced into the heart of the empire. [39]

[Footnote 37: Panegyr. Vet. vii. 21.]

[Footnote 38: There was a settlement of the Sarmatians in the neighborhood of Treves, which seems to have been deserted by those lazy barbarians. Ausonius speaks of them in his Mosella:— "Unde iter ingrediens nemorosa per avia solum, Et nulla humani spectans vestigia cultus; .... Arvaque Sauromatum nuper metata colonis."]

[Footnote 39: There was a town of the Carpi in the Lower Maesia. See the rhetorical exultation of Eumenius.]

While the Caesars exercised their valor on the banks of the Rhine and Danube, the presence of the emperors was required on the southern confines of the Roman world. From the Nile to Mount Atlas Africa was in arms. A confederacy of five Moorish nations issued from their deserts to invade the peaceful provinces. [40] Julian had assumed the purple at Carthage. [41] Achilleus at Alexandria, and even the Blemmyes, renewed, or rather continued, their incursions into the Upper Egypt. Scarcely any circumstances have been preserved of the exploits of Maximian in the western parts of Africa; but it appears, by the event, that the progress of his arms was rapid and decisive, that he vanquished the fiercest barbarians of Mauritania, and that he removed them from the mountains, whose inaccessible strength had inspired their inhabitants with a lawless confidence, and habituated them to a life of rapine and violence. [42] Diocletian, on his side, opened the campaign in Egypt by the siege of Alexandria, cut off the aqueducts which conveyed the waters of the Nile into every quarter of that immense city, [43] and rendering his camp impregnable to the sallies of the besieged multitude, he pushed his reiterated attacks with caution and vigor. After a siege of eight months, Alexandria, wasted by the sword and by fire, implored the clemency of the conqueror, but it experienced the full extent of his severity. Many thousands of the citizens perished in a promiscuous slaughter, and there were few obnoxious persons in Egypt who escaped a sentence either of death or at least of exile. [44] The fate of Busiris and of Coptos was still more melancholy than that of Alexandria: those proud cities, the former distinguished by its antiquity, the latter enriched by the passage of the Indian trade, were utterly destroyed by the arms and by the severe order of Diocletian. [45] The character of the Egyptian nation, insensible to kindness, but extremely susceptible of fear, could alone justify this excessive rigor. The seditions of Alexandria had often affected the tranquillity and subsistence of Rome itself. Since the usurpation of Firmus, the province of Upper Egypt, incessantly relapsing into rebellion, had embraced the alliance of the savages of Aethiopia. The number of the Blemmyes, scattered between the Island of Meroe and the Red Sea, was very inconsiderable, their disposition was unwarlike, their weapons rude and inoffensive. [46] Yet in the public disorders, these barbarians, whom antiquity, shocked with the deformity of their figure, had almost excluded from the human species, presumed to rank themselves among the enemies of Rome. [47] Such had been the unworthy allies of the Egyptians; and while the attention of the state was engaged in more serious wars, their vexations inroads might again harass the repose of the province. With a view of opposing to the Blemmyes a suitable adversary, Diocletian persuaded the Nobatae, or people of Nubia, to remove from their ancient habitations in the deserts of Libya, and resigned to them an extensive but unprofitable territory above Syene and the cataracts of the Nile, with the stipulation, that they should ever respect and guard the frontier of the empire. The treaty long subsisted; and till the establishment of Christianity introduced stricter notions of religious worship, it was annually ratified by a solemn sacrifice in the Isle of Elephantine, in which the Romans, as well as the barbarians, adored the same visible or invisible powers of the universe. [48]

[Footnote 40: Scaliger (Animadvers. ad Euseb. p. 243) decides, in his usual manner, that the Quinque gentiani, or five African nations, were the five great cities, the Pentapolis of the inoffensive province of Cyrene.]

[Footnote 41: After his defeat, Julian stabbed himself with a dagger, and immediately leaped into the flames. Victor in Epitome.]

[Footnote 42: Tu ferocissimos Mauritaniae populos inaccessis montium jugis et naturali munitione fidentes, expugnasti, recepisti, transtulisti. Panegyr Vet. vi. 8.]

[Footnote 43: See the description of Alexandria, in Hirtius de Bel. Alexandrin c. 5.]

[Footnote 44: Eutrop. ix. 24. Orosius, vii. 25. John Malala in Chron. Antioch. p. 409, 410. Yet Eumenius assures us, that Egypt was pacified by the clemency of Diocletian.]

[Footnote 45: Eusebius (in Chron.) places their destruction several years sooner and at a time when Egypt itself was in a state of rebellion against the Romans.]

[Footnote 46: Strabo, l. xvii. p. 172. Pomponius Mela, l. i. c. 4. His words are curious: "Intra, si credere libet vix, homines magisque semiferi Aegipanes, et Blemmyes, et Satyri."]

[Footnote 47: Ausus sese inserere fortunae et provocare arma Romana.]

[Footnote 48: See Procopius de Bell. Persic. l. i. c. 19. Note: Compare, on the epoch of the final extirpation of the rites of Paganism from the Isle of Philae, (Elephantine,) which subsisted till the edict of Theodosius, in the sixth century, a dissertation of M. Letronne, on certain Greek inscriptions. The dissertation contains some very interesting observations on the conduct and policy of Diocletian in Egypt. Mater pour l'Hist. du Christianisme en Egypte, Nubie et Abyssinie, Paris 1817—M.]

At the same time that Diocletian chastised the past crimes of the Egyptians, he provided for their future safety and happiness by many wise regulations, which were confirmed and enforced under the succeeding reigns. [49] One very remarkable edict which he published, instead of being condemned as the effect of jealous tyranny, deserves to be applauded as an act of prudence and humanity. He caused a diligent inquiry to be made "for all the ancient books which treated of the admirable art of making gold and silver, and without pity, committed them to the flames; apprehensive, as we are assumed, lest the opulence of the Egyptians should inspire them with confidence to rebel against the empire." [50] But if Diocletian had been convinced of the reality of that valuable art, far from extinguishing the memory, he would have converted the operation of it to the benefit of the public revenue. It is much more likely, that his good sense discovered to him the folly of such magnificent pretensions, and that he was desirous of preserving the reason and fortunes of his subjects from the mischievous pursuit. It may be remarked, that these ancient books, so liberally ascribed to Pythagoras, to Solomon, or to Hermes, were the pious frauds of more recent adepts. The Greeks were inattentive either to the use or to the abuse of chemistry. In that immense register, where Pliny has deposited the discoveries, the arts, and the errors of mankind, there is not the least mention of the transmutation of metals; and the persecution of Diocletian is the first authentic event in the history of alchemy. The conquest of Egypt by the Arabs diffused that vain science over the globe. Congenial to the avarice of the human heart, it was studied in China as in Europe, with equal eagerness, and with equal success. The darkness of the middle ages insured a favorable reception to every tale of wonder, and the revival of learning gave new vigor to hope, and suggested more specious arts of deception. Philosophy, with the aid of experience, has at length banished the study of alchemy; and the present age, however desirous of riches, is content to seek them by the humbler means of commerce and industry. [51]

[Footnote 49: He fixed the public allowance of corn, for the people of Alexandria, at two millions of medimni; about four hundred thousand quarters. Chron. Paschal. p. 276 Procop. Hist. Arcan. c. 26.]

[Footnote 50: John Antioch, in Excerp. Valesian. p. 834. Suidas in Diocletian.]

[Footnote 51: See a short history and confutation of Alchemy, in the works of that philosophical compiler, La Mothe le Vayer, tom. i. p. 32—353.]

The reduction of Egypt was immediately followed by the Persian war. It was reserved for the reign of Diocletian to vanquish that powerful nation, and to extort a confession from the successors of Artaxerxes, of the superior majesty of the Roman empire.

We have observed, under the reign of Valerian, that Armenia was subdued by the perfidy and the arms of the Persians, and that, after the assassination of Chosroes, his son Tiridates, the infant heir of the monarchy, was saved by the fidelity of his friends, and educated under the protection of the emperors. Tiridates derived from his exile such advantages as he could never have obtained on the throne of Armenia; the early knowledge of adversity, of mankind, and of the Roman discipline. He signalized his youth by deeds of valor, and displayed a matchless dexterity, as well as strength, in every martial exercise, and even in the less honorable contests of the Olympian games. [52] Those qualities were more nobly exerted in the defence of his benefactor Licinius. [53] That officer, in the sedition which occasioned the death of Probus, was exposed to the most imminent danger, and the enraged soldiers were forcing their way into his tent, when they were checked by the single arm of the Armenian prince. The gratitude of Tiridates contributed soon afterwards to his restoration. Licinius was in every station the friend and companion of Galerius, and the merit of Galerius, long before he was raised to the dignity of Caesar, had been known and esteemed by Diocletian. In the third year of that emperor's reign Tiridates was invested with the kingdom of Armenia. The justice of the measure was not less evident than its expediency. It was time to rescue from the usurpation of the Persian monarch an important territory, which, since the reign of Nero, had been always granted under the protection of the empire to a younger branch of the house of Arsaces. [54]

[Footnote 52: See the education and strength of Tiridates in the Armenian history of Moses of Chorene, l. ii. c. 76. He could seize two wild bulls by the horns, and break them off with his hands.]

[Footnote 53: If we give credit to the younger Victor, who supposes that in the year 323 Licinius was only sixty years of age, he could scarcely be the same person as the patron of Tiridates; but we know from much better authority, (Euseb. Hist. Ecclesiast. l. x. c. 8,) that Licinius was at that time in the last period of old age: sixteen years before, he is represented with gray hairs, and as the contemporary of Galerius. See Lactant. c. 32. Licinius was probably born about the year 250.]

[Footnote 54: See the sixty-second and sixty-third books of Dion Cassius.]

When Tiridates appeared on the frontiers of Armenia, he was received with an unfeigned transport of joy and loyalty. During twenty-six years, the country had experienced the real and imaginary hardships of a foreign yoke. The Persian monarchs adorned their new conquest with magnificent buildings; but those monuments had been erected at the expense of the people, and were abhorred as badges of slavery. The apprehension of a revolt had inspired the most rigorous precautions: oppression had been aggravated by insult, and the consciousness of the public hatred had been productive of every measure that could render it still more implacable. We have already remarked the intolerant spirit of the Magian religion. The statues of the deified kings of Armenia, and the sacred images of the sun and moon, were broke in pieces by the zeal of the conqueror; and the perpetual fire of Ormuzd was kindled and preserved upon an altar erected on the summit of Mount Bagavan. [55] It was natural, that a people exasperated by so many injuries, should arm with zeal in the cause of their independence, their religion, and their hereditary sovereign. The torrent bore down every obstacle, and the Persian garrisons retreated before its fury. The nobles of Armenia flew to the standard of Tiridates, all alleging their past merit, offering their future service, and soliciting from the new king those honors and rewards from which they had been excluded with disdain under the foreign government. [56] The command of the army was bestowed on Artavasdes, whose father had saved the infancy of Tiridates, and whose family had been massacred for that generous action. The brother of Artavasdes obtained the government of a province. One of the first military dignities was conferred on the satrap Otas, a man of singular temperance and fortitude, who presented to the king his sister [57] and a considerable treasure, both of which, in a sequestered fortress, Otas had preserved from violation. Among the Armenian nobles appeared an ally, whose fortunes are too remarkable to pass unnoticed. His name was Mamgo, [57/1] his origin was Scythian, and the horde which acknowledge his authority had encamped a very few years before on the skirts of the Chinese empire, [58] which at that time extended as far as the neighborhood of Sogdiana. [59] Having incurred the displeasure of his master, Mamgo, with his followers, retired to the banks of the Oxus, and implored the protection of Sapor. The emperor of China claimed the fugitive, and alleged the rights of sovereignty. The Persian monarch pleaded the laws of hospitality, and with some difficulty avoided a war, by the promise that he would banish Mamgo to the uttermost parts of the West, a punishment, as he described it, not less dreadful than death itself. Armenia was chosen for the place of exile, and a large district was assigned to the Scythian horde, on which they might feed their flocks and herds, and remove their encampment from one place to another, according to the different seasons of the year.

They were employed to repel the invasion of Tiridates; but their leader, after weighing the obligations and injuries which he had received from the Persian monarch, resolved to abandon his party.

The Armenian prince, who was well acquainted with this merit as well as power of Mamgo, treated him with distinguished respect; and, by admitting him into his confidence, acquired a brave and faithful servant, who contributed very effectually to his restoration. [60]

[Footnote 55: Moses of Chorene. Hist. Armen. l. ii. c. 74. The statues had been erected by Valarsaces, who reigned in Armenia about 130 years before Christ, and was the first king of the family of Arsaces, (see Moses, Hist. Armen. l. ii. 2, 3.) The deification of the Arsacides is mentioned by Justin, (xli. 5,) and by Ammianus Marcellinus, (xxiii. 6.)]

[Footnote 56: The Armenian nobility was numerous and powerful. Moses mentions many families which were distinguished under the reign of Valarsaces, (l. ii. 7,) and which still subsisted in his own time, about the middle of the fifth century. See the preface of his Editors.]

[Footnote 57: She was named Chosroiduchta, and had not the os patulum like other women. (Hist. Armen. l. ii. c. 79.) I do not understand the expression. Note: Os patulum signifies merely a large and widely opening mouth. Ovid (Metam. xv. 513) says, speaking of the monster who attacked Hippolytus, patulo partem maris evomit ore. Probably a wide mouth was a common defect among the Armenian women.—G.]

[Footnote 57/1: Mamgo (according to M. St. Martin, note to Le Beau. ii. 213) belonged to the imperial race of Hon, who had filled the throne of China for four hundred years. Dethroned by the usurping race of Wei, Mamgo found a hospitable reception in Persia in the reign of Ardeschir. The emperor of china having demanded the surrender of the fugitive and his partisans, Sapor, then king, threatened with war both by Rome and China, counselled Mamgo to retire into Armenia. "I have expelled him from my dominions, (he answered the Chinese ambassador;) I have banished him to the extremity of the earth, where the sun sets; I have dismissed him to certain death." Compare Mem. sur l'Armenie, ii. 25.—M.]

[Footnote 58: In the Armenian history, (l. ii. 78,) as well as in the Geography, (p. 367,) China is called Zenia, or Zenastan. It is characterized by the production of silk, by the opulence of the natives, and by their love of peace, above all the other nations of the earth. Note: See St. Martin, Mem. sur l'Armenie, i. 304.]

[Footnote 59: Vou-ti, the first emperor of the seventh dynasty, who then reigned in China, had political transactions with Fergana, a province of Sogdiana, and is said to have received a Roman embassy, (Histoire des Huns, tom. i. p. 38.) In those ages the Chinese kept a garrison at Kashgar, and one of their generals, about the time of Trajan, marched as far as the Caspian Sea. With regard to the intercourse between China and the Western countries, a curious memoir of M. de Guignes may be consulted, in the Academie des Inscriptions, tom. xxii. p. 355. Note: The Chinese Annals mention, under the ninth year of Yan-hi, which corresponds with the year 166 J. C., an embassy which arrived from Tathsin, and was sent by a prince called An-thun, who can be no other than Marcus Aurelius Antoninus, who then ruled over the Romans. St. Martin, Mem. sur l'Armaenic. ii. 30. See also Klaproth, Tableaux Historiques de l'Asie, p. 69. The embassy came by Jy-nan, Tonquin.—M.]

[Footnote 60: See Hist. Armen. l. ii. c. 81.]

For a while, fortune appeared to favor the enterprising valor of Tiridates. He not only expelled the enemies of his family and country from the whole extent of Armenia, but in the prosecution of his revenge he carried his arms, or at least his incursions, into the heart of Assyria. The historian, who has preserved the name of Tiridates from oblivion, celebrates, with a degree of national enthusiasm, his personal prowess: and, in the true spirit of eastern romance, describes the giants and the elephants that fell beneath his invincible arm. It is from other information that we discover the distracted state of the Persian monarchy, to which the king of Armenia was indebted for some part of his advantages. The throne was disputed by the ambition of contending brothers; and Hormuz, after exerting without success the strength of his own party, had recourse to the dangerous assistance of the barbarians who inhabited the banks of the Caspian Sea. [61] The civil war was, however, soon terminated, either by a victor or by a reconciliation; and Narses, who was universally acknowledged as king of Persia, directed his whole force against the foreign enemy. The contest then became too unequal; nor was the valor of the hero able to withstand the power of the monarch, Tiridates, a second time expelled from the throne of Armenia, once more took refuge in the court of the emperors. [611] Narses soon reestablished his authority over the revolted province; and loudly complaining of the protection afforded by the Romans to rebels and fugitives, aspired to the conquest of the East. [62]

[Footnote 61: Ipsos Persas ipsumque Regem ascitis Saccis, et Russis, et Gellis, petit frater Ormies. Panegyric. Vet. iii. 1. The Saccae were a nation of wandering Scythians, who encamped towards the sources of the Oxus and the Jaxartes. The Gelli where the inhabitants of Ghilan, along the Caspian Sea, and who so long, under the name of Dilemines, infested the Persian monarchy. See d'Herbelot, Bibliotheque]

[Footnote 611: M St. Martin represents this differently. Le roi de Perse profits d'un voyage que Tiridate avoit fait a Rome pour attaquer ce royaume. This reads like the evasion of the national historians to disguise the fact discreditable to their hero. See Mem. sur l'Armenie, i. 304.—M.]

[Footnote 62: Moses of Chorene takes no notice of this second revolution, which I have been obliged to collect from a passage of Ammianus Marcellinus, (l. xxiii. c. 5.) Lactantius speaks of the ambition of Narses: "Concitatus domesticis exemplis avi sui Saporis ad occupandum orientem magnis copiis inhiabat." De Mort. Persecut. c. 9.]

Neither prudence nor honor could permit the emperors to forsake the cause of the Armenian king, and it was resolved to exert the force of the empire in the Persian war. Diocletian, with the calm dignity which he constantly assumed, fixed his own station in the city of Antioch, from whence he prepared and directed the military operations. [63] The conduct of the legions was intrusted to the intrepid valor of Galerius, who, for that important purpose, was removed from the banks of the Danube to those of the Euphrates. The armies soon encountered each other in the plains of Mesopotamia, and two battles were fought with various and doubtful success; but the third engagement was of a more decisive nature; and the Roman army received a total overthrow, which is attributed to the rashness of Galerius, who, with an inconsiderable body of troops, attacked the innumerable host of the Persians. [64] But the consideration of the country that was the scene of action, may suggest another reason for his defeat. The same ground on which Galerius was vanquished, had been rendered memorable by the death of Crassus, and the slaughter of ten legions. It was a plain of more than sixty miles, which extended from the hills of Carrhae to the Euphrates; a smooth and barren surface of sandy desert, without a hillock, without a tree, and without a spring of fresh water. [65] The steady infantry of the Romans, fainting with heat and thirst, could neither hope for victory if they preserved their ranks, nor break their ranks without exposing themselves to the most imminent danger. In this situation they were gradually encompassed by the superior numbers, harassed by the rapid evolutions, and destroyed by the arrows of the barbarian cavalry.

The king of Armenia had signalized his valor in the battle, and acquired personal glory by the public misfortune. He was pursued as far as the Euphrates; his horse was wounded, and it appeared impossible for him to escape the victorious enemy. In this extremity Tiridates embraced the only refuge which appeared before him: he dismounted and plunged into the stream. His armor was heavy, the river very deep, and at those parts at least half a mile in breadth; [66] yet such was his strength and dexterity, that he reached in safety the opposite bank. [67] With regard to the Roman general, we are ignorant of the circumstances of his escape; but when he returned to Antioch, Diocletian received him, not with the tenderness of a friend and colleague, but with the indignation of an offended sovereign. The haughtiest of men, clothed in his purple, but humbled by the sense of his fault and misfortune, was obliged to follow the emperor's chariot above a mile on foot, and to exhibit, before the whole court, the spectacle of his disgrace. [68]

[Footnote 63: We may readily believe, that Lactantius ascribes to cowardice the conduct of Diocletian. Julian, in his oration, says, that he remained with all the forces of the empire; a very hyperbolical expression.]

[Footnote 64: Our five abbreviators, Eutropius, Festus, the two Victors, and Orosius, all relate the last and great battle; but Orosius is the only one who speaks of the two former.]

[Footnote 65: The nature of the country is finely described by Plutarch, in the life of Crassus; and by Xenophon, in the first book of the Anabasis]

[Footnote 66: See Foster's Dissertation in the second volume of the translation of the Anabasis by Spelman; which I will venture to recommend as one of the best versions extant.]

[Footnote 67: Hist. Armen. l. ii. c. 76. I have transferred this exploit of Tiridates from an imaginary defeat to the real one of Galerius.]

[Footnote 68: Ammian. Marcellin. l. xiv. The mile, in the hands of Eutropoius, (ix. 24,) of Festus (c. 25,) and of Orosius, (vii 25), easily increased to several miles]

As soon as Diocletian had indulged his private resentment, and asserted the majesty of supreme power, he yielded to the submissive entreaties of the Caesar, and permitted him to retrieve his own honor, as well as that of the Roman arms. In the room of the unwarlike troops of Asia, which had most probably served in the first expedition, a second army was drawn from the veterans and new levies of the Illyrian frontier, and a considerable body of Gothic auxiliaries were taken into the Imperial pay. [69] At the head of a chosen army of twenty-five thousand men, Galerius again passed the Euphrates; but, instead of exposing his legions in the open plains of Mesopotamia he advanced through the mountains of Armenia, where he found the inhabitants devoted to his cause, and the country as favorable to the operations of infantry as it was inconvenient for the motions of cavalry. [70] Adversity had confirmed the Roman discipline, while the barbarians, elated by success, were become so negligent and remiss, that in the moment when they least expected it, they were surprised by the active conduct of Galerius, who, attended only by two horsemen, had with his own eyes secretly examined the state and position of their camp. A surprise, especially in the night time, was for the most part fatal to a Persian army. "Their horses were tied, and generally shackled, to prevent their running away; and if an alarm happened, a Persian had his housing to fix, his horse to bridle, and his corselet to put on, before he could mount." [71] On this occasion, the impetuous attack of Galerius spread disorder and dismay over the camp of the barbarians. A slight resistance was followed by a dreadful carnage, and, in the general confusion, the wounded monarch (for Narses commanded his armies in person) fled towards the deserts of Media. His sumptuous tents, and those of his satraps, afforded an immense booty to the conqueror; and an incident is mentioned, which proves the rustic but martial ignorance of the legions in the elegant superfluities of life. A bag of shining leather, filled with pearls, fell into the hands of a private soldier; he carefully preserved the bag, but he threw away its contents, judging that whatever was of no use could not possibly be of any value. [72] The principal loss of Narses was of a much more affecting nature. Several of his wives, his sisters, and children, who had attended the army, were made captives in the defeat. But though the character of Galerius had in general very little affinity with that of Alexander, he imitated, after his victory, the amiable behavior of the Macedonian towards the family of Darius. The wives and children of Narses were protected from violence and rapine, conveyed to a place of safety, and treated with every mark of respect and tenderness, that was due from a generous enemy to their age, their sex, and their royal dignity. [73]

[Footnote 69: Aurelius Victor. Jornandes de Rebus Geticis, c. 21.]

[Footnote 70: Aurelius Victor says, "Per Armeniam in hostes contendit, quae fermo sola, seu facilior vincendi via est." He followed the conduct of Trajan, and the idea of Julius Caesar.]

[Footnote 71: Xenophon's Anabasis, l. iii. For that reason the Persian cavalry encamped sixty stadia from the enemy.]

[Footnote 72: The story is told by Ammianus, l. xxii. Instead of saccum, some read scutum.]

[Footnote 73: The Persians confessed the Roman superiority in morals as well as in arms. Eutrop. ix. 24. But this respect and gratitude of enemies is very seldom to be found in their own accounts.]

PART III

While the East anxiously expected the decision of this great contest, the emperor Diocletian, having assembled in Syria a strong army of observation, displayed from a distance the resources of the Roman power, and reserved himself for any future emergency of the war. On the intelligence of the victory he condescended to advance towards the frontier, with a view of moderating, by his presence and counsels, the pride of Galerius. The interview of the Roman princes at Nisibis was accompanied with every expression of respect on one side, and of esteem on the other. It was in that city that they soon afterwards gave audience to the ambassador of the Great King. [74] The power, or at least the spirit, of Narses, had been broken by his last defeat; and he considered an immediate peace as the only means that could stop the progress of the Roman arms. He despatched Apharban, a servant who possessed his favor and confidence, with a commission to negotiate a treaty, or rather to receive whatever conditions the conqueror should impose. Apharban opened the conference by expressing his master's gratitude for the generous treatment of his family, and by soliciting the liberty of those illustrious captives. He celebrated the valor of Galerius, without degrading the reputation of Narses, and thought it no dishonor to confess the superiority of the victorious Caesar, over a monarch who had surpassed in glory all the princes of his race. Notwithstanding the justice of the Persian cause, he was empowered to submit the present differences to the decision of the emperors themselves; convinced as he was, that, in the midst of prosperity, they would not be unmindful of the vicissitudes of fortune. Apharban concluded his discourse in the style of eastern allegory, by observing that the Roman and Persian monarchies were the two eyes of the world, which would remain imperfect and mutilated if either of them should be put out.

[Footnote 74: *The account of the negotiation is taken from the fragments of Peter the Patrician, in the Excerpta Legationum, published in the Byzantine Collection. Peter lived under Justinian; but it is very evident, by the nature of his materials, that they are drawn from the most authentic and respectable writers.*]

"It well becomes the Persians," replied Galerius, with a transport of fury, which seemed to convulse his whole frame, "it well becomes the Persians to expatiate on the vicissitudes of fortune, and calmly to read us lectures on the virtues of moderation. Let them remember their own moderation, towards the unhappy Valerian. They vanquished him by fraud, they treated him with indignity. They detained him till the last moment of his life in shameful captivity, and after his death they exposed his body to perpetual ignominy." Softening, however, his tone, Galerius insinuated to the ambassador, that it had never been the practice of the Romans to trample on a prostrate enemy; and that, on this occasion, they should consult their own dignity rather than the Persian merit. He dismissed Apharban with a hope that Narses would soon be informed on what conditions he might obtain, from the clemency of the emperors, a lasting peace, and the restoration of his wives and children. In this conference we may discover the fierce passions of Galerius, as well as his deference to the superior wisdom and authority of Diocletian. The ambition of the former grasped at the conquest of the East, and had proposed to reduce Persia into the state of a province. The prudence of the latter, who adhered to the moderate policy of Augustus and the Antonines, embraced the favorable opportunity of terminating a successful war by an honorable and advantageous peace. [75]

[Footnote 75: *Adeo victor (says Aurelius) ut ni Valerius, cujus nutu omnis gerebantur, abnuisset, Romani fasces in provinciam novam ferrentur Verum pars terrarum tamen nobis utilior quaesita.*]

In pursuance of their promise, the emperors soon afterwards appointed Sicorius Probus, one of their secretaries, to acquaint the Persian court with their final resolution. As the minister of peace, he was received with every mark of politeness and friendship; but, under the pretence of allowing him the necessary repose after so long a journey, the audience of Probus was deferred from day to day; and he attended the slow motions of the king, till at length he was admitted to his presence, near the River Asprudus in Media. The secret motive of Narses, in this delay, had been to collect such a military force as might enable him, though sincerely desirous of peace, to negotiate with the greater weight and dignity. Three persons only assisted at this important conference, the minister Apharban, the praefect of the guards, and an officer who had commanded on the Armenian frontier. [76] The first condition proposed by the ambassador is not at present of a very intelligible nature; that the city of Nisibis might be established for the place of mutual exchange, or, as we should formerly have termed it, for the staple of trade, between the two empires. There is no difficulty in conceiving the intention of the Roman princes to improve their revenue by some restraints upon commerce; but as Nisibis was situated within their own dominions, and as they were masters both of the imports and exports, it should seem that such restraints were the objects of an internal law, rather than of a foreign treaty. To render them more effectual, some stipulations were probably required on the side of the king of Persia, which appeared so very repugnant either to his interest or to his dignity, that Narses could not be persuaded to subscribe them. As this was the only article to which he refused his consent, it was no longer insisted on; and the emperors either suffered the trade to flow in its natural channels, or contented themselves with such restrictions, as it depended on their own authority to establish.

[Footnote 76: He had been governor of Sumium, (Pot. Patricius in Excerpt. Legat. p. 30.) This province seems to be mentioned by Moses of Chorene, (Geograph. p. 360,) and lay to the east of Mount Ararat. Note: The Siounikh of the Armenian writers St. Martin i. 142.—M.]

As soon as this difficulty was removed, a solemn peace was concluded and ratified between the two nations. The conditions of a treaty so glorious to the empire, and so necessary to Persia Persian, may deserve a more peculiar attention, as the history of Rome presents very few transactions of a similar nature; most of her wars having either been terminated by absolute conquest, or waged against barbarians ignorant of the use of letters. I. The Aboras, or, as it is called by Xenophon, the Araxes, was fixed as the boundary between the two monarchies. [77] That river, which rose near the Tigris, was increased, a few miles below Nisibis, by the little stream of the Mygdonius, passed under the walls of Singara, and fell into the Euphrates at Circesium, a frontier town, which, by the care of Diocletian, was very strongly fortified. [78] Mesopotomia, the object of so many wars, was ceded to the empire; and the Persians, by this treaty, renounced all pretensions to that great province. II. They relinquished to the Romans five provinces beyond the Tigris. [79] Their situation formed a very useful barrier, and their natural strength was soon improved by art and military skill. Four of these, to the north of the river, were districts of obscure fame and inconsiderable extent; Intiline, Zabdicene, Arzanene, and Moxoene; [79/1] but on the east of the Tigris, the empire acquired the large and mountainous territory of Carduene, the ancient seat of the Carduchians, who preserved for many ages their manly freedom in the heart of the despotic monarchies of Asia. The ten thousand Greeks traversed their country, after a painful march, or rather engagement, of seven days; and it is confessed by their leader, in his incomparable relation of the retreat, that they suffered more from the arrows of the Carduchians, than from the power of the Great King. [80] Their posterity, the Curds, with very little alteration either of name or manners, [80/1] acknowledged the nominal sovereignty of the Turkish sultan. III. It is almost needless to observe, that Tiridates, the faithful ally of Rome, was restored to the throne of his fathers, and that the rights of the Imperial supremacy were fully asserted and secured. The limits of Armenia were extended as far as the fortress of Sintha in Media, and this increase of dominion was not so much an act of liberality as of justice. Of the provinces already mentioned beyond the Tigris, the four first had been dismembered by the Parthians from the crown of Armenia; [81] and when the Romans acquired the possession of them, they stipulated, at the expense of the usurpers, an ample compensation, which invested their ally with the extensive and fertile country of Atropatene. Its principal city, in the same situation perhaps as the modern Tauris, was frequently honored by the residence of Tiridates; and as it sometimes bore the name of Ecbatana, he imitated, in the buildings and fortifications, the splendid capital of the Medes. [82] IV. The country of Iberia was barren, its inhabitants rude and savage. But they were accustomed to the use of arms, and they separated from the empire barbarians much fiercer and more formidable than themselves. The narrow defiles of Mount Caucasus were in their hands, and it was in their choice, either to admit or to exclude the wandering tribes of Sarmatia, whenever a rapacious spirit urged them to penetrate into the richer climes of the South. [83] The nomination of the kings of Iberia, which was resigned by the Persian monarch to the emperors, contributed to the strength and security of the Roman power in Asia. [84] The East enjoyed a profound tranquillity during forty years; and the treaty between the rival monarchies was strictly observed till the death of Tiridates; when a new generation, animated with different views and different passions, succeeded to the government of the world; and the grandson of Narses undertook a long and memorable war against the princes of the house of Constantine.

[Footnote 77: By an error of the geographer Ptolemy, the position of Singara is removed from the Aboras to the Tigris, which may have produced the mistake of Peter, in assigning the latter river for the boundary, instead of the former. The line of the Roman frontier traversed, but never followed, the course of the Tigris. Note: There are here several errors. Gibbon has confounded the streams, and the towns which they pass. The Aboras, or rather the Chaboras, the Araxes of Xenophon, has its source above Ras-Ain or Re-Saina, (Theodosiopolis,) about twenty-seven leagues from the Tigris; it receives the waters of the Mygdonius, or Saocoras, about thirty-three leagues below Nisibis. at a town now called Al Nahraim; it does not pass under the walls of Singara; it is the Saocoras that washes the walls of that town: the latter river has its source near Nisibis. at five leagues from the Tigris. See D'Anv. l'Euphrate et le Tigre, 46, 49, 50, and the map.— To the east of the Tigris is another less considerable river, named also the Chaboras, which D'Anville calls the Centrites, Khabour, Nicephorius, without quoting the authorities on which he gives those names. Gibbon did not mean to speak of this river, which does not pass by Singara, and does not fall into the Euphrates. See Michaelis, Supp. ad Lex. Hebraica. 3d part, p. 664, 665.—G.]

[Footnote 78: Procopius de Edificiis, l. ii. c. 6.]

[Footnote 79: Three of the provinces, Zabdicene, Arzanene, and Carduene, are allowed on all sides. But instead of the other two, Peter (in Excerpt. Leg. p. 30) inserts Rehimene and Sophene. I have preferred Ammianus, (l. xxv. 7,) because it might be proved that Sophene was never in the hands of the Persians, either before the reign of Diocletian, or after that of Jovian. For want of correct maps, like those of M. d'Anville, almost all the moderns, with Tillemont and Valesius at their head, have imagined, that it was in respect to Persia, and not to Rome, that the five provinces were situate beyond the Tigris.]

[Footnote 79/1: See St. Martin, note on Le Beau, i. 380. He would read, for Intiline, Ingeleme, the name of a small province of Armenia, near the sources of the Tigris, mentioned by St. Epiphanius, (Haeres, 60;) for the unknown name Arzacene, with Gibbon, Arzanene. These provinces do not appear to have made an integral part of the Roman empire; Roman garrisons replaced those of Persia, but the sovereignty remained in the hands of the feudatory princes of Armenia. A prince of Carduene, ally or dependent on the empire, with the Roman name of Jovianus, occurs in the reign of Julian.—M.]

[Footnote 80: Xenophon's Anabasis, l. iv. Their bows were three cubits in length, their arrows two; they rolled down stones that were each a wagon load. The Greeks found a great many villages in that rude country.]

[Footnote 80/1: I travelled through this country in 1810, and should judge, from what I have read and seen of its inhabitants, that they have remained unchanged in their appearance and character for more than twenty centuries Malcolm, note to Hist. of Persia, vol. i. p. 82.—M.]

[Footnote 81: According to Eutropius, (vi. 9, as the text is represented by the best Mss.,) the city of Tigranocerta was in Arzanene. The names and situation of the other three may be faintly traced.]

[Footnote 82: Compare Herodotus, l. i. c. 97, with Moses Choronens. Hist Armen. l. ii. c. 84, and the map of Armenia given by his editors.]

[Footnote 83: Hiberi, locorum potentes, Caspia via Sarmatam in Armenios raptim effundunt. Tacit. Annal. vi. 34. See Strabon. Geograph. l. xi. p. 764, edit. Casaub.]

[Footnote 84: Peter Patricius (in Excerpt. Leg. p. 30) is the only writer who mentions the Iberian article of the treaty.]

The arduous work of rescuing the distressed empire from tyrants and barbarians had now been completely achieved by a succession of Illyrian peasants. As soon as Diocletian entered into the twentieth year of his reign, he celebrated that memorable aera, as well as the success of his arms, by the pomp of a Roman triumph. [85] Maximian, the equal partner of his power, was his only companion in the glory of that day. The two Caesars had fought and conquered, but the merit of their exploits was ascribed, according to the rigor of ancient maxims, to the auspicious influence of their fathers and emperors. [86] The triumph of Diocletian and Maximian was less magnificent, perhaps, than those of Aurelian and Probus, but it was dignified by several circumstances of superior fame and good fortune. Africa and Britain, the Rhine, the Danube, and the Nile, furnished their respective trophies; but the most distinguished ornament was of a more singular nature, a Persian victory followed by an important conquest. The representations of rivers, mountains, and provinces, were carried before the Imperial car. The images of the captive wives, the sisters, and the children of the Great King, afforded a new and grateful spectacle to the vanity of the people. [87] In the eyes of posterity, this triumph is remarkable, by a distinction of a less honorable kind. It was the last that Rome ever beheld. Soon after this period, the emperors ceased to vanquish, and Rome ceased to be the capital of the empire.

[Footnote 85: Euseb. in Chron. Pagi ad annum. Till the discovery of the treatise De Mortibus Persecutorum, it was not certain that the triumph and the Vicennalia was celebrated at the same time.]

[Footnote 86: At the time of the Vicennalia, Galerius seems to have kept station on the Danube. See Lactant. de M. P. c. 38.]

[Footnote 87: Eutropius (ix. 27) mentions them as a part of the triumph. As the persons had been restored to Narses, nothing more than their images could be exhibited.]

The spot on which Rome was founded had been consecrated by ancient ceremonies and imaginary miracles. The presence of some god, or the memory of some hero, seemed to animate every part of the city, and the empire of the world had been promised to the Capitol. [88] The native Romans felt and confessed the power of this agreeable illusion. It was derived from their ancestors, had grown up with their earliest habits of life, and was protected, in some measure, by the opinion of political utility. The form and the seat of government were intimately blended together, nor was it esteemed possible to transport the one without destroying the other. [89] But the sovereignty of the capital was gradually annihilated in the extent of conquest; the provinces rose to the same level, and the vanquished nations acquired the name and privileges, without imbibing the partial affections, of Romans. During a long period, however, the remains of the ancient constitution, and the influence of custom, preserved the dignity of Rome. The emperors, though perhaps of African or Illyrian extraction, respected their adopted country, as the seat of their power, and the centre of their extensive dominions. The emergencies of war very frequently required their presence on the frontiers; but Diocletian and Maximian were the first Roman princes who fixed, in time of peace, their ordinary residence in the provinces; and their conduct, however it might be suggested by private motives, was justified by very specious considerations of policy. The court of the emperor of the West was, for the most part, established at Milan, whose situation, at the foot of the Alps, appeared far more convenient than that of Rome, for the important purpose of watching the motions of the barbarians of Germany. Milan soon assumed the splendor of an Imperial city. The houses are described as numerous and well built; the manners of the people as polished and liberal. A circus, a theatre, a mint, a palace, baths, which bore the name of their founder Maximian; porticos adorned with statues, and a double circumference of walls, contributed to the beauty of the new capital; nor did it seem oppressed even by the proximity of Rome. [90] To rival the majesty of Rome was the ambition likewise of Diocletian, who employed his leisure, and the wealth of the East, in the embellishment of Nicomedia, a city placed on the verge of Europe and Asia, almost at an equal distance between the Danube and the Euphrates. By the taste of the monarch, and at the expense of the people, Nicomedia acquired, in the space of a few years, a degree of magnificence which might appear to have required the labor of ages, and became inferior only to Rome, Alexandria, and Antioch, in extent of populousness. [91] The life of Diocletian and Maximian was a life of action, and a considerable portion of it was spent in camps, or in the long and frequent marches; but whenever the public business allowed them any relaxation, they seemed to have retired with pleasure to their favorite residences of Nicomedia and Milan. Till Diocletian, in the twentieth year of his reign, celebrated his Roman triumph, it is extremely doubtful whether he ever visited the ancient capital of the empire. Even on that memorable occasion his stay did not exceed two months. Disgusted with the licentious familiarity of the people, he quitted Rome with precipitation thirteen days before it was expected that he should have appeared in the senate, invested with the ensigns of the consular dignity. [92]

[Footnote 88: Livy gives us a speech of Camillus on that subject, (v. 51—55,) full of eloquence and sensibility, in opposition to a design of removing the seat of government from Rome to the neighboring city of Veii.]

[Footnote 89: Julius Caesar was reproached with the intention of removing the empire to Ilium or Alexandria. See Sueton. in Caesar. c. 79. According to the ingenious conjecture of Le Fevre and Dacier, the ode of the third book of Horace was intended to divert from the execution of a similar design.]

[Footnote 90: See Aurelius Victor, who likewise mentions the buildings erected by Maximian at Carthage, probably during the Moorish war. We shall insert some verses of Ausonius de Clar. Urb. v.— Et Mediolani miraeomnia: copia rerum; Innumerae cultaeque domus; facunda virorum Ingenia, et mores laeti: tum duplice muro Amplificata loci species; populique voluptas Circus; et inclusi moles cuneata Theatri; Templa, Palatinaeque arces, opulensque Moneta, Et regio Herculei celebris sub honore lavacri. Cunctaque marmoreis ornata Peristyla signis; Moeniaque in valli formam circumdata labro, Omnia quae magnis operum velut aemula formis Excellunt: nec juncta premit vicinia Romae.]

[Footnote 91: Lactant. de M. P. c. 17. Libanius, Orat. viii. p. 203.]

[Footnote 92: Lactant. de M. P. c. 17. On a similar occasion, Ammianus mentions the dicacitas plebis, as not very agreeable to an Imperial ear. (See l. xvi. c. 10.)]

The dislike expressed by Diocletian towards Rome and Roman freedom, was not the effect of momentary caprice, but the result of the most artful policy. That crafty prince had framed a new system of Imperial government, which was afterwards completed by the family of Constantine; and as the image of the old constitution was religiously preserved in the senate, he resolved to deprive that order of its small remains of power and consideration. We may recollect, about eight years before the elevation, of Diocletian the transient greatness, and the ambitious hopes, of the Roman senate. As long as that enthusiasm prevailed, many of the nobles imprudently displayed their zeal in the cause of freedom; and after the successes of Probus had withdrawn their countenance from the republican party, the senators were unable to disguise their impotent resentment. As the sovereign of Italy, Maximian was intrusted with the care of extinguishing this troublesome, rather than dangerous spirit, and the task was perfectly suited to his cruel temper. The most illustrious members of the senate, whom Diocletian always affected to esteem, were involved, by his colleague, in the accusation of imaginary plots; and the possession of an elegant villa, or a well-cultivated estate, was interpreted as a convincing evidence of guilt. [93] The camp of the Praetorians, which had so long oppressed, began to protect, the majesty of Rome; and as those haughty troops were conscious of the decline of their power, they were naturally disposed to unite their strength with the authority of the senate. By the prudent measures of Diocletian, the numbers of the Praetorians were insensibly reduced, their privileges abolished, [94] and their place supplied by two faithful legions of Illyricum, who, under the new titles of Jovians and Herculians, were appointed to perform the service of the Imperial guards. [95] But the most fatal though secret wound, which the senate received from the hands of Diocletian and Maximian, was inflicted by the inevitable operation of their absence. As long as the emperors resided at Rome, that assembly might be oppressed, but it could scarcely be neglected. The successors of Augustus exercised the power of dictating whatever laws their wisdom or caprice might suggest; but those laws were ratified by the sanction of the senate. The model of ancient freedom was preserved in its deliberations and decrees; and wise princes, who respected the prejudices of the Roman people, were in some measure obliged to assume the language and behavior suitable to the general and first magistrate of the republic. In the armies and in the provinces, they displayed the dignity of monarchs; and when they fixed their residence at a distance from the capital, they forever laid aside the dissimulation which Augustus had recommended to his successors. In the exercise of the legislative as well as the executive power, the sovereign advised with his ministers, instead of consulting the great council of the nation. The name of the senate was mentioned with honor till the last period of the empire; the vanity of its members was still flattered with honorary distinctions; [96] but the assembly which had so long been the source, and so long the instrument of power, was respectfully suffered to sink into oblivion. The senate of Rome, losing all connection with the Imperial court and the actual constitution, was left a venerable but useless monument of antiquity on the Capitoline hill.

[Footnote 93: Lactantius accuses Maximian of destroying fictis criminationibus lumina senatus, (De M. P. c. 8.) Aurelius Victor speaks very doubtfully of the faith of Diocletian towards his friends.]

[Footnote 94: Truncatae vires urbis, imminuto praetoriarum cohortium atque in armis vulgi numero. Aurelius Victor. Lactantius attributes to Galerius the prosecution of the same plan, (c. 26.)]

[Footnote 95: They were old corps stationed in Illyricum; and according to the ancient establishment, they each consisted of six thousand men. They had acquired much reputation by the use of the plumbatoe, or darts loaded with lead. Each soldier carried five of these, which he darted from a considerable distance, with great strength and dexterity. See Vegetius, i. 17.]

[Footnote 96: See the Theodosian Code, l. vi. tit. ii. with Godefroy's commentary.]

PART IV

When the Roman princes had lost sight of the senate and of their ancient capital, they easily forgot the origin and nature of their legal power. The civil offices of consul, of proconsul, of censor, and of tribune, by the union of which it had been formed, betrayed to the people its republican extraction. Those modest titles were laid aside; [97] and if they still distinguished their high station by the appellation of Emperor, or Imperator, that word was understood in a new and more dignified sense, and no longer denoted the general of the Roman armies, but the sovereign of the Roman world. The name of Emperor, which was at first of a military nature, was associated with another of a more servile kind. The epithet of Dominus, or Lord, in its primitive signification, was expressive, not of the authority of a prince over his subjects, or of a commander over his soldiers, but of the despotic power of a master over his domestic slaves. [98] Viewing it in that odious light, it had been rejected with abhorrence by the first Caesars. Their resistance insensibly became more feeble, and the name less odious; till at length the style of our Lord and Emperor was not only bestowed by flattery, but was regularly admitted into the laws and public monuments. Such lofty epithets were sufficient to elate and satisfy the most excessive vanity; and if the successors of Diocletian still declined the title of King, it seems to have been the effect not so much of their moderation as of their delicacy. Wherever the Latin tongue was in use, (and it was the language of government throughout the empire,) the Imperial title, as it was peculiar to themselves, conveyed a more respectable idea than the name of king, which they must have shared with a hundred barbarian chieftains; or which, at the best, they could derive only from Romulus, or from Tarquin. But the sentiments of the East were very different from those of the West. From the earliest period of history, the sovereigns of Asia had been celebrated in the Greek language by the title of Basileus, or King; and since it was considered as the first distinction among men, it was soon employed by the servile provincials of the East, in their humble addresses to the Roman throne. [99] Even the attributes, or at least the titles, of the Divinity, were usurped by Diocletian and Maximian, who transmitted them to a succession of Christian emperors. [100] Such extravagant compliments, however, soon lose their impiety by losing their meaning; and when the ear is once accustomed to the sound, they are heard with indifference, as vague though excessive professions of respect.

[Footnote 97: See the 12th dissertation in Spanheim's excellent work de Usu Numismatum. From medals, inscriptions, and historians, he examines every title separately, and traces it from Augustus to the moment of its disappearing.]

[Footnote 98: Pliny (in Panegyr. c. 3, 55, &c.) speaks of Dominus with execration, as synonymous to Tyrant, and opposite to Prince. And the same Pliny regularly gives that title (in the tenth book of the epistles) to his friend rather than master, the virtuous Trajan. This strange contradiction puzzles the commentators, who think, and the translators, who can write.]

[Footnote 99: Synesius de Regno, edit. Petav. p. 15. I am indebted for this quotation to the Abbe de la Bleterie.]

[Footnote 100: Soe Vandale de Consecratione, p. 354, &c. It was customary for the emperors to mention (in the preamble of laws) their numen, sacreo majesty, divine oracles, &c. According to Tillemont, Gregory Nazianzen complains most bitterly of the profanation, especially when it was practised by an Arian emperor. Note: In the time of the republic, says Hegewisch, when the consuls, the praetors, and the other magistrates appeared in public, to perform the functions of their office, their dignity was announced both by the symbols which use had consecrated, and the brilliant cortege by which they were accompanied. But this dignity belonged to the office, not to the individual; this pomp belonged to the magistrate, not to the man. The consul, followed, in the comitia, by all the senate, the praetors, the quaestors, the aediles, the lictors, the apparitors, and the heralds, on reentering his house, was served only by freedmen and by his slaves. The first emperors went no further. Tiberius had, for his personal attendance, only a moderate number of slaves, and a few freedmen. (Tacit. Ann. iv. 7.) But in proportion as the republican forms disappeared, one after another, the inclination of the emperors to environ themselves with personal pomp, displayed itself more and more. The magnificence and the ceremonial of the East were entirely introduced by Diocletian, and were consecrated by Constantine to the Imperial use. Thenceforth the palace, the court, the table, all the personal attendance, distinguished the emperor from his subjects, still more than his superior dignity. The organization which Diocletian gave to his new court, attached less honor and distinction to rank than to services performed towards the members of the Imperial family. Hegewisch, Essai, Hist. sur les Finances Romains. Few historians have characterized,

in a more philosophic manner, the influence of a new institution.—G.—It is singular that the son of a slave reduced the haughty aristocracy of Home to the offices of servitude.—M.]

From the time of Augustus to that of Diocletian, the Roman princes, conversing in a familiar manner among their fellow-citizens, were saluted only with the same respect that was usually paid to senators and magistrates. Their principal distinction was the Imperial or military robe of purple; whilst the senatorial garment was marked by a broad, and the equestrian by a narrow, band or stripe of the same honorable color. The pride, or rather the policy, of Diocletian, engaged that artful prince to introduce the stately magnificence of the court of Persia. [101] He ventured to assume the diadem, an ornament detested by the Romans as the odious ensign of royalty, and the use of which had been considered as the most desperate act of the madness of Caligula. It was no more than a broad white fillet set with pearls, which encircled the emperor's head. The sumptuous robes of Diocletian and his successors were of silk and gold; and it is remarked with indignation, that even their shoes were studded with the most precious gems. The access to their sacred person was every day rendered more difficult by the institution of new forms and ceremonies. The avenues of the palace were strictly guarded by the various schools, as they began to be called, of domestic officers. The interior apartments were intrusted to the jealous vigilance of the eunuchs, the increase of whose numbers and influence was the most infallible symptom of the progress of despotism. When a subject was at length admitted to the Imperial presence, he was obliged, whatever might be his rank, to fall prostrate on the ground, and to adore, according to the eastern fashion, the divinity of his lord and master. [102] Diocletian was a man of sense, who, in the course of private as well as public life, had formed a just estimate both of himself and of mankind: nor is it easy to conceive, that in substituting the manners of Persia to those of Rome, he was seriously actuated by so mean a principle as that of vanity. He flattered himself, that an ostentation of splendor and luxury would subdue the imagination of the multitude; that the monarch would be less exposed to the rude license of the people and the soldiers, as his person was secluded from the public view; and that habits of submission would insensibly be productive of sentiments of veneration. Like the modesty affected by Augustus, the state maintained by Diocletian was a theatrical representation; but it must be confessed, that of the two comedies, the former was of a much more liberal and manly character than the latter. It was the aim of the one to disguise, and the object of the other to display, the unbounded power which the emperors possessed over the Roman world.

[Footnote 101: See Spanheim de Usu Numismat. Dissert. xii.]

[Footnote 102: Aurelius Victor. Eutropius, ix. 26. It appears by the Panegyrists, that the Romans were soon reconciled to the name and ceremony of adoration.]

Ostentation was the first principle of the new system instituted by Diocletian. The second was division. He divided the empire, the provinces, and every branch of the civil as well as military administration. He multiplied the wheels of the machine of government, and rendered its operations less rapid, but more secure. Whatever advantages and whatever defects might attend these innovations, they must be ascribed in a very great degree to the first inventor; but as the new frame of policy was gradually improved and completed by succeeding princes, it will be more satisfactory to delay the consideration of it till the season of its full maturity and perfection. [103] Reserving, therefore, for the reign of Constantine a more exact picture of the new empire, we shall content ourselves with describing the principal and decisive outline, as it was traced by the hand of Diocletian. He had associated three colleagues in the exercise of the supreme power; and as he was convinced that the abilities of a single man were inadequate to the public defence, he considered the joint administration of four princes not as a temporary expedient, but as a fundamental law of the constitution. It was his intention, that the two elder princes should be distinguished by the use of the diadem, and the title of Augusti; that, as affection or esteem might direct their choice, they should regularly call to their assistance two subordinate colleagues; and that the Coesars, rising in their turn to the first rank, should supply an uninterrupted succession of emperors. The empire was divided into four parts. The East and Italy were the most honorable, the Danube and the Rhine the most laborious stations. The former claimed the presence of the Augusti, the latter were intrusted to the administration of the Coesars. The strength of the legions was in the hands of the four partners of sovereignty, and the despair of successively vanquishing four formidable rivals might intimidate the ambition of an aspiring general. In their civil government, the emperors were supposed to exercise the undivided power of the monarch, and their edicts, inscribed with their joint names, were received in all the provinces, as promulgated by their mutual councils and authority. Notwithstanding these precautions, the political union of the Roman world was gradually dissolved, and a principle of division was introduced, which, in the course of a few years, occasioned the perpetual separation of the Eastern and Western Empires.

[Footnote 103: The innovations introduced by Diocletian are chiefly deduced, 1st, from some very strong passages in Lactantius; and, 2dly, from the new and various offices which, in the Theodosian code, appear already established in the beginning of the reign of Constantine.]

The system of Diocletian was accompanied with another very material disadvantage, which cannot even at present be totally overlooked; a more expensive establishment, and consequently an increase of taxes, and the oppression of the people. Instead of a modest family of slaves and freedmen, such as had contented the simple greatness of Augustus and Trajan, three or four magnificent courts were established in the various parts of the empire, and as many Roman kings contended with each other and with the Persian monarch for the vain superiority of pomp and luxury. The number of ministers, of magistrates, of officers, and of servants, who filled the different departments of the state, was multiplied beyond the example of former times; and (if we may borrow the warm expression of a contemporary) "when the proportion of those who received, exceeded the proportion of those who contributed, the provinces were oppressed by the weight of tributes." [104] From this period to the extinction of the empire, it would be easy to deduce an uninterrupted series of clamors and complaints. According to his religion and situation, each writer chooses either Diocletian, or Constantine, or Valens, or Theodosius, for the object of his invectives; but they unanimously agree in representing the burden of the public impositions, and particularly the land tax and capitation, as the intolerable and increasing grievance of their own times. From such a concurrence, an impartial historian, who is obliged to extract truth from satire, as well as from panegyric, will be inclined to divide the blame among the princes whom they accuse, and to ascribe their exactions much less to their personal vices, than to the uniform system of their administration. [1041] The emperor Diocletian was indeed the author of that system; but during his reign, the growing evil was confined within the bounds of modesty and discretion, and he deserves the reproach of establishing pernicious precedents, rather than of exercising actual oppression. [105] It may be added, that his revenues were managed with prudent economy; and that after all the current expenses were discharged, there still remained in the Imperial treasury an ample provision either for judicious liberality or for any emergency of the state.

[Footnote 104: Lactant. de M. P. c. 7.]

[Footnote 104/1: The most curious document which has come to light since the publication of Gibbon's History, is the edict of Diocletian, published from an inscription found at Eskihissar, (Stratoniccia,) by Col. Leake. This inscription was first copied by Sherard, afterwards much more completely by Mr. Bankes. It is confirmed and illustrated by a more imperfect copy of the same edict, found in the Levant by a gentleman of Aix, and brought to this country by M. Vescovali. This edict was issued in the name of the four Caesars, Diocletian, Maximian, Constantius, and Galerius. It fixed a maximum of prices throughout the empire, for all the necessaries and commodities of life. The preamble insists, with great vehemence on the extortion and inhumanity of the venders and merchants. Quis enim adeo obtunisi (obtusi) pectores (is) et a sensu inhumanitatis extorris est qui ignorare potest immo non senserit in venalibus rebus quaevel in mercimoniis aguntur vel diurna urbium conversatione tractantur, in tantum se licen liam defusisse, ut effraenata libido rapien—rum copia nec annorum ubertatibus mitigaretur. The edict, as Col. Leake clearly shows, was issued A. C. 303. Among the articles of which the maximum value is assessed, are oil, salt, honey, butchers' meat, poultry, game, fish, vegetables, fruit the wages of laborers and artisans, schoolmasters and skins, boots and shoes, harness, timber, corn, wine, and beer, (zythus.) The depreciation in the value of money, or the rise in the price of commodities, had been so great during the past century, that butchers' meat, which, in the second century of the empire, was in Rome about two denaril the pound, was now fixed at a maximum of eight. Col. Leake supposes the average price could not be less than four: at the same time the maximum of the wages of the agricultural laborers was twenty-five. The whole edict is, perhaps, the most gigantic effort of a blind though well-intentioned despotism, to control that which is, and ought to be, beyond the regulation of the government. See an Edict of Diocletian, by Col. Leake, London, 1826. Col. Leake has not observed that this Edict is expressly named in the treatise de Mort. Persecut. ch. vii. Idem cum variis iniquitatibus immensam faceret caritatem, legem pretiis rerum venalium statuere conatus.—M]

[Footnote 105: Indicta lex nova quae sane illorum temporum modestia tolerabilis, in perniciem processit. Aurel. Victor., who has treated the character of Diocletian with good sense, though in bad Latin.]

It was in the twenty first year of his reign that Diocletian executed his memorable resolution of abdicating the empire; an action more naturally to have been expected from the elder or the younger Antoninus, than from a prince who had never practised the lessons of philosophy either in the attainment or in the use of supreme power. Diocletian acquired the glory of giving to the world the first example of a resignation, [106] which has not been very frequently imitated by succeeding monarchs. The parallel of Charles the Fifth, however, will naturally offer itself to our mind, not only since the eloquence of a modern historian has rendered that name so familiar to an English reader, but from the very striking resemblance between the characters of the two emperors, whose political abilities were superior to their military genius, and whose specious virtues were much less the effect of nature than of art. The abdication of Charles appears to have been hastened by the vicissitude of fortune; and the disappointment of his favorite schemes urged him to relinquish a power which he found inadequate to his ambition. But the reign of Diocletian had flowed with a tide of uninterrupted success; nor was it till after he had vanquished all his enemies, and accomplished all his designs, that he seems to have entertained any serious thoughts of resigning the empire. Neither Charles nor Diocletian were arrived at a very advanced period of life; since the one was only fifty-five, and the other was no more than fifty-nine years of age; but the active life of those princes, their wars and journeys, the cares of royalty, and their application to business, had already impaired their constitution, and brought on the infirmities of a premature old age. [107]

[Footnote 106: Solus omnium post conditum Romanum Imperium, qui extanto fastigio sponte ad privatae vitae statum civilitatemque remearet, Eutrop. ix. 28.]

[Footnote 107: The particulars of the journey and illness are taken from Laclantius, c. 17, who may sometimes be admitted as an evidence of public facts, though very seldom of private anecdotes.]

Notwithstanding the severity of a very cold and rainy winter, Diocletian left Italy soon after the ceremony of his triumph, and began his progress towards the East round the circuit of the Illyrian provinces. From the inclemency of the weather, and the fatigue of the journey, he soon contracted a slow illness; and though he made easy marches, and was generally carried in a close litter, his disorder, before he arrived at Nicomedia, about the end of the summer, was become very serious and alarming. During the whole winter he was confined to his palace: his danger inspired a general and unaffected concern; but the people could only judge of the various alterations of his health, from the joy or consternation which they discovered in the countenances and behavior of his attendants. The rumor of his death was for some time universally believed, and it was supposed to be concealed with a view to prevent the troubles that might have happened during the absence of the Caesar Galerius. At length, however, on the first of March, Diocletian once more appeared in public, but so pale and emaciated, that he could scarcely have been recognized by those to whom his person was the most familiar. It was time to put an end to the painful struggle, which he had sustained during more than a year, between the care of his health and that of his dignity. The former required indulgence and relaxation, the latter compelled him to direct, from the bed of sickness, the administration of a great empire. He resolved to pass the remainder of his days in honorable repose, to place his glory beyond the reach of fortune, and to relinquish the theatre of the world to his younger and more active associates. [108]

[Footnote 108: Aurelius Victor ascribes the abdication, which had been so variously accounted for, to two causes: 1st, Diocletian's contempt of ambition; and 2dly, His apprehension of impending troubles. One of the panegyrists (vi. 9) mentions the age and infirmities of Diocletian as a very natural reason for his retirement. Note: Constantine (Orat. ad Sanct. c. 401) more than insinuated that derangement of mind, connected with the conflagration of the palace at Nicomedia by lightning, was the cause of his abdication. But Heinichen. in a very sensible note on this passage in Eusebius, while he admits that his long illness might produce a temporary depression of spirits, triumphantly appeals to the philosophical conduct of Diocletian in his retreat, and the influence which he still retained on public affairs.—M.]

The ceremony of his abdication was performed in a spacious plain, about three miles from Nicomedia. The emperor ascended a lofty throne, and in a speech, full of reason and dignity, declared his intention, both to the people and to the soldiers who were assembled on this extraordinary occasion. As soon as he had divested himself of his purple, he withdrew from the gazing multitude; and traversing the city in a covered chariot, proceeded, without delay, to the favorite retirement which he had chosen in his native country of Dalmatia. On the same day, which was the first of May, [109] Maximian, as it had been previously concerted, made his resignation of the Imperial dignity at Milan.

Even in the splendor of the Roman triumph, Diocletian had meditated his design of abdicating the government. As he wished to secure the obedience of Maximian, he exacted from him either a general assurance that he would submit his actions to the authority of his benefactor, or a particular promise that he would descend from the throne, whenever he should receive the advice and the example. This engagement, though it was confirmed by the solemnity of an oath before the altar of the Capitoline Jupiter, [110] would have proved a feeble restraint on the fierce temper of Maximian, whose passion was the love of power, and who neither desired present tranquility nor future reputation. But he yielded, however reluctantly, to the ascendant which his wiser colleague had acquired over him, and retired, immediately after his abdication, to a villa in Lucania, where it was almost impossible that such an impatient spirit could find any lasting tranquility.

[Footnote 109: The difficulties as well as mistakes attending the dates both of the year and of the day of Diocletian's abdication are perfectly cleared up by Tillemont, Hist. des Empereurs, tom. iv. p 525, note 19, and by Pagi ad annum.]

[Footnote 110: See Panegyr. Veter. vi. 9. The oration was pronounced after Maximian had resumed the purple.]

Diocletian, who, from a servile origin, had raised himself to the throne, passed the nine last years of his life in a private condition. Reason had dictated, and content seems to have accompanied, his retreat, in which he enjoyed, for a long time, the respect of those princes to whom he had resigned the possession of the world. [111] It is seldom that minds long exercised in business have formed the habits of conversing with themselves, and in the loss of power they principally regret the want of occupation. The amusements of letters and of devotion, which afford so many resources in solitude, were incapable of fixing the attention of Diocletian; but he had preserved, or at least he soon recovered, a taste for the most innocent as well as natural pleasures, and his leisure hours were sufficiently employed in building, planting, and gardening. His answer to Maximian is deservedly celebrated. He was solicited by that restless old man to reassume the reins of government, and the Imperial purple. He rejected the temptation with a smile of pity, calmly observing, that if he could show Maximian the cabbages which he had planted with his own hands at Salona, he should no longer be urged to relinquish the enjoyment of happiness for the pursuit of power. [112] In his conversations with his friends, he frequently acknowledged, that of all arts, the most difficult was the art of reigning; and he expressed himself on that favorite topic with a degree of warmth which could be the result only of experience. "How often," was he accustomed to say, "is it the interest of four or five ministers to combine together to deceive their sovereign! Secluded from mankind by his exalted dignity, the truth is concealed from his knowledge; he can see only with their eyes, he hears nothing but their misrepresentations. He confers the most important offices upon vice and weakness, and disgraces the most virtuous and deserving among his subjects. By such infamous arts," added Diocletian, "the best and wisest princes are sold to the venal corruption of their courtiers." [113] A just estimate of greatness, and the assurance of immortal fame, improve our relish for the pleasures of retirement; but the Roman emperor had filled too important a character in the world, to enjoy without alloy the comforts and security of a private condition. It was impossible that he could remain ignorant of the troubles which afflicted the empire after his abdication. It was impossible that he could be indifferent to their consequences. Fear, sorrow, and discontent, sometimes pursued him into the solitude of Salona. His tenderness, or at least his pride, was deeply wounded by the misfortunes of his wife and daughter; and the last moments of Diocletian were imbittered by some affronts, which Licinius and Constantine might have spared the father of so many emperors, and the first author of their own fortune. A report, though of a very doubtful nature, has reached our times, that he prudently withdrew himself from their power by a voluntary death. [114]

[Footnote 111: Eumenius pays him a very fine compliment: "At enim divinum illum virum, qui primus imperium et participavit et posuit, consilii et fact isui non poenitet; nec amisisse se putat quod sponte transcripsit. Felix beatusque vere quem vestra, tantorum principum, colunt privatum." Panegyr. Vet. vii. 15.]

[Footnote 112: We are obliged to the younger Victor for this celebrated item. Eutropius mentions the thing in a more general manner.]

[Footnote 113: Hist. August. p. 223, 224. Vopiscus had learned this conversation from his father.]

[Footnote 114: The younger Victor slightly mentions the report. But as Diocletian had disobliged a powerful and successful party, his memory has been loaded with every crime and misfortune. It has been affirmed that he died raving mad, that he was condemned as a criminal by the Roman senate, &c.]

Before we dismiss the consideration of the life and character of Diocletian, we may, for a moment, direct our view to the place of his retirement. Salona, a principal city of his native province of Dalmatia, was near two hundred Roman miles (according to the measurement of the public highways) from Aquileia and the confines of Italy, and about two hundred and seventy from Sirmium, the usual residence of the emperors whenever they visited the Illyrian frontier. [115] A miserable village still preserves the name of Salona; but so late as the sixteenth century, the remains of a theatre, and a confused prospect of broken arches and marble columns, continued to attest its ancient splendor. [116] About six or seven miles from the city, Diocletian constructed a magnificent palace, and we may infer, from the greatness of the work, how long he had meditated his design of abdicating the empire. The choice of a spot which united all that could contribute either to health or to luxury, did not require the partiality of a native. "The soil was dry and fertile, the air is pure and wholesome, and though extremely hot during the summer months, this country seldom feels those sultry and noxious winds, to which the coasts of Istria and some parts of Italy are exposed. The views from the palace are no less beautiful than the soil and climate were inviting. Towards the west lies the fertile shore that stretches along the Adriatic, in which a number of small islands are scattered in such a manner, as to give this part of the sea the appearance of a great lake. On the north side lies the bay, which led to the ancient city of Salona; and the country beyond it, appearing in sight, forms a proper contrast to that more extensive prospect of water, which the Adriatic presents both to the south and to the east. Towards the north, the view is terminated by high and irregular mountains, situated at a proper distance, and in many places covered with villages, woods, and vineyards." [117]

[Footnote 115: See the Itiner. p. 269, 272, edit. Wessel.]

[Footnote 116: The Abate Fortis, in his Viaggio in Dalmazia, p. 43, (printed at Venice in the year 1774, in two small volumes in quarto,) quotes a Ms account of the antiquities of Salona, composed by Giambattista Giustiniani about the middle of the xvith century.]

[Footnote 117: Adam's Antiquities of Diocletian's Palace at Spalatro, p. 6. We may add a circumstance or two from the Abate Fortis: the little stream of the Hyader, mentioned by Lucan, produces most exquisite trout, which a sagacious writer, perhaps a monk, supposes to have been one of the principal reasons that determined Diocletian in the choice of his retirement. Fortis, p. 45. The same author (p. 38) observes, that a taste for agriculture is reviving at Spalatro; and that an experimental farm has lately been established near the city, by a society of gentlemen.]

Though Constantine, from a very obvious prejudice, affects to mention the palace of Diocletian with contempt, [118] yet one of their successors, who could only see it in a neglected and mutilated state, celebrates its magnificence in terms of the highest admiration. [119] It covered an extent of ground consisting of between nine and ten English acres. The form was quadrangular, flanked with sixteen towers. Two of the sides were near six hundred, and the other two near seven hundred feet in length. The whole was constructed of a beautiful freestone, extracted from the neighboring quarries of Trau, or Tragutium, and very little inferior to marble itself. Four streets, intersecting each other at right angles, divided the several parts of this great edifice, and the approach to the principal apartment was from a very stately entrance, which is still denominated the Golden Gate. The approach was terminated by a peristylium of granite columns, on one side of which we discover the square temple of Aesculapius, on the other the octagon temple of Jupiter. The latter of those deities Diocletian revered as the patron of his fortunes, the former as the protector of his health. By comparing the present remains with the precepts of Vitruvius, the several parts of the building, the baths, bed-chamber, the atrium, the basilica, and the Cyzicene, Corinthian, and Egyptian halls have been described with some degree of precision, or at least of probability. Their forms were various, their proportions just; but they all were attended with two imperfections, very repugnant to our modern notions of taste and conveniency. These stately rooms had neither windows nor chimneys. They were lighted from the top, (for the building seems to have consisted of no more than one story,) and they received their heat by the help of pipes that were conveyed along the walls. The range of principal apartments was protected towards the south-west by a portico five hundred and seventeen feet long, which must have formed a very noble and delightful walk, when the beauties of painting and sculpture were added to those of the prospect.

[Footnote 118: Constantin. Orat. ad Coetum Sanct. c. 25. In this sermon, the emperor, or the bishop who composed it for him, affects to relate the miserable end of all the persecutors of the church.]

[Footnote 119: Constantin. Porphyr. de Statu Imper. p. 86.]

Had this magnificent edifice remained in a solitary country, it would have been exposed to the ravages of time; but it might, perhaps, have escaped the rapacious industry of man. The village of Aspalathus, [120] and, long afterwards, the provincial town of Spalatro, have grown out of its ruins. The Golden Gate now opens into the market-place. St. John the Baptist has usurped the honors of Aesculapius; and the temple of Jupiter, under the protection of the Virgin, is converted into the cathedral church.

For this account of Diocletian's palace we are principally indebted to an ingenious artist of our own time and country, whom a very liberal curiosity carried into the heart of Dalmatia. [121] But there is room to suspect that the elegance of his designs and engraving has somewhat flattered the objects which it was their purpose to represent. We are informed by a more recent and very judicious traveller, that the awful ruins of Spalatro are not less expressive of the decline of the art than of the greatness of the Roman empire in the time of Diocletian. [122] If such was indeed the state of architecture, we must naturally believe that painting and sculpture had experienced a still more sensible decay. The practice of architecture is directed by a few general and even mechanical rules. But sculpture, and above all, painting, propose to themselves the imitation not only of the forms of nature, but of the characters and passions of the human soul. In those sublime arts, the dexterity of the hand is of little avail, unless it is animated by fancy, and guided by the most correct taste and observation.

[Footnote 120: D'Anville, Geographie Ancienne, tom. i. p. 162.]

[Footnote 121: Messieurs Adam and Clerisseau, attended by two draughtsmen visited Spalatro in the month of July, 1757. The magnificent work which their journey produced was published in London seven years afterwards.]

[Footnote 122: I shall quote the words of the Abate Fortis. "E'bastevolmente agli amatori dell' Architettura, e dell' Antichita, l'opera del Signor Adams, che a donato molto a que' superbi vestigi coll'abituale eleganza del suo toccalapis e del bulino. In generale la rozzezza del scalpello, e'l cattivo gusto del secolo vi gareggiano colla magnificenz del fabricato." See Viaggio in Dalmazia, p. 40.]

It is almost unnecessary to remark, that the civil distractions of the empire, the license of the soldiers, the inroads of the barbarians, and the progress of despotism, had proved very unfavorable to genius, and even to learning. The succession of Illyrian princes restored the empire without restoring the sciences. Their military education was not calculated to inspire them with the love of letters; and even the mind of Diocletian, however active and capacious in business, was totally uninformed by study or speculation. The professions of law and physic are of such common use and certain profit, that they will always secure a sufficient number of practitioners, endowed with a reasonable degree of abilities and knowledge; but it does not appear that the students in those two faculties appeal to any celebrated masters who have flourished within that period. The voice of poetry was silent. History was reduced to dry and confused abridgments, alike destitute of amusement and instruction. A languid and affected eloquence was still retained in the pay and service of the emperors, who encouraged not any arts except those which contributed to the gratification of their pride, or the defence of their power. [123]

[Footnote 123: The orator Eumenius was secretary to the emperors Maximian and Constantius, and Professor of Rhetoric in the college of Autun. His salary was six hundred thousand sesterces, which, according to the lowest computation of that age, must have exceeded three thousand pounds a year. He generously requested the permission of employing it in rebuilding the college. See his Oration De Restaurandis Scholis; which, though not exempt from vanity, may atone for his panegyrics.]

The declining age of learning and of mankind is marked, however, by the rise and rapid progress of the new Platonists. The school of Alexandria silenced those of Athens; and the ancient sects enrolled themselves under the banners of the more fashionable teachers, who recommended their system by the novelty of their method, and the austerity of their manners. Several of these masters, Ammonius, Plotinus, Amelius, and Porphyry, [124] were men of profound thought and intense application; but by mistaking the true object of philosophy, their labors contributed much less to improve than to corrupt the human understanding. The knowledge that is suited to our situation and powers, the whole compass of moral, natural, and mathematical science, was neglected by the new Platonists; whilst they exhausted their strength in the verbal disputes of metaphysics, attempted to explore the secrets of the invisible world, and studied to reconcile Aristotle with Plato, on subjects of which both these philosophers were as ignorant as the rest of mankind. Consuming their reason in these deep but unsubstantial meditations, their minds were exposed to illusions of fancy. They flattered themselves that they possessed the secret of disengaging the soul from its corporal prison; claimed a familiar intercourse with demons and spirits; and, by a very singular revolution, converted the study of philosophy into that of magic. The ancient sages had derided the popular superstition; after disguising its extravagance by the thin pretence of allegory, the disciples of Plotinus and Porphyry became its most zealous defenders. As they agreed with the Christians in a few mysterious points of faith, they attacked the remainder of their theological system with all the fury of civil war. The new Platonists would scarcely deserve a place in the history of science, but in that of the church the mention of them will very frequently occur.

[Footnote 124: Porphyry died about the time of Diocletian's abdication. The life of his master Plotinus, which he composed, will give us the most complete idea of the genius of the sect, and the manners of its professors. This very curious piece is inserted in Fabricius Bibliotheca Graeca tom. iv. p. 88—148.]

CHAPTER XIV

SIX EMPERORS AT THE SAME TIME, REUNION OF THE EMPIRE

PART I

TROUBLES AFTER THE ABDICATION OF DIOCLETIAN—DEATH OF CONSTANTIUS—ELEVATION OF CONSTANTINE AND MAXENTIUS—SIX EMPERORS AT THE SAME TIME—DEATH OF MAXIMIAN AND GALERIUS—VICTORIES OF CONSTANTINE OVER MAXENTIUS AND LICINUS—REUNION OF THE EMPIRE UNDER THE AUTHORITY OF CONSTANTINE

The balance of power established by Diocletian subsisted no longer than while it was sustained by the firm and dexterous hand of the founder. It required such a fortunate mixture of different tempers and abilities, as could scarcely be found or even expected a second time; two emperors without jealousy, two Caesars without ambition, and the same general interest invariably pursued by four independent princes. The abdication of Diocletian and Maximian was succeeded by eighteen years of discord and confusion. The empire was afflicted by five civil wars; and the remainder of the time was not so much a state of tranquillity as a suspension of arms between several hostile monarchs, who, viewing each other with an eye of fear and hatred, strove to increase their respective forces at the expense of their subjects.

As soon as Diocletian and Maximian had resigned the purple, their station, according to the rules of the new constitution, was filled by the two Caesars, Constantius and Galerius, who immediately assumed the title of Augustus. [1]

[Footnote 1: M. de Montesquieu (Considerations sur la Grandeur et La Decadence des Romains, c. 17) supposes, on the authority of Orosius and Eusebius, that, on this occasion, the empire, for the first time, was really divided into two parts. It is difficult, however, to discover in what respect the plan of Galerius differed from that of Diocletian.]

The honors of seniority and precedence were allowed to the former of those princes, and he continued under a new appellation to administer his ancient department of Gaul, Spain, and Britain.

The government of those ample provinces was sufficient to exercise his talents and to satisfy his ambition. Clemency, temperance, and moderation, distinguished the amiable character of Constantius, and his fortunate subjects had frequently occasion to compare the virtues of their sovereign with the passions of Maximian, and even with the arts of Diocletian. [2] Instead of imitating their eastern pride and magnificence, Constantius preserved the modesty of a Roman prince. He declared, with unaffected sincerity, that his most valued treasure was in the hearts of his people, and that, whenever the dignity of the throne, or the danger of the state, required any extraordinary supply, he could depend with confidence on their gratitude and liberality. [3] The provincials of Gaul, Spain, and Britain, sensible of his worth, and of their own happiness, reflected with anxiety on the declining health of the emperor Constantius, and the tender age of his numerous family, the issue of his second marriage with the daughter of Maximian.

[Footnote 2: Hic non modo amabilis, sed etiam venerabilis Gallis fuit; praecipuc quod Diocletiani suspectam prudentiam, et Maximiani sanguinariam violentiam imperio ejus evaserant. Eutrop. Breviar. x. i.]

[Footnote 3: Divitiis Provincialium (mel. provinciarum) ac privatorum studens, fisci commoda non admodum affectans; ducensque melius publicas opes a privatis haberi, quam intra unum claustrum reservari. Id. ibid. He carried this maxim so far, that whenever he gave an entertainment, he was obliged to borrow a service of plate.]

The stern temper of Galerius was cast in a very different mould; and while he commanded the esteem of his subjects, he seldom condescended to solicit their affections. His fame in arms, and, above all, the success of the Persian war, had elated his haughty mind, which was naturally impatient of a superior, or even of an equal. If it were possible to rely on the partial testimony of an injudicious writer, we might ascribe the abdication of Diocletian to the menaces of Galerius, and relate the particulars of a private conversation between the two princes, in which the former discovered as much pusillanimity as the latter displayed ingratitude and arrogance. [4] But these obscure anecdotes are sufficiently refuted by an impartia view of the character and conduct of Diocletian. Whatever might otherwise have been his intentions, if he had apprehended any danger from the violence of Galerius, his good sense would have instructed him to prevent the ignominious contest; and as he had held the sceptre with glory, he would have resigned it without disgrace.

[Footnote 4: Lactantius de Mort. Persecur. c. 18. Were the particulars of this conference more consistent with truth and decency, we might still ask how they came to the knowledge of an obscure rhetorician. But there are many historians who put us in mind of the admirable saying of the great Conde to Cardinal de Retz: "Ces coquins nous font parlor et agir, comme ils auroient fait eux-memes a notre place." Note: This attack upon Lactantius is unfounded. Lactantius was so far from having been an obscure rhetorician, that he had taught rhetoric publicly, and with the greatest success, first in Africa, and afterwards in Nicomedia. His reputation obtained him the esteem of Constantine, who invited him to his court, and intrusted to him the education of his son Crispus. The facts which he relates took place during his own time; he cannot be accused of dishonesty or imposture. Satis me vixisse arbitrabor et officium hominis implesse si labor meus aliquos homines, ab erroribus iberatos, ad iter coeleste direxerit. De Opif. Dei, cap. 20. The eloquence of Lactantius has caused him to be called the Christian Cicero. Annon Gent.—G. —Yet no unprejudiced person can read this coarse and particular private conversation of the two emperors, without assenting to the justice of Gibbon's severe sentence. But the authorship of the treatise is by no means certain. The fame of Lactantius for eloquence as well as for truth, would suffer no loss if it should be adjudged to some more "obscure rhetorician." Manso, in his Leben Constantins des Grossen, concurs on this point with Gibbon Beylage, iv. —M.]

After the elevation of Constantius and Galerius to the rank of Augusti, two new Coesars were required to supply their place, and to complete the system of the Imperial government. Diocletian, was sincerely desirous of withdrawing himself from the world; he considered Galerius, who had married his daughter, as the firmest support of his family and of the empire; and he consented, without reluctance, that his successor should assume the merit as well as the envy of the important nomination. It was fixed without consulting the interest or inclination of the princes of the West. Each of them had a son who was arrived at the age of manhood, and who might have been deemed the most natural candidates for the vacant honor. But the impotent resentment of Maximian was no longer to be dreaded; and the moderate Constantius, though he might despise the dangers, was humanely apprehensive of the calamities, of civil war. The two persons whom Galerius promoted to the rank of Caesar, were much better suited to serve the views of his ambition; and their principal recommendation seems to have consisted in the want of merit or personal consequence. The first of these was Daza, or, as he was afterwards called, Maximin, whose mother was the sister of Galerius. The unexperienced youth still betrayed, by his manners and language, his rustic education, when, to his own astonishment, as well as that of the world, he was invested by Diocletian with the purple, exalted to the dignity of Caesar, and intrusted with the sovereign command of Egypt and Syria. [5] At the same time, Severus, a faithful servant, addicted to pleasure, but not incapable of business, was sent to Milan, to receive, from the reluctant hands of Maximian, the Caesarian ornaments, and the possession of Italy and Africa. According to the forms of the constitution,

Severus acknowledged the supremacy of the western emperor; but he was absolutely devoted to the commands of his benefactor Galerius, who, reserving to himself the intermediate countries from the confines of Italy to those of Syria, firmly established his power over three fourths of the monarchy. In the full confidence that the approaching death of Constantius would leave him sole master of the Roman world, we are assured that he had arranged in his mind a long succession of future princes, and that he meditated his own retreat from public life, after he should have accomplished a glorious reign of about twenty years. [7]

[Footnote 5: Sublatus nuper a pecoribus et silvis (says Lactantius de M. P. c. 19) statim Scutarius, continuo Protector, mox Tribunus, postridie Caesar, accepit Orientem. Aurelius Victor is too liberal in giving him the whole portion of Diocletian.]

[Footnote 6: His diligence and fidelity are acknowledged even by Lactantius, de M. P. c. 18.]

[Footnote 7: These schemes, however, rest only on the very doubtful authority of Lactantius de M. P. c. 20.]

But within less than eighteen months, two unexpected revolutions overturned the ambitious schemes of Galerius. The hopes of uniting the western provinces to his empire were disappointed by the elevation of Constantine, whilst Italy and Africa were lost by the successful revolt of Maxentius.

I. The fame of Constantine has rendered posterity attentive to the most minute circumstances of his life and actions. The place of his birth, as well as the condition of his mother Helena, have been the subject, not only of literary, but national disputes. Notwithstanding the recent tradition, which assigns for her father a British king, [8] we are obliged to confess, that Helena was the daughter of an innkeeper; but at the same time, we may defend the legality of her marriage, against those who have represented her as the concubine of Constantius. [9] The great Constantine was most probably born at Naissus, in Dacia; [10] and it is not surprising that, in a family and province distinguished only by the profession of arms, the youth should discover very little inclination to improve his mind by the acquisition of knowledge. [11] He was about eighteen years of age when his father was promoted to the rank of Caesar; but that fortunate event was attended with his mother's divorce; and the splendor of an Imperial alliance reduced the son of Helena to a state of disgrace and humiliation. Instead of following Constantius in the West, he remained in the service of Diocletian, signalized his valor in the wars of Egypt and Persia, and gradually rose to the honorable station of a tribune of the first order. The figure of Constantine was tall and majestic; he was dexterous in all his exercises, intrepid in war, affable in peace; in his whole conduct, the active spirit of youth was tempered by habitual prudence; and while his mind was engrossed by ambition, he appeared cold and insensible to the allurements of pleasure. The favor of the people and soldiers, who had named him as a worthy candidate for the rank of Caesar, served only to exasperate the jealousy of Galerius; and though prudence might restrain him from exercising any open violence, an absolute monarch is seldom at a loss now to execute a sure and secret revenge. [12] Every hour increased the danger of Constantine, and the anxiety of his father, who, by repeated letters, expressed the warmest desire of embracing his son. For some time the policy of Galerius supplied him with delays and excuses; but it was impossible long to refuse so natural a request of his associate, without maintaining his refusal by arms. The permission of the journey was reluctantly granted, and whatever precautions the emperor might have taken to intercept a return, the consequences of which he, with so much reason, apprehended, they were effectually disappointed by the incredible diligence of Constantine. [13] Leaving the palace of Nicomedia in the night, he travelled post through Bithynia,

Thrace, Dacia, Pannonia, Italy, and Gaul, and, amidst the joyful acclamations of the people, reached the port of Boulogne in the very moment when his father was preparing to embark for Britain. [14]

[Footnote 8: This tradition, unknown to the contemporaries of Constantine was invented in the darkness of monestaries, was embellished by Jeffrey of Monmouth, and the writers of the xiith century, has been defended by our antiquarians of the last age, and is seriously related in the ponderous History of England, compiled by Mr. Carte, (vol. i. p. 147.) He transports, however, the kingdom of Coil, the imaginary father of Helena, from Essex to the wall of Antoninus.]

[Footnote 9: Eutropius (x. 2) expresses, in a few words, the real truth, and the occasion of the error "ex obscuriori matrimonio ejus filius." Zosimus (l. ii. p. 78) eagerly seized the most unfavorable report, and is followed by Orosius, (vii. 25,) whose authority is oddly enough overlooked by the indefatigable, but partial Tillemont. By insisting on the divorce of Helena, Diocletian acknowledged her marriage.]

[Footnote 10: There are three opinions with regard to the place of Constantine's birth. 1. Our English antiquarians were used to dwell with rapture on the words of his panegyrist, "Britannias illic oriendo nobiles fecisti." But this celebrated passage may be referred with as much propriety to the accession, as to the nativity of Constantine. 2. Some of the modern Greeks have ascribed the honor of his birth to Drepanum, a town on the Gulf of Nicomedia, (Cellarius, tom. ii. p. 174,) which Constantine dignified with the name of Helenopolis, and Justinian adorned with many splendid buildings, (Procop. de Edificiis, v. 2.) It is indeed probable enough, that Helena's father kept an inn at Drepanum, and that Constantius might lodge there when he returned from a Persian embassy, in the reign of Aurelian. But in the wandering life of a soldier, the place of his marriage, and the places where his children are born, have very little connection with each other. 3. The claim of Naissus is supported by the anonymous writer, published at the end of Ammianus, p. 710, and who in general copied very good materials; and it is confirmed by Julius Firmicus, (de Astrologia, l. i. c. 4,) who flourished under the reign of Constantine himself. Some objections have been raised against the integrity of the text, and the application of the passage of Firmicus but the former is established by the best Mss., and the latter is very ably defended by Lipsius de Magnitudine Romana, l. iv. c. 11, et Supplement.]

[Footnote 11: Literis minus instructus. Anonym. ad Ammian. p. 710.]

[Footnote 12: Galerius, or perhaps his own courage, exposed him to single combat with a Sarmatian, (Anonym. p. 710,) and with a monstrous lion. See Praxagoras apud Photium, p. 63. Praxagoras, an Athenian philosopher, had written a life of Constantine in two books, which are now lost. He was a contemporary.]

[Footnote 13: Zosimus, l. ii. p. 78, 79. Lactantius de M. P. c. 24. The former tells a very foolish story, that Constantine caused all the post-horses which he had used to be hamstrung. Such a bloody execution, without preventing a pursuit, would have scattered suspicions, and might have stopped his journey. Note: Zosimus is not the only writer who tells this story. The younger Victor confirms it. Ad frustrandos insequentes, publica jumenta, quaqua iter ageret, interficiens. Aurelius Victor de Caesar says the same thing, G. as also the Anonymus Valesii.— M. —Manso, (Leben Constantins,) p. 18, observes that the story has been exaggerated; he took this precaution during the first stage of his journey.—M.]

[Footnote 14: Anonym. p. 710. Panegyr. Veter. vii. 4. But Zosimus, l. ii. p. 79, Eusebius de Vit. Constant. l. i. c. 21, and Lactantius de M. P. c. 24. suppose, with less accuracy, that he found his father on his death-bed.]

The British expedition, and an easy victory over the barbarians of Caledonia, were the last exploits of the reign of Constantius. He ended his life in the Imperial palace of York, fifteen months after he had received the title of Augustus, and almost fourteen years and a half after he had been promoted to the rank of Caesar. His death was immediately succeeded by the elevation of Constantine. The ideas of inheritance and succession are so very familiar, that the generality of mankind consider them as founded, not only in reason, but in nature itself. Our imagination readily transfers the same principles from private property to public dominion: and whenever a virtuous father leaves behind him a son whose merit seems to justify the esteem, or even the hopes, of the people, the joint influence of prejudice and of affection operates with irresistible weight. The flower of the western armies had followed Constantius into Britain, and the national troops were reenforced by a numerous body of Alemanni, who obeyed the orders of Crocus, one of their hereditary chieftains. [15] The opinion of their own importance, and the assurance that Britain, Gaul, and Spain would acquiesce in their nomination, were diligently inculcated to the legions by the adherents of Constantine. The soldiers were asked, whether they could hesitate a moment between the honor of placing at their head the worthy son of their beloved emperor, and the ignominy of tamely expecting the arrival of some obscure stranger, on whom it might please the sovereign of Asia to bestow the armies and provinces of the West. It was insinuated to them, that gratitude and liberality held a distinguished place among the virtues of Constantine; nor did that artful prince show himself to the troops, till they were prepared to salute him with the names of Augustus and Emperor. The throne was the object of his desires; and had he been less actuated by ambition, it was his only means of safety. He was well acquainted with the character and sentiments of Galerius, and sufficiently apprised, that if he wished to live he must determine to reign. The decent and even obstinate resistance which he chose to affect, [16] was contrived to justify his usurpation; nor did he yield to the acclamations of the army, till he had provided the proper materials for a letter, which he immediately despatched to the emperor of the East. Constantine informed him of the melancholy event of his father's death, modestly asserted his natural claim to the succession, and respectfully lamented, that the affectionate violence of his troops had not permitted him to solicit the Imperial purple in the regular and constitutional manner. The first emotions of Galerius were those of surprise, disappointment, and rage; and as he could seldom restrain his passions, he loudly threatened, that he would commit to the flames both the letter and the messenger. But his resentment insensibly subsided; and when he recollected the doubtful chance of war, when he had weighed the character and strength of his adversary, he consented to embrace the honorable accommodation which the prudence of Constantine had left open to him. Without either condemning or ratifying the choice of the British army, Galerius accepted the son of his deceased colleague as the sovereign of the provinces beyond the Alps; but he gave him only the title of Caesar, and the fourth rank among the Roman princes, whilst he conferred the vacant place of Augustus on his favorite Severus. The apparent harmony of the empire was still preserved, and Constantine, who already possessed the substance, expected, without impatience, an opportunity of obtaining the honors, of supreme power. [17]

[Footnote 15: Cunctis qui aderant, annitentibus, sed praecipue Croco (alii Eroco) [Erich?] Alamannorum Rege, auxilii gratia Constantium comitato, imperium capit. Victor Junior, c. 41. This is perhaps the first instance of a barbarian king, who assisted the Roman arms with an independent body of his own subjects. The practice grew familiar and at last became fatal.]

[Footnote 16: His panegyrist Eumenius (vii. 8) ventures to affirm in the presence of Constantine, that he put spurs to his horse, and tried, but in vain, to escape from the hands of his soldiers.]

[Footnote 17: Lactantius de M. P. c. 25. Eumenius (vii. 8.) gives a rhetorical turn to the whole transaction.]

The children of Constantius by his second marriage were six in number, three of either sex, and whose Imperial descent might have solicited a preference over the meaner extraction of the son of Helena. But Constantine was in the thirty-second year of his age, in the full vigor both of mind and body, at the time when the eldest of his brothers could not possibly be more than thirteen years old. His claim of superior merit had been allowed and ratified by the dying emperor. [18] In his last moments Constantius bequeathed to his eldest son the care of the safety as well as greatness of the family; conjuring him to assume both the authority and the sentiments of a father with regard to the children of Theodora. Their liberal education, advantageous marriages, the secure dignity of their lives, and the first honors of the state with which they were invested, attest the fraternal affection of Constantine; and as those princes possessed a mild and grateful disposition, they submitted without reluctance to the superiority of his genius and fortune. [19]

[Footnote 18: The choice of Constantine, by his dying father, which is warranted by reason, and insinuated by Eumenius, seems to be confirmed by the most unexceptionable authority, the concurring evidence of Lactantius (de M. P. c. 24) and of Libanius, (Oratio i.,) of Eusebius (in Vit. Constantin. l. i. c. 18, 21) and of Julian, (Oratio i)]

[Footnote 19: Of the three sisters of Constantine, Constantia married the emperor Licinius, Anastasia the Caesar Bassianus, and Eutropia the consul Nepotianus. The three brothers were, Dalmatius, Julius Constantius, and Annibalianus, of whom we shall have occasion to speak hereafter.]

II. The ambitious spirit of Galerius was scarcely reconciled to the disappointment of his views upon the Gallic provinces, before the unexpected loss of Italy wounded his pride as well as power in a still more sensible part. The long absence of the emperors had filled Rome with discontent and indignation; and the people gradually discovered, that the preference given to Nicomedia and Milan was not to be ascribed to the particular inclination of Diocletian, but to the permanent form of government which he had instituted. It was in vain that, a few months after his abdication, his successors dedicated, under his name, those magnificent baths, whose ruins still supply the ground as well as the materials for so many churches and convents. [20] The tranquility of those elegant recesses of ease and luxury was disturbed by the impatient murmurs of the Romans, and a report was insensibly circulated, that the sums expended in erecting those buildings would soon be required at their hands. About that time the avarice of Galerius, or perhaps the exigencies of the state, had induced him to make a very strict and rigorous inquisition into the property of his subjects, for the purpose of a general taxation, both on their lands and on their persons. A very minute survey appears to have been taken of their real estates; and wherever there was the slightest suspicion of concealment, torture was very freely employed to obtain a sincere declaration of their personal wealth. [21] The privileges which had exalted Italy above the rank of the provinces were no longer regarded: [211] and the officers of the revenue already began to number the Roman people, and to settle the proportion of the new taxes. Even when the spirit of freedom had been utterly extinguished, the tamest subjects have sometimes ventured to resist an unprecedented invasion of their property; but on this occasion the injury was aggravated by the insult, and the sense of private interest was quickened by that of national honor. The conquest of Macedonia, as we have already observed, had delivered the Roman people from the weight of personal taxes.

Though they had experienced every form of despotism, they had now enjoyed that exemption near five hundred years; nor could they patiently brook the insolence of an Illyrian peasant, who, from his distant residence in Asia, presumed to number Rome among the tributary cities of his empire. The rising fury of the people was encouraged by the authority, or at least the connivance, of the senate; and the feeble remains of the Praetorian guards, who had reason to apprehend their own dissolution, embraced so honorable a pretence, and declared their readiness to draw their swords in the service of their oppressed country. It was the wish, and it soon became the hope, of every citizen, that after expelling from Italy their foreign tyrants, they should elect a prince who, by the place of his residence, and by his maxims of government, might once more deserve the title of Roman emperor. The name, as well as the situation, of Maxentius determined in his favor the popular enthusiasm.

[Footnote 20: See Gruter. Inscrip. p. 178. The six princes are all mentioned, Diocletian and Maximian as the senior Augusti, and fathers of the emperors. They jointly dedicate, for the use of their own Romans, this magnificent edifice. The architects have delineated the ruins of these Thermoe, and the antiquarians, particularly Donatus and Nardini, have ascertained the ground which they covered. One of the great rooms is now the Carthusian church; and even one of the porter's lodges is sufficient to form another church, which belongs to the Feuillans.]

[Footnote 21: See Lactantius de M. P. c. 26, 31.]

[Footnote 211: Saviguy, in his memoir on Roman taxation, (Mem. Berl. Academ. 1822, 1823, p. 5,) dates from this period the abolition of the Jus Italicum. He quotes a remarkable passage of Aurelius Victor. Hinc denique parti Italiae invec tum tributorum ingens malum. Aur. Vict. c. 39. It was a necessary consequence of the division of the empire: it became impossible to maintain a second court and executive, and leave so large and fruitful a part of the territory exempt from contribution.—M.]

Maxentius was the son of the emperor Maximian, and he had married the daughter of Galerius. His birth and alliance seemed to offer him the fairest promise of succeeding to the empire; but his vices and incapacity procured him the same exclusion from the dignity of Caesar, which Constantine had deserved by a dangerous superiority of merit. The policy of Galerius preferred such associates as would never disgrace the choice, nor dispute the commands, of their benefactor. An obscure stranger was therefore raised to the throne of Italy, and the son of the late emperor of the West was left to enjoy the luxury of a private fortune in a villa a few miles distant from the capital. The gloomy passions of his soul, shame, vexation, and rage, were inflamed by envy on the news of Constantine's success; but the hopes of Maxentius revived with the public discontent, and he was easily persuaded to unite his personal injury and pretensions with the cause of the Roman people. Two Praetorian tribunes and a commissary of provisions undertook the management of the conspiracy; and as every order of men was actuated by the same spirit, the immediate event was neither doubtful nor difficult. The praefect of the city, and a few magistrates, who maintained their fidelity to Severus, were massacred by the guards; and Maxentius, invested with the Imperial ornaments, was acknowledged by the applauding senate and people as the protector of the Roman freedom and dignity. It is uncertain whether Maximian was previously acquainted with the conspiracy; but as soon as the standard of rebellion was erected at Rome, the old emperor broke from the retirement where the authority of Diocletian had condemned him to pass a life of melancholy and solitude, and concealed his returning ambition under the disguise of paternal tenderness. At the request of his son and of the senate, he condescended to reassume the purple. His ancient dignity, his experience, and his fame in arms, added strength as well as reputation to the party of Maxentius. [22]

[Footnote 22: The sixth Panegyric represents the conduct of Maximian in the most favorable light, and the ambiguous expression of Aurelius Victor, "retractante diu," may signify either that he contrived, or that he opposed, the conspiracy. See Zosimus, l. ii. p. 79, and Lactantius de M. P. c. 26.]

According to the advice, or rather the orders, of his colleague, the emperor Severus immediately hastened to Rome, in the full confidence, that, by his unexpected celerity, he should easily suppress the tumult of an unwarlike populace, commanded by a licentious youth. But he found on his arrival the gates of the city shut against him, the walls filled with men and arms, an experienced general at the head of the rebels, and his own troops without spirit or affection. A large body of Moors deserted to the enemy, allured by the promise of a large donative; and, if it be true that they had been levied by Maximian in his African war, preferring the natural feelings of gratitude to the artificial ties of allegiance. Anulinus, the Praetorian praefect, declared himself in favor of Maxentius, and drew after him the most considerable part of the troops, accustomed to obey his commands.

Rome, according to the expression of an orator, recalled her armies; and the unfortunate Severus, destitute of force and of counsel, retired, or rather fled, with precipitation, to Ravenna.

Here he might for some time have been safe. The fortifications of Ravenna were able to resist the attempts, and the morasses that surrounded the town, were sufficient to prevent the approach, of the Italian army. The sea, which Severus commanded with a powerful fleet, secured him an inexhaustible supply of provisions, and gave a free entrance to the legions, which, on the return of spring, would advance to his assistance from Illyricum and the East. Maximian, who conducted the siege in person, was soon convinced that he might waste his time and his army in the fruitless enterprise, and that he had nothing to hope either from force or famine. With an art more suitable to the character of Diocletian than to his own, he directed his attack, not so much against the walls of Ravenna, as against the mind of Severus. The treachery which he had experienced disposed that unhappy prince to distrust the most sincere of his friends and adherents. The emissaries of Maximian easily persuaded his credulity, that a conspiracy was formed to betray the town, and prevailed upon his fears not to expose himself to the discretion of an irritated conqueror, but to accept the faith of an honorable capitulation. He was at first received with humanity and treated with respect. Maximian conducted the captive emperor to Rome, and gave him the most solemn assurances that he had secured his life by the resignation of the purple. But Severus, could obtain only an easy death and an Imperial funeral. When the sentence was signified to him, the manner of executing it was left to his own choice; he preferred the favorite mode of the ancients, that of opening his veins; and as soon as he expired, his body was carried to the sepulchre which had been constructed for the family of Gallienus. [23]

[Footnote 23: The circumstances of this war, and the death of Severus, are very doubtfully and variously told in our ancient fragments, (see Tillemont, Hist. des Empereurs, tom. iv. part i. p. 555.) I have endeavored to extract from them a consistent and probable narration. Note: Manso justly observes that two totally different narratives might be formed, almost upon equal authority. Beylage, iv.—M.]

PART II

Though the characters of Constantine and Maxentius had very little affinity with each other, their situation and interest were the same; and prudence seemed to require that they should unite their forces against the common enemy. Notwithstanding the superiority of his age and dignity, the indefatigable Maximian passed the Alps, and, courting a personal interview with the sovereign of Gaul, carried with him his daughter Fausta as the pledge of the new alliance. The marriage was celebrated at Arles with every circumstance of magnificence; and the ancient colleague of Diocletian, who again asserted his claim to the Western empire, conferred on his son-in-law and ally the title of Augustus. By consenting to receive that honor from Maximian, Constantine seemed to embrace the cause of Rome and of the senate; but his professions were ambiguous, and his assistance slow and ineffectual. He considered with attention the approaching contest between the masters of Italy and the emperor of the East, and was prepared to consult his own safety or ambition in the event of the war. [24]

[Footnote 24: The sixth Panegyric was pronounced to celebrate the elevation of Constantine; but the prudent orator avoids the mention either of Galerius or of Maxentius. He introduces only one slight allusion to the actual troubles, and to the majesty of Rome. Note: Compare Manso, Beylage, iv. p. 302. Gibbon's account is at least as probable as that of his critic.—M.]

The importance of the occasion called for the presence and abilities of Galerius. At the head of a powerful army, collected from Illyricum and the East, he entered Italy, resolved to revenge the death of Severus, and to chastise the rebellions Romans; or, as he expressed his intentions, in the furious language of a barbarian, to extirpate the senate, and to destroy the people by the sword. But the skill of Maximian had concerted a prudent system of defence. The invader found every place hostile, fortified, and inaccessible; and though he forced his way as far as Narni, within sixty miles of Rome, his dominion in Italy was confined to the narrow limits of his camp. Sensible of the increasing difficulties of his enterprise, the haughty Galerius made the first advances towards a reconciliation, and despatched two of his most considerable officers to tempt the Roman princes by the offer of a conference, and the declaration of his paternal regard for Maxentius, who might obtain much more from his liberality than he could hope from the doubtful chance of war. [25] The offers of Galerius were rejected with firmness, his perfidious friendship refused with contempt, and it was not long before he discovered, that, unless he provided for his safety by a timely retreat, he had some reason to apprehend the fate of Severus. The wealth which the Romans defended against his rapacious tyranny, they freely contributed for his destruction. The name of Maximian, the popular arts of his son, the secret distribution of large sums, and the promise of still more liberal rewards, checked the ardor and corrupted the fidelity of the Illyrian legions; and when Galerius at length gave the signal of the retreat, it was with some difficulty that he could prevail on his veterans not to desert a banner which had so often conducted them to victory and honor. A contemporary writer assigns two other causes for the failure of the expedition; but they are both of such a nature, that a cautious historian will scarcely venture to adopt them. We are told that Galerius, who had formed a very imperfect notion of the greatness of Rome by the cities of the East with which he was acquainted, found his forces inadequate to the siege of that immense capital.

But the extent of a city serves only to render it more accessible to the enemy: Rome had long since been accustomed to submit on the approach of a conqueror; nor could the temporary enthusiasm of the people have long contended against the discipline and valor of the legions. We are likewise informed that the legions themselves were struck with horror and remorse, and that those pious sons of the republic refused to violate the sanctity of their venerable parent. [26] But when we recollect with how much ease, in the more ancient civil wars, the zeal of party and the habits of military obedience had converted the native citizens of Rome into her most implacable enemies, we shall be inclined to distrust this extreme delicacy of strangers and barbarians, who had never beheld Italy till they entered it in a hostile manner. Had they not been restrained by motives of a more interested nature, they would probably have answered Galerius in the words of Caesar's veterans: "If our general wishes to lead us to the banks of the Tyber, we are prepared to trace out his camp. Whatsoever walls he has determined to level with the ground, our hands are ready to work the engines: nor shall we hesitate, should the name of the devoted city be Rome itself." These are indeed the expressions of a poet; but of a poet who has been distinguished, and even censured, for his strict adherence to the truth of history. [27]

[Footnote 25: With regard to this negotiation, see the fragments of an anonymous historian, published by Valesius at the end of his edition of Ammianus Marcellinus, p. 711. These fragments have furnished with several curious, and, as it should seem, authentic anecdotes.]

[Footnote 26: Lactantius de M. P. c. 28. The former of these reasons is probably taken from Virgil's Shepherd: "Illam ego huic notra similem, Meliboee, putavi," &c. Lactantius delights in these poetical illusions.]

[Footnote 27: Castra super Tusci si ponere Tybridis undas; (jubeus) Hesperios audax veniam metator in agros. Tu quoscunque voles in planum effundere muros, His aries actus disperget saxa lacertis; Illa licet penitus tolli quam jusseris urbem Roma sit. Lucan. Pharsal. i. 381.]

The legions of Galerius exhibited a very melancholy proof of their disposition, by the ravages which they committed in their retreat. They murdered, they ravished, they plundered, they drove away the flocks and herds of the Italians; they burnt the villages through which they passed, and they endeavored to destroy the country which it had not been in their power to subdue. During the whole march, Maxentius hung on their rear, but he very prudently declined a general engagement with those brave and desperate veterans. His father had undertaken a second journey into Gaul, with the hope of persuading Constantine, who had assembled an army on the frontier, to join in the pursuit, and to complete the victory. But the actions of Constantine were guided by reason, and not by resentment. He persisted in the wise resolution of maintaining a balance of power in the divided empire, and he no longer hated Galerius, when that aspiring prince had ceased to be an object of terror. [28]

[Footnote 28: Lactantius de M. P. c. 27. Zosim. l. ii. p. 82. The latter, that Constantine, in his interview with Maximian, had promised to declare war against Galerius.]

The mind of Galerius was the most susceptible of the sterner passions, but it was not, however, incapable of a sincere and lasting friendship. Licinius, whose manners as well as character, were not unlike his own, seems to have engaged both his affection and esteem. Their intimacy had commenced in the happier period perhaps of their youth and obscurity. It had been cemented by the freedom and dangers of a military life; they had advanced almost by equal steps through the successive honors of the service; and as soon as Galerius was invested with the Imperial dignity, he seems to have conceived the design of raising his companion to the same rank with himself. During the short period of his prosperity, he considered the rank of Caesar as unworthy of the age and merit of Licinius, and rather chose to reserve for him the place of Constantius, and the empire of the West. While the emperor was employed in the Italian war, he intrusted his friend with the defence of the Danube; and immediately after his return from that unfortunate expedition, he invested Licinius with the vacant purple of Severus, resigning to his immediate command the provinces of Illyricum. [29] The news of his promotion was no sooner carried into the East, than Maximin, who governed, or rather oppressed, the countries of Egypt and Syria, betrayed his envy and discontent, disdained the inferior name of Caesar, and, notwithstanding the prayers as well as arguments of Galerius, exacted, almost by violence, the equal title of Augustus. [30] For the first, and indeed for the last time, the Roman world was administered by six emperors. In the West, Constantine and Maxentius affected to reverence their father Maximian. In the East, Licinius and Maximin honored with more real consideration their benefactor Galerius. The opposition of interest, and the memory of a recent war, divided the empire into two great hostile powers; but their mutual fears produced an apparent tranquillity, and even a feigned reconciliation, till the death of the elder princes, of Maximian, and more particularly of Galerius, gave a new direction to the views and passions of their surviving associates.

[Footnote 29: M. de Tillemont (Hist. des Empereurs, tom. iv. part i. p. 559) has proved that Licinius, without passing through the intermediate rank of Caesar, was declared Augustus, the 11th of November, A. D. 307, after the return of Galerius from Italy.]

[Footnote 30: Lactantius de M. P. c. 32. When Galerius declared Licinius Augustus with himself, he tried to satisfy his younger associates, by inventing for Constantine and Maximin (not Maxentius; see Baluze, p. 81) the new title of sons of the Augusti. But when Maximin acquainted him that he had been saluted Augustus by the army, Galerius was obliged to acknowledge him as well as Constantine, as equal associates in the Imperial dignity.]

When Maximian had reluctantly abdicated the empire, the venal orators of the times applauded his philosophic moderation. When his ambition excited, or at least encouraged, a civil war, they returned thanks to his generous patriotism, and gently censured that love of ease and retirement which had withdrawn him from the public service. [31] But it was impossible that minds like those of Maximian and his son could long possess in harmony an undivided power. Maxentius considered himself as the legal sovereign of Italy, elected by the Roman senate and people; nor would he endure the control of his father, who arrogantly declared that by his name and abilities the rash youth had been established on the throne. The cause was solemnly pleaded before the Praetorian guards; and those troops, who dreaded the severity of the old emperor, espoused the party of Maxentius. [32] The life and freedom of Maximian were, however, respected, and he retired from Italy into Illyricum, affecting to lament his past conduct, and secretly contriving new mischiefs. But Galerius, who was well acquainted with his character, soon obliged him to leave his dominions, and the last refuge of the disappointed Maximian was the court of his son-in-law Constantine. [33] He was received with respect by that artful prince, and with the appearance of filial tenderness by the empress Fausta. That he might remove every suspicion, he resigned the Imperial purple a second time, [34] professing himself at length convinced of the vanity of greatness and ambition. Had he persevered in this resolution, he might have ended his life with less dignity, indeed, than in his first retirement, yet, however, with comfort and reputation. But the near prospect of a throne brought back to his remembrance the state from whence he was fallen, and he resolved, by a desperate effort either to reign or to perish. An incursion of the Franks had summoned Constantine, with a part of his army, to the banks of the Rhine; the remainder of the troops were stationed in the southern provinces of Gaul, which lay exposed to the enterprises of the Italian emperor, and a considerable treasure was deposited in the city of Arles. Maximian either craftily invented, or easily credited, a vain report of the death of Constantine. Without hesitation he ascended the throne, seized the treasure, and scattering it with his accustomed profusion among the soldiers, endeavored to awake in their minds the memory of his ancient dignity and exploits. Before he could establish his authority, or finish the negotiation which he appears to have entered into with his son Maxentius, the celerity of Constantine defeated all his hopes. On the first news of his perfidy and ingratitude, that prince returned by rapid marches from the Rhine to the Saone, embarked on the last mentioned river at Chalons, and at Lyons trusting himself to the rapidity of the Rhone, arrived at the gates of Arles, with a military force which it was impossible for Maximian to resist, and which scarcely permitted him to take refuge in the neighboring city of Marseilles. The narrow neck of land which joined that place to the continent was fortified against the besiegers, whilst the sea was open, either for the escape of Maximian, or for the succor of Maxentius, if the latter should choose to disguise his invasion of Gaul under the honorable pretence of defending a distressed, or, as he might allege, an injured father. Apprehensive of the fatal consequences of delay, Constantine gave orders for an immediate assault; but the scaling-ladders were found too short for the height of the walls, and Marseilles might have sustained as long a siege as it formerly did against the arms of Caesar, if the garrison, conscious either of their fault or of their danger, had not purchased their pardon by delivering up the city and the person of Maximian. A secret but irrevocable sentence of death was pronounced against the usurper; he obtained only the same favor which he had indulged to Severus, and it was published to the world, that, oppressed by the remorse of his repeated crimes, he strangled himself with his own hands. After he had lost the assistance, and disdained the moderate counsels of Diocletian, the second period of his active life was a series of public calamities and personal mortifications, which were terminated, in about three years, by an ignominious death. He deserved his fate; but we should find more reason to applaud the humanity of Constantine, if he had spared an old man, the benefactor of his father, and the father of his wife. During the whole of this melancholy transaction, it appears that Fausta sacrificed the sentiments of nature to her conjugal duties. [35]

[Footnote 31: See Panegyr. Vet. vi. 9. Audi doloris nostri liberam vocem, &c. The whole passage is imagined with artful flattery, and expressed with an easy flow of eloquence.]

[Footnote 32: Lactantius de M. P. c. 28. Zosim. l. ii. p. 82. A report was spread, that Maxentius was the son of some obscure Syrian, and had been substituted by the wife of Maximian as her own child. See Aurelius Victor, Anonym. Valesian, and Panegyr. Vet. ix. 3, 4.]

[Footnote 33: Ab urbe pulsum, ab Italia fugatum, ab Illyrico repudiatum, provinciis, tuis copiis, tuo palatio recepisti. Eumen. in Panegyr Vet. vii. 14.]

[Footnote 34: Lactantius de M. P. c. 29. Yet, after the resignation of the purple, Constantine still continued to Maximian the pomp and honors of the Imperial dignity; and on all public occasions gave the right hand place to his father-in-law. Panegyr. Vet. viii. 15.]

[Footnote 35: Zosim. l. ii. p. 82. Eumenius in Panegyr. Vet. vii. 16—21. The latter of these has undoubtedly represented the whole affair in the most favorable light for his sovereign. Yet even from this partial narrative we may conclude, that the repeated clemency of Constantine, and the reiterated treasons of Maximian, as they are described by Lactantius, (de M. P. c. 29, 30,) and copied by the moderns, are destitute of any historical foundation. Note: Yet some pagan authors relate and confirm them. Aurelius Victor speaking of Maximin, says, cumque specie officii, dolis compositis, Constantinum generum tentaret acerbe, jure tamen interierat. Aur. Vict. de Caesar l. p. 623. Eutropius also says, inde ad Gallias profectus est (Maximianus) composito tamquam a filio esset expulsus, ut Constantino genero jun geretur: moliens tamen Constantinum, reperta occasione, interficere, dedit justissimo exitu. Eutrop. x. p. 661. (Anon. Gent.)—G. — These writers hardly confirm more than Gibbon admits; he denies the repeated clemency of Constantine, and the reiterated treasons of Maximian Compare Manso, p. 302.—M.]

The last years of Galerius were less shameful and unfortunate; and though he had filled with more glory the subordinate station of Caesar than the superior rank of Augustus, he preserved, till the moment of his death, the first place among the princes of the Roman world. He survived his retreat from Italy about four years; and wisely relinquishing his views of universal empire, he devoted the remainder of his life to the enjoyment of pleasure, and to the execution of some works of public utility, among which we may distinguish the discharging into the Danube the superfluous waters of the Lake Pelso, and the cutting down the immense forests that encompassed it; an operation worthy of a monarch, since it gave an extensive country to the agriculture of his Pannonian subjects. [36] His death was occasioned by a very painful and lingering disorder. His body, swelled by an intemperate course of life to an unwieldy corpulence, was covered with ulcers, and devoured by innumerable swarms of those insects which have given their name to a most loathsome disease; [37] but as Galerius had offended a very zealous and powerful party among his subjects, his sufferings, instead of exciting their compassion, have been celebrated as the visible effects of divine justice. [38] He had no sooner expired in his palace of Nicomedia, than the two emperors who were indebted for their purple to his favors, began to collect their forces, with the intention either of disputing, or of dividing, the dominions which he had left without a master. They were persuaded, however, to desist from the former design, and to agree in the latter. The provinces of Asia fell to the share of Maximin, and those of Europe augmented the portion of Licinius. The Hellespont and the Thracian Bosphorus formed their mutual boundary, and the banks of those narrow seas, which flowed in the midst of the Roman world, were covered with soldiers, with arms, and with fortifications. The deaths of Maximian and of Galerius reduced the number of emperors to four. The sense of their true interest soon connected Licinius and Constantine; a secret alliance was concluded between Maximin and Maxentius, and their unhappy subjects expected with terror the bloody consequences of their inevitable dissensions, which were no longer restrained by the fear or the respect which they had entertained for Galerius. [39]

[Footnote 36: Aurelius Victor, c. 40. But that lake was situated on the upper Pannonia, near the borders of Noricum; and the province of Valeria (a name which the wife of Galerius gave to the drained country) undoubtedly lay between the Drave and the Danube, (Sextus Rufus, c. 9.) I should therefore suspect that Victor has confounded the Lake Pelso with the Volocean marshes, or, as they are now called, the Lake Sabaton. It is placed in the heart of Valeria, and its present extent is not less than twelve Hungarian miles (about seventy English) in length, and two in breadth. See Severini Pannonia, l. i. c. 9.]

[Footnote 37: Lactantius (de M. P. c. 33) and Eusebius (l. viii. c. 16) describe the symptoms and progress of his disorder with singular accuracy and apparent pleasure.]

[Footnote 38: If any (like the late Dr. Jortin, Remarks on Ecclesiastical History, vol. ii. p. 307—356) still delight in recording the wonderful deaths of the persecutors, I would recommend to their perusal an admirable passage of Grotius (Hist. l. vii. p. 332) concerning the last illness of Philip II. of Spain.]

[Footnote 39: See Eusebius, l. ix. 6, 10. Lactantius de M. P. c. 36. Zosimus is less exact, and evidently confounds Maximian with Maximin.]

Among so many crimes and misfortunes, occasioned by the passions of the Roman princes, there is some pleasure in discovering a single action which may be ascribed to their virtue. In the sixth year of his reign, Constantine visited the city of Autun, and generously remitted the arrears of tribute, reducing at the same time the proportion of their assessment from twenty-five to eighteen thousand heads, subject to the real and personal capitation. [40] Yet even this indulgence affords the most unquestionable proof of the public misery. This tax was so extremely oppressive, either in itself or in the mode of collecting it, that whilst the revenue was increased by extortion, it was diminished by despair: a considerable part of the territory of Autun was left uncultivated; and great numbers of the provincials rather chose to live as exiles and outlaws, than to support the weight of civil society. It is but too probable, that the bountiful emperor relieved, by a partial act of liberality, one among the many evils which he had caused by his general maxims of administration. But even those maxims were less the effect of choice than of necessity. And if we except the death of Maximian, the reign of Constantine in Gaul seems to have been the most innocent and even virtuous period of his life.

The provinces were protected by his presence from the inroads of the barbarians, who either dreaded or experienced his active valor. After a signal victory over the Franks and Alemanni, several of their princes were exposed by his order to the wild beasts in the amphitheatre of Treves, and the people seem to have enjoyed the spectacle, without discovering, in such a treatment of royal captives, any thing that was repugnant to the laws of nations or of humanity. [41]

[Footnote 40: See the viiith Panegyr., in which Eumenius displays, in the presence of Constantine, the misery and the gratitude of the city of Autun.]

[Footnote 41: Eutropius, x. 3. Panegyr. Veter. vii. 10, 11, 12. A great number of the French youth were likewise exposed to the same cruel and ignominious death.]

[Footnote 41: Yet the panegyric assumes something of an apologetic tone. Te vero Constantine, quantumlibet oderint hoses, dum perhorrescant. Haec est enim vera virtus, ut non ament et quiescant. The orator appeals to the ancient ideal of the republic.—M.]

The virtues of Constantine were rendered more illustrious by the vices of Maxentius. Whilst the Gallic provinces enjoyed as much happiness as the condition of the times was capable of receiving, Italy and Africa groaned under the dominion of a tyrant, as contemptible as he was odious. The zeal of flattery and faction has indeed too frequently sacrificed the reputation of the vanquished to the glory of their successful rivals; but even those writers who have revealed, with the most freedom and pleasure, the faults of Constantine, unanimously confess that Maxentius was cruel, rapacious, and profligate. [42] He had the good fortune to suppress a slight rebellion in Africa. The governor and a few adherents had been guilty; the province suffered for their crime. The flourishing cities of Cirtha and Carthage, and the whole extent of that fertile country, were wasted by fire and sword. The abuse of victory was followed by the abuse of law and justice. A formidable army of sycophants and delators invaded Africa; the rich and the noble were easily convicted of a connection with the rebels; and those among them who experienced the emperor's clemency, were only punished by the confiscation of their estates. [43] So signal a victory was celebrated by a magnificent triumph, and Maxentius exposed to the eyes of the people the spoils and captives of a Roman province. The state of the capital was no less deserving of compassion than that of Africa. The wealth of Rome supplied an inexhaustible fund for his vain and prodigal expenses, and the ministers of his revenue were skilled in the arts of rapine. It was under his reign that the method of exacting a free gift from the senators was first invented; and as the sum was insensibly increased, the pretences of levying it, a victory, a birth, a marriage, or an imperial consulship, were proportionably multiplied. [44] Maxentius had imbibed the same implacable aversion to the senate, which had characterized most of the former tyrants of Rome; nor was it possible for his ungrateful temper to forgive the generous fidelity which had raised him to the throne, and supported him against all his enemies. The lives of the senators were exposed to his jealous suspicions, the dishonor of their wives and daughters heightened the gratification of his sensual passions. [45] It may be presumed, that an Imperial lover was seldom reduced to sigh in vain; but whenever persuasion proved ineffectual, he had recourse to violence; and there remains one memorable example of a noble matron, who preserved her chastity by a voluntary death. The soldiers were the only order of men whom he appeared to respect, or studied to please. He filled Rome and Italy with armed troops, connived at their tumults, suffered them with impunity to plunder, and even to massacre, the defenceless people; [46] and indulging them in the same licentiousness which their emperor enjoyed, Maxentius often bestowed on his military favorites the splendid villa, or the beautiful wife, of a senator. A prince of such a character, alike incapable of governing, either in peace or in war, might purchase the support, but he could never obtain the esteem, of the army. Yet his pride was equal to his other vices. Whilst he passed his indolent life either within the walls of his palace, or in the neighboring gardens of Sallust, he was repeatedly heard to declare, that he alone was emperor, and that the other princes were no more than his lieutenants, on whom he had devolved the defence of the frontier provinces, that he might enjoy without interruption the elegant luxury of the capital. Rome, which had so long regretted the absence, lamented, during the six years of his reign, the presence of her sovereign. [47]

[Footnote 42: Julian excludes Maxentius from the banquet of the Caesars with abhorrence and contempt; and Zosimus (l. ii. p. 85) accuses him of every kind of cruelty and profligacy.]

[Footnote 43: Zosimus, l. ii. p. 83—85. Aurelius Victor.]

[Footnote 44: The passage of Aurelius Victor should be read in the following manner: Primus instituto pessimo, munerum specie, Patres Oratores que pecuniam conferre prodigenti sibi cogeret.]

[Footnote 45: Panegyr. Vet. ix. 3. Euseb. Hist Eccles. viii. 14, et in Vit. Constant i. 33, 34. Rufinus, c. 17. The virtuous matron who stabbed herself to escape the violence of Maxentius, was a Christian, wife to the praefect of the city, and her name was Sophronia. It still remains a question among the casuists, whether, on such occasions, suicide is justifiable.]

[Footnote 46: Praetorianis caedem vulgi quondam annueret, is the vague expression of Aurelius Victor. See more particular, though somewhat different, accounts of a tumult and massacre which happened at Rome, in Eusebius, (l. viii. c. 14,) and in Zosimus, (l. ii. p. 84.)]

[Footnote 47: See, in the Panegyrics, (ix. 14,) a lively description of the indolence and vain pride of Maxentius. In another place the orator observes that the riches which Rome had accumulated in a period of 1060 years, were lavished by the tyrant on his mercenary bands; redemptis ad civile latrocinium manibus in gesserat.]

Though Constantine might view the conduct of Maxentius with abhorrence, and the situation of the Romans with compassion, we have no reason to presume that he would have taken up arms to punish the one or to relieve the other. But the tyrant of Italy rashly ventured to provoke a formidable enemy, whose ambition had been hitherto restrained by considerations of prudence, rather than by principles of justice. [48] After the death of Maximian, his titles, according to the established custom, had been erased, and his statues thrown down with ignominy. His son, who had persecuted and deserted him when alive, effected to display the most pious regard for his memory, and gave orders that a similar treatment should be immediately inflicted on all the statues that had been erected in Italy and Africa to the honor of Constantine.

That wise prince, who sincerely wished to decline a war, with the difficulty and importance of which he was sufficiently acquainted, at first dissembled the insult, and sought for redress by the milder expedient of negotiation, till he was convinced that the hostile and ambitious designs of the Italian emperor made it necessary for him to arm in his own defence. Maxentius, who openly avowed his pretensions to the whole monarchy of the West, had already prepared a very considerable force to invade the Gallic provinces on the side of Rhaetia; and though he could not expect any assistance from Licinius, he was flattered with the hope that the legions of Illyricum, allured by his presents and promises, would desert the standard of that prince, and unanimously declare themselves his soldiers and subjects. [49] Constantine no longer hesitated. He had deliberated with caution, he acted with vigor. He gave a private audience to the ambassadors, who, in the name of the senate and people, conjured him to deliver Rome from a detested tyrant; and without regarding the timid remonstrances of his council, he resolved to prevent the enemy, and to carry the war into the heart of Italy. [50]

[Footnote 48: After the victory of Constantine, it was universally allowed, that the motive of delivering the republic from a detested tyrant, would, at any time, have justified his expedition into Italy. Euseb in Vi'. Constantin. l. i. c. 26. Panegyr. Vet. ix. 2.]

[Footnote 49: Zosimus, l. ii. p. 84, 85. Nazarius in Panegyr. x. 7—13.]

[Footnote 50: See Panegyr. Vet. ix. 2. Omnibus fere tuis Comitibus et Ducibus non solum tacite mussantibus, sed etiam aperte timentibus; contra consilia hominum, contra Haruspicum monita, ipse per temet liberandae arbis tempus venisse sentires. The embassy of the Romans is mentioned only by Zonaras, (l. xiii.,) and by Cedrenus, (in Compend. Hist. p. 370;) but those modern Greeks had the opportunity of consulting many writers which have since been lost, among which we may reckon the life of Constantine by Praxagoras. Photius (p. 63) has made a short extract from that historical work.]

The enterprise was as full of danger as of glory; and the unsuccessful event of two former invasions was sufficient to inspire the most serious apprehensions. The veteran troops, who revered the name of Maximian, had embraced in both those wars the party of his son, and were now restrained by a sense of honor, as well as of interest, from entertaining an idea of a second desertion. Maxentius, who considered the Praetorian guards as the firmest defence of his throne, had increased them to their ancient establishment; and they composed, including the rest of the Italians who were enlisted into his service, a formidable body of fourscore thousand men. Forty thousand Moors and Carthaginians had been raised since the reduction of Africa. Even Sicily furnished its proportion of troops; and the armies of Maxentius amounted to one hundred and seventy thousand foot and eighteen thousand horse. The wealth of Italy supplied the expenses of the war; and the adjacent provinces were exhausted, to form immense magazines of corn and every other kind of provisions.

The whole force of Constantine consisted of ninety thousand foot and eight thousand horse; [51] and as the defence of the Rhine required an extraordinary attention during the absence of the emperor, it was not in his power to employ above half his troops in the Italian expedition, unless he sacrificed the public safety to his private quarrel. [52] At the head of about forty thousand soldiers he marched to encounter an enemy whose numbers were at least four times superior to his own. But the armies of Rome, placed at a secure distance from danger, were enervated by indulgence and luxury. Habituated to the baths and theatres of Rome, they took the field with reluctance, and were chiefly composed of veterans who had almost forgotten, or of new levies who had never acquired, the use of arms and the practice of war. The hardy legions of Gaul had long defended the frontiers of the empire against the barbarians of the North; and in the performance of that laborious service, their valor was exercised and their discipline confirmed. There appeared the same difference between the leaders as between the armies. Caprice or flattery had tempted Maxentius with the hopes of conquest; but these aspiring hopes soon gave way to the habits of pleasure and the consciousness of his inexperience. The intrepid mind of Constantine had been trained from his earliest youth to war, to action, and to military command.

[Footnote 51: Zosimus (l. ii. p. 86) has given us this curious account of the forces on both sides. He makes no mention of any naval armaments, though we are assured (Panegyr. Vet. ix. 25) that the war was *carried on by sea as well as by land; and that the fleet of Constantine took possession of Sardinia, Corsica, and the ports of Italy.]*

[Footnote 52: Panegyr. Vet. ix. 3. It is not surprising that the orator should diminish the numbers with which his sovereign achieved the conquest of Italy; but it appears somewhat singular that he should esteem the tyrant's army at no more than 100,000 men.]

PART III

When Hannibal marched from Gaul into Italy, he was obliged, first to discover, and then to open, a way over mountains, and through savage nations, that had never yielded a passage to a regular army. [53] The Alps were then guarded by nature, they are now fortified by art. Citadels, constructed with no less skill than labor and expense, command every avenue into the plain, and on that side render Italy almost inaccessible to the enemies of the king of Sardinia. [54] But in the course of the intermediate period, the generals, who have attempted the passage, have seldom experienced any difficulty or resistance. In the age of Constantine, the peasants of the mountains were civilized and obedient subjects; the country was plentifully stocked with provisions, and the stupendous highways, which the Romans had carried over the Alps, opened several communications between Gaul and Italy. [55] Constantine preferred the road of the Cottian Alps, or, as it is now called, of Mount Cenis, and led his troops with such active diligence, that he descended into the plain of Piedmont before the court of Maxentius had received any certain intelligence of his departure from the banks of the Rhine. The city of Susa, however, which is situated at the foot of Mount Cenis, was surrounded with walls, and provided with a garrison sufficiently numerous to check the progress of an invader; but the impatience of Constantine's troops disdained the tedious forms of a siege. The same day that they appeared before Susa, they applied fire to the gates, and ladders to the walls; and mounting to the assault amidst a shower of stones and arrows, they entered the place sword in hand, and cut in pieces the greatest part of the garrison. The flames were extinguished by the care of Constantine, and the remains of Susa preserved from total destruction. About forty miles from thence, a more severe contest awaited him. A numerous army of Italians was assembled under the lieutenants of Maxentius, in the plains of Turin. Its principal strength consisted in a species of heavy cavalry, which the Romans, since the decline of their discipline, had borrowed from the nations of the East. The horses, as well as the men, were clothed in complete armor, the joints of which were artfully adapted to the motions of their bodies. The aspect of this cavalry was formidable, their weight almost irresistible; and as, on this occasion, their generals had drawn them up in a compact column or wedge, with a sharp point, and with spreading flanks, they flattered themselves that they could easily break and trample down the army of Constantine. They might, perhaps, have succeeded in their design, had not their experienced adversary embraced the same method of defence, which in similar circumstances had been practised by Aurelian. The skilful evolutions of Constantine divided and baffled this massy column of cavalry. The troops of Maxentius fled in confusion towards Turin; and as the gates of the city were shut against them, very few escaped the sword of the victorious pursuers. By this important service, Turin deserved to experience the clemency and even favor of the conqueror. He made his entry into the Imperial palace of Milan, and almost all the cities of Italy between the Alps and the Po not only acknowledged the power, but embraced with zeal the party, of Constantine. [56]

[Footnote 53: The three principal passages of the Alps between Gaul and Italy, are those of Mount St. Bernard, Mount Cenis, and Mount Genevre. Tradition, and a resemblance of names, (Alpes Penninoe,) had assigned the first of these for the march of Hannibal, (see Simler de Alpibus.) The Chevalier de Folard

(Polyp. tom. iv.) and M. d'Anville have led him over Mount Genevre. But notwithstanding the authority of an experienced officer and a learned geographer, the pretensions of Mount Cenis are supported in a specious, not to say a convincing, manner, by M. Grosley. Observations sur l'Italie, tom. i. p. 40, &c. — The dissertation of Messrs. Cramer and Wickham has clearly shown that the Little St. Bernard must claim the honor of Hannibal's passage. Mr. Long (London, 1831) has added some sensible corrections re Hannibal's march to the Alps.—M]

[Footnote 54: La Brunette near Suse, Demont, Exiles, Fenestrelles, Coni, &c.]

[Footnote 55: See Ammian. Marcellin. xv. 10. His description of the roads over the Alps is clear, lively, and accurate.]

[Footnote 56: Zosimus as well as Eusebius hasten from the passage of the Alps to the decisive action near Rome. We must apply to the two Panegyrics for the intermediate actions of Constantine.]

From Milan to Rome, the Aemilian and Flaminian highways offered an easy march of about four hundred miles; but though Constantine was impatient to encounter the tyrant, he prudently directed his operations against another army of Italians, who, by their strength and position, might either oppose his progress, or, in case of a misfortune, might intercept his retreat. Ruricius Pompeianus, a general distinguished by his valor and ability, had under his command the city of Verona, and all the troops that were stationed in the province of Venetia. As soon as he was informed that Constantine was advancing towards him, he detached a large body of cavalry which was defeated in an engagement near Brescia, and pursued by the Gallic legions as far as the gates of Verona. The necessity, the importance, and the difficulties of the siege of Verona, immediately presented themselves to the sagacious mind of Constantine. [57] The city was accessible only by a narrow peninsula towards the west, as the other three sides were surrounded by the Adige, a rapid river, which covered the province of Venetia, from whence the besieged derived an inexhaustible supply of men and provisions. It was not without great difficulty, and after several fruitless attempts, that Constantine found means to pass the river at some distance above the city, and in a place where the torrent was less violent. He then encompassed Verona with strong lines, pushed his attacks with prudent vigor, and repelled a desperate sally of Pompeianus. That intrepid general, when he had used every means of defence that the strength of the place or that of the garrison could afford, secretly escaped from Verona, anxious not for his own, but for the public safety. With indefatigable diligence he soon collected an army sufficient either to meet Constantine in the field, or to attack him if he obstinately remained within his lines. The emperor, attentive to the motions, and informed of the approach of so formidable an enemy, left a part of his legions to continue the operations of the siege, whilst, at the head of those troops on whose valor and fidelity he more particularly depended, he advanced in person to engage the general of Maxentius. The army of Gaul was drawn up in two lines, according to the usual practice of war; but their experienced leader, perceiving that the numbers of the Italians far exceeded his own, suddenly changed his disposition, and, reducing the second, extended the front of his first line to a just proportion with that of the enemy. Such evolutions, which only veteran troops can execute without confusion in a moment of danger, commonly prove decisive; but as this engagement began towards the close of the day, and was contested with great obstinacy during the whole night, there was less room for the conduct of the generals than for the courage of the soldiers. The return of light displayed the victory of Constantine, and a field of carnage covered with many thousands of the vanquished Italians. Their general, Pompeianus, was found among the slain; Verona immediately surrendered at discretion, and the garrison was made prisoners of war. [58] When the officers of the victorious army congratulated their master on this important success, they ventured to add some respectful complaints, of such a nature, however, as the most jealous monarchs will listen to without displeasure. They represented to Constantine, that, not contented with all the duties of a commander, he had exposed his own person with an excess of valor which almost degenerated into rashness; and they conjured him for the future to pay more regard to the preservation of a life in which the safety of Rome and of the empire was involved. [59]

[Footnote 57: The Marquis Maffei has examined the siege and battle of Verona with that degree of attention and accuracy which was due to a memorable action that happened in his native country. The fortifications of that city, constructed by Gallienus, were less extensive than the modern walls, and the amphitheatre was not included within their circumference. See Verona Illustrata, part i. p. 142 150.]

[Footnote 58: They wanted chains for so great a multitude of captives; and the whole council was at a loss; but the sagacious conqueror imagined the happy expedient of converting into fetters the swords of the vanquished. Panegyr. Vet. ix. 11.]

[Footnote 59: Panegyr. Vet. ix. 11.]

While Constantine signalized his conduct and valor in the field, the sovereign of Italy appeared insensible of the calamities and danger of a civil war which reigned in the heart of his dominions. Pleasure was still the only business of Maxentius. Concealing, or at least attempting to conceal, from the public knowledge the misfortunes of his arms, [60] he indulged himself in a vain confidence which deferred the remedies of the approaching evil, without deferring the evil itself. [61] The rapid progress of Constantine [62] was scarcely sufficient to awaken him from his fatal security; he flattered himself, that his well-known liberality, and the majesty of the Roman name, which had already delivered him from two invasions, would dissipate with the same facility the rebellious army of Gaul. The officers of experience and ability, who had served under the banners of Maximian, were at length compelled to inform his effeminate son of the imminent danger to which he was reduced; and, with a freedom that at once surprised and convinced him, to urge the necessity of preventing his ruin, by a vigorous exertion of his remaining power. The resources of Maxentius, both of men and money, were still considerable. The Praetorian guards felt how strongly their own interest and safety were connected with his cause; and a third army was soon collected, more numerous than those which had been lost in the battles of Turin and Verona. It was far from the intention of the emperor to lead his troops in person. A stranger to the exercises of war, he trembled at the apprehension of so dangerous a contest; and as fear is commonly superstitious, he listened with melancholy attention to the rumors of omens and presages which seemed to menace his life and empire. Shame at length supplied the place of courage, and forced him to take the field. He was unable to sustain the contempt of the Roman people. The circus resounded with their indignant clamors, and they tumultuously besieged the gates of the palace, reproaching the pusillanimity of their indolent sovereign, and celebrating the heroic spirit of Constantine. [63] Before Maxentius left Rome, he consulted the Sibylline books. The guardians of these ancient oracles were as well versed in the arts of this world as they were ignorant of the secrets of fate; and they returned him a very prudent answer, which might adapt itself to the event, and secure their reputation, whatever should be the chance of arms. [64]

[Footnote 60: Literas calamitatum suarum indices supprimebat. Panegyr Vet. ix. 15.]

[Footnote 61: Remedia malorum potius quam mala differebat, is the fine censure which Tacitus passes on the supine indolence of Vitellius.]

[Footnote 62: The Marquis Maffei has made it extremely probable that Constantine was still at Verona, the 1st of September, A.D. 312, and that the memorable aera of the indications was dated from his conquest of the Cisalpine Gaul.]

[Footnote 63: See Panegyr. Vet. xi. 16. Lactantius de M. P. c. 44.]

[Footnote 64: Illo die hostem Romanorum esse periturum. The vanquished became of course the enemy of Rome.]

The celerity of Constantine's march has been compared to the rapid conquest of Italy by the first of the Caesars; nor is the flattering parallel repugnant to the truth of history, since no more than fifty-eight days elapsed between the surrender of Verona and the final decision of the war. Constantine had always apprehended that the tyrant would consult the dictates of fear, and perhaps of prudence; and that, instead of risking his last hopes in a general engagement, he would shut himself up within the walls of Rome. His ample magazines secured him against the danger of famine; and as the situation of Constantine admitted not of delay, he might have been reduced to the sad necessity of destroying with fire and sword the Imperial city, the noblest reward of his victory, and the deliverance of which had been the motive, or rather indeed the pretence, of the civil war. [65] It was with equal surprise and pleasure, that on his arrival at a place called Saxa Rubra, about nine miles from Rome, [66] he discovered the army of Maxentius prepared to give him battle. [67] Their long front filled a very spacious plain, and their deep array reached to the banks of the Tyber, which covered their rear, and forbade their retreat. We are informed, and we may believe, that Constantine disposed his troops with consummate skill, and that he chose for himself the post of honor and danger. Distinguished by the splendor of his arms, he charged in person the cavalry of his rival; and his irresistible attack determined the fortune of the day. The cavalry of Maxentius was principally composed either of unwieldy cuirassiers, or of light Moors and Numidians. They yielded to the vigor of the Gallic horse, which possessed more activity than the one, more firmness than the other. The defeat of the two wings left the infantry without any protection on its flanks, and the undisciplined Italians fled without reluctance from the standard of a tyrant whom they had always hated, and whom they no longer feared. The Praetorians, conscious that their offences were beyond the reach of mercy, were animated by revenge and despair. Notwithstanding their repeated efforts, those brave veterans were unable to recover the victory: they obtained, however, an honorable death; and it was observed that their bodies covered the same ground which had been occupied by their ranks. [68] The confusion then became general, and the dismayed troops of Maxentius, pursued by an implacable enemy, rushed by thousands into the deep and rapid stream of the Tyber. The emperor himself attempted to escape back into the city over the Milvian bridge; but the crowds which pressed together through that narrow passage forced him into the river, where he was immediately drowned by the weight of his armor. [69] His body, which had sunk very deep into the mud, was found with some difficulty the next day. The sight of his head, when it was exposed to the eyes of the people, convinced them of their deliverance, and admonished them to receive with acclamations of loyalty and gratitude the fortunate Constantine, who thus achieved by his valor and ability the most splendid enterprise of his life. [70]

[Footnote 65: See Panegyr. Vet. ix. 16, x. 27. The former of these orators magnifies the hoards of corn, which Maxentius had collected from Africa and the Islands. And yet, if there is any truth in the scarcity mentioned by Eusebius, (in Vit. Constantin. l. i. c. 36,) the Imperial granaries must have been open only to the soldiers.]

[Footnote 66: Maxentius... tandem urbe in Saxa Rubra, millia ferme novem aegerrime progressus. Aurelius Victor. See Cellarius Geograph. Antiq. tom. i. p. 463. Saxa Rubra was in the neighborhood of the Cremera, a trifling rivulet, illustrated by the valor and glorious death of the three hundred Fabii.]

[Footnote 67: The post which Maxentius had taken, with the Tyber in his rear is very clearly described by the two Panegyrists, ix. 16, x. 28.]

[Footnote 68: Exceptis latrocinii illius primis auctoribus, qui desperata venia ocum quem pugnae sumpserant texere corporibus. Panegyr. Vet 17.]

[Footnote 69: A very idle rumor soon prevailed, that Maxentius, who had not taken any precaution for his own retreat, had contrived a very artful snare to destroy the army of the pursuers; but that the wooden bridge, which was to have been loosened on the approach of Constantine, unluckily broke down under the weight of the flying Italians. M. de Tillemont (Hist. des Empereurs, tom. iv. part i. p. 576) very seriously examines whether, in contradiction to common sense, the testimony of Eusebius and Zosimus ought to prevail over the silence of Lactantius, Nazarius, and the anonymous, but contemporary orator, who composed the ninth Panegyric. Note: Manso (Beylage, vi.) examines the question, and adduces two manifest allusions to the bridge, from the Life of Constantine by Praxagoras, and from Libanius. Is it not very probable that such a bridge was thrown over the river to facilitate the advance, and to secure the retreat, of the army of Maxentius? In case of defeat, orders were given for destroying it, in order to check the pursuit: it broke down accidentally, or in the confusion was destroyed, as has not unfrequently been the case, before the proper time.—M.]

[Footnote 70: Zosimus, l. ii. p. 86-88, and the two Panegyrics, the former of which was pronounced a few months afterwards, afford the clearest notion of this great battle. Lactantius, Eusebius, and even the Epitomes, supply several useful hints.]

In the use of victory, Constantine neither deserved the praise of clemency, nor incurred the censure of immoderate rigor. [71] He inflicted the same treatment to which a defeat would have exposed his own person and family, put to death the two sons of the tyrant, and carefully extirpated his whole race. The most distinguished adherents of Maxentius must have expected to share his fate, as they had shared his prosperity and his crimes; but when the Roman people loudly demanded a greater number of victims, the conqueror resisted with firmness and humanity, those servile clamors, which were dictated by flattery as well as by resentment. Informers were punished and discouraged; the innocent, who had suffered under the late tyranny, were recalled from exile, and restored to their estates. A general act of oblivion quieted the minds and settled the property of the people, both in Italy and in Africa. [72] The first time that Constantine honored the senate with his presence, he recapitulated his own services and exploits in a modest oration, assured that illustrious order of his sincere regard, and promised to reestablish its ancient dignity and privileges. The grateful senate repaid these unmeaning professions by the empty titles of honor, which it was yet in their power to bestow; and without presuming to ratify the authority of Constantine, they passed a decree to assign him the first rank among the three Augusti who governed the Roman world. [73] Games and festivals were instituted to preserve the fame of his victory, and several edifices, raised at the expense of Maxentius, were dedicated to the honor of his successful rival. The triumphal arch of Constantine still remains a melancholy proof of the decline of the arts, and a singular testimony of the meanest vanity. As it was not possible to find in the capital of the empire a sculptor who was capable of adorning that public monument, the arch of Trajan, without any respect either for his memory or for the rules of propriety, was stripped of its most elegant figures. The difference of times and persons, of actions and characters, was totally disregarded. The Parthian captives appear prostrate at the feet of a prince who never carried his arms beyond the Euphrates; and curious antiquarians can still discover the head of Trajan on the trophies of Constantine. The new ornaments which it was necessary to introduce between the vacancies of ancient sculpture are executed in the rudest and most unskillful manner. [74]

[Footnote 71: Zosimus, the enemy of Constantine, allows (l. ii. p. 88) that only a few of the friends of Maxentius were put to death; but we may remark the expressive passage of Nazarius, (Panegyr. Vet. x. 6.) Omnibus qui labefactari statum ejus poterant cum stirpe deletis. The other orator (Panegyr. Vet. ix. 20, 21) contents himself with observing, that Constantine, when he entered Rome, did not imitate the cruel massacres of Cinna, of Marius, or of Sylla. Note: This may refer to the son or sons of Maxentius.—M.]

[Footnote 72: See the two Panegyrics, and the laws of this and the ensuing year, in the Theodosian Code.]

[Footnote 73: Panegyr. Vet. ix. 20. Lactantius de M. P. c. 44. Maximin, who was confessedly the eldest Caesar, claimed, with some show of reason, the first rank among the Augusti.]

[Footnote 74: Adhuc cuncta opera quae magnifice construxerat, urbis fanum atque basilicam, Flavii meritis patres sacravere. Aurelius Victor. With regard to the theft of Trajan's trophies, consult Flaminius Vacca, apud Montfaucon, Diarium Italicum, p. 250, and l'Antiquite Expliquee of the latter, tom. iv. p. 171.]

The final abolition of the Praetorian guards was a measure of prudence as well as of revenge. Those haughty troops, whose numbers and privileges had been restored, and even augmented, by Maxentius, were forever suppressed by Constantine. Their fortified camp was destroyed, and the few Praetorians who had escaped the fury of the sword were dispersed among the legions, and banished to the frontiers of the empire, where they might be serviceable without again becoming dangerous. [75] By suppressing the troops which were usually stationed in Rome, Constantine gave the fatal blow to the dignity of the senate and people, and the disarmed capital was exposed without protection to the insults or neglect of its distant master. We may observe, that in this last effort to preserve their expiring freedom, the Romans, from the apprehension of a tribute, had raised Maxentius to the throne. He exacted that tribute from the senate under the name of a free gift. They implored the assistance of Constantine. He vanquished the tyrant, and converted the free gift into a perpetual tax. The senators, according to the declaration which was required of their property, were divided into several classes. The most opulent paid annually eight pounds of gold, the next class paid four, the last two, and those whose poverty might have claimed an exemption, were assessed, however, at seven pieces of gold. Besides the regular members of the senate, their sons, their descendants, and even their relations, enjoyed the vain privileges, and supported the heavy burdens, of the senatorial order; nor will it any longer excite our surprise, that Constantine should be attentive to increase the number of persons who were included under so useful a description. [76] After the defeat of Maxentius, the victorious emperor passed no more than two or three months in Rome, which he visited twice during the remainder of his life, to celebrate the solemn festivals of the tenth and of the twentieth years of his reign. Constantine was almost perpetually in motion, to exercise the legions, or to inspect the state of the provinces. Treves, Milan, Aquileia, Sirmium, Naissus, and Thessalonica, were the occasional places of his residence, till he founded a new Rome on the confines of Europe and Asia. [77]

[Footnote 75: Praetoriae legiones ac subsidia factionibus aptiora quam urbi Romae, sublata penitus; simul arma atque usus indumenti militaris Aurelius Victor. Zosimus (l. ii. p. 89) mentions this fact as an historian, and it is very pompously celebrated in the ninth Panegyric.]

[Footnote 76: Ex omnibus provinciis optimates viros Curiae tuae pigneraveris ut Senatus dignitas.... ex totius Orbis flore consisteret. Nazarius in Panegyr. Vet x. 35. The word pigneraveris might almost seem maliciously chosen. Concerning the senatorial tax, see Zosimus, l. ii. p. 115, the second title of the sixth book of the Theodosian Code, with Godefroy's Commentary, and Memoires de l'Academic des Inscriptions, tom. xxviii. p. 726.]

[Footnote 77: From the Theodosian Code, we may now begin to trace the motions of the emperors; but the dates both of time and place have frequently been altered by the carelessness of transcribers.]

Before Constantine marched into Italy, he had secured the friendship, or at least the neutrality, of Licinius, the Illyrian emperor. He had promised his sister Constantia in marriage to that prince; but the celebration of the nuptials was deferred till after the conclusion of the war, and the interview of the two emperors at Milan, which was appointed for that purpose, appeared to cement the union of their families and interests. [78] In the midst of the public festivity they were suddenly obliged to take leave of each other. An inroad of the Franks summoned Constantine to the Rhime, and the hostile approach of the sovereign of Asia demanded the immediate presence of Licinius. Maximin had been the secret ally of Maxentius, and without being discouraged by his fate, he resolved to try the fortune of a civil war. He moved out of Syria, towards the frontiers of Bithynia, in the depth of winter. The season was severe and tempestuous; great numbers of men as well as horses perished in the snow; and as the roads were broken up by incessant rains, he was obliged to leave behind him a considerable part of the heavy baggage, which was unable to follow the rapidity of his forced marches. By this extraordinary effort of diligence, he arrived with a harassed but formidable army, on the banks of the Thracian Bosphorus before the lieutenants of Licinius were apprised of his hostile intentions. Byzantium surrendered to the power of Maximin, after a siege of eleven days. He was detained some days under the walls of Heraclea; and he had no sooner taken possession of that city, than he was alarmed by the intelligence, that Licinius had pitched his camp at the distance of only eighteen miles. After a fruitless negotiation, in which the two princes attempted to seduce the fidelity of each other's adherents, they had recourse to arms. The emperor of the East commanded a disciplined and veteran army of above seventy thousand men; and Licinius, who had collected about thirty thousand Illyrians, was at first oppressed by the superiority of numbers. His military skill, and the firmness of his troops, restored the day, and obtained a decisive victory. The incredible speed which Maximin exerted in his flight is much more celebrated than his prowess in the battle. Twenty-four hours afterwards he was seen, pale, trembling, and without his Imperial ornaments, at Nicomedia, one hundred and sixty miles from the place of his defeat. The wealth of Asia was yet unexhausted; and though the flower of his veterans had fallen in the late action, he had still power, if he could obtain time, to draw very numerous levies from Syria and Egypt. But he survived his misfortune only three or four months. His death, which happened at Tarsus, was variously ascribed to despair, to poison, and to the divine justice. As Maximin was alike destitute of abilities and of virtue, he was lamented neither by the people nor by the soldiers. The provinces of the East, delivered from the terrors of civil war, cheerfully acknowledged the authority of Licinius. [79]

[Footnote 78: Zosimus (l. ii. p. 89) observes, that before the war the sister of Constantine had been betrothed to Licinius. According to the younger Victor, Diocletian was invited to the nuptials; but having ventured to plead his age and infirmities, he received a second letter, filled with reproaches for his supposed partiality to the cause of Maxentius and Maximin.]

[Footnote 79: Zosimus mentions the defeat and death of Maximin as ordinary events; but Lactantius expatiates on them, (de M. P. c. 45-50,) ascribing them to the miraculous interposition of Heaven. Licinius at that time was one of the protectors of the church.]

The vanquished emperor left behind him two children, a boy of about eight, and a girl of about seven, years old. Their inoffensive age might have excited compassion; but the compassion of Licinius was a very feeble resource, nor did it restrain him from extinguishing the name and memory of his adversary. The death of Severianus will admit of less excuse, as it was dictated neither by revenge nor by policy. The conqueror had never received any injury from the father of that unhappy youth, and the short and obscure reign of Severus, in a distant part of the empire, was already forgotten. But the execution of Candidianus was an act of the blackest cruelty and ingratitude. He was the natural son of Galerius, the friend and benefactor of Licinius. The prudent father had judged him too young to sustain the weight of a diadem; but he hoped that, under the protection of princes who were indebted to his favor for the Imperial purple, Candidianus might pass a secure and honorable life. He was now advancing towards the twentieth year of his age, and the royalty of his birth, though unsupported either by merit or ambition, was sufficient to exasperate the jealous mind of Licinius. [80] To these innocent and illustrious victims of his tyranny, we must add the wife and daughter of the emperor Diocletian. When that prince conferred on Galerius the title of Caesar, he had given him in marriage his daughter Valeria, whose melancholy adventures might furnish a very singular subject for tragedy. She had fulfilled and even surpassed the duties of a wife. As she had not any children herself, she condescended to adopt the illegitimate son of her husband, and invariably displayed towards the unhappy Candidianus the tenderness and anxiety of a real mother. After the death of Galerius, her ample possessions provoked the avarice, and her personal attractions excited the desires, of his successor, Maximin. [81] He had a wife still alive; but divorce was permitted by the Roman law, and the fierce passions of the tyrant demanded an immediate gratification. The answer of Valeria was such as became the daughter and widow of emperors; but it was tempered by the prudence which her defenceless condition compelled her to observe. She represented to the persons whom Maximin had employed on this occasion, "that even if honor could permit a woman of her character and dignity to entertain a thought of second nuptials, decency at least must forbid her to listen to his addresses at a time when the ashes of her husband, and his benefactor were still warm, and while the sorrows of her mind were still expressed by her mourning garments. She ventured to declare, that she could place very little confidence in the professions of a man whose cruel inconstancy was capable of repudiating a faithful and affectionate wife." [82] On this repulse, the love of Maximin was converted into fury; and as witnesses and judges were always at his disposal, it was easy for him to cover his fury with an appearance of legal proceedings, and to assault the reputation as well as the happiness of Valeria. Her estates were confiscated, her eunuchs and domestics devoted to the most inhuman tortures; and several innocent and respectable matrons, who were honored with her friendship, suffered death, on a false accusation of adultery. The empress herself, together with her mother Prisca, was condemned to exile; and as they were ignominiously hurried from place to place before they were confined to a sequestered village in the deserts of Syria, they exposed their shame and distress to the provinces of the East, which, during thirty years, had respected their august dignity. Diocletian made several ineffectual efforts to alleviate the misfortunes of his daughter; and, as the last return that he expected for the Imperial purple, which he had conferred upon Maximin, he entreated that Valeria might be permitted to share his retirement of Salona, and to close the eyes of her afflicted father. [83] He entreated; but as he could no longer threaten, his prayers were received with coldness and disdain; and the pride of Maximin was gratified, in treating Diocletian as a suppliant, and his daughter as a criminal. The death of Maximin seemed to assure the empresses of a favorable alteration in their fortune. The public disorders relaxed the vigilance of their guard, and they easily found means to escape from the place of their exile, and to repair, though with some precaution, and in disguise, to the court of Licinius. His behavior, in the first days of his reign, and the honorable reception which he gave to young Candidianus, inspired Valeria with a secret satisfaction, both on her own account and on that of her adopted son. But these grateful prospects were soon succeeded by horror and astonishment; and the bloody executions which stained the palace of Nicomedia sufficiently convinced her that the throne of Maximin was filled by a tyrant more inhuman than himself. Valeria consulted her safety by a hasty flight, and, still accompanied by her mother Prisca, they wandered above fifteen months [84] through the provinces, concealed in the disguise of plebeian habits. They were at length discovered at Thessalonica; and as the sentence of their death was already pronounced, they were immediately beheaded, and their bodies thrown into the sea. The people gazed on the melancholy spectacle; but their grief and indignation were suppressed by the terrors of a military guard. Such was the unworthy fate of the wife and daughter of Diocletian. We lament their misfortunes, we cannot discover their crimes; and whatever idea we may justly entertain of the cruelty of Licinius, it remains a matter of surprise that he was not contented with some more secret and decent method of revenge. [85]

[Footnote 80: Lactantius de M. P. c. 50. Aurelius Victor touches on the different conduct of Licinius, and of Constantine, in the use of victory.]

[Footnote 81: The sensual appetites of Maximin were gratified at the expense of his subjects. His eunuchs, who forced away wives and virgins, examined their naked charms with anxious curiosity, lest any part of their body should be found unworthy of the royal embraces. Coyness and disdain were considered as treason, and the obstinate fair one was condemned to be drowned. A custom was gradually introduced, that no person should marry a wife without the permission of the emperor, "ut ipse in omnibus nuptiis praegustator esset." Lactantius de M. P. c. 38.]

[Footnote 82: Lactantius de M. P. c. 39.]

[Footnote 83: Diocletian at last sent cognatum suum, quendam militarem ae potentem virum, to intercede in favor of his daughter, (Lactantius de M. P. c. 41.) We are not sufficiently acquainted with the history of these times to point out the person who was employed.]

[Footnote 84: Valeria quoque per varias provincias quindecim mensibus plebeio cultu pervagata. Lactantius de M. P. c. 51. There is some doubt whether we should compute the fifteen months from the moment of her exile, or from that of her escape. The expression of parvagata seems to denote the latter; but in that case we must suppose that the treatise of Lactantius was written after the first civil war between Licinius and Constantine. See Cuper, p. 254.]

[Footnote 85: Ita illis pudicitia et conditio exitio fuit. Lactantius de M. P. c. 51. He relates the misfortunes of the innocent wife and daughter of Discletian with a very natural mixture of pity and exultation.]

The Roman world was now divided between Constantine and Licinius, the former of whom was master of the West, and the latter of the East. It might perhaps have been expected that the conquerors, fatigued with civil war, and connected by a private as well as public alliance, would have renounced, or at least would have suspended, any further designs of ambition. And yet a year had scarcely elapsed after the death of Maximin, before the victorious emperors turned their arms against each other. The genius, the success, and the aspiring temper of Constantine, may seem to mark him out as the aggressor; but the perfidious character of Licinius justifies the most unfavorable suspicions, and by the faint light which history reflects on this transaction, [86] we may discover a conspiracy fomented by his arts against the authority of his colleague. Constantine had lately given his sister Anastasia in marriage to Bassianus, a man of a considerable family and fortune, and had elevated his new kinsman to the rank of Caesar. According to the system of government instituted by Diocletian, Italy, and perhaps Africa, were designed for his department in the empire. But the performance of the promised favor was either attended with so much delay, or accompanied with so many unequal conditions, that the fidelity of Bassianus was alienated rather than secured by the honorable distinction which he had obtained. His nomination had been ratified by the consent of Licinius; and that artful prince, by the means of his emissaries, soon contrived to enter into a secret and dangerous correspondence with the new Caesar, to irritate his discontents, and to urge him to the rash enterprise of extorting by violence what he might in vain solicit from the justice of Constantine. But the vigilant emperor discovered the conspiracy before it was ripe for execution; and after solemnly renouncing the alliance of Bassianus, despoiled him of the purple, and inflicted the deserved punishment on his treason and ingratitude. The haughty refusal of Licinius, when he was required to deliver up the criminals who had taken refuge in his dominions, confirmed the suspicions already entertained of his perfidy; and the indignities offered at Aemona, on the frontiers of Italy, to the statues of Constantine, became the signal of discord between the two princes. [87]

[Footnote 86: The curious reader, who consults the Valesian fragment, p. 713, will probably accuse me of giving a bold and licentious paraphrase; but if he considers it with attention, he will acknowledge that my interpretation is probable and consistent.]

[Footnote 87: The situation of Aemona, or, as it is now called, Laybach, in Carniola, (D'Anville, Geographie Ancienne, tom. i. p. 187,) may suggest a conjecture. As it lay to the north-east of the Julian Alps, that important territory became a natural object of dispute between the sovereigns of Italy and of Illyricum.]

The first battle was fought near Cibalis, a city of Pannonia, situated on the River Save, about fifty miles above Sirmium. [88] From the inconsiderable forces which in this important contest two such powerful monarchs brought into the field, it may be inferred that the one was suddenly provoked, and that the other was unexpectedly surprised. The emperor of the West had only twenty thousand, and the sovereign of the East no more than five and thirty thousand, men. The inferiority of number was, however, compensated by the advantage of the ground. Constantine had taken post in a defile about half a mile in breadth, between a steep hill and a deep morass, and in that situation he steadily expected and repulsed the first attack of the enemy. He pursued his success, and advanced into the plain. But the veteran legions of Illyricum rallied under the standard of a leader who had been trained to arms in the school of Probus and Diocletian. The missile weapons on both sides were soon exhausted; the two armies, with equal valor, rushed to a closer engagement of swords and spears, and the doubtful contest had already lasted from the dawn of the day to a late hour of the evening, when the right wing, which Constantine led in person, made a vigorous and decisive charge. The judicious retreat of Licinius saved the remainder of his troops from a total defeat; but when he computed his loss, which amounted to more than twenty thousand men, he thought it unsafe to pass the night in the presence of an active and victorious enemy. Abandoning his camp and magazines, he marched away with secrecy and diligence at the head of the greatest part of his cavalry, and was soon removed beyond the danger of a pursuit. His diligence preserved his wife, his son, and his treasures, which he had deposited at Sirmium. Licinius passed through that city, and breaking down the bridge on the Save, hastened to collect a new army in Dacia and Thrace. In his flight he bestowed the precarious title of Caesar on Valens, his general of the Illyrian frontier. [89]

[Footnote 88: Cibalis or Cibalae (whose name is still preserved in the obscure ruins of Swilei) was situated about fifty miles from Sirmium, the capital of Illyricum, and about one hundred from Taurunum, or Belgrade, and the conflux of the Danube and the Save. The Roman garrisons and cities on those rivers are finely illustrated by M. d'Anville in a memoir inserted in l'Academie des Inscriptions, tom. xxviii.]

[Footnote 89: Zosimus (l. ii. p. 90, 91) gives a very particular account of this battle; but the descriptions of Zosimus are rhetorical rather than military]

PART IV

The plain of Mardia in Thrace was the theatre of a second battle no less obstinate and bloody than the former. The troops on both sides displayed the same valor and discipline; and the victory was once more decided by the superior abilities of Constantine, who directed a body of five thousand men to gain an advantageous height, from whence, during the heat of the action, they attacked the rear of the enemy, and made a very considerable slaughter. The troops of Licinius, however, presenting a double front, still maintained their ground, till the approach of night put an end to the combat, and secured their retreat towards the mountains of Macedonia. [90] The loss of two battles, and of his bravest veterans, reduced the fierce spirit of Licinius to sue for peace. His ambassador Mistrianus was admitted to the audience of Constantine: he expatiated on the common topics of moderation and humanity, which are so familiar to the eloquence of the vanquished; represented in the most insinuating language, that the event of the war was still doubtful, whilst its inevitable calamities were alike pernicious to both the contending parties; and declared that he was authorized to propose a lasting and honorable peace in the name of the two emperors his masters. Constantine received the mention of Valens with indignation and contempt. "It was not for such a purpose," he sternly replied, "that we have advanced from the shores of the western ocean in an uninterrupted course of combats and victories, that, after rejecting an ungrateful kinsman, we should accept for our colleague a contemptible slave. The abdication of Valens is the first article of the treaty." [91] It was necessary to accept this humiliating condition; and the unhappy Valens, after a reign of a few days, was deprived of the purple and of his life. As soon as this obstacle was removed, the tranquillity of the Roman world was easily restored. The successive defeats of Licinius had ruined his forces, but they had displayed his courage and abilities. His situation was almost desperate, but the efforts of despair are sometimes formidable, and the good sense of Constantine preferred a great and certain advantage to a third trial of the chance of arms. He consented to leave his rival, or, as he again styled Licinius, his friend and brother, in the possession of Thrace, Asia Minor, Syria, and Egypt; but the provinces of Pannonia, Dalmatia, Dacia, Macedonia, and Greece, were yielded to the Western empire, and the dominions of Constantine now extended from the confines of Caledonia to the extremity of Peloponnesus. It was stipulated by the same treaty, that three royal youths, the sons of emperors, should be called to the hopes of the succession. Crispus and the young Constantine were soon afterwards declared Caesars in the West, while the younger Licinius was invested with the same dignity in the East. In this double proportion of honors, the conqueror asserted the superiority of his arms and power. [92]

[Footnote 90: Zosimus, l. ii. p. 92, 93. Anonym. Valesian. p. 713. The Epitomes furnish some circumstances; but they frequently confound the two wars between Licinius and Constantine.]

[Footnote 91: Petrus Patricius in Excerpt. Legat. p. 27. If it should be thought that signifies more properly a son-in-law, we might conjecture that Constantine, assuming the name as well as the duties of a father, had adopted his younger brothers and sisters, the children of Theodora. But in the best authors sometimes signifies a husband, sometimes a father-in-law, and sometimes a kinsman in general. See Spanheim, Observat. ad Julian. Orat. i. p. 72.]

[Footnote 92: Zosimus, l. ii. p. 93. Anonym. Valesian. p. 713. Eutropius, x. v. Aurelius Victor, Euseb. in Chron. Sozomen, l. i. c. 2. Four of these writers affirm that the promotion of the Caesars was an article of the treaty. It is, however, certain, that the younger Constantine and Licinius were not yet born; and it is highly probable that the promotion was made the 1st of March, A. D. 317. The treaty had probably stipulated that the two Caesars might be created by the western, and one only by the eastern emperor; but each of them reserved to himself the choice of the persons.]

The reconciliation of Constantine and Licinius, though it was imbittered by resentment and jealousy, by the remembrance of recent injuries, and by the apprehension of future dangers, maintained, however, above eight years, the tranquility of the Roman world. As a very regular series of the Imperial laws commences about this period, it would not be difficult to transcribe the civil regulations which employed the leisure of Constantine. But the most important of his institutions are intimately connected with the new system of policy and religion, which was not perfectly established till the last and peaceful years of his reign. There are many of his laws, which, as far as they concern the rights and property of individuals, and the practice of the bar, are more properly referred to the private than to the public jurisprudence of the empire; and he published many edicts of so local and temporary a nature, that they would ill deserve the notice of a general history. Two laws, however, may be selected from the crowd; the one for its importance, the other for its singularity; the former for its remarkable benevolence, the latter for its excessive severity. 1. The horrid practice, so familiar to the ancients, of exposing or murdering their new-born infants, was become every day more frequent in the provinces, and especially in Italy. It was the effect of distress; and the distress was principally occasioned by the intolerant burden of taxes, and by the vexatious as well as cruel prosecutions of the officers of the revenue against their insolvent debtors. The less opulent or less industrious part of mankind, instead of rejoicing in an increase of family, deemed it an act of paternal tenderness to release their children from the impending miseries of a life which they themselves were unable to support. The humanity of Constantine; moved, perhaps, by some recent and extraordinary instances of despair, engaged him to address an edict to all the cities of Italy, and afterwards of Africa, directing immediate and sufficient relief to be given to those parents who should produce before the magistrates the children whom their own poverty would not allow them to educate. But the promise was too liberal, and the provision too vague, to effect any general or permanent benefit. [93] The law, though it may merit some praise, served rather to display than to alleviate the public distress. It still remains an authentic monument to contradict and confound those venal orators, who were too well satisfied with their own situation to discover either vice or misery under the government of a generous sovereign. [94] 2. The laws of Constantine against rapes were dictated with very little indulgence for the most amiable weaknesses of human nature; since the description of that crime was applied not only to the brutal violence which compelled, but even to the gentle seduction which might persuade, an unmarried woman, under the age of twenty-five, to leave the house of her parents. "The successful ravisher was punished with death;" and as if simple death was inadequate to the enormity of his guilt, he was either burnt alive, or torn in pieces by wild beasts in the amphitheatre. The virgin's declaration, that she had been carried away with her own consent, instead of saving her lover, exposed her to share his fate. The duty of a public prosecution was intrusted to the parents of the guilty or unfortunate maid; and if the sentiments of nature prevailed on them to dissemble the injury, and to repair by a subsequent marriage the honor of their family, they were themselves punished by exile and confiscation. The slaves, whether male or female, who were convicted of having been accessory to rape or seduction, were burnt alive, or put to death by the ingenious torture of pouring down their throats a quantity of melted lead. As the crime was of a public kind, the accusation was permitted even to strangers.[94/1]

[Footnote 94/1: This explanation appears to me little probable. Godefroy has made a much more happy conjecture, supported by all the historical circumstances which relate to this edict. It was published the 12th of May, A. D. 315. at Naissus in Pannonia, the birthplace of Constantine. The 8th of October, in that year, Constantine gained the victory of Cibalis over Licinius. He was yet uncertain as to the fate of the war: the Christians, no doubt, whom he favored, had prophesied his victory. Lactantius, then preceptor of Crispus, had just written his work upon Christianity, (his Divine Institutes;) he had dedicated it to Constantine. In this book he had inveighed with great force against infanticide, and the exposure of infants, (l. vi. c. 20.) Is it not probable that Constantine had read this work, that he had conversed on the subject with Lactantius, that he was moved, among other things, by the passage to which I have referred, and in the first transport of his enthusiasm, he published the edict in question? The whole of the edict bears the character of precipitation, of excitement, (entrainement,) rather than of deliberate reflection—the extent of the promises, the indefiniteness of the means, of the conditions, and of the time during which the parents might have a right to the succor of the state. Is there not reason to believe that the humanity of Constantine was excited by the influence of Lactantius, by that of the principles of Christianity, and of the Christians themselves, already in high esteem with the emperor, rather than by some "extraordinary instances of despair"? See Hegewisch, Essai Hist. sur les Finances Romaines. The edict for Africa was not published till 322: of that we may say in truth that its origin was in the misery of the times. Africa had suffered much from the cruelty of Maxentius. Constantine says expressly, that he had learned that parents, under the pressure of distress, were there selling their children. This decree is more distinct, more maturely deliberated than the former; the succor which was to be given to the parents, and the source from which it was to be derived, are determined. (Code Theod. l. xi. tit. 27, c 2.) If the direct utility of these laws may not have been very extensive, they had at least the great and happy effect of establishing a decisive opposition between the principles of the government and those which, at this time, had prevailed among the subjects of the empire.—G.]

The commencement of the action was not limited to any term of years, and the consequences of the sentence were extended to the innocent offspring of such an irregular union. [95] But whenever the offence inspires less horror than the punishment, the rigor of penal law is obliged to give way to the common feelings of mankind. The most odious parts of this edict were softened or repealed in the subsequent reigns; [96] and even Constantine himself very frequently alleviated, by partial acts of mercy, the stern temper of his general institutions. Such, indeed, was the singular humor of that emperor, who showed himself as indulgent, and even remiss, in the execution of his laws, as he was severe, and even cruel, in the enacting of them. It is scarcely possible to observe a more decisive symptom of weakness, either in the character of the prince, or in the constitution of the government. [97]

[Footnote 93: Codex Theodosian. l. xi. tit. 27, tom. iv. p. 188, with Godefroy's observations. See likewise l. v. tit. 7, 8.]

[Footnote 94: Omnia foris placita, domi prospera, annonae ubertate, fructuum copia, &c. Panegyr. Vet. x. 38. This oration of Nazarius was pronounced on the day of the Quinquennalia of the Caesars, the 1st of March, A. D. 321.]

[Footnote 95: See the edict of Constantine, addressed to the Roman people, in the Theodosian Code, l. ix. tit. 24, tom. iii. p. 189.]

[Footnote 96: His son very fairly assigns the true reason of the repeal: "Na sub specie atrocioris judicii aliqua in ulciscendo crimine dilatio nae ceretur." Cod. Theod. tom. iii. p. 193]

[Footnote 97: Eusebius (in Vita Constant. l. iii. c. 1) chooses to affirm, that in the reign of this hero, the sword of justice hung idle in the hands of the magistrates. Eusebius himself, (l. iv. c. 29, 54,) and the Theodosian Code, will inform us that this excessive lenity was not owing to the want either of atrocious criminals or of penal laws.]

The civil administration was sometimes interrupted by the military defence of the empire. Crispus, a youth of the most amiable character, who had received with the title of Caesar the command of the Rhine, distinguished his conduct, as well as valor, in several victories over the Franks and Alemanni, and taught the barbarians of that frontier to dread the eldest son of Constantine, and the grandson of Constantius. [98] The emperor himself had assumed the more difficult and important province of the Danube. The Goths, who in the time of Claudius and Aurelian had felt the weight of the Roman arms, respected the power of the empire, even in the midst of its intestine divisions. But the strength of that warlike nation was now restored by a peace of near fifty years; a new generation had arisen, who no longer remembered the misfortunes of ancient days; the Sarmatians of the Lake Maeotis followed the Gothic standard either as subjects or as allies, and their united force was poured upon the countries of Illyricum. Campona, Margus, and Benonia, [981] appear to have been the scenes of several memorable sieges and battles; [99] and though Constantine encountered a very obstinate resistance, he prevailed at length in the contest, and the Goths were compelled to purchased an ignominious retreat, by restoring the booty and prisoners which they had taken. Nor was this advantage sufficient to satisfy the indignation of the emperor. He resolved to chastise as well as to repulse the insolent barbarians who had dared to invade the territories of Rome. At the head of his legions he passed the Danube after repairing the bridge which had been constructed by Trajan, penetrated into the strongest recesses of Dacia, [100] and when he had inflicted a severe revenge, condescended to give peace to the suppliant Goths, on condition that, as often as they were required, they should supply his armies with a body of forty thousand soldiers. [101] Exploits like these were no doubt honorable to Constantine, and beneficial to the state; but it may surely be questioned, whether they can justify the exaggerated assertion of Eusebius, that All Scythia, as far as the extremity of the North, divided as it was into so many names and nations of the most various and savage manners, had been added by his victorious arms to the Roman empire. [102]

[Footnote 98: Nazarius in Panegyr. Vet. x. The victory of Crispus over the Alemanni is expressed on some medals. Note: Other medals are extant, the legends of which commemorate the success of Constantine over the Sarmatians and other barbarous nations, Sarmatia Devicta. Victoria Gothica. Debellatori Gentium Barbarorum. Exuperator Omnium Gentium. St. Martin, note on Le Beau, i. 148.—M.]

[Footnote 98/1]: Campona, Old Buda in Hungary; Margus, Benonia, Widdin, in Maesia—G and M.]

[Footnote 99: See Zosimus, l. ii. p. 93, 94; though the narrative of that historian is neither clear nor consistent. The Panegyric of Optatianus (c. 23) mentions the alliance of the Sarmatians with the Carpi and Getae, and points out the several fields of battle. It is supposed that the Sarmatian games, celebrated in the month of November, derived their origin from the success of this war.]

[Footnote 100: In the Caesars of Julian, (p. 329. Commentaire de Spanheim, p. 252.) Constantine boasts, that he had recovered the province (Dacia) which Trajan had subdued. But it is insinuated by Silenus, that the conquests of Constantine were like the gardens of Adonis, which fade and wither almost the moment they appear.]

[Footnote 101: Jornandes de Rebus Geticis, c. 21. I know not whether we may entirely depend on his authority. Such an alliance has a very recent air, and scarcely is suited to the maxims of the beginning of the fourth century.]

[Footnote 102: Eusebius in Vit. Constantin. l. i. c. 8. This passage, however, is taken from a general declamation on the greatness of Constantine, and not from any particular account of the Gothic war.]

In this exalted state of glory, it was impossible that Constantine should any longer endure a partner in the empire. Confiding in the superiority of his genius and military power, he determined, without any previous injury, to exert them for the destruction of Licinius, whose advanced age and unpopular vices seemed to offer a very easy conquest. [103] But the old emperor, awakened by the approaching danger, deceived the expectations of his friends, as well as of his enemies. Calling forth that spirit and those abilities by which he had deserved the friendship of Galerius and the Imperial purple, he prepared himself for the contest, collected the forces of the East, and soon filled the plains of Hadrianople with his troops, and the Straits of the Hellespont with his fleet. The army consisted of one hundred and fifty thousand foot, and fifteen thousand horse; and as the cavalry was drawn, for the most part, from Phrygia and Cappadocia, we may conceive a more favorable opinion of the beauty of the horses, than of the courage and dexterity of their riders. The fleet was composed of three hundred and fifty galleys of three ranks of oars. A hundred and thirty of these were furnished by Egypt and the adjacent coast of Africa. A hundred and ten sailed from the ports of Phoenicia and the Isle of Cyprus; and the maritime countries of Bithynia, Ionia, and Caria, were likewise obliged to provide a hundred and ten galleys. The troops of Constantine were ordered to a rendezvous at Thessalonica; they amounted to above a hundred and twenty thousand horse and foot. [104] Their emperor was satisfied with their martial appearance, and his army contained more soldiers, though fewer men, than that of his eastern competitor. The legions of Constantine were levied in the warlike provinces of Europe; action had confirmed their discipline, victory had elevated their hopes, and there were among them a great number of veterans, who, after seventeen glorious campaigns under the same leader, prepared themselves to deserve an honorable dismission by a last effort of their valor. [105] But the naval preparations of Constantine were in every respect much inferior to those of Licinius. The maritime cities of Greece sent their respective quotas of men and ships to the celebrated harbor of Piraeus, and their united forces consisted of no more than two hundred small vessels—a very feeble armament, if it is compared with those formidable fleets which were equipped and maintained by the republic of Athens during the Peloponnesian war. [106] Since Italy was no longer the seat of government, the naval establishments of Misenum and Ravenna had been gradually neglected; and as the shipping and mariners of the empire were supported by commerce rather than by war, it was natural that they should the most abound in the industrious provinces of Egypt and Asia. It is only surprising that the eastern emperor, who possessed so great a superiority at sea, should have neglected the opportunity of carrying an offensive war into the centre of his rival's dominions.

[Footnote 103: Constantinus tamen, vir ingens, et omnia efficere nitens quae animo praeparasset, simul principatum totius urbis affectans, Licinio bellum intulit. Eutropius, x. 5. Zosimus, l. ii. p 89. The reasons which they have assigned for the first civil war, may, with more propriety, be applied to the second.]

[Footnote 104: Zosimus, l. ii. p. 94, 95.]

[Footnote 105: Constantine was very attentive to the privileges and comforts of his fellow-veterans, (Conveterani,) as he now began to style them. See the Theodosian Code, l. vii. tit. 10, tom. ii. p. 419, 429.]

[Footnote 106: Whilst the Athenians maintained the empire of the sea, their fleet consisted of three, and afterwards of four, hundred galleys of three ranks of oars, all completely equipped and ready for immediate service. The arsenal in the port of Piraeus had cost the republic a thousand talents, about two hundred and sixteen thousand pounds. See Thucydides de Bel. Pelopon. l. ii. c. 13, and Meursius de Fortuna Attica, c. 19.]

Instead of embracing such an active resolution, which might have changed the whole face of the war, the prudent Licinius expected the approach of his rival in a camp near Hadrianople, which he had fortified with an anxious care, that betrayed his apprehension of the event. Constantine directed his march from Thessalonica towards that part of Thrace, till he found himself stopped by the broad and rapid stream of the Hebrus, and discovered the numerous army of Licinius, which filled the steep ascent of the hill, from the river to the city of Hadrianople. Many days were spent in doubtful and distant skirmishes; but at length the obstacles of the passage and of the attack were removed by the intrepid conduct of Constantine. In this place we might relate a wonderful exploit of Constantine, which, though it can scarcely be paralleled either in poetry or romance, is celebrated, not by a venal orator devoted to his fortune, but by an historian, the partial enemy of his fame. We are assured that the valiant emperor threw himself into the River Hebrus, accompanied only by twelve horsemen, and that by the effort or terror of his invincible arm, he broke, slaughtered, and put to flight a host of a hundred and fifty thousand men. The credulity of Zosimus prevailed so strongly over his passion, that among the events of the memorable battle of Hadrianople, he seems to have selected and embellished, not the most important, but the most marvellous. The valor and danger of Constantine are attested by a slight wound which he received in the thigh; but it may be discovered even from an imperfect narration, and perhaps a corrupted text, that the victory was obtained no less by the conduct of the general than by the courage of the hero; that a body of five thousand archers marched round to occupy a thick wood in the rear of the enemy, whose attention was diverted by the construction of a bridge, and that Licinius, perplexed by so many artful evolutions, was reluctantly drawn from his advantageous post to combat on equal ground on the plain. The contest was no longer equal. His confused multitude of new levies was easily vanquished by the experienced veterans of the West. Thirty-four thousand men are reported to have been slain. The fortified camp of Licinius was taken by assault the evening of the battle; the greater part of the fugitives, who had retired to the mountains, surrendered themselves the next day to the discretion of the conqueror; and his rival, who could no longer keep the field, confined himself within the walls of Byzantium. [107]

[Footnote 107: Zosimus, l. ii. p. 95, 96. This great battle is described in the Valesian fragment, (p. 714,) in a clear though concise manner. "Licinius vero circum Hadrianopolin maximo exercitu latera ardui montis impleverat; illuc toto agmine Constantinus inflexit. Cum bellum terra marique traheretur, quamvis per arduum suis nitentibus, attamen disciplina militari et felicitate, Constantinus Licinu confusum et sine ordine agentem vicit exercitum; leviter femore sau ciatus."]

The siege of Byzantium, which was immediately undertaken by Constantine, was attended with great labor and uncertainty. In the late civil wars, the fortifications of that place, so justly considered as the key of Europe and Asia, had been repaired and strengthened; and as long as Licinius remained master of the sea, the garrison was much less exposed to the danger of famine than the army of the besiegers. The naval commanders of Constantine were summoned to his camp, and received his positive orders to force the passage of the Hellespont, as the fleet of Licinius, instead of seeking and destroying their feeble enemy, continued inactive in those narrow straits, where its superiority of numbers was of little use or advantage. Crispus, the emperor's eldest son, was intrusted with the execution of this daring enterprise, which he performed with so much courage and success, that he deserved the esteem, and most probably excited the jealousy, of his father. The engagement lasted two days; and in the evening of the first, the contending fleets, after a considerable and mutual loss, retired into their respective harbors of Europe and Asia. The second day, about noon, a strong south wind [108] sprang up, which carried the vessels of Crispus against the enemy; and as the casual advantage was improved by his skilful intrepidity, he soon obtained a complete victory. A hundred and thirty vessels were destroyed, five thousand men were slain, and Amandus, the admiral of the Asiatic fleet, escaped with the utmost difficulty to the shores of Chalcedon. As soon as the Hellespont was open, a plentiful convoy of provisions flowed into the camp of Constantine, who had already advanced the operations of the siege. He constructed artificial mounds of earth of an equal height with the ramparts of Byzantium. The lofty towers which were erected on that foundation galled the besieged with large stones and darts from the military engines, and the battering rams had shaken the walls in several places. If Licinius persisted much longer in the defence, he exposed himself to be involved in the ruin of the place. Before he was surrounded, he prudently removed his person and treasures to Chalcedon in Asia; and as he was always desirous of associating companions to the hopes and dangers of his fortune, he now bestowed the title of Caesar on Martinianus, who exercised one of the most important offices of the empire. [109]

[Footnote 108: Zosimus, l. ii. p. 97, 98. The current always sets out of the Hellespont; and when it is assisted by a north wind, no vessel can attempt the passage. A south wind renders the force of the current almost imperceptible. See Tournefort's Voyage au Levant, Let. xi.]

[Footnote 109: Aurelius Victor. Zosimus, l. ii. p. 93. According to the latter, Martinianus was Magister Officiorum, (he uses the Latin appellation in Greek.) Some medals seem to intimate, that during his short reign he received the title of Augustus.]

Such were still the resources, and such the abilities, of Licinius, that, after so many successive defeats, he collected in Bithynia a new army of fifty or sixty thousand men, while the activity of Constantine was employed in the siege of Byzantium. The vigilant emperor did not, however, neglect the last struggles of his antagonist. A considerable part of his victorious army was transported over the Bosphorus in small vessels, and the decisive engagement was fought soon after their landing on the heights of Chrysopolis, or, as it is now called, of Scutari. The troops of Licinius, though they were lately raised, ill armed, and worse disciplined, made head against their conquerors with fruitless but desperate valor, till a total defeat, and a slaughter of five and twenty thousand men, irretrievably determined the fate of their leader. [110] He retired to Nicomedia, rather with the view of gaining some time for negotiation, than with the hope of any effectual defence. Constantia, his wife, and the sister of Constantine, interceded with her brother in favor of her husband, and obtained from his policy, rather than from his compassion, a solemn promise, confirmed by an oath, that after the sacrifice of Martinianus, and the resignation of the purple, Licinius himself should be permitted to pass the remainder of this life in peace and affluence. The behavior of Constantia, and her relation to the contending parties, naturally recalls the remembrance of that virtuous matron who was the sister of Augustus, and the wife of Antony. But the temper of mankind was altered, and it was no longer esteemed infamous for a Roman to survive his honor and independence. Licinius solicited and accepted the pardon of his offences, laid himself and his purple at the feet of his lord and master, was raised from the ground with insulting pity, was admitted the same day to the Imperial banquet, and soon afterwards was sent away to Thessalonica, which had been chosen for the place of his confinement. [111] His confinement was soon terminated by death, and it is doubtful whether a tumult of the soldiers, or a decree of the senate, was suggested as the motive for his execution. According to the rules of tyranny, he was accused of forming a conspiracy, and of holding a treasonable correspondence with the barbarians; but as he was never convicted, either by his own conduct or by any legal evidence, we may perhaps be allowed, from his weakness, to presume his innocence. [112] The memory of Licinius was branded with infamy, his statues were thrown down, and by a hasty edict, of such mischievous tendency that it was almost immediately corrected, all his laws, and all the judicial proceedings of his reign, were at once abolished. [113] By this victory of Constantine, the Roman world was again united under the authority of one emperor, thirty-seven years after Diocletian had divided his power and provinces with his associate Maximian.

[Footnote 110: Eusebius (in Vita Constantin. l. ii. c. 16, 17) ascribes this decisive victory to the pious prayers of the emperor. The Valesian fragment (p. 714) mentions a body of Gothic auxiliaries, under their chief Aliquaca, who adhered to the party of Licinius.]

[Footnote 111: Zosimus, l. ii. p. 102. Victor Junior in Epitome. Anonym. Valesian. p. 714.]

[Footnote 112: Contra religionem sacramenti Thessalonicae privatus occisus est. Eutropius, x. 6; and his evidence is confirmed by Jerome (in Chronic.) as well as by Zosimus, l. ii. p. 102. The Valesian writer is the only one who mentions the soldiers, and it is Zonaras alone who calls in the assistance of the senate. Eusebius prudently slides over this delicate transaction. But Sozomen, a century afterwards, ventures to assert the treasonable practices of Licinius.]

[Footnote 113: See the Theodosian Code, l. xv. tit. 15, tom. v. p 404, 405. These edicts of Constantine betray a degree of passion and precipitation very unbecoming the character of a lawgiver.]

The successive steps of the elevation of Constantine, from his first assuming the purple at York, to the resignation of Licinius, at Nicomedia, have been related with some minuteness and precision, not only as the events are in themselves both interesting and important, but still more, as they contributed to the decline of the empire by the expense of blood and treasure, and by the perpetual increase, as well of the taxes, as of the military establishment. The foundation of Constantinople, and the establishment of the Christian religion, were the immediate and memorable consequences of this revolution.

CHAPTER XV

PROGRESS OF THE CHRISTIAN RELIGION

PART I

THE PROGRESS OF THE CHRISITAN RELIGION, AND THE SENTIMENTS, MANNERS, NUMBERS, AND CONDITION OF THE PRIMITIVE CHRISTIANS [101]

[Footnote 101: In spite of my resolution, Lardner led me to look through the famous fifteenth and sixteenth chapters of Gibbon. I could not lay them down without finishing them. The causes assigned, in the fifteenth chapter, for the diffusion of Christianity, must, no doubt, have contributed to it materially; but I doubt whether he saw them all. Perhaps those which he enumerates are among the most obvious. They might all be safely adopted by a Christian writer, with some change in the language and manner. Mackintosh see Life, i. p. 244.—M.]

A candid but rational inquiry into the progress and establishment of Christianity may be considered as a very essential part of the history of the Roman empire. While that great body was invaded by open violence, or undermined by slow decay, a pure and humble religion gently insinuated itself into the minds of men, grew up in silence and obscurity, derived new vigor from opposition, and finally erected the triumphant banner of the Cross on the ruins of the Capitol. Nor was the influence of Christianity confined to the period or to the limits of the Roman empire. After a revolution of thirteen or fourteen centuries, that religion is still professed by the nations of Europe, the most distinguished portion of human kind in arts and learning as well as in arms. By the industry and zeal of the Europeans, it has been widely diffused to the most distant shores of Asia and Africa; and by the means of their colonies has been firmly established from Canada to Chili, in a world unknown to the ancients.

But this inquiry, however useful or entertaining, is attended with two peculiar difficulties. The scanty and suspicious materials of ecclesiastical history seldom enable us to dispel the dark cloud that hangs over the first age of the church. The great law of impartiality too often obliges us to reveal the imperfections of the uninspired teachers and believers of the gospel; and, to a careless observer, their faults may seem to cast a shade on the faith which they professed. But the scandal of the pious Christian, and the fallacious triumph of the Infidel, should cease as soon as they recollect not only by whom, but likewise to whom, the Divine Revelation was given. The theologian may indulge the pleasing task of describing Religion as she descended from Heaven, arrayed in her native purity. A more melancholy duty is imposed on the historian. He must discover the inevitable mixture of error and corruption, which she contracted in a long residence upon earth, among a weak and degenerate race of beings. [102]

[Footnote 102: The art of Gibbon, or at least the unfair impression produced by these two memorable chapters, consists in confounding together, in one undistinguishable mass, the origin and apostolic propagation of the Christian religion with its later progress. The main question, the divine origin of the religion, is dexterously eluded or speciously conceded; his plan enables him to commence his account, in most parts, below the apostolic times; and it is only by the strength of the dark coloring with which he has brought out the failings and the follies of succeeding ages, that a shadow of doubt and suspicion is thrown back on the primitive period of Christianity. Divest this whole passage of the latent sarcasm betrayed by the subsequent one of the whole disquisition, and it might commence a Christian history, written in the most Christian spirit of candor.—M.]

Our curiosity is naturally prompted to inquire by what means the Christian faith obtained so remarkable a victory over the established religions of the earth. To this inquiry, an obvious but satisfactory answer may be returned; that it was owing to the convincing evidence of the doctrine itself, and to the ruling providence of its great Author. But as truth and reason seldom find so favorable a reception in the world, and as the wisdom of Providence frequently condescends to use the passions of the human heart, and the general circumstances of mankind, as instruments to execute its purpose, we may still be permitted, though with becoming submission, to ask, not indeed what were the first, but what were the secondary causes of the rapid growth of the Christian church. It will, perhaps, appear, that it was most effectually favored and assisted by the five following causes: I. The inflexible, and if we may use the expression, the intolerant zeal of the Christians, derived, it is true, from the Jewish religion, but purified from the narrow and unsocial spirit, which, instead of inviting, had deterred the Gentiles from embracing the law of Moses.

II. The doctrine of a future life, improved by every additional circumstance which could give weight and efficacy to that important truth. III. The miraculous powers ascribed to the primitive church. IV. The pure and austere morals of the Christians.

V. The union and discipline of the Christian republic, which gradually formed an independent and increasing state in the heart of the Roman empire.

[Footnote!: Though we are thus far agreed with respect to the inflexibility and intolerance of Christian zeal, yet as to the principle from which it was derived, we are, toto coelo, divided in opinion. You deduce it from the Jewish religion; I would refer it to a more adequate and a more obvious source, a full persuasion of the truth of Christianity. Watson. Letters Gibbon, i. 9.—M.]

I. We have already described the religious harmony of the ancient world, and the facility [104] with which the most different and even hostile nations embraced, or at least respected, each other's superstitions. A single people refused to join in the common intercourse of mankind. The Jews, who, under the Assyrian and Persian monarchies, had languished for many ages the most despised portion of their slaves, [1] emerged from obscurity under the successors of Alexander; and as they multiplied to a surprising degree in the East, and afterwards in the West, they soon excited the curiosity and wonder of other nations. [2] The sullen obstinacy with which they maintained their peculiar rites and unsocial manners, seemed to mark them out as a distinct species of men, who boldly professed, or who faintly disguised, their implacable habits to the rest of human kind. [3] Neither the violence of Antiochus, nor the arts of Herod, nor the example of the circumjacent nations, could ever persuade the Jews to associate with the institutions of Moses the elegant mythology of the Greeks. [4] According to the maxims of universal toleration, the Romans protected a superstition which they despised. [5] The polite Augustus condescended to give orders, that sacrifices should be offered for his prosperity in the temple of Jerusalem; [6] whilst the meanest of the posterity of Abraham, who should have paid the same homage to the Jupiter of the Capitol, would have been an object of abhorrence to himself and to his brethren.

But the moderation of the conquerors was insufficient to appease the jealous prejudices of their subjects, who were alarmed and scandalized at the ensigns of paganism, which necessarily introduced themselves into a Roman province. [7] The mad attempt of Caligula to place his own statue in the temple of Jerusalem was defeated by the unanimous resolution of a people who dreaded death much less than such an idolatrous profanation. [8] Their attachment to the law of Moses was equal to their detestation of foreign religions. The current of zeal and devotion, as it was contracted into a narrow channel, ran with the strength, and sometimes with the fury, of a torrent.

[Footnote 102: This facility has not always prevented intolerance, which seems inherent in the religious spirit, when armed with authority. The separation of the ecclesiastical and civil power, appears to be the only means of at once maintaining religion and tolerance: but this is a very modern notion. The passions, which mingle themselves with opinions, made the Pagans very often intolerant and persecutors; witness the Persians, the Egyptians even the Greeks and Romans.

1st. The Persians.—Cambyses, conqueror of the Egyptians, condemned to death the magistrates of Memphis, because they had offered divine honors to their god. Apis: he caused the god to be brought before him, struck him with his dagger, commanded the priests to be scourged, and ordered a general massacre of all the Egyptians who should be found celebrating the festival of the statues of the gods to be burnt. Not content with this intolerance, he sent an army to reduce the Ammonians to slavery, and to set on fire the temple in which Jupiter delivered his oracles. See Herod. iii. 25—29, 37. Xerxes, during his invasion of Greece, acted on the same principles: l c destroyed all the temples of Greece and Ionia, except that of Ephesus. See Paus. l. vii. p. 533, and x. p. 887.

Strabo, l. xiv. b. 941. 2d. The Egyptians.—They thought themselves defiled when they had drunk from the same cup or eaten at the same table with a man of a different belief from their own. "He who has voluntarily killed any sacred animal is punished with death; but if any one, even involuntarily, has killed a cat or an ibis, he cannot escape the extreme penalty: the people drag him away, treat him in the most cruel manner, sometimes without waiting for a judicial sentence. Even at the time when King Ptolemy was not yet the acknowledged friend of the Roman people, while the multitude were paying court with all possible attention to the strangers who came from Italy * * a Roman having killed a cat, the people rushed to his house, and neither the entreaties of the nobles, whom the king sent to them, nor the terror of the Roman name, were sufficiently powerful to rescue the man from punishment, though he had committed the crime involuntarily." Diod. Sic. i 83. Juvenal, in his 13th Satire, describes the sanguinary conflict between the inhabitants of Ombos and of Tentyra, from religious animosity. The fury was carried so far, that the conquerors tore and devoured the quivering limbs of the conquered.

Ardet adhuc Ombos et Tentyra, summus utrinque Inde furor vulgo, quod numina vicinorum Odit uterque locus; quum solos credat habendos Esse Deos quos ipse colit. Sat. xv. v. 85.

3d. The Greeks.—"Let us not here," says the Abbe Guenee, "refer to the cities of Peloponnesus and their severity against atheism; the Ephesians prosecuting Heraclitus for impiety; the Greeks armed one against the other by religious zeal, in the Amphictyonic war. Let us say nothing either of the frightful cruelties inflicted by three successors of Alexander upon the Jews, to force them to abandon their religion, nor of Antiochus expelling the philosophers from his states. Let us not seek our proofs of intolerance so far off. Athens, the polite and learned Athens, will supply us with sufficient examples. Every citizen made a public and solemn vow to conform to the religion of his country, to defend it, and to cause it to be respected. An express law severely punished all discourses against the gods, and a rigid decree ordered the denunciation of all who should deny their existence. The practice was in unison with the severity of the law. The proceedings commenced against Protagoras; a price set upon the head of Diagoras; the danger of Alcibiades; Aristotle obliged to fly; Stilpo banished; Anaxagoras hardly escaping death; Pericles himself, after all his services to his country, and all the glory he had acquired, compelled to appear before the tribunals and make his defence; a priestess executed for having introduced strange gods; Socrates condemned and drinking the hemlock, because he was accused of not recognizing those of his country, &c.; these facts attest too loudly, to be called in question, the religious intolerance of the most humane and enlightened people in Greece." Lettres de quelques Juifs a Mons. Voltaire, i. p. 221. (Compare Bentley on Freethinking, from which much of this is derived.)—M.

4th. The Romans.—The laws of Rome were not less express and severe. The intolerance of foreign religions reaches, with the Romans, as high as the laws of the twelve tables; the prohibitions were afterwards renewed at different times. Intolerance did not discontinue under the emperors; witness the counsel of Maecenas to Augustus. This counsel is so remarkable, that I think it right to insert it entire. "Honor the gods yourself," says Maecenas to Augustus, "in every way according to the usage of your ancestors, and compel others to worship them. Hate and punish those who introduce strange gods, not only for the sake of the gods, (he who despises them will respect no one,) but because those who introduce new gods engage a multitude of persons in foreign laws and customs. From hence arise unions bound by oaths and confederacies, and associations, things dangerous to a monarchy." Dion

Cass. l. ii. c. 36. (But, though some may differ from it, see Gibbon's just observation on this passage in Dion Cassius, ch. xvi. note 117; impugned, indeed, by M. Guizot, note in loc.)—M.

Even the laws which the philosophers of Athens and of Rome wrote for their imaginary republics are intolerant. Plato does not leave to his citizens freedom of religious worship; and Cicero expressly prohibits them from having other gods than those of the state. Lettres de quelques Juifs a Mons. Voltaire, i. p. 226.—G.

According to M. Guizot's just remarks, religious intolerance will always ally itself with the passions of man, however different those passions may be. In the instances quoted above, with the Persians it was the pride of despotism; to conquer the gods of a country was the last mark of subjugation. With the Egyptians, it was the gross Fetichism of the superstitious populace, and the local jealousy of neighboring towns. In Greece, persecution was in general connected with political party; in Rome, with the stern supremacy of the law and the interests of the state. Gibbon has been mistaken in attributing to the tolerant spirit of Paganism that which arose out of the peculiar circumstances of the times. 1st. The decay of the old Polytheism, through the progress of reason and intelligence, and the prevalence of philosophical opinions among the higher orders.

2d. The Roman character, in which the political always predominated over the religious party. The Romans were contented with having bowed the world to a uniformity of subjection to their power, and cared not for establishing the (to them) less important uniformity of religion.—M.

[Footnote 1: Dum Assyrios penes, Medosque, et Persas Oriens fuit, despectissima pars servientium. Tacit. Hist. v. 8. Herodotus, who visited Asia whilst it obeyed the last of those empires, slightly mentions the Syrians of Palestine, who, according to their own confession, had received from Egypt the rite of circumcision. See l. ii. c. 104.]

[Footnote 2: Diodorus Siculus, l. xl. Dion Cassius, l. xxxvii. p. 121. Tacit Hist. v. 1—9. Justin xxxvi. 2, 3.]

[Footnote 3: Tradidit arcano quaecunque volumine Moses, Non monstrare vias cadem nisi sacra colenti, Quaesitum ad fontem solos deducere verpas. The letter of this law is not to be found in the present volume of Moses. But the wise, the humane Maimonides openly teaches that if an idolater fall into the water, a Jew ought not to save him from instant death. See Basnage, Histoire des Juifs, l. vi. c. 28. Note: It is diametrically opposed to its spirit and to its letter, see, among other passages, Deut. v. 18. 19, (God) "loveth the stranger in giving him food and raiment. Love ye, therefore, the stranger: for ye were strangers in the land of Egypt." Comp. Lev. xxiii. 25. Juvenal is a satirist, whose strong expressions can hardly be received as historic evidence; and he wrote after the horrible cruelties of the Romans, which, during and after the war, might give some cause for the complete isolation of the Jew from the rest of the world. The Jew was a bigot, but his religion was not the only source of his bigotry. After how many centuries of mutual wrong and hatred, which had still further estranged the Jew from mankind, did Maimonides write?—M.]

[Footnote 4: A Jewish sect, which indulged themselves in a sort of occasional conformity, derived from Herod, by whose example and authority they had been seduced, the name of Herodians. But their numbers were so inconsiderable, and their duration so short, that Josephus has not thought them worthy of his notice. See Prideaux's Connection, vol. ii. p. 285. Note: The Herodians were probably more of a political party than a religious sect, though Gibbon is most likely right as to their occasional conformity. See Hist. of the Jews, ii. 108.—M.]

[Footnote 5: Cicero pro Flacco, c. 28. Note: The edicts of Julius Caesar, and of some of the cities in Asia Minor (Krebs. Decret. pro Judaeis,) in favor of the nation in general, or of the Asiatic Jews, speak a different language.—M.]

[Footnote 6: Philo de Legatione. Augustus left a foundation for a perpetual sacrifice. Yet he approved of the neglect which his grandson Caius expressed towards the temple of Jerusalem. See Sueton. in August. c. 93, and Casaubon's notes on that passage.]

[Footnote 7: See, in particular, Joseph. Antiquitat. xvii. 6, xviii. 3; and de Bell. Judiac. i. 33, and ii. 9, edit. Havercamp. Note: This was during the government of Pontius Pilate. (Hist. of Jews, ii. 156.) Probably in part to avoid this collision, the Roman governor, in general, resided at Caesarea.—M.]

[Footnote 8: Jussi a Caio Caesare, effigiem ejus in templo locare, arma potius sumpsere. Tacit. Hist. v. 9. Philo and Josephus gave a very circumstantial, but a very rhetorical, account of this transaction, which exceedingly perplexed the governor of Syria. At the first mention of this idolatrous proposal, King Agrippa fainted away; and did not recover his senses until the third day. (Hist. of Jews, ii. 181, &c.)]

This inflexible perseverance, which appeared so odious or so ridiculous to the ancient world, assumes a more awful character, since Providence has deigned to reveal to us the mysterious history of the chosen people. But the devout and even scrupulous attachment to the Mosaic religion, so conspicuous among the Jews who lived under the second temple, becomes still more surprising, if it is compared with the stubborn incredulity of their forefathers. When the law was given in thunder from Mount Sinai, when the tides of the ocean and the course of the planets were suspended for the convenience of the Israelites, and when temporal rewards and punishments were the immediate consequences of their piety or disobedience, they perpetually relapsed into rebellion against the visible majesty of their Divine King, placed the idols of the nations in the sanctuary of Jehovah, and imitated every fantastic ceremony that was practised in the tents of the Arabs, or in the cities of Phoenicia. [9] As the protection of Heaven was deservedly withdrawn from the ungrateful race, their faith acquired a proportionable degree of vigor and purity.

The contemporaries of Moses and Joshua had beheld with careless indifference the most amazing miracles. Under the pressure of every calamity, the belief of those miracles has preserved the Jews of a later period from the universal contagion of idolatry; and in contradiction to every known principle of the human mind, that singular people seems to have yielded a stronger and more ready assent to the traditions of their remote ancestors, than to the evidence of their own senses. [10]

[Footnote 9: For the enumeration of the Syrian and Arabian deities, it may be observed, that Milton has comprised in one hundred and thirty very beautiful lines the two large and learned syntagmas which Selden had composed on that abstruse subject.]

[Footnote 10: "How long will this people provoke me? and how long will it be ere they believe me, for all the signs which I have shown among them?" (Numbers xiv. 11.) It would be easy, but it would be unbecoming, to justify the complaint of the Deity from the whole tenor of the Mosaic history. Note: Among a rude and barbarous people, religious impressions are easily made, and are as soon effaced. The ignorance which multiplies imaginary wonders, would weaken and destroy the effect of real miracle. At the period of the Jewish history, referred to in the passage from Numbers, their fears predominated over their faith,—the fears of an unwarlike people, just rescued from debasing slavery, and commanded to

attack a fierce, a well-armed, a gigantic, and a far more numerous race, the inhabitants of Canaan. As to the frequent apostasy of the Jews, their religion was beyond their state of civilization. Nor is it uncommon for a people to cling with passionate attachment to that of which, at first, they could not appreciate the value. Patriotism and national pride will contend, even to death, for political rights which have been forced upon a reluctant people. The Christian may at least retort, with justice, that the great sign of his religion, the resurrection of Jesus, was most ardently believed, and most resolutely asserted, by the eye witnesses of the fact.—M.]

The Jewish religion was admirably fitted for defence, but it was never designed for conquest; and it seems probable that the number of proselytes was never much superior to that of apostates. The divine promises were originally made, and the distinguishing rite of circumcision was enjoined, to a single family. When the posterity of Abraham had multiplied like the sands of the sea, the Deity, from whose mouth they received a system of laws and ceremonies, declared himself the proper and as it were the national God of Israel and with the most jealous care separated his favorite people from the rest of mankind. The conquest of the land of Canaan was accompanied with so many wonderful and with so many bloody circumstances, that the victorious Jews were left in a state of irreconcilable hostility with all their neighbors. They had been commanded to extirpate some of the most idolatrous tribes, and the execution of the divine will had seldom been retarded by the weakness of humanity.

With the other nations they were forbidden to contract any marriages or alliances; and the prohibition of receiving them into the congregation, which in some cases was perpetual, almost always extended to the third, to the seventh, or even to the tenth generation. The obligation of preaching to the Gentiles the faith of Moses had never been inculcated as a precept of the law, nor were the Jews inclined to impose it on themselves as a voluntary duty.

In the admission of new citizens, that unsocial people was actuated by the selfish vanity of the Greeks, rather than by the generous policy of Rome. The descendants of Abraham were flattered by the opinion that they alone were the heirs of the covenant, and they were apprehensive of diminishing the value of their inheritance by sharing it too easily with the strangers of the earth. A larger acquaintance with mankind extended their knowledge without correcting their prejudices; and whenever the God of Israel acquired any new votaries, he was much more indebted to the inconstant humor of polytheism than to the active zeal of his own missionaries. [11] The religion of Moses seems to be instituted for a particular country as well as for a single nation; and if a strict obedience had been paid to the order, that every male, three times in the year, should present himself before the Lord Jehovah, it would have been impossible that the Jews could ever have spread themselves beyond the narrow limits of the promised land. [12] That obstacle was indeed removed by the destruction of the temple of Jerusalem; but the most considerable part of the Jewish religion was involved in its destruction; and the Pagans, who had long wondered at the strange report of an empty sanctuary, [13] were at a loss to discover what could be the object, or what could be the instruments, of a worship which was destitute of temples and of altars, of priests and of sacrifices.

Yet even in their fallen state, the Jews, still asserting their lofty and exclusive privileges, shunned, instead of courting, the society of strangers. They still insisted with inflexible rigor on those parts of the law which it was in their power to practise. Their peculiar distinctions of days, of meats, and a variety of trivial though burdensome observances, were so many objects of disgust and aversion for the other nations, to whose habits and prejudices they were diametrically opposite. The painful and even dangerous rite of circumcision was alone capable of repelling a willing proselyte from the door of the synagogue. [14]

[Footnote 11: All that relates to the Jewish proselytes has been very ably by Basnage, Hist. des Juifs, l. vi. c. 6, 7.]

[Footnote 12: See Exod. xxiv. 23, Deut. xvi. 16, the commentators, and a very sensible note in the Universal History, vol. i. p. 603, edit. fol.]

[Footnote 13: When Pompey, using or abusing the right of conquest, entered into the Holy of Holies, it was observed with amazement, "Nulli intus Deum effigie, vacuam sedem et inania arcana." Tacit. Hist. v. 9. It was a popular saying, with regard to the Jews, "Nil praeter nubes et coeli numen adorant."]

[Footnote 14: A second kind of circumcision was inflicted on a Samaritan or Egyptian proselyte. The sullen indifference of the Talmudists, with respect to the conversion of strangers, may be seen in Basnage Histoire des Juifs, l. xi. c. 6.]

Under these circumstances, Christianity offered itself to the world, armed with the strength of the Mosaic law, and delivered from the weight of its fetters. An exclusive zeal for the truth of religion, and the unity of God, was as carefully inculcated in the new as in the ancient system: and whatever was now revealed to mankind concerning the nature and designs of the Supreme Being, was fitted to increase their reverence for that mysterious doctrine. The divine authority of Moses and the prophets was admitted, and even established, as the firmest basis of Christianity. From the beginning of the world, an uninterrupted series of predictions had announced and prepared the long-expected coming of the Messiah, who, in compliance with the gross apprehensions of the Jews, had been more frequently represented under the character of a King and Conqueror, than under that of a Prophet, a Martyr, and the Son of God. By his expiatory sacrifice, the imperfect sacrifices of the temple were at once consummated and abolished. The ceremonial law, which consisted only of types and figures, was succeeded by a pure and spiritual worship, equally adapted to all climates, as well as to every condition of mankind; and to the initiation of blood was substituted a more harmless initiation of water. The promise of divine favor, instead of being partially confined to the posterity of Abraham, was universally proposed to the freeman and the slave, to the Greek and to the barbarian, to the Jew and to the Gentile. Every privilege that could raise the proselyte from earth to heaven, that could exalt his devotion, secure his happiness, or even gratify that secret pride which, under the semblance of devotion, insinuates itself into the human heart, was still reserved for the members of the Christian church; but at the same time all mankind was permitted, and even solicited, to accept the glorious distinction, which was not only proffered as a favor, but imposed as an obligation. It became the most sacred duty of a new convert to diffuse among his friends and relations the inestimable blessing which he had received, and to warn them against a refusal that would be severely punished as a criminal disobedience to the will of a benevolent but all-powerful Deity.

PART II

The enfranchisement of the church from the bonds of the synagogue was a work, however, of some time and of some difficulty. The Jewish converts, who acknowledged Jesus in the character of the Messiah foretold by their ancient oracles, respected him as a prophetic teacher of virtue and religion; but they obstinately adhered to the ceremonies of their ancestors, and were desirous of imposing them on the Gentiles, who continually augmented the number of believers. These Judaizing Christians seem to have argued with some degree of plausibility from the divine origin of the Mosaic law, and from the immutable perfections of its great Author. They affirmed, that if the Being, who is the same through all eternity, had designed to abolish those sacred rites which had served to distinguish his chosen people, the repeal of them would have been no less clear and solemn than their first promulgation: that, instead of those frequent declarations, which either suppose or assert the perpetuity of the Mosaic religion, it would have been represented as a provisionary scheme intended to last only to the coming of the Messiah, who should instruct mankind in a more perfect mode of faith and of worship: [15] that the Messiah himself, and his disciples who conversed with him on earth, instead of authorizing by their example the most minute observances of the Mosaic law, [16] would have published to the world the abolition of those useless and obsolete ceremonies, without suffering Christianity to remain during so many years obscurely confounded among the sects of the Jewish church. Arguments like these appear to have been used in the defence of the expiring cause of the Mosaic law; but the industry of our learned divines has abundantly explained the ambiguous language of the Old Testament, and the ambiguous conduct of the apostolic teachers. It was proper gradually to unfold the system of the gospel, and to pronounce, with the utmost caution and tenderness, a sentence of condemnation so repugnant to the inclination and prejudices of the believing Jews.

[Footnote 15: These arguments were urged with great ingenuity by the Jew Orobio, and refuted with equal ingenuity and candor by the Christian Limborch. See the Amica Collatio, (it well deserves that name,) or account of the dispute between them.]

[Footnote 16: Jesus... circumcisus erat; cibis utebatur Judaicis; vestitu simili; purgatos scabie mittebat ad sacerdotes; Paschata et alios dies festos religiose observabat: Si quos sanavit sabbatho, ostendit non tantum ex lege, sed et exceptis sententiis, talia opera sabbatho non interdicta. Grotius de Veritate Religionis Christianae, l. v. c. 7. A little afterwards, (c. 12,) he expatiates on the condescension of the apostles.]

The history of the church of Jerusalem affords a lively proof of the necessity of those precautions, and of the deep impression which the Jewish religion had made on the minds of its sectaries. The first fifteen bishops of Jerusalem were all circumcised Jews; and the congregation over which they presided united the law of Moses with the doctrine of Christ. [17] It was natural that the primitive tradition of a church which was founded only forty days after the death of Christ, and was governed almost as many years under the immediate inspection of his apostle, should be received as the standard of orthodoxy. [18] The distant churches very frequently appealed to the authority of their venerable Parent, and relieved her distresses by a liberal contribution of alms. But when numerous and opulent societies were established in the great cities of the empire, in Antioch, Alexandria, Ephesus, Corinth, and Rome, the reverence which Jerusalem had inspired to all the Christian colonies insensibly diminished. The Jewish converts, or, as they were afterwards called, the Nazarenes, who had laid the foundations of the church, soon found themselves overwhelmed by the increasing multitudes, that from all the various religions of polytheism enlisted under the banner of Christ: and the Gentiles, who, with the approbation of their peculiar apostle, had rejected the intolerable weight of the Mosaic ceremonies, at length refused to their more scrupulous brethren the same toleration which at first they had humbly solicited for their own practice. The ruin of the temple of the city, and of the public religion of the Jews, was severely felt by the Nazarenes; as in their manners, though not in their faith, they maintained so intimate a connection with their impious countrymen, whose misfortunes were attributed by the Pagans to the contempt, and more justly ascribed by the Christians to the wrath, of the Supreme Deity. The Nazarenes retired from the ruins of Jerusalem [18] to the little town of Pella beyond the Jordan, where that ancient church languished above sixty years in solitude and obscurity. [19] They still enjoyed the comfort of making frequent and devout visits to the Holy City, and the hope of being one day restored to those seats which both nature and religion taught them to love as well as to revere. But at length, under the reign of Hadrian, the desperate fanaticism of the Jews filled up the measure of their calamities; and the Romans, exasperated by their repeated rebellions, exercised the rights of victory with unusual rigor. The emperor founded, under the name of Aelia Capitolina, a new city on Mount Sion, [20] to which he gave the privileges of a colony; and denouncing the severest penalties against any of the Jewish people who should dare to approach its precincts, he fixed a vigilant garrison of a Roman cohort to enforce the execution of his orders. The Nazarenes had only one way left to escape the common proscription, and the force of truth was on this occasion assisted by the influence of temporal advantages. They elected Marcus for their bishop, a prelate of the race of the Gentiles, and most probably a native either of Italy or of some of the Latin provinces. At his persuasion, the most considerable part of the congregation renounced the Mosaic law, in the practice of which they had persevered above a century. By this sacrifice of their habits and prejudices, they purchased a free admission into the colony of Hadrian, and more firmly cemented their union with the Catholic church. [21]

[Footnote 17: Paene omnes Christum Deum sub legis observatione credebant Sulpicius Severus, ii. 31. See Eusebius, Hist. Ecclesiast. l. iv. c. 5.]

[Footnote 18: Mosheim de Rebus Christianis ante Constantinum Magnum, page 153. In this masterly performance, which I shall often have occasion to quote he enters much more fully into the state of the primitive church than he has an opportunity of doing in his General History.]

[Footnote 18: This is incorrect: all the traditions concur in placing the abandonment of the city by the Christians, not only before it was in ruins, but before the seige had commenced. Euseb. loc. cit., and Le Clerc.—M.]

[Footnote 19: Eusebius, l. iii. c. 5. Le Clerc, Hist. Ecclesiast. p. 605. During this occasional absence, the bishop and church of Pella still retained the title of Jerusalem. In the same manner, the Roman pontiffs resided seventy years at Avignon; and the patriarchs of Alexandria have long since transferred their episcopal seat to Cairo.]

[Footnote 20: Dion Cassius, l. lxix. The exile of the Jewish nation from Jerusalem is attested by Aristo of Pella, (apud Euseb. l. iv. c. 6,) and is mentioned by several ecclesiastical writers; though some of them too hastily extend this interdiction to the whole country of Palestine.]

[Footnote 21: Eusebius, l. iv. c. 6. Sulpicius Severus, ii. 31. By comparing their unsatisfactory accounts, Mosheim (p. 327, &c.) has drawn out a very distinct representation of the circumstances and motives of this revolution.]

When the name and honors of the church of Jerusalem had been restored to Mount Sion, the crimes of heresy and schism were imputed to the obscure remnant of the Nazarenes, which refused to accompany their Latin bishop. They still preserved their former habitation of Pella, spread themselves into the villages adjacent to Damascus, and formed an inconsiderable church in the city of Beroea, or, as it is now called, of Aleppo, in Syria. [22] The name of Nazarenes was deemed too honorable for those Christian Jews, and they soon received, from the supposed poverty of their understanding, as well as of their condition, the contemptuous epithet of Ebionites. [23] In a few years after the return of the church of Jerusalem, it became a matter of doubt and controversy, whether a man who sincerely acknowledged Jesus as the Messiah, but who still continued to observe the law of Moses, could possibly hope for salvation. The humane temper of Justin Martyr inclined him to answer this question in the affirmative; and though he expressed himself with the most guarded diffidence, he ventured to determine in favor of such an imperfect Christian, if he were content to practise the Mosaic ceremonies, without pretending to assert their general use or necessity. But when Justin was pressed to declare the sentiment of the church, he confessed that there were very many among the orthodox Christians, who not only excluded their Judaizing brethren from the hope of salvation, but who declined any intercourse with them in the common offices of friendship, hospitality, and social life. [24] The more rigorous opinion prevailed, as it was natural to expect, over the milder; and an eternal bar of separation was fixed between the disciples of Moses and those of Christ. The unfortunate Ebionites, rejected from one religion as apostates, and from the other as heretics, found themselves compelled to assume a more decided character; and although some traces of that obsolete sect may be discovered as late as the fourth century, they insensibly melted away, either into the church or the synagogue. [25]

[Footnote 22: Le Clerc (Hist. Ecclesiast. p. 477, 535) seems to have collected from Eusebius, Jerome, Epiphanius, and other writers, all the principal circumstances that relate to the Nazarenes or Ebionites. The nature of their opinions soon divided them into a stricter and a milder sect; and there is some reason to conjecture, that the family of Jesus Christ remained members, at least, of the latter and more moderate party.]

[Footnote 23: Some writers have been pleased to create an Ebion, the imaginary author of their sect and name. But we can more safely rely on the learned Eusebius than on the vehement Tertullian, or the credulous Epiphanius. According to Le Clerc, the Hebrew word Ebjonim may be translated into Latin by that of Pauperes. See Hist. Ecclesiast. p. 477. Note: The opinion of Le Clerc is generally admitted; but Neander has suggested some good reasons for supposing that this term only applied to poverty of condition. The obscure history of their tenets and divisions, is clearly and rationally traced in his History of the Church, vol. i. part ii. p. 612, &c., Germ. edit.—M.]

[Footnote 24: See the very curious Dialogue of Justin Martyr with the Jew Tryphon. The conference between them was held at Ephesus, in the reign of Antoninus Pius, and about twenty years after the return of the church of Pella to Jerusalem. For this date consult the accurate note of Tillemont, Memoires Ecclesiastiques, tom. ii. p. 511. Note: Justin Martyr makes an important distinction, which Gibbon has neglected to notice. There were some who were not content with observing the Mosaic law themselves, but enforced the same observance, as necessary to salvation, upon the heathen converts, and refused all social intercourse with them if they did not conform to the law. Justin Martyr himself freely admits those who kept the law themselves to Christian communion, though he acknowledges that some, not the Church, thought otherwise; of the other party, he himself thought less favorably. The former by some are considered the Nazarenes the atter the Ebionites—G and M.]

[Footnote 25: Of all the systems of Christianity, that of Abyssinia is the only one which still adheres to the Mosaic rites. (Geddes's Church History of Aethiopia, and Dissertations de La Grand sur la Relation du P. Lobo.) The eunuch of the queen Candace might suggest some suspicious; but as we are assured (Socrates, i. 19. Sozomen, ii. 24. Ludolphus, p. 281) that the Aethiopians were not converted till the fourth century, it is more reasonable to believe that they respected the sabbath, and distinguished the forbidden meats, in imitation of the Jews, who, in a very early period, were seated on both sides of the Red Sea. Circumcision had been practised by the most ancient Aethiopians, from motives of health and cleanliness, which seem to be explained in the Recherches Philosophiques sur les Americains, tom. ii. p. 117.]

While the orthodox church preserved a just medium between excessive veneration and improper contempt for the law of Moses, the various heretics deviated into equal but opposite extremes of error and extravagance. From the acknowledged truth of the Jewish religion, the Ebionites had concluded that it could never be abolished. From its supposed imperfections, the Gnostics as hastily inferred that it never was instituted by the wisdom of the Deity. There are some objections against the authority of Moses and the prophets, which too readily present themselves to the sceptical mind; though they can only be derived from our ignorance of remote antiquity, and from our incapacity to form an adequate judgment of the divine economy. These objections were eagerly embraced and as petulantly urged by the vain science of the Gnostics. [26] As those heretics were, for the most part, averse to the pleasures of sense, they morosely arraigned the polygamy of the patriarchs, the gallantries of David, and the seraglio of Solomon. The conquest of the land of Canaan, and the extirpation of the unsuspecting natives, they were at a loss how to reconcile with the common notions of humanity and justice. [26/1] But when they recollected the sanguinary list of murders, of executions, and of massacres, which stain almost every page of the Jewish annals, they acknowledged that the barbarians of Palestine had exercised as much compassion towards their idolatrous enemies, as they had ever shown to their friends or countrymen. [27] Passing from the sectaries of the law to the law itself, they asserted that it was impossible that a religion which consisted only of bloody sacrifices and trifling ceremonies, and whose rewards as well as punishments were all of a carnal and temporal nature, could inspire the love of virtue, or restrain the impetuosity of passion. The Mosaic account of the creation and fall of man was treated with profane derision by the Gnostics, who would not listen with patience to the repose of the Deity after six days' labor, to the rib of Adam, the garden of Eden, the trees of life and of knowledge, the speaking serpent, the forbidden fruit, and the condemnation pronounced against human kind for the venial offence of their first progenitors. [28] The God of Israel was impiously represented by the Gnostics as a being liable to passion and to error, capricious in his favor, implacable in his resentment, meanly jealous of his superstitious worship, and confining his partial providence to a single people, and to this transitory life. In such a character they could discover none of the features of the wise and omnipotent Father of the universe. [29] They allowed that the religion of the Jews was somewhat less criminal than the idolatry of the Gentiles; but it was their fundamental doctrine, that the Christ whom they adored as the first and brightest emanation of the Deity appeared upon earth to rescue mankind from their various errors, and to reveal a new system of truth and perfection. The most learned of the fathers, by a very singular condescension, have imprudently admitted the sophistry of the Gnostics. [29/1] Acknowledging that the literal sense is repugnant to every principle of faith as well as reason, they deem themselves secure and invulnerable behind the ample veil of allegory, which they carefully spread over every tender part of the Mosaic dispensation. [30]

[Footnote 26: Beausobre, Histoire du Manicheisme, l. i. c. 3, has stated their objections, particularly those of Faustus, the adversary of Augustin, with the most learned impartiality.]

[Footnote 26/1: On the "war law" of the Jews, see Hist. of Jews, i. 137.—M.]

[Footnote 27: Apud ipsos fides obstinata, misericordia in promptu: adversus amnes alios hostile odium. Tacit. Hist. v. 4. Surely Tacitus had seen the Jews with too favorable an eye. The perusal of Josephus must have destroyed the antithesis. Note: Few writers have suspected Tacitus of partiality towards the Jews. The whole later history of the Jews illustrates as well their strong feelings of humanity to their brethren, as their hostility to the rest of mankind. The character and the position of Josephus with the Roman authorities, must be kept in mind during the perusal of his History. Perhaps he has not exaggerated the ferocity and fanaticism of the Jews at that time; but insurrectionary warfare is not the best school for the *humaner virtues, and much must be allowed for the grinding tyranny of the later Roman governors. See Hist. of Jews, ii. 254.—M.]*

[Footnote 28: Dr. Burnet (Archaeologia, l. ii. c. 7) has discussed the first chapters of Genesis with too much wit and freedom. Note: Dr. Burnet apologized for the levity with which he had conducted some of his arguments, by the excuse that he wrote in a learned language for scholars alone, not for the vulgar. Whatever may be thought of his success in tracing an Eastern allegory in the first chapters of Genesis, his other works prove him to have been a man of great genius, and of sincere piety.—M]

[Footnote 29: The milder Gnostics considered Jehovah, the Creator, as a Being of a mixed nature between God and the Daemon. Others confounded him with an evil principle. Consult the second century of the general history of Mosheim, which gives a very distinct, though concise, account of their strange opinions on this subject.]

[Footnote 29/1: The Gnostics, and the historian who has stated these plausible objections with so much force as almost to make them his own, would have shown a more considerate and not less reasonable philosophy, if they had considered the religion of Moses with reference to the age in which it was promulgated; if they had done justice to its sublime as well as its more imperfect views of the divine nature; the humane and civilizing provisions of the Hebrew law, as well as those adapted for an infant and barbarous people. See Hist of Jews, i. 36, 37, &c.—M.]

[Footnote 30: See Beausobre, Hist. du Manicheisme, l. i. c. 4. Origen and St. Augustin were among the allegorists.]

It has been remarked with more ingenuity than truth, that the virgin purity of the church was never violated by schism or heresy before the reign of Trajan or Hadrian, about one hundred years after the death of Christ. [31] We may observe with much more propriety, that, during that period, the disciples of the Messiah were indulged in a freer latitude, both of faith and practice, than has ever been allowed in succeeding ages. As the terms of communion were insensibly narrowed, and the spiritual authority of the prevailing party was exercised with increasing severity, many of its most respectable adherents, who were called upon to renounce, were provoked to assert their private opinions, to pursue the consequences of their mistaken principles, and openly to erect the standard of rebellion against the unity of the church. The Gnostics were distinguished as the most polite, the most learned, and the most wealthy of the Christian name; and that general appellation, which expressed a superiority of knowledge, was either assumed by their own pride, or ironically bestowed by the envy of their adversaries. They were almost without exception of the race of the Gentiles, and their principal founders seem to have been natives of Syria or Egypt, where the warmth of the climate disposes both the mind and the body to indolent and contemplative devotion. The Gnostics blended with the faith of Christ many sublime but obscure tenets, which they derived from oriental philosophy, and even from the religion of Zoroaster, concerning the eternity of matter, the existence of two principles, and the mysterious hierarchy of the invisible world. [32] As soon as they launched out into that vast abyss, they delivered themselves to the guidance of a disordered imagination; and as the paths of error are various and infinite, the Gnostics were imperceptibly divided into more than fifty particular sects, [33] of whom the most celebrated appear to have been the Basilidians, the Valentinians, the Marcionites, and, in a still later period, the Manichaeans. Each of these sects could boast of its bishops and congregations, of its doctors and martyrs; [34] and, instead of the Four Gospels adopted by the church, [341] the heretics produced a multitude of histories, in which the actions and discourses of Christ and of his apostles were adapted to their respective tenets. [35] The success of the Gnostics was rapid and extensive. [36] They covered Asia and Egypt, established themselves in Rome, and sometimes penetrated into the provinces of the West. For the most part they arose in the second century, flourished during the third, and were suppressed in the fourth or fifth, by the prevalence of more fashionable controversies, and by the superior ascendant of the reigning power. Though they constantly disturbed the peace, and frequently disgraced the name, of religion, they contributed to assist rather than to retard the progress of Christianity. The Gentile converts, whose strongest objections and prejudices were directed against the law of Moses, could find admission into many Christian societies, which required not from their untutored mind any belief of an antecedent revelation. Their faith was insensibly fortified and enlarged, and the church was ultimately benefited by the conquests of its most inveterate enemies. [37]

[Footnote 31: Hegesippus, ap. Euseb. l. iii. 32, iv. 22. Clemens Alexandrin Stromat. vii. 17. Note: The assertion of Hegesippus is not so positive: it is sufficient to read the whole passage in Eusebius, to see that the former part is modified by the matter. Hegesippus adds, that up to this period the church had remained pure and immaculate as a virgin. Those who labored to corrupt the doctrines of the gospel worked as yet in obscurity—G]

[Footnote 32: In the account of the Gnostics of the second and third centuries, Mosheim is ingenious and candid; Le Clerc dull, but exact; Beausobre almost always an apologist; and it is much to be feared that the primitive fathers are very frequently calumniators. Note The Histoire du Gnosticisme of M. Matter is at once the fairest and most complete account of these sects.—M.]

[Footnote 33: See the catalogues of Irenaeus and Epiphanius. It must indeed be allowed, that those writers were inclined to multiply the number of sects which opposed the unity of the church.]

[Footnote 34: Eusebius, l. iv. c. 15. Sozomen, l. ii. c. 32. See in Bayle, in the article of Marcion, a curious detail of a dispute on that subject. It should seem that some of the Gnostics (the Basilidians) declined, and even refused the honor of Martyrdom. Their reasons were singular and abstruse. See Mosheim, p. 539.]

[Footnote 34/1: M. Hahn has restored the Marcionite Gospel with great ingenuity. His work is reprinted in Thilo. Codex. Apoc. Nov. Test. vol. i.—M.]

[Footnote 35: See a very remarkable passage of Origen, (Proem. ad Lucam.) That indefatigable writer, who had consumed his life in the study of the Scriptures, relies for their authenticity on the inspired authority of the church. It was impossible that the Gnostics could receive our present Gospels, many parts of which (particularly in the resurrection of Christ) are directly, and as it might seem designedly, pointed against their favorite tenets. It is therefore somewhat singular that Ignatius (Epist. ad Smyrn. Patr. Apostol. tom. ii. p. 34) should choose to employ a vague and doubtful tradition, instead of quoting the certain testimony of the evangelists. Note: Bishop Pearson has attempted very happily to explain this singularity.' The first Christians were acquainted with a number of sayings of Jesus Christ, which are not related in our Gospels, and indeed have never been written. Why might not St. Ignatius, who had lived with the apostles or their disciples, repeat in other words that which St. Luke has related, particularly at a time when, being in prison, he could have the Gospels at hand? Pearson, Vind Ign. pp. 2, 9 p. 396 in tom. ii. Patres Apost. ed. Coteler—G.]

[Footnote 36: Faciunt favos et vespae; faciunt ecclesias et Marcionitae, is the strong expression of Tertullian, which I am obliged to quote from memory. In the time of Epiphanius (advers. Haereses, p. 302) the Marcionites were very numerous in Italy, Syria, Egypt, Arabia, and Persia.]

[Footnote 37: *Augustin is a memorable instance of this gradual progress from reason to faith. He was, during several years, engaged in the Manichaear sect.*]

But whatever difference of opinion might subsist between the Orthodox, the Ebionites, and the Gnostics, concerning the divinity or the obligation of the Mosaic law, they were all equally animated by the same exclusive zeal; and by the same abhorrence for idolatry, which had distinguished the Jews from the other nations of the ancient world. The philosopher, who considered the system of polytheism as a composition of human fraud and error, could disguise a smile of contempt under the mask of devotion, without apprehending that either the mockery, or the compliance, would expose him to the resentment of any invisible, or, as he conceived them, imaginary powers. But the established religions of Paganism were seen by the primitive Christians in a much more odious and formidable light. It was the universal sentiment both of the church and of heretics, that the daemons were the authors, the patrons, and the objects of idolatry. [38] Those rebellious spirits who had been degraded from the rank of angels, and cast down into the infernal pit, were still permitted to roam upon earth, to torment the bodies, and to seduce the minds, of sinful men. The daemons soon discovered and abused the natural propensity of the human heart towards devotion, and artfully withdrawing the adoration of mankind from their Creator, they usurped the place and honors of the Supreme Deity. By the success of their malicious contrivances, they at once gratified their own vanity and revenge, and obtained the only comfort of which they were yet susceptible, the hope of involving the human species in the participation of their guilt and misery. It was confessed, or at least it was imagined, that they had distributed among themselves the most important characters of polytheism, one daemon assuming the name and attributes of Jupiter, another of Aesculapius, a third of Venus, and a fourth perhaps of Apollo; [39] and that, by the advantage of their long experience and aerial nature, they were enabled to execute, with sufficient skill and dignity, the parts which they had undertaken. They lurked in the temples, instituted festivals and sacrifices, invented fables, pronounced oracles, and were frequently allowed to perform miracles. The Christians, who, by the interposition of evil spirits, could so readily explain every preternatural appearance, were disposed and even desirous to admit the most extravagant fictions of the Pagan mythology. But the belief of the Christian was accompanied with horror. The most trifling mark of respect to the national worship he considered as a direct homage yielded to the daemon, and as an act of rebellion against the majesty of God.

[Footnote 38: *The unanimous sentiment of the primitive church is very clearly explained by Justin Martyr, Apolog. Major, by Athenagoras, Legat. c. 22. &c., and by Lactantius, Institut. Divin. ii. 14—19.*]

[Footnote 39: *Tertullian (Apolog. c. 23) alleges the confession of the daemons themselves as often as they were tormented by the Christian exorcists*]

PART III

In consequence of this opinion, it was the first but arduous duty of a Christian to preserve himself pure and undefiled by the practice of idolatry. The religion of the nations was not merely a speculative doctrine professed in the schools or preached in the temples. The innumerable deities and rites of polytheism were closely interwoven with every circumstance of business or pleasure, of public or of private life; and it seemed impossible to escape the observance of them, without, at the same time, renouncing the commerce of mankind, and all the offices and amusements of society. [40] The important transactions of peace and war were prepared or concluded by solemn sacrifices, in which the magistrate, the senator, and the soldier, were obliged to preside or to participate. [41] The public spectacles were an essential part of the cheerful devotion of the Pagans, and the gods were supposed to accept, as the most grateful offering, the games that the prince and people celebrated in honor of their peculiar festivals. [42] The Christians, who with pious horror avoided the abomination of the circus or the theatre, found himself encompassed with infernal snares in every convivial entertainment, as often as his friends, invoking the hospitable deities, poured out libations to each other's happiness. [43] When the bride, struggling with well-affected reluctance, was forced into hymenaeal pomp over the threshold of her new habitation, [44] or when the sad procession of the dead slowly moved towards the funeral pile; [45] the Christian, on these interesting occasions, was compelled to desert the persons who were the dearest to him, rather than contract the guilt inherent to those impious ceremonies. Every art and every trade that was in the least concerned in the framing or adorning of idols was polluted by the stain of idolatry; [46] a severe sentence, since it devoted to eternal misery the far greater part of the community, which is employed in the exercise of liberal or mechanic professions. If we cast our eyes over the numerous remains of antiquity, we shall perceive, that besides the immediate representations of the gods, and the holy instruments of their worship, the elegant forms and agreeable fictions consecrated by the imagination of the Greeks, were introduced as the richest ornaments of the houses, the dress, and the furniture of the Pagan. [47] Even the arts of music and painting, of eloquence and poetry, flowed from the same impure origin. In the style of the fathers, Apollo and the Muses were the organs of the infernal spirit; Homer and Virgil were the most eminent of his servants; and the beautiful mythology which pervades and animates the compositions of their genius, is destined to celebrate the glory of the daemons. Even the common language of Greece and Rome abounded with familiar but impious expressions, which the imprudent Christian might too carelessly utter, or too patiently hear. [48]

[Footnote 40: Tertullian has written a most severe treatise against idolatry, to caution his brethren against the hourly danger of incurring that guilt. Recogita sylvam, et quantae latitant spinae. De Corona Militis, c. 10.]

[Footnote 41: The Roman senate was always held in a temple or consecrated place. (Aulus Gellius, xiv. 7.) Before they entered on business, every senator dropped some wine and frankincense on the altar. Sueton. in August. c. 35.]

[Footnote 42: See Tertullian, De Spectaculis. This severe reformer shows no more indulgence to a tragedy of Euripides, than to a combat of gladiators. The dress of the actors particularly offends him. By the use of the lofty buskin, they impiously strive to add a cubit to their stature. c. 23.]

[Footnote 43: The ancient practice of concluding the entertainment with libations, may be found in every classic. Socrates and Seneca, in their last moments, made a noble application of this custom. Postquam stagnum, calidae aquae introiit, respergens proximos servorum, addita voce, libare se liquorem illum Jovi Liberatori. Tacit. Annal. xv. 64.]

[Footnote 44: See the elegant but idolatrous hymn of Catullus, on the nuptials of Manlius and Julia. O Hymen, Hymenaee Io! Quis huic Deo comparari ausit?]

[Footnote 45: The ancient funerals (in those of Misenus and Pallas) are no less accurately described by Virgil, than they are illustrated by his commentator Servius. The pile itself was an altar, the flames were fed with the blood of victims, and all the assistants were sprinkled with lustral water.]

[Footnote 46: Tertullian de Idololatria, c. 11. Note: The exaggerated and declamatory opinions of Tertullian ought not to be taken as the general sentiment of the early Christians. Gibbon has too often allowed himself to consider the peculiar notions of certain Fathers of the Church as inherent in Christianity. This is not accurate.—G.]

[Footnote 47: See every part of Montfaucon's Antiquities. Even the reverses of the Greek and Roman coins were frequently of an idolatrous nature. Here indeed the scruples of the Christian were suspended by a stronger passion. Note: All this scrupulous nicety is at variance with the decision of St. Paul about meat offered to idols, 1, Cor. x. 21— 32.—M.]

[Footnote 48: Tertullian de Idololatria, c. 20, 21, 22. If a Pagan friend (on the occasion perhaps of sneezing) used the familiar expression of "Jupiter bless you," the Christian was obliged to protest against the divinity of Jupiter.]

The dangerous temptations which on every side lurked in ambush to surprise the unguarded believer, assailed him with redoubled violence on the days of solemn festivals. So artfully were they framed and disposed throughout the year, that superstition always wore the appearance of pleasure, and often of virtue. Some of the most sacred festivals in the Roman ritual were destined to salute the new calends of January with vows of public and private felicity; to indulge the pious remembrance of the dead and living; to ascertain the inviolable bounds of property; to hail, on the return of spring, the genial powers of fecundity; to perpetuate the two memorable areas of Rome, the foundation of the city and that of the republic, and to restore, during the humane license of the Saturnalia, the primitive equality of mankind. Some idea may be conceived of the abhorrence of the Christians for such impious ceremonies, by the scrupulous delicacy which they displayed on a much less alarming occasion. On days of general festivity, it was the custom of the ancients to adorn their doors with lamps and with branches of laurel, and to crown their heads with a garland of flowers. This innocent and elegant practice might perhaps have been tolerated as a mere civil institution. But it most unluckily happened that the doors were under the protection of the household gods, that the laurel was sacred to the lover of Daphne, and that garlands of flowers, though frequently worn as a symbol of joy or mourning, had been dedicated in their first origin to the service of superstition. The trembling Christians, who were persuaded in this instance to comply with the fashion of their country, and the commands of the magistrate, labored under the most gloomy apprehensions, from the reproaches of his own conscience, the censures of the church, and the denunciations of divine vengeance. [50]

[Footnote 49: Consult the most labored work of Ovid, his imperfect Fasti. He finished no more than the first six months of the year. The compilation of Macrobius is called the Saturnalia, but it is only a small part of the first book that bears any relation to the title.]

[Footnote 50: Tertullian has composed a defence, or rather panegyric, of the rash action of a Christian soldier, who, by throwing away his crown of laurel, had exposed himself and his brethren to the most imminent danger. By the mention of the emperors, (Severus and Caracalla,) it is evident, notwithstanding the wishes of M. de Tillemont, that Tertullian composed his treatise De Corona long before he was engaged in the errors of the Montanists. See Memoires Ecclesiastiques, tom. iii. p. 384. Note: The soldier did not tear off his crown to throw it down with contempt; he did not even throw it away; he held it in his hand, while others were it on their heads. Solus libero capite, ornamento in manu otioso.—G Note: Tertullian does not expressly name the two emperors, Severus and Caracalla: he speaks only of two emperors, and of a long peace which the church had enjoyed. It is generally agreed that Tertullian *became a Montanist about the year 200: his work, de Corona Militis, appears to have been written, at the earliest about the year 202 before the persecution of Severus: it may be maintained, then, that it is subsequent to the Montanism of the author. See Mosheim, Diss. de Apol. Tertull. p. 53. Biblioth. Amsterd. tom. x. part ii. p. 292. Cave's Hist. Lit. p. 92, 93. —G. —The state of Tertullian's opinions at the particular period is almost an idle question. "The fiery African" is not at any time to be considered a fair representative of Christianity. —M.]*

Such was the anxious diligence which was required to guard the chastity of the gospel from the infectious breath of idolatry. The superstitious observances of public or private rites were carelessly practised, from education and habit, by the followers of the established religion. But as often as they occurred, they afforded the Christians an opportunity of declaring and confirming their zealous opposition. By these frequent protestations their attachment to the faith was continually fortified; and in proportion to the increase of zeal, they combated with the more ardor and success in the holy war, which they had undertaken against the empire of the demons.

II. The writings of Cicero [51] represent in the most lively colors the ignorance, the errors, and the uncertainty of the ancient philosophers with regard to the immortality of the soul. When they are desirous of arming their disciples against the fear of death, they inculcate, as an obvious, though melancholy position, that the fatal stroke of our dissolution releases us from the calamities of life; and that those can no longer suffer, who no longer exist. Yet there were a few sages of Greece and Rome who had conceived a more exalted, and, in some respects, a juster idea of human nature, though it must be confessed, that in the sublime inquiry, their reason had been often guided by their imagination, and that their imagination had been prompted by their vanity. When they viewed with complacency the extent of their own mental powers, when they exercised the various faculties of memory, of fancy, and of judgment, in the most profound speculations, or the most important labors, and when they reflected on the desire of fame, which transported them into future ages, far beyond the bounds of death and of the grave, they were unwilling to confound themselves with the beasts of the field, or to suppose that a being, for whose dignity they entertained the most sincere admiration, could be limited to a spot of earth, and to a few years of duration. With this favorable prepossession they summoned to their aid the science, or rather the language, of Metaphysics. They soon discovered, that as none of the properties of matter will apply to the operations of the mind, the human soul must consequently be a substance distinct from the body, pure, simple, and spiritual, incapable of dissolution, and susceptible of a much higher degree of virtue and happiness after the release from its corporeal prison. From these specious and noble principles, the philosophers who trod in the footsteps of Plato deduced a very unjustifiable conclusion, since they asserted, not only the future immortality, but the past eternity, of the human soul, which they were too apt to consider as a portion of the infinite and self-existing spirit, which pervades and sustains the universe. [52] A doctrine thus removed beyond the senses and the experience of mankind, might serve to amuse the leisure of a philosophic mind; or, in the silence of solitude, it might sometimes impart a ray of comfort to desponding virtue; but the faint impression which had been received in the schools, was soon obliterated by the commerce and business of active life. We are sufficiently acquainted with the eminent persons who flourished in the age of Cicero, and of the first Caesars, with their actions, their characters, and their motives, to be assured that their conduct in this life was never regulated by any serious conviction of the rewards or punishments of a future state. At the bar and in the senate of Rome the ablest orators were not apprehensive of giving offence to their hearers, by exposing that doctrine as an idle and extravagant opinion, which was rejected with contempt by every man of a liberal education and understanding. [53]

[Footnote 51: In particular, the first book of the Tusculan Questions, and the treatise De Senectute, and the Somnium Scipionis, contain, in the most beautiful language, every thing that Grecian philosophy, on Roman good sense, could possibly suggest on this dark but important object.]

[Footnote 52: The preexistence of human souls, so far at least as that doctrine is compatible with religion, was adopted by many of the Greek and Latin fathers. See Beausobre, Hist. du Manicheisme, l. vi. c. 4.]

[Footnote 53: See Cicero pro Cluent. c. 61. Caesar ap. Sallust. de Bell. Catilis n 50. Juvenal. Satir. ii. 149. — Esse aliquid manes, et subterranea regna, —Nec pueri credunt, nisi qui nondum aeree lavantae.]

Since therefore the most sublime efforts of philosophy can extend no further than feebly to point out the desire, the hope, or, at most, the probability, of a future state, there is nothing, except a divine revelation, that can ascertain the existence, and describe the condition, of the invisible country which is destined to receive the souls of men after their separation from the body. But we may perceive several defects inherent to the popular religions of Greece and Rome, which rendered them very unequal to so arduous a task. 1. The general system of their mythology was unsupported by any solid proofs; and the wisest among the Pagans had already disclaimed its usurped authority. 2. The description of the infernal regions had been abandoned to the fancy of painters and of poets, who peopled them with so many phantoms and monsters, who dispensed their rewards and punishments with so little equity, that a solemn truth, the most congenial to the human heart, was opposed and disgraced by the absurd mixture of the wildest fictions. [54] 3. The doctrine of a future state was scarcely considered among the devout polytheists of Greece and Rome as a fundamental article of faith. The providence of the gods, as it related to public communities rather than to private individuals, was principally displayed on the visible theatre of the present world. The petitions which were offered on the altars of Jupiter or Apollo, expressed the anxiety of their worshippers for temporal happiness, and their ignorance or indifference concerning a future life. [55] The important truth of the of the immortality of the soul was inculcated with more diligence, as well as success, in India, in Assyria, in Egypt, and in Gaul; and since we cannot attribute such a difference to the superior knowledge of the barbarians, we we must ascribe it to the influence of an established priesthood, which employed the motives of virtue as the instrument of ambition. [56]

[Footnote 54: The xith book of the Odyssey gives a very dreary and incoherent account of the infernal shades. Pindar and Virgil have embellished the picture; but even those poets, though more correct than their great model, are guilty of very strange inconsistencies. See Bayle, Responses aux Questions d'un Provincial, part iii. c. 22.]

[Footnote 55: See xvith epistle of the first book of Horace, the xiiith Satire of Juvenal, and the iid Satire of Persius: these popular discourses express the sentiment and language of the multitude.]

[Footnote 56: If we confine ourselves to the Gauls, we may observe, that they intrusted, not only their lives, but even their money, to the security of another world. Vetus ille mos Gallorum occurrit (says Valerius Maximus, l. ii. c. 6, p. 10) quos, memoria proditum est pecunias montuas, quae his apud inferos redderentur, dare solitos. The same custom is more darkly insinuated by Mela, l. iii. c. 2. It is almost needless to add, that the profits of trade hold a just proportion to the credit of the merchant, and that the Druids derived from their holy profession a character of responsibility, which could scarcely be claimed by any other order of men.]

We might naturally expect that a principle so essential to religion, would have been revealed in the clearest terms to the chosen people of Palestine, and that it might safely have been intrusted to the hereditary priesthood of Aaron. It is incumbent on us to adore the mysterious dispensations of Providence, [57] when we discover that the doctrine of the immortality of the soul is omitted in the law of Moses it is darkly insinuated by the prophets; and during the long period which clasped between the Egyptian and the Babylonian servitudes, the hopes as well as fears of the Jews appear to have been confined within the narrow compass of the present life. [58] After Cyrus had permitted the exiled nation to return into the promised land, and after Ezra had restored the ancient records of their religion, two celebrated sects, the Sadducees and the Pharisees, insensibly arose at Jerusalem. [59] The former, selected from the more opulent and distinguished ranks of society, were strictly attached to the literal sense of the Mosaic law, and they piously rejected the immortality of the soul, as an opinion that received no countenance from the divine book, which they revered as the only rule of their faith. To the authority of Scripture the Pharisees added that of tradition, and they accepted, under the name of traditions, several speculative tenets from the philosophy or religion of the eastern nations. The doctrines of fate or predestination, of angels and spirits, and of a future state of rewards and punishments, were in the number of these new articles of belief; and as the Pharisees, by the austerity of their manners, had drawn into their party the body of the Jewish people, the immortality of the soul became the prevailing sentiment of the synagogue, under the reign of the Asmonaean princes and pontiffs. The temper of the Jews was incapable of contenting itself with such a cold and languid assent as might satisfy the mind of a Polytheist; and as soon as they admitted the idea of a future state, they embraced it with the zeal which has always formed the characteristic of the nation. Their zeal, however, added nothing to its evidence, or even probability: and it was still necessary that the doctrine of life and immortality, which had been dictated by nature, approved by reason, and received by superstition, should obtain the sanction of divine truth from the authority and example of Christ.

[Footnote 57: The right reverend author of the Divine Legation of Moses as signs a very curious reason for the omission, and most ingeniously retorts it on the unbelievers. Note: The hypothesis of Warburton concerning this remarkable fact, which, as far as the Law of Moses, is unquestionable, made few disciples; and it is difficult to suppose that it could be intended by the author himself for more than a display of intellectual strength. Modern writers have accounted in various ways for the silence of the Hebrew legislator on the immortality of the soul. According to Michaelis, "Moses wrote as an historian and as a lawgiver; he regulated the ecclesiastical discipline, rather than the religious belief of his people; and the sanctions of the law being temporal, he had no occasion, and as a civil legislator could not with propriety, threaten punishments in another world." See Michaelis, Laws of Moses, art. 272, vol. iv. p. 209, Eng. Trans.; and Syntagma Commentationum, p. 80, quoted by Guizot. M. Guizot adds, the "ingenious conjecture of a philosophic theologian," which approximates to an opinion long entertained by the Editor. That writer believes, that in the state of civilization at the time of the legislator, this doctrine, become popular among the Jews, would necessarily have given birth to a multitude of idolatrous superstitions which he wished to prevent. His primary object was to establish a firm theocracy, to make his people the conservators of the doctrine of the Divine Unity, the basis upon which Christianity was hereafter to rest. He carefully excluded everything which could obscure or weaken that doctrine. Other nations had strangely abused their notions on the immortality of the soul; Moses wished to prevent this abuse: hence he forbade the Jews from consulting necromancers, (those who evoke the spirits of the dead.) Deut. xviii. 11. Those who reflect on the state of the Pagans and the Jews, and on the facility with which idolatry crept in on every side, will not be astonished that Moses has not developed a doctrine of which the influence might be more pernicious than useful to his people. Orat. Fest. de Vitae Immort. Spe., &c., auct. Ph. Alb. Stapfer, p. 12 13, 20. Berne, 1787. —Moses, as well from the intimations scattered in his writings, the passage relating to the translation of Enoch, (Gen. v. 24,) the prohibition of necromancy, (Michaelis believes him to be the author of the Book of Job though this opinion is in general rejected; other learned writers consider this Book to be coeval with and known to Moses,) as from his long residence in Egypt, and his acquaintance with Egyptian wisdom, could not be ignorant of the doctrine of the immortality of the soul. But this doctrine if popularly known among the Jews, must have been purely Egyptian, and as so, intimately connected with the whole religious system of that country. It was no doubt moulded up with the tenet of the transmigration of the soul, perhaps with notions analogous to the emanation system of India in which the human soul was an efflux from or indeed a part of, the Deity. The Mosaic religion drew a wide and impassable interval between the Creator and created human beings: in this it differed from the Egyptian and all the Eastern religions. As then the immortality of the soul was thus inseparably blended with those foreign religions which were altogether to be effaced from the minds of the people, and by no means necessary for the establishment of the theocracy, Moses maintained silence on this point and a purer notion of it was left to be developed at a more favorable period in the history of man.—M.]

[Footnote 58: See Le Clerc (Prolegomena ad Hist. Ecclesiast. sect. 1, c. 8) His authority seems to carry the greater weight, as he has written a learned and judicious commentary on the books of the Old Testament.]

[Footnote 59: Joseph. Antiquitat. l. xiii. c. 10. De Bell. Jud. ii. 8. According to the most natural interpretation of his words, the Sadducees admitted only the Pentateuch; but it has pleased some modern critics to add the Prophets to their creed, and to suppose that they contented themselves with rejecting the traditions of the Pharisees. Dr. Jortin has argued that point in his Remarks on Ecclesiastical History, vol. ii. p. 103.]

When the promise of eternal happiness was proposed to mankind on condition of adopting the faith, and of observing the precepts, of the gospel, it is no wonder that so advantageous an offer should have been accepted by great numbers of every religion, of every rank, and of every province in the Roman empire. The ancient Christians were animated by a contempt for their present existence, and by a just confidence of immortality, of which the doubtful and imperfect faith of modern ages cannot give us any adequate notion. In the primitive church, the influence of truth was very powerfully strengthened by an opinion, which, however it may deserve respect for its usefulness and antiquity, has not been found agreeable to experience. It was universally believed, that the end of the world, and the kingdom of heaven, were at hand. [591] The near approach of this wonderful event had been predicted by the apostles; the tradition of it was preserved by their earliest disciples, and those who understood in their literal senses the discourse of Christ himself, were obliged to expect the second and glorious coming of the Son of Man in the clouds, before that generation was totally extinguished, which had beheld his humble condition upon earth, and which might still be witness of the calamities of the Jews under Vespasian or Hadrian. The revolution of seventeen centuries has instructed us not to press too closely the mysterious language of prophecy and revelation; but as long as, for wise purposes, this error was permitted to subsist in the church, it was productive of the most salutary effects on the faith and practice of Christians, who lived in the awful expectation of that moment, when the globe itself, and all the various race of mankind, should tremble at the appearance of their divine Judge. [60]

[Footnote 591: This was, in fact, an integral part of the Jewish notion of the Messiah, from which the minds of the apostles themselves were but gradually detached. See Bertholdt, Christologia Judaeorum, concluding chapters—M.]

[Footnote 60: This expectation was countenanced by the twenty-fourth chapter of St. Matthew, and by the first epistle of St. Paul to the Thessalonians. Erasmus removes the difficulty by the help of allegory and metaphor; and the learned Grotius ventures to insinuate, that, for wise purposes, the pious deception was permitted to take place. Note: Some modern theologians explain it without discovering either allegory or deception. They say, that Jesus Christ, after having proclaimed the ruin of Jerusalem and of the Temple, speaks of his second coming and the sings which were to precede it; but those who believed that the moment was near deceived themselves as to the sense of two words, an error which still subsists in our versions of the Gospel according to St. Matthew, xxiv. 29, 34. In verse 29, we read, "Immediately after the tribulation of those days shall the sun be darkened," &c. The Greek word signifies all at once, suddenly, not immediately; so that it signifies only the sudden appearance of the signs which Jesus Christ announces not the shortness of the interval which was to separate them from the "days of tribulation," of which he was speaking. The verse 34 is this "Verily I say unto you, This generation shall not pass till all these things shall be fulfilled." Jesus, speaking to his disciples, uses these words, which the translators have rendered by this generation, but which means the race, the filiation of my disciples; that is, he speaks of a class of men, not of a generation. The true sense then, according to these learned men, is, In truth I tell you that this race of men, of which you are the commencement, shall not pass away till this shall take place; that is to say, the succession of Christians shall not cease till his coming. See Commentary of M. Paulus on the New Test., edit. 1802, tom. iii. p. 445,—446.—G. —Others, as Rosenmuller and Kuinoel, in loc., confine this passage to a highly figurative description of the ruins of the Jewish city and polity.—M.]

PART IV

The ancient and popular doctrine of the Millennium was intimately connected with the second coming of Christ. As the works of the creation had been finished in six days, their duration in their present state, according to a tradition which was attributed to the prophet Elijah, was fixed to six thousand years. [61] By the same analogy it was inferred, that this long period of labor and contention, which was now almost elapsed, [62] would be succeeded by a joyful Sabbath of a thousand years; and that Christ, with the triumphant band of the saints and the elect who had escaped death, or who had been miraculously revived, would reign upon earth till the time appointed for the last and general resurrection. So pleasing was this hope to the mind of believers, that the New Jerusalem, the seat of this blissful kingdom, was quickly adorned with all the gayest colors of the imagination. A felicity consisting only of pure and spiritual pleasure would have appeared too refined for its inhabitants, who were still supposed to possess their human nature and senses. A garden of Eden, with the amusements of the pastoral life, was no longer suited to the advanced state of society which prevailed under the Roman empire. A city was therefore erected of gold and precious stones, and a supernatural plenty of corn and wine was bestowed on the adjacent territory; in the free enjoyment of whose spontaneous productions, the happy and benevolent people was never to be restrained by any jealous laws of exclusive property. [63] The assurance of such a Millennium was carefully inculcated by a succession of fathers from Justin Martyr, [64] and Irenaeus, who conversed with the immediate disciples of the apostles, down to Lactantius, who was preceptor to the son of Constantine. [65] Though it might not be universally received, it appears to have been the reigning sentiment of the orthodox believers; and it seems so well adapted to the desires and apprehensions of mankind, that it must have contributed in a very considerable degree to the progress of the Christian faith. But when the edifice of the church was almost completed, the temporary support was laid aside. The doctrine of Christ's reign upon earth was at first treated as a profound allegory, was considered by degrees as a doubtful and useless opinion, and was at length rejected as the absurd invention of heresy and fanaticism. [66] A mysterious prophecy, which still forms a part of the sacred canon, but which was thought to favor the exploded sentiment, has very narrowly escaped the proscription of the church. [67]

[Footnote 61: See Burnet's Sacred Theory, part iii. c. 5. This tradition may be traced as high as the the author of Epistle of Barnabas, who wrote in the first century, and who seems to have been half a Jew. Note: In fact it is purely Jewish. See Mosheim, De Reb. Christ. ii. 8. Lightfoot's Works, 8vo. edit. vol. iii. p. 37. Bertholdt, Christologia Judaeorum ch. 38.—M.]

[Footnote 62: The primitive church of Antioch computed almost 6000 years from the creation of the world to the birth of Christ. Africanus, Lactantius, and the Greek church, have reduced that number to 5500, and Eusebius has contented himself with 5200 years. These calculations were formed on the Septuagint, which was universally received during the six first centuries. The authority of the vulgate and of the Hebrew text has determined the moderns, Protestants as well as Catholics, to prefer a period of about 4000 years; though, in the study of profane antiquity, they often find themselves straitened by those narrow limits. Note: Most of the more learned modern English Protestants, Dr. Hales, Mr. Faber, Dr. Russel, as well as the Continental writers, adopt the larger chronology. There is little doubt that the narrower system was framed by the Jews of Tiberias; it was clearly neither that of St. Paul, nor of Josephus, nor of the Samaritan Text. It is greatly to be regretted that the chronology of the earlier Scriptures should ever have been made a religious question—M.]

[Footnote 63: Most of these pictures were borrowed from a misrepresentation of Isaiah, Daniel, and the Apocalypse. One of the grossest images may be found in Irenaeus, (l. v. p. 455,) the disciple of Papias, who had seen the apostle St. John.]

[Footnote 64: See the second dialogue of Justin with Triphon, and the seventh book of Lactantius. It is unnecessary to allege all the intermediate fathers, as the fact is not disputed. Yet the curious reader may consult Daille de Uus Patrum, l. ii. c. 4.]

[Footnote 65: The testimony of Justin of his own faith and that of his orthodox brethren, in the doctrine of a Millennium, is delivered in the clearest and most solemn manner, (Dialog. cum Tryphonte Jud. p. 177, 178, edit. Benedictin.) If in the beginning of this important passage there is any thing like an inconsistency, we may impute it, as we think proper, either to the author or to his transcribers. Note: The Millenium is described in what once stood as the XLIst Article of the English Church (see Collier, Eccles. Hist., for Articles of Edw. VI.) as "a fable of Jewish dotage." The whole of these gross and earthly images may be traced in the works which treat on the Jewish traditions, in Lightfoot, Schoetgen, and Eisenmenger; "Das enthdeckte Judenthum" t. ii 809; and briefly in Bertholdt, i. c. 38, 39.—M.]

[Footnote 66: Dupin, Bibliotheque Ecclesiastique, tom. i. p. 223, tom. ii. p. 366, and Mosheim, p. 720; though the latter of these learned divines is not altogether candid on this occasion.]

[Footnote 67: In the council of Laodicea, (about the year 360,) the Apocalypse was tacitly excluded from the sacred canon, by the same churches of Asia to which it is addressed; and we may learn from the complaint of Sulpicius Severus, that their sentence had been ratified by the greater number of Christians of his time. From what causes then is the Apocalypse at present so generally received by the Greek, the Roman, and the Protestant churches? The following ones may be assigned. 1. The Greeks were subdued by the authority of an impostor, who, in the sixth century, assumed the character of Dionysius the Areopagite. 2. A just apprehension that the grammarians might become more important than the *theologians, engaged the council of Trent to fix the seal of their infallibility on all the books of Scripture contained in the Latin Vulgate, in the number of which the Apocalypse was fortunately included. (Fr. Paolo, Istoria del Concilio Tridentino, l. ii.) 3. The advantage of turning those mysterious prophecies against the See of Rome, inspired the Protestants with uncommon veneration for so useful an ally. See the ingenious and elegant discourses of the present bishop of Litchfield on that unpromising subject. Note: The exclusion of the Apocalypse is not improbably assigned to its obvious unfitness to be read in churches. It is to be feared that a history of the interpretation of the Apocalypse would not give a very favorable view either of the wisdom or the charity of the successive ages of Christianity. Wetstein's interpretation, differently modified, is adopted by most Continental scholars.—M.]*

Whilst the happiness and glory of a temporal reign were promised to the disciples of Christ, the most dreadful calamities were denounced against an unbelieving world. The edification of a new Jerusalem was to advance by equal steps with the destruction of the mystic Babylon; and as long as the emperors who reigned before Constantine persisted in the profession of idolatry, the epithet of babylon was applied to the city and to the empire of Rome. A regular series was prepared of all the moral and physical evils which can afflict a flourishing nation; intestine discord, and the invasion of the fiercest barbarians from the unknown regions of the North; pestilence and famine, comets and eclipses, earthquakes and inundations. [68] All these were only so many preparatory and alarming signs of the great catastrophe of Rome, when the country of the Scipios and Caesars should be consumed by a flame from Heaven, and the city of the seven hills, with her palaces, her temples, and her triumphal arches, should be buried in a vast lake of fire and brimstone. It might, however, afford some consolation to Roman vanity, that the period of their empire would be that of the world itself; which, as it had once perished by the element of water, was destined to experience a second and a speedy destruction from the element of fire. In the opinion of a general conflagration, the faith of the Christian very happily coincided with the tradition of the East, the philosophy of the Stoics, and the analogy of Nature; and even the country, which, from religious motives, had been chosen for the origin and principal scene of the conflagration, was the best adapted for that purpose by natural and physical causes; by its deep caverns, beds of sulphur, and numero is volcanoes, of which those of Aetna, of Vesuvius, and of Lipari, exhibit a very imperfect representation. The calmest and most intrepid sceptic could not refuse to acknowledge that the destruction of the present system of the world by fire, was in itself extremely probable. The Christian, who founded his belief much less on the fallacious arguments of reason than on the authority of tradition and the interpretation of Scripture, expected it with terror and confidence as a certain and approaching event; and as his mind was perpetually filled with the solemn idea, he considered every disaster that happened to the empire as an infallible symptom of an expiring world. [69]

[Footnote 68: Lactantius (Institut. Divin. vii. 15, &c.) relates the dismal talk of futurity with great spirit and eloquence. Note: Lactantius had a notion of a great Asiatic empire, which was previously to rise on the ruins of the Roman: quod Romanum nomen animus dicere, sed dicam. quia futurum est tolletur de terra, et impere. Asiam revertetur.—M.]

[Footnote 69: On this subject every reader of taste will be entertained with the third part of Burnet's Sacred Theory. He blends philosophy, Scripture, and tradition, into one magnificent system; in the description of which he displays a strength of fancy not inferior to that of Milton himself.]

The condemnation of the wisest and most virtuous of the Pagans, on account of their ignorance or disbelief of the divine truth, seems to offend the reason and the humanity of the present age. [70] But the primitive church, whose faith was of a much firmer consistence, delivered over, without hesitation, to eternal torture, the far greater part of the human species. A charitable hope might perhaps be indulged in favor of Socrates, or some other sages of antiquity, who had consulted the light of reason before that of the gospel had arisen. [71] But it was unanimously affirmed, that those who, since the birth or the death of Christ, had obstinately persisted in the worship of the daemons, neither deserved nor could expect a pardon from the irritated justice of the Deity. These rigid sentiments, which had been unknown to the ancient world, appear to have infused a spirit of bitterness into a system of love and harmony. The ties of blood and friendship were frequently torn asunder by the difference of religious faith; and the Christians, who, in this world, found themselves oppressed by the power of the Pagans, were sometimes seduced by resentment and spiritual pride to delight in the prospect of their future triumph. "You are fond of spectacles," exclaims the stern Tertullian; "expect the greatest of all spectacles, the last and eternal judgment of the universe. How shall I admire, how laugh, how rejoice, how exult, when I behold so many proud monarchs, so many fancied gods, groaning in the lowest abyss of darkness; so many magistrates, who persecuted the name of the Lord, liquefying in fiercer fires than they ever kindled against the Christians; so many sage philosophers blushing in red-hot flames with their deluded scholars; so many celebrated poets trembling before the tribunal, not of Minos, but of Christ; so many tragedians, more tuneful in the expression of their own sufferings; so many dancers."

[71/1] But the humanity of the reader will permit me to draw a veil over the rest of this infernal description, which the zealous African pursues in a long variety of affected and unfeeling witticisms. [72]

[Footnote 70: *And yet whatever may be the language of individuals, it is still the public doctrine of all the Christian churches; nor can even our own refuse to admit the conclusions which must be drawn from the viiith and the xviiith of her Articles. The Jansenists, who have so diligently studied the works of the fathers, maintain this sentiment with distinguished zeal; and the learned M. de Tillemont never dismisses a virtuous emperor without pronouncing his damnation. Zuinglius is perhaps the only leader of a party who has ever adopted the milder sentiment, and he gave no less offence to the Lutherans than to the Catholics. See Bossuet, Histoire des Variations des Eglises Protestantes, l. ii. c. 19—22.*]

[Footnote 71: *Justin and Clemens of Alexandria allow that some of the philosophers were instructed by the Logos; confounding its double signification of the human reason, and of the Divine Word.*]

[Footnote 71/1: *This translation is not exact: the first sentence is imperfect. Tertullian says, Ille dies nationibus insperatus, ille derisus, cum tanta sacculi vetustas et tot ejus nativitates uno igne haurientur. The text does not authorize the exaggerated expressions, so many magistrates, so many sago philosophers, so many poets, &c.; but simply magistrates, philosophers, poets.—G. —It is not clear that Gibbon's version or paraphrase is incorrect: Tertullian writes, tot tantosque reges item praesides, &c.—M.*]

[Footnote 72: *Tertullian, de Spectaculis, c. 30. In order to ascertain the degree of authority which the zealous African had acquired it may be sufficient to allege the testimony of Cyprian, the doctor and guide of all the western churches. (See Prudent. Hym. xiii. 100.) As often as he applied himself to his daily study of the writings of Tertullian, he was accustomed to say, "Da mihi magistrum, Give me my master." (Hieronym. de Viris Illustribus, tom. i. p. 284.) The object of Tertullian's vehemence in his Treatise, was to keep the Christians away from the secular games celebrated by the Emperor Severus: It has not prevented him from showing himself in other places full of benevolence and charity towards unbelievers: the spirit of the gospel has sometimes prevailed over the violence of human passions: Qui ergo putaveris nihil nos de salute Caesaris curare (he says in his Apology) inspice Dei voces, literas nostras. Scitote ex illis praeceptum esse nobis ad redudantionem, benignitates etiam pro inimicis Deum orare, et pro persecutoribus cona precari. Sed etiam nominatim atque manifeste orate inquit (Christus) pro regibus et pro principibus et potestatibus ut omnia sint tranquilla vobis Tert. Apol. c. 31.—G. —It would be wiser for Christianity, retreating upon its genuine records in the New Testament, to disclaim this fierce African, than to identify itself with his furious invectives by unsatisfactory apologies for their unchristian fanaticism.—M.]*

Doubtless there were many among the primitive Christians of a temper more suitable to the meekness and charity of their profession. There were many who felt a sincere compassion for the danger of their friends and countrymen, and who exerted the most benevolent zeal to save them from the impending destruction.

The careless Polytheist, assailed by new and unexpected terrors, against which neither his priests nor his philosophers could afford him any certain protection, was very frequently terrified and subdued by the menace of eternal tortures. His fears might assist the progress of his faith and reason; and if he could once persuade himself to suspect that the Christian religion might possibly be true, it became an easy task to convince him that it was the safest and most prudent party that he could possibly embrace.

III. The supernatural gifts, which even in this life were ascribed to the Christians above the rest of mankind, must have conduced to their own comfort, and very frequently to the conviction of infidels. Besides the occasional prodigies, which might sometimes be effected by the immediate interposition of the Deity when he suspended the laws of Nature for the service of religion, the Christian church, from the time of the apostles and their first disciples, [73] has claimed an uninterrupted succession of miraculous powers, the gift of tongues, of vision, and of prophecy, the power of expelling daemons, of healing the sick, and of raising the dead. The knowledge of foreign languages was frequently communicated to the contemporaries of Irenaeus, though Irenaeus himself was left to struggle with the difficulties of a barbarous dialect, whilst he preached the gospel to the natives of Gaul. [74] The divine inspiration, whether it was conveyed in the form of a waking or of a sleeping vision, is described as a favor very liberally bestowed on all ranks of the faithful, on women as on elders, on boys as well as upon bishops. When their devout minds were sufficiently prepared by a course of prayer, of fasting, and of vigils, to receive the extraordinary impulse, they were transported out of their senses, and delivered in ecstasy what was inspired, being mere organs of the Holy Spirit, just as a pipe or flute is of him who blows into it. [75] We may add, that the design of these visions was, for the most part, either to disclose the future history, or to guide the present administration, of the church. The expulsion of the daemons from the bodies of those unhappy persons whom they had been permitted to torment, was considered as a signal though ordinary triumph of religion, and is repeatedly alleged by the ancient apologists, as the most convincing evidence of the truth of Christianity. The awful ceremony was usually performed in a public manner, and in the presence of a great number of spectators; the patient was relieved by the power or skill of the exorcist, and the vanquished daemon was heard to confess that he was one of the fabled gods of antiquity, who had impiously usurped the adoration of mankind. [76] But the miraculous cure of diseases of the most inveterate or even preternatural kind, can no longer occasion any surprise, when we recollect, that in the days of Iranaeus, about the end of the second century, the resurrection of the dead was very far from being esteemed an uncommon event; that the miracle was frequently performed on necessary occasions, by great fasting and the joint supplication of the church of the place, and that the persons thus restored to their prayers had lived afterwards among them many years. [77] At such a period, when faith could boast of so many wonderful victories over death, it seems difficult to account for the scepticism of those philosophers, who still rejected and derided the doctrine of the resurrection. A noble Grecian had rested on this important ground the whole controversy, and promised Theophilus, Bishop of Antioch, that if he could be gratified with the sight of a single person who had been actually raised from the dead, he would immediately embrace the Christian religion. It is somewhat remarkable, that the prelate of the first eastern church, however anxious for the conversion of his friend, thought proper to decline this fair and reasonable challenge. [78]

[Footnote 73: Notwithstanding the evasions of Dr. Middleton, it is impossible to overlook the clear traces of visions and inspiration, which may be found in the apostolic fathers. Note: Gibbon should have noticed the distinct and remarkable passage from Chrysostom, quoted by Middleton, (Works, vol. i. p. 105,) in which he affirms the long discontinuance of miracles as a notorious fact.—M.]

[Footnote 74: Irenaeus adv. Haeres. Proem. p.3 Dr. Middleton (Free Inquiry, p. 96, &c.) observes, that as this pretension of all others was the most difficult to support by art, it was the soonest given up. The observation suits his hypothesis. Note: This passage of Irenaeus contains no allusion to the gift of tongues; it is merely an apology for a rude and unpolished Greek style, which could not be expected from one who passed his life in a remote and barbarous province, and was continually obliged to speak the Celtic language.—M. Note: Except in the life of Pachomius, an Egyptian monk of the fourth century. (see Jortin, Ecc. Hist. i. p. 368, edit. 1805,) and the latter (not earlier) lives of Xavier, there is no claim laid to the gift of tongues since the time of Irenaeus; and of this claim, Xavier's own letters are profoundly silent. See Douglas's Criterion, p. 76 edit. 1807.—M.]

[Footnote 75: Athenagoras in Legatione. Justin Martyr, Cohort. ad Gentes Tertullian advers. Marcionit. l. iv. These descriptions are not very unlike the prophetic fury, for which Cicero (de Divinat.ii. 54) expresses so little reverence.]

[Footnote 76: Tertullian (Apolog. c. 23) throws out a bold defiance to the Pagan magistrates. Of the primitive miracles, the power of exorcising is the only one which has been assumed by Protestants. Note: But by Protestants neither of the most enlightened ages nor most reasoning minds.—M.]

[Footnote 77: Irenaeus adv. Haereses, l. ii. 56, 57, l. v. c. 6. Mr. Dodwell (Dissertat. ad Irenaeum, ii. 42) concludes, that the second century was still more fertile in miracles than the first. Note: It is difficult to answer Middleton's objection to this statement of Irenae us: "It is very strange, that from the time of the apostles there is not a single instance of this miracle to be found in the three first centuries; except a single case, slightly intimated in Eusebius, from the Works of Papias; which he seems to rank among the other fabulous stories delivered by that weak man." Middleton, Works, vol. i. p. 59. Bp. Douglas (Criterion, p 389) would consider Irenaeus to speak of what had "been performed formerly." not in his own time.—M.]

[Footnote 78: Theophilus ad Autolycum, l. i. p. 345. Edit. Benedictin. Paris, 1742. Note: A candid sceptic might discern some impropriety in the Bishop being called upon to perform a miracle on demand.—M.]

The miracles of the primitive church, after obtaining the sanction of ages, have been lately attacked in a very free and ingenious inquiry, [79] which, though it has met with the most favorable reception from the public, appears to have excited a general scandal among the divines of our own as well as of the other Protestant churches of Europe. [80] Our different sentiments on this subject will be much less influenced by any particular arguments, than by our habits of study and reflection; and, above all, by the degree of evidence which we have accustomed ourselves to require for the proof of a miraculous event. The duty of an historian does not call upon him to interpose his private judgment in this nice and important controversy; but he ought not to dissemble the difficulty of adopting such a theory as may reconcile the interest of religion with that of reason, of making a proper application of that theory, and of defining with precision the limits of that happy period, exempt from error and from deceit, to which we might be disposed to extend the gift of supernatural powers. From the first of the fathers to the last of the popes, a succession of bishops, of saints, of martyrs, and of miracles, is continued without interruption; and the progress of superstition was so gradual, and almost imperceptible, that we know not in what particular link we should break the chain of tradition. Every age bears testimony to the wonderful events by which it was distinguished, and its testimony appears no less weighty and respectable than that of the preceding generation, till we are insensibly led on to accuse our own inconsistency, if in the eighth or in the twelfth century we deny to the venerable Bede, or to the holy Bernard, the same degree of confidence which, in the second century, we had so liberally granted to Justin or to Irenaeus. [81] If the truth of any of those miracles is appreciated by their apparent use and propriety, every age had unbelievers to convince, heretics to confute, and idolatrous nations to convert; and sufficient motives might always be produced to justify the interposition of Heaven. And yet, since every friend to revelation is persuaded of the reality, and every reasonable man is convinced of the cessation, of miraculous powers, it is evident that there must have been some period in which they were either suddenly or gradually withdrawn from the Christian church. Whatever aera is chosen for that purpose, the death of the apostles, the conversion of the Roman empire, or the extinction of the Arian heresy, [82] the insensibility of the Christians who lived at that time will equally afford a just matter of surprise. They still supported their pretensions after they had lost their power. Credulity performed the office of faith; fanaticism was permitted to assume the language of inspiration, and the effects of accident or contrivance were ascribed to supernatural causes. The recent experience of genuine miracles should have instructed the Christian world in the ways of Providence, and habituated their eye (if we may use a very inadequate expression) to the style of the divine artist. Should the most skilful painter of modern Italy presume to decorate his feeble imitations with the name of Raphael or of Correggio, the insolent fraud would be soon discovered, and indignantly rejected.

[Footnote 79: Dr. Middleton sent out his Introduction in the year 1747, published his Free Inquiry in 1749, and before his death, which happened in 1750, he had prepared a vindication of it against his numerous adversaries.]

[Footnote 80: The university of Oxford conferred degrees on his opponents. From the indignation of Mosheim, (p. 221,) we may discover the sentiments of the Lutheran divines. Note: Yet many Protestant divines will now without reluctance confine miracles to the time of the apostles, or at least to the first century.—M]

[Footnote 81: It may seem somewhat remarkable, that Bernard of Clairvaux, who records so many miracles of his friend St. Malachi, never takes any notice of his own, which, in their turn, however, are carefully related by his companions and disciples. In the long series of ecclesiastical history, does there exist a single instance of a saint asserting that he himself possessed the gift of miracles?]

[Footnote 82: The conversion of Constantine is the aera which is most usually fixed by Protestants. The more rational divines are unwilling to admit the miracles of the ivth, whilst the more credulous are unwilling to reject those of the vth century. Note: All this appears to proceed on the principle that any distinct line can be drawn in an unphilosophic age between wonders and miracles, or between what piety, from their unexpected and extraordinary nature, the marvellous concurrence of secondary causes to some remarkable end, may consider providential interpositions, and miracles strictly so called, in which the laws of nature are suspended or violated. It is impossible to assign, on one side, limits to human credulity, on the other, to the influence of the imagination on the bodily frame; but some of the miracles recorded in the Gospels are such palpable impossibilities, according to the known laws and *operations of nature, that if recorded on sufficient evidence, and the evidence we believe to be that of eye-witnesses, we cannot reject them, without either asserting, with Hume, that no evidence can prove a miracle, or that the Author of Nature has no power of suspending its ordinary laws. But which of the post-apostolic miracles will bear this test?—M.]*

Whatever opinion may be entertained of the miracles of the primitive church since the time of the apostles, this unresisting softness of temper, so conspicuous among the believers of the second and third centuries, proved of some accidental benefit to the cause of truth and religion. In modern times, a latent and even involuntary scepticism adheres to the most pious dispositions. Their admission of supernatural truths is much less an active consent than a cold and passive acquiescence. Accustomed long since to observe and to respect the variable order of Nature, our reason, or at least our imagination, is not sufficiently prepared to sustain the visible action of the Deity.

But, in the first ages of Christianity, the situation of mankind was extremely different. The most curious, or the most credulous, among the Pagans, were often persuaded to enter into a society which asserted an actual claim of miraculous powers. The primitive Christians perpetually trod on mystic ground, and their minds were exercised by the habits of believing the most extraordinary events. They felt, or they fancied, that on every side they were incessantly assaulted by daemons, comforted by visions, instructed by prophecy, and surprisingly delivered from danger, sickness, and from death itself, by the supplications of the church. The real or imaginary prodigies, of which they so frequently conceived themselves to be the objects, the instruments, or the spectators, very happily disposed them to adopt with the same ease, but with far greater justice, the authentic wonders of the evangelic history; and thus miracles that exceeded not the measure of their own experience, inspired them with the most lively assurance of mysteries which were acknowledged to surpass the limits of their understanding. It is this deep impression of supernatural truths, which has been so much celebrated under the name of faith; a state of mind described as the surest pledge of the divine favor and of future felicity, and recommended as the first, or perhaps the only merit of a Christian. According to the more rigid doctors, the moral virtues, which may be equally practised by infidels, are destitute of any value or efficacy in the work of our justification.

PART V

IV. But the primitive Christian demonstrated his faith by his virtues; and it was very justly supposed that the divine persuasion, which enlightened or subdued the understanding, must, at the same time, purify the heart, and direct the actions, of the believer. The first apologists of Christianity who justify the innocence of their brethren, and the writers of a later period who celebrate the sanctity of their ancestors, display, in the most lively colors, the reformation of manners which was introduced into the world by the preaching of the gospel. As it is my intention to remark only such human causes as were permitted to second the influence of revelation, I shall slightly mention two motives which might naturally render the lives of the primitive Christians much purer and more austere than those of their Pagan contemporaries, or their degenerate successors; repentance for their past sins, and the laudable desire of supporting the reputation of the society in which they were engaged. [83]

[Footnote 83: These, in the opinion of the editor, are the most uncandid paragraphs in Gibbon's History. He ought either, with manly courage, to have denied the moral reformation introduced by Christianity, or fairly to have investigated all its motives; not to have confined himself to an insidious and sarcastic

description of the less pure and generous elements of the Christian character as it appeared even at that early time.—M.]

It is a very ancient reproach, suggested by the ignorance or the malice of infidelity, that the Christians allured into their party the most atrocious criminals, who, as soon as they were touched by a sense of remorse, were easily persuaded to wash away, in the water of baptism, the guilt of their past conduct, for which the temples of the gods refused to grant them any expiation. But this reproach, when it is cleared from misrepresentation, contributes as much to the honor as it did to the increase of the church. [83] The friends of Christianity may acknowledge without a blush, that many of the most eminent saints had been before their baptism the most abandoned sinners. Those persons, who in the world had followed, though in an imperfect manner, the dictates of benevolence and propriety, derived such a calm satisfaction from the opinion of their own rectitude, as rendered them much less susceptible of the sudden emotions of shame, of grief, and of terror, which have given birth to so many wonderful conversions. After the example of their divine Master, the missionaries of the gospel disdained not the society of men, and especially of women, oppressed by the consciousness, and very often by the effects, of their vices. As they emerged from sin and superstition to the glorious hope of immortality, they resolved to devote themselves to a life, not only of virtue, but of penitence. The desire of perfection became the ruling passion of their soul; and it is well known, that while reason embraces a cold mediocrity, our passions hurry us, with rapid violence, over the space which lies between the most opposite extremes.

[Footnote 83: The imputations of Celsus and Julian, with the defence of the fathers, are very fairly stated by Spanheim, Commentaire sur les Cesars de Julian, p. 468.]

When the new converts had been enrolled in the number of the faithful, and were admitted to the sacraments of the church, they found themselves restrained from relapsing into their past disorders by another consideration of a less spiritual, but of a very innocent and respectable nature. Any particular society that has departed from the great body of the nation, or the religion to which it belonged, immediately becomes the object of universal as well as invidious observation. In proportion to the smallness of its numbers, the character of the society may be affected by the virtues and vices of the persons who compose it; and every member is engaged to watch with the most vigilant attention over his own behavior, and over that of his brethren, since, as he must expect to incur a part of the common disgrace, he may hope to enjoy a share of the common reputation. When the Christians of Bithynia were brought before the tribunal of the younger Pliny, they assured the proconsul, that, far from being engaged in any unlawful conspiracy, they were bound by a solemn obligation to abstain from the commission of those crimes which disturb the private or public peace of society, from theft, robbery, adultery, perjury, and fraud. [84] [841] Near a century afterwards, Tertullian with an honest pride, could boast, that very few Christians had suffered by the hand of the executioner, except on account of their religion. [85] Their serious and sequestered life, averse to the gay luxury of the age, inured them to chastity, temperance, economy, and all the sober and domestic virtues. As the greater number were of some trade or profession, it was incumbent on them, by the strictest integrity and the fairest dealing, to remove the suspicions which the profane are too apt to conceive against the appearances of sanctity. The contempt of the world exercised them in the habits of humility, meekness, and patience. The more they were persecuted, the more closely they adhered to each other. Their mutual charity and unsuspecting confidence has been remarked by infidels, and was too often abused by perfidious friends. [86]

[Footnote 84: Plin. Epist. x. 97. Note: Is not the sense of Tertullian rather, if guilty of any other offence, he had thereby ceased to be a Christian?—M.]

[Footnote 841: And this blamelessness was fully admitted by the candid and enlightened Roman.—M.]

[Footnote 85: Tertullian, Apolog. c. 44. He adds, however, with some degree of hesitation, "Aut si aliud, jam non Christianus." Note: Tertullian says positively no Christian, nemo illic Christianus; for the rest, the limitation which he himself subjoins, and which Gibbon quotes in the foregoing note, diminishes the force of this assertion, and appears to prove that at least he knew none such.—G.]

[Footnote 86: The philosopher Peregrinus (of whose life and death Lucian has left us so entertaining an account) imposed, for a long time, on the credulous simplicity of the Christians of Asia.]

It is a very honorable circumstance for the morals of the primitive Christians, that even their faults, or rather errors, were derived from an excess of virtue. The bishops and doctors of the church, whose evidence attests, and whose authority might influence, the professions, the principles, and even the practice of their contemporaries, had studied the Scriptures with less skill than devotion; and they often received, in the most literal sense, those rigid precepts of Christ and the apostles, to which the prudence of succeeding commentators has applied a looser and more figurative mode of interpretation. Ambitious to exalt the perfection of the gospel above the wisdom of philosophy, the zealous fathers have carried the duties of self-mortification, of purity, and of patience, to a height which it is scarcely possible to attain, and much less to preserve, in our present state of weakness and corruption. A doctrine so extraordinary and so sublime must inevitably command the veneration of the people; but it was ill calculated to obtain the suffrage of those worldly philosophers, who, in the conduct of this transitory life, consult only the feelings of nature and the interest of society. [87]

[Footnote 87: See a very judicious treatise of Barbeyrac sur la Morale des Peres.]

There are two very natural propensities which we may distinguish in the most virtuous and liberal dispositions, the love of pleasure and the love of action. If the former is refined by art and learning, improved by the charms of social intercourse, and corrected by a just regard to economy, to health, and to reputation, it is productive of the greatest part of the happiness of private life. The love of action is a principle of a much stronger and more doubtful nature. It often leads to anger, to ambition, and to revenge; but when it is guided by the sense of propriety and benevolence, it becomes the parent of every virtue, and if those virtues are accompanied with equal abilities, a family, a state, or an empire, may be indebted for their safety and prosperity to the undaunted courage of a single man. To the love of pleasure we may therefore ascribe most of the agreeable, to the love of action we may attribute most of the useful and respectable, qualifications. The character in which both the one and the other should be united and harmonized, would seem to constitute the most perfect idea of human nature. The insensible and inactive disposition, which should be supposed alike destitute of both, would be rejected, by the common consent of mankind, as utterly incapable of procuring any happiness to the individual, or any public benefit to the world. But it was not in this world, that the primitive Christians were desirous of making themselves either agreeable or useful. [87/1]

[Footnote 87/1: El que me fait cette homelie semi-stoicienne, semi-epicurienne? t'on jamais regarde l'amour du plaisir comme l'un des principes de la perfection morale? Et de quel droit faites vous de l'amour de l'action, et de l'amour du plaisir, les seuls elemens de l'etre humain? Est ce que vous faites abstraction de la verite en elle-meme, de la conscience et du sentiment du devoir? Est ce que vous ne

sentez point, par exemple, que le sacrifice du moi a la justice et a la verite, est aussi dans le coeur de l'homme: que tout n'est pas pour lui action ou plaisir, et que dans le bien ce n'est pas le mouvement, mais la verite, qu'il cherche? Et puis Thucy dide et Tacite. ces maitres de l'histoire, ont ils jamais introduits dans leur recits un fragment de dissertation sur le plaisir et sur l'action. Villemain Cours de Lit. Franc part ii. Lecon v.—M.]

The acquisition of knowledge, the exercise of our reason or fancy, and the cheerful flow of unguarded conversation, may employ the leisure of a liberal mind. Such amusements, however, were rejected with abhorrence, or admitted with the utmost caution, by the severity of the fathers, who despised all knowledge that was not useful to salvation, and who considered all levity of discours eas a criminal abuse of the gift of speech. In our present state of existence the body is so inseparably connected with the soul, that it seems to be our interest to taste, with innocence and moderation, the enjoyments of which that faithful companion is susceptible. Very different was the reasoning of our devout predecessors; vainly aspiring to imitate the perfection of angels, they disdained, or they affected to disdain, every earthly and corporeal delight. [88] Some of our senses indeed are necessary for our preservation, others for our subsistence, and others again for our information; and thus far it was impossible to reject the use of them. The first sensation of pleasure was marked as the first moment of their abuse. The unfeeling candidate for heaven was instructed, not only to resist the grosser allurements of the taste or smell, but even to shut his ears against the profane harmony of sounds, and to view with indifference the most finished productions of human art. Gay apparel, magnificent houses, and elegant furniture, were supposed to unite the double guilt of pride and of sensuality; a simple and mortified appearance was more suitable to the Christian who was certain of his sins and doubtful of his salvation. In their censures of luxury, the fathers are extremely minute and circumstantial; [89] and among the various articles which excite their pious indignation, we may enumerate false hair, garments of any color except white, instruments of music, vases of gold or silver, downy pillows, (as Jacob reposed his head on a stone,) white bread, foreign wines, public salutations, the use of warm baths, and the practice of shaving the beard, which, according to the expression of Tertullian, is a lie against our own faces, and an impious attempt to improve the works of the Creator. [90] When Christianity was introduced among the rich and the polite, the observation of these singular laws was left, as it would be at present, to the few who were ambitious of superior sanctity. But it is always easy, as well as agreeable, for the inferior ranks of mankind to claim a merit from the contempt of that pomp and pleasure which fortune has placed beyond their reach. The virtue of the primitive Christians, like that of the first Romans, was very frequently guarded by poverty and ignorance.

[Footnote 88: Lactant. Institut. Divin. l. vi. c. 20, 21, 22.]

[Footnote 89: Consult a work of Clemens of Alexandria, entitled The Paedagogue, which contains the rudiments of ethics, as they were taught in the most celebrated of the Christian schools.]

[Footnote 90: Tertullian, de Spectaculis, c. 23. Clemens Alexandrin. Paedagog. l. iii. c. 8.]

The chaste severity of the fathers, in whatever related to the commerce of the two sexes, flowed from the same principle; their abhorrence of every enjoyment which might gratify the sensual, and degrade the spiritual, nature of man. It was their favorite opinion, that if Adam had preserved his obedience to the Creator, he would have lived forever in a state of virgin purity, and that some harmless mode of vegetation might have peopled paradise with a race of innocent and immortal beings. [91] The use of marriage was permitted only to his fallen posterity, as a necessary expedient to continue the human species, and as a restraint, however imperfect, on the natural licentiousness of desire. The hesitation of the orthodox casuists on this interesting subject, betrays the perplexity of men, unwilling to approve an institution which they were compelled to tolerate. [92] The enumeration of the very whimsical laws, which they most circumstantially imposed on the marriage-bed, would force a smile from the young and a blush from the fair. It was their unanimous sentiment, that a first marriage was adequate to all the purposes of nature and of society. The sensual connection was refined into a resemblance of the mystic union of Christ with his church, and was pronounced to be indissoluble either by divorce or by death. The practice of second nuptials was branded with the name of a egal adultery; and the persons who were guilty of so scandalous an offence against Christian purity, were soon excluded from the honors, and even from the alms, of the church. [93] Since desire was imputed as a crime, and marriage was tolerated as a defect, it was consistent with the same principles to consider a state of celibacy as the nearest approach to the divine perfection. It was with the utmost difficulty that ancient Rome could support the institution of six vestals; [94] but the primitive church was filled with a great number of persons of either sex, who had devoted themselves to the profession of perpetual chastity. [95] A few of these, among whom we may reckon the learned Origen, judged it the most prudent to disarm the tempter. [96] Some were insensible and some were invincible against the assaults of the flesh. Disdaining an ignominious flight, the virgins of the warm climate of Africa encountered the enemy in the closest engagement; they permitted priests and deacons to share their bed, and gloried amidst the flames in their unsullied purity. But insulted Nature sometimes vindicated her rights, and this new species of martyrdom served only to introduce a new scandal into the church. [97] Among the Christian ascetics, however, (a name which they soon acquired from their painful exercise,) many, as they were less presumptuous, were probably more successful. The loss of sensual pleasure was supplied and compensated by spiritual pride. Even the multitude of Pagans were inclined to estimate the merit of the sacrifice by its apparent difficulty; and it was in the praise of these chaste spouses of Christ that the fathers have poured forth the troubled stream of their eloquence. [98] Such are the early traces of monastic principles and institutions, which, in a subsequent age, have counterbalanced all the temporal advantages of Christianity. [99]

[Footnote 91: Beausobro, Hist. Critique du Manicheisme, l. vii. c. 3. Justin, Gregory of Nyssa, Augustin, &c., strongly incline to this opinion. Note: But these were Gnostic or Manichean opinions. Beausobre distinctly describes Autustine's bias to his recent escape from Manicheism; and adds that he afterwards changed his views.—M.]

[Footnote 92: Some of the Gnostic heretics were more consistent; they rejected the use of marriage.]

[Footnote 93: See a chain of tradition, from Justin Martyr to Jerome, in the Morale des Peres, c. iv. 6—26.]

[Footnote 94: See a very curious Dissertation on the Vestals, in the Memoires de l'Academie des Inscriptions, tom. iv. p. 161—227. Notwithstanding the honors and rewards which were bestowed on those virgins, it was difficult to procure a sufficient number; nor could the dread of the most horrible death always restrain their incontinence.]

[Footnote 95: Cupiditatem procreandi aut unam scimus aut nullam. Minutius Faelix, c. 31. Justin. Apolog. Major. Athenagoras in Legat. c 28. Tertullian de Cultu Foemin. l. ii.]

[Footnote 96: Eusebius, l. vi. 8. Before the fame of Origen had excited envy and persecution, this extraordinary action was rather admired than censured. As it was his general practice to allegorize Scripture, it seems unfortunate that in this instance only, he should have adopted the literal sense.]

[Footnote 97: Cyprian. Epist. 4, and Dodwell, Dissertat. Cyprianic. iii. Something like this rash attempt was long afterwards imputed to the founder of the order of Fontevrault. Bayle has amused himself and his readers on that very delicate subject.]

[Footnote 98: Dupin (Bibliotheque Ecclesiastique, tom. i. p. 195) gives a particular account of the dialogue of the ten virgins, as it was composed by Methodius, Bishop of Tyre. The praises of virginity are excessive.]

[Footnote 99: The Ascetics (as early as the second century) made a public profession of mortifying their bodies, and of abstaining from the use of flesh and wine. Mosheim, p. 310.]

The Christians were not less averse to the business than to the pleasures of this world. The defence of our persons and property they knew not how to reconcile with the patient doctrine which enjoined an unlimited forgiveness of past injuries, and commanded them to invite the repetition of fresh insults. Their simplicity was offended by the use of oaths, by the pomp of magistracy, and by the active contention of public life; nor could their humane ignorance be convinced that it was lawful on any occasion to shed the blood of our fellow-creatures, either by the sword of justice, or by that of war; even though their criminal or hostile attempts should threaten the peace and safety of the whole community. [100] It was acknowledged, that, under a less perfect law, the powers of the Jewish constitution had been exercised, with the approbation of Heaven, by inspired prophets and by anointed kings. The Christians felt and confessed that such institutions might be necessary for the present system of the world, and they cheerfully submitted to the authority of their Pagan governors. But while they inculcated the maxims of passive obedience, they refused to take any active part in the civil administration or the military defence of the empire. Some indulgence might, perhaps, be allowed to those persons who, before their conversion, were already engaged in such violent and sanguinary occupations; [101] but it was impossible that the Christians, without renouncing a more sacred duty, could assume the character of soldiers, of magistrates, or of princes. [102] This indolent, or even criminal disregard to the public welfare, exposed them to the contempt and reproaches of the Pagans who very frequently asked, what must be the fate of the empire, attacked on every side by the barbarians, if all mankind should adopt the pusillanimous sentiments of the new sect. [103] To this insulting question the Christian apologists returned obscure and ambiguous answers, as they were unwilling to reveal the secret cause of their security; the expectation that, before the conversion of mankind was accomplished, war, government, the Roman empire, and the world itself, would be no more. It may be observed, that, in this instance likewise, the situation of the first Christians coincided very happily with their religious scruples, and that their aversion to an active life contributed rather to excuse them from the service, than to exclude them from the honors, of the state and army.

[Footnote 100: See the Morale des Peres. The same patient principles have been revived since the Reformation by the Socinians, the modern Anabaptists, and the Quakers. Barclay, the Apologist of the Quakers, has protected his brethren by the authority of the primitive Christian; p. 542-549]

[Footnote 101: Tertullian, Apolog. c. 21. De Idololatria, c. 17, 18. Origen contra Celsum, l. v. p. 253, l. vii. p. 348, l. viii. p. 423-428.]

[Footnote 102: Tertullian (de Corona Militis, c. 11) suggested to them the expedient of deserting; a counsel which, if it had been generally known, was not very proper to conciliate the favor of the emperors towards the Christian sect. Note: There is nothing which ought to astonish us in the refusal of the primitive Christians to take part in public affairs; it was the natural consequence of the contrariety of their principles to the customs, laws, and active life of the Pagan world. As Christians, they could not enter into the senate, which, according to Gibbon himself, always assembled in a temple or consecrated place, and where each senator, before he took his seat, made a libation of a few drops of wine, and burnt incense on the altar; as Christians, they could not assist at festivals and banquets, which always terminated with libations, &c.; finally, as "the innumerable deities and rites of polytheism were closely interwoven with every circumstance of public and private life," the Christians could not participate in them without incurring, according to their principles, the guilt of impiety. It was then much less by an effect of their doctrine, than by the consequence of their situation, that they stood aloof from public business. Whenever this situation offered no impediment, they showed as much activity as the Pagans. Proinde, says Justin Martyr, (Apol. c. 17,) nos solum Deum adoramus, et vobis in rebus aliis laeti inservimus.—G. —This latter passage, M. Guizot quotes in Latin; if he had consulted the original, he would have found it to be altogether irrelevant: it merely relates to the payment of taxes.—M. —Tertullian does not suggest to the soldiers the expedient of deserting; he says that they ought to be constantly on their guard to do nothing during their service contrary to the law of God, and to resolve to suffer martyrdom rather than submit to a base compliance, or openly to renounce the service. (De Cor. Mil. ii. p. 127.) He does not positively decide that the military service is not permitted to Christians; he ends, indeed, by saying, Puta denique licere militiam usque ad causam coronae.—G. —M. Guizot is. I think, again unfortunate in his defence of Tertullian. That father says, that many Christian soldiers had deserted, aut deserendum statim sit, ut a multis actum. The latter sentence, Puta, &c, &c., is a concession for the sake of argument: wha follows is more to the purpose.—M. Many other passages of Tertullian prove that the army was full of Christians, Hesterni sumus et vestra omnia implevimus, urbes, insulas, castella, municipia, conciliabula, castra ipsa. (Apol. c. 37.) Navigamus et not vobiscum et militamus. (c. 42.) Origen, in truth, appears to have maintained a more rigid opinion, (Cont. Cels. l. viii.;) but he has often renounced this exaggerated severity, perhaps necessary to produce great results, and he speaks of the profession of arms as an honorable one. (l. iv. c. 218.)— G. —On these points Christian opinion, it should seem, was much divided Tertullian, when he wrote the De Cor. Mil., was evidently inclining to more ascetic opinions, and Origen was of the same class. See Neander, vol. I part ii. p. 305, edit. 1828.—M.]

[Footnote 103: As well as we can judge from the mutilated representation of Origen, (1. viii. p. 423,) his adversary, Celsus, had urged his objection with great force and candor.]

PART VI

V. But the human character, however it may be exalted or depressed by a temporary enthusiasm, will return by degrees to its proper and natural level, and will resume those passions that seem the most adapted to its present condition. The primitive Christians were dead to the business and pleasures of the world; but their love of action, which could never be entirely extinguished, soon revived, and found a new occupation in the government of the church. A separate society, which attacked the established religion of the empire, was obliged to adopt some form of internal policy, and to appoint a sufficient number of ministers, intrusted not only with the spiritual functions, but even with the temporal direction of the Christian commonwealth. The safety of that society, its honor, its aggrandizement, were productive, even in the most pious minds, of a spirit of patriotism, such as the first of the Romans had felt for the republic, and sometimes of a similar indifference, in the use of whatever means might probably conduce to so desirable an end. The ambition of raising themselves or their friends to the honors and offices of the church, was disguised by the laudable intention of devoting to the public benefit the power and consideration, which, for that purpose only, it became their duty to solicit. In the exercise of their functions, they were frequently called upon to detect the errors of heresy or the arts of faction, to oppose the designs of perfidious brethren, to stigmatize their characters with deserved infamy, and to expel them from the bosom of a society whose peace and happiness they had attempted to disturb. The ecclesiastical governors of the Christians were taught to unite the wisdom of the serpent with the innocence of the dove; but as the former was refined, so the latter was insensibly corrupted, by the habits of government. If the church as well as in the world, the persons who were placed in any public station rendered themselves considerable by their eloquence and firmness, by their knowledge of mankind, and by their dexterity in business; and while they concealed from others, and perhaps from themselves, the secret motives of their conduct, they too frequently relapsed into all the turbulent passions of active life, which were tinctured with an additional degree of bitterness and obstinacy from the infusion of spiritual zeal.

The government of the church has often been the subject, as well as the prize, of religious contention. The hostile disputants of Rome, of Paris, of Oxford, and of Geneva, have alike struggled to reduce the primitive and apostolic model [104] to the respective standards of their own policy. The few who have pursued this inquiry with more candor and impartiality, are of opinion, [105] that the apostles declined the office of legislation, and rather chose to endure some partial scandals and divisions, than to exclude the Christians of a future age from the liberty of varying their forms of ecclesiastical government according to the changes of times and circumstances. The scheme of policy, which, under their approbation, was adopted for the use of the first century, may be discovered from the practice of Jerusalem, of Ephesus, or of Corinth. The societies which were instituted in the cities of the Roman empire, were united only by the ties of faith and charity. Independence and equality formed the basis of their internal constitution. The want of discipline and human learning was supplied by the occasional assistance of the prophets, [106] who were called to that function without distinction of age, of sex, [106/1] or of natural abilities, and who, as often as they felt the divine impulse, poured forth the effusions of the Spirit in the assembly of the faithful. But these extraordinary gifts were frequently abused or misapplied by the prophetic teachers. They displayed them at an improper season, presumptuously disturbed the service of the assembly, and, by their pride or mistaken zeal, they introduced, particularly into the apostolic church of Corinth, a long and melancholy train of disorders. [107] As the institution of prophets became useless, and even pernicious, their powers were withdrawn, and their office abolished. The public functions of religion were solely intrusted to the established ministers of the church, the bishops and the presbyters; two appellations which, in their first origin, appear to have distinguished the same office and the same order of persons. The name of Presbyter was expressive of their age, or rather of their gravity and wisdom. The title of Bishop denoted their inspection over the faith and manners of the Christians who were committed to their pastoral care. In proportion to the respective numbers of the faithful, a larger or smaller number of these episcopal presbyters guided each infant congregation with equal authority and with united counsels. [108]

[Footnote 104: The aristocratical party in France, as well as in England, has strenuously maintained the divine origin of bishops. But the Calvinistical presbyters were impatient of a superior; and the Roman Pontiff refused to acknowledge an equal. See Fra Paolo.]

[Footnote 105: In the history of the Christian hierarchy, I have, for the most part, followed the learned and candid Mosheim.]

[Footnote 106: For the prophets of the primitive church, see Mosheim, Dissertationes ad Hist. Eccles. pertinentes, tom. ii. p. 132—208.]

[Footnote 106/1: St. Paul distinctly reproves the intrusion of females into the prophets office. 1 Cor. xiv. 34, 35. 1 Tim. ii. 11.—M.]

[Footnote 107: See the epistles of St. Paul, and of Clemens, to the Corinthians. Note: The first ministers established in the church were the deacons, appointed at Jerusalem, seven in number; they were charged with the distribution of the alms; even females had a share in this employment. After the deacons came the elders or priests, charged with the maintenance of order and decorum in the community, and to act every where in its name. The bishops were afterwards charged to watch over the faith and the instruction of the disciples: the apostles themselves appointed several bishops. Tertullian, (adv. Marium, c. v.,) Clement of Alexandria, and many fathers of the second and third century, do not permit us to doubt this fact. The equality of rank between these different functionaries did not prevent their functions being, even in their origin, distinct; they became subsequently still more so. See Plank, Geschichte der Christ. Kirch. Verfassung., vol. i. p. 24.—G. On this extremely obscure subject, which has been so much perplexed by passion and interest, it is impossible to justify any opinion without entering into long and controversial details.—It must be admitted, in opposition to Plank, that in the New Testament, several words are sometimes indiscriminately used. (Acts xx. v. 17, comp. with 28 Tit. i. 5 and 7. Philip. i. 1.) But it is as clear, that as soon as we can discern the form of church government, at a period closely bordering upon, if not within, the apostolic age, it appears with a bishop at the head of each community, holding some superiority over the presbyters. Whether he was, as Gibbon from Mosheim supposes, merely an elective head of the College of Presbyters, (for this we have, in fact, no valid authority,) or whether his distinct functions were established on apostolic authority, is still contested. The universal submission to this episcopacy, in every part of the Christian world appears to me strongly to favor the latter view.—M.]

[Footnote 108: Hooker's Ecclesiastical Polity, l. vii.]

But the most perfect equality of freedom requires the directing hand of a superior magistrate: and the order of public deliberations soon introduces the office of a president, invested at least with the authority of collecting the sentiments, and of executing the resolutions, of the assembly. A regard for the public tranquillity, which would so frequently have been interrupted by annual or by occasional elections, induced the primitive Christians to constitute an honorable and perpetual magistracy, and to choose one of the wisest and most holy among their presbyterians to execute, during his life, the duties of their ecclesiastical governor. It was under these circumstances that the lofty title of Bishop began to raise itself above the humble appellation of Presbyter; and while the latter remained the most natural distinction for the members of every Christian senate, the former was appropriated to the dignity of its new president. [109] The advantages of this episcopal form of government, which appears to have been introduced before the end of the first century, [110] were so obvious, and so important for the future greatness, as well as the present peace, of Christianity, that it was adopted without delay by all the societies which were already scattered over the empire, had acquired in a very early period the sanction of antiquity, [111] and is still revered by the most powerful churches, both of the East and of the West, as a primitive and even as a divine establishment. [112] It is needless to observe, that the pious and humble presbyters, who were first dignified with the episcopal title, could not possess, and would probably have rejected, the power and pomp which now encircles the tiara of the Roman pontiff, or the mitre of a German prelate. But we may define, in a few words, the narrow limits of their original jurisdiction, which was chiefly of a spiritual, though in some instances of a temporal nature. [113] It consisted in the administration of the sacraments and discipline of the church, the superintendency of religious ceremonies, which imperceptibly increased in number and variety, the consecration of ecclesiastical ministers, to whom the bishop assigned their respective functions, the management of the public fund, and the determination of all such differences as the faithful were unwilling to expose before the tribunal of an idolatrous judge. These powers, during a short period, were exercised according to the advice of the presbyteral college, and with the consent and approbation of the assembly of Christians. The primitive bishops were considered only as the first of their equals, and the honorable servants of a free people. Whenever the episcopal chair became vacant by death, a new president was chosen among the presbyters by the suffrages of the whole congregation, every member of which supposed himself invested with a sacred and sacerdotal character. [114]

[Footnote 109: See Jerome and Titum, c. i. and Epistol. 85, (in the Benedictine edition, 101,) and the elaborate apology of Blondel, pro sententia Hieronymi. The ancient state, as it is described by Jerome, of the bishop and presbyters of Alexandria, receives a remarkable confirmation from the patriarch Eutychius, (Annal. tom. i. p. 330, Vers Pocock;) whose testimony I know not how to reject, in spite of all the objections of the learned Pearson in his Vindiciae Ignatianae, part i. c. 11.]

[Footnote 110: See the introduction to the Apocalypse. Bishops, under the name of angels, were already instituted in the seven cities of Asia. And yet the epistle of Clemens (which is probably of as ancient a date) does not lead us to discover any traces of episcopacy either at Corinth or Rome.]

[Footnote 111: Nulla Ecclesia sine Episcopo, has been a fact as well as a maxim since the time of Tertullian and Irenaeus.]

[Footnote 112: After we have passed the difficulties of the first century, we find the episcopal government universally established, till it was interrupted by the republican genius of the Swiss and German reformers.]

[Footnote 113: See Mosheim in the first and second centuries. Ignatius (ad Smyrnaeos, c. 3, &c.) is fond of exalting the episcopal dignity. Le Clerc (Hist. Eccles. p. 569) very bluntly censures his conduct, Mosheim, with a more critical judgment, (p. 161,) suspects the purity even of the smaller epistles.]

[Footnote 114: Nonne et Laici sacerdotes sumus? Tertullian, Exhort. ad Castitat. c. 7. As the human heart is still the same, several of the observations which Mr. Hume has made on Enthusiasm, (Essays, vol. i. p. 76, quarto edit.) may be applied even to real inspiration. Note: This expression was employed by the earlier Christian writers in the sense used by St. Peter, 1 Ep ii. 9. It was the sanctity and virtue not the power of priesthood, in which all Christians were to be equally distinguished.—M.]

Such was the mild and equal constitution by which the Christians were governed more than a hundred years after the death of the apostles. Every society formed within itself a separate and independent republic; and although the most distant of these little states maintained a mutual as well as friendly intercourse of letters and deputations, the Christian world was not yet connected by any supreme authority or legislative assembly. As the numbers of the faithful were gradually multiplied, they discovered the advantages that might result from a closer union of their interest and designs. Towards the end of the second century, the churches of Greece and Asia adopted the useful institutions of provincial synods, [114/1] and they may justly be supposed to have borrowed the model of a representative council from the celebrated examples of their own country, the Amphictyons, the Achaean league, or the assemblies of the Ionian cities. It was soon established as a custom and as a law, that the bishops of the independent churches should meet in the capital of the province at the stated periods of spring and autumn. Their deliberations were assisted by the advice of a few distinguished presbyters, and moderated by the presence of a listening multitude. [115] Their decrees, which were styled Canons, regulated every important controversy of faith and discipline; and it was natural to believe that a liberal effusion of the Holy Spirit would be poured on the united assembly of the delegates of the Christian people. The institution of synods was so well suited to private ambition, and to public interest, that in the space of a few years it was received throughout the whole empire. A regular correspondence was established between the provincial councils, which mutually communicated and approved their respective proceedings; and the catholic church soon assumed the form, and acquired the strength, of a great foederative republic. [116]

[Footnote 114/1: The synods were not the first means taken by the insulated churches to enter into communion and to assume a corporate character. The dioceses were first formed by the union of several country churches with a church in a city: many churches in one city uniting among themselves, or joining a more considerable church, became metropolitan. The dioceses were not formed before the beginning of the second century: before that time the Christians had not established sufficient churches in the country to stand in need of that union. It is towards the middle of the same century that we discover the first traces of the metropolitan constitution. (Probably the country churches were founded in general by missionaries from those in the city, and would preserve a natural connection with the parent church.)— M. —The provincial synods did not commence till towards the middle of the third century, and were not the first synods. History gives us distinct notions of the synods, held towards the end of the second century, at Ephesus at Jerusalem, at Pontus, and at Rome, to put an end to the disputes which had arisen between the Latin and Asiatic churches about the celebration of Easter. But these synods were not subject to any regular form or periodical return; this regularity was first established with the provincial synods, which were formed by a union of the bishops of a district, subject to a metropolitan. Plank, p. 90. Geschichte der Christ. Kirch. Verfassung—G]

[Footnote 115: Acta Concil. Carthag. apud Cyprian. edit. Fell, p. 158. This council was composed of eighty-seven bishops from the provinces of Mauritania, Numidia, and Africa; some presbyters and deacons assisted at the assembly; praesente plebis maxima parte.]

[Footnote 116: Aguntur praeterea per Graecias illas, certis in locis concilia, &c Tertullian de Jejuniis, c. 13. The African mentions it as a recent and foreign institution. The coalition of the Christian churches is very ably explained by Mosheim, p. 164 170.]

As the legislative authority of the particular churches was insensibly superseded by the use of councils, the bishops obtained by their alliance a much larger share of executive and arbitrary power; and as soon as they were connected by a sense of their common interest, they were enabled to attack with united vigor, the original rights of their clergy and people. The prelates of the third century imperceptibly changed the language of exhortation into that of command, scattered the seeds of future usurpations, and supplied, by scripture allegories and declamatory rhetoric, their deficiency of force and of reason. They exalted the unity and power of the church, as it was represented in the Episcopal Office, of which every bishop enjoyed an equal and undivided portion. [117] Princes and magistrates, it was often repeated, might boast an earthly claim to a transitory dominion; it was the episcopal authority alone which was derived from the Deity, and extended itself over this and over another world. The bishops were the vicegerents of Christ, the successors of the apostles, and the mystic substitutes of the high priest of the Mosaic law. Their exclusive privilege of conferring the sacerdotal character, invaded the freedom both of clerical and of popular elections; and if, in the administration of the church, they still consulted the judgment of the presbyters, or the inclination of the people, they most carefully inculcated the merit of such a voluntary condescension. The bishops acknowledged the supreme authority which resided in the assembly of their brethren; but in the government of his peculiar diocese, each of them exacted from his flock the same implicit obedience as if that favorite metaphor had been literally just, and as if the shepherd had been of a more exalted nature than that of his sheep. [118] This obedience, however, was not imposed without some efforts on one side, and some resistance on the other. The democratical part of the constitution was, in many places, very warmly supported by the zealous or interested opposition of the inferior clergy. But their patriotism received the ignominious epithets of faction and schism; and the episcopal cause was indebted for its rapid progress to the labors of many active prelates, who, like Cyprian of Carthage, could reconcile the arts of the most ambitious statesman with the Christian virtues which seem adapted to the character of a saint and martyr. [119]

[Footnote 117: Cyprian, in his admired treatise De Unitate Ecclesiae. p. 75—86]

[Footnote 118: We may appeal to the whole tenor of Cyprian's conduct, of his doctrine, and of his epistles. Le Clerc, in a short life of Cyprian, (Bibliotheque Universelle, tom. xii. p. 207—378,) has laid him open with great freedom and accuracy.]

[Footnote 119: If Novatus, Felicissimus, &c., whom the Bishop of Carthage expelled from his church, and from Africa, were not the most detestable monsters of wickedness, the zeal of Cyprian must occasionally have prevailed over his veracity. For a very just account of these obscure quarrels, see Mosheim, p. 497—512.]

The same causes which at first had destroyed the equality of the presbyters introduced among the bishops a preeminence of rank, and from thence a superiority of jurisdiction. As often as in the spring and autumn they met in provincial synod, the difference of personal merit and reputation was very sensibly felt among the members of the assembly, and the multitude was governed by the wisdom and eloquence of the few. But the order of public proceedings required a more regular and less invidious distinction; the office of perpetual presidents in the councils of each province was conferred on the bishops of the principal city; and these aspiring prelates, who soon acquired the lofty titles of Metropolitans and Primates, secretly prepared themselves to usurp over their episcopal brethren the same authority which the bishops had so lately assumed above the college of presbyters. [120] Nor was it long before an emulation of preeminence and power prevailed among the Metropolitans themselves, each of them affecting to display, in the most pompous terms, the temporal honors and advantages of the city over which he presided; the numbers and opulence of the Christians who were subject to their pastoral care; the saints and martyrs who had arisen among them; and the purity with which they preserved the tradition of the faith, as it had been transmitted through a series of orthodox bishops from the apostle or the apostolic disciple, to whom the foundation of their church was ascribed. [121] From every cause, either of a civil or of an ecclesiastical nature, it was easy to foresee that Rome must enjoy the respect, and would soon claim the obedience of the provinces. The society of the faithful bore a just proportion to the capital of the empire; and the Roman church was the greatest, the most numerous, and, in regard to the West, the most ancient of all the Christian establishments, many of which had received their religion from the pious labors of her missionaries. Instead of one apostolic founder, the utmost boast of Antioch, of Ephesus, or of Corinth, the banks of the Tyber were supposed to have been honored with the preaching and martyrdom of the two most eminent among the apostles; [122] and the bishops of Rome very prudently claimed the inheritance of whatsoever prerogatives were attributed either to the person or to the office of St. Peter. [123] The bishops of Italy and of the provinces were disposed to allow them a primacy of order and association (such was their very accurate expression) in the Christian aristocracy. [124] But the power of a monarch was rejected with abhorrence, and the aspiring genius of Rome experienced from the nations of Asia and Africa a more vigorous resistance to her spiritual, than she had formerly done to her temporal, dominion. The patriotic Cyprian, who ruled with the most absolute sway the church of Carthage and the provincial synods, opposed with resolution and success the ambition of the Roman pontiff, artfully connected his own cause with that of the eastern bishops, and, like Hannibal, sought out new allies in the heart of Asia. [125] If this Punic war was carried on without any effusion of blood, it was owing much less to the moderation than to the weakness of the contending prelates. Invectives and excommunications were their only weapons; and these, during the progress of the whole controversy, they hurled against each other with equal fury and devotion. The hard necessity of censuring either a pope, or a saint and martyr, distresses the modern Catholics whenever they are obliged to relate the particulars of a dispute in which the champions of religion indulged such passions as seem much more adapted to the senate or to the camp. [126]

[Footnote 120: Mosheim, p. 269, 574. Dupin, Antiquae Eccles. Disciplin. p. 19, 20.]

[Footnote 121: Tertullian, in a distinct treatise, has pleaded against the heretics the right of prescription, as it was held by the apostolic churches.]

[Footnote 122: The journey of St. Peter to Rome is mentioned by most of the ancients, (see Eusebius, ii. 25,) maintained by all the Catholics, allowed by some Protestants, (see Pearson and Dodwell de Success. Episcop. Roman,) but has been vigorously attacked by Spanheim, (Miscellanes Sacra, iii. 3.) According to Father Hardouin, the monks of the thirteenth century, who composed the Aeneid, represented St. Peter under the allegorical character of the Trojan hero. Note: It is quite clear that, strictly speaking, the church of Rome was not founded by either of these apostles. St. Paul's Epistle to the Romans proves undeniably the flourishing state of the church before his visit to the city; and many Roman Catholic writers have given up the impracticable task of reconciling with chronology any visit of St. Peter to Rome before the end of the reign of Claudius, or the beginning of that of Nero.—M.]

[Footnote 123: It is in French only that the famous allusion to St. Peter's name is exact. Tu es Pierre, et sur cette pierre.—The same is imperfect in Greek, Latin, Italian, &c., and totally unintelligible in our Tentonic languages. Note: It is exact in Syro-Chaldaic, the language in which it was spoken by Jesus Christ. (St. Matt. xvi. 17.) Peter was called Cephas; and cepha signifies base, foundation, rock—G.]

[Footnote 124: Irenaeus adv. Haereses, iii. 3. Tertullian de Praescription. c. 36, and Cyprian, Epistol. 27, 55, 71, 75. Le Clere (Hist. Eccles. p. 764) and Mosheim (p. 258, 578) labor in the interpretation of these passages. But the loose and rhetorical style of the fathers often appears favorable to the pretensions of Rome.]

[Footnote 125: See the sharp epistle from Firmilianus, bishop of Caesarea, to Stephen, bishop of Rome, ap. Cyprian, Epistol. 75.]

[Footnote 126: Concerning this dispute of the rebaptism of heretics, see the epistles of Cyprian, and the seventh book of Eusebius.]

The progress of the ecclesiastical authority gave birth to the memorable distinction of the laity and of the clergy, which had been unknown to the Greeks and Romans. [127] The former of these appellations comprehended the body of the Christian people; the latter, according to the signification of the word, was appropriated to the chosen portion that had been set apart for the service of religion; a celebrated order of men, which has furnished the most important, though not always the most edifying, subjects for modern history. Their mutual hostilities sometimes disturbed the peace of the infant church, but their zeal and activity were united in the common cause, and the love of power, which (under the most artful disguises) could insinuate itself into the breasts of bishops and martyrs, animated them to increase the number of their subjects, and to enlarge the limits of the Christian empire. They were destitute of any temporal force, and they were for a long time discouraged and oppressed, rather than assisted, by the civil magistrate; but they had acquired, and they employed within their own society, the two most efficacious instruments of government, rewards and punishments; the former derived from the pious liberality, the latter from the devout apprehensions, of the faithful.

[Footnote 127: For the origin of these words, see Mosheim, p. 141. Spanheim, Hist. Ecclesiast. p. 633. The distinction of Clerus and laicus was established before the time of Tertullian.]

PART VII

I. The community of goods, which had so agreeably amused the imagination of Plato, [128] and which subsisted in some degree among the austere sect of the Essenians, [129] was adopted for a short time in the primitive church. The fervor of the first proselytes prompted them to sell those worldly possessions, which they despised, to lay the price of them at the feet of the apostles, and to content themselves with receiving an equal share out of the general distribution. [130] The progress of the Christian religion relaxed, and gradually abolished, this generous institution, which, in hands less pure than those of the apostles, would too soon have been corrupted and abused by the returning selfishness of human nature; and the converts who embraced the new religion were permitted to retain the possession of their patrimony, to receive legacies and inheritances, and to increase their separate property by all the lawful means of trade and industry. Instead of an absolute sacrifice, a moderate proportion was accepted by the ministers of the gospel; and in their weekly or monthly assemblies, every believer, according to the exigency of the occasion, and the measure of his wealth and piety, presented his voluntary offering for the use of the common fund. [131] Nothing, however inconsiderable, was refused; but it was diligently inculcated; that, in the article of Tithes, the Mosaic law was still of divine obligation; and that since the Jews, under a less perfect discipline, had been commanded to pay a tenth part of all that they possessed, it would become the disciples of Christ to distinguish themselves by a superior degree of liberality, [132] and to acquire some merit by resigning a superfluous treasure, which must so soon be annihilated with the world itself. [133] It is almost unnecessary to observe, that the revenue of each particular church, which was of so uncertain and fluctuating a nature, must have varied with the poverty or the opulence of the faithful, as they were dispersed in obscure villages, or collected in the great cities of the empire. In the time of the emperor Decius, it was the opinion of the magistrates, that the Christians of Rome were possessed of very considerable wealth; that vessels of gold and silver were used in their religious worship, and that many among their proselytes had sold their lands and houses to increase the public riches of the sect, at the expense, indeed, of their unfortunate children, who found themselves beggars, because their parents had been saints. [134] We should listen with distrust to the suspicions of strangers and enemies: on this occasion, however, they receive a very specious and probable color from the two following circumstances, the only ones that have reached our knowledge, which define any precise sums, or convey any distinct idea. Almost at the same period, the bishop of Carthage, from a society less opulent than that of Rome, collected a hundred thousand sesterces, (above eight hundred and fifty pounds sterling,) on a sudden call of charity to redeem the brethren of Numidia, who had been carried away captives by the barbarians of the desert. [135] About a hundred years before the reign of Decius, the Roman church had received, in a single donation, the sum of two hundred thousand sesterces from a stranger of Pontus, who proposed to fix his residence in the capital. [136] These oblations, for the most part, were made in money; nor was the society of Christians either desirous or capable of acquiring, to any considerable degree, the encumbrance of landed property. It had been provided by several laws, which were enacted with the same design as our statutes of mortmain, that no real estates should be given or bequeathed to any corporate body, without either a special privilege or a particular dispensation from the emperor or from the senate; [137] who were seldom disposed to grant them in favor of a sect, at first the object of their contempt, and at last of their fears and jealousy. A transaction, however, is related under the reign of Alexander Severus, which discovers that the restraint was sometimes eluded or suspended, and that the Christians were permitted to claim and to possess lands within the limits of Rome itself. [138] The progress of Christianity, and the civil confusion of the empire, contributed to relax the severity of the laws; and before the close of the third century many considerable estates were bestowed on the opulent churches of Rome, Milan, Carthage, Antioch, Alexandria, and the other great cities of Italy and the provinces.

[Footnote 128: The community instituted by Plato is more perfect than that which Sir Thomas More had imagined for his Utopia. The community of women, and that of temporal goods, may be considered as inseparable parts of the same system.]

[Footnote 129: Joseph. Antiquitat. xviii. 2. Philo, de Vit. Contemplativ.]

[Footnote 130: See the Acts of the Apostles, c. 2, 4, 5, with Grotius's Commentary. Mosheim, in a particular dissertation, attacks the common opinion with very inconclusive arguments. Note: This is not the general judgment on Mosheim's learned dissertation. There is no trace in the latter part of the New Testament of this community of goods, and many distinct proofs of the contrary. All exhortations to almsgiving would have been unmeaning if property had been in common—M.]

[Footnote 131: Justin Martyr, Apolog. Major, c. 89. Tertullian, Apolog. c. 39.]

[Footnote 132: Irenaeus ad Haeres. l. iv. c. 27, 34. Origen in Num. Hom. ii Cyprian de Unitat. Eccles. Constitut. Apostol. l. ii. c. 34, 35, with the notes of Cotelerius. The Constitutions introduce this divine precept, by declaring that priests are as much above kings as the soul is above the body. Among the tithable articles, they enumerate corn, wine, oil, and wool. On this interesting subject, consult Prideaux's History of Tithes, and Fra Paolo delle Materie Beneficiarie; two writers of a very different character.]

[Footnote 133: The same opinion which prevailed about the year one thousand, was productive of the same effects. Most of the Donations express their motive, "appropinquante mundi fine." See Mosheim's General History of the Church, vol. i. p. 457.]

[Footnote 134: Tum summa cura est fratribus (Ut sermo testatur loquax.) Offerre, fundis venditis Sestertiorum millia. Addicta avorum praedia Foedis sub auctionibus, Successor exheres gemit Sanctis egens Parentibus. Haec occuluntur abditis Ecclesiarum in angulis. Et summa pietas creditur Nudare dulces liberos.—Prudent. Hymn 2. The subsequent conduct of the deacon Laurence only proves how proper a use was made of the wealth of the Roman church; it was undoubtedly very considerable; but Fra Paolo (c. 3) appears to exaggerate, when he supposes that the successors of Commodus were urged to persecute the Christians by their own avarice, or that of their Praetorian praefects.]

[Footnote 135: Cyprian, Epistol. 62.]

[Footnote 136: Tertullian de Praescriptione, c. 30.]

[Footnote 137: Diocletian gave a rescript, which is only a declaration of the old law; "Collegium, si nullo speciali privilegio subnixum sit, haereditatem capere non posse, dubium non est." Fra Paolo (c. 4) thinks that these regulations had been much neglected since the reign of Valerian.]

[Footnote 138: Hist. August. p. 131. The ground had been public; and was row disputed between the society of Christians and that of butchers. Note : Carponarii, rather victuallers.—M.]

The bishop was the natural steward of the church; the public stock was intrusted to his care without account or control; the presbyters were confined to their spiritual functions, and the more dependent order of the deacons was solely employed in the management and distribution of the ecclesiastical revenue. [139] If we may give credit to the vehement declamations of Cyprian, there were too many among his African brethren, who, in the execution of their charge, violated every precept, not only of evangelical perfection, but even of moral virtue. By some of these unfaithful stewards the riches of the church were lavished in sensual pleasures; by others they were perverted to the purposes of private gain, of fraudulent purchases, and of rapacious usury. [140] But as long as the contributions of the Christian people were free and unconstrained, the abuse of their confidence could not be very frequent, and the general uses to which their liberality was applied reflected honor on the religious society. A decent portion was reserved for the maintenance of the bishop and his clergy; a sufficient sum was allotted for the expenses of the public worship, of which the feasts of love, the agapoe, as they were called, constituted a very pleasing part. The whole remainder was the sacred patrimony of the poor. According to the discretion of the bishop, it was distributed to support widows and orphans, the lame, the sick, and the aged of the community; to comfort strangers and pilgrims, and to alleviate the misfortunes of prisoners and captives, more especially when their sufferings had been occasioned by their firm attachment to the cause of religion. [141] A generous intercourse of charity united the most distant provinces, and the smaller congregations were cheerfully assisted by the alms of their more opulent brethren. [142] Such an institution, which paid less regard to the merit than to the distress of the object, very materially conduced to the progress of Christianity. The Pagans, who were actuated by a sense of humanity, while they derided the doctrines, acknowledged the benevolence, of the new sect. [143] The prospect of immediate relief and of future protection allured into its hospitable bosom many of those unhappy persons whom the neglect of the world would have abandoned to the miseries of want, of sickness, and of old age. There is some reason likewise to believe that great numbers of infants, who, according to the inhuman practice of the times, had been exposed by their parents, were frequently rescued from death, baptized, educated, and maintained by the piety of the Christians, and at the expense of the public treasure. [144]

[Footnote 139: Constitut. Apostol. ii. 35.]

[Footnote 140: Cyprian de Lapsis, p. 89. Epistol. 65. The charge is confirmed by the 19th and 20th canon of the council of Illiberis.]

[Footnote 141: See the apologies of Justin, Tertullian, &c.]

[Footnote 142: The wealth and liberality of the Romans to their most distant brethren is gratefully celebrated by Dionysius of Corinth, ap. Euseb. l. iv. c. 23.]

[Footnote 143: See Lucian iu Peregrin. Julian (Epist. 49) seems mortified that the Christian charity maintains not only their own, but likewise the heathen poor.]

[Footnote 144: Such, at least, has been the laudable conduct of more modern missionaries, under the same circumstances. Above three thousand new-born infants are annually exposed in the streets of Pekin. See Le Comte, Memoires sur la Chine, and the Recherches sur les Chinois et les Egyptians, tom. i. p. 61.]

II. It is the undoubted right of every society to exclude from its communion and benefits such among its members as reject or violate those regulations which have been established by general consent. In the exercise of this power, the censures of the Christian church were chiefly directed against scandalous sinners, and particularly those who were guilty of murder, of fraud, or of incontinence; against the authors or the followers of any heretical opinions which had been condemned by the judgment of the episcopal order; and against those unhappy persons, who, whether from choice or compulsion, had polluted themselves after their baptism by any act of idolatrous worship. The consequences of excommunication were of a temporal as well as a spiritual nature. The Christian against whom it was pronounced, was deprived of any part in the oblations of the faithful. The ties both of religious and of private friendship were dissolved: he found himself a profane object of abhorrence to the persons whom he the most esteemed, or by whom he had been the most tenderly beloved; and as far as an expulsion from a respectable society could imprint on his character a mark of disgrace, he was shunned or suspected by the generality of mankind. The situation of these unfortunate exiles was in itself very painful and melancholy; but, as it usually happens, their apprehensions far exceeded their sufferings. The benefits of the Christian communion were those of eternal life; nor could they erase from their minds the awful opinion, that to those ecclesiastical governors by whom they were condemned, the Deity had committed the keys of Hell and of Paradise. The heretics, indeed, who might be supported by the consciousness of their intentions, and by the flattering hope that they alone had discovered the true path of salvation, endeavored to regain, in their separate assemblies, those comforts, temporal as well as spiritual, which they no longer derived from the great society of Christians. But almost all those who had reluctantly yielded to the power of vice or idolatry were sensible of their fallen condition, and anxiously desirous of being restored to the benefits of the Christian communion.

With regard to the treatment of these penitents, two opposite opinions, the one of justice, the other of mercy, divided the primitive church. The more rigid and inflexible casuists refused them forever, and without exception, the meanest place in the holy community, which they had disgraced or deserted; and leaving them to the remorse of a guilty conscience, indulged them only with a faint ray of hope that the contrition of their life and death might possibly be accepted by the Supreme Being. [145] A milder sentiment was embraced in practice as well as in theory, by the purest and most respectable of the Christian churches. [146] The gates of reconciliation and of heaven were seldom shut against the returning penitent; but a severe and solemn form of discipline was instituted, which, while it served to expiate his crime, might powerfully deter the spectators from the imitation of his example. Humbled by a public confession, emaciated by fasting and clothed in sackcloth, the penitent lay prostrate at the door of the assembly, imploring with tears the pardon of his offences, and soliciting the prayers of the faithful. [147] If the fault was of a very heinous nature, whole years of penance were esteemed an inadequate satisfaction to the divine justice; and it was always by slow and painful gradations that the sinner, the heretic, or the apostate, was readmitted into the bosom of the church. A sentence of perpetual excommunication was, however, reserved for some crimes of an extraordinary magnitude, and particularly for the inexcusable relapses of those penitents who had already experienced and abused the clemency of their ecclesiastical superiors. According to the circumstances or the number of the guilty, the exercise of the Christian discipline was varied by the discretion of the bishops. The councils of Ancyra and Illiberis were held about the same time, the one in Galatia, the other in Spain; but their respective canons, which are still extant, seem to breathe a very different spirit. The Galatian, who after his baptism had repeatedly sacrificed to idols, might obtain his pardon by a penance of seven years; and if he had seduced others to imitate his example, only three years more were added to the term of his exile. But the unhappy Spaniard, who had committed the same offence, was deprived of the hope of reconciliation, even in the article of death; and his idolatry was placed at the head of a list of seventeen other crimes, against which a sentence no less terrible was pronounced. Among these we may distinguish the inexpiable guilt of calumniating a bishop, a presbyter, or even a deacon. [148]

[Footnote 145: The Montanists and the Novatians, who adhered to this opinion with the greatest rigor and obstinacy, found themselves at last in the number of excommunicated heretics. See the learned and copious Mosheim, Secul. ii. and iii.]

[Footnote 146: Dionysius ap. Euseb. iv. 23. Cyprian, de Lapsis.]

[Footnote 147: Cave's Primitive Christianity, part iii. c. 5. The admirers of antiquity regret the loss of this public penance.]

[Footnote 148: See in Dupin, Bibliotheque Ecclesiastique, tom. ii. p. 304—313, a short but rational exposition of the canons of those councils, which were assembled in the first moments of tranquillity, after the persecution of Diocletian. This persecution had been much less severely felt in Spain than in Galatia; a difference which may, in some measure account for the contrast of their regulations.]

The well-tempered mixture of liberality and rigor, the judicious dispensation of rewards and punishments, according to the maxims of policy as well as justice, constituted the human strength of the church. The Bishops, whose paternal care extended itself to the government of both worlds, were sensible of the importance of these prerogatives; and covering their ambition with the fair pretence of the love of order, they were jealous of any rival in the exercise of a discipline so necessary to prevent the desertion of those troops which had enlisted themselves under the banner of the cross, and whose numbers every day became more considerable. From the imperious declamations of Cyprian, we should naturally conclude that the doctrines of excommunication and penance formed the most essential part of religion; and that it was much less dangerous for the disciples of Christ to neglect the observance of the moral duties, than to despise the censures and authority of their bishops. Sometimes we might imagine that we were listening to the voice of Moses, when he commanded the earth to open, and to swallow up, in consuming flames, the rebellious race which refused obedience to the priesthood of Aaron; and we should sometimes suppose that we hear a Roman consul asserting the majesty of the republic, and declaring his inflexible resolution to enforce the rigor of the laws. "If such irregularities are suffered with impunity," (it is thus that the bishop of Carthage chides the lenity of his colleague,) "if such irregularities are suffered, there is an end of Episcopal Vigor; [149] an end of the sublime and divine power of governing the Church, an end of Christianity itself." Cyprian had renounced those temporal honors, which it is probable he would never have obtained; but the acquisition of such absolute command over the consciences and understanding of a congregation, however obscure or despised by the world, is more truly grateful to the pride of the human heart, than the possession of the most despotic power, imposed by arms and conquest on a reluctant people. [Footnote 149/1]: Gibbon has been accused of injustice to the character of Cyprian, as exalting the "censures and authority of the church above the observance of the moral duties." Felicissimus had been condemned by a synod of bishops, (non tantum mea, sed plurimorum coepiscorum, sententia condemnatum,) on the charge not only of schism, but of embezzlement of public money, the debauching of virgins, and frequent acts of adultery. His violent menaces had extorted his readmission into the church, against which Cyprian protests with much vehemence: ne pecuniae commissae sibi fraudator, ne stuprator virginum, ne matrimoniorum multorum depopulator et corruptor, ultra adhuc sponsam Christi incorruptam praesentiae suae dedecore, et impudica atque incesta contagione, violaret. See Chelsum's Remarks, p. 134. If these charges against Felicissimus were true, they were something more than "irregularities," A Roman censor would have been a fairer subject of comparison than a consul. On the other hand, it must be admitted that the charge of adultery deepens very rapidly as the controversy becomes more violent. It is first represented as a single act, recently detected, and which men of character were prepared to substantiate: adulterii etiam crimen accedit. quod patres nostri graves viri deprehendisse se nuntiaverunt, et probaturos se asseverarunt. Epist. xxxviii. The heretic has now darkened into a man of notorious and general profligacy. Nor can it be denied that of the whole long epistle, very far the larger and the more passionate part dwells on the breach of ecclesiastical unity rather than on the violation of Christian holiness.—M.]

[Footnote 149: Cyprian Epist. 69.]

[Footnote 149/1: This supposition appears unfounded: the birth and the talents of Cyprian might make us presume the contrary. Thascius Caecilius Cyprianus, Carthaginensis, artis oratoriae professione clarus, magnam sibi gloriam, opes, honores acquisivit, epularibus caenis et largis dapibus assuetus, pretiosa veste conspicuus, auro atque purpura fulgens, fascibus oblectatus et honoribus, stipatus clientium cuneis, frequentiore comitatu officii agminis honestatus, ut ipse de se loquitur in Epistola ad Donatum. See De Cave, Hist. Liter. b. i. p. 87.—G. Cave has rather embellished Cyprian's language.—M.]

In the course of this important, though perhaps tedious inquiry, I have attempted to display the secondary causes which so efficaciously assisted the truth of the Christian religion. If among these causes we have discovered any artificial ornaments, any accidental circumstances, or any mixture of error and passion, it cannot appear surprising that mankind should be the most sensibly affected by such motives as were suited to their imperfect nature. It was by the aid of these causes, exclusive zeal, the immediate expectation of another world, the claim of miracles, the practice of rigid virtue, and the constitution of the primitive church, that Christianity spread itself with so much success in the Roman empire. To the first of these the Christians were indebted for their invincible valor, which disdained to capitulate with the enemy whom they were resolved to vanquish. The three succeeding causes supplied their valor with the most formidable arms. The last of these causes united their courage, directed their arms, and gave their efforts that irresistible weight, which even a small band of well-trained and intrepid volunteers has so often possessed over an undisciplined multitude, ignorant of the subject, and careless of the event of the war. In the various religions of Polytheism, some wandering fanatics of Egypt and Syria, who addressed themselves to the credulous superstition of the populace, were perhaps the only order of priests [150] that derived their whole support and credit from their sacerdotal profession, and were very deeply affected by a personal concern for the safety or prosperity of their tutelar deities. The ministers of Polytheism, both in Rome and in the provinces, were, for the most part, men of a noble birth, and of an affluent fortune, who received, as an honorable distinction, the care of a celebrated temple, or of a public sacrifice, exhibited, very frequently at their own expense, the sacred games, [151] and with cold indifference performed the ancient rites, according to the laws and fashion of their country. As they were engaged in the ordinary occupations of life, their zeal and devotion were seldom animated by a sense of interest, or by the habits of an ecclesiastical character. Confined to their respective temples and cities, they remained without any connection of discipline or government; and whilst they acknowledged the supreme jurisdiction of the senate, of the college of pontiffs, and of the emperor, those civil magistrates contented themselves with the easy task of maintaining in peace and dignity the general worship of mankind. We have already seen how various, how loose, and how uncertain were the religious sentiments of Polytheists. They were abandoned, almost without control, to the natural workings of a superstitious fancy. The accidental circumstances of their life and situation determined the object as well as the degree of their devotion; and as long as their adoration was successively prostituted to a thousand deities, it was scarcely possible that their hearts could be susceptible of a very sincere or lively passion for any of them.

[Footnote 150: The arts, the manners, and the vices of the priests of the Syrian goddess are very humorously described by Apuleius, in the eighth book of his Metamorphosis.]

[Footnote 151: The office of Asiarch was of this nature, and it is frequently mentioned in Aristides, the Inscriptions, &c. It was annual and elective. None but the vainest citizens could desire the honor; none but the most wealthy could support the expense. See, in the Patres Apostol. tom. ii. p. 200, with how much indifference Philip the Asiarch conducted himself in the martyrdom of Polycarp. There were likewise Bithyniarchs, Lyciarchs, &c.]

When Christianity appeared in the world, even these faint and imperfect impressions had lost much of their original power. Human reason, which by its unassisted strength is incapable of perceiving the mysteries of faith, had already obtained an easy triumph over the folly of Paganism; and when Tertullian or Lactantius employ their labors in exposing its falsehood and extravagance, they are obliged to transcribe the eloquence of Cicero or the wit of Lucian. The contagion of these sceptical writings had been diffused far beyond the number of their readers. The fashion of incredulity was communicated from the philosopher to the man of pleasure or business, from the noble to the plebeian, and from the master to the menial slave who waited at his table, and who eagerly listened to the freedom of his conversation. On public occasions the philosophic part of mankind affected to treat with respect and decency the religious institutions of their country; but their secret contempt penetrated through the thin and awkward disguise; and even the people, when they discovered that their deities were rejected and derided by those whose rank or understanding they were accustomed to reverence, were filled with doubts and apprehensions concerning the truth of those doctrines, to which they had yielded the most implicit belief. The decline of ancient prejudice exposed a very numerous portion of human kind to the danger of a painful and comfortless situation. A state of scepticism and suspense may amuse a few inquisitive minds. But the practice of superstition is so congenial to the multitude, that if they are forcibly awakened, they still regret the loss of their pleasing vision. Their love of the marvellous and supernatural, their curiosity with regard to future events, and their strong propensity to extend their hopes and fears beyond the limits of the visible world, were the principal causes which favored the establishment of Polytheism. So urgent on the vulgar is the necessity of believing, that the fall of any system of mythology will most probably be succeeded by the introduction of some other mode of superstition. Some deities of a more recent and fashionable cast might soon have occupied the deserted temples of Jupiter and Apollo, if, in the decisive moment, the wisdom of Providence had not interposed a genuine revelation, fitted to inspire the most rational esteem and conviction, whilst, at the same time, it was adorned with all that could attract the curiosity, the wonder, and the veneration of the people. In their actual disposition, as many were almost disengaged from their artificial prejudices, but equally susceptible and desirous of a devout attachment; an object much less deserving would have been sufficient to fill the vacant place in their hearts, and to gratify the uncertain eagerness of their passions. Those who are inclined to pursue this reflection, instead of viewing with astonishment the rapid progress of Christianity, will perhaps be surprised that its success was not still more rapid and still more universal. It has been observed, with truth as well as propriety, that the conquests of Rome prepared and facilitated those of Christianity. In the second chapter of this work we have attempted to explain in what manner the most civilized provinces of Europe, Asia, and Africa were united under the dominion of one sovereign, and gradually connected by the most intimate ties of laws, of manners, and of language. The Jews of Palestine, who had fondly expected a temporal deliverer, gave so cold a reception to the miracles of the divine prophet, that it was found unnecessary to publish, or at least to preserve, any Hebrew gospel. [152] The authentic histories of the actions of Christ were composed in the Greek language, at a considerable distance from Jerusalem, and after the Gentile converts were grown extremely numerous. [153] As soon as those histories were translated into the Latin tongue, they were perfectly intelligible to all the subjects of Rome, excepting only to the peasants of Syria and Egypt, for whose benefit particular versions were afterwards made. The public highways, which had been constructed for the use of the legions, opened an easy passage for the Christian missionaries from Damascus to Corinth, and from Italy to the extremity of Spain or Britain; nor did those spiritual conquerors encounter any of the obstacles which usually retard or prevent the introduction of a foreign religion into a distant country. There is the strongest reason to believe, that before the reigns of Diocletian and Constantine, the faith of Christ had been preached in every province, and in all the great cities of the empire; but the foundation of the several congregations, the numbers of the faithful who composed them, and their proportion to the unbelieving multitude, are now buried in obscurity, or disguised by fiction and declamation. Such imperfect circumstances, however, as have reached our knowledge concerning the increase of the Christian name in Asia and Greece, in Egypt, in Italy, and in the West, we shall now proceed to relate, without neglecting the real or imaginary acquisitions which lay beyond the frontiers of the Roman empire.

[Footnote 152: The modern critics are not disposed to believe what the fathers almost unanimously assert, that St. Matthew composed a Hebrew gospel, of which only the Greek translation is extant. It seems, however, dangerous to reject their testimony. Note: Strong reasons appear to confirm this testimony. Papias, contemporary of the Apostle St. John, says positively that Matthew had written the discourses of Jesus Christ in Hebrew, and that each interpreted them as he could. This Hebrew was the Syro-Chaldaic dialect, then in use at Jerusalem: Origen, Irenaeus, Eusebius, Jerome, Epiphanius, confirm this statement. Jesus Christ preached himself in Syro-Chaldaic, as is proved by many words which he used, and which the Evangelists have taken the pains to translate. St. Paul, addressing the Jews, used the same language: Acts xxi. 40, xxii. 2, xxvi. 14. The opinions of some critics prove nothing against such undeniable testimonies. Moreover, their principal objection is, that St. Matthew quotes the Old Testament according to the Greek version of the LXX., which is inaccurate; for of ten quotations, found in his Gospel, seven are evidently taken from the Hebrew text; the threo others offer little that differ: moreover, the latter are not literal quotations. St. Jerome says positively, that, according to a copy which he had seen in the library of Caesarea, the quotations were made in Hebrew (in Catal.) More modern critics, among others Michaelis, do not entertain a doubt on the subject. The Greek version appears to have been made in the time of the apostles, as St. Jerome and St. Augustus affirm, perhaps by one of them.—G. —Among modern critics, Dr. Hug has asserted the Greek original of St. Matthew, but the general opinion of the most learned biblical writer, supports the view of M. Guizot.—M.]

[Footnote 153: Under the reigns of Nero and Domitian, and in the cities of Alexandria, Antioch, Rome, and Ephesus. See Mill. Prolegomena ad Nov. Testament, and Dr. Lardner's fair and extensive collection, vol. xv. Note: This question has, it is well known, been most elaborately discussed since the time of Gibbon. The Preface to the Translation of Schleier Macher's Version of St. Luke contains a very able summary of the various theories.—M.]

PART VIII

The rich provinces that extend from the Euphrates to the Ionian Sea, were the principal theatre on which the apostle of the Gentiles displayed his zeal and piety. The seeds of the gospel, which he had scattered in a fertile soil, were diligently cultivated by his disciples; and it should seem that, during the two first centuries, the most considerable body of Christians was contained within those limits. Among the societies which were instituted in Syria, none were more ancient or more illustrious than those of Damascus, of Berea or Aleppo, and of Antioch. The prophetic introduction of the Apocalypse has described and immortalized the seven churches of Asia; Ephesus, Smyrna, Pergamus, Thyatira, [154] Sardes, Laodicea and Philadelphia; and their colonies were soon diffused over that populous country. In a very early period, the islands of Cyprus and Crete, the provinces of Thrace and Macedonia, gave a favorable reception to the new religion; and Christian republics were soon founded in the cities of Corinth, of Sparta, and of Athens. [155] The antiquity of the Greek and Asiatic churches allowed a sufficient space of time for their increase and multiplication; and even the swarms of Gnostics and other heretics serve to display the flourishing condition of the orthodox church, since the appellation of hereties has always been applied to the less numerous party. To these domestic testimonies we may add the confession, the complaints, and the apprehensions of the Gentiles themselves. From the writings of Lucian, a philosopher who had studied mankind, and who describes their manners in the most lively colors, we may learn that, under the reign of Commodus, his native country of Pontus was filled with Epicureans and Christians. [156] Within fourscore years after the death of Christ, [157] the humane Pliny laments the magnitude of the evil which he vainly attempted to eradicate. In his very curious epistle to the emperor Trajan, he affirms, that the temples were almost deserted, that the sacred victims scarcely found any purchasers, and that the superstition had not only infected the cities, but had even spread itself into the villages and the open country of Pontus and Bithynia. [158]

[Footnote 154: The Alogians (Epiphanius de Haeres. 51) disputed the genuineness of the Apocalypse, because the church of Thyatira was not yet founded. Epiphanius, who allows the fact, extricates himself from the difficulty by ingeniously supposing that St. John wrote in the spirit of prophecy. See Abauzit, Discours sur l'Apocalypse.]

[Footnote 155: The epistles of Ignatius and Dionysius (ap. Euseb. iv. 23) point out many churches in Asia and Greece. That of Athens seems to have been one of the least flourishing.]

[Footnote 156: Lucian in Alexandro, c. 25. Christianity however, must have been very unequally diffused over Pontus; since, in the middle of the third century, there was no more than seventeen believers in the extensive diocese of Neo-Caesarea. See M. de Tillemont, Memoires Ecclesiast. tom. iv. p. 675, from Basil and Gregory of Nyssa, who were themselves natives of Cappadocia. Note: Gibbon forgot the conclusion of this story, that Gregory left only seventeen heathens in his diocese. The antithesis is suspicious, and both numbers may have been chosen to magnify the spiritual fame of the wonder-worker.—M.]

[Footnote 157: According to the ancients, Jesus Christ suffered under the consulship of the two Gemini, in the year 29 of our present aera. Pliny was sent into Bithynia (according to Pagi) in the year 110.]

[Footnote 158: Plin. Epist. x. 97.]

Without descending into a minute scrutiny of the expressions or of the motives of those writers who either celebrate or lament the progress of Christianity in the East, it may in general be observed, that none of them have left us any grounds from whence a just estimate might be formed of the real numbers of the faithful in those provinces. One circumstance, however, has been fortunately preserved, which seems to cast a more distinct light on this obscure but interesting subject. Under the reign of Theodosius, after Christianity had enjoyed, during more than sixty years, the sunshine of Imperial favor, the ancient and illustrious church of Antioch consisted of one hundred thousand persons, three thousand of whom were supported out of the public oblations. [159] The splendor and dignity of the queen of the East, the acknowledged populousness of Caesarea, Seleucia, and Alexandria, and the destruction of two hundred and fifty thousand souls in the earthquake which afflicted Antioch under the elder Justin, [160] are so many convincing proofs that the whole number of its inhabitants was not less than half a million, and that the Christians, however multiplied by zeal and power, did not exceed a fifth part of that great city. How different a proportion must we adopt when we compare the persecuted with the triumphant church, the West with the East, remote villages with populous towns, and countries recently converted to the faith with the place where the believers first received the appellation of Christians! It must not, however, be dissembled, that, in another passage, Chrysostom, to whom we are indebted for this useful information, computes the multitude of the faithful as even superior to that of the Jews and Pagans. [161] But the solution of this apparent difficulty is easy and obvious. The eloquent preacher draws a parallel between the civil and the ecclesiastical constitution of Antioch; between the list of Christians who had acquired heaven by baptism, and the list of citizens who had a right to share the public liberality. Slaves, strangers, and infants were comprised in the former; they were excluded from the latter.

[Footnote 159: Chrysostom. Opera, tom. vii. p. 658, 810, (edit. Savil. ii. 422, 329.)]

[Footnote 160: John Malala, tom. ii. p. 144. He draws the same conclusion with regard to the populousness of antioch.]

[Footnote 161: Chrysostom. tom. i. p. 592. I am indebted for these passages, though not for my inference, to the learned Dr. Lardner. Credibility of the Gospel of History, vol. xii. p. 370. Note: The statements of Chrysostom with regard to the population of Antioch, whatever may be their accuracy, are perfectly consistent. In one passage he reckons the population at 200,000. In a second the Christians at 100,000. In a third he states that the Christians formed more than half the population. Gibbon has neglected to notice the first passage, and has drawn by estimate of the population of Antioch from other sources. The 8000 maintained by alms were widows and virgins alone—M.]

The extensive commerce of Alexandria, and its proximity to Palestine, gave an easy entrance to the new religion. It was at first embraced by great numbers of the Theraputae, or Essenians, of the Lake Mareotis, a Jewish sect which had abated much of its reverence for the Mosaic ceremonies. The austere life of the Essenians, their fasts and excommunications, the community of goods, the love of celibacy, their zeal for martyrdom, and the warmth though not the purity of their faith, already offered a very lively image of the primitive discipline. [162] It was in the school of Alexandria that the Christian theology appears to have assumed a regular and scientific form; and when Hadrian visited Egypt, he found a church composed of Jews and of Greeks, sufficiently important to attract the notice of that inquisitive prince. [163] But the progress of Christianity was for a long time confined within the limits of a single city, which was itself a foreign colony, and till the close of the second century the predecessors of Demetrius were the only prelates of the Egyptian church. Three bishops were consecrated by the hands of Demetrius, and the number was increased to twenty by his successor Heraclas. [164] The body of the natives, a people distinguished by a sullen inflexibility of temper, [165] entertained the new doctrine with coldness and reluctance; and even in the time of Origen, it was rare to meet with an

Egyptian who had surmounted his early prejudices in favor of the sacred animals of his country. [166] As soon, indeed, as Christianity ascended the throne, the zeal of those barbarians obeyed the prevailing impulsion; the cities of Egypt were filled with bishops, and the deserts of Thebais swarmed with hermits.

[Footnote 162: Basnage, Histoire des Juifs, l. 2, c. 20, 21, 22, 23, has examined with the most critical accuracy the curious treatise of Philo, which describes the Therapeutae. By proving that it was composed as early as the time of Augustus, Basnage has demonstrated, in spite of Eusebius (l. ii. c. 17) and a crowd of modern Catholics, that the Therapeutae were neither Christians nor monks. It still remains probable that they changed their name, preserved their manners, adopted some new articles of faith, and gradually became the fathers of the Egyptian Ascetics.]

[Footnote 163: See a letter of Hadrian in the Augustan History, p. 245.]

[Footnote 164: For the succession of Alexandrian bishops, consult Renaudot's History, p. 24, &c. This curious fact is preserved by the patriarch Eutychius, (Annal. tom. i. p. 334, Vers. Pocock,) and its internal evidence would alone be a sufficient answer to all the objections which Bishop Pearson has urged in the Vindiciae Ignatianae.]

[Footnote 165: Ammian. Marcellin. xxii. 16.]

[Footnote 166: Origen contra Celsum, l. i. p. 40.]

A perpetual stream of strangers and provincials flowed into the capacious bosom of Rome. Whatever was strange or odious, whoever was guilty or suspected, might hope, in the obscurity of that immense capital, to elude the vigilance of the law. In such a various conflux of nations, every teacher, either of truth or falsehood, every founder, whether of a virtuous or a criminal association, might easily multiply his disciples or accomplices. The Christians of Rome, at the time of the accidental persecution of Nero, are represented by Tacitus as already amounting to a very great multitude, [167] and the language of that great historian is almost similar to the style employed by Livy, when he relates the introduction and the suppression of the rites of Bacchus. After the Bacchanals had awakened the severity of the senate, it was likewise apprehended that a very great multitude, as it were another people, had been initiated into those abhorred mysteries. A more careful inquiry soon demonstrated, that the offenders did not exceed seven thousand; a number indeed sufficiently alarming, when considered as the object of public justice. [168] It is with the same candid allowance that we should interpret the vague expressions of Tacitus, and in a former instance of Pliny, when they exaggerate the crowds of deluded fanatics who had forsaken the established worship of the gods. The church of Rome was undoubtedly the first and most populous of the empire; and we are possessed of an authentic record which attests the state of religion in that city about the middle of the third century, and after a peace of thirty-eight years. The clergy, at that time, consisted of a bishop, forty-six presbyters, seven deacons, as many sub-deacons, forty-two acolythes, and fifty readers, exorcists, and porters. The number of widows, of the infirm, and of the poor, who were maintained by the oblations of the faithful, amounted to fifteen hundred. [169] From reason, as well as from the analogy of Antioch, we may venture to estimate the Christians of Rome at about fifty thousand. The populousness of that great capital cannot perhaps be exactly ascertained; but the most modest calculation will not surely reduce it lower than a million of inhabitants, of whom the Christians might constitute at the most a twentieth part. [170]

[Footnote 167: Ingens multitudo is the expression of Tacitus, xv. 44.]

[Footnote 168: T. Liv. xxxix. 13, 15, 16, 17. Nothing could exceed the horror and consternation of the senate on the discovery of the Bacchanalians, whose depravity is described, and perhaps exaggerated, by Livy.]

[Footnote 169: Eusebius, l. vi. c. 43. The Latin translator (M. de Valois) has thought proper to reduce the number of presbyters to forty-four.]

[Footnote 170: This proportion of the presbyters and of the poor, to the rest of the people, was originally fixed by Burnet, (Travels into Italy, p. 168,) and is approved by Moyle, (vol. ii. p. 151.) They were both unacquainted with the passage of Chrysostom, which converts their conjecture almost into a fact.]

The western provincials appeared to have derived the knowledge of Christianity from the same source which had diffused among them the language, the sentiments, and the manners of Rome.

In this more important circumstance, Africa, as well as Gaul, was gradually fashioned to the imitation of the capital. Yet notwithstanding the many favorable occasions which might invite the Roman missionaries to visit their Latin provinces, it was late before they passed either the sea or the Alps; [171] nor can we discover in those great countries any assured traces either of faith or of persecution that ascend higher than the reign of the Antonines. [172] The slow progress of the gospel in the cold climate of Gaul, was extremely different from the eagerness with which it seems to have been received on the burning sands of Africa. The African Christians soon formed one of the principal members of the primitive church. The practice introduced into that province of appointing bishops to the most inconsiderable towns, and very frequently to the most obscure villages, contributed to multiply the splendor and importance of their religious societies, which during the course of the third century were animated by the zeal of Tertullian, directed by the abilities of Cyprian, and adorned by the eloquence of Lactantius.

But if, on the contrary, we turn our eyes towards Gaul, we must content ourselves with discovering, in the time of Marcus Antoninus, the feeble and united congregations of Lyons and Vienna; and even as late as the reign of Decius, we are assured, that in a few cities only, Arles, Narbonne, Thoulouse, Limoges, Clermont, Tours, and Paris, some scattered churches were supported by the devotion of a small number of Christians. [173] Silence is indeed very consistent with devotion; but as it is seldom compatible with zeal, we may perceive and lament the languid state of Christianity in those provinces which had exchanged the Celtic for the Latin tongue, since they did not, during the three first centuries, give birth to a single ecclesiastical writer. From Gaul, which claimed a just preeminence of learning and authority over all the countries on this side of the Alps, the light of the gospel was more faintly reflected on the remote provinces of Spain and Britain; and if we may credit the vehement assertions of Tertullian, they had already received the first rays of the faith, when he addressed his apology to the magistrates of the emperor Severus. [174] But the obscure and imperfect origin of the western churches of Europe has been so negligently recorded, that if we would relate the time and manner of their foundation, we must supply the silence of antiquity by those legends which avarice or superstition long afterwards dictated to the monks in the lazy gloom of their convents. [175] Of these holy romances, that of the apostle St. James can alone, by its singular extravagance, deserve to be mentioned. From a peaceful fisherman of the Lake of Gennesareth, he was transformed into a valorous knight, who charged at the head of the Spanish chivalry in their battles against the Moors. The gravest historians have celebrated his exploits; the miraculous shrine of Compostella displayed his power; and the sword of a military order, assisted by the terrors of the Inquisition, was sufficient to remove every objection of profane criticism. [176]

[Footnote 171: Serius trans Alpes, religione Dei suscepta. Sulpicius Severus, l. ii. With regard to Africa, see Tertullian ad Scapulam, c. 3. It is imagined that the Scyllitan martyrs were the first, (Acta Sincera Rumart. p. 34.) One of the adversaries of Apuleius seems to have been a Christian. Apolog. p. 496, 497, edit. Delphin.]

[Footnote 172: Tum primum intra Gallias martyria visa. Sulp. Severus, l. ii. These were the celebrated martyrs of Lyons. See Eusebius, v. i. Tillemont, Mem. Ecclesiast. tom. ii. p. 316. According to the Donatists, whose assertion is confirmed by the tacit acknowledgment of Augustin, Africa was the last of the provinces which received the gospel. Tillemont, Mem. Ecclesiast. tom. i. p. 754.]

[Footnote 173: Rarae in aliquibus civitatibus ecclesiae, paucorum Christianorum devotione, resurgerent. Acta Sincera, p. 130. Gregory of Tours, l i. c. 28. Mosheim, p. 207, 449. There is some reason to believe that in the beginning of the fourth century, the extensive dioceses of Liege, of Treves, and of Cologne, composed a single bishopric, which had been very recently founded. See Memoires de Tillemont, tom vi. part i. p. 43, 411.]

[Footnote 174: The date of Tertullian's Apology is fixed, in a dissertation of Mosheim, to the year 198.]

[Footnote 175: In the fifteenth century, there were few who had either inclination or courage to question, whether Joseph of Arimathea founded the monastery of Glastonbury, and whether Dionysius the Areopagite preferred the residence of Paris to that of Athens.]

[Footnote 176: The stupendous metamorphosis was performed in the ninth century. See Mariana, (Hist. Hispan. l. vii. c. 13, tom. i. p. 285, edit. Hag. Com. 1733,) who, in every sense, imitates Livy, and the honest detection of the legend of St. James by Dr. Geddes, Miscellanies, vol. ii. p. 221.]

The progress of Christianity was not confined to the Roman empire; and according to the primitive fathers, who interpret facts by prophecy, the new religion, within a century after the death of its divine Author, had already visited every part of the globe. "There exists not," says Justin Martyr, "a people, whether Greek or Barbarian, or any other race of men, by whatsoever appellation or manners they may be distinguished, however ignorant of arts or agriculture, whether they dwell under tents, or wander about in covered wagons, among whom prayers are not offered up in the name of a crucified Jesus to the Father and Creator of all things." [177] But this splendid exaggeration, which even at present it would be extremely difficult to reconcile with the real state of mankind, can be considered only as the rash sally of a devout but careless writer, the measure of whose belief was regulated by that of his wishes. But neither the belief nor the wishes of the fathers can alter the truth of history. It will still remain an undoubted fact, that the barbarians of Scythia and Germany, who afterwards subverted the Roman monarchy, were involved in the darkness of paganism; and that even the conversion of Iberia, of Armenia, or of Aethiopia, was not attempted with any degree of success till the sceptre was in the hands of an orthodox emperor. [178] Before that time, the various accidents of war and commerce might indeed diffuse an imperfect knowledge of the gospel among the tribes of Caledonia, [179] and among the borderers of the Rhine, the Danube, and the Euphrates. [180] Beyond the last-mentioned river, Edessa was distinguished by a firm and early adherence to the faith. [181] From Edessa the principles of Christianity were easily introduced into the Greek and Syrian cities which obeyed the successors of Artaxerxes; but they do not appear to have made any deep impression on the minds of the Persians, whose religious system, by the labors of a well disciplined order of priests, had been constructed with much more art and solidity than the uncertain mythology of Greece and Rome. [182]

[Footnote 177: Justin Martyr, Dialog. cum Tryphon. p. 341. Irenaeus adv. Haeres. l. i. c. 10. Tertullian adv. Jud. c. 7. See Mosheim, p. 203.]

[Footnote 178: See the fourth century of Mosheim's History of the Church. Many, though very confused circumstances, that relate to the conversion of Iberia and Armenia, may be found in Moses of Chorene, l. ii. c. 78—89. Note: Mons. St. Martin has shown that Armenia was the first nation that embraced Christianity. Memoires sur l'Armenie, vol. i. p. 306, and notes to Le Beae. Gibbon, indeed had expressed his intention of withdrawing the words "of Armenia" from the text of future editions. (Vindication, Works, iv. 577.) He was bitterly taunted by Person for neglecting or declining to fulfil his promise. Preface to Letters to Travis.—M.]

[Footnote 179: According to Tertullian, the Christian faith had penetrated into parts of Britain inaccessible to the Roman arms. About a century afterwards, Ossian, the son of Fingal, is said to have disputed, in his extreme old age, with one of the foreign missionaries, and the dispute is still extant, in verse, and in the Erse language. See Mr. Macpherson's Dissertation on the Antiquity of Ossian's Poems, p. 10.]

[Footnote 180: The Goths, who ravaged Asia in the reign of Gallienus, carried away great numbers of captives; some of whom were Christians, and became missionaries. See Tillemont, Memoires Ecclesiast. tom. iv. p. 44.]

[Footnote 181: The legends of Abgarus, fabulous as it is, affords a decisive proof, that many years before Eusebius wrote his history, the greatest part of the inhabitants of Edessa had embraced Christianity. Their rivals, the citizens of Carrhae, adhered, on the contrary, to the cause of Paganism, as late as the sixth century.]

[Footnote 182: According to Bardesanes (ap. Euseb. Praepar. Evangel.) there were some Christians in Persia before the end of the second century. In the time of Constantine (see his epistle to Sapor, Vit. l. iv. c. 13) they composed a flourishing church. Consult Beausobre, Hist. Cristique du Manicheisme, tom. i. p. 180, and the Bibliotheca Orietalis of Assemani.]

PART IX

From this impartial though imperfect survey of the progress of Christianity, it may perhaps seem probable, that the number of its proselytes has been excessively magnified by fear on the one side, and by devotion on the other. According to the irreproachable testimony of Origen, [183] the proportion of the faithful was very inconsiderable, when compared with the multitude of an unbelieving world; but, as we are left without any distinct information, it is impossible to determine, and it is difficult even to conjecture, the real numbers of the primitive Christians. The most favorable calculation, however, that can be deduced from the examples of Antioch and of Rome, will not permit us to imagine that more than a themselves under the banner of the cross before the important conversion of Constantine. But their habits of faith, of zeal, and of union, seemed to multiply their numbers; and the same causes which contributed to their future increase, served to render their actual strength more apparent and more formidable.

[Footnote 183: Origen contra Celsum, l. viii. p. 424.]

Such is the constitution of civil society, that whilst a few persons are distinguished by riches, by honors, and by knowledge, the body of the people is condemned to obscurity, ignorance and poverty. The Christian religion, which addressed itself to the whole human race, must consequently collect a far greater number of proselytes from the lower than from the superior ranks of life. This innocent and natural circumstance has been improved into a very odious imputation, which seems to be less strenuously denied by the apologists, than it is urged by the adversaries, of the faith; that the new sect of Christians was almost entirely composed of the dregs of the populace, of peasants and mechanics, of boys and women, of beggars and slaves, the last of whom might sometimes introduce the missionaries into the rich and noble families to which they belonged. These obscure teachers (such was the charge of malice and infidelity) are as mute in public as they are loquacious and dogmatical in private. Whilst they cautiously avoid the dangerous encounter of philosophers, they mingle with the rude and illiterate crowd, and insinuate themselves into those minds, whom their age, their sex, or their education, has the best disposed to receive the impression of superstitious terrors. [184]

[Footnote 184: Minucius Felix, c. 8, with Wowerus's notes. Celsus ap. Origen, l. iii. p. 138, 142. Julian ap. Cyril. l. vi. p. 206, edit. Spanheim.]

This unfavorable picture, though not devoid of a faint resemblance, betrays, by its dark coloring and distorted features, the pencil of an enemy. As the humble faith of Christ diffused itself through the world, it was embraced by several persons who derived some consequence from the advantages of nature or fortune. Aristides, who presented an eloquent apology to the emperor Hadrian, was an Athenian philosopher. [185] Justin Martyr had sought divine knowledge in the schools of Zeno, of Aristotle, of Pythagoras, and of Plato, before he fortunately was accosted by the old man, or rather the angel, who turned his attention to the study of the Jewish prophets. [186] Clemens of Alexandria had acquired much various reading in the Greek, and Tertullian in the Latin, language. Julius Africanus and Origen possessed a very considerable share of the learning of their times; and although the style of Cyprian is very different from that of Lactantius, we might almost discover that both those writers had been public teachers of rhetoric. Even the study of philosophy was at length introduced among the Christians, but it was not always productive of the most salutary effects; knowledge was as often the parent of heresy as of devotion, and the description which was designed for the followers of Artemon, may, with equal propriety, be applied to the various sects that resisted the successors of the apostles. "They presume to alter the Holy Scriptures, to abandon the ancient rule of faith, and to form their opinions according to the subtile precepts of logic. The science of the church is neglected for the study of geometry, and they lose sight of heaven while they are employed in measuring the earth. Euclid is perpetually in their hands. Aristotle and Theophrastus are the objects of their admiration; and they express an uncommon reverence for the works of Galen. Their errors are derived from the abuse of the arts and sciences of the infidels, and they corrupt the simplicity of the gospel by the refinements of human reason." [187]

[Footnote 185: Euseb. Hist. Eccles. iv. 3. Hieronym. Epist. 83.]

[Footnote 186: The story is prettily told in Justin's Dialogues. Tillemont, (Mem Ecclesiast. tom. ii. p. 384,) who relates it after him is sure that the old man was a disguised angel.]

[Footnote 187: Eusebius, v. 28. It may be hoped, that none, except the heretics, gave occasion to the complaint of Celsus, (ap. Origen, l. ii. p. 77,) that the Christians were perpetually correcting and altering

their Gospels. Note: Origen states in reply, that he knows of none who had altered the Gospels except the Marcionites, the Valentinians, and perhaps some followers of Lucanus.—M.]

Nor can it be affirmed with truth, that the advantages of birth and fortune were always separated from the profession of Christianity. Several Roman citizens were brought before the tribunal of Pliny, and he soon discovered, that a great number of persons of every order of men in Bithynia had deserted the religion of their ancestors. [188] His unsuspected testimony may, in this instance, obtain more credit than the bold challenge of Tertullian, when he addresses himself to the fears as well as the humanity of the proconsul of Africa, by assuring him, that if he persists in his cruel intentions, he must decimate Carthage, and that he will find among the guilty many persons of his own rank, senators and matrons of nobles' extraction, and the friends or relations of his most intimate friends. [189] It appears, however, that about forty years afterwards the emperor Valerian was persuaded of the truth of this assertion, since in one of his rescripts he evidently supposes, that senators, Roman knights, and ladies of quality, were engaged in the Christian sect. [190] The church still continued to increase its outward splendor as it lost its internal purity; and, in the reign of Diocletian, the palace, the courts of justice, and even the army, concealed a multitude of Christians, who endeavored to reconcile the interests of the present with those of a future life.

[Footnote 188: Plin. Epist. x. 97. Fuerunt alii similis amentiae, cives Romani—Multi enim omnis aetatis, omnis ordinis, utriusque sexus, etiam vocuntur in periculum et vocabuntur.]

[Footnote 189: Tertullian ad Scapulum. Yet even his rhetoric rises no higher than to claim a tenth part of Carthage.]

[Footnote 190: Cyprian. Epist. 70.]

And yet these exceptions are either too few in number, or too recent in time, entirely to remove the imputation of ignorance and obscurity which has been so arrogantly cast on the first proselytes of Christianity. [190/1] Instead of employing in our defence the fictions of later ages, it will be more prudent to convert the occasion of scandal into a subject of edification. Our serious thoughts will suggest to us, that the apostles themselves were chosen by Providence among the fishermen of Galilee, and that the lower we depress the temporal condition of the first Christians, the more reason we shall find to admire their merit and success. It is incumbent on us diligently to remember, that the kingdom of heaven was promised to the poor in spirit, and that minds afflicted by calamity and the contempt of mankind, cheerfully listen to the divine promise of future happiness; while, on the contrary, the fortunate are satisfied with the possession of this world; and the wise abuse in doubt and dispute their vain superiority of reason and knowledge.

[Footnote 190/1: This incomplete enumeration ought to be increased by the names of several Pagans converted at the dawn of Christianity, and whose conversion weakens the reproach which the historian appears to support. Such are, the Proconsul Sergius Paulus, converted at Paphos, (Acts xiii. 7—12.) Dionysius, member of the Areopagus, converted with several others, al Athens, (Acts xvii. 34;) several persons at the court of Nero, (Philip. iv 22;) Erastus, receiver at Corinth, (Rom. xvi.23;) some Asiarchs, (Acts xix. 31) As to the philosophers, we may add Tatian, Athenagoras, Theophilus of Antioch, Hegesippus, Melito, Miltiades, Pantaenus, Ammenius, all distinguished for their genius and learning.—G.]

We stand in need of such reflections to comfort us for the loss of some illustrious characters, which in our eyes might have seemed the most worthy of the heavenly present. The names of Seneca, of the elder and the younger Pliny, of Tacitus, of Plutarch, of Galen, of the slave Epictetus, and of the emperor Marcus Antoninus, adorn the age in which they flourished, and exalt the dignity of human nature. They filled with glory their respective stations, either in active or contemplative life; their excellent understandings were improved by study; Philosophy had purified their minds from the prejudices of the popular superstition; and their days were spent in the pursuit of truth and the practice of virtue. Yet all these sages (it is no less an object of surprise than of concern) overlooked or rejected the perfection of the Christian system. Their language or their silence equally discover their contempt for the growing sect, which in their time had diffused itself over the Roman empire. Those among them who condescended to mention the Christians, consider them only as obstinate and perverse enthusiasts, who exacted an implicit submission to their mysterious doctrines, without being able to produce a single argument that could engage the attention of men of sense and learning. [191]

[Footnote 191: Dr. Lardner, in his first and second volumes of Jewish and Christian testimonies, collects and illustrates those of Pliny the younger, of Tacitus, of Galen, of Marcus Antoninus, and perhaps of Epictetus, (for it is doubtful whether that philosopher means to speak of the Christians.) The new sect is totally unnoticed by Seneca, the elder Pliny, and Plutarch.]

It is at least doubtful whether any of these philosophers perused the apologies [191/1] which the primitive Christians repeatedly published in behalf of themselves and of their religion; but it is much to be lamented that such a cause was not defended by abler advocates. They expose with superfluous with and eloquence the extravagance of Polytheism. They interest our compassion by displaying the innocence and sufferings of their injured brethren. But when they would demonstrate the divine origin of Christianity, they insist much more strongly on the predictions which announced, than on the miracles which accompanied, the appearance of the Messiah. Their favorite argument might serve to edify a Christian or to convert a Jew, since both the one and the other acknowledge the authority of those prophecies, and both are obliged, with devout reverence, to search for their sense and their accomplishment. But this mode of persuasion loses much of its weight and influence, when it is addressed to those who neither understand nor respect the Mosaic dispensation and the prophetic style. [192] In the unskilful hands of Justin and of the succeeding apologists, the sublime meaning of the Hebrew oracles evaporates in distant types, affected conceits, and cold allegories; and even their authenticity was rendered suspicious to an unenlightened Gentile, by the mixture of pious forgeries, which, under the names of Orpheus, Hermes, and the Sibyls, [193] were obtruded on him as of equal value with the genuine inspirations of Heaven. The adoption of fraud and sophistry in the defence of revelation too often reminds us of the injudicious conduct of those poets who load their invulnerable heroes with a useless weight of cumbersome and brittle armor.

[Footnote 191/1: The emperors Hadrian, Antoninus &c., read with astonishment the apologies of Justin Martyr, of Aristides, of Melito, &c. (See St. Hieron. ad mag. orat. Orosius, lviii. c. 13.) Eusebius says expressly, that the cause of Christianity was defended before the senate, in a very elegant discourse, by Apollonius the Martyr.—G. —Gibbon, in his severer spirit of criticism, may have questioned the authority of Jerome and Eusebius. There are some difficulties about Apollonius, which Heinichen (note in loc. Eusebii) would solve, by suppose lag him to have been, as Jerome states, a senator.—M.]

[Footnote 192: If the famous prophecy of the Seventy Weeks had been alleged to a Roman philosopher, would he not have replied in the words of Cicero, "Quae tandem ista auguratio est, annorum potius quam aut raensium aut dierum?" De Divinatione, ii. 30. Observe with what irreverence Lucian, (in

Alexandro, c. 13.) and his friend Celsus ap. Origen, (l. vii. p. 327,) express themselves concerning the Hebrew prophets.]

[Footnote 193: The philosophers who derided the more ancient predictions of the Sibyls, would easily have detected the Jewish and Christian forgeries, which have been so triumphantly quoted by the fathers, from Justin Martyr to Lactantius. When the Sibylline verses had performed their appointed task, they, like the system of the millennium, were quietly laid aside. The Christian Sybil had unluckily fixed the ruin of Rome for the year 195, A. U. C. 948.]

But how shall we excuse the supine inattention of the Pagan and philosophic world, to those evidences which were represented by the hand of Omnipotence, not to their reason, but to their senses? During the age of Christ, of his apostles, and of their first disciples, the doctrine which they preached was confirmed by innumerable prodigies. The lame walked, the blind saw, the sick were healed, the dead were raised, daemons were expelled, and the laws of Nature were frequently suspended for the benefit of the church. But the sages of Greece and Rome turned aside from the awful spectacle, and, pursuing the ordinary occupations of life and study, appeared unconscious of any alterations in the moral or physical government of the world. Under the reign of Tiberius, the whole earth, [194] or at least a celebrated province of the Roman empire, [195] was involved in a preternatural darkness of three hours. Even this miraculous event, which ought to have excited the wonder, the curiosity, and the devotion of mankind, passed without notice in an age of science and history. [196] It happened during the lifetime of Seneca and the elder Pliny, who must have experienced the immediate effects, or received the earliest intelligence, of the prodigy. Each of these philosophers, in a laborious work, has recorded all the great phenomena of Nature, earthquakes, meteors comets, and eclipses, which his indefatigable curiosity could collect. [197] Both the one and the other have omitted to mention the greatest phenomenon to which the mortal eye has been witness since the creation of the globe. A distinct chapter of Pliny [198] is designed for eclipses of an extraordinary nature and unusual duration; but he contents himself with describing the singular defect of light which followed the murder of Caesar, when, during the greatest part of a year, the orb of the sun appeared pale and without splendor. The season of obscurity, which cannot surely be compared with the preternatural darkness of the Passion, had been already celebrated by most of the poets [199] and historians of that memorable age. [200]

[Footnote 194: The fathers, as they are drawn out in battle array by Dom Calmet, (Dissertations sur la Bible, tom. iii. p. 295—308,) seem to cover the whole earth with darkness, in which they are followed by most of the moderns.]

[Footnote 195: Origen ad Matth. c. 27, and a few modern critics, Beza, Le Clerc, Lardner, &c., are desirous of confining it to the land of Judea.]

[Footnote 196: The celebrated passage of Phlegon is now wisely abandoned. When Tertullian assures the Pagans that the mention of the prodigy is found in Arcanis (not Archivis) vestris, (see his Apology, c. 21,) he probably appeals to the Sibylline verses, which relate it exactly in the words of the Gospel. Note: According to some learned theologians a misunderstanding of the text in the Gospel has given rise to this mistake, which has employed and wearied so many laborious commentators, though Origen had already taken the pains to preinform them. The expression does not mean, they assert, an eclipse, but any kind of obscurity occasioned in the atmosphere, whether by clouds or any other cause. As this obscuration of the sun rarely took place in Palestine, where in the middle of April the sky was usually clear, it assumed, in the eyes of the Jews and Christians, an importance conformable to the received notion, that the sun concealed at midday was a sinister presage. See Amos viii. 9, 10. The word is often taken in this sense by

contemporary writers; the Apocalypse says the sun was concealed, when speaking of an obscuration caused by smoke and dust. (Revel. ix. 2.) Moreover, the Hebrew word ophal, which in the LXX. answers to the Greek, signifies any darkness; and the Evangelists, who have modelled the sense of their expressions by those of the LXX., must have taken it in the same latitude. This darkening of the sky usually precedes earthquakes. (Matt. xxvii. 51.) The Heathen authors furnish us a number of examples, of which a miraculous explanation was given at the time. See Ovid. ii. v. 33, l. xv. v. 785. Pliny, Hist. Nat. l. ii. c 30. Wetstein has collected all these examples in his edition of the New Testament. We need not, then, be astonished at the silence of the Pagan authors concerning a phenomenon which did not extend beyond Jerusalem, and which might have nothing contrary to the laws of nature; although the Christians and the Jews may have regarded it as a sinister presage. See Michaelia Notes on New Testament, v. i. p. 290. Paulus, Commentary on New Testament, iii. p. 760.—G.]

[Footnote 197: Seneca, Quaest. Natur. l. i. 15, vi. l. vii. 17. Plin. Hist. Natur. l. ii.]

[Footnote 198: Plin. Hist. Natur. ii. 30.]

[Footnote 199: Virgil. Georgic. i. 466. Tibullus, l. i. Eleg. v. ver. 75. Ovid Metamorph. xv. 782. Lucan. Pharsal. i. 540. The last of these poets places this prodigy before the civil war.]

[Footnote 200: See a public epistle of M. Antony in Joseph. Antiquit. xiv. 12. Plutarch in Caesar. p. 471. Appian. Bell. Civil. l. iv. Dion Cassius, l. xlv. p. 431. Julius Obsequens, c. 128. His little treatise is an abstract of Livy's prodigies.]

EDWARD GIBBON – A SHORT BIOGRAPHY

Edward Gibbon was born on 8th May, 1737, the son of Edward and Judith Gibbon at Lime Grove, in the town of Putney, Surrey. He had six siblings, all of whom died in infancy. His grandfather, also named Edward, had lost everything as a result of the South Sea Bubble collapse in 1720, but eventually regained much of his wealth, so that Gibbon's father was able to inherit a substantial estate.

As a youth, Gibbon's health was under constant threat. He described himself as "a puny child, neglected by my Mother, starved by my nurse". At age nine, he was sent to Dr. Woddeson's school at Kingston-upon-Thames, shortly after which his mother died. He was then moved to the Westminster School boarding house, owned by his adored "Aunt Kitty", Catherine Porten.

By 1751, Gibbon's reading was already extensive and certainly pointed toward his future pursuits having covered such works as Laurence Echard's Roman History (1713), William Howell's An Institution of General History (1680–85), and several of the 65 volumes of the acclaimed Universal History from the Earliest Account of Time (1747–1768).

Following a stay at Bath, at age 15, in 1752 to improve his health, Gibbon was sent by his father to Magdalen College, Oxford, where he was enrolled as a gentleman-commoner (a rank of student above commoners i.e. normal students who paid the normal rate for tuition and boarding but below noblemen. They paid double the tuition fee and enjoyed more privileges). He was ill-suited, however, to the college atmosphere and later rued his 14 months there as the "most idle and unprofitable" of his life. Because of his autobiography, it used to be thought that his penchant for "theological controversy" (his aunt's influence) fully bloomed when he came under the spell of the deist or rationalist theologian Conyers Middleton, the author of Free Inquiry into the Miraculous Powers (1749). In that tract, Middleton denied the validity of such powers; Gibbon promptly objected, or so the argument used to run. The product of that disagreement, with some assistance from the work of Catholic Bishop Jacques-Bénigne Bossuet, and that of the Elizabethan Jesuit Robert Parsons, yielded the most memorable event of his time at Oxford: his conversion to Roman Catholicism on 8th June 1753. He was further 'corrupted' by the 'free thinking' deism of the playwright/poet couple David and Lucy Mallet; and finally Gibbon's father, already deeply in despair, had had enough.

However, this story has fallen somewhat into disrepute only being introduced to the final draft of Gibbon's "Memoirs" in 1792–93. There are also other accounts as to why Gibbons may have given a new 'backstory' to his conversion.

Within weeks of his conversion, the Gibbons was removed from Oxford and sent to live under the care and tutelage of Daniel Pavillard, Reformed pastor of Lausanne in Switzerland.

Here he made great friendships with Jacques Georges Deyverdun (the French-language translator of Goethe's The Sorrows of Young Werther), and John Baker Holroyd (later Lord Sheffield).

Just a year and a half later, after his father threatened to disinherit him, on Christmas Day, 1754, he reconverted to Protestantism. "The various articles of the Romish creed," he wrote, "disappeared like a dream".

He remained in Lausanne for five intellectually productive years, a period that greatly enriched Gibbon's already immense aptitude for scholarship and erudition: he read Latin literature; travelled throughout Switzerland studying its cantons' constitutions; and studied the works of Hugo Grotius, Samuel von Pufendorf, John Locke, Pierre Bayle, and Blaise Pascal.

He also met the one love in his life: the daughter of the pastor of Crassy; Suzanne Curchod. As the two developed an ever-closer relationship; Gibbon raised the question of marriage, but ultimately wedlock was out of the question, blocked both by his father's staunch disapproval and Curchod's refusal to leave Switzerland.

Gibbon returned to England in August 1758 to face his father. There was to be no refusal of his wishes. Gibbon put it rather poetically: "I sighed as a lover, I obeyed as a son." He proceeded to cut off all contact with Suzanne, even as she vowed to wait for him.

Upon his return to England, Gibbon published his first book, Essai sur l'Étude de la Littérature in 1761, which produced an initial taste of celebrity and distinguished him, in Paris at least, as a man of letters.

Interestingly to add to his interests and talents he had, from 1759 to 1770, served on active duty and then in reserve with the South Hampshire militia, his deactivation in December 1762 coinciding with the militia's dispersal after the Seven Years' War.

In 1763, he began as many men of privilege of class then did to round out and embellish their education on the Grand Tour, which included a visit to Rome. In his autobiography Gibbon vividly records his rapture when he finally neared "the great object of my pilgrimage": ...at the distance of twenty-five years I can neither forget nor express the strong emotions which agitated my mind as I first approached and entered the eternal City. After a sleepless night, I trod, with a lofty step the ruins of the Forum; each memorable spot where Romulus stood, or Tully spoke, or Caesar fell, was at once present to my eye; and several days of intoxication were lost or enjoyed before I could descend to a cool and minute investigation.

And it was here that Gibbon first conceived the idea of composing a history of the city, later extended to the entire empire, a moment known to history as the Capitoline vision: "It was at Rome, on the 15th of October 1764, as I sat musing amidst the ruins of the Capitol, while the barefooted fryars were singing Vespers in the temple of Jupiter, that the idea of writing the decline and fall of the City first started to my mind".

In June 1765, Gibbon returned to his father's house. He would remain there for the following five years until his father's death. He always considered this span of time as the worst of his life. He busied himself with various writing projects which failed to reach fruition. His first historical narrative, the History of Switzerland, was neither published nor finished. Gibbon had become too self-critical and abandoned the work a mere 60 pages in.

His second work, Memoires Litteraires de la Grande Bretagne, in two volumes, described both the literary and the social conditions of England at the time. When published it failed to gain any traction.

With the death of his father and the settling of the estate Gibbon had enough of a legacy to be free of any financial problems. He moved to Bentinck Street in London and began to live the life that suited him. He joined a number of clubs, including Dr. Johnson's Literary Club. He succeeded Oliver Goldsmith at the Royal Academy as 'professor in ancient history' (honorary but nonetheless prestigious). And he was writing. The work for which he would gain worldwide fame was under way.

But still other interests would divert his attention.

In late 1774, he was initiated a freemason of the Premier Grand Lodge of England. That same year he was returned to Parliament for the seat of Liskeard in Cornwall through the intervention of his relative and patron, Edward Eliot. Gibbon became a typical backbencher, mute and indifferent to his responsibilities, apart from routinely voting for the Whig Administration.

After several rewrites usually brought on by self-doubt and seven years of work the first volume of The History of the Decline and Fall of the Roman Empire, was published on 17th February 1776.

It was an immediate success. Within a year it had gone through three editions and the royalties were very handsome indeed.

Further volumes followed quickly and with the same measure of success; Volumes II and III were published on 1st March 1781, and volume IV was released in June 1784. Volumes V and VI were completed during a second Lausanne sojourn (September 1783 to August 1787) where Gibbon reunited with his friend Deyverdun. By early 1787, he was "straining for the goal" and with great relief the project was finished in June. Gibbon later wrote: "It was on the day, or rather the night, of 27th June 1787, between the hours of eleven and twelve, that I wrote the last lines of the last page in a summer-house in my garden...I will not dissemble the first emotions of joy on the recovery of my freedom, and perhaps the establishment of my fame. But my pride was soon humbled, and a sober melancholy was spread over my mind by the idea that I had taken my everlasting leave of an old and agreeable companion, and that, whatsoever might be the future date of my history, the life of the historian must be short and precarious".

Volumes V, and VI finally reached the press in May 1788, their publication having been delayed since March, so it could coincide with a dinner party on the 8th celebrating Gibbon's 51st birthday.

Praise came from all directions. Leading it were such contemporary luminaries as Adam Smith, Lord Camden, and Horace Walpole. Smith remarked that Gibbon's triumph had positioned him "at the very head of Europe's literary tribe."

In November of that year, he was elected a Fellow of the Royal Society, the main proposer being his good friend Lord Sheffield.

But the high-water mark had been reached and for Gibbon the following years were of sorrow and increasing health problems.

In 1789 he returned to Lausanne only to learn of and be "deeply affected" by the death of Deyverdun, who had willed Gibbon his home, La Grotte. He resided there with little commotion, took in the local society, received a visit from Sheffield in 1791, and "shared the common abhorrence" of the French Revolution.

In a letter to Lord Sheffield on 5th February 1791, Gibbon praised Burke's Reflections on the Revolution in France: "Burke's book is a most admirable medicine against the French disease, which has made too much progress even in this happy country. I admire his eloquence, I approve his politics, I adore his chivalry, and I can even forgive his superstition...The French spread so many lyes about the sentiments of the English nation, that I wish the most considerable men of all parties and descriptions would join in some public act declaring themselves satisfied with, and resolved to support, our present constitution."

In 1793, word came of Lady Sheffield's death; Gibbon immediately left Lausanne and set sail to comfort a grieving but composed Sheffield. But for Gibbon too, time was failing. His health began to fail critically in December, and at the turn of the new year, he was in rapid decline.

Gibbon is believed to have suffered from an extreme case of scrotal swelling, probably a hydrocele testis, a condition in which the scrotum swell with fluid in a compartment overlying either testicle. In an age when close-fitting clothes were fashionable, his condition led to a chronic and disfiguring inflammation that left Gibbon a lonely figure. As his condition worsened, he underwent numerous procedures to alleviate the condition, but with no enduring success. In early January, the last of a series of three operations caused an unremitting peritonitis to set in and spread, from which he died.

Edward Gibbon, the "English giant of the Enlightenment" finally succumbed at 12:45 pm, 16 January 1794 at age 56. He was buried in the Sheffield Mausoleum attached to the north transept of the Church of St Mary and St Andrew, Fletching, East Sussex.

EDWARD GIBBON – A CONCISE BIBLIOGRAPHY

Essai sur l'Étude de la Littérature (1761)

Critical Observations on the Sixth Book of Vergil's 'The Aeneid' (1770)
The History of the Decline and Fall of the Roman Empire (Vol. I, 1776; Vols. II, III, 1781; Vols. IV, V, VI, 1788–1789)
A Vindication of some passages in the fifteenth and sixteenth chapters of the History of the Decline and Fall of the Roman Empire (1779)
Mémoire Justificatif pour servir de Réponse à l'Exposé, etc. de la Cour de France (1779)
Mémoires Littéraires de la Grande-Bretagne. co-author: Georges Deyverdun (2 vols: vol. 1, 1767; vol. 2, 1768)
Miscellaneous Works of Edward Gibbon, Esq., ed. John Lord Sheffield (2 vols., 1796; 5 vols., 1814; 3 vols., 1815) Includes Memoirs of the Life and Writings of Edward Gibbon, Esq.
Autobiographies of Edward Gibbon, ed. John Murray (1896). Edward Gibbon's complete memoirs (six drafts) from the original manuscripts.
The Private Letters of Edward Gibbon, 2 vols., ed. Rowland E. Prothero (1896)
The works of Edward Gibbon (Volume 3, 1906)
Gibbon's Journal to 28 January 1763, ed. D.M. Low (1929)
Le Journal de Gibbon à Lausanne, ed. Georges A. Bonnard (1945)
Miscellanea Gibboniana, eds. G.R. de Beer, L. Junod, G.A. Bonnard (1952)
The Letters of Edward Gibbon, 3 vols., ed. J.E. Norton (1956). vol. 1: 1750–1773; vol. 2: 1774–1784; vol. 3: 1784–1794. cited as 'Norton, Letters'
Gibbon's Journey from Geneva to Rome, ed. G.A. Bonnard (1961) Journal
Edward Gibbon: Memoirs of My Life, ed. G.A. Bonnard (1969; 1966). portions of Edward Gibbon's memoirs arranged chronologically, omitting repetition.
The English Essays of Edward Gibbon, ed. Patricia Craddock (1972)

www.ingramcontent.com/pod-product-compliance
Lightning Source LLC
Chambersburg PA
CBHW050119170426
43197CB00011B/1646